MODERN SOFTWARE DEVELOPMENT USING JAVA™

A TEXT FOR THE SECOND COURSE IN COMPUTER SCIENCE

Paul T. Tymann
Rochester Institute of Technology

G. Michael Schneider
Macalester College

THOMSON

BROOKS/COLE

Australia • Canada • Mexico • Singapore • Spain • United Kingdom • United States

Publisher: *Bill Stenquist*
Acquisitions Editor: *Kallie Swanson*
Editorial Assistants: *Aarti Jayaraman, Carla Vera*
Technology Project Manager: *Burke Taft*
Executive Marketing Manager: *Tom Ziolkowski*
Marketing Communications Team: *Margaret Parks,*
 Vicky Chao
Editorial Production Project Manager: *Kelsey McGee*

Print/Media Buyer: *Jessica Reed*
Permissions Editor: *Sue Ewing*
Production Service: *Matrix Productions*
Copy Editor: *Frank Hubert*
Cover Designer: *Ross Carron Design*
Cover Image: *Chad Baker/Ryan McVay*
Cover Printing, Printing and Binding: *Phoenix Color Corp.*
Compositor: *Scratchgravel Publishing Services*

Printed in the United States of America
1 2 3 4 5 6 7 06 05 04 03

For more information about our products, contact us at:
Thomson Learning Academic Resource Center
1-800-423-0563
For permission to use material from this text,
contact us by:
Phone: 1-800-730-2214
Fax: 1-800-730-2215
Web: http://www.thomsonrights.com

Library of Congress Control Number: 2002027652

ISBN 0-534-38449-8

Brooks/Cole–Thomson Learning
511 Forest Lodge Road
Pacific Grove, CA 93950
USA

Asia
Thomson Learning
5 Shenton Way #01-01
UIC Building
Singapore 068808

Australia
Nelson Thomson Learning
102 Dodds Street
South Melbourne, Victoria 3205
Australia

Canada
Nelson Thomson Learning
1120 Birchmount Road
Toronto, Ontario M1K 5G4
Canada

Europe/Middle East/Africa
Thomson Learning
High Holborn House
50/51 Bedford Row
London WC1R 4LR
United Kingdom

Latin America
Thomson Learning
Seneca, 53
Colonia Polanco
11560 Mexico D.F.
Mexico

Spain
Paraninfo Thomson Learning
Calle/Magallanes, 25
28015 Madrid, Spain

To my parents who made my life possible,
to Lisa, Heidi, and James who make my life worth living,
and to my students who taught me everything I know.

P. T. T.

To my wife Ruthann, my son Benjamin,
and my daughter Rebecca.

G. M. S.

CONTENTS

PART I

OBJECT-ORIENTED SOFTWARE DEVELOPMENT   33

CHAPTER 4

Case Study in Object-Oriented Software Development   150

PART II

ALGORITHMS AND DATA STRUCTURES   207

CHAPTER 5

The Analysis of Algorithms   209

CHAPTER 6

Linear Data Structures   239

CHAPTER 7

Hierarchical Data Structures   352

PART III

MODERN PROGRAMMING TECHNIQUES   597

CHAPTER 10

Exceptions and Streams   599

CHAPTER 11

Threads   642

CHAPTER 12

Graphical User Interfaces   709

CHAPTER 13

Networking   771

APPENDIX

Basic Java Syntax   820

PREFACE

This is a text for a second course in computer science. This class is often referred to in curricular recommendations as "CS 2," including the recently released *ACM/IEEE Computing Curriculum 2001* (CC2001). CS 2 traditionally follows the introductory programming and problem solving course that is the starting point for the great majority of computer science undergraduates.

In this book we take a rather different view from other texts regarding appropriate topics to include in CS 2. This is because of the many differences between software development today and the not so distant past, as well as recommendations contained in the CC2001 report. The field of computing is changing dramatically with new hardware and software developments announced almost daily. The computer science curricula must adapt if they are to remain current with these new developments as well as the changing background of our students. For example, CS 0, the service course for non-majors, was often a class in the applications of computing—for example, databases, spreadsheets, Web browsing. However, it is rare today for students to be unfamiliar with these packages, so many schools changed their service courses to cover more modern topics such as multimedia or social and ethical issues in information technology. Similarly, CS 1, the first programming course, evolved in response to improved language environments, initially from Pascal to C++ and, more recently, to Java and object-oriented programming. The authors feel quite strongly that the time is right for another curricular evolution, this time in CS 2.

For many years, beginning with *ACM Curriculum '78*, CS 2 was understood to be a course on data structures, with some supporting material on algorithm analysis, sorting, and searching. For 20 years it was an accepted fact that it would cover topics like linked lists, stacks, trees, hash tables, and graphs. For more than two decades, computer science students dutifully learned to implement a queue using circular arrays, update pointers in a doubly linked list, and work through algorithms for balancing a B-tree. Recent versions of CS 2 have made changes, often to expand the coverage of object-oriented programming. However, the great majority of time, sometimes as much as 70 to 80 percent, is still dedicated to designing and implementing the classic data structures of computer science. In spite of the enormous changes in computing and software design in the last two decades, the syllabi of many CS 2 classes could, with the exception of Java, have been written in 1980. This represents what we believe to be an outmoded view. Just as other courses adapted to present a more modern outlook, it is now time for CS 2 to change to address important new concepts in computer science and software development.

The basic precept of our text is that the topic of data structures, while certainly important, should no longer be the central focus of CS 2. Instead, it is time to recognize and address some fundamental changes in software development. The three concerns that we feel will have the greatest impact on the curriculum are:

- the need to introduce students, as early as possible, to *all* aspects of the software life cycle, including requirements, specification, and design
- the existence of languages like Java that contain extensive libraries that provide the functionality required to use a wide range of data structures
- topics that were often delayed until junior or senior level classes are becoming an increasingly important part of the software development landscape and need to be introduced much earlier in the curriculum.

This text addresses all three of these issues in order to provide a more modern view of software design and development.

Part I. Object-Oriented Design and Development (Chapters 1–4)

The first section, Chapters 1–4, reviews the overall software life cycle. All too often students focus so heavily on implementation-related issues that they develop the mistaken impression that "software development = programming." CS 1, the first programming course, usually introduces the basic concepts of object-oriented programming but, because of limited class time, this coverage is often quite brief. Students are exposed to classes, objects, and methods but have little experience using these ideas to solve complex problems. In Part I of the text we expand on this initial presentation and introduce students to all aspects of the problem solving process.

Chapter 1 overviews the phases of the software life cycle, especially those that must precede implementation—requirements, specification, and design. In Chapter 2 we look more closely at program design as we investigate the following questions:

- How can the classes to include in our design be inferred from the problem specification document?
- How can we determine the appropriate states and behaviors for these classes?
- How can we use a formal notation such as UML to clearly and unambiguously represent our proposed design?

This chapter also takes an in-depth look at inheritance. It presents different models of inheritance, such as specialization, specification, and limitation, and shows how each of these models enhances the problem solving process. While Chapter 2 discusses object-oriented design in a conceptual, language-independent way, Chapter 3 looks at how these features are realized in Java. This chapter provides a full treatment of the facilities available in the language, including abstract classes, interfaces, public/private/protected visibility, method overloading, and dynamic binding. Finally, Chapter 4 is an extended case study that follows the solution of a problem through its life cycle, from user requirements to implementation and testing. This case study ties together the object-oriented concepts presented in the previous three chapters and allows the student to see how they form a coherent design philosophy.

Part II. Algorithms and Data Structures (Chapters 5–9)

The second part of the text, Chapters 5–9, addresses the topics of algorithms and data structures, what has been the central focus of the second course for so many years. As we said earlier, this is still an important subject, and students must be familiar with the classic data structures of computer science. However, our coverage focuses more on their behavior, their strengths and weaknesses, and their best-case/worst-case performance than on the nitty-gritty details of their implementation. The appearance of data structure libraries in languages like Java has dramatically changed the way we approach this topic in the classroom. It is no longer as important for a student to *build* every data structure they use; however, it is vital that they be able to *understand*, *analyze*, and intelligently *select* and *use* the most appropriate data structures to solve a given problem.

Chapter 5 covers the mathematical tools needed to analyze the properties of data structures, namely, the asymptotic analysis of algorithms, also called Big-O notation. Next we begin our investigation of the most widely used data structures. It is important that students not view the many structures presented in these chapters as disparate and unrelated issues. Instead, they must see this discussion as an integrated topic with many closely related ideas. To achieve this, we first present a taxonomy that categorizes all data structures into one of four fundamental groupings. Then, in the succeeding chapters, we individually investigate each of these classifications. Chapter 6 looks at the linear, or *(one:one)*, grouping that includes lists, stacks, queues, and priority queues. We show why these structures can all be considered as belonging to the same classification and differ only in the types of operations permitted or excluded. We also discuss the conditions under which each of these linear structures can be a useful representation. Chapter 7 looks at the hierarchical, or *(one: many)*, grouping that includes binary trees, search trees, and heaps. Chapter 8 covers the final two classifications in the taxonomy—graphs, or *(many:many)*, structures, and sets. This latter discussion focuses on the set types that are most important to the computer scientist, namely maps and hash tables. In all cases, our coverage centers on providing an understanding of the performance, behaviors, and characteristics of each type.

Chapter 9, one of the most important, provides in-depth coverage of the Java Collection Framework, a set of classes that provides functionality for the data structures discussed in the previous three chapters. This framework includes multiple implementations of each structure along with methods for creating, accessing, and modifying them. Students today no longer need to always build these structures from scratch; instead, they can reuse existing code. Code reuse is one of the real benefits of object-oriented programming, but students rarely get to exploit this important characteristic. With the Java Collection Framework, students can take advantage of the existence of class libraries to experience the enormous improvements in productivity that come from the intelligent use of object-oriented programming, inheritance, and code reuse.

Part III. Modern Programming Practices (Chapters 10–13)

Not so long ago, topics such as recursion and algorithmic analysis were considered too advanced for a first class. Today, they are routinely included in CS 1, and it is not unusual to see them in a high school program. That is the way it is with many ideas in computer science—they enter the curriculum as advanced subject matter but quickly migrate to earlier courses.

This is now ready to happen in the second course as well. Today, a computer science student involved in developing software must know about and be comfortable with topics previously covered only in advanced classes, including:

- Exception handling
- Streams
- Threads
- Graphical user interfaces and event-driven programming
- Networking
- Security

Many of these topics are not part of the typical CS 2 course but are delayed until junior or senior electives in operating systems, networks, and computer graphics. However, most modern software projects involve a visual front-end, access to a network, and multiple threads of control. Therefore, we believe it is much more important today for beginning students to be introduced to exception handling, human-computer interaction, multithreaded software, and client/server programming than it is for them to implement a tournament tree or adjust pointers in a doubly linked list. While our treatment will be elementary and not intended to replace advanced courses, introducing these topics in our early courses can be very beneficial. By working with these ideas at the very beginning of their studies, rather than only at the end, students should feel more comfortable when they see them again in later courses. This is fully consistent with the CC2001 report, which recommends inclusion of such topics as event-driven programming, human-computer interaction, principles of networking, graphics, and fault tolerant computing in the second course.

Chapter 10 discusses how to write robust software and shows how the Java exception handling mechanism can be used to achieve this goal. This chapter also covers the topic of streams. This will allow students to build software that, without change, can take its input from an I/O device, a file, or a network connection. Chapter 11 looks at threads and how to write multithreaded code. It demonstrates, using the `java.threads` class, such basic operations as creating, scheduling, running, and coordinating threads. Chapter 12 introduces graphical user interfaces and asynchronous (i.e., event-driven) programming. It uses both the Abstract Window Toolkit (`java.awt`) and Swing (`javax.swing`) to present these ideas. It cannot possibly cover everything contained in these two massive packages; instead, it focuses on the most important concepts in interface design—the GUI class hierarchy, containers, components, layout, event listeners, and event handlers. By the end of the chapter, students should be able to build simple graphical interfaces and, most important, be prepared to read the Java documentation and learn more about the components not treated in this chapter. Finally, Chapter 13 covers TCP/IP networking using the `java.net` package. It again focuses on the key ideas of networking, such as sockets, connections, hosts, IP addresses, and datagrams. At the conclusion of this discussion, students will be able to write simple, but fully functional, client/server applications. This chapter also includes a short introduction to the topic of network security.

To summarize, the basic philosophy of this text is to build upon the foundation laid in CS 1 and present the concepts and techniques essential for working in a modern software development environment. These include the software life cycle, requirements and specification, object-oriented design, formal design notations, object-oriented programming, algorithmic analysis, data structures and data structure libraries, exception handling, streams, threads, graphical user interfaces, and network computing. This will provide students with an up-to-date view of computer science and software design while addressing the concerns of the CC2001 committee for inclusion of modern software design principles and practices in introductory courses.

Although this is not a book on Java programming, we have chosen to illustrate our ideas using Java. This is because of its enormous popularity as well as the expressive power of the language and the libraries it provides to developers. There is no other programming language that would allow us to so clearly and easily present the range of topics that we cover. For those students not familiar with Java, we have included an Appendix that covers the basic procedural aspects of the language—data types and declarations, assignment, conditionals, iteration, procedures, parameters, and program structure. Together with the material in the main body of the text, this will allow students to read and understand the examples presented in the book.

We strongly recommend that Part I be covered first, before any other material. To fully understand and appreciate the ideas contained in later chapters, students need a solid grasp of object-oriented concepts such as classes, interfaces, and inheritance. However, the material in Parts II and III can be presented in whatever order is deemed best. For example, instructors who wish to utilize exception handling during their discussion of data structures should first cover Chapter 10, "Exceptions and Streams," before diving into Part II. Similarly, if instructors want students to build visual front-ends for their software, then they should present the material in Chapter 12, "Graphical User Interfaces," early on in the course. The order of presentation of chapters in Parts II and III will depend on the interests and goals of the instructor and the particular class.

We would like to recognize a number of people who have provided invaluable assistance in the preparation of this book. We wish to thank the many reviewers of the original proposal: Jim Ball of Indiana State University, Essam El-Kwae of the University of North Carolina at Charlotte, Steven Huss-Lederman of Beloit College, Daniel G. Schwartz of Florida State University, and Henry Walker of Grinnell College. They helped us to organize our thoughts and create a more well-structured and useful text. We also want to thank those people who read the early drafts of chapters and provided valuable comments and criticisms—Hans-Peter Bischof, Jorge Díaz-Herrera,

Hank Etlinger, Jim Fink, Edith Hemaspaandra, Mike Lutz, Fernando Naveda, Laura Neureuter, Rod Tosten, and Jim Vallino. Many thanks to our editor, Kallie Swanson of Brooks/Cole, who was there with support whenever we asked for it, and who was invaluable in seeing this project through to its successful completion. A special thanks goes to Mr. John Mikucki. Originally hired to assist in writing code, he became much more—a programmer, a sounding board for ideas, and a thoughtful critic whenever he felt that we were not living up to our own high standards of software development. To all of these individuals, we say many thanks for helping us with the enormous undertaking.

Paul T. Tymann
G. Michael Schneider

CHAPTER 1

Overview of Modern Software Development

1.1 INTRODUCTION

This is a text on modern topics in software development, and it is intended for use in a second course in computer science. The first questions we must ask ourselves are: What does the phrase "modern software development" mean? What are the appropriate topics to include in such a text, and why are they important?

In your first computer science course, you probably spent a good deal of time learning some basic algorithmic concepts and the syntax and semantics of a programming language—perhaps C++, Visual Basic®, Scheme, or Java—in which to code and execute algorithms. You wrote a number of small programs, struggled to get them working correctly, and in the process, learned a lot about problem solving and programming, including such fundamental concepts as variables, scope, conditionals, iteration, recursion, functions, and parameters. You also gained valuable experience with algorithms to solve interesting problems in computer science such as searching, sorting, pattern matching, and root finding.

This emphasis (some might say overemphasis) on programming languages in a first course often leads to the mistaken impression that coding and debugging are the most important steps in software development and the most intellectually challenging part of modern software design. Nothing could be further from the truth. In fact, coding and debugging together may occupy as little as 15 to 20 percent of the overall time involved in the development of production software. Why is there this huge discrepancy between what occurs in the classroom and what actually happens in the real world?

The reason can be summarized in a single word—*size*. The programs written in a first computer science course usually contain about 100 to 300 lines of code, depending on the programming language and the problem being solved. Even by the end of the semester, it is unusual to develop a program larger than 500 lines. When writing programs of this limited size, it is possible to keep all necessary implementation details in your head. You can easily remember what has been finished, what is in progress, and what still needs to be done; in a sense, you can keep the entire project in your mind. With small programs, you do not need a technical strategy or a management plan anymore than children need a business plan to run a neighborhood lemonade stand. Instead, you dive directly into the coding, making decisions about how to address problems as they occur and debugging on the fly.

The problem, however, is that software packages that solve important tasks are not a few hundred lines long, and the strategy used for writing small programs will not work as you move to larger and larger jobs. Just as the informal approach to running a lemonade stand does not work for a chain of franchised juice bars, the technique of coding immediately does not scale; that is, it is not workable with large projects, and it inevitably leads to frustration, errors, and unusable software. Figure 1.1 is a table of size categories for software along with the typical number of programmers for that size project and its duration from initial specification to delivery of the finished product. Although the numbers are only rough approximations, they do give a reasonably good idea of the enormous size of most modern software packages.

As you can see in Figure 1.1, the overwhelming majority of programs developed in a first course would be categorized as trivial. (Although try telling that to the student who has just spent many late-night hours in a computer lab struggling to get his

Category	Programmers	Duration	Product Size (Lines of Code)
Trivial	1	1–4 weeks	<500
Small	1–2	1–6 months	500–3,000
Medium	2–5	6 months–2 years	3,000–20,000
Large	5–20	2–3 years	20,000–100,000
Very large	20–200	3–6 years	100,000–1,000,000
Extremely large	>200	>6 years	> 1,000,000

FIGURE 1.1 Size categories of software products

or her program working!) Even by the end of a student's 4-year computer science program, it would be unusual to develop a program beyond the small category. However, virtually all real-world software is neither trivial nor small but falls into the medium, large, very large, and even extremely large categories of Figure 1.1. It would contain tens or hundreds of thousands of lines of code and occupy dozens or more programmers for periods of months or years. This includes such well-known packages as compilers, operating systems, productivity software, telecommunications protocols, database programs, and e-commerce applications.

How do we approach problems of such enormous magnitude? How can we implement correct, efficient, user-friendly software, which contains thousands or even millions of lines, and do it in a way that allows it to be quickly and easily modified when we are faced with unexpected errors or proposed changes? Indeed, the answers to these difficult but important questions will occupy us for the remainder of the text.

While we will not ask you to develop software containing tens of thousands of lines of code (and we assume that neither will your instructor), the ideas presented here, unlike the methods used in a first course, *will* scale and *will* allow you to intellectually manage the massive projects that you will almost certainly encounter in your future activities.

1.2 THE SOFTWARE LIFE CYCLE

The first point to realize is that there is a great deal of preparatory work that must be done, and done well, before we even think about writing code. This preparatory work involves specifying the problem, designing the overall structure of the proposed solution, and selecting and analyzing the algorithms and data structures that we will use in our solution. This is not dissimilar to the task of building a new house. It would be foolhardy to immediately pick up hammer, nails, and lumber and start putting up walls. One can only imagine what would be produced. Instead, there is a great deal of thinking, budgeting, planning, and designing that must be done first, culminating in a set of detailed architectural blueprints that lay out the exact project specifications.

Similarly, there is a good deal of work that must be done after the software has been completed. This work involves activities such as testing, documentation, support, and maintenance. Again, using our housing example, these follow-up steps are

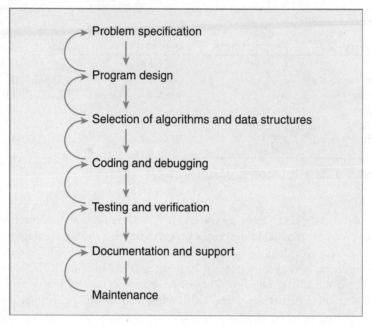

FIGURE 1.2 Software life cycle

equivalent to inspecting the house to ensure there are no construction flaws and making additions or modifications to the original home as your family size increases.

There is no universal agreement on the exact sequence of steps involved in software development, but there is general agreement on certain essential operations that must be successfully completed to produce correct, efficient, and user-friendly software. This sequence of operations is called the **software life cycle**, and it is diagrammed in Figure 1.2. The following sections will discuss each of the phases included in Figure 1.2 and identify the chapters in this text that treat each topic in more detail.

◆ 1.2.1 Problem Specifications

The **problem specification phase** involves the creation of a complete, accurate, and unambiguous statement of the exact problem to be solved. There is an old saying in computer science that it is not enough to solve the problem *correctly*; you must also solve the *correct problem*. Before starting any design work, it is imperative that you know exactly what to do, and there must be complete and total agreement between user and developer about exactly what will be produced. It doesn't do anyone any good to build a working program if it does not provide the desired results.

What does it mean to "specify a problem"? How do we clearly and unambiguously describe what tasks must be done? The answer is that we describe a problem by listing the *inputs* that will be provided to the program and, for each of these inputs, exactly what *output* the program will produce. Thus, a **problem specification document** is simply an *input/output document* that says, "If you give me *X*, I will give you

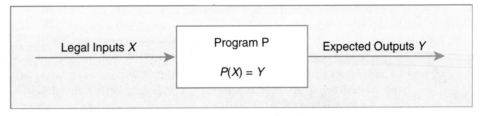

FIGURE 1.3(a) Basic structure of a problem specification document

back Y," as diagrammed in Figure 1.3(a). Notice that the specification document says nothing at all about how X is transformed into Y.

In addition to input/output specifications, this document also contains information on delivery date, budget constraints, performance requirements, and acceptance criteria.

In an academic environment, you should be quite familiar with the concept of a specification document, although in this context you are more likely to call it a homework assignment. A typical classroom project is, just like Figure 1.3(a), a document that describes some inputs and tells you to write a program that produces specific outputs from these given inputs and do it by a given date. Thus, in a classroom setting, the first phase of software development is not done by students but by the instructor who individually determines the exact problem to be solved. In real life, that is of course not the case, and it will be necessary for you to flesh out a complete problem statement through meetings and interviews with potential users.

Unfortunately, although it is easy to describe what a problem specification document is, it is difficult to create a good one. In fact, an enormous number of software errors occur because of incomplete, inaccurate, and ambiguous specifications. There are at least three reasons for these problems.

Problem 1: The persons specifying the problem may not describe it accurately and may frequently change their mind about what they want done.

Problem specifications are created by talking with users to find out what they want. Some users will be very certain about their needs, and they will be able to describe the problem thoroughly and accurately. Unfortunately, most users are not like that. They will forget essential details, give misleading or incorrect information, and repeatedly change their mind about how the software should function. This makes it extremely difficult to create accurate specifications and leads to errors, omissions, cost overruns, and missed deadlines.

A technique called **rapid prototyping** is often used to help users decide what they really want. The software developer constructs a model, or prototype, of the planned software. The prototype contains a user interface that simulates the look and feel of the software when completed, but it has no functionality. It is only a "false front." However, seeing an actual interface along with a proposed set of operations can help users identify in their own mind what functions they really want, what may be missing, and what might be done in a better way. These prototypes can usually be built quite quickly, and they can help produce a more accurate description of program behavior.

The problem specification document is a contract between user and developer. The developer agrees to build software that operates exactly as described in this document, and the user agrees to accept it. Changes made after the specifications have been accepted will be difficult and expensive to fix—much like changes in the design of a new home after the blueprints have been drawn or, even worse, after the walls have started going up. It is absolutely critical that, before any design work begins, everyone is satisfied with the problem description contained in the specification document.

Problem 2: It is necessary to include a description of the program's behavior for every possible input, not just the expected ones.

When giving directions or guidelines to a person, we can assume a certain level of common sense and omit instructions that anyone would obviously know how to handle. For example, when describing how to drive a car, we usually don't include the commands "open the door" and "get into the driver's seat" before instructing you on how to start the engine. Similarly we do not provide information on what to do if someone has lost his or her keys. However, computer programs do not have common sense, and it is necessary to describe the desired behavior of the software for *all* inputs, even the most unexpected ones. For example, if you are developing a program to sort a set of numbers, you need to know exactly what to do if one or more inputs is nonnumeric (e.g., three point five, XXVII) or if there is no input at all. It is not unusual for the majority of pages in a problem specification document to be devoted to describing unusual, unexpected, and illegal inputs and specifying the appropriate response to each. This leads to the more realistic diagram of a problem specification document shown in Figure 1.3(b).

Problem 3: Natural language (English, in our case) is a poor choice of representations for producing accurate specifications, but it is the one almost universally used.

English (or Spanish, Chinese, Swahili, . . .) is a rich language full of contextual nuances, multiple meanings, and shades of interpretation. That is wonderful if you are writing poetry or fiction, but it is horrible if you are trying to produce accurate specifications. For example, assume that a problem specification document contains

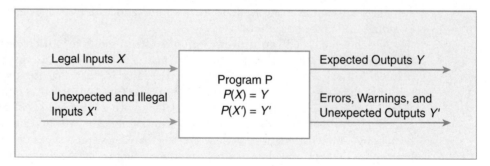

FIGURE 1.3(b) More realistic diagram of a problem specification document

the phrase, "Sum up all values in the N-element list L that are between 1 and 100." Does that include the numbers 1 and 100 themselves? Is the first element in the list L_0 or L_1? The answers to these questions are not clear from the preceding statement, and that can lead to incorrect results. It would have been more accurate to write this problem statement as:

$$\sum_{i=0}^{N-1} L_i \ni [(L_i \geq 1) \wedge (L_i \leq 100)]$$

Now the problem statement is clear and unambiguous if you understand the mathematical notation. In fact, that is the main problem with **formal specification languages,** such as the mathematical notation shown. They are much more precise than natural languages, but they may be more difficult for people to read and interpret. On the other hand, natural languages are easy to read, but they lack the high level of precision so necessary for writing good specifications. In this text, we will use a formalized notation called **UML,** for **Unified Modeling Language,** as a way to visually diagram the relationships and dependencies between the various sections in our programs.

Let's do an example that illustrates the problems involved in writing clear and unambiguous problems specifications. Here is a simple statement of a problem, not unlike what you might have been asked to do as a project in your first computer science class:

> *You will be given an N-element array of numbers A and a key value X. If X occurs anywhere within the array A, then return the position in A where X occurs. If X does not occur anywhere within A, then return the position of the entry in A whose value is closest to that of X.*

It may seem simple enough, but there are a number of uncertainties lurking within this problem statement. For example:

1. We are asked to return the "position" of a value within the list A. But are the positions within the list numbered 0, 1, 2, . . . as in C++ and Java, or are they numbered 1, 2, 3, . . . as they are in BASIC?

2. What if X occurs multiple times within A? Assume $X = 8$ and the list A contains the six values 24, 7, 8, 13, 6, 8. Should we return a 2 (assuming the first item in A is position 0)? Should we return a 5? Should we return both 2 and 5?

3. In the last sentence, what does the word *closest* mean? Does it mean *lexicographically* closest—that is, the greatest number of identical digits in the same position? In that case, the number 999 is closer to 899 than 1,000 because there are two of three matching digits. Or does it mean *numerically* closest—that is, the smallest value of $|A_i - X|$. In that case, 999 is closer to 1,000 than 899 because there is a difference of only 1 rather than 100.

4. What if the list A is empty—that is, $N = 0$? Then nothing in A can be closest to X regardless of the meaning of the word *closest.*

In this simple problem statement, we identified at least four uncertainties or ambiguities, each of which could, if not further clarified, lead to errors in the finished program. (Exercise 3 at the end of the chapter asks you to identify additional problems that may exist in the original specification.) Imagine the number of problems that could occur in a real-world specification document containing dozens or hundreds of pages.

Writing good specifications is a difficult but essential first step in software development, although it is beyond the scope of this text. Instead, we will assume that all the programs you are asked to develop are based on complete and accurate specifications; there will never be uncertainty about what you are supposed to do. Future classes in software engineering will address this important issue in much greater detail.

◆ 1.2.2 Program Design

When the specification document is completed and approved, we can move on to the next phase in the software development process called **program design**. This is where we specify an integrated set of components that will solve the problem contained in the specification document of Section 1.2.1. By the term **component** we mean a separately compiled program unit. Depending on the language, a component may go by such names as function, procedure, class, template, package, or interface. However, regardless of what it is called, it serves the same purpose: helping to organize, plan, and manage the upcoming coding task. Program design is a **divide and conquer** operation in which a single large problem is divided into a number of smaller and simpler subproblems. It is exactly like outlining a paper before writing it. This modularization step is essential because it is virtually impossible to implement a program containing thousands of lines without some type of "master plan" to help us understand what needs to be done.

For each component in our solution, we must include the following three items:

- ◆ the **interface**: How this component is invoked by other units.
- ◆ the **preconditions**: What conditions must initially be true when this component is invoked by another unit.
- ◆ the **postconditions**: What conditions will be true when the component finishes, assuming that all the preconditions have been met.

The collection of all component specifications is called a **program design document**.

Just as the problem specification document is a contract between user and developer, the pre- and postconditions are a contract between this program unit and any other unit that calls it. The contract says if you guarantee that all preconditions are true, I guarantee that when I finish execution and return, all postconditions will be true.

Here is an example of what a typical module specification might look like:

```
/* preconditions:  X has been assigned a positive real value > 0.0 and
                    n has been assigned a positive integer value ≥ 1.
   postconditions: If the preconditions have been met, positivePower
                   returns the floating point value Xⁿ. Otherwise it
                   returns -1.0.
*/

    public static float positivePower(float x, int n);
```

The most interesting question about program design is how we approach this decomposition process. How can we take problem P and subdivide it into pieces A, B, C, and D that, together, solve the problem? How do we know that this choice of units is better than subdividing P into W, X, Y, and Z instead?

There are a number of different ways to carry out this design process. In the early days of programming, the most widely used approach to program design was called **top-down design**, and it was based on decomposing the problem *functionally*. That is, we carefully examine the activities taking place and then design program units that are each responsible for a single, coherent, well-defined task. For example, assume that we are designing a program to simulate a banking environment in which customers enter the bank, stand in a waiting line, carry out some transactions, and then leave. The bank plans to use this program to determine how many tellers to hire in its new branch office to provide the highest level of customer service at the lowest cost.

From a purely functional point of view, we might see the problem as composed of four basic functions: customer arrivals, transaction processing, customer departures, and printing the final results. Thus, our first-level design might look like this:

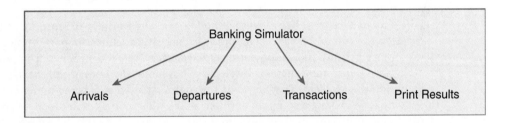

When we have specified the components at this level, we further subdivide the second-level routines based on the functions they perform. For example, the Arrivals routine might input the type and amount of the transaction and validate that this transaction is legal. The Transaction handler might include Process Deposit and Process Withdrawal units to handle these two transaction types. Now our software design will have expanded to the following:

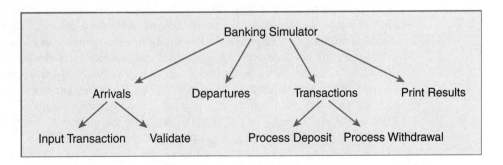

This refinement process continues until we have described the entire problem in terms of a collection of small, simple, and easily understood components that do not need to be further decomposed. We would then be ready to begin the next phase.

The top-down design process does work, and indeed, it was the methodology used in software design for many years. Unfortunately, it suffers from a serious problem: a difficulty in modifying the final program to meet new and unexpected needs. For example, what if, after our banking simulator was completed, we added a new transaction type—say, loan payments—which caused us to change how we represent transactions. Looking at the design document we have created, let's ask ourselves which routines might possibly be affected by this change. Certainly, we will need to modify both Input Transaction and Validate because they both check the transaction type. The Transaction handler needs to be aware of all the different kinds of transactions to activate the correct program, so we will probably need to make some modifications here. Finally, the details of loan payments will probably be included in the final output, so Print Results may have to undergo modification as well.

The point is that when you decompose a problem along functional lines, many different program units need to have knowledge of the internal details of the data being manipulated. In our case, since many different units examined the transaction type field, all of them needed to know how transactions were represented internally. Therefore, our change to the transaction code propagated throughout the program. This makes modifications difficult, and even tiny changes can cause massive headaches.

Since the early 1990s, a new methodology, called **object-oriented design**, has replaced the top-down approach, and it is currently the most important and widely used design technique. In object-oriented design, the program is decomposed not along the lines of the functions carried out but along the lines of the *entities* that exist within the problem. That is, we do not look first at what is being done, but at who is doing it. We create a component called a **class** that models each distinct type of entity in our problem. Then we instantiate specific instances of these classes called **objects**. In the case of our banking simulation, we might choose to decompose our program into the following four classes:

```
Customers

Waiting Lines

Tellers

Transactions
```

Once we have decided on the classes in our design, we then describe the functionality of these classes—that is, the operations that every object in that class is capable of performing. For example, every waiting line must be able to add a new customer to the end of the line and remove its first customer. It must also be able to respond to the questions "Are you empty?" and "Are you full?" These operations are called **methods** in object-oriented terminology, and selecting the appropriate set of methods for each class is one of the key parts of object-oriented design.

Figure 1.4 lists some of the operations that might be included in an object-oriented design approach to our banking simulation problem.

We can now begin to see the advantages of an object-based decomposition of a problem. Information about transactions is obtained not by looking into the internal structure of the data items but by asking the transaction object to tell you this information. For example, if we need to print a report listing the type and amount of a transaction T, it might be done like this:

Class:	`WaitingLine`	
Methods:	`putAtEnd(c)`	Put a new customer c at the end of this line.
	`c = getFirstCustomer()`	Remove the first customer in this line; return it in c.
	`isEmpty()`	True if this line is empty; false otherwise.
	`isFull()`	True if this line is full; false otherwise.
Class:	`Teller`	
Methods:	`isBusy()`	True if this teller is busy; false otherwise.
	`serve(c)`	This teller begins serving customer c.
Class:	`Customer`	
Methods:	`depart()`	A customer leaves the bank.
Class:	`Transaction`	
Method:	`t = transactionType()`	Return the type of this transaction.
	`a = transactionAmount()`	Return the dollar amount of this transaction.

FIGURE 1.4 Example of object-oriented design

```
type = T.transactionType();   // Ask T for its type
amt = T.transactionAmount();  // Ask T for its amount
printResults(type, amt);      // Output the results
```

The component requesting this information is isolated from any knowledge of the internal workings of how we choose to represent transactions. Furthermore, if we change that internal representation, the preceding three lines of code would not be affected in any way.

Similarly, if we want to know if waiting line *w* is or is not empty, we do not look to see if some linked list pointer is **null** or an array index is 0. These operations would again leave us vulnerable to a change in the way that the programmer has chosen to implement the waiting line w. Instead, we simply ask the waiting line itself to tell us if it is or is not empty:

```
boolean b = w.isEmpty();    // ask w if it is or is not empty
```

As both of these examples demonstrate, the basic style of programming in an object-oriented environment is by exchanging information between objects. Figure 1.5 shows a typical piece of object-oriented code as it might appear using some of the methods listed in Figure 1.4.

Even though you may be unfamiliar with the Java syntax in Figure 1.5, you should be able to appreciate the clarity of the object-oriented programming style. Each of the objects in the system—c, w, joe—can send messages to other objects and respond either to inquiries about its current state or to requests to change state. Only the object itself knows how it carries out these requests; the other objects are simply given a response.

```
Customer c;            // c will refer to a customer
WaitingLine w;         // w is where customers wait for a teller
Teller joe;            // joe will be our bank teller

w = new WaitingLine(); // w refers to a new waiting line
joe = new Teller();    // joe refers to a new teller object
c = new Customer();    // c refers to a newly-created customer

// Is the teller serving someone right now?

if ( joe.isBusy() ) {
    // See if there is room in the line

    if ( w.isFull() ) {
        // The line is full, so the customer can't wait
        // instead the customer must leave.
        c.depart();
    }
    else {
        // The line is not full, so the customer can wait.
        // Put the customer at the end of the line.
        w.putAtEnd(c);
    }
}
else {
    // The teller is not busy so the customer can be served.
    joe.serve(c); // serve the customer
    c.depart();   // after service, the customer leaves the bank
}
```

FIGURE 1.5 Example of object-oriented programming style

Part I, Chapters 2–4, will spend a good deal of time looking at the object-oriented design philosophy. Chapter 2 investigates object-oriented design, including such fundamental concepts as classes, objects, behavior, state, and inheritance. Chapter 3 looks at object-oriented programming—specifically, those features of the Java programming language that support the ideas and concepts first presented in Chapter 2. Java is a true object-oriented programming language designed from the very start to support the object-oriented design philosophy. Finally, Chapter 4 will put these ideas together in a case study that uses the object-oriented design and programming techniques that have been presented. This case study will clearly demonstrate how a large, complex software project (although still small according to Figure 1.1) can be organized and managed using a modern software design strategy.

◆ 1.2.3 Algorithms and Data Structures

Our task is now laid out before us. The problem has been decomposed into a set of classes, each one representing a distinct entity in our solution. Each class has a set of methods representing the operations that objects of this class are able to perform, and each of these methods is clearly specified in terms of its pre- and postconditions.

For example, the waiting line class mentioned in Figure 1.4 includes a method called putAtEnd() that might behave as follows:

```
/**
 * Preconditions:   The waiting line carrying out this operation is not
 *                  full, and c refers to a customer object.
 * Postconditions:  If the line is not full, then customer c has been
 *                  added to the end of the line. If the line is full,
 *                  then the method throws a LineFullException.
 */

public void putAtEnd( Customer c ) throws LineFullException;
```

There may be hundreds or thousands of such module specifications in a typical design document, and each one must be implemented and tested for correctness.

An important decision that needs to be made before we start coding is selecting the data structures we will use to represent our data objects and choosing the algorithms that will access and modify these data structures. As you will learn in Chapter 5, software efficiency is most strongly influenced by the data structures and algorithms selected to manipulate the data, not by our choice of programming language, not by how well the code is written, and not by the speed of the machine on which the program is run. An efficient algorithm will remain efficient no matter how inelegantly it is written, and no amount of programming cleverness or machine speed can turn an inefficient method into an efficient one. That is why we will spend a good deal of time on the topic of data structures and the different techniques available for storing and representing information.

For example, referring to the previous specification of putAtEnd(), we could choose to implement the waiting line as an array, as shown in Figure 1.6(a) or we

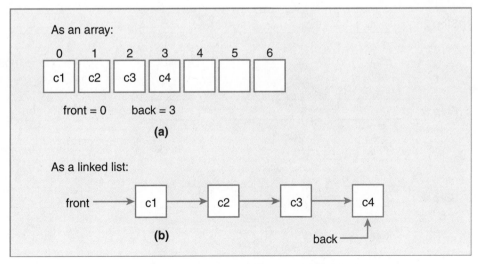

FIGURE 1.6 Different ways of implementing a waiting line

might opt to implement it as a linked list, as shown in Figure 1.6(b). Both diagrams show a waiting line containing four individuals, c1, c2, c3, and c4, in just that order.

If we choose to represent our waiting line as an array, then the `putAtEnd()` operation can, if there is room, be easily implemented in only two steps:

```
back = (back + 1) % arraySize; // add 1 to back,
                               // modulo the array size
a[back] = c;        // put customer c at the end of the line
```

However, if the array is full, then we have made a bad choice. An array is a static data structure that cannot be dynamically enlarged beyond the number of spaces allocated when it was first created.

If the maximum size of the waiting line is not known, then we might be better off selecting the linked list representation, which does not place an upper bound on the maximum number of customers as long as memory is available. Now our `putAtEnd()` algorithm would behave as shown in Figure 1.7:

Step 1: Get a new node to hold this customer.

Step 2: Put the customer object c into the data field of this new node and a null (Λ) into the next field, where null means it is not pointing at anything.

Step 3: Reset the next field of the node currently pointed at by back so that it now points at this new node

Step 4: Reset the back pointer so that it now points at this new node.

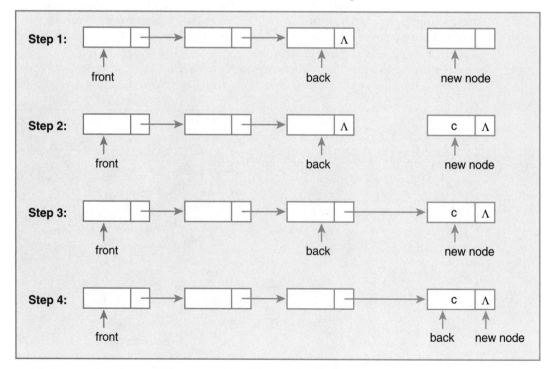

FIGURE 1.7 Implementing `putAtEnd()` using a list

This is still an efficient operation that takes only four steps, but notice how much more memory is required to represent the waiting line. For every customer in the list, we now need a field that points to the next customer in line. This field was not needed when we used an array. If there are only a few individuals in line, it is a trivial amount of memory and would not be a problem. However, if the line contained tens or hundreds of thousands of customers (e.g., a list of people waiting to access a popular Web site), then this choice will require a great deal of extra memory.

Is there another way to represent a waiting line that does not suffer from either the problem of fixed size or extra memory but that still allows the putAtEnd() operation to be implemented in an efficient manner? These are exactly the questions that we will study in Part II, Chapters 5–9, which investigate different methods of data representation, including linear data structures (Chapter 6), hierarchical structures (Chapter 7), and set and graph structures (Chapter 8). Finally, Chapter 9 will introduce a set of Java classes, called the **Java Collection Framework**, that automatically provides many of these data structures, including such important representations as maps, lists, sets, and tables.

◆ 1.2.4 Coding and Debugging

Coding is the software development phase with which you are undoubtedly most familiar, as it is covered extensively in a first computer science course. In this text, we will be using Java, which may or may not be the programming language you studied in the first course. If it is, then you will have no problem understanding the code. If your first language was something other than Java, we have included an Appendix, entitled Basic Java Syntax, which covers the basic "procedural" concepts of the language—declarations, assignment, input/output, conditionals, iteration, functions, and parameters. If you are not familiar with Java, you should carefully review that material before continuing with the remainder of the text.

Java was first developed in 1991 by James Gosling of Sun® Microsystems Inc. It was not originally conceived as a programming vehicle for traditional applications. Instead, Sun wanted to create a "platform-independent" environment to control **embedded systems**—microprocessors located inside consumer devices such as televisions, microwaves, and coffeemakers. Unfortunately, the programmable consumer electronics market of the early 1990s was not as lucrative as Sun had expected, and the Java language project was in danger of being cancelled. At about the same time, however, another application exploded onto the marketplace—the World Wide Web. Sun quickly realized that Java's architecturally neutral design made it a perfect language for getting dynamic content into Web pages. Using Java, it is possible to write a small program (called an **applet**) and embed it into a Web page. When someone later accesses this page, the applet is transmitted along with the HTML commands and is executed on the client's computer regardless of its make or model.

Sun announced Java to the world in May 1995, and it quickly generated enormous interest because of its commercial possibilities. In the years since that initial appearance, it has become one of the most widely used programming languages in the world, in both the commercial and the academic marketplaces.

If it were only a question of using Java to build applets and "sexy" Web pages, the language would hold little interest in academic computer science. However, there are other reasons Java has become such an important classroom tool for teaching modern software development:

> *Java is a true object-oriented language designed from the start to support the concepts of object-oriented design.*

Object-oriented design became popular in the early to mid-1980s, well after the appearance of popular languages from the 1950s, 60s, and 70s such as Fortran, COBOL, BASIC, Pascal, and C. Therefore, if programmers in these older languages wanted to use these new object-oriented design principles, they would have to discard the language they currently used and learn a new one. (There was an object-oriented language available at that time called Smalltalk.) Most programmers did not want to learn a totally new language, so designers took these existing languages and created object-oriented versions of them by tacking on features. This is exactly what happened with Objective C and C++, both object-oriented extensions to C. However, it was usually quite obvious that these were quick-and-dirty "patch jobs," created to allow object-oriented principles to be grafted onto existing procedural languages.

Java, however, is a true object-oriented language, not a hastily crafted extension, and the class concept is central to the design of the entire language. With Java, you will be learning a modern programming language created from the start to fully incorporate the capabilities and techniques of object-oriented design. (Java is not the only modern object-oriented programming language. However, it is certainly the most popular and widely used.)

> *Java includes an enormous number of standard classes that automatically provide a range of important and useful services.*

One of the issues studied by computer scientists is **software productivity**—investigating ways to increase the amount of correct, working code that can be produced by a programmer in a given time period. In the early days of computing, say 1950 through about 1980, the operational principle of software design was: "Machines are costly, programmers are cheap, so optimize for computer efficiency." In this environment, it would be appropriate to throw dozens or hundreds of programmers at a task and let them take as long as necessary, as long as their programs fully and efficiently utilized the multimillion-dollar computer on which they were run.

That situation is totally reversed. Computers now cost as little as $500 or $1,000, but the salary of the people who develop the software for these machines may exceed $100,000 per year. In this environment, our new goal is to maximize the productivity of each of those highly trained and very expensive individuals.

How can we increase a programmer's productivity? One way is through **software reuse**—making use of software that already exists rather than developing it from scratch. It is certainly a lot faster and more efficient to take a finished program out of a library than to design and code it yourself. Unfortunately, while software reuse is a highly desirable goal, it has not yet made much of an impact. One reason is that complete programs are not always an easily sharable "chunk" of code because they may incorporate application-specific material not transferable to other situations. The time it might take to modify an existing program to fit your specific needs may be more than it would take to develop a totally new program.

However, classes are an ideal unit of sharing, as they do not address the entire problem but only a small component of a problem that typically occurs repeatedly in computing applications. Using the banking simulation example discussed earlier, if we have already developed a waiting line class and placed it in a library, then we could reuse that class with any future application that included a waiting line data structure, greatly simplifying our task and reducing development time.

The Java environment includes a huge library of classes that address a number of commonly occurring aspects of programming, such as error handling, graphics, user interface design, file input/output, networking, security, multitasking, and cryptography, to name just a few. Java 1.0, the first public version of the language, contained 212 distinct classes, and Java 1.1 raised that number to 504. Java 1.2 (later renamed Java 2) had 1,520 classes in 59 different packages. The most recent version, the 1.4 release of Java 2 Standard Edition, includes 2,757 classes in 135 packages—a truly monumental amount of already available software, and future releases will almost certainly expand on these numbers. We have already mentioned one of these groups of classes—the Java Collection Framework—and we will make use of many more built-in classes throughout the remainder of this text.

Although there is no possible way to discuss all of these classes, or even a fraction, we will be highlighting some of the important and useful services provided automatically within the standard Java libraries. Our goal will be to make you realize that, in terms of modern software development, your first thought during the coding phase should not necessarily be "How do I write it?" but, instead, "Where can I find it?" If you are able to use code that has already been written, debugged, and tested, your productivity will increase manyfold, and the cost of software development will be dramatically reduced.

Java contains a wide range of language features that are vitally important in modern software development practices.

Because Java was created in the 1990s, rather than the 60s, 70s, or 80s, its designers had an opportunity to think about what new features would be needed by software developers in the 21st century, and then include those features in the initial design of the language and its environment. In most cases, they were absolutely correct, and Java contains many features not found in other languages, which are becoming more and more important in the design of correct, cost-efficient, maintainable code. We will be looking at these features in Part III of this text, Chapters 10–13, entitled Contemporary Programming Techniques. Here are some of these important new ideas.

1. Exceptions. You know how frustrated you become when a program crashes or halts with a weird, unfathomable error message. Computing is becoming more and more critical to the proper functioning of society, and software failures are no longer just frustrating; they can lead to financial ruin or even catastrophic disasters. (Imagine a business without the ability to handle customer inputs or an airplane unable to fly.) All modern software must be able to deal with faults (errors, failure, and unexpected consequences) in a planned, orderly way. It is no longer considered acceptable to write:

```
if (code < 0)      // transaction code is illegal
    errorFlag = true;
else {
    errorFlag = false;
    activateHandler(code); // code is legal
}
```

and then hope and pray that the person who invoked your program remembers to check the value of errorFlag before assuming that the transaction has been correctly processed.

Exception handling is a powerful and effective way to deal with errors, failures, and other unexpected circumstances that occur during the execution of a program. Java includes a number of built-in exceptions to deal with common error conditions as well as the capability for users to define and handle their own exception conditions. Exceptions will be discussed in detail in Chapter 10.

2. Streams. As commercial and business applications become more "information centered," it becomes increasingly important for programming languages to deal with data transmitted to and from external files for the purposes of archival storage. Java contains a powerful set of classes for handling file input and output in many different formats. Java lets the programmer view the stored information as streams of either bytes or characters. It also provides classes to deal with random access storage, buffering, data compression, type conversion, and data encryption. We will take an in-depth look at how Java deals with streams and external files in Chapter 10.

3. Threads. Most existing languages are sequential in nature, and their programs execute serially, one statement at a time, from beginning to end. That has been the standard mode of computing from its very earliest days. However, this situation is changing, and to a greater degree, modern high-speed desktop computers have the ability to carry out multiple tasks at once. You use this capability whenever you start up a print job and then, instead of waiting for it to complete, immediately begin reading your email or surfing the Web.

A **thread** is a program unit in execution, and the capability of having more than one thread executing at the same time is called, naturally enough, **multithreading.** If your computer has more than one processor, then each thread can execute in **parallel,** with each one running on its own separate processor. If your computer has only a single processor, we can still do multithreading, but the threads have to "take turns." Each thread runs for a while and then stops to allow the other thread to execute for a while. This "round-robin" mode of execution is called **concurrent processing**.

In the "olden days" of computing (prior to the 1990s) statements for supporting concurrency and parallelism were rarely included as part of a programming language or its environment. The only way to implement these services was by accessing complex operating system primitives that were available to only the most advanced and experienced of programmers. It was certainly not a topic that would be introduced to first-year computer science students. However, most modern software packages make extensive use of both concurrency and parallelism, and threads are no longer a topic appropriate only for advanced students. Instead, they should be introduced in first-year programming classes so that students have seen these concepts and feel comfortable with them when discussed more fully in later classes.

Java includes an extensive set of library operations for creating, scheduling, executing, suspending, and terminating threads. These operations are included in the **Thread** class, and they will be discussed in Chapter 11. Our goal is not to make you an expert in multithreading but to introduce you to the concepts and capabilities of parallelism and concurrency. These ideas will be discussed at much greater length in later computer science classes such as operating systems, distributed systems, and parallel processing.

4. Graphical User Interfaces. Most software applications developed in the last few years use a **graphical user interface** (GUI, pronounced goo-eey) to interact with users. No programming environment can claim to be modern and up-to-date if it does not include an extensive array of components for building high-quality user interfaces like the one shown in Figure 1.8. These components allow users to create visual features such as windows, buttons, text fields, labels, choice boxes, check boxes, and lists. In addition, the components allow you to control the placement, size, and color of these components to customize the "look and feel" of your interface.

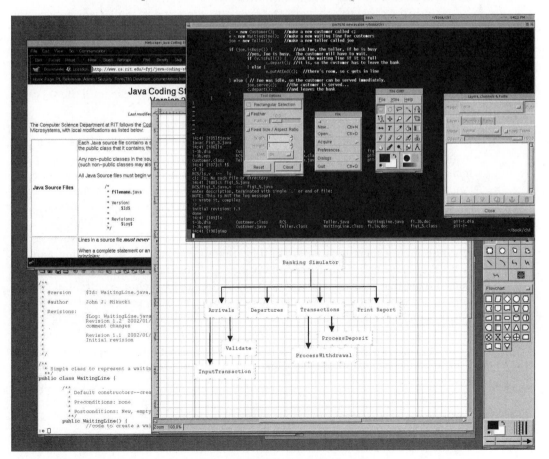

FIGURE 1.8 Example of a modern graphical user interface

Java includes a powerful collection of routines called the **Abstract Window Toolkit,** which is found in the package **java.awt.** This package, containing literally dozens of classes, allows users to create and manipulate the types of interfaces shown in Figure 1.8. There is a second package of classes called **Swing** that contains an even more powerful set of visual components. These GUI toolkits will be discussed at length in Chapter 12.

5. Networking. Many programs today are "net-centric," which means that they work in tandem with a computer network such as the Internet. We are all familiar with email, file transfer, and Web browsers, which have been around for a while. More recently, we have seen an explosion of new applications like search engines, online access to remote data bases, dynamic Web pages, chat rooms, Internet TV and telephone, remote sensing, and a host of other client/server applications. In addition, e-commerce and e-banking, which would not exist without networks, are multibillion-dollar industries. Today it is rare for a software application to function in a standalone fashion without regard for or concern with issues of data communications. Even a simple word processing application must be designed to produce files that can be attached to an email message and transmitted across a network.

As was the case with threads, statements to support and implement networking and data communications were generally not part of older programming languages or environments, and it was necessary to access the operating system to obtain these services. Therefore, it was a topic that was again seen as appropriate only for advanced students and was not part of the beginning curriculum. Students were not introduced to the underlying software and hardware technologies of networks until the very end of their computer science studies.

However, Java includes the package **java.net** that allows users to easily develop powerful client/server network applications using the TCP/IP and UDP network protocols. These classes are easy to explain and understand, and it is now appropriate to include these ideas in the very first year of study. As before, our goal is not to make you networking experts, but we do want to introduce you to topics that are becoming critically important in modern software development—topics such as sockets, connections, packets, datagrams, clients, servers, and protocols. This will allow you to be familiar and comfortable with these ideas when they reappear in classes such as networking, data communications, and distributed computing. Networking and the java.net package will be discussed in Chapter 13. This chapter will also briefly introduce a topic that is closely related to networking, and which is an essential component of any modern networking software package, the concept of **security**.

In summary, we are using Java because it is a true object-oriented language, it has class libraries that provide an enormous range of important services, and it has many new language features that allow us to develop fault-tolerant, visually oriented, multithreaded, net-centric programs. Now that really does represent a modern software development environment!

◆ **1.2.5** Testing and Verification

You have written your program, debugged it, and gotten it to work correctly on a single data case. Does that mean it is correct? Of course not. It means that you are ready to begin the next phase of software development—testing and verification—where you demonstrate that the program is indeed correct and performs exactly as described in the problem specification document of Section 1.2.1. There are two quite different ways of demonstrating that correctness. One is very powerful but difficult and controversial, and the other is easier but much less powerful.

Program verification is a technique of formally proving the correctness of a program, much as you would prove the truth of a geometric theorem or an algebraic formula. You develop the correctness proof of the program at the same time as you write the code itself. As you develop the code, you formally argue that given input I, the output O of that code segment is identical to the output required by the specification document for that input. As you can imagine, this is a difficult task, but if it can be done, you have essentially proved that the program is correct—that is, it will work properly for every input, even those not tested.

Let's do a small example. The following is a code segment that is supposed to sum the values in array A from A[1] to A[N], for any $N \geq 1$. Let's formally prove that it does what it is supposed to do.

```
j = 1;
sum = A[1];
while (j < N) {
    j = j + 1;
    sum = sum + A[j];
}
```

First, we will add preconditions, as comments to the code, that describe what must be true initially for this code to operate correctly. In our case, N must be greater than or equal to 1, and the elements of A from A[1] to A[N] must all have been assigned a value.

```
// N ≥ 1 and A[1] , . . . , A[N] are defined
j = 1;
sum = A[1];
while (j < N) {
    j = j + 1;
    sum = sum + A[j];
}
```

Next, we will specify the **loop invariant**—a condition that is true when the loop is first entered and that remains true after every iteration. In this case, the loop invariant is that the variable sum holds the sum of the first j elements in the array:

```
// N ≥ 1 and A[1] , . . . , A[N] are defined
j = 1;
sum = A[1];

// The loop invariant:
// sum = A[1] + A[2] + . . . + A[j], and (j ≤ N)
while (j < N) {
    j = j + 1;
```

```
    sum = sum + A[j];
    // sum = A[1] + A[2] + . . . + A[j], and (j ≤ N)
}
```

This invariant is obviously true on loop entry because j is initialized to 1 (which is less than or equal to N, given the precondition), and sum is set to A[1]. This condition remains true after each iteration, since the loop increments the value of j by 1 and adds the next array element to sum. We also know that (j ≤ N) because j must be strictly less than N before beginning the loop, and we add 1 to j, which can only make j less than or equal to N. Finally, we know that the loop must terminate since j is initialized to the integer 1, and N must be an integer value greater than or equal to 1. There are only a finite number of integer values between 1 and any finite value of N greater than or equal to 1. Therefore, the loop can only execute a finite number of times. When it exits, the condition (j < N) will be false. That is, j will be greater than or equal to N. This is called the **postcondition** of the loop, and we add this to our commentary.

```
// N ≥ 1 and A[1] , . . . , A[N] are defined
j = 1;
sum = A[1];

// The loop invariant:
// sum = A[1] + A[2] + . . . + A[j], and (j ≤ N)
while (j < N) {
    j = j + 1;
    sum = sum + A[j];
    // sum = A[1] + A[2] + . . . + A[j], and (j ≤ N)
}
// (j ≥ N)
```

However, the loop invariant said that (j ≤ N) after every pass through the loop, and now we have shown that on loop termination we have the postcondition (j ≥ N). The only way that both conditions can be true is if (j = N). For (j = N) our loop invariant, which said that sum = A[1] + A[2] + . . . + A[j] and (j ≤ N), reduces to:

```
// N ≥ 1 and A[1] , . . . , A[N] are defined
j = 1;
sum = A[1];

// The loop invariant:
// sum = A[1] + A[2] + . . . + A[j], and (j ≤ N)
while (j < N) {
    j = j + 1;
    sum = sum + A[j];
    // sum = A[1] + A[2] + . . . + A[j], and (j ≤ N)
}
// (j ≥ N)
// Therefore, (j = N) and sum = A[1] + A[2] + . . . + A[N]
```

We have formally proven that the code fragment shown does correctly compute the sum of the first N elements in the area for any positive, nonzero value of N. Whew!

Now you may be able to see why this method is considered somewhat controversial. It took a great deal of argumentation to prove the correctness of a six-line code fragment. Imagine how long it would take to prove the correctness of a 100- or 200-line function that carries out some highly intricate operation. There is as much likelihood of an error in the proof as there is of an error in the program itself.

There are many people who believe that program verification will never become an important software tool because of this complexity. But other computer scientists believe that it will become important as we learn more about how to develop formal proofs, and we create programming languages designed to support formal verification. (One example might be a functional language such as LISP or Scheme.) It is hard now to determine which of these arguments will prevail. However, it is fair to say that program verification is not widely used and has not made much of an impact on the development of real-world production software. We will not be discussing it any further in this text.

Instead, most software designers demonstrate the correctness of their programs through **empirical testing**. With empirical testing, we test our program using a number of carefully selected test cases and see if the program works correctly for all of them. If it does, then we argue that the program will indeed work properly for all data sets, even those that we did not test. Now, of course, that statement is not true. There still could be an error that was not detected because none of our test cases revealed its presence. However, if we are careful in how we choose our test data and we thoroughly and completely test everything we have written, we can have a reasonable amount of confidence that the overwhelming majority of errors will have been located and corrected.

Empirical testing usually proceeds in three steps. The first phase is **unit testing**. As we finish writing each program unit, we thoroughly test it before placing it into our library. Extensive and thorough unit testing is one of the central characteristics of the new software development model called **eXtreme Programming**, often abbreviated XP. When using XP, you write your testing programs at the same time as you are developing the code itself. The idea is to create a "mesh" of extensive, well-crafted testing procedures and then wrap it around every single module as soon as it is developed. The goal is to immediately locate every error that is present, correct it, and ensure that it will never get into the code a second time.

When developing test suites, you must be sure to test every flow path through the program at least once, and preferably more than once. A **flow path** is a unique execution sequence through the program unit. For example, if B_i represents a Boolean condition and S_i represents a Java statement, then the following code fragment:

```
S1
while (B1)     {
    if (B2)
      S2
    else
      S3
}
```

contains the following seven flow paths:

S_1 The path we take when we do not execute the loop at all.

S_1, S_2 The path we take when we execute the loop once and do the true branch of the conditional.

S_1, S_3 The path we take when we execute the loop once and do the false branch of the conditional.

S_1, S_2, S_3 The two paths we could take if we execute the loop twice

S_1, S_3, S_2 and execute a different branch each time.

S_1, S_2, S_2 The two paths we could take if we execute the loop twice

S_1, S_3, S_3 and execute the same branch each time.

There are an infinite number of flow paths in this example, and that is why exhaustive testing of a program unit is generally impossible. However, your goal during unit testing is to make sure than every statement in the program unit is executed at least once and that we have included data sets that test as many of the important flow paths as possible. For example, if we tested our code fragment with the seven examples shown, we would have executed every statement in the fragment (the `while`, `if`, and S_1, S_2, S_3) and we would have included test cases in which (a) the loop is not executed, (b) it is executed once, (c) it is executed more than once, and (d) both the true and false branches of the conditional are executed. That is the type of careful selection process that should be used during the empirical testing process. Thorough and complete testing of every module as soon as it is written is a critically important step in the software development process.

The second level of testing is **integration testing**, and it is where you test the correctness of a group of routines working together. That is, assume you are given the following group of three program units:

It is possible for A, B, and C to work properly by themselves but not when grouped together as a unit. For example, when testing A, its builder may have assumed that we call B with parameters X and Y by writing B(X,Y). Similarly, the person who coded B may have believed that the correct parameter order was B(Y,X). Each of the individual tests will work exactly as its designer thinks its should. However, when the two units attempt to operate together, there will be an error. This error will only reveal itself when units A and B are executed as a group.

Integration testing usually proceeds from the bottom-up, in ever increasing group sizes. For example:

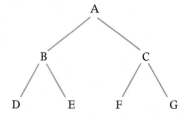

After empirical testing of each individual unit, we might choose to test the BDE cluster followed by the CFG cluster. Only when both of these integration tests have been completed satisfactorily would we proceed to test the entire seven-unit collection.

Both unit testing and integration testing are examples of what is called **clear box testing**, or **alpha testing**. That term means we are allowed to look inside the code to decide what test cases are needed. We carefully examine the program and its structure to ensure that we have tested all of the flow paths and all of the individual units. However, the third and final phase of testing is quite different. It is called **black box testing**, also referred to as **beta testing** or **acceptance testing**.

Rather than selecting test data on the basis of examining the program's structure, we place the program into the environment in which it will ultimately be used, and we run it. The test data are now related to actual user needs rather than an artificial stream of inputs created to exercise specific sections of code. We see if the program operates correctly in this real environment and measure whether or not it meets the performance criteria given in the problem specification document. These performance criteria will be statements like:

The program must operate with a mean time between failures of 24 hours.

The program must process a minimum of 1,000 transactions/hour.

The program must respond to 99.9 percent of customer requests in less than 1 second.

If the beta tests show that the program is operating correctly and meets all performance criteria, then we have met the requirements laid out in the problem specification document. The software project has been completed, and the finished program can now be delivered to the user.

◆ 1.2.6 Postproduction Phases

The phrase "the software project has been completed" is somewhat misleading. In the classroom, once a program has been written, debugged, and tested, it is rarely ever used again. It is handed in to the instructor for grading, and we move on to the next assignment. In the real world, however, programs have a very long shelf life. It is not unusual for the initial development phase of a piece of software to last 1 to 3 years, but the program itself might remain in use for 5 to 15 years. It is expensive to develop software, so once it has been successfully completed, it will be maintained and exploited for as long as possible.

Therefore, in the software life cycle, there are a number of important steps that continue after completion of the program. Although you will have little opportunity to carry out these steps in the academic environment, we mention them for the sake of completeness.

1.2.6.1 Documentation and Support

Documentation involves producing the information needed by both users and the technical support staff who maintain the program.

User documentation usually means a complete and well-written user's manual. With most modern software packages, it also may include online documentation, such as a searchable database of helpful information. In addition to both printed and online documentation, many users today expect an extensive support environment. This might include such features as phone and email support, a Web site with useful information and frequently asked questions (FAQs), downloads of the most recent versions of the software, and chat rooms where users of this package can exchange ideas and get help.

Technical documentation is a collection of all the written materials produced during the software life cycle. This will include the problem specification document (Section 1.2.1), the program design document (Section 1.2.2), a description of the algorithms and data structures (Section 1.2.3), a listing of the program along with inline comments (Section 1.2.4), and finally, a description of the testing and acceptance procedures to which the program was subjected (Section 1.2.5).

The designers of Java realized the importance of high-quality technical documentation, so they developed a special tool to assist in its preparation. It is a special type of inline comment called a **Javadoc comment**. These comments are identified by placing them within the symbols /** and */. They contain technical information, called **tags,** that provide useful information about this program unit. The tags are preceded by the special symbol @, and they can be extracted by a special Javadoc processor and displayed in HTML format. There are more than a dozen different types of tags. Four of the more important ones are:

@author *name*	identifies the author of this code
@version *text*	specifies the version number of this code
@param *name description*	gives information about all of the parameters
@return *description*	describes the value returned by this method

The @author and @version provide important historical information about this program unit. The @param and @return behave much like the pre- and postcondition comments described in Section 1.2.2.

For example, referring to the `Customer` class included in the bank simulation example of Figure 1.4, if we included the Javadoc tags just given, we could produce documentation that would look like the output in Figure 1.9.

Not only is this documentation both highly readable and in a standardized format, but it is also in HTML format, which means that it is easy to place on the Web for all developers to access. All code developed in this text will include Javadoc comments that will allow us to produce documentation like that shown in Figure 1.9.

1.2.6.2 Program Maintenance

The last step in software development is program maintenance. This is not really a separate phase but a realization that programs are not static entities that, once completed, never change. As mentioned earlier, it is not uncommon for programs to be in use 5, 10, or even 15 years after they were initially developed. During that time, new errors will almost certainly be uncovered, faster hardware and newer peripherals will be purchased, and user needs and marketplace whims will fluctuate. For all these reasons, the original program will need to be modified to meet changing conditions.

Program maintenance is the process of adapting existing software to maintain its correctness and keep it current with changing specifications and/or new equipment. In a sense, program maintenance implies that the software life cycle is truly a cycle that will have to be repeated more than once. For example, if new errors are uncovered, we may need to rewrite code, test it, update the documentation, and distribute the modifications to all our users. When newer, faster hardware is announced, we may wish to modify both the program design and the code to exploit this new equip-

---

Class Customer   file://F:/Book/John/ch1/code/javadoc/Customer.html

Class Tree Deprecated Index Help
PREV CLASS NEXT CLASS   FRAMES NO FRAMES
SUMMARY: INNER | FIELD | CONSTR | METHOD   DETAIL: FIELD | CONSTR | METHOD

Class Customer

```
java.lang.Object
  |
  • --Customer
```

public class **Customer**
extends java.lang.Object

A simple class to represent a bank customer. Doesn't do much yet.

Constructor Summary

Customer ()
        Default constructor--create 'bare minimum' Customer

Method Summary

void depart ()
            Customer leaves the bank.

Methods inherited from class java.lang.Object

clone, equals, finalize, getClass, hashCode, notify, notifyAll, toString, wait,
wait, wait

Constructor Detail

Customer

public **Customer()**

        Default constructor--create 'bare minimum' Customer

        Preconditions: none

        Postconditions: Default customer object has been created.

1 of 2

FIGURE 1.9 Example of Javadoc documentation

ment. If the user has new and unexpected needs or the marketplace is demanding new capabilities, we may decide to redo the specification document and then implement a totally new version of the software.

If our software package has been accurately specified, organized using the object-oriented design philosophy, elegantly coded in Java using good object-oriented programming techniques, and thoroughly tested and documented, then program maintenance will be a much less difficult task. Given the highly modular nature of object-oriented software, program maintenance should, at least theoretically, be similar to the job of a modern TV repairperson. When there is a problem with the TV, the repairperson checks the components one by one, locates the defective one, and then snaps in a new one. To fix or update our software, we should, in theory, be able to locate the desired class that needs to be adapted, unplug the current code, plug in the new code, and have a correct working version. It is important to follow the software life cycle guidelines described in this section not only to get the program working correctly initially but also to ensure that future maintenance will not be a difficult and expensive task.

1.3 SUMMARY

As we have tried to show in this chapter, there is much more to programming than coding. Recent studies on the time spent by software developers in various stages of initial program development show that a relatively small amount is spent on implementation (coding and debugging), with a much larger amount of time spent on the necessary preparatory work of specification, design, and algorithmic planning. Figure 1.10 lists the approximate percentage of time spent on each of the major phases of initial software development. Furthermore, Figure 1.10 describes only the time allocation for initial development. Over the 5- to 15-year life of a software package, 60 percent or more of the total time and money will be spent maintaining the software after it has been initially released for general use.

Software development is an extremely complex task made up of many phases, each of which is important and each of which contributes to the overall solution. Do not equate the topics of software development and coding. Remember that coding must be preceded by a good deal of preparatory work clarifying, specifying, and designing the solution, and it must be followed by an extensive amount of testing, verifying, measuring, and documenting to guarantee the quality of the final product.

This text will follow the outline of the software life cycle first diagrammed in Figure 1.2. Part I focuses on the design phase as it reviews the object-oriented design philosophy (Chapter 2) and the object-oriented programming features provided in

Phase	Approximate Percentage of Time
Specification, design, and planning	30–40
Coding and debugging	15–20
Testing, reviewing, and fixing	30–40
Documentation and support	10–15

FIGURE 1.10 Approximate percentage of time spent on the different phases of software development

Java (Chapter 3). It closes with a case study (Chapter 4) that demonstrates how the object-oriented methodology can address and solve a large-scale program.

Part II looks at the algorithm and data structure selection phase of the software life cycle. It initially presents the mathematical tools needed to analyze the efficiency of the algorithms you have selected (Chapter 5). Then it introduces the four fundamental categories of data representation. This taxonomy forms the basis for the following discussion of data structures, as it presents first the linear data structures (Chapter 6), then the hierarchical structures (Chapter 7), and finally set and graph structures (Chapter 8). Then it introduces the Java Collection Framework and the rich library of classes provided automatically to all Java software developers (Chapter 9).

Part III looks at some modern programming techniques supported in Java. These include exceptions and streams (Chapter 10), threads (Chapter 11), graphical user interfaces (Chapter 12), and networking and security (Chapter 13).

Our goal in this text is to begin the process of turning an individual who knows coding into a "modern software developer," someone who understands and appreciates the range of skills required to build correct, efficient, high-quality software. Although that will take far more than one class and one textbook, we hope that the ideas presented in the following pages will start you down this interesting path.

EXERCISES

1. See if you can find out (possibly from your computing center staff) the total number of lines of code in some of the popular software packages that are used on campus (e.g., word processing, email, Web browsing, compiler, or operating system). Using the table in Figure 1.1, what category does each package fit into? How does this compare to the size of the programs that you wrote in your first computer science class?

2. Here is a simple problem specification statement:

   You are given N numbers as input. Sort these numbers into order and then print them.

   a. Clearly identify what important information is missing from this problem statement that could lead to errors and faults in the program you develop. These omissions would include the necessary information required to make sure that the program runs correctly in all circumstances, not just the expected ones.

   b. Make reasonable assumptions about the omissions that you identified in part a and then write a more thorough, complete, and unambiguous set of problem specifications.

3. Looking over the problem statement on page 7, can you identify any additional problems with this statement besides the four that are described in the body of the text?

4. Would either of the following changes affect the code fragment shown in Figure 1.5?

    a. The implementation of the waiting line w is changed from an array to a linked list.

    b. We change from a Boolean value (true, false) to an integer value (0, 1) for keeping track of whether or not a teller was busy.

What do your responses to these changes say about the maintainability of object-oriented code?

5. Propose some additional methods that you think might be appropriate for the Teller and WaitingLine classes that were discussed in Section 1.2.2 and listed in Figure 1.4.

6. Describe some situations in everyday life (other than software development) where you use the idea of divide and conquer to attack and solve a large, complex problem.

7. Assume that you are working on a spelling checker program. One of the most important data structures in that program is the *dictionary*. The program will look up words in your dictionary to see if they are there. If so, we assume that the word is correctly spelled; if not, it is incorrectly spelled. In addition, we will allow users to add new words to the dictionary to customize it for their specific needs.

    We have lots of choices on how we store the words in the dictionary and how we will search it. This choice will significantly affect the performance of our spell checking software. Discuss what you think might be the main advantages and disadvantages of each of the following choices:

    a. a sorted array of words

    b. an unsorted array of words

    c. an unsorted linked list of words

8. Browse the set of packages available in the Java class library. They can be found at:

http://java.sun.com/j2se/1.3/docs/api/index.html

Look at the operations performed by some of these packages and think about how they could be helpful in creating applications in such areas as:

    a. games

    b. client/server network applications

    c. e-commerce

9. Do you agree or disagree with the following statements? Explain your answers.

    a. Empirical testing is an adequate testing technique because all you need to do is exhaustively test all possible input sequences.

    b. Empirical testing allows you to determine both the presence of errors and the absence of errors in a program unit.

    c. Empirical testing can prove the presence of errors but never their absence.

10. Assume you are given the following sequence of statements, where the B_i are any Boolean expressions and the S_i are any Java statements:

```java
while (B₁) {
    S₁;
    if (B₂)
        S₂;
    else
        if (B₃)
                while (B₄) S₃;
        else
                S₄;
}
```

Explain exactly how you would plan to empirically test this code fragment to ensure that it is correct. What does your answer say about the issue of testing quite large methods that contain dozens or hundreds of lines of code?

11. Interview one or two professional software developers (possibly from your computing center) to find out what proportion of their time is spent on each of the software development phases listed in Figure 1.2. Compare what they tell you with an estimate of how much time you spent in each phase when you were writing programs for your first class in computer science.

PART I

OBJECT-ORIENTED SOFTWARE DEVELOPMENT

CHAPTER 2

Object-Oriented Design and Programming

2.1 INTRODUCTION

Take a few minutes to look around the place where you are reading this book. For example, I am writing this chapter in the dining room of my home. I am sitting on a chair in front of a table that holds my computer. As I look around, I can see windows and doors on every wall. In the center of the ceiling is a large fan controlled by two switches on the far wall. There is also a thermostat that controls the temperature in the room by turning on and off the heaters located beneath the windows on the opposite wall. The place where you are located is probably not identical to my dining room, although there will be many similarities, such as windows, lights, and controls for lighting and temperature.

Although the exact things we see in our environment may differ, what is similar is the way that we describe, and ultimately interact with, our environment. As human beings, we make sense of our environment by trying to identify and understand the things, or *objects*, that surround us. According to Webster's online dictionary, an **object** is "something material that may be perceived by the senses." Chairs, desks, computers, and thermostats are all examples of things that we perceive through our senses.

In fact, we do much more than perceive objects around us. We also interact with objects, and objects interact with each other, to get things done. For example, at this instant, I am interacting with my computer to write these words. You are interacting with a printed version of this book by reading it. We describe and understand the world around us by (a) identifying the objects in our world, (b) understanding what these objects can do, and (c) interacting with these objects to accomplish a specific task. For example, to increase the temperature in my dining room, I first need to know that an object called a thermostat accomplishes this task. Then I need to find the thermostat and learn how to use it. Finally, I need to adjust it in the proper way. The thermostat will then interact with the room to determine the current temperature and then interact with the heaters to change the temperature as necessary.

Objects by their nature hide, or *encapsulate*, their inner workings. If you look up the word **encapsulation** in a dictionary, you will learn that it means "to enclose in as if in a capsule." Placing this definition in an object-oriented context, encapsulation is a method by which information can be confined or hidden inside objects so it is not visible to the outside world. Using objects to encapsulate information makes it possible to view a complex system only in terms of its external interface, without regard for its internal structure. I do not need to know, nor do I really care about, the inner workings of the thermostat in my dining room. All I need to know is that if the room is too cold, I can warm it by raising the temperature setting, and if the room is too warm, then I can cool it by lowering the setting. I have no need to know exactly how the thermostat accomplishes these feats. In addition, should the internal structure of the thermostat be changed, it will in no way affect my ability to use it because I will still operate it in exactly the same way. Encapsulation enables us to build and understand complex systems that consist of large collections of objects, and it makes it possible to replace an old object with a new one without the need to rebuild the entire system in which the object is located.

To help us understand what objects can do and how we interact with them, objects with similar properties are grouped together into sets called **classes**. The Webster online dictionary defines a class as "a group, set, or kind sharing common attributes."

In the description of my dining room, I described a thermostat that controls the temperature. Although you may never have seen this exact make and model (an Aube TH101D), you probably would be able to use it because you understand, in general, what a thermostat is and what it does. You expect that there will be a button or dial on the front, along with some temperature markings, and you use the dial to set the desired room temperature. This level of understanding allows you to walk into almost any room and adjust the temperature to your liking. Even though there are thousands of different types of thermostats, and you do not know exactly which one will be in a specific room, you will almost certainly be able to use it in the correct manner. That is because all thermostat objects belong to the same class, and they share a set of common functions and attributes.

Computers, unlike human beings, do not describe their world in terms of objects but, instead, focus on the sequence of steps required to complete a given task. A **procedure** is "a series of steps followed in a regular definite order," and at the machine level, a program is a collection of procedures and statements that are executed in a predetermined order. This fetching, decoding and executing of instructions in a well-defined sequence is the very essence of the von Neumann architecture. To make this distinction between human and computer thought processes a little clearer, think for a moment how you would explain the behavior of a thermostat. You would describe it as a device that consists of a dial, a temperature sensor, and a connection to a heating unit. The dial records the desired room temperature. The temperature sensor monitors both the setting on the dial and the current room temperature and turns on the heater when the room temperature falls below the setting on the dial. Your description has been given in terms of entities, their functions, and their communications with each other. This type of description is called an **object-oriented view** of the problem, and it is diagrammed in Figure 2.1a.

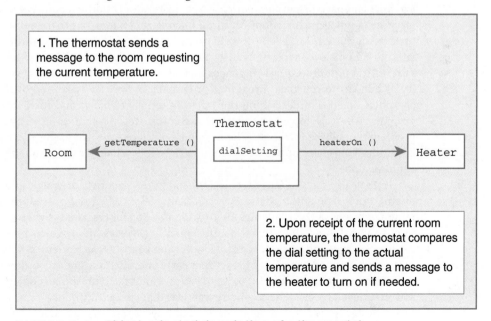

FIGURE 2.1a Object-oriented description of a thermostat

1. Obtain the current temperature of the room.
2. Obtain the current setting on the dial.
3. If the room temperature is less than the setting on the dial, turn on the heater.
4. If the room temperature is greater than or equal to the setting on the dial, turn off the heater.
5. Go back to Step 1.

FIGURE 2.1b Procedure-oriented description of a thermostat

A computer, on the other hand, would take a much more procedural, step-by-step view of the problem. It might describe a thermostat as a device that carries out the five-step algorithm in Figure 2.1b.

This is called a **procedure-oriented view** of the problem. Although both descriptions are similar, and both explain what a thermostat does, most people would be more comfortable with the object-oriented view of Figure 2.1a that describes a collection of interacting objects, whereas the computer would prefer the procedural, step-by-step description in Figure 2.1b.

Since human beings are generally most comfortable dealing with objects, you might think that all high-level programming languages would allow programmers to use objects to describe their programs. In fact, this is not the case. The earliest high-level programming languages (FORTRAN, COBOL, ALGOL, Pascal) were all strictly procedural languages. They provided programmers with the tools required to produce a sequence of steps to solve a given task, much like the algorithm of Figure 2.1b. Essentially, what these programming languages did was make programming easier by providing powerful high-level procedural constructs to replace cumbersome low-level machine language primitives. For example, instead of thinking about the dozen or so machine language instructions required to construct a loop, a programmer could use the high-level `for`, `while`, or `do` constructs instead. The compiler would then translate these high-level constructs into the actual machine code executed by the computer. Although procedural languages increased productivity and improved the ability of humans to construct programs, programmers were still required to *think* like a computer. Instead of describing the world in terms of objects and their interactions, programmers were forced to construct a step-by-step procedural description of the problem they wished to solve. The designers of these early languages did not change the underlying *mode* of problem solving. They only changed the ease with which it could be done.

In the early days of language design, computer scientists did not explore object-oriented programming models for two reasons. First, when the procedural programming languages of the 1950s and 1960s were developed, researchers were only beginning to understand the syntactic and semantic theories upon which programming language design and compiler construction were based. Object-oriented languages require sophisticated compiler support that early compiler designers could not yet provide. The technology of the 1950s and 1960s was not ready to support object-oriented software development. The second reason was that computing was very new, and language designers were gaining an understanding of the basic principles of programming. It is quite natural to build upon what you know and what you have seen, which in this case, was the procedural approach of machine languages. Thus, most of the early language design work focused on programming models that were closely related to that of the underlying von Neumann architecture.

In 1962, Ole-Johan Dahl and Kristen Nygaard at the Norwegian Computing Center in Oslo started work on the design of the first object-based programming language, Simula. Simula was a special-purpose language designed for discrete event simulation, and it focused on modeling rather than general-purpose computing. This change in focus forced the use of several innovative computing techniques, and Simula was the first language that enabled programmers to describe computational constructs using objects. Simula never was widely used, but it had a significant influence on the future design and development of modern object-oriented languages.

Two important design projects were based on that early work with Simula. In 1972, Alan Kay of the Xerox Palo Alto Research Center (PARC) created a language called Smalltalk in an attempt to improve the novel ideas he saw in Simula. Kay was intrigued by the "promise of an entirely new way to structure computations." It took Kay several years to develop his insights and devise efficient mechanisms to implement them on the primitive computer systems of the early 1970s. In 1980 Smalltalk become one of the first commercially available object-oriented programming languages, and it set the standard for the languages that followed. The class libraries included with the Smalltalk environment were the basis for libraries provided with many modern object-oriented languages.

Bjarne Stroustrup used Simula while working on his Ph.D. thesis at Cambridge University in England. He was studying distributed systems and felt that the object-oriented features of Simula would be an ideal tool for his work. Stroustrup was impressed by the way "the concepts of the language helped me to think about the problems in my application." He was also intrigued by the fact that the mechanisms provided by Simula became even more helpful as the size of his program increased. In other words, he felt that the ideas embodied in Simula might be a useful way to manage the complexity found in huge software projects. After completing his Ph.D., Stroustrup went to work for Bell Laboratories and worked on a project to analyze how the UNIX® operating system could be distributed over a network of computers. He decided the best way to attack this problem was to devise a new language that added Simula's class concept to C. At that time, C was the most widely used systems implementation language. In 1979, Stroustrup began work on a new language he initially called "C with classes" but which later evolved into the programming language we now know as C++, the first widely used object-oriented programming language. By the mid-1980s, C++ was becoming a popular development language in the United States, clearly demonstrating the benefits of the object-oriented view of software design and development.

In 1991, Sun Microsystems embarked on a variety of projects to branch out into new areas of computing technology. One of these projects, code-named Green, was formed to explore the use of inexpensive microprocessors in a variety of consumer electronics devices, including personal digital assistants (PDAs) and television set-top boxes. The software to drive these devices would have to run on a variety of different platforms, fit into a small amount of memory, and be both robust and secure. The team at Sun had planned on using C++, but they encountered a number of problems that caused the team to think about designing a new and different language.

James Gosling began the development of a language to address the problems faced by the Sun team. Since most programmers at that time were using either C or C++, a decision was made to make the structure of this new language similar to C++. This would make it easier for programmers to understand and eliminate the need for extreme retraining. Since the language would be used to develop software that could run on many different types of simple devices, the goals of the new language were to keep it small, robust, and highly portable. The language was initially named Oak, after the tree growing outside Gosling's office window. It was eventually renamed Java because of trademark conflicts with an existing Oak product. Sun's consumer electronics initiative failed, but by 1994, the World Wide Web was becoming increasingly popular. Java, although designed for a totally different purpose, turned out to be quite well suited for Web-based applications because it was platform independent, secure, and robust. The Web had made distributed, secure programming in high demand, and Java had found a new lease on life. By the beginning of the 21st century, Java was well on its way to displacing C++.

Regardless of whether you use Smalltalk, C++, or Java, there is no doubt that the object-oriented paradigm is the most widely used model for the design and implementation of large software systems. The next section of this chapter will introduce objects, classes, and inheritance, which are the fundamental concepts of object-oriented programming. The last section of the chapter discusses techniques and tools that can be used to design object-oriented programs. After reading this chapter, you will understand what object-oriented programming is and how to design simple object-oriented programs.

2.2 OBJECT-ORIENTED PROGRAMMING

◆ 2.2.1 Objects

Although we all have an intuitive understanding of the concept of an object in the real world, exactly what is an object in an object-oriented programming language? You might think this question would be easy to answer. But surprisingly, it is not, and there are several different definitions in current usage. Grady Booch, a well-known author and computer scientist, has proposed the following widely used definition:

> *An object is an entity that has state, behavior, and identity.*

For many, that definition may not be very helpful. In fact, it may leave you even more confused and uncertain. So let's take it apart and look at it piece by piece.

Referring back to the thermostat example discussed in Section 2.1, we saw that there are certain values that a thermostat needs to remember to function properly. For example, it has to know the desired room temperature and whether or not it has turned on the heaters in the room. The information that an object needs to remember makes up what is called its **state**. More formally, the state of an object is composed of the properties that the object possesses and the current values of those properties. A **property** is a characteristic, trait, quality, or feature that contributes to making an object uniquely that object. For example, the desired temperature setting is a property of a thermostat but not a property of an elevator. An elevator would have properties such as the state of its doors, its direction of travel, and its current location. The **value** of a property is the specific quantity stored in it at a given instant of time. For our elevator example, its current values might be (doors closed, going up, on the 10th floor). The properties of an object are fixed, or static, whereas the values of these properties are dynamic and will almost certainly vary over time. A thermostat will always need to know the desired room temperature, but at night this setting may be 63 degrees, whereas during the day it may be 68 degrees.

The second characteristic in Booch's definition of an object is behavior. The **behavior** of an object describes how it reacts in terms of state changes and interactions with other objects. Using the thermostat example again, one of the behaviors exhibited by a thermostat is that the heater will be turned on when the current room temperature falls below the desired temperature. Here the thermostat is changing state in reaction to a change in temperature. Another example of behavior is reflected in the fact that an elevator will close its doors and move in an upward direction when it is on the ground floor and someone presses the button labeled 23. All objects exhibit a variety of different behaviors, which may be used by other objects to achieve a desired result.

Object-oriented programming languages model behaviors in one of two ways. A **message** is a unit of information that can be sent from one object to another to cause a certain behavior to be invoked. Languages that model behavior using messages, such as Smalltalk, provide the programmer with a means of defining the different messages that an object is willing to receive and the specific behaviors that will be associated with the arrival of each message type. An object then sends the appropriate message to invoke a particular behavior. For example, a furnace will accept messages from a thermostat that instruct it to turn on or off as shown in Figure 2.1a.

Languages such as Java use a different approach. They model behavior by providing procedures, called **methods**, which are associated with a specific type of object. These methods can be called, or **invoked**, by other objects to achieve certain behavior. Although they represent different viewpoints, "sending a message" and "invoking a method" do essentially the same thing. They both cause an object to perform a specific action or behavior.

Conventional parameter-passing mechanisms provide a way to pass information to the procedure that implements this behavior. Using methods, for example, a furnace would have an `activateFurnace()` method that takes a Boolean parameter specifying whether the furnace should be turned on or off. A thermostat object could then indicate that the furnace should be turned on by invoking the `activateFurnace()` method with the Boolean value true as the argument. When this method is invoked, the furnace object will have all the information it requires to determine whether or not to activate the heating unit. The methods associated with an object will, of course, depend on the object type. A thermostat object will include `activateHeaters()` and `temperaturechange()` methods, whereas an elevator object would contain the methods `openDoor()`, `closeDoor()`, `goDown()`, and `goUp()`.

The methods associated with an object can be grouped into four categories based on the type of response by the object. These four categories are summarized in Table 2.1. The first two categories, accessors and mutators, provide the ability to obtain or change the state of an object. An **accessor** is used to query but not change the state of an object, whereas a **mutator** provides a way to change the state of an object. It is relatively easy to see real-world examples of both of these method types.

TABLE 2.1 Types of Methods

Method Type	Action Performed
Accessor	Return some information about the object's state but do not change the object's state.
Mutator	Change the object's state.
Constructor	Create and initialize a new object.
Destructor	Remove an object currently in the system. Free up any resources associated with the object.

For example, a thermostat can display its current temperature setting, an accessor, and it provides a mechanism whereby that setting can be changed, a mutator.

In programming, as in the real world, objects must be created and destroyed. **Constructors** provide a mechanism whereby a new object can be created and initialization operations can be carried out on that object. A **destructor**, on the other hand, provides a way for an existing object to be removed from the system when it is no longer needed.

Identity is the third and last part of Booch's definition of an object. An object-oriented language must provide a mechanism to distinguish one object from another. If I were to write a program that created two thermostats, I must have a way of specifying which thermostat I wish to work with. I must have the ability to say something like, "I want to adjust the setting of the thermostat on the east wall of the dining room, not the one in the bedroom."

Most object-oriented programming languages use **reference** variables to identify objects. A reference variable is a variable that references, or points to, a specific object. For example, I may define the reference variables `DiningRoom` and `Bedroom` in my program and arrange to have them refer to the objects that model the thermostats in the dining room and bedroom, respectively. If I wish to change the setting of the thermostat in the bedroom, I would do so by specifying that the object referred to by the variable `Bedroom` should change its desired temperature. Note that a reference variable can refer to only one object at a time, but it is possible that two or more reference variables may refer to the same object as shown in Figure 2.2.

The concept of identity is closely related to that of **equality**. Equality attempts to answer the question: Are two objects equal? At first glance, this seems like a simple concept; however, it is complicated by the fact that objects can be identified and distinguished in two different ways.

Imagine yourself standing on the bank of a river on two different days. Did you see the *same* river on both days even though the water that flowed through the river at those two times was different? In other words, do we identify a river by its location or by its contents? If we identify the river by content, then clearly you saw two different rivers on those two days even though you were in the exact same location.

Object-oriented programming languages typically provide the ability to compare objects by name (location) and by content. Two variables are said to be **name equivalent** if they both refer to the exact same object. The variables `Bedroom` and `MainBedroom` in Figure 2.2 are name equivalent because they both refer to the same thermostat object. When comparing objects by name, we are only interested in determining if two objects are in fact the exact same object. Name equivalence is often im-

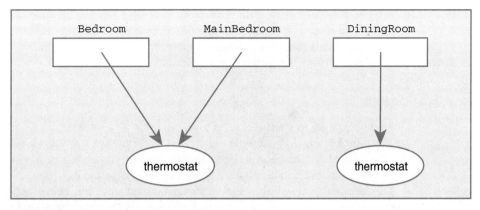

FIGURE 2.2 Reference variables

plemented by comparing the memory addresses of the two objects. In this "shallow" way of identifying objects, two objects are considered the same if they occupy the exact same memory locations. That is, they are the exact same object.

Two objects are said to be **content equivalent** if the objects are both from the same class, and the state information stored in each object is exactly the same. To determine content equivalence, the programmer must understand the structure of the objects being compared and determine if the state of both objects is exactly the same.

Figure 2.3 shows three distinct thermostat objects identified using the four reference variables T1, T2, T3, and T4. The variables T2 and T3 refer to the same object and are therefore considered name-equivalent. The objects referenced by T1 and T4 are

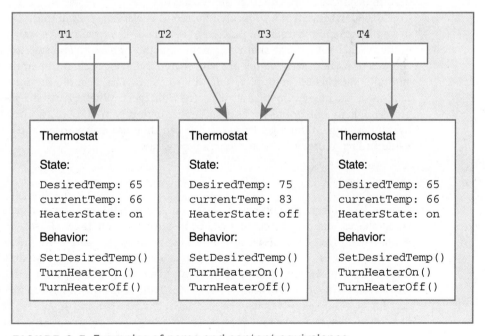

FIGURE 2.3 Examples of name and content equivalence

content equivalent because they have the exact same state, but they are not name equivalent because the objects occupy different areas in memory. Finally, T1 and T2 are neither name equivalent, as they occupy different areas of memory, nor content equivalent, as they have different state values.

◆ 2.2.2 Classes

Human beings group similar objects together to help us understand what the objects are capable of doing. For example, when I say "thermostat," you think about a device used to control the temperature setting. Not only do you have a general idea of what the object does, but you also have a good idea of how to use it.

A **class** is a group of objects that share common state and behavior. A class is an abstraction or description of an object. An object, on the other hand, is a concrete entity that exists in space and time. Object-oriented programming languages use classes to define the state and behavior associated with objects and to provide a means to create the objects that make up a program. You can think of a class as a blueprint, a template, a "cookie cutter," or a factory from which objects can be created or, to use the object-oriented terminology, **instantiated**. While Car is a class, my 1993 Toyota Corolla is a specific instance, or object, of that class.

For example, to write a program that models the heating system in my dining room, I might start out by defining three classes: Room, Thermostat, and Heater. I could then use these classes to instantiate as many distinct room, thermostat, and heater objects as required. Even though my dining room has two heaters, I only need to define a single heater class, from which I can instantiate two (or more) distinct heater objects. We saw this situation in Figure 2.3 where a single thermostat class was used to instantiate three distinct thermostat objects.

Although they are not typically referred to as classes, you can think of a data type in a conventional programming language as a class. The term *integer* is the name for a group of data values that share common state and behavior. The state of an integer consists of its numerical value, and the shared behavior includes operations such as addition, subtraction, multiplication, and division. The term *integer* does not represent a specific integer; instead it refers to *all* integers. When we need a specific integer variable in a program, we use the integer data type to declare an integer variable (instantiation) and initialize its value. We can then use accessor methods to print its value and mutator methods to assign a new value.

◆ 2.2.3 Inheritance

Classes, like objects, do not exist in isolation. It is possible to infer useful information about classes, and the objects that can be instantiated from these classes, based on the relationships that exist between classes. For example, consider the following three classes: ProgrammableThermostat, AnalogThermostat, and Thermostat. Given our understanding of these names, we can infer that both a ProgrammableThermostat and an AnalogThermostat are Thermostats. This means that anything a Thermostat can do, we would expect that a ProgrammableThermostat and an AnalogThermostat can do as well. You should be able to replace a Thermostat with either a ProgrammableThermostat or an AnalogThermostat and expect the heating system to still function correctly. The heating system may exhibit additional functionality (e.g.,

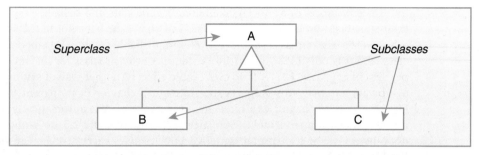

FIGURE 2.4 Inheritance

it may now be programmable), and the techniques used to monitor and adjust the temperature may have changed, but the state and behavior present in the original thermostat are still present in the new system.

When the state and behavior of one class are a subset of the state and behavior of another more general class, the classes are related by **inheritance**. The more general class (i.e., Thermostat) is referred to as a **superclass**, or **parent**, of a second, more specialized class (i.e., ProgrammableThermostat). The second class is called a **subclass** of the superclass and is said to inherit the state and behavior of the superclass. The inheritance relationship can be diagrammed as shown in the Figure 2.4.

When a subclass such a B or C in Figure 2.4 inherits from a superclass, it means that the state and behavior of the subclass are an extension of the state and behavior associated with the parent class. The subclass is thus a more specialized form of the superclass.

When two classes are related by inheritance, the *is-a* relationship will apply to the classes. The is-a relationship holds between two classes when one class is a specialized instance of the second. For example, a ProgrammableThermostat *is a* Thermostat, and thus, it is an appropriate subclass. Similarly, a sports car *is a* car and a minivan *is a* car, so both would be appropriate subclasses of the superclass car. A train is certainly not a car, and a car is not a train, so it would be inappropriate to place them in a subclass/superclass relationship. However, both cars and trains are forms of transportation, so the inheritance hierarchy in Figure 2.5 might be entirely appropriate.

The *has-a* relationship, on the other hand, holds when one class is a component of the second. For example, a car has a steering wheel, but a car is not a steering wheel. Therefore, it would not be appropriate to make steering wheel a subclass of car.

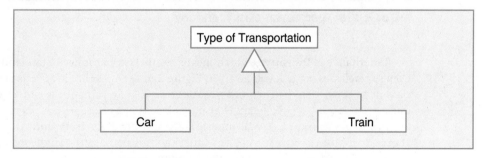

FIGURE 2.5 Is-a relationship

Since instances of a subclass contain all of the state and behavior associated with their superclass, an instance of a subclass can mimic the behavior of the superclass. In other words, the subclass should be indistinguishable from an instance of the superclass, and it is possible to substitute instances of the subclass for instances of the superclass in any situation with no observable effect. Another way of saying this is that a subclass automatically inherits the state and behavior of its parent. Referring to Figure 2.4, any behavior exhibited by an instance of A is automatically available to instances of the classes B and C. Similarly, referring to Figure 2.5, anything that can be done by a type of transportation (e.g., move people, carry things) can be done by both cars and trains, although not necessarily in the same way.

When used properly, inheritance provides a means by which a programmer can create a new class that exhibits slightly different behavior than its superclass. A side benefit of using inheritance is code reuse. For example, if I have developed some complex behavior describing the operation of a car, it would be foolish and time-consuming for me to rewrite the same code for sports cars and minivans. Instead, by making these subclasses of car, all sports car objects and all minivan objects will inherit this code and exhibit exactly the same behavior with no additional work. Inheritance is a way to increase programmer productivity via code sharing.

Inheritance allows us to organize classes into hierarchies based on their inheritance relationships. The class hierarchy of the thermostat classes discussed earlier is shown in Figure 2.6.

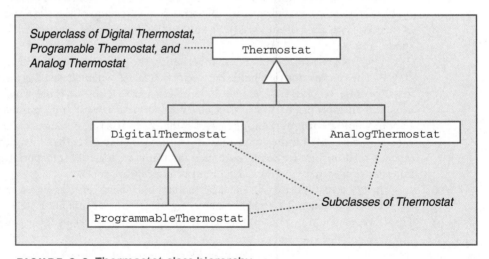

FIGURE 2.6 Thermostat class hierarchy

Inheritance is transitive, which means a subclass can inherit state and behavior from superclasses many levels away. In Figure 2.6, `ProgrammableThermostat` is a subclass of `DigitalThermostat`, and `DigitalThermostat` is a subclass of `Thermostat`; thus, `ProgrammableThermostat` is also a subclass of `Thermostat`. This means that a `ProgrammableThermostat` will inherit state and behavior from both the `DigitalThermostat` and `Thermostat` classes. Inheritance is perhaps the single most powerful tool provided by object-oriented programming languages.

TABLE 2.2 Five Forms of Inheritance

Form of Inheritance	Description
Specification	The superclass defines behavior that is implemented in the subclass but not in the superclass. This provides a way to guarantee that the subclass implements the same behavior.
Specialization	The subclass is a specialized form of the superclass but satisfies the specifications of the parent class in all relevant aspects.
Extension	The subclass adds new functionality to the parent class but does not change any inherited behavior.
Limitation	The subclass restricts the use of some of the behavior inherited from the superclass.
Combination	The subclass inherits features from more than one superclass (i.e., multiple inheritance).

Not surprisingly, in an object-oriented program, inheritance can take on different forms and can be used in different ways. Five of the most common forms of inheritance are summarized in Table 2.2.

To make the differences between the five forms of inheritance given in Table 2.2 more concrete, consider a class called Clock that defines the functionality of a simple clock. The state defined by Clock includes the current time and two behaviors that provide the ability to set the time and ask what the time is. The state and behavior defined by the Clock class are summarized in Figure 2.7.

The **specification** form of inheritance described in Table 2.2 specifies the required set of behaviors that any of its subclasses must provide. When using the specification form of inheritance, the subclass inherits the specification of the behavior of its superclass, and it is up to the subclass to provide the implementation for all of these behaviors. In a sense, the specification form of inheritance specifies what the subclass must do but not how it will do it. This form of inheritance is useful in situations where you have a highly generalized type of object, such as the class Timepiece. What is important to the superclass are the specific behaviors that every object must exhibit, not the details of the implementation. In essence, what is being inherited by the subclass is only the behavioral specification. The specification form of inheritance says that you cannot be considered a type of Timepiece or Clock unless you provide the behaviors that both determine and set the time. These are the two essential behaviors of all clocks; however, the details of how a particular type of clock either sets or determines the time are not as important and can be specified by the subclass.

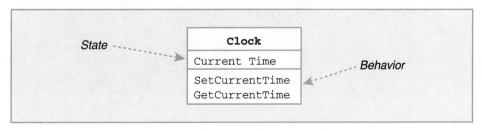

FIGURE 2.7 Clock class

The **specialization** form of inheritance is most easily defined in terms of the is-a relationship. The subclass is a more specialized form of the superclass. What makes the specialization form of inheritance different from the specification form is that in specialization the subclass inherits both the specification of a behavior and the implementation of some or all of the behaviors provided by the superclass. Now the parent states not only what you must do but, for at least some of the behaviors, how you will do it. This form of inheritance is useful when you are implementing a group of objects that are related in some way. For example, consider the classes `DigitalClock` and `AnalogClock`. Both of these classes define clocks. They differ in the way they display the time but not in how they update and store the time. Therefore, it would make sense to place the code required to implement that common behavior in the superclass and let it be inherited by the subclass. Now any subclass of `Clock` will automatically have the capability of keeping track of the time; that is, it inherits the two behaviors "set current time" and "get current time" from the parent. How a clock is able to display the time is only specified in the superclass, and it is implemented differently in the two subclasses as shown in Figure 2.8.

There are times when inheritance can expand the existing function of a superclass. This is the **extension** form of inheritance, and it is used to add totally new capabilities to the subclass. In the specialization form of inheritance, subclasses have the same behavioral properties as the superclass, but in each subclass, these behaviors may be implemented quite differently. In the extension form of inheritance, the subclass will have behaviors that are not present in the superclass. For example, it is possible to purchase an atomic clock that automatically sets itself based on radio signals broadcast from Fort Collins, Colorado. These clocks are typically accurate to within a few milliseconds, and you do not have to adjust them when daylight-savings time takes effect. Clearly, an

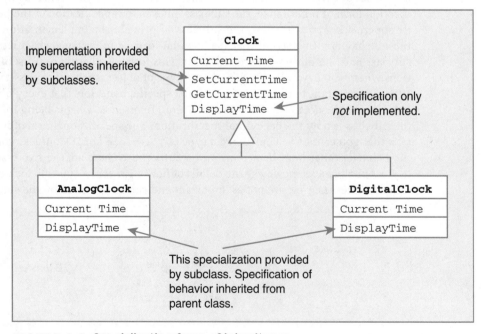

FIGURE 2.8 Specialization form of inheritance

atomic clock is a clock that has the added ability to automatically set itself. This behavior is an extension to the set of behaviors provided by a standard clock. You would certainly not want to require that every clock provide this functionality.

If you think about the atomic clock described in the previous paragraph, you realize that there might not ever be a need to provide a way to set the time manually on this type of clock. In fact, since it is likely that an atomic clock can determine the time more accurately than any human, you may not want to permit humans to set the time by hand on an atomic clock. This is an example of the **limitation** form of inheritance. The strict definition of the limitation form of inheritance says that you remove a behavior that is inherited from a superclass to the subclass. Notice that this violates the is-a relationship. If we remove the ability to set the time on an atomic clock, it is no longer a clock because it does not exhibit all of the behaviors of the superclass. Therefore, when using this form of inheritance, a behavior is not actually removed but simply implemented as a "no operation." An atomic clock would still provide a set time method, but invoking that method will have no effect on the state of the clock.

In **single inheritance,** a subclass has at most one direct superclass from which it inherits behavior. **Combination** is a form of inheritance in which a subclass inherits directly from two or more superclasses.

Consider the inheritance relationship between the classes `Clock`, `AlarmClock`, `Radio`, and `AlarmClockRadio` in Figure 2.9. The `AlarmClockRadio` class has both `Radio` and `AlarmClock` as direct superclasses. This means that an `AlarmClockRadio` can act as both a `Radio` and an `AlarmClock` at the same time. The term **multiple inheritance** is commonly used to describe the combination form of inheritance in programming languages. Not all object-oriented programming languages allow multiple inheritance.

Inheritance is a technique that, when used correctly, can help solve some of the problems associated with the development of extremely large software systems such as those described in Chapter 1. For example, let's say you are a programmer working for a software company that develops programs that analyze the efficiency of residential home heating systems. Given that there are literally hundreds of thermostats that could be used in a home, how can this software be designed to analyze all of the existing thermostats currently on the market as well as the new ones that will be developed in the future?

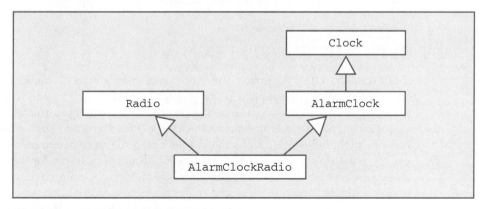

FIGURE 2.9 Multiple inheritance

One way to solve this problem is to define a generic thermostat class that defines the state and behavior associated with any thermostat that the system might be expected to simulate. The software could then be written in terms of a generic thermostat class. When the time comes to add a specific model of thermostat to the system, we would design a subclass for that thermostat type that inherits from the generic thermostat superclass. Since the program cannot distinguish between an object of the subclass and an object of the superclass, the software will continue to work properly.

This is an example of the specification form of inheritance described in Table 2.2, which provides a consistent interface for a group of classes within the system. This enables a programmer to develop programs using standard software components, just as computer engineers build computers using standard hardware components. Once a thermostat class has been written, it is very easy to reuse that class in a completely different program. It is also possible to provide functionality in the generic thermostat class that can be used in all of its subclasses—the specialization form of inheritance. Finally, if this type of thermostat has certain unique features, we can use the extension and limitation forms of inheritance to customize its behavior.

Chapter 3 will demonstrate how these inheritance concepts are realized in Java, and Chapter 4 will implement this home heating system as a case study so that you can see the power and capability of the object-oriented design approach.

This section has discussed the basic concepts of object-oriented programming. An object-oriented program consists of a number of objects that have state, behavior, and identity that interact to accomplish some task. Objects are instantiated from classes, which are like cookie cutters in the sense that they describe the general structure of an object. Classes that define similar state and behavior can be organized into a hierarchical structure using subclasses and inheritance. A subclass automatically inherits the state and behavior of its superclass. Inheritance is an extremely powerful tool that can increase programmer productivity and help solve some of the problems associated with the development of large software systems.

The next section of this chapter looks at the steps that precede the actual coding effort: the specification and design phases of the software life cycle of Figure 1.2. It looks at how software is designed based on information contained in the user requirements and problem specifications described in Section 1.2.1. The chapter concludes by introducing the basics of the Unified Modeling Language (UML), a tool commonly used to document the design of object-oriented systems.

2.3 OBJECT-ORIENTED DESIGN

If you think back to your junior and senior years in high school, you will realize that there was a very important process that you had to go through to get to where you are today: beginning your college career. The process started when you and your guidance counselor discussed career options and worked to identify some possible career paths that you might follow after high school. Your next goal was to determine exactly what you wanted to do and then identify colleges that would prepare you for the career path that you selected. You had to determine the specific type of college you wished to attend and whether you wanted to live on or off campus. At this stage, you were trying to determine exactly what your educational experience would be like. You asked questions like: "Given my SAT scores, will I be accepted to this school?" and "How long will it take to earn my degree?" It was almost as if you were treating your future college experience as a computer program and were attempting to define the output of the process based on the input. In the end you found a college that met your educational needs and prepared you for the career path that you selected.

Software development, like selecting a college, is not a single step but rather a process consisting of many steps. A common misunderstanding among students is that software development begins and ends with programming. Nothing could be further from the truth. Writing code is a significant part of the software life cycle, but there are important steps, called the requirements, specification, and design phases, that must take place *before* the coding effort can begin. These important steps were diagrammed in Figure 1.2.

During the **requirements phase** of the software life cycle, the user's needs are identified and documented. The **requirements document**, which is the end result of this effort, describes the behavior of the proposed software from the user's perspective. The focus of the requirements document is to describe what the program will *do* rather than explaining *how* the program will be implemented. The information in the requirements document is similar to the information you collected during the initial stages of your college search process. At that time, you were more concerned about determining what your needs were rather than how you would achieve them. For example, you may have known that you wanted to pursue a career in computer science, but you were not sure how you would attain this goal.

The **specification** phase of the software life cycle is concerned with defining the explicit behavior of a program. The **specification document**, produced during this phase, focuses on identifying the specific outputs of the program for all possible inputs, as shown in Figure 1.3b. If a specific type of hardware environment, programming language, or algorithm must be used, that information will be documented during the specification phase. The requirements document describes the desired effects to be produced by the software, whereas the specification document defines the behavior of the software that produces those effects. For example, during the requirements phase, we may learn that the user requires a program that can solve polynomial equations. This is the result that we wish to achieve. During the specification phase, we describe the specific behavior to achieve that result. That is, the program will input the $n+1$ coefficients of an nth degree polynomial as floating-point numbers and will output the n real roots of the equation to two decimal places. If some or all of the roots are imaginary, the specification document must describe how to handle them. Taken together, the requirement and specification documents provide the information that the system analyst needs to design a program to solve the problem.

Once the requirements and specification phases are completed, the **design phase** can begin. The design phase is guided by the information contained in the requirements and specification documents. The object-oriented design process focuses on identifying and defining the classes, the behaviors of each class, and the interactions that take place between the classes. The focus is on the functionality provided by the classes, not on the details of how the classes are implemented. The code that implements the classes will be written during the **implementation phase**. The design document serves as a guide to the programmers responsible for implementing the software.

Design is one of the most difficult but also most interesting phases in the software development process. Learning and mastering a new programming language is challenging, but a programming language is only a tool used to realize a design. Consider, for example, the role a hammer plays in the process of building a new home. The hammer is a tool that plays a crucial role in the construction process; however, it is a very small part of the process. Sure there are different types of hammers, and you need to pick the correct hammer for the task at hand, but the construction process is being guided by the blueprints prepared by the architect, not by the hammer. The role of coding in the software development process is very similar to the role of the hammer in the construction process. Coding is an important and critical part of the process, and knowing how to code is an important skill, but it is not the central focus or the driving force behind the development effort.

Several different designs for a software system can evolve from a single set of requirement and specification documents. The trick is to produce a design that will allow the programmers to develop software that is efficient, easy to build, and easy to maintain. This task is not as easy as you might think. You may find that there are several "good" designs for a particular piece of software, each of which has its advantages and disadvantages. You need to consider each design and objectively determine which one is right for the task at hand. Producing a design is a highly creative task, and there is no single "correct answer" that can be checked at the end of the process, anymore than there is a single "correct home design" that can be produced by an architect from a user's statement of likes and dislikes. The process you follow to select the right design for a software system cannot always be clearly stated, and you often must rely on intuition or experience to determine which design is the best.

Even though the focus of this text is on implementation issues, it will also provide some of the experience needed to master the art of software design. The case study presented in Chapter 4 illustrates how to derive a design given the requirements and specifications for a simple software system. When you read this case study, keep in mind that several different designs could have been used. Study the specific design that is presented and the decisions that were made. Then consider some of the alternative designs that were possible and discuss these alternatives with your instructor and other members of the class. These steps will give you experience with some of the basic steps in the software design process.

The next section of this chapter introduces a technique to identify the classes needed in a software system based on the information contained in the requirements and specifications documents. The chapter concludes with a discussion of the Unified Modeling Language (UML), a graphical modeling language used to express and represent designs.

◆ 2.3.1 Finding Classes

The primary goals of the design phase are to identify the classes that will be used in the system and to determine the relationships that exist between the classes in the system. Making the correct decisions in this phase of the design process requires talent and experience. There are no algorithms that can guarantee you will extract the best set of classes to use in your design based on the contents of the requirements document. The purpose of this section of the text is to describe a simple technique that can help you identify some of the classes that will be part of the final design.

The identities of the vast majority of classes needed in a system actually appear in the requirements and specification documents. The trick is learning how to read these documents so that you can identify the classes and their interrelationships. Objects, whether in a program or in the real world, are the things that we interact with to do work. In English, a noun is a part of speech that refers to an entity, quality, state, action, or concept. In an object-oriented view, nouns give names to objects. Therefore, the nouns that appear in the requirements and specification documents can help identify candidates for classes in our object-oriented solution. In the same sense, the verbs that appear in a requirements document often provide clues as to the behaviors that the classes will exhibit.

Recall the words at the beginning of this chapter that describe my dining room: "I am sitting on a chair in front of a table that holds my computer. As I look around, I can see windows and doors on every wall. In the center of the ceiling is a large fan controlled by two switches on the far wall. There is also a thermostat that controls the temperature in the room by turning on and off the heaters located beneath the windows on the opposite wall." The nouns that appear in this text include room, thermostat, and heaters. These are the exact objects that make up the heating system discussed at the beginning of this chapter.

You probably have noticed that there are far more than three nouns in the description of my dining room. The words wall, windows, ceiling, and door also appear in the description, yet there are no wall, window, ceiling, or door classes in our home heating system software design. There is not a one-to-one relationship between the nouns that appear in the requirements document and the classes that end up in the final design of the system. Using nouns to identify classes is a way to *start* the design process. The nouns in a requirements document provide a list of potential classes, but this list needs to be refined until you arrive at the set of classes that makes up your design.

EXAMPLE 2.1 ◆ An Inventory Program

Consider the requirements and specifications for the inventory system shown in Figure 2.10. The nouns in the requirements section are printed in boldface.

Requirements:
Every **department** is required to maintain an **inventory** of the **items** it is responsible for. For any **item** in the **inventory**, the **program** must be able to report the **name, serial number, cost,** and **location** of the **item. Users** must have the ability to add, delete, and locate any **item** contained in the **inventory.** The **program** provides a reporting feature that produces a **list** of all **items** in the **inventory** or a **list** of **items** for a single **location.**

Specifications:
◆ The information must be stored in an ASCII text file on a magnetic disk.
◆ The interface to the program must be menu driven.
◆ The name and serial number of an item may each contain up to 40 characters.
◆ The cost of an item ranges from $0 to $1,000.
◆ Up to 15 users will be able to use the system simultaneously.

FIGURE 2.10 Inventory system requirements and specifications

There are a total of 10 unique nouns in this description: department, inventory, item, program, name, serial number, cost, location, users, list. For each of these nouns, we need to ask the question: Does this noun represent a class that is relevant to the design of the system and should be included in the software? Remember that our goal is to develop an object-oriented model for this one program; we are not trying to create a model of the entire world. Clearly, the words *inventory* and *item* are central to the program because we are designing an inventory system to manage items. The term *department* also seems central to our software since departments maintain the inventory. What about the word *users*? Certainly, a user is necessary to run the program, but a user does not need to be modeled by our software, so it can be removed from our list. What about the word *program*? Users will run the program, and the system will be packaged as a program, but like the word *users,* the word *program* refers to an entity that we really do not need to include in our design. Finally, we can eliminate the word *list* because it refers to the physical output that users will obtain if they utilize the reporting feature of the system. The words *name, serial number, cost,* and *location* refer not to unique classes but, instead, to the state of an item, so they can also be removed from our list of candidates.

That leaves us with three potential classes: department, inventory, and item. Based on the description of the problem, it is clear that this system must contain at least two classes: Inventory and Item. The Inventory class will act as a repository of items. The information about each of the physical items will be stored as state information in the Item class. What about Department? Is it a separate class or part of the state of an item? If department is a class, then an inventory object (along with the items in that inventory) would be associated with the department. For example, the item "bowling shirt" would be associated with the inventory of the Sporting Goods department. This might make it difficult for a user to determine if a particular item is contained in the inventory of another department, assuming that the user only has access to their department object. For example, someone in the Men's Clothing department would be able to look up the price of a shirt but would not be able to look up the price of a bowling shirt since that item is in the inventory of a different department. Making department part of the state of an item would mean that one inventory object could be used to store all the items owned by the corporation.

Which is the correct approach? Based on the information in Figure 2.10, we cannot decide, and if we were doing this design in real life, we would need to consult with the owner of the store to determine how they wish the program to function, modify the requirements, and then select the appropriate design. For the purposes of this discussion, assume that department is part of the state information of an item, so our final design will consist of two classes: Inventory and Item.

Now that we have identified the classes how do we define the state and the behavior for each of these classes? As you have seen, the state of an object may be derived from some of the nouns that appear in the requirements. We know that an item object has the following state: department, name, serial number, cost, and location. We have also decided that an inventory object will have a collection of items as part of its state. What about the behavior of these classes? The Item class is fairly straightforward since its role in this system is to maintain the information associated with each item. Accessor and mutator methods that provide the ability to obtain and change these values are probably all that are required. For example, getDepartment() and setDepartment() methods would provide the ability to obtain or modify the department where the item is located.

The Inventory class is a different story, and the clues for its behavior come from the verbs in the requirements document that describe what operations users perform on the inventory. The document states, "Users must have the ability to add, delete, and locate any item contained in the inventory." This implies that an inventory object would have the methods listed in Table 2.3 that will make these operations possible. Additional behaviors would be required to list the contents of the inventory.

TABLE 2.3 Inventory Methods

Method	Description
void add(SerialNumber sn, Item it)	Add the item it identified by the serial number sn to the inventory.
boolean delete (SerialNumber sn)	Delete the item identified by the serial number sn from the inventory. Return true if the item was deleted and false otherwise.
Item locate(SerialNumber sn)	Locate the item identified by the serial number sn. Return a reference to the item if it is in the inventory or null if the item is not found.

We have presented the criteria used in selecting the nouns that identify classes that will appear in the final design. Since this process is not exact, it might be helpful to discuss criteria used to eliminate nouns from consideration.

The principle of object-oriented programming is to build software based on objects rather than functionality. A common mistake is calling something a class when in reality it is a function or behavior of a class. Classes whose names end with *er,* such as Lister or Finder, are a good example of this type of mistake. A class is not supposed to do one thing but to provide a set of behaviors that act on or modify the state of the object. If the class really only does one thing, it is probably not a class, but instead a behavior that should be associated with some class in your design.

EXAMPLE 2.2 ◆ A Banking System

The requirements and specifications for a simple banking system are given in Figure 2.11. As before, the nouns in the requirements section are printed in boldface.

Clearly, the purpose of this system is similar to the inventory system of Figure 2.10, but instead of storing items, the bank stores accounts. The good news is that we will be able to reuse some of the ideas developed in the design of the inventory system. So as before, one class, Bank, will be responsible for storing all of the account information. Like the Inventory class from the previous example, the Bank class will provide the ability to add, delete, and locate accounts as shown in Table 2.4.

So far, everything seems reasonable except for the fact that the bank has three different types of accounts. If you think about a checking, a savings, or a money market

Requirements:
A **bank** offers **customers** three types of **accounts: checking, savings,** and **money market. Checking accounts** pay 3 percent **interest, savings accounts** have a minimum **balance** of $150 and pay 5 percent **interest,** and **money market accounts** have a minimum **balance** of $1,000 and pay 10 percent **interest.** The **system** is to provide a **report** feature that will list all of the **accounts** and the **interest** that they have accrued during the current **period** (principal * interest / 12). The **system** will also provide **auditor** feature that, when invoked, will print all **accounts** whose **balance** falls below the minimum required for that type of **account.**

For each **account,** the **system** will record the **account number, name, current balance,** and **interest rate.**

Specifications:
Account numbers contain only numeric characters and are exactly 10 characters in length.
Names may contain up to 30 characters.
Balances may range from $0 to $1,000,000.
There will never be more that 2,500 accounts in the bank.
The user will interact with the system using a graphical user interface.

FIGURE 2.11 Banking system requirements and specifications

TABLE 2.4 Bank Methods

Method	Description
`void add( String an, Account a)`	Add the account `a`, identified by the account number `an`, to the bank.
`boolean delete (String an)`	Delete the account identified by the account number `an` from the bank. Return true if the item was deleted and false otherwise.
`Account locate( String an)`	Locate the account identified by the account number `an`. Return a reference to the account if it is in the bank or null if the account is not found.

account, you will realize that they are all accounts. In other words, a checking account is-a account, a savings account is-a account, and a money market account is-a account. The only differences are their interest rates and the minimum balances required. Since the specific account types are only specialized forms of an account, it seems reasonable to use the concept of inheritance first presented in Section 2.2.3. The superclass Account will provide the attributes (account number, name, current balance, interest rate) and behaviors (accessors and mutators) common to all accounts. The specialized rules regarding minimum balances and the computation of interest will be delegated to the subclasses defining that account type. The Bank class will then store Accounts and not worry about the specific types of accounts it is storing (Figure 2.12).

Consider for a moment how the design of the banking system would change if you were asked to add a no interest checking account to the system. Using inheri-

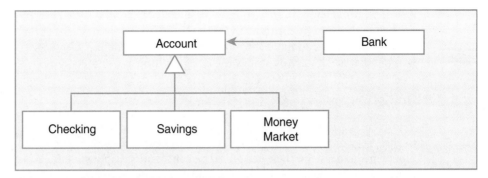

FIGURE 2.12 Banking system design

tance, this is an extremely easy task. You would only have to create a new subclass that captures the details of the new account type. All of the other standard behaviors will be inherited directly from the superclass `Account`. Since the new account type is an `Account`, the `Bank` class will already know how to work with the new class. Thus, the only modification to the existing code would be the addition of the new class. In a procedural language, the changes would be much more substantial.

The last design issue that needs to be dealt with is the "auditor" feature. You might be tempted to create an `Auditor` class that would go through all the accounts stored in the bank and check to see if they satisfy the minimum requirements. The problem with this decision is that you are creating a class consisting of a single method and whose primary purpose is to provide functionality. This is exactly the problem discussed earlier in this section. A better way to deal with the auditing feature is to provide an audit method in the `Bank`, `Account`, `Checking`, `Savings`, and `MoneyMarket` classes. The `audit()` method in `Bank` would step through the accounts it manages invoking, one by one, the specialized audit methods for each type of account. The `audit()` method in the `Checking`, `Savings`, and `MoneyMarket` classes would verify that the minimum requirements have been met for this account type and, if not, print an appropriate message. Note that the end result is the same for both auditor designs. The difference is that the second design is much easier to extend. Once again, ask yourself what is needed to add a new account type. For the second design, all you have to do is add a new subclass to the system that describes the new account and make sure that it includes its own specialized audit method. In the first design, you must not only add a new subclass, but you must also remember to modify the `Auditor` class to handle this new account type.

One of the marks of a good design is that when a change is made to the specification of the problem, the change to the design is localized to a single class rather than propagating through many classes. When you find yourself saying things like, "We must add a new subclass A, and also modify classes B, C, and D to deal with this new subclass," you greatly increase the likelihood for error and complicate the maintenance process.

By working through these two designs, you should have an idea of how to start the design of an object-oriented system. Clearly, in a few pages, it is impossible to give you all the information and experience that you need to build large robust systems.

Another problem that these two examples have highlighted is that a natural language, English in our case, is entirely too ambiguous to precisely describe the design of software. In the next section, we introduce the Unified Modeling Language (UML), which is a tool that accurately describes the design of object-oriented systems.

◆ 2.3.2 Unified Modeling Language (UML)

A software design is useless if it cannot be clearly, concisely, and correctly described to the programmers writing the code. In the construction industry, architects use blueprints to describe their design to the contractors responsible for constructing the building. Software architects need a similar form of "software blueprints"—that is, a standard way of clearly describing the system to be built. This section introduces the **Unified Modeling Language (UML),** a graphical modeling language used to visually express the design of a software system. UML provides a way for a software architect to represent a design in a standard format so that a team of programmers can correctly implement the system.

Prior to the development of UML, there were many different and incompatible techniques that software architects used to express their designs. Since there was no one universally accepted method, it was difficult for software architects to share their designs with each other and, more important, with the programming teams responsible for implementing the software. In 1994, Grady Booch, James Rumbaugh, and Ivar Jacobson (this group of computer scientists is often referred to as the "three amigos") started work on UML. One of the goals of UML was to provide a unified way of modeling any large system, not just software, using object-oriented design techniques. For UML to be widely used, it was important that the language be available to everyone. Therefore, the resulting language is a nonproprietary industrial standard and open to all.

There are several aspects of a system that need to be described in a design. For example, the functional aspects of a system describe the static structure and the dynamic interactions between components in the system, whereas nonfunctional aspects include items such as timing requirements, reliability, or deployment strategies. To describe all of the relevant aspects of a software system, UML provides five different views that document the various aspects of a system. A **view** is an abstraction consisting of a number of diagrams that highlight a particular aspect of the system. Four of the views provided by UML are summarized in Table 2.5.

In addition to the four views of Table 2.5, UML defines nine different **diagram types** that describe specific aspects of the system. Since a single diagram cannot possibly capture all the information required to describe a system, each separate UML view will consist of several diagrams that describe various aspects of the system. The names of the nine types of UML diagrams, a brief description of each type, and the view in which the diagram is typically used are given in Table 2.6.

UML is a powerful tool that has many features, and it can express very complicated designs. In this text, we are only interested in the logical view (the static structure and dynamic behavior) of a system. Therefore, we will make extensive use of class, object, state, and sequence diagrams when expressing our designs.

Unlike a programming language, UML does not have rigid rules regarding what must or must not be included in a diagram, and it allows the software architect to determine how much detail to include in the final diagram. When writing up your designs,

TABLE 2.5 UML Views

View	Description
Use-Case	Describes the functionality that the system should deliver as perceived by external actors (users). Used to document the requirements and specifications of a system.
Logical	Illustrates how the functionality of the system will be implemented in terms of the system's static structure and dynamic behavior.
Component	Shows the organization of the code components.
Deployment	Illustrates the deployment of the system into physical architecture with computers and devices called nodes.

keep in mind what you are trying to illustrate and who will be using your diagrams. A programmer will require very detailed information regarding the state and behavior of an object, whereas a system analyst may only require a general description of the

TABLE 2.6 UML Diagrams

Name	Description	Views
Use-case	Captures a typical interaction between a user and a computing system. Useful when defining the user's view of the system.	Use-case
Class	Describes the classes that make up a system and the various kinds of static relationships that exist among them.	Logical
Object	A variant of the class diagram except that an object diagram shows a number of instances of classes instead of the actual classes.	Logical
State	Describes all the possible states that a particular object can get into and how the object's state changes as a result of messages sent to the object.	Logical, Concurrency
Sequence	Describes how a group of objects collaborates in some behavior concentrating on the messages sent to elicit that behavior.	Logical, Concurrency
Collaboration	Describes how a group of objects collaborates in some behavior concentrating on the static connections between the objects.	Logical, Concurrency
Activity	Shows a sequential flow of activities performed in an operation.	Logical, Concurrency
Component	Describes the physical structure of the code in terms of code components.	Concurrency, Component
Deployment	Shows the physical architecture of the software and hardware components that make up a system.	Concurrency, Deployment

classes that make up the system. Your diagram should provide enough information to illustrate your design but not so much detail that a reader gets lost. The structure of the UML should be based on the needs of the individuals reading the document.

2.3.2.1 Class Diagrams

A class diagram in UML (see Table 2.6) describes the static structure of a system in terms of its classes and the relationships among those classes. Class diagrams are the most common way to describe the design of an object-oriented system, and you will find yourself using them all the time. Class diagrams, like UML, are very expressive and provide ways to describe even the subtlest aspects of a class. To avoid becoming lost in the details, we will only describe the more commonly used features of class diagrams. As you gain more experience, you will almost certainly want to read more about the advanced features of class diagrams, as they can be very useful. There are many excellent references on UML.

It may not be possible, or even desirable, to use a single class diagram to describe a complete system. It is better to concentrate on key areas of the design and then document these ideas with different class diagrams. Keeping the diagrams simple and using them to convey key concepts of a design can be much more effective than using the "shotgun" approach of describing everything in as compact a space as possible.

A class in a class diagram is drawn as a rectangle that can be divided into three compartments (Figure 2.13). The name of the class appears in bold text centered in the compartment at the top of the rectangle. The compartments that describe the state and behavior of the class are optional, as shown in Figure 2.14a. Type information for the methods that make up the behavior of the class is also optional; however, the names of routines that take parameters must be followed by opening and closing parentheses (even if you choose not to put anything inside of them). Parameter and return types for behaviors may be specified using the colon notation shown in Figures 2.14b and 2.14c.

When drawing a class diagram, you want to include only as much information as a reader needs to understand your design. You do not want to overwhelm a reader with trivial detail when it is not required. For example, most class diagrams do not contain obvious behaviors, such as accessors or mutators, so that the nonobvious behaviors in the class are easier to recognize. Similarly, we may choose to omit such relatively unimportant details as `void` return values, as we did in Figure 2.14b. Classes

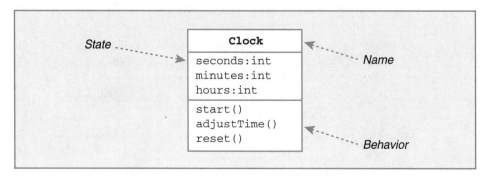

FIGURE 2.13 Clock class diagram

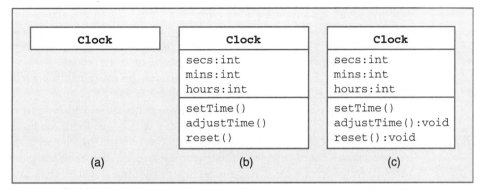

FIGURE 2.14 UML model of a clock class

whose behaviors are well known, such as classes provided in a system library, will either be drawn as a single rectangle with no compartments, as in Figure 2.14a, or omitted from the diagram altogether.

Describing the classes that are present in a software system does not provide enough information for a programmer to understand how these classes work together in a program. For example, if you were asked to describe a family, it would not be enough to say, "A family consists of parents and children." Additional information must be provided to describe the nature of the relationship between parents and children. To completely specify the static structure of a system, the classes and the nature of the relationships between the classes must be defined.

A relationship exists between two classes if one class "knows" about the other. In most object-oriented programming languages, a relationship exists between two classes if an instance of one class invokes a method or accesses the state of an instance of the other class. Knowing that a relationship exists between two classes does not provide any information about the *nature* of the relationship. For example, the relationship that exists between the parents in a family is considerably different from the relationship that exists between the parents and the children. UML defines several different types of relationships that can describe the way in which two or more classes are related in a class diagram. This text uses three different types of relationships: associations, dependencies, and generalizations.

An **association** is a relationship that ties two or more classes together and represents a structural relationship between instances of a class. An association indicates that objects of one class are connected to objects of another. This connection is permanent and makes up part of the state of one of the associated classes. From a programming perspective, two classes are associated if the state of one class contains a reference to an instance of the other class.

In the home heating system, relationships exist between the thermostat, heater, and users of the system. The relationship that exists between the thermostat and heater makes up the structure of the system. At any time while the heating system is in existence, the thermostat will know about the heater. This type of relationship, which represents a permanent structural relationship between two classes, would be classified as an association. The relationship between the thermostat and heater is clearly different from the relationship that exists between a user and the thermostat.

A user is an important part of the system and "uses" the thermostat to adjust the temperature in the room; however, a user does not make up part of the structure of the system nor is the system always associated with a user. The heating system in my dining room continues to function whether or not I am in the room.

For another example of association, consider the relationship between instances of the Engine and Car classes in an automotive simulation program. The relationship that exists between instances of the Engine and Car classes forms part of the structure of a Car. As long as a Car exists, the Car will know about, or be in a relationship with, the Engine. This is not true of the relationship between the Car and Driver classes. At night when I am sleeping and my van is in the garage, my van can still function as a car. On the other hand, should someone break into my garage and remove the engine from my van, it will no longer be capable of functioning as a car. Therefore, although relationships exist among these classes, there is an association between the Engine and Car classes but not between the Driver and Car classes.

In UML, a solid line is drawn between two classes to represent an association. The UML class diagram in Figure 2.15 specifies that the relationship between the Car and Engine classes in the automotive simulation program is an association.

Car	Engine
running:boolean myEngine:Engine	curRPM:int running:boolean
start() lock() accelerate()	accelerate() decelerate() stop()

FIGURE 2.15 UML association

The association between the Car and Engine of Figure 2.15 goes in both directions; the Car knows about the Engine, and the Engine knows about the Car. Associations, however, are not always bidirectional. Consider the relationship between the Engine and GasPedal classes. This relationship can be described as an association because it is permanent and is part of the structure of a Car. Unlike the association between the Car and Engine classes, the association between the GasPedal and the Engine does not go in both directions. The GasPedal knows about the Engine because it invokes the accelerate() method of the Engine; however, the Engine does not know about the GasPedal because it never invokes a method on that class.

Navigability information can be included in a UML class diagram to clarify the nature of the relationship between two classes. As shown in Figure 2.16, an arrow is added to the solid line that represents an association to indicate the *direction* of a relationship. In Figure 2.16, the arrow indicates that the GasPedal knows about the Engine, but the Engine does not know about the GasPedal.

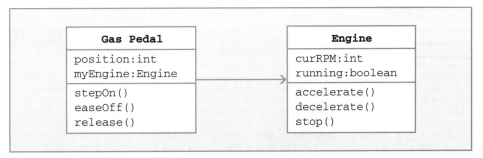

FIGURE 2.16 Adding navigability information to an association

In addition to navigability, **multiplicity** can be used to describe the nature of a relationship between classes. Consider the relationship between the automated-teller machine (ATM) and Bank classes in an electronic banking system. This relationship is an association because it is structural and permanent (i.e., the ATM always needs to know about the Bank). Furthermore, the association is one way because the ATM knows about (i.e., invokes methods on) the Bank, but the Bank does not invoke methods on the ATM. However, there are likely to be several instances of the ATM class, whereas there will only be one instance of the Bank class. This last bit of information can be included in a UML class diagram by adding multiplicity information to the association.

Multiplicity information has been added to the UML diagram in Figure 2.17. The * indicates there may be zero, one, or more instances of the ATM class. The 1 next to the Bank class indicates there is exactly one bank in the system.

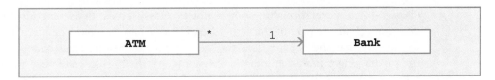

FIGURE 2.17 Multiplicity information added to an association

Let's use association, navigability, and multiplicity to model the inventory system, described in Figure 2.10, and designed in the previous section. Recall that the design consisted of two classes: Inventory and Item. The Inventory class was responsible for storing items and providing methods to add, delete, locate, and modify items in the collection. The Item class captured the state associated with the items owned by each department. The UML class diagram, shown in Figure 2.18, models this design.

The class diagram in Figure 2.18 includes a description of the two classes, Inventory and Item, which make up the inventory system. Since the behaviors that are associated with the Item class consist exclusively of accessors and mutators (e.g., getName(), getCost()), the type of methods that you would expect to find in a class such as this, they have been omitted from the diagram for clarity. Furthermore, the type of data structure used to implement the Inventory class will not affect the design of the system, so it has been omitted to make the diagram easier to understand.

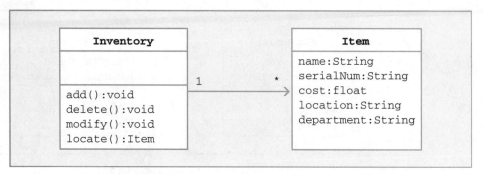

FIGURE 2.18 Inventory system

The relationship between the `Inventory` and `Item` classes is drawn as an association because it describes the structure of the system (i.e., the inventory contains items). In this case, the `Inventory` will not invoke methods of the `Item` class, but clearly, the `Inventory` must know about the items. The navigation information specifies that the `Inventory` knows about the items, but that the items do not know about the `Inventory`. Finally, the multiplicity information specifies that a single `Inventory` will hold zero, one, or more items and that the system consists of exactly one inventory object.

The second type of relationship that will be used in this text is called a **dependency**. A dependency is a using relationship that specifies that a change in one class may affect another class that uses it. A dependency is inherently a one-way relationship where one class is dependent on the other. Returning to the automotive simulation program, clearly a relationship exists between the `Car` and `Driver` classes, but this relationship should not be classified as an association because it does not constitute part of the structure of the system. It would be more descriptive to indicate that the `Driver` uses the `Car` because if the `Car` class changes (perhaps the car no longer has an automatic transmission), the `Driver` may need to change in order to use the `Car`.

The difference between an association and a dependency can be made a little clearer by looking at the way these relationships are implemented in a program. Associations are usually implemented as part of the state of one of the classes. For example, in the code that implements the state of the `GasPedal` class, you would expect to find a variable that refers to the `Engine` object that the `GasPedal` controls. As long as the `Car` is in existence, a `GasPedal` object will always be associated with a specific `Engine` object. The state variable provides a mechanism whereby the `GasPedal` can access the `Engine`.

A dependency typically takes the form of a local variable, parameter, or return value in the methods that implement the behavior of the object. These types of variables are often referred to as **automatic** because they are created and destroyed as needed. They do not represent a permanent structural relationship. If the variable is in scope (in other words, if it exists), one class has a way to access another class it depends on. So at some point in the lifetime of the object, it may know about an instance of a class with which it related, and at other times, it will not. This reflects the transient, or nonpermanent, nature of a dependency. In an automotive simulation program, you

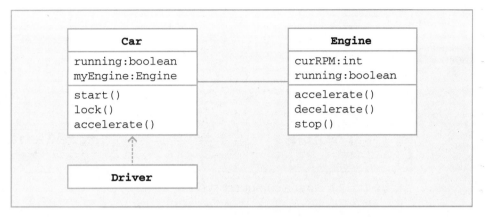

FIGURE 2.19 UML association and dependency

would expect that the `Driver` has a method named `driveCar()` that takes as a parameter a reference to the `Car` that is to be driven. The `Car` is clearly not part of the state of the `Driver`. Furthermore, a `Driver` only knows about a specific `Car` when physically driving it. When the `Driver` is finished with that `Car`, the relationship ends.

In a UML class diagram, a dependency is drawn as a dashed line (Figure 2.19). The arrow on the line points to the independent element. In Figure 2.19, the arrow captures the fact that if the `Car` changes, the `Driver` may need to change, but if the `Driver` changes, the `Car` will not be affected.

Generalization, or inheritance, is the third type of relationship that will be used in this text. In an inheritance relationship, a subclass is a specialized form of the superclass. If you look at the relationship from the superclass' perspective, you could say that the superclass is a generalization of its subclasses. This generalization relationship is denoted by a triangle connecting a subclass to its parent class. The triangle is connected to and points at the parent class as shown in Figure 2.20.

Both associations and generalizations (inheritance) can be illustrated in a single diagram as shown in Figure 2.21. This diagram describes the relationships between a processor, disk controller, and disk drive. Here the CPU is associated with the class `Controller` that describes all controllers. `SCSIController`, a subclass of `Controller`,

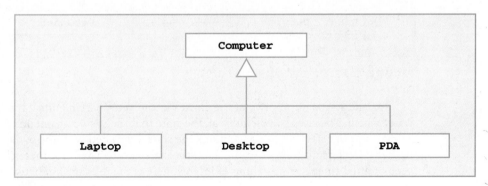

Figure 2.20. Generalization (inheritance)

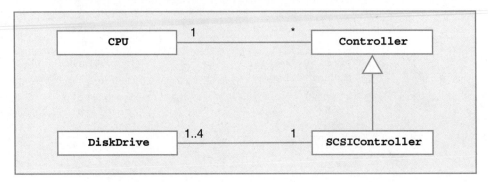

FIGURE 2.21 Simple computer system

is the class that is associated with DiskDrive. In a class diagram, associations should only be shown at the highest possible level. For example, in Figure 2.21, the association is between the CPU and Controller (the superclass) and not between the CPU and the SCSIController (the subclass). This indicates that the CPU is designed to work with any Controller, not just a SCSIController.

2.3.2.2 Example Class Diagrams

The best way to master the basics of class diagrams is to use them to model simple systems. This section presents four different UML class diagrams along with a description of the system that each diagram models. To improve your understanding of class diagrams, take a few minutes to review each UML class diagram before reading the description of the diagram in the text. Write down what you believe is the description of the system being modeled. Then read the description of the system that follows and reconcile your description with that in the text.

EXAMPLE 2.3 ♦ Veterinary System

The first class diagram models two classes in a system used by a veterinarian to track patients (i.e., pets), and it is given in Figure 2.22.

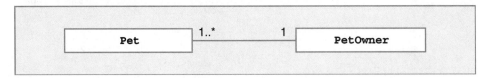

FIGURE 2.22 Pets and pet owners

Pet and PetOwner are two of the classes in the veterinarian animal tracking software system. The class Pet includes all the state that the system maintains for a single animal, and the class PetOwner contains the state associated with the owner of a Pet. In the UML class diagram of Figure 2.22, the state and behavior for these classes have been omitted since the only thing of interest here is the relationship between the two classes. The state of every Pet object contains a reference to its owner. Since this relationship provides structural information and instances of the `Pet` class will always contain a reference to a `PetOwner`, the relationship is modeled as an association.

The absence of the navigability information in the drawing indicates that the association is bidirectional. In other words, a `Pet` knows about its owner, and a `PetOwner` knows about its pet. Finally, the multiplicity information shows that every `Pet` has exactly one owner, and every `PetOwner` has one or more `Pets`. If the multiplicity information was omitted, nothing can be said about the number of `PetOwners` associated with a `Pet` and the number of `Pets` associated with a `PetOwner`.

EXAMPLE 2.4 ◆ Library System

The class diagram in Figure 2.23 describes the relationships that exists between books, pages of a book, shelves, and the patrons of a typical library. This diagram indicates that a `Book` contains one or more pages. This relationship has been modeled as an association because the pages are actually part of the book. If we rip the pages out of the book, that book is no longer a book. Note, however, that whether the pages are in the book or not, they are still pages. This is why the solid line that specifies the association between the `Book` and `Page` classes has an arrow that points to the `Page` class. Compare this to the relationship that exists between the `Shelf` and `Book` classes. Clearly, a book is not part of a shelf, and a shelf is not part of a book; however, should the properties of a book change (becomes taller, heavier, etc.), the shelf may have to change to accommodate the book. This means that in this relationship, the `Shelf` class is dependent on the `Book` class. The arrow specifies the independent class (i.e., the class that does not have to change).

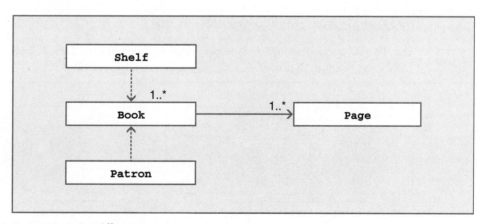

FIGURE 2.23 Library

EXAMPLE 2.5 ◆ Banking System

In this system, shown in Figure 2.24, a single bank is associated with, or has, one or more accounts. The lack of navigability information indicates that the association goes in both directions. Clearly, the bank knows about its accounts, but the accounts also

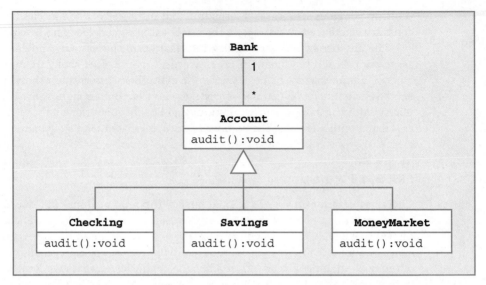

FIGURE 2.24 Banking system

know about the bank. This means that an account can utilize the services provided by its bank, such as obtaining the current interest rate set by the Federal Reserve Bank. An account is a generalization of three classes: Checking, Savings, and MoneyMarket. The audit() method is defined in the Account class and is a behavior that all of its subclasses will have.

EXAMPLE 2.6 ◆ Home Heating System

Finally, this section would not be complete without Figure 2.25, which contains a UML class diagram that models a simple home heating system.

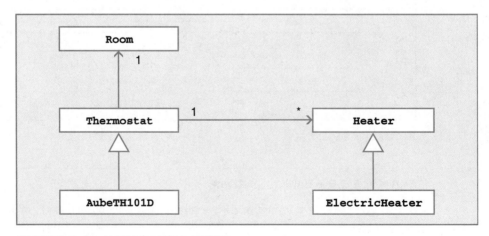

FIGURE 2.25 Home heating system

UML class diagrams are an excellent tool for capturing the static aspects of a system, namely, the classes in the system and the relationships between classes. What we have not discussed yet is how we capture the dynamic aspects of a system. Using a class diagram, it is not possible to document that in the home heating system of Figure 2.25 the thermostat queries the room for the current temperature and turns on the heaters if necessary. A class diagram can show that a thermostat knows about a room and knows about the heaters, but it cannot say anything about what specific interactions the thermostat has with these items. In the next section, we introduce UML sequence diagrams that are used to describe the dynamic behavior of an object-oriented system.

2.3.2.3 Sequence Diagrams

Sequence diagrams describe how groups of objects dynamically collaborate with each other. Typically, a single sequence diagram describes a single behavior. It diagrams a number of objects and the messages passed between these objects. Sequence diagrams provide a way to describe the dynamic behavior of a system.

To illustrate some of the basic features of sequence diagrams, in this section of the text we model the behavior of a printing system. The system consists of a number of printers, each of which has different resources: the size and type of paper it is currently holding or the ability to print in color. Each printer is serviced by a print queue that holds the jobs for this printer. Information about the printer resources and the location of the queues that service the printers is maintained by the printer registry. The class diagram for this system is given in Figure 2.26.

Although the class diagram in Figure 2.26 explains the static structure of the printing system, it does not explain how the objects collaborate to achieve a specific

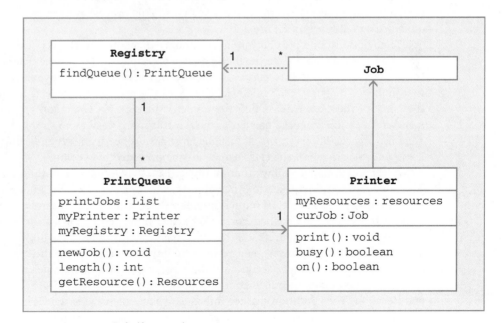

FIGURE 2.26 Printing system

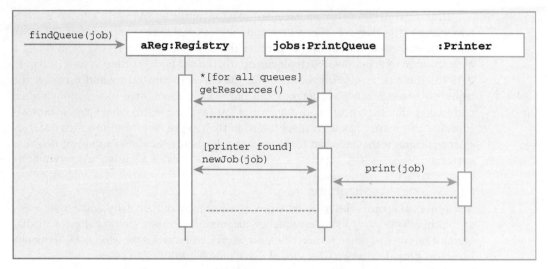

FIGURE 2.27 Sequence diagram for the printing system of Figure 2.26

behavior. For example, a question that a programmer needs to ask when implementing this system is: How does a job find a printer with exactly the set of resources it requires? The answer is that when a print job needs to be sent to a printer, a message findQueue() is sent to the registry that contains the job to be printed and a list of the required resources. The registry then searches each of its print queues looking for the first printer that has the resources required to print this job. If such a printer exists, the registry sends a newJob() message to the print queue, which in turn will send a print() message to the correct Printer. This process is described in the sequence diagram given in Figure 2.27.

Time flows from top to bottom in a sequence diagram, and the vertical lines that run down the diagram denote the lifetime of an object. Since a sequence diagram illustrates objects as opposed to classes, a slightly different labeling convention is used. In a sequence diagram, each line is labeled with the name of the object, followed by the name of the class from which the object is instantiated. A colon separates the name of the object from the name of the class. It is not necessary to supply names for all of the objects; however, the class name must always be given. When labeling a line using only a class name, the class name must be preceded by a colon.

A vertical rectangle shows that an object is active—that is, handling a request. The object can send requests to other objects, which is indicated by a horizontal arrow. An object can send itself requests, which is indicated with an arrow that points back to the object. The dashed horizontal arrow indicates a return from a message, not a new message. In Figure 2.27, the PrintQueue sends the print(job) message to a Printer, which is followed by a return. Note that after handling the message, the Printer object is no longer active, and therefore, the vertical rectangle ends.

Two forms of control information can be placed in a sequence diagram: condition and iteration. The condition marker indicates when a message is sent. The condition appears in square brackets above the message—for example, [printer found]. The message is only sent if the condition is true. The iteration marker indicates that a message is sent many times to multiple receiver objects. The basis of the iteration appears within square brackets immediately preceded by an asterisk (*). In Figure 2.27, the control information *[for all queues] indicates that the Registry will send a getResources() message to each of the PrintQueue objects that it is managing. The condition marker [printer found] specifies that the print job will be sent to a printer only if a printer with the correct resources is located.

A sequence diagram illustrates the sequencing of events in an object-oriented system. It does not show the algorithms that are involved; it only shows the order in which messages are sent. Each of the classes that appears in a sequence diagram should be described in a separate class diagram. Note that if a sequence diagram indicates that an object sends a message to another object, then in the corresponding class diagram, there must be a relationship, either an association or dependency, between those two classes. You should include a separate sequence diagram for each of the major behaviors in the system being modeled. What is a "major" behavior? It depends on your audience and what information you are trying to convey in your drawing, but as a guideline, you should include those behaviors that are central to an understanding of the software being developed. For example, in our home heating system, it would be essential to understand the behaviors associated with obtaining the room temperature and activating the heaters. However, the behaviors associated with testing the thermostat or putting it into "vacation mode" would be less important. You must be very careful not to hide the central aspects of the the design by including a great deal of unnecessary information.

2.4 SUMMARY

As was mentioned in Chapter 1, there is a great deal of preparatory work that must be done, and done well, before we even think about starting to write code. This preparatory work is called problem specification and program design.

This chapter has looked more closely at these specification and design phases and introduced some fundamental principles of one development method called object-oriented design. This technique allows us to design and build software in a manner more closely related to how people organize and think about systems in their own mind. Instead of a step-by-step procedural approach, the object-oriented model allows designers to think in terms of entities encapsulated with their external behaviors. Users do not need to know exactly how these behaviors are implemented, only that they are provided. This allows the internal implementation of a behavior to change without affecting a user's program, greatly facilitating program maintenance. In addition, the object-oriented model provides a concept called inheritance, which allows classes to automatically acquire existing functionality from other classes, enhancing programmer productivity. Encapsulation and inheritance are two of the most important characteristics of this object-oriented design method.

The chapter also introduced a formalized notation for expressing and representing our object-oriented designs: the Unified Modeling Language, or UML for short. UML is an industrial standard that can express the design of a software system in the same way that blueprints can describe the design of a building. UML provides an expressive tool that can be used by a software architect to convey a design to a team of

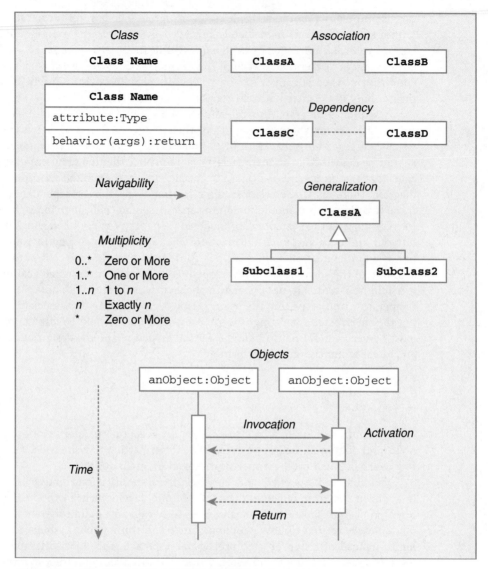

FIGURE 2.28 Summary of UML modeling elements

programmers. We will be using UML throughout the text, including the case study done in Chapter 4. The features of UML introduced in this section are summarized in Figure 2.28.

Our discussions in this chapter have been at a rather abstract level, using such lofty concepts as classes, behaviors, states, associations, and dependencies. However, once the design of our software has been completed, we would like to reflect this design in our actual code by using an object-oriented programming language that linguistically supports the design ideas presented in this chapter: classes, objects, methods, encapsulation, and inheritance.

Chapter 3 will show how these basic object-oriented concepts are realized and implemented in the Java programming language. Chapter 4 presents a significant case study that will use the concepts introduced in this chapter, along with the Java programming techniques from Chapter 3, to design and implement an object-oriented solution to our home heating problem.

EXERCISES

1. Review the design of some of the earliest object-oriented programming languages such as Simula and Smalltalk. Discuss the influence they had on the C++ and Java languages.

2. Consider one process or task you do every day such as making toast, buying groceries, brushing your teeth, and so forth. Identify at least two nontrivial objects involved in the process and detail their classes' data members and methods. Draw class diagrams for each of the classes you found.

3. Explain the distinction between the is-a and has-a relationships.

4. Determine whether or not the following groups would or would not be related by inheritance. If so, state which are the superclasses and which are the subclasses: car/truck/vehicle, car/bicycle, rock/paper/scissors, and car/driver/tire.

5. List common methods of finding classes in a requirements document.

6. List and discuss differences between the design processes for an object-oriented program and a procedural program.

7. Define the term *object* in the context of the object-oriented programming paradigm. Justify your definition by explaining how building "your" objects allows you to develop better code.

8. List the phases of the software life cycle and give a brief description of each. List common processes, the deliverables they produce, and the uses for those deliverables.

9. Write detailed and precise English instructions to perform a moderately complicated task. Write a procedural and an object-oriented solution to solve this task. Describe the differences in the way you would use (and reuse) the code that would be used to implement the procedural solution with the code that would be used to implement the object-oriented solution.

10. List and explain differences between an Integer object and an integer variable.

11. Create a UML diagram for the most basic (operational) chair you can think of. Call the class ChairA. Create two new types of chair called ChairB and ChairC. Let ChairB and ChairC each extend ChairA, adding new functionality and/or features to the basic design of ChairA. Draw a UML diagram that describes Chairs A, B, and C and illustrates their relationship. Derive ChairD from ChairB, adding at least one new feature and modifying the way in which one of ChairB's methods works. Write pseudocode for the original ChairB method and its modified ChairD version. Add ChairD to the UML diagram for part B.

12. A requirements document for a medium-sized project could contain hundreds of nouns. Some of those nouns will become core classes of your software solution. The rest, while important, don't figure into the design quite so directly. Your solution's correctness, budget, and profit margin depend on finding those core nouns quickly and reliably. What characteristics will you look for to help distinguish the nouns that will become your classes? Write up a short (one- to three-page) requirements document describing the desired operation of a program. Draw a class diagram for this program.

13. Two friends have decided to rent an apartment together. They work in different locations, with coordinates X1, Y1 and X2, Y2. Given coordinates for local towns, design and diagram an object-oriented program that minimizes and equalizes the distance they must each commute. Design the solution so that cities may be ranked by additional criteria. Your design should maximize (or minimize, as appropriate) these preferences as well.

14. Big Oil Inc. has developed a new technique for locating undersea oil. By analyzing information from two different types of sensors, sonar and teledensitometer (TD), Big Oil scientists can pinpoint undersea oil fields. In an effort to lower risk to their employees, Big Oil plans to use robotic drones to explore interesting areas of the seabed. The drones can physically mount one sensor module each. Drones can be instructed to move about on the ocean surface, report their position via a Global Positioning System, and hold their position while measurements are being taken. All sensor modules provide the ability to retrieve the data they have collected, but the differing nature of the sensor types leads to differing controls, as follows:

    a. A sonar sensor generates a pulse of sonic energy and listens for the echoes. Sonar readings are very storage intensive, and so sonar modules cannot store more than one reading at a time. The current reading may be retrieved by the operator or overwritten by a new one.

    b. A teledensitometer sensor generates readings using a continuous process. The TD sensor is switched on when it is over an area of interest. While switched on, data generated with confidence values past a certain threshold are added to the TD's temporary buffer. After collection, the operator can instruct the TD to verify that the buffer contains sufficient data for an accurate measurement. Depending on the result, the operator must either discard the buffer data, retain it to add more (by reactivating the TD sensor), or archive it to one of five of the TD module's long-term storage locations (thus emptying the buffer). Appending data from one target point to a buffer containing data from another target point corrupts the buffer's data.

    Write English instruction for using each of the two types of drones to survey an area for the presence of oil. Based on the instructions that you have written, design a class for a drone and each of the two sensor types. Document your design using a UML class diagram.

15. Describe in simple English the systems represented by the following four UML diagrams:

a.

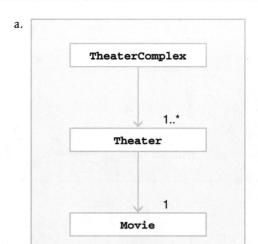

b.

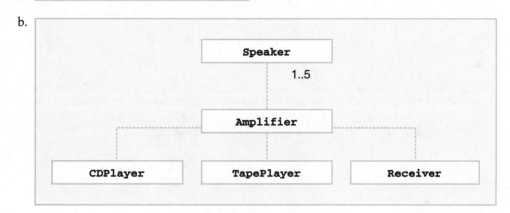

c.

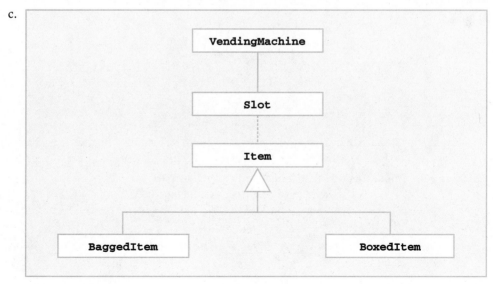

d.

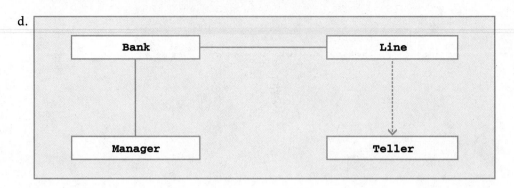

CHAPTER 3

Object-Oriented Programming Using Java

3.1 INTRODUCTION

After reading Chapters 1 and 2, it should be quite clear that there is much more to software development than writing a program. In Chapter 1, you learned that the first step in the software life cycle is to describe the behavior of the proposed software and to document that behavior formally in the requirements and specifications documents. In Chapter 2, you learned how to use object-oriented techniques to develop a design that, when implemented, satisfies the conditions spelled out in the requirements and specifications documents. This chapter focuses on those aspects of Java that will enable you to write a correct and efficient object-oriented program. Although the focus of this chapter is on implementation, it is important to keep in mind that coding is only one step in the software life cycle. A considerable amount of work must be done both before and after the coding phase commences.

We have made two important decisions regarding this chapter. First, it only discusses those aspects of Java necessary to write object-oriented programs. Java provides many additional features useful in the development of software. Although important, we will defer discussion of these features until later in the text. Second, we assume that you already have learned to program in some high-level language and therefore understand fundamental programming concepts such as types, variables, parameter passing, and control structures. You probably studied these concepts in your first programming course. However, if these concepts are new to you or if you are not fully comfortable with them, you should spend a few minutes reviewing the Appendix, which contains a brief introduction to basic procedural programming concepts in Java. You may also want to consider reviewing an introductory programming text before reading this chapter.

As we mentioned in Chapter 2, an object-oriented program consists of a number of objects that interact to accomplish a specified task. Since objects are instantiated from classes, the primary activity of an object-oriented programmer is to write class definitions that can then be used to instantiate the objects in a program. Given the importance of class definitions in an object-oriented program, this chapter begins with a discussion of how to write classes and utilize inheritance. This is followed by a discussion of the nuts and bolts of running a Java program.

3.2 CLASS DEFINITIONS IN JAVA

In Java, a class declaration defines a new class from which objects can be instantiated. The purpose of the class declaration is to define the state and behavior that will be exhibited by instances of the class. Variables defined within the class model the state of objects, and the methods defined in the class provide an implementation of the behavior exhibited by the object. A Java program is a collection of one or more class declarations.

Classes in Java are organized into packages. A **package** is a collection of related classes. Every class definition in Java, whether written by you or supplied in a class library, is a member of a package. It is important to understand that every class is a member of a package and that if a class does not name the package to which it belongs, the class automatically becomes a member of the "unnamed" package. All Java

```
ClassModifier class identifier {
    Class State . . .
    Class Behavior . . .
}
```

FIGURE 3.1 General form of a top-level class declaration

systems must support at least one unnamed package. Understanding the concept of package membership will become important later when we discuss accessibility.

A Java class can be declared as either a top-level class or as one of four different types of nested classes. As the name implies, a **nested class** is defined inside another class. Nested classes are often referred to as **inner classes** in the Java literature. The general form of a top-level class declaration is given in Figure 3.1.

The *identifier* specifies the name of the class. In Java, a name consists of an arbitrary number of letters (including _ and $) and digits. The first character of an identifier must be a letter. Identifiers cannot have the same spelling as any of the keywords or literals used in the Java language. By convention, the first letters of the names of classes are capitalized, and the first letters of the names of variables are not. If a name contains multiple words, the first letter of each word in the name is capitalized with the exception of the first word if the name refers to a variable. For example, the names counter, xCoordinate, and numberOfSides are all examples of variable names. The names Rectangle, Thermostat, and GasFurnace are examples of class names. This naming style is a coding convention and is not a requirement of the Java language. Coding conventions are used by programmers to make their code easier to read.

Class declarations are placed into source files. Each Java source file contains a single public class. The name of the file and the name of the public class that it contains must be the same. By convention, files that contain Java source code use the suffix .java. For example, Figure 3.2 contains the skeleton of a class definition that defines a point. Since the name of this class is Point, the file that contains this class definition must be named Point.java.

In a top-level class, the *ClassModifier* is most often used to determine what classes are allowed to access the class declaration. The *ClassModifier* is optional, and if it is omitted, the class is defined as having **package scope**. Package scope means that only classes that are members of the same package can access the declaration and create

```
/**
 * A class that defines a point.
 */

public class Point {
/* This class defines points in 2 dimensional space */
    // State of a Point
    // Behavior of a Point
} // Point
```

FIGURE 3.2 Skeleton definition of a Point class

instances of the class. If a top-level class is defined as `public`, any class, regardless of the package in which it is defined, can access the declaration and use it to create instances of the class. Most of the classes that you will write have public access.

As illustrated in Figure 3.2, Java permits programmers to use two types of comments to document their code. Multiline comments begin with the characters `/*` and end with `*/`. Anything between the starting `/*` and the terminating `*/` is ignored by the compiler. Single-line comments start with the character `//` and terminate at the end of the line. Everything on the line following the `//` is ignored by the compiler. Comments do not nest, which means that the character sequences `/*` and `//` have no special meaning inside a comment.

If you look closely at the comments in Figure 3.2, you will notice that some of the multiline comments start with `/**` instead of `/*`. The extra asterisk at the end of the `/*` is a flag that indicates that the comment contains information that should be processed by the Javadoc program. These are often referred to as **Javadoc comments**. In Chapter 1, you learned that Javadoc is a program that is included with the standard Java distribution and can be used to generate HTML-based documentation. The Javadoc program processes the information within a Javadoc comment. This information will be incorporated into the documentation generated by the program. Table 3.1 lists the Javadoc tags that appear in this chapter. However, there are many more tags that can be used to create an extensive set of online documentation for a Java program.

TABLE 3.1 Javadoc Tags

Tag	Description
@author	Identifies the author(s) of the code:
	`@author Paul Tymann...`
@param	Provides information about method and constructor parameters. The tag is followed by a parameter name and a comment:
	`@param count number of elements...`
@return	Description of return value for nonvoid methods

The body of the class definition contains declarations that define the state and behavior associated with the class. In the next section, we will look at how state information is declared in a Java class definition.

◆ 3.2.1 State

The state of a Java object is represented by variables. The variables that define the state associated with instances of a class are referred to as **instance variables**. The format for the declaration of an instance variable is given in Figure 3.3.

Modifiers Type VariableName;

FIGURE 3.3 General form of an instance variable declaration

```
/**
 * A Class that defines a point.
 */

public class Point {
    // State of a Point
    private int xCoordinate;    // The x coordinate
    private int yCoordinate;    // The y coordinate

    // Behavior of a point

}   // Point
```

FIGURE 3.4 Adding state to the Point class

In Figure 3.4, two instance variables, xCoordinate and yCoordinate, have been added to the Point class. These variables are used to store the *X* and *Y* coordinates of a point.

Every time a new instance of a class is created, a new set of instance variables will be created for that object. The instance variables are permanently associated with the object in which they are declared and represent the state of that object. As long as the object exists, its instance variables exist, which means it has state. If you assign a value to an instance variable, that value will remain stored in the instance variable until you either change it or the object is destroyed. This is considerably different from the way in which local variables are created and destroyed. Local variables are automatically created when the method in which they are defined is invoked, and they are destroyed when the method returns. One of the consequences of this occurs if you assign a value to both an instance variable and a local variable during an invocation of a method. The next time the method is invoked, the instance variable will still contain the value that was assigned in the previous invocation, whereas the local variable will not. This happens because local variables are created "fresh" every time the method is invoked, whereas the instance variables are created only once when the object is instantiated.

Like a class definition, every instance variable has an associated accessibility that determines the visibility of the variable. Instance variables with public accessibility can be accessed by instances of any class. The use of public instance variables should be avoided because they break the encapsulation provided by the class structure. Private instance variables can be accessed by any instance of the same class. The scope of a private variable is not restricted to a single instance of the class. Any instance of the same class can access the private instance variables of other instances of the same class. In terms of the Point class of Figure 3.4, this means that any Point object can access the xCoordinate and yCoordinate of any other Point object.

In Java, the modifiers public and private specify the access of an instance variable. The modifiers appear in the declaration of the instance variable before the keyword that specifies the type of the variable. Only one access modifier can appear in the declaration of an instance variable. In Figure 3.4, the instance variables xCoordinate

```
/**

 * Illustrate how to specify the scope of instance variables.
 */

public class InstanceScope {

    // x is private which means x can only be accessed by
    // instances of the InstanceScope class.
    private int x;

    // y is public which means y can be accessed by any
    // instance of any class.
    public int y;

     // z has package scope which means z can be accessed
     // by any instance of a class that is in the same
     // package as InstanceScope.
    int z;

} // InstanceScope
```

FIGURE 3.5 Specifying the access of instance variables

and yCoordinate have private access. Package access is the default for an instance variable. So if you do not provide an access modifier for an instance variable, that variable will have package scope. The class definition in Figure 3.5 shows how to declare instance variables with private, public, and package access.

The state of an object is normally private and accessed using methods that are provided by the class. Finally, any class in the same package can access instance variables with package access. Like public instance variables, instance variables with package access should be avoided.

Instance variables are associated with an instance of a class. It is possible to associate a state variable with a Java class by declaring the variable as static. **Static variables** represent state that is associated with the entire class, not with individual instances of the class. This means that there is exactly one copy of the static variable whether zero, six, or a thousand instances of the class have been created. Since these variables are associated with the class and not with instances of the class, they are referred to as **class variables**. All instances of a class can access the class variables associated with the class. You can almost think of a class variable as a global variable that is associated with a class. Whether or not instances of other classes can access a class variable depends on the access modifier that is associated with the variable. The accessibility of a class variable is specified in the same way as the accessibility of an instance variable is specified. The keyword static in the declaration of a state variable specifies that the variable is a class variable. If a modifier specifies the access of the class variable, it should precede the static modifier. The class definition in Figure 3.6 illustrates how class variables can be declared.

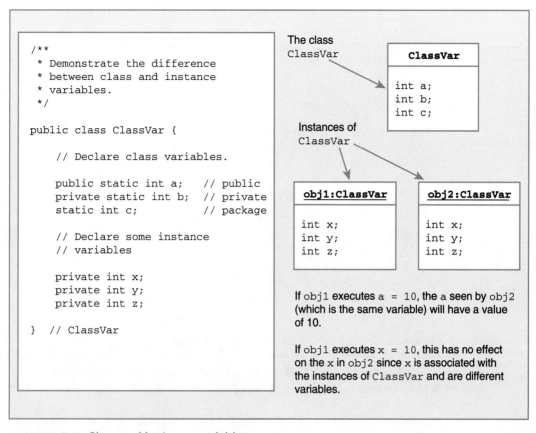

```
/**
 * Demonstrate the difference
 * between class and instance
 * variables.
 */

public class ClassVar {

    // Declare class variables.

    public static int a;     // public
    private static int b;    // private
    static int c;            // package

    // Declare some instance
    // variables

    private int x;
    private int y;
    private int z;

}  // ClassVar
```

The class
ClassVar

ClassVar

int a;
int b;
int c;

Instances of
ClassVar

obj1:ClassVar

int x;
int y;
int z;

obj2:ClassVar

int x;
int y;
int z;

If obj1 executes a = 10, the a seen by obj2 (which is the same variable) will have a value of 10.

If obj1 executes x = 10, this has no effect on the x in obj2 since x is associated with the instances of ClassVar and are different variables.

FIGURE 3.6 Class and instance variables

Both instance and class variables can be initialized at the time they are declared by adding an initialization expression to the declaration of the variable. The initialization expression takes the form of an assignment statement in which the variable declaration appears on the left side of the assignment operator and an expression appears on the right side.

After the memory for the variables has been allocated, the expression on the right side of the assignment operator is evaluated, and the result is stored in the variable. An initialization expression for a class variable is executed exactly once, when the class is initialized. If the initialization expression is for an instance variable, it will be executed every time an instance of the class is created. Initialization expressions can also appear in the declaration of local variables. Figure 3.7 illustrates initialization expressions in a class definition.

The use of initialization expressions is optional. By default, all instance and class variables are initialized (numerical variables are initialized to 0, character variables are initialized to the null character, Boolean variables are initialized to false, and reference variables are initialized to null). Even though the variables that represent the state of an object are initialized by default, it is considered good coding practice to explicitly initialize these variables either when they are declared or in the constructor for the class (preferably in the constructor).

```
/**
 * Illustrate how to use initializers in a class
 * definition.
 */

public class Initializers {

    private static int a = 13;      // a is initialized to 13

    private static int b = a * 2;   // b is initialized to 26

    private int x = a;              // a copy of the value
                                    // in a is placed in x

    private int y = 0;              // y is initialized to 0

} // Initializers
```

FIGURE 3.7 Initialization statements in a class declaration

The default initialization rules apply only to instance and class variables; local variables are not automatically initialized. All variables in a Java class must be initialized before they can be used. This means that local variables must be explicitly initialized before they can be used. A good habit is to explicitly initialize all local variables as soon as they are declared.

The standard programming rules apply to the expressions in initialization statements. The type of the expression must match the type of the variable, and any variables in the expression must already have been declared and initialized. What might not be as obvious is that instance variables cannot initialize the value of a class variable. Recall that a class variable is initialized when the class is initialized, which happens before any instances of the class are created. If there are no instances of the class, then the instance variables do not exist yet. If the instance variables do not exist, they cannot be used in an initialization expression. Even if instances of the class existed, how would the compiler know which instance variable to use to initialize the class variables if multiple instances exist?

final is the last modifier that we will discuss that can be applied to a variable. A final variable can only be assigned a value when it is declared. Any attempt to change the value of the variable, except during initialization, will be flagged as an error. In essence, when you declare a state variable as final, it behaves as a constant. final applies to the contents of the state variable and not to any object that the variable may be referring to. For reference types, this means that the reference stored in the variable cannot be changed, but the object that the reference is referring to may be changed.

To make this last point a little clearer, recall from the Appendix that variables in Java can be divided into two broad groups: primitives and references. Primitive variables are declared to be one of the following eight types: char, byte, short, int, long, float, double, or boolean. If a variable is defined to be of any type other than

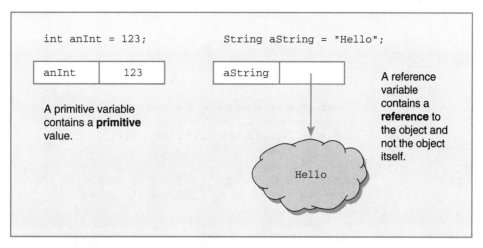

FIGURE 3.8 Primitive and reference variables

the eight just listed, then it is a reference variable. In terms of memory, a primitive variable holds one of the eight basic types, whereas a reference variable holds a reference to an object as illustrated in Figure 3.8.

If the variables in Figure 3.8 were declared as `final`, it would not be possible to change the contents of either variable. The compiler would reject any statement that attempted to change the 123 stored in `anInt` or a statement that tried to change the reference (i.e., the arrow in Figure 3.8) stored in the variable `aString` so that it referred to a different object. In other words, the statements `anInt = 456` or `aString = "World"` would be rejected by the compiler. However, an attempt to change the object that the variable `aString` is referring to would not be considered an error (assuming that `aString` can be changed).

The most common use of the `static` and `final` modifiers in variable declarations is in the creation of symbolic constants in a Java program. By convention, the name associated with a symbolic constant is all uppercase and the underscore (_) character separates words within the name. For example, the name `MAX_VALUE` is a valid name for a symbolic constant. Like the conventions associated with the naming of classes and variables, the compiler does not enforce naming conventions for symbolic constants. Note that a symbolic constant does not have to be declared as `static`. A copy of a nonstatic constant will be present in each instance of the class. If the variable is a constant, it is a slightly more efficient use of space to declare the constant as `static`. The `Point` class in Figure 3.9 has been modified to include a symbolic constant named `MAX_VALUE`, which can be used to determine the maximum value that may be assigned to either of the coordinate values.

In this section, we looked at how the state associated with an object is modeled in Java using variables. State information in Java is stored in instance and class variables. Instance variables are associated with an instance of a class, which means there is a different copy of an instance variable in each instance of a class. Class variables, on the other hand, belong to the class, which means there is only one copy of the variable that is shared by all instances of the class. Class variables are declared as `static`, whereas instance variables are not. Every state variable has an associated accessibility.

```
/**
 * A Class that defines a point.
 */

public class Point {
    // Constant that gives the maximum value that may
    // be assigned to either the x or y coordinates
    public final static int MAX_VALUE = 1024;

    // State of a Point
    private int xCoordinate;   // The x coordinate
    private int yCoordinate;   // The y coordinate

  // Behavior of a Point

} // Point
```

FIGURE 3.9 Adding a symbolic constant to the Point class

Members of any class can access public variables, but only members of the same class can access private variables. Variables without an explicit access modifier have package accessibility, meaning that only classes in the same package can access the variable. The modifier final can create read-only variables that are often used to create symbolic constants in a class.

State is only one part of the definition of a class. In Chapter 2, we stated that an object has state, behavior, and identity. In the next section, we will discuss how to add methods to a class definition that will define the behavior associated with an object.

◆ 3.2.2 Behavior

The behavior of an object is modeled in Java using **methods**. You can think of a method as a procedure, or function, associated with a particular class or object. To call, or invoke, the method, you must have a reference to the class or object that the method is associated with. The general form of a method declaration appears in Figure 3.10.

{MethodModifiers ReturnType MethodName(FormalParameterList)}

FIGURE 3.10 General form of a method declaration

In Chapter 2 we defined four categories of methods that can be associated with an object: accessors, mutators, constructors, and destructors. The Point class in Figure 3.11 has been modified to include two accessors: getXCoordinate() and getYCoordinate(). The getXCoordinate() method returns the value stored in the xCoordinate instance variable, and similarly, the getYCoordinate() returns the value currently stored in the yCoordinate instance variable. Using these methods, it

```
/**
 * A Class that defines a point.
 */

public class Point {
    // Constant that gives the maximum value that may
    // be assigned to either the x or y coordinates
    public final static int MAX_VALUE = 1024;

    // State of a Point
    private int xCoordinate;   // The x coordinate
    private int yCoordinate;   // The y coordinate

    /**
     * Return the x coordinate of this point.
     * @return the x coordinate of this point.
     */
    public int getXCoordinate() {
        return xCoordinate;
    }

    /**
     * Return the y coordinate of this point.
     * @return the y coordinate of this point.
     */
    public int getYCoordinate() {
        return yCoordinate;
    }

} // Point
```

FIGURE 3.11 Adding accessor methods to the Point class

is possible to access the state of a Point object. By convention, the name of an accessor method starts with the word get. This convention is not enforced by the compiler but rather is stated in a coding standard.

If you look at the general form of a method declaration in Figure 3.10 and then look at the method declarations in Figure 3.11, you should come to the conclusion that the method modifiers for both the getXCoordinate() and getYCoordinate() methods are public and that their return type is int.

A method modifier specifies the accessibility of a method in the same way that the modifier associated with class or instance variables specifies the accessibility of the variable. The method modifier specifies the accessibility of the method and determines which objects can see and subsequently invoke the method. The accessibility rules for methods are essentially the same as that of class and instance variable declarations. Any object, regardless of the class from which it was instantiated, can invoke methods that have been declared as public. Only objects that are members of the same class are allowed to invoke private methods. And finally, methods that do not specify a modifier have package scope, which means that they can only be invoked by objects that are members of same package.

The return type in a method declaration determines the type of value, if any, the method will return when it is invoked. In nonobject-oriented programming languages, methods that return values are referred to as functions. Every method, with the exception of a constructor, must specify a return type. If a method does not return a value (i.e., a procedure in nonobject-oriented languages), the return type is specified as void. The methods in Figure 3.11 are all defined as returning integer values when they are invoked. This is specified in the method declaration by the appearance of the keyword int before the name of the method. In other words, the declaration public int getXCoordinate() specifies that the getXCoordinate() method returns an integer value when it is invoked. A method can return a single value of any known type. If a method is defined to return a value, then a return statement that specifies a value of the correct type must appear somewhere in the method. Typically but not always, the return statement will be the last statement in a method. When a return statement is executed, the method has completed.

Mutators, which are defined in Table 2.1, change the state (i.e., change the value of an instance variable) of an object. Mutators typically do not return a value and are declared using the void return type. A mutator often requires additional information that specifies how the state of the object is to be changed. The methods setXCoordinate(), setYCoordinate(), and setXY() in Figure 3.12 are all mutator methods in the Point class. The setXCoordinate() method changes the value of the xCoordinate instance variable, whereas the setYCoordinate() method changes the value of the yCoordinate instance variable. The setXY() method changes both the X and the Y coordinate values at the same time. By convention, the names of mutator methods start with set.

Mutators, unlike accessors, usually do not return a value when they are invoked. The void return type in the declaration of the method setXCoordinate() specifies that the method does not return a value. Additionally, a mutator method must be provided with additional information to change the state of the object. For example, the setXCoordinate() method must be provided with the new value of the X coordinate. These values, which are specified when the method is invoked, are referred to as **arguments**. A method's **formal parameters** define the number and types of arguments that must be passed to a method when it is invoked. The formal parameters are specified as a list of comma-separated variable declarations that appear inside the parentheses following the name of the method. For example, the declaration int newX in the definition of the setXCoordinate() method of Figure 3.12 specifies that when the method is invoked, the programmer must provide a single integer value as an argument. The comma-separated list int newX, int newY in the definition of the setXY() method of Figure 3.12 specifies that the programmer must provide two integer arguments when invoking the method. The fact that the formal parameter list in the getXCoordinate() method in Figure 3.11 is empty specifies that no arguments are required when invoking the method.

Every method, whether it is an accessor or a mutator, has an associated signature. The **signature** of a method consists of the name of the method and the types of the formal parameters to the method. For example, the getXCoordinate() method in Figure 3.11 has the signature getXCoordinate(void), where the word void indicates

```java
/**
 * A Class that defines a point.
 */

public class Point {
    // Constant that gives the maximum value that may
    // be assigned to either the x or y coordinates
    public final static int MAX_VALUE = 1024;

    // State of a Point
    private int xCoordinate;  // The x coordinate
    private int yCoordinate;  // The y coordinate

  // public int getXCoordinate()...
  // public int getYCoordinate()...

  /**
   * Set the x coordinate of this point.
   * @param newX the new x coordinate.
   */
  public void setXCoordinate( int newX ) {
      xCoordinate = newX;
  }

  /**
   * Set the y coordinate of this point.
   * @param newY the new y coordinate.
   */
  public void setYCoordinate( int newY ) {
      yCoordinate = newY;
  }

  /**
   * Set both the X and Y coordinates of this point.
   *
   * @param newX the new x coordinate.
   * @param newY the new y coordinate.
   */
  public void setXY( int newX, int newY ) {
      xCoordinate = newX;
      yCoordinate = newY;
  }

} // Point
```

FIGURE 3.12 Mutators for the Point class

that the method has no formal parameters, whereas the setXY() method in Figure 3.12 has the signature setXY(int, int). The Java language specification requires that all of the methods in a class have different signatures.

Since the signature of a method includes the number of and the types of the formal parameters to the method, you may have two or more methods that have the same name in a class, provided that their signatures (i.e., their formal parameter lists) are different. Consider the second version of the `setXY()` method that has been added to the `Point` class in Figure 3.13. The first form of the `setXY()` requires two integer parameters that specify the new X and Y coordinates of the point. The second form of the `setXY()` requires only a single integer parameter that specifies the new value of both the X and Y coordinates of the point. Although the names of these methods are the same, their signatures `setXY(int,int)` and `setXY(int)` are different; thus, both forms of the method may be defined in the same class. The compiler can determine which form of the method to use based on the number and types of the arguments.

Providing multiple forms of a method is a common practice when writing a class. A method that appears in multiple forms in the same class is an **overloaded** method. At first glance, overloading a method seems like a strange thing to do, but in fact, you have been using overloaded methods in other programming languages. Consider, for example, the addition operator, +. There is only one name (symbol) for the addition operation, and yet the same symbol can add two integer values or two real values. The compiler determines which version of + to use based on the parameters that are passed to it when it is called. Note that since a method's signature in Java does not include the return type, it is not possible to overload the return type of a method. This is not the case in all programming languages.

In the `Point` class of Figure 3.9, the comment before the constant MAX_VALUE states that the x and y coordinate values will never be greater than the value stored in the constant. As the `Point` class is currently written, invoking the method `setXCoordinate()` with the argument 4096 is valid, although the value 4096 is outside the range of valid values for coordinates. Invoking the method in this way will result in an object whose internal state is inconsistent with its specification. Fortunately, correcting this is a simple matter; the mutator methods can be modified so that a check is made to ensure the value of the argument is valid before assigning that value, to the appropriate instance variable. Only if the argument is within the range of valid values will it be assigned to the instance variable. The `setXCoordinate()` and `setYCoordinate()` mutators in Figure 3.14 have been written so that it is no longer possible to set either the x or y coordinates to invalid values.

The mutators in Figure 3.14 illustrate why using `public` instance variables to store the state of an object is a bad programming practice. If an instance variable is `public`, then any object can change the value of the instance variable to any value it desires, which might result in an object whose state is invalid. On the other hand, if instance variables are declared `private`, then the only way to change the values of these variables is to use a mutator method. The mutator method, as shown in Figure 3.14, can verify that the new value is valid and make the change only if it is appropriate. By declaring instance variables as `private`, and allowing access to these variables through accessors or mutators, you can control the way in which the corresponding instance variables can be accessed and thus assure that the state of the object is valid.

Currently, neither version of the `setXY()` mutators in Figure 3.14 checks its parameters to ensure that they do not exceed the maximum value for a point. Changing these methods to make these checks is a trivial matter; essentially, all that needs to be done is copy the code that was added to the `setXCoordinate()` and `setYCoordinate()` methods that perform the checks. However, it is rarely a good

```
/**
 * A Class that defines a point.
 */

public class Point {
    // Constant that gives the maximum value that may
    // be assigned to either the x or y coordinates
    public final static int MAX_VALUE = 1024;

    // State of a Point
    private int xCoordinate;   // The x coordinate
    private int yCoordinate;   // The y coordinate

    // public int getXCoordinate()...
    // public int getYCoordinate()...
    // public void setXCoordinate( int newX )...
    // public void setYCoordinate( int newY )...

    /**
     * Set both the X and Y coordinates of this point.
     * @param newX the new x coordinate.
     * @param newY the new y coordinate.
     */
    public void setXY( int newX, int newY ) {
        xCoordinate = newX;
        yCoordinate = newY;
    }

    /**
     * Set the X and Y coordinate to the same value.
     * @param value the value to set the X and Y coordinate to.
     */
    public void setXY( int value ) {
        xCoordinate = value;
        yCoordinate = value;
    }

} // Point
```

FIGURE 3.13 Overloaded methods in the `Point` class

idea to copy code from one method to another; a better practice is to place code that is commonly used by several methods in a single method and then invoke this method to have the work done. By isolating the code to a single method, if there is something wrong with the code or if the code needs to be modified, you only need to make the changes in one method rather than searching through the program for all occurrences of the code that has been duplicated and needs to be fixed.

In the `Point` class, the methods `setXCoordinate()` and `setYCoordinate()` have already been modified to check their parameter before assigning it the appropriate instance variable. Ideally, what we would like to do for the `setXY()` methods is to use

```java
/**
 * A Class that defines a point.
 */

public class Point {
    // Constant that gives the maximum value that may
    // be assigned to either the x or y coordinates
    public final static int MAX_VALUE = 1024;

    // State of a Point
    private int xCoordinate;   // The x coordinate
    private int yCoordinate;   // The y coordinate

    // public int getXCoordinate()...
    // public int getYCoordinate()...

    /**
     * Set the x coordinate of this point.
     * @param newX the new x coordinate.
     */
    public void setXCoordinate( int newX ) {
        if ( newX > MAX_VALUE ) {
            xCoordinate = MAX_VALUE;
        }
        else {
            xCoordinate = newX;
        }
    }

    /**
     * Set the y coordinate of this point.
     * @param newY the new y coordinate.
     */
    public void setYCoordinate( int newY ) {
        if ( newY > MAX_VALUE ) {
            yCoordinate = MAX_VALUE;
        }
        else {
            yCoordinate = newY;
        }
    }

    // public void setXY( int newX, int newY )...
    // public void setXY( int value )...

} // Point
```

FIGURE 3.14 Safe mutators for the Point class

the `setXCoordintate()` and `setYCoordinate()` methods to change the values of the `xCoordinate` and `yCoordinate` instance variables instead of changing the variables directly. In this way, should an invalid coordinate value be passed to either one of the `setXY()` methods, the value will be checked before assigning it to the state of the object.

The methods that we have been discussing up to this point in this chapter are referred to as instance methods. An **instance method** is associated with an instance of a class and is always invoked with respect to an object. To invoke an instance method, you must specify both the name of the method that you wish to invoke and the object upon which the method will be executed. In other words, it is not enough to specify that I want to invoke the `setXCoordinate()` method. I must also specify the object whose state will be changed as a result of executing the method. The general form of instance method invocation appears in Figure 3.15.

ObjectReference.MethodName(ArgumentList);

FIGURE 3.15 Instance method invocation in Java

The *ObjectReference* in Figure 3.15 identifies the object upon which the method *MethodName* will be executed. The *Argumentlist* specifies the actual arguments that will be passed to the method when it is invoked. The type and number of the actual arguments must match the type and number of the formal parameters in the method definition.

Within a class definition, it is possible to invoke methods within the same class without explicitly specifying the object that the methods will be invoked on. In other words, should the *ObjectReference* be omitted, the compiler assumes that the method being invoked can be found in the class whose definition contains the method invocation and that the method will be invoked on the current object. The `setXY()` mutators, in Figure 3.16 have been modified to invoke the `setXCoordinate()` and `setYCoordinate()` methods to change the appropriate instance variables within the object.

The third type of method that was defined in Table 2.1 is a constructor. A **constructor** initializes the state of an object. In the `Point` class, the constructor would be used to initialize the values of the `xCoordinate` and `yCoordinate` instance variables because these variables make up the state of the object.

All Java classes have constructors that initialize instances of the class. A constructor will always have the same name as the class and cannot return a value. Java supports overloaded constructors so that a class can have any number of constructors. Overloaded constructors are often provided to give the user of the class flexibility in the way in which the instances of the class can be created. The `Point` class in Figure 3.17 contains two constructors: The first constructor requires two integer arguments that are used to initialize the x and y coordinates of the new `Point` object, and the second constructor initializes the x and y coordinates to the same value (similar in function to the overloaded version of the `setXY()` method in Figure 3.13). The compiler has no problem determining which constructor to use in a program because the signatures of both constructors, `Point(int, int)` and `Point(int)`, are different.

```
/**
 * A Class that defines a point.
 */

public class Point {
    // Constant that gives the maximum value that may
    // be assigned to either the x or y coordinates
    public final static int MAX_VALUE = 1024;

    // State of a Point
    private int xCoordinate;   // The x coordinate
    private int yCoordinate;   // The y coordinate

    // public int getXCoordinate()...
    // public int getYCoordinate()...
    // public void setXCoordinate( int newX )...
    // public void setYCoordinate( int newY )...

    /**
     * Set both the x and y coordinates of this point.
     * @param newX the new x coordinate.
     * @param newY the new y coordinate.
     */
    public void setXY( int newX, int newY ) {
        setXCoordinate( newX );
        setYCoordinate( newY );
    }

    /**
     * Set the x and y coordinates to the same value.
     * @param value the value to set the x and y coordinate to.
     */
    public void setXY( int value ) {
        setXCoordinate( value );
        setYCoordinate( value );
    }

} // Point
```

FIGURE 3.16 Invoking "a" method

The modifier associated with a constructor determines what objects can use that constructor to create instances of the class. A class with a public constructor can be instantiated by any object, whereas a private constructor specifies that only objects that are members of the same class may create instances of the class using the private constructor. Since the constructors in Figure 3.17 are public, any class can create Point objects.

A constructor that takes no parameters is called the **default constructor** of the class. If you do not explicitly write a constructor for a class, the Java compiler will

```
/**
 * A Class that defines a point.
 */

public class Point {
    // Constant that gives the maximum value that may
    // be assigned to either the x or y coordinates
    public final static int MAX_VALUE = 1024;

    // State of a Point
    private int xCoordinate;  // The x coordinate
    private int yCoordinate;  // The y coordinate

    /**
     * Create a new point at the specified location.
     *
     * @param x the x coordinate.
     * @param y the y coordinate.
     */
    public Point( int x, int y ) {
        setXY( x, y );
    }

    /**
     * Create a new point at (value,value).
     *
     * @param value the value to set the x and y coordinates to.
     */
    public Point( int value ) {
            setXY( value );
    }

    // public int getXCoordinate()...
    // public int getYCoordinate()...
    // public void setXCoordinate( int newX )...
    // public void setYCoordinate( int newY )...
    // public void setXY( int newX, int newY )...
    // public void setXY( int value )...

} // Point
```

FIGURE 3.17 Adding constructors to the Point class

automatically create a default constructor. The default constructor initializes all instance variables to default values as specified in Section 3.2.1. The compiler will add a default constructor to a class only if a constructor for that class has not been specified. In this way, Java guarantees that every class will have a constructor. Note that the Point class in Figure 3.16 will have a default constructor automatically added to its definition, whereas the Point class of Figure 3.17 will not. Since two constructors were defined for the class in Figure 3.17, the Java compiler will not provide a default (i.e., a no argument) constructor. The only way to instantiate an object from the `Point` class of Figure 3.17 is to invoke a constructor that requires a parameter.

In Java and in other object-oriented programming languages, memory is allocated whenever a new object is created. When an object is no longer needed in a program, the run-time system should be informed so that the memory allocated for that object can be used for other purposes. Failing to release the memory that is allocated by the program as it is running leads to a problem that is referred to as a **memory leak**. A program that has a memory leak will, over time, monopolize all of the memory resources in a computer.

Keeping track of memory that has been allocated in a program so that it can be reused when it is no longer needed is not difficult, but it is tedious. The programmer must be very careful to write classes in such a way that whenever an object is no longer needed, all of the memory resources required by that object are released. Most object-oriented programming languages assist the programmer in this effort by guaranteeing that any memory allocated by the compiler is released, but it is often not possible for the compiler to do this for memory that has been dynamically allocated by the object during its lifetime.

A **destructor**, the fourth type of method introduced in Chapter 2, provides a mechanism for a programmer to release any system resources, including memory, that were allocated by an object before it is removed from the system. Given the important role that a destructor plays in an object-oriented system, you might be surprised to learn that there are no destructors in Java. The closest thing in Java to a destructor is the `finalize()` method that will be discussed in Section 3.3.4.

The Java run-time system automatically tracks the use of memory and releases memory resources when it determines that they are no longer needed. The Java run-time system uses a technique called **garbage collection** to manage memory. In addition to keeping track of all the objects in existence while a program is running, the Java run-time system keeps track of the number of references to every object. Since the only way to access an object is through a reference, when the reference count of an object goes to zero, it means that no other object in the program can access the object. An object that can no longer be accessed is called garbage, and from time to time, the Java run-time system will make a sweep through memory and delete any objects that have been marked as garbage.

In Section 3.2.1, we made a distinction between instance and class variables. Instance variables are associated with an instance of a class, whereas class variables are associated with a class. In a similar fashion, a distinction can be made between instance methods, which are associated with an instance of a class, and class methods. **Class methods**, like class variables, are associated with a class and not an instance of a class. The class method `getNumPoints()` has been added to the `Point` class in Figure 3.18.

The class method `getNumPoints()` is an accessor method that returns the current value of the class variable `numPoints`. The constructors in the `Point` class of Figure 3.18 have been modified so that they add 1 to the current value of the class variable `numPoints` every time a constructor is invoked. Because `numPoints` is a class variable and not an instance variable, there is exactly one copy of `numPoints` regardless of how many `Point` objects have been instantiated. Since the constructors increment the same copy of `numPoints`, this variable indicates how many times the constructors have been

```java
/**
 * A Class that defines a point.
 */

public class Point {
    // Constant that gives the maximum value that may
    // be assigned to either the x or y coordinates
    public final static int MAX_VALUE = 1024;

    // The number of Point objects created so far
    private static int numPoints = 0;

    // State of a Point
    private int xCoordinate;   // The x coordinate
    private int yCoordinate;   // The y coordinate

    /**
     * Return the number of Point objects that have been created
     * thus far.
     *
     * @param the number of Point objects that have been created.
     */
    public static int getNumPoints() {
        return numPoints;
    }

    /**
     * Create a new point at the specified location.
     *
     * @param x the X coordinate.
     * @param y the Y coordinate.
     */
    public Point( int x, int y ) {
        setXY( x, y );
        numPoints = numPoints + 1;
    }

    /**
     * Create a new point at(value,value).
     *
     * @param value the value to set the X and Y coordinates to.
     */
    public Point( int value ) {
        setXY( value );
        numPoints = numPoints + 1;
    }

    // public int getXCoordinate()...
    // public int getYCoordinate()...
    // public void setXCoordinate( int newX )...
    // public void setYCoordinate( int newY )...
    // public void setXY( int newX, int newY )...
    // public void setXY( int value )...

} // Point
```

FIGURE 3.18 Adding a class method to the Point class

invoked. This means that numPoints keeps track of the number of Point objects that have been created. Note that numPoints does not indicate how many Point objects are still in existence (i.e., not garbage collected); it only indicates how many times the constructors to the class have been invoked.

Class methods are invoked just like instance methods, but instead of specifying the object upon which the method will be executed, you must specify the class that the method is associated with. If you do not specify a class when invoking a class method, the compiler will assume that the method is defined in the same class in which it is being invoked.

Whenever an instance method is invoked, the method is executed upon an object, which means that the method can access the state of the object on which it was executed. Since a class method is associated with the class and not one of its instances, the class method cannot access the state of an object without specifying the object whose state it wishes to access. Likewise, a class method cannot invoke an instance method without specifying the object upon which the method should be executed.

In the context of the Point class, the class method getNumPoints() cannot access the getXCoordinate() method, nor can it access the xCoordinate instance variable without specifying an object reference. This makes perfect sense if you think about the nature of a class method. Since a class method is associated with a class and not with an instance, you can access a class method before any instances of the class have been instantiated. A class method, however, cannot access an instance of its own class without specifying a reference to an object, because it is possible that no such instances exist.

You may be wondering why an object-oriented programming language, such as Java, would include the ability to define class methods. As it turns out, class methods are a very useful tool when writing class definitions. Consider, for example, writing a class that consists exclusively of static variables and static methods. It would be possible to access any of the members of this class without ever creating an instance of the class. A class defined in this way could be viewed as a repository of methods. Any object that knew the name of the class could use the methods that are defined within it. Probably the best example of this type of class is the Math class provided by the standard Java application programming interface (API) in the java.lang package. Table 3.2 lists a few of the methods defined in java.lang.Math. The Javadoc page for the class provides a list of all of the methods in the class.

TABLE 3.2 Some useful methods defined in `java.lang.Math`

Method	Description
`static double abs( double a )`	Returns the absolute value of the argument.
`static double cos( double a )`	Returns the cosine of an angle.
`static double max( double a, double b )`	Returns the largest argument.
`static double pow( double a, double b )`	Returns the result of raising the first argument to the power of the second.
`static double sqrt( double a )`	Returns the square root of the argument.

The class `java.lang.Math` contains more than 30 methods that provide implementations of the most common math functions that might be needed in a Java program. The instance method `distanceFrom()` in Figure 3.19 shows how two of the methods in the `Math` class can be used to determine the distance between a `Point` object and the origin.

We have spent a considerable amount of time talking about classes and objects in this chapter, but we have not yet discussed how to write a Java program. In Section 3.1, we stated that an object-oriented program consisted of a number of objects that interact to accomplish a specified task. You now know how to create the classes that can instantiate the objects that will interact in the program, but what you still do not know is how to get this process started. It would seem that to run a Java program, you would have to identify a class that the Java run-time system would use to instantiate the first object that would start the program. There are problems with this approach: How do you pass the parameters to the constructors of the class, and how do

```java
/**
 * A Class that defines a point.
 */

public class Point {
    // Constant that gives the maximum value that may
    // be assigned to either the x or y coordinates
    public final static int MAX_VALUE = 1024;

    // The maximum number of points created so far
    private static int numPoints = 0;

    // State of a Point
    private int xCoordinate;   // The x coordinate
    private int yCoordinate;   // The y coordinate

    // public static int getNumPoints()...
    // public Point( int x, int y )...
    // public Point( int value )...
    // public int getXCoordinate()...
    // public int getYCoordinate()...
    // public void setXCoordinate( int newX )...
    // public void setYCoordinate( int newY )...
    // public void setXY( int newX, int newY )...
    // public void setXY( int value )...

    public double distanceFrom() {
        return Math.sqrt( Math.pow( xCoordinate, 2 ) +
                          Math.pow( yCoordinate, 2 ) );
    }

} // Point
```

FIGURE 3.19 Computing the distance between a point and the origin

you specify which method should be invoked once the object has been created? What is really needed is a special method that could be invoked by the Java run-time system without having to instantiate an object. If you give this a little thought, you will realize that a class method will fill this role quite effectively.

In Java, the class method main() provides an entry point into a class to start a Java program. When the Java run-time system is started, it is provided with the name of a class that contains a main() method. After the run-time system has initialized its environment, it invokes the main() method in the class that was specified on the command line. Figure 3.20 contains an example of a class that contains a main() method. If this class is passed to the Java run-time system, the program will print the string "Hello World" and terminate.

Even though the class in Figure 3.20 can be executed from the command line, it is defined in the same way as any other class in Java. The class just happens to have a main() method that will be invoked by the Java run-time system to start the program. It is also important to note that there is nothing special about the method main(). It is nothing more than a public class method that does not return a value when it is invoked. What makes main() different from all other class methods is that the Java run-time system will invoke this particular method to start a program. For the run-time system to be able to invoke main(), the method must be defined exactly as shown in Figure 3.20 (i.e., it must have the signature void main(String[])). Finally, any class can have a main() method. Adding a main() method to a class does not in any way force you to "run" that class from the command line.

Based on the signature of the method main(), the method must be provided with an array that contains references to String objects. When the Java run-time system invokes main(), it passes an array that contains references to the command arguments that were specified by the user. The arguments that are passed to main() include

```
/**
 * A Hello World Program in Java
 */

public class HelloWorld {

    /**
     * The entry point for this class.  When executed the
     * program will simply print "Hello World" and terminate.
     *
     * @param args command line arguments.
     */

    public static void main( String args[] ) {
        System.out.println( "Hello World" );
    }

} // HelloWorld
```

FIGURE 3.20 Using main() in Java

```
/**
 * A program that echos the command line.
 */

public class EchoCommandLine {

    /**
     * Print out the contents of the args array that is
     * passed to the method when it is invoked.
     *
     * @param args the command line arguments.
     */

    public static void main( String args[] ) {

        // Print out args

        for ( int i = 0; i < args.length; i++ ) {
        System.out.println( args[ i ] );
        }

    }

} // EchoCommandLine
```

FIGURE 3.21 Program that will print the contents of the `args` array

everything that is typed on the command line after the class name. The `main()` method in the class of Figure 3.21 prints the contents of the array passed as an argument to the method.

The `main()` method in Figure 3.21 uses a simple loop to iterate over the elements in the array it is passed as a parameter. Note that there is no need to pass the number of arguments to the `main()` method because this information can be obtained from the array using the `length` instance variable. Figure 3.22 shows the output that will be generated by this program.

This section has illustrated how the behavior of an object is modeled in Java using methods. A method is nothing more than a function, or a procedure, that is associated

```
% java EchoCommandLine arg1 arg2 arg3
arg1
arg2
arg3
%java EchoCommandLine
%
```

FIGURE 3.22 Execution of the `EchoCommandLine` program

with a class or an object. Like instance variables, methods have an accessibility that is used to determine how they can be accessed. As in other programming languages, the definition of a method specifies the type of the value returned by the method, if any, and the number and type of formal parameters that must be provided when the method is invoked.

Every method in Java has associated with it a signature, which consists of the name of the method followed by the number and types of the formal parameters the method requires when it is invoked. All of the methods in a Java class must have unique signatures. Overloaded methods are methods in a single class that have the same name but different signatures.

Finally, methods, again like instance variables, can be declared as static. Class methods, or static methods, are associated with a class and not an object. One of the most common uses of a static method is to write a `main()` method that can be invoked by the Java run-time system and serves as the starting point of execution for most Java programs.

Up to this point in this chapter, we have discussed how the state and behavior of an object are defined, but you have not yet learned how to access the state of an object or invoke its methods. In the next section, we will discuss how objects are created from classes and how the state and behavior of these objects can be accessed.

◆ 3.2.3 Identity

Once a class definition is available, the Java operator `new` can be used to create instances of the class. Operator `new` takes as parameters the arguments, if any, that will be passed to the appropriate constructor and returns a reference to the newly instantiated object. At compile time, the compiler checks to make sure that there is a constructor that matches the arguments to operator `new`. If no such constructor can be found, the compiler will generate an error message. The program in Figure 3.23 illustrates how the operator `new` can create several points at different locations.

Instantiating an object is a three-step process: (a) the memory required to store the object is allocated, (b) the default initialization rules and/or initialization expressions, if any, are applied to the instance variables, and (c) the appropriate constructor is invoked to initialize the state of the object. Operator `new` performs all of these steps: allocating memory, initializing instance variables, and invoking the constructor. The instantiation process is illustrated in Figure 3.24.

As you can see from Figure 3.24, the Java run-time system uses the default initialization rules described in Section 3.2.1 to initialize the instance variables of a class before the constructor is invoked. So although it is not strictly necessary to initialize the state of an instance variable using an initialization expression or within a constructor, it is considered a good programming practice to explicitly initialize the instance variables of a class. In this way, it is absolutely clear what the initial value of the instance variable will be.

Now that we know how to create objects, we can invoke methods on these objects using the method invocation syntax in Figure 3.15 from the previous section. You will recall that we said to invoke an instance method you have to specify the object upon which the method will be executed and the name of the method to invoke.

```
/**
 * This program creates several points at different
 * locations.
 */

public class CreatePoints {

    /**
     * The main method.
     *
     * @param args command line arguments (ignored).
     */

    public static void main( String args[] ) {
      Point p1, p2, p3;

      p1 = new Point( 10, 45 );   // Create a point at (10,45)
      p2 = new Point( 10, 10 );   // Create a point at (10,10)
      p3 = new Point( 10, 10 );   // Create a point at (10,10)


    }

}   // CreatePoints
```

FIGURE 3.23 Using operator new

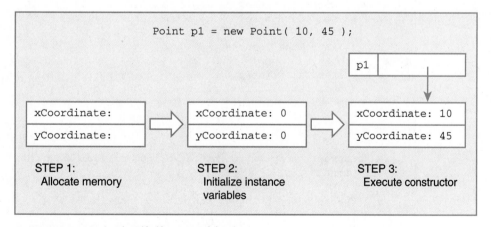

FIGURE 3.24 Instantiating an object

The program in Figure 3.25 creates three Point objects, invokes mutators on some of the points to modify their state, and then prints the resulting coordinates by invoking the appropriate accessor methods. The output generated by this program is given in Figure 3.26.

```java
/**
 * This program creates several points at different
 * locations.
 */

public class CreatePoints {

    /**
     * The main method.
     *
     * @param args command line arguments (ignored).
     */

    public static void main( String args[] ) {
        Point p1, p2, p3;

        p1 = new Point( 10, 45 );  // Create a point at (10,45)
        p2 = new Point( 10, 10 );  // Create a point at (10,10)
        p3 = new Point( 10, 10 );  // Create a point at (10,10)

        // Place p1 at the origin
        p1.setXY( 0 );

        // Locate p2 at the same location as p1
        p2.setXCoordinate( p1.getXCoordinate() );
        p2.setYCoordinate( p1.getYCoordinate() );

        // Place p3 10 units away from p2 in each dimension
        p3.setXCoordinate( p2.getXCoordinate() + 10 );
        p3.setYCoordinate( p2.getYCoordinate() + 10 );

        // Print the results

        System.out.println( "p1 -> " + pointToString( p1 ) );
        System.out.println( "p2 -> " + pointToString( p2 ) );
        System.out.println( "p3 -> " + pointToString( p3 ) );
    }

    /**
     * Convert the given point to string form suitable for
     * printing.
     *
     * @param p the point to convert to a string.
     */

    public static String pointToString( Point p ) {
        return "(" + p.getXCoordinate() + "," +
                    p.getYCoordinate() + ")";
    }

}  // CreatePoints
```

FIGURE 3.25 Invoking methods

```
p1 -> (0,0)
p2 -> (0,0)
p3 -> (10,10)
```

FIGURE 3.26 Output generated by CreatePoints program in Figure 3.25

The variables p1, p2, and p3 in the program in Figure 3.25 hold references to the objects that were created by operator new. The references serve as a means of identity for an object; using a reference you can specify the object on which you wish to invoke a method. It is important to remember that p1, p2, and p3 are not points; they are reference variables that hold references to different Point objects as illustrated in Figure 3.27. A common misunderstanding is to not distinguish the fact that reference variables contain references to objects and not the objects themselves.

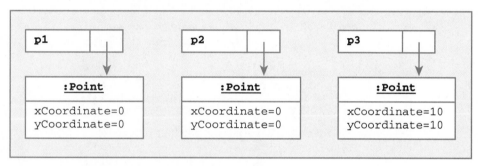

FIGURE 3.27 Reference variables

Consider the program in Figure 3-28. Like the program in Figure 3.25, it creates three points. In Figure 3.28, however, notice that the reference variable p3 is initialized using the assignment operator.

You would think that the output from the program in Figure 3.28 would be the same as that produced by the program in Figure 3.25 since the only thing that was changed in this program was the way in which the variable p3 was initialized. The output from this program is given in Figure 3.29.

The key to understanding the output produced by the program in Figure 3.28 is to remember that a reference variable contains a reference to an object and not the object itself. The reference variable holds the identity, or name, of the object. When the assignment operator is applied to a reference variable, it is the identity of the object that is duplicated, not the object that the name identifies. This is an example of the shallow copy operation that was discussed in Chapter 2. The assignment operation, when applied to reference types, performs a shallow copy. It only affects the reference, or name, of the object and not the object itself.

Consider the effect of executing the statement p3 = p2 in the program in Figure 3.28. The assignment operator copies the contents of the variable on the right side of the assignment operator into the variable on the left side. If these variables were primitive types, the assignment operation creates a new primitive *value* that is placed into the variable on the left side. In the case of reference variables, the assignment operator

```java
/**
 * This program creates several points at different
 * locations.
 */

public class AssignPoint {
    /**
     * The main method.
     *
     * @param args command line arguments (ignored).
     */
    public static void main( String args[] ) {
        Point p1, p2, p3;

        p1 = new Point( 10, 45 );  // Create a point at (10,45)
        p2 = new Point( 10, 10 );  // Create a point at (10,10)
        p3 = p2;         // Use assignment to initialize p3 so
                         // that it refers to a point at (10,10)

        // Place p1 at the origin
        p1.setXY( 0 );

        // Place p2 at the same location as p1
        p2.setXCoordinate( p1.getXCoordinate() );
        p2.setYCoordinate( p1.getYCoordinate() );

        // Place p3 10 units away from p2 in each dimension
        p3.setXCoordinate( p2.getXCoordinate() + 10 );
        p3.setYCoordinate( p2.getYCoordinate() + 10 );

        // Print the results
        System.out.println( "p1 -> " + pointToString( p1 ) );
        System.out.println( "p2 -> " + pointToString( p2 ) );
        System.out.println( "p3 -> " + pointToString( p3 ) );
    }

    /**
     * Convert the point to a form suitable for printing.
     *
     * @param p the point to convert to a string.
     */
    public static String pointToString( Point p ) {
        return "(" + p.getXCoordinate() + "," +
                    p.getYCoordinate() + ")";
    }

}  // AssignPoint
```

FIGURE 3.28 Using assignment to initialize a `Point` variable

```
p1 -> (0,0)
p2 -> (10,10)
p3 -> (10,10)
```

FIGURE 3.29 Output produced by the program of Figure 3.28

performs the same operation, but here the *reference* to the object on the right side of the operator is copied and not the object itself. The results are shown in Figure 3.30.

After the assignment has been executed, p2 and p3 contain a reference to the same object. Assignment does not create a new object; it only copies the value of one reference variable and places it in a second reference variable. The only way to create a completely new object in Java is by using the operator new. After the assignment operation has been completed, the variables p2 and p3 are **name equivalent.** The program in Figure 3.28 only creates two objects and initializes the reference variables p2 and p3 so that they refer to the same object. Any attempt to invoke a method on the object referred to by p2 will have the same effect as invoking the same method using p3. The invocation of the setXCoordinate() and setYCoordinate() methods changes the state of the object that is referred to by both the variables p2 and p3 even though only the reference variable p2 is used when the methods are invoked. In fact, although the output in Figure 3.29 appears to list the state of three Point objects, it only lists the state of two objects. The last two lines in the output refer to the same Point object. When two variables reference the same object they are said to be **aliases.**

The Java assignment operation performs a shallow copy since it only operates on the contents of the variables and not the objects that they might be referring to. There is no "deep assignment" operator in Java; however, it is possible to add methods to a class definition that make it possible to create duplicates of an object. Consider the constructor that has been added to the Point class in Figure 3.31.

The constructor that was added to the Point class in Figure 3.31 initializes the state of the new Point object using the state of an existing Point object. This type of constructor is sometimes referred to as a **copy constructor** because it provides a mechanism that can create new objects that are copies of existing objects. The program in Figure 3.32 uses the copy constructor to initialize the reference variable p3. Note that this program creates three distinct Point objects because new is invoked three times.

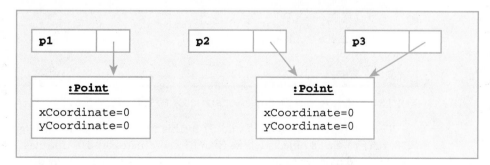

FIGURE 3.30 Object diagram after executing p3 = p2

```
/**
 * A Class that defines a point.
 */

public class Point {
    // Constant that gives the maximum value that may
    // be assigned to either the x or y coordinates
    public final static int MAX_VALUE = 1024;

    // The maximum number of points created so far
    private static int numPoints = 0;

    // State of a Point
    private int xCoordinate;   // The x coordinate
    private int yCoordinate;   // The y coordinate

    // public static int getNumPoints()...
    // public Point( int x, int y )...
    // public Point( int value )...

    /**
      * Create a duplicate point object.
      *
      * @param p the point to duplicate.
      */

    public Point( Point p ) {
        xCoordinate = p.xCoordinate;
        // OR xCoordinate = p.getXCoordinate()

        yCoordinate = p.yCoordinate;
        // OR yCoordinate = p.getYCoordinate()

        numPoints = numPoints + 1;
    }

    // public int getXCoordinate()...
    // public int getYCoordinate()...
    // public void setXCoordinate( int newX )...
    // public void setYCoordinate( int newY )...
    // public void setXY( int newX, int newY )...
    // public void setXY( int value )...
    // public double distanceFrom()...

} // Point
```

FIGURE 3.31 Adding a copy constructor to the Point class

The reference variables p2 and p3 in this program, like the program in Figure 3.28, refer to Point objects whose X and Y coordinates are 10. However, in this program, p2 and p3 refer to *different* Point objects. So if a change is made to the state of

```
/**
 * This program creates several points at different
 * locations.
 */

public class AssignPoint {
    /**
     * The main method.
     *
     * @param args command line arguments (ignored).
     */
    public static void main( String args[] ) {
        Point p1, p2, p3;

        p1 = new Point( 10, 45 );  // Create a point at (10,45)
        p2 = new Point( 10, 10 );  // Create a point at (10,10)

        p3 = new Point( p2 );        // Use a copy constructor so p3
                                     // refers to a point at (10,10)

        // Place p1 at the origin
        p1.setXY( 0 );

        // Place p2 at the same location as p1
        p2.setXCoordinate( p1.getXCoordinate() );
        p2.setYCoordinate( p1.getYCoordinate() );

        // Place p3 10 units away from p2 in each dimension
        p3.setXCoordinate( p2.getXCoordinate() + 10 );
        p3.setYCoordinate( p2.getYCoordinate() + 10 );

        // Print the results
        System.out.println( "p1 -> " + pointToString( p1 ) );
        System.out.println( "p2 -> " + pointToString( p2 ) );
        System.out.println( "p3 -> " + pointToString( p3 ) );
    }

    /**
     * Convert the point to a form suitable for printing.
     *
     * @param p the point to convert to a string.
     */
    public static String pointToString( Point p ) {
        return "(" + p.getXCoordinate() + "," +
                    p.getYCoordinate() + ")";
    }

}   // AssignPoint
```

FIGURE 3.32 Using the copy constructor to initialize a Point variable

the object that is referred to by the variable p2, it will not cause a change in the state of the object referred to by the variable p3. Therefore, the output from this program will be the same as the output from the program in Figure 3.25.

Now that you understand how assignment works in Java, we can discuss the details of parameter passing. Parameter passing refers to the process by which Java associates the arguments that are specified in a method invocation with the parameters in the definition of the method being invoked. In Java, parameters are **passed by value**, which means that whenever an argument is passed to a Java method, a copy of the value that is stored in the argument is made, and the copy is what is passed to the method. Since the parameters of the method are copies of the arguments, changes made to the parameters during the execution of the method are not seen outside the method (i.e., the changes do not affect the values of the corresponding arguments).

One way to understand how parameters are passed is to view the parameters of a method as local variables that have been defined within the method. Parameters, like local variables, are created when the method is invoked, and they are destroyed when the method returns. Unlike a local variable, the initial value of a parameter depends on the value of the corresponding argument. When a method is invoked, the values of the arguments are assigned to the corresponding parameter.

Consider the main() method in the program of Figure 3.33, which invokes the move() method to move the Point object referred to by the variable aPoint 16 units in the X direction and 67 units in the Y direction.

When the main() method invokes the move() method, the compiler copies the values in the arguments (aPoint, x, and y) to the parameters (p, deltaX, and deltaY) using the basic assignment operation as shown in Figure 3.34.

Since assignment is used to initialize the values of the parameters to a method, the copies are shallow, which means if a reference variable is passed to a method, the reference is duplicated and not the object that is referred to. So although changes made to the reference variable will not be seen outside the method, if the method uses the reference variable to change the state of the object to which it refers, that change will be seen by any method that has a reference to the affected object (Figure 3.35).

The equality operator (==), like assignment, is a shallow operator that compares the references stored in the variable and not the objects the variables are referring to. The equality operator, when applied to reference variables, returns true if the references stored in the two variables being compared are the same. In other words, the equality operator returns true when two reference variables refer to the same object. It returns false when two reference variables refer to different objects, even if the state of the objects is the same. Consider the program in Figure 3.36.

The object diagram in Figure 3.37 illustrates the reference variables and objects that are created by the program in Figure 3.36. Clearly, since p1 and p3 are the only two reference variables in the program that refer to the same object, then p1==p3 will return true. Any other statements that compare p1 to any other variables in the program (i.e., p2 and p4) will return false, even though the state of the objects referred to by the variables p1 and p4 is the same.

The last piece of Java syntax that we will discuss that concerns identity is the keyword this. The keyword this may only be used in the body of an instance method, in a constructor, or in the initializer of an instance variable of a class. When used in an expression, this acts as a reference variable that contains a reference to the object upon

```java
/**
 * A simple program to demonstrate parameter passing in Java.
 */

public class Param {

    /**
     * Create and initialize a Point and some int values. Print
     * the values of these variables before and after invoking the
     * method move().
     *
     * @param args command line arguments (ignored).
     */

    public static void main( String args[] ) {
        int x = 16;
        int y = 67;
        Point aPoint = new Point( 0, 0 );

        // Before...
        System.out.println( "x=" + x );
        System.out.println( "y=" + y );
        System.out.println( "aPoint=" + pointToString( aPoint ) );

        move( aPoint, x, y );

        // After...
        System.out.println( "x=" + x );
        System.out.println( "y=" + y );
        System.out.println( "aPoint=" + pointToString( aPoint ) );
    }

    /**
     * Move a point.
     *
     * @param p the point to move.
     * @param deltaX movement of the X coordinate.
     * @param deltaY movement of the Y coordinate.
     */

    public static void move( Point p, int deltaX, int deltaY ) {
        p.setXCoordinate( p.getXCoordinate() + deltaX );
        p.setYCoordinate( p.getYCoordinate() + deltaY );
    }

    /**
     * Convert the given point to string form suitable for
     * printing.
     *
     * @param p the point to convert to a string.
     */

    public static String pointToString( Point p ) {
        return "(" + p.getXCoordinate() + "," +
                     p.getYCoordinate() + ")";
    }

} // Param
```

FIGURE 3.33 Parameter passing in Java

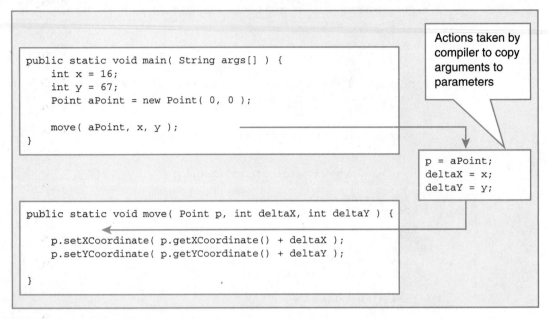

```
public static void main( String args[] ) {
    int x = 16;
    int y = 67;
    Point aPoint = new Point( 0, 0 );

    move( aPoint, x, y );
}
```

Actions taken by compiler to copy arguments to parameters

```
p = aPoint;
deltaX = x;
deltaY = y;
```

```
public static void move( Point p, int deltaX, int deltaY ) {

    p.setXCoordinate( p.getXCoordinate() + deltaX );
    p.setYCoordinate( p.getYCoordinate() + deltaY );

}
```

FIGURE 3.34 Parameter passing

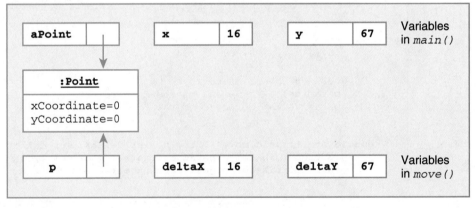

FIGURE 3.35 Object diagram during invocation of move()

which the method was invoked or to the object that is being constructed. The keyword this is automatically declared and initialized by the Java compiler.

Before we discuss how you can use the keyword this in a program, let's take a minute to explain the method invocation syntax discussed earlier in this chapter. In Figure 3.15, we implied that whenever you invoke a method, you place a reference to the object whose method you wish to invoke on the left side of the dot (.) and the name of the method on the right side of the dot. You will certainly have noticed that in all of the Point class examples, we have left out the object reference and the dot whenever invoking a method within the same object. In an instance method, whenever Java sees

```
/**
 * Test the results of applying the equality operator (==)
 * to different points.
 */

public class Equality {
    /**
     * The main method.
     *
     * @param args command line arguments (ignored).
     */
    public static void main( String args[] ) {
        // Create some points
        Point p1 = new Point( 12, 34 );
        Point p2 = new Point( 56, 78 );
        Point p3 = p1;
        Point p4 = new Point( 12, 34 );

        // False - two different points
        System.out.println( p1 == p2 );

        // True - both refer to the same object
        System.out.println( p1 == p3 );

        // False - two different objects that with identical state
        System.out.println( p1 == p4 );

    }

} // Equality
```

FIGURE 3.36 Using the equality operator

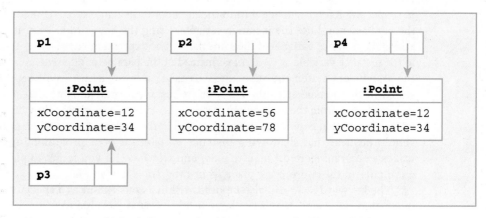

FIGURE 3.37 Object diagram for the program in Figure 3.36

```
public void setXY( int newX, int newY ) {
    setXCoordinate( newX );
    setYCoordinate( newY );
}
```

⬇ Becomes . . .

```
public void setXY( int newX, int newY ) {
    this.setXCoordinate( newX );
    this.setYCoordinate( newY );
}
```

FIGURE 3.38 Implicit this placed in front of method invocations

a method invocation that does not specify an object, it automatically inserts an implicit this. in front of the method invocation, as shown in Figure 3.38, which conforms to the method invocation syntax in Figure 3.15.

When writing Java programs, the keyword this comes in handy in a couple of common situations. The first occurs whenever an object needs to pass a reference to itself as an argument to a method, or needs to return a reference to itself from a method. Another very common situation occurs when the names of parameters to a method, or local variables defined in a method, have the same name as instance variables in the class. Consider the setXCoordinate() method in Figure 3.39. The parameter list for this method has been changed so that the name of the parameter is the same as the name of one of the instance variables of the class.

Within the setXCoordinate() method, the parameter xCoordinate shadows or hides the instance variable with the same name from view. As long as the parameter is in scope, any reference made within the method to the name xCoordinate will refer to the parameter and not the instance variable. Using the keyword this, it is possible to access the instance variable of the same name. The expression this.xCoordinate refers to the instance variable xCoordinate instead of the parameter xCoordinate. Therefore, the assignment statement this.xCoordinate = xCoordinate will copy the valve stored in the parameter to the appropriate instance variable. Note that omitting the keyword this from the assignment statement, while still syntactically valid, results in an expression that copies the reference stored in the parameter xCoordinate to itself. It should be clear that shadowing instance variables is poor programming. It clearly makes a program more difficult to read, and worse yet, if you forget to place the keyword this in the appropriate place, your program is likely to fail.

The keyword this can also be used within a constructor as a special constructor invocation statement. Using the keyword this, it is possible to write a constructor that invokes another constructor. If you think about the constructors that were added

```
/**
 * A Class that defines a point.
 */

public class Point {
    // Constant that gives the maximum value that may
    // be assigned to either the x or y coordinates
    public final static int MAX_VALUE = 1024;

    // State of a Point
    private int xCoordinate;   // The x coordinate
    private int yCoordinate;   // The y coordinate

    // public int getXCoordinate()...
    // public int getYCoordinate()...

    /**
     * Set the x coordinate of this point.
     * @param xCoordinate the new x coordinate.
     */

    public void setXCoordinate( int xCoordinate ) {
        if ( xCoordinate > MAX_VALUE ) {
            this.xCoordinate = MAX_VALUE;
        }
        else {
            this.xCoordinate = xCoordinate;
        }
    }

    // public void setYCoordinate( int newY )...
    // public void setXY( int newX, int newY )...
    // public void setXY( int value )...

} // Point
```

FIGURE 3.39 Using `this` in an expression

to the `Point` class in Figure 3.17, you will realize that each constructor does basically the same thing; the only difference is how the initial x and y values are passed as parameters. A common strategy when writing constructors for a class is to write one constructor that actually does the initialization and to write other constructors that simply call the real constructor with the appropriate arguments. Consider the constructors in the `Point` class of Figure 3.40.

In Figure 3.40, the constructor with the signature `Point(int, int)` is the one that does the actual work of initializing the class. The other constructors use the keyword `this` to invoke the `Point(int, int)` constructor with the appropriate arguments to initialize the class. When used as a constructor invocation statement, the keyword `this` must be the first statement within the body of the constructor. Using the keyword `this`

```java
/**
 * A Class that defines a point.
 */

public class Point {
    // Constant that gives the maximum value that may
    // be assigned to either the x or y coordinates
    public final static int MAX_VALUE = 1024;

    // State of a Point
    private int xCoordinate;  // The x coordinate
    private int yCoordinate;  // The y coordinate

    /**
     * Create a new point at the origin.
     */

    public Point() {
        this( 0, 0 );
    }

    /**
     * Create a new point at (value,value).
     *
     * @param value the value to set the X and Y coordinates to.
     */


    public Point( int value ) {
        this( value, value );
    }
    /**
     * Create a new point at the specified location.
     *
     * @param x the X coordinate.
     * @param y the Y coordinate.
     */
    public Point( int x, int y ) {
        setXY( x, y );
    }

    // public int getXCoordinate(). . .
    // public int getYCoordinate(). . .
    // public void setXCoordinate( int newX ). . .
    // public void setYCoordinate( int newY ). . .
    // public void setXY( int newX, int newY ). . .
    // public void setXY( int value ). . .

} // Point
```

FIGURE 3.40 Using this in constructors

to invoke constructors has the benefit of reducing the amount of duplicate code that you will need to write in a class and places all of the real initialization work in a single method, which makes debugging and maintaining the class easier.

In this section, we have discussed how the third component in the definition of an object, identity, is implemented in Java. Objects are created in Java by invoking operator new, which returns a reference to the newly created object and serves as the identity of the object. In the next section, we will tie together the basic objected-oriented syntax of Java that has been introduced in this chapter by way of an example.

◆ 3.2.4 Example: Square Class

Consider writing a program that provides a user with the tools necessary to draw and manipulate simple two-dimensional shapes (e.g., circles, squares, rectangles, triangles, etc). After performing an object-oriented analysis of the specifications and requirements for this program, you would likely determine that you would need classes to represent each of the shapes that the program can manipulate. The program would include classes that defined objects such as circles, squares, rectangles, and triangles. In this section, we develop a design and implementation of a class that could be used to represent squares within the program.

Before we can write the code that will implement the Square class, we need to determine the state and behavior of a square within this program. The state of a square is simple: We only need to store the length of one of the sides of the square and the location of the square on the drawing surface. We will use an integer value to represent the length of one of the sides of the square and an instance of the Point class to keep track of the location of the center of the square.

Since we know very little about how a square will be used in this program, defining the behavior for the square is a little more difficult. If we were developing an actual program, it would be necessary to review the specifications and requirements for the program to understand the behavior that a square would be required to exhibit. Since this is only an example, we will simply define typical behaviors exhibited by all squares. The UML diagram in Figure 3.41 defines the state and behavior to be exhibited by a square object.

The UML diagram in Figure 3.41 shows two classes: Square and Point. The arrow that connects these two classes indicates that a relationship exists between the classes. In other words, a Square knows about a Point. The arrow indicates that the relationship does not go in both directions. The Square knows about the Point, but the Point does not know about the Square. The relationship between the Square and the Point represents part of the structure of a Square; a Square consists of a Point that gives the location of the Square. This is the reason the relationship that exists between the Square and Point classes has been drawn as an association. This indicates that the connection is permanent and makes up part of the state of a Square. From a programming perspective, this means that the Square class will contain an instance variable that refers to the Point object that specifies the current location of the center of the Square.

Note that the state and behavior for the Point class have not been included in the UML diagram. Recall from Chapter 2 that when drawing an UML diagram, you only want to include as much information as the reader needs to understand the system.

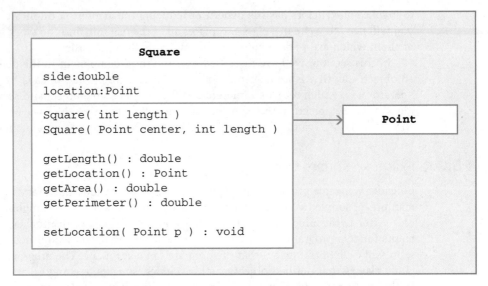

FIGURE 3.41 Design of the Square class

After reading the previous section of this chapter, you already know what the state and behavior of a Point object is, so there is no need to clutter the diagram with this information.

Based on the UML diagram of Figure 3.41, you can determine that the state of a square consists of a double value that gives the length of one of the sides of the square and a reference to a Point object that gives the location of the square. The Square class provides two constructors and several methods that can be used to obtain information about the square and manipulate its state. The Square class provides two accessors, getLength() and getLocation(), that can be used to determine the current values associated with the state of the square. The Square class also provides one mutator, setLocation(), that can change the location of a square object. Finally, there are two methods, getArea() and getPerimeter(), that can determine the area and perimeter of the square.

Based only on the information provided in the UML diagram, it is possible to write programs that use square objects. The program in Figure 3.42 illustrates how to instantiate a square object and then print the length, location, area, and perimeter of the square. The Java code that implements the Square class is given in Figure 3.43.

Consider for a moment the words that we used to describe the example classes that were discussed in the previous section: "Write a program that provides a user with the tools necessary to draw and manipulate simple two-dimensional shapes (i.e., circles, squares, rectangles, triangles, etc.)." Notice that we described the classes that we were planning to write, not individually but collectively by using the word *shape*. Using the word shape and your understanding of what shape means, we were able to convey some basic information about every class we were planning to write. For example, you would expect that all shapes know about their location and provide behaviors that allow a programmer to determine and set the location of a specific shape object.

```java
/**
 * A simple program to illustrate how to use the square class.
 */

public class TestSquare {
    /**
     * Create a square and then print its length, location,
     * perimeter, and area.
     */

    public static void main( String args[] ) {
        Square aSquare = new Square( 10 );

        System.out.println( "Square:" );
        System.out.println(
            " Length == "+aSquare.getLength() );
        System.out.println(
            " Location == (" +
            aSquare.getLocation().getXCoordinate() + "," +
            aSquare.getLocation().getYCoordinate() + ")" );

        System.out.println(
            " Perimeter == " + aSquare.getPerimeter() );
        System.out.println( " Area == " + aSquare.getArea() );
    }

} // TestSquare
```

FIGURE 3.42 Using the Square class

```java
/**
 * A class that represents a square.  The state of a
 * square consists of the length of its side and a point
 * object.  The point object specifies the location of
 * the center of the square.
 */
public class Square {
    private double side;      // Length of a side
    private Point location;   // Location of the square

    /**
     * Create a new square at location (0,0).
     *
     * @param length the length of one of the sides of the square.
     */
```

(continued)

FIGURE 3.43 Square class

```java
    public Square( double length ) {
        this( new Point( 0, 0 ), length );
    }

    /**
     * Create a square at the specified location with the given
     * length.
     *
     * @param center the location of the center of the square.
     * @param length the length of one of the sides of the square.
     */

    public Square( Point center, double length ) {
        side = length;
        location = new Point( center );
    }

    /**
     * Determine the length of one of the sides of the square.
     *
     * @return the length of one of the sides of the sqaure.
     */

    public double getLength() {
        return side;
    }

    /**
     * Determine the location of the center of the sqaure.
     *
     * @return a point that gives the location of the center of
     * the square.
     */

    public Point getLocation() {
        return location;
    }

    /**
     * Determine the area of the square.
     *
     * @return the area of the square.
     */

    public double getArea() {
        return side * side;
    }
```

FIGURE 3.43 Square class *(continued)*

```
    /**
     * Determine the perimeter of the square.

     *
     * @return the perimeter of the square.
     */

    public double getPerimeter() {
        return 4 * side;
    }

    /**
     * Set the location of the center of this square to the
     * coordinates specified by the given point.
     *
     * @param p the location of the center of the square.
     */

    public void setLocation( Point p ) {
        location.setXY( p );
    }

} // Square
```

FIGURE 3.43 Square class *(continued)*

Inheritance in an object-oriented programming language provides the same expressive power we used in the previous paragraph, but instead of collecting together a group of related words, in a programming language, we can group together related classes. In the next section of this chapter, we will discuss how to use inheritance in a Java program.

3.3 INHERITANCE

Now that you have written the Square class for the drawing application, you might want to write the class that represents a circle. Circles are different from squares, but you will find that some of the methods in the Circle class also appear in the Square class. In particular, anything in the Square class that deals with location will have to be included in the Circle class as well.

You might start thinking about writing a Shape class that could represent the state and behavior that are common to all shapes rather than duplicating the code in each class. This makes perfect sense because a circle and a square are shapes. The class definition in Figure 3.44 contains the state and behavior that are common to all shapes.

Since a circle and a square are shapes, it makes sense to make the Circle and Square classes subclasses of the Shape class. In Chapter 2, we stated that two classes are related by inheritance when the state and behavior of one class are a subset of the state and behavior of another. The more general class (i.e., Shape) is referred to as the **superclass** of the second more specialized class (i.e., Circle or Square). The second class is called a **subclass** of the superclass and is said to inherit the state and behavior

```java
/**
 * The base class for shape objects.
 */

public class Shape {

    private Point location;  // Location of the shape

    /**
     * Create a new shape at location (0,0).
     */

    public Shape() {
        this( new Point( 0, 0 ) );
    }

    /**
     * Create a shape at the specified location.
     *
     * @param center the location of the center of the shape.
     */
    public Shape( Point center ) {
        location = new Point( center );
    }

    /**
     * Determine the location of the center of the shape.
     *
     * @return a point that gives the location of the center of
     *         the shape.
     */

    public Point getLocation() {
        return location;
    }

    /**
     * Set the location of the center of this shape to the
     * coordinates specified by the given point.
     *
     * @param p the location of the center of the shape.
     */

    public void setLocation( Point p ) {
        location.setXY( p );
    }

} // Shape
```

FIGURE 3.44 Shape class

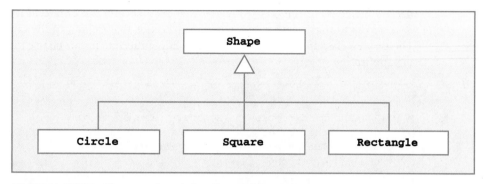

FIGURE 3.45 Shape class inheritance hierarchy

of the superclass. The UML diagram of Figure 3.45 illustrates the inheritance relationship between the classes in the drawing program.

A subclass is a more specialized form of the superclass. It satisfies the basic specifications of the superclass and can differentiate itself from the parent by adding to, or extending, the behavior of the superclass in some way. For example, in the drawing application, both the Circle and Square classes provide the state and behavior needed to manage their location, but they also add state and behavior specific to their class. For example, the Square class includes a variable that allows an instance of the class to determine the length of one of its sides, and it provides behaviors that allow a programmer to determine the area or perimeter of a square.

In Table 2.2, we introduced five forms of inheritance. In the next section, we will look at how you can use the specialization form of inheritance in a Java program.

◆ 3.3.1 Extending a Class

A subclass specifies the class that it is inheriting from using the keyword extends. A subclass can extend any public class that is not final. The general form of a subclass is given in Figure 3.46. At most one class name can be listed after the keyword extends. Java does not support inheritance from multiple superclasses. This capability is called **multiple inheritance** in other object-oriented programming languages.

A subclass inherits all of the public and protected state and behavior of the class that it *extends*. Constructors, which are not considered members of a class, are not inherited by a subclass. Note that any member of a class with protected access is accessible not only to the classes in the same package as the superclass but also to any of its subclasses, regardless of the package to which the subclass belongs. Thus, if you

```
modifier class subClassName extends superClassName {
   Class state...
   Class behavior...
}
```

FIGURE 3.46 General form of a subclass

declare members of the class to have `protected` access, not only will its subclasses have access to that member but so will any classes that belong to the same package. The `Square` class in Figure 3.47 illustrates how inheritance can be used in the drawing application.

```java
/**
 * A class that represents a square. The state of a
 * square consists of the length of its side and a point
 * object. The point object specifies the location of
 * the center of the square.
 */

public class Square extends Shape {
    private double side;      // Length of a side

    /**
     * Create a new square at location (0,0).
     *
     * @param length the length of one of the sides of the square.
     */

    public Square( double length ) {
        this( new Point( 0, 0 ), length );
    }

    /**
     * Create a square at the specified location with the given
     * length.
     *
     * @param center the location of the center of the square.
     * @param length the length of one of the sides of the square.
     */

    public Square( Point center, double length ) {
        super( center );
        side = length;
    }

    /**
     * Determine the length of one of the sides of the square.
     *
     * @return the length of one of the sides of the square.
     */

    public double getLength() {
        return side;
    }
```

FIGURE 3.47 `Square` subclass

```
    /**
     * Determine the area of the square.
     *
     * @return the area of the square.
     */

    public double getArea() {
        return side * side;
    }

    /**
     * Determine the perimeter of the square.
     *
     * @return the perimeter of the square.
     */

    public double getPerimeter() {
        return 4 * side;
    }

} // Square
```

FIGURE 3.47 Square subclass *(continued)*

A class can be extended as many times as desired. There is no limit on the number of subclasses that a single class can have. In terms of the drawing application, the Shape class can have as many subclasses as needed, but it is not valid for Circle to extend both Shape and some other class. A class can inherit from superclasses many levels away. For example, if Dog is a subclass of Mammal, and Mammal is a subclass of Animal, then Dog inherits from both the Mammal and Animal classes. This is not an example of multiple inheritance because each class in the inheritance hierarchy has at most a single parent as shown in the UML diagram in Figure 3.48.

When a class is extended, the accessibility rules are still enforced. This means a subclass cannot access the private members of any of its superclasses. Since the class Square is a subclass of Shape, it inherits all of the public state and behavior of Shape. This means that it is valid to invoke the getLocation() and setLocation() methods on an instance of the Square class even though these methods are not explicitly defined in the class. Also note that since location is a private member of the Shape class, it is not inherited by Square. Because the getLocation() and setLocation() methods are members of the Shape class, they are permitted to access the private instance variable location.

In the second constructor in the Square class of Figure 3.47, you will notice the use of the keyword super. The keyword super provides a reference to the superclass of a class in much the same way that the keyword this provides access to the object in which it is used. The keyword super can be used by a subclass to directly access the state or behavior of its immediate superclass, or it can be used in a constructor to

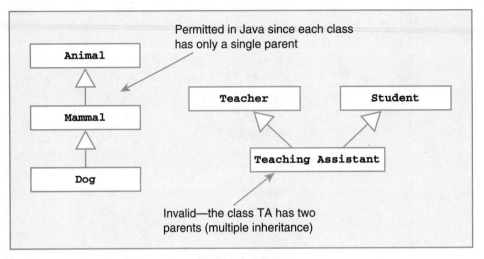

FIGURE 3.48 Single versus multiple inheritance

invoke a superclass constructor as shown in Figure 3.47. The keyword super can only be used to invoke the constructor of a superclass inside the body of a constructor for a subclass, and as was the case with this, it must be the first statement in the body of the constructor.

Given that a superclass may have state that is inaccessible to a subclass, you may wonder how the state of the superclasses is initialized when an instance of the subclass is created. Unless the programmer has specified differently, when a subclass is instantiated, Java will attempt to invoke the default constructors of all the superclasses, starting with the constructor in the highest superclass in the inheritance hierarchy down to the lowest (Figure 3.49). The output generated by executing the main() method in the class Subclass clearly indicates the order in which the superclass constructors are invoked.

What happens if a superclass does not have a default constructor or if you wish to use a constructor other than the default? The answer is to use super to specify the constructor that you wish to have invoked. This is exactly what was done in the second constructor for the Square class of Figure 3.47. Since this constructor takes as a parameter the location of the square that is being created, the super(Point) constructor of the Shape class must be invoked to properly initialize the instance variable location. The use of super in the Square constructor invokes the appropriate superclass constructor because the argument in super matches the parameter list in the nondefault constructor of the Shape class. Note that if you are extending a class that does not provide a default constructor, you must use super in the constructor of the subclass to indicate which superclass constructor to invoke. If you fail to do so, the program will not compile. This makes perfect sense because if you do not specify in the subclass what superclass constructor to invoke, Java will attempt to invoke the default constructor and the superclass does not have one.

Inheritance increases the number of classes that need to be searched when an attempt is made to access either a variable or a method. Java will search the local scope first, then check the class scope, and then check the scope of each superclass in turn

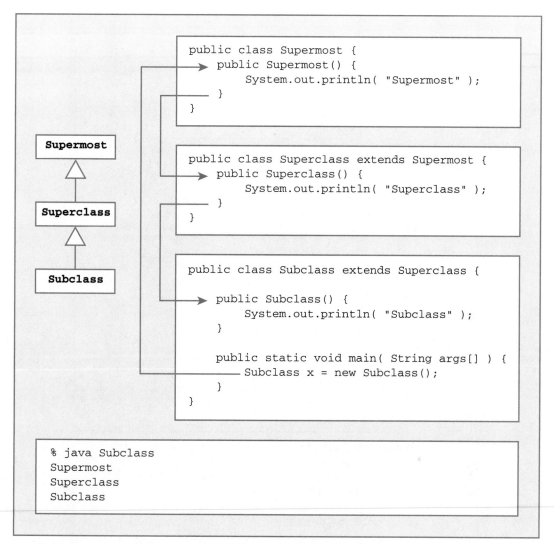

FIGURE 3.49 Superclass constructor invocation

up to the top of the inheritance hierarchy. If a variable or method with the same name is declared in several scopes, the first one that is found is used.

Consider how Java resolves the reference to the instance variable x in the constructor for ClassC in Figure 3.50. Java will start by searching the local scope in which x is used. In this case, since there are no local variables or parameters named x in the constructor, the class scope is checked next. There is an instance variable named x defined within the class. So the x in the constructor for ClassC resolves to the instance variable x defined in ClassC. The variable y in the constructor resolves to the instance variable y that is defined in ClassB. In this situation, y is not declared in either the constructor or in ClassC. The search then moves up the inheritance chain to ClassB, which contains a definition for an instance variable y.

```
public class ClassC extends ClassB {
    private int x;

    public ClassC() {
        x = -1;
        y = -2;
        z = -3;
    }
}
```

```
class ClassB extends ClassA {
    protected int y;

    public ClassB() {
        y = 1;
        z = 2;
    }

}
```

```
class ClassA {
    protected int x;
    protected int y;
    protected int z;

    public ClassA() {
        x = 123;
        y = 456;
        z = 789;
    }
}
```

FIGURE 3.50 Scope and inheritance

Similarly the variable z in the constructor refers to the instance variable z defined in ClassA.

Earlier in this chapter, we discussed overloaded methods. These are methods with the same name but different parameters. A subclass also has the ability to **override** superclass methods. A subclass overrides a superclass method by providing an implementation of that method with the same signature in the subclass. The definition in the subclass overrides the method in the superclass. Note that this is not the same as overloading a method. When a method is overloaded, both versions of the method are still accessible. When a method is overridden, an object outside of the class no longer has the ability to access the version of the method that is defined in the superclass. The method in the subclass always overrides the superclass version.

You can change the inheritance hierarchy that we have been using in this section. Instead of having a Shape class, imagine writing a class named Polygon. The state of a polygon would consist of an array that contains the vertices of the polygon. Figure 3.51 contains the code to implement a very basic Polygon class.

```
/**
 * A very simple implementation of a polygon.
 */

public class Polygon {

    private Point vertices[];   // The vertices of the polygon
    private int numPoints;      // Number of points in the array

    /**
     * Create a new polygon.
     *
     * @param numVertices the number of vertices in the polygon
     */

    public Polygon( int numVertices ) {
        vertices = new Point[ numVertices ];
        numVertices = 0;
    }

    /**
     * Add a new vertex to the polygon.
     *
     * @param p a point that represent the vertex to be added.
     */

    public void addVertex( Point p ) {
        // Cannot add more vertices than the array will hold.
        if ( numPoints < vertices.length ) {
            vertices[ numPoints ] = p;
            numPoints = numPoints + 1;
        }
    }
```

(continued)

FIGURE 3.51 Polygon class

```
/**
 * Compute the perimeter of the polygon.
 *

 * @return the perimeter of the polygon.
 */

public double getPerimeter() {
    double retVal = 0;

    // Compute the perimeter of the polygon by stepping
    // through the vertices and computing the distance
    // of each side.
    for ( int i = 0; i < numPoints; i++ ) {
        Point p1 = vertices[ i ];
        Point p2 = vertices[ ( i + 1 ) % numPoints ];
        retVal = p1.distanceFrom( p2 );

    }

    return retVal;
}

} // Polygon
```

FIGURE 3.51 Polygon class *(continued)*

Now you can consider writing a Square class that extends the Polygon class. The Square class could use all of the methods that it inherits from the Polygon class; however, we know that we can calculate the perimeter of the square much more efficiently than the perimeter of an arbitrary polygon. Instead of stepping through the array of vertices and summing the distances between each pair of vertices, we can return four times the length of one side. In this situation, it would definitely make sense to override the getPerimeter() method Square inherited from Polygon as shown in Figure 3.52.

Notice that the getPerimeter() method in the Square class of Figure 3.52 has the exact same signature as the getPerimeter() method in the Polygon class of Figure 3.51. Thus, when an attempt is made to invoke getPerimeter() on a square, the version of the method that is defined in the Square class will be executed.

Once a method has been overridden, it is no longer possible for an object to access that method. Within a subclass, however, it is possible using the keyword super to access an overridden version of a method in the superclass.

There are times when you may not want a class to be extended or you may not want a particular method in a superclass to be overridden. Perhaps it does not make any sense for a class to have subclasses. Another reason might be for security. Declaring a class as final prevents that class from being extended. The keyword final is placed before the class keyword in the class declaration. If you want to allow a class to be extended, but there are methods in the class that you do not want overridden, you can declare those methods as final. When the final keyword is in the declaration of a method, it prevents that method from being overridden. You might

```
public class Square extends Polygon {

    /**
     * Create a new square.
     */
    public Square() {
        super( 4 );   // A square has 4 vertices
    }

    /**
     * Return the perimeter of the square.
     *
     * @return the perimeter of the square.
     */

    public double getPerimeter() {
        return 4 * vertices[ 0 ].distanceFrom( vertices[ 1 ] );
    }

} // Square
```

FIGURE 3.52 Overriding the `getPerimeter()` method in `Polygon`

wish to make a method `final` if it has an implementation that should not be changed and is critical to the consistent state of the object.

In this section, you have seen how to use the keyword `extends` in Java to use the specialization form of inheritance. There are times when you want to specify that a subclass must have a particular behavior but it is not possible to provide an implementation for that behavior in the superclass. In the next section, we will discuss how abstract classes can be used to specify the behavior that a subclass should exhibit.

◆ 3.3.2 Abstract Classes

If you give a little bit of thought to the behavior that should be included in every subclass of the `Shape` class, you would probably include the ability to determine the area and perimeter of the shape. Although it is possible to compute the area and perimeter of all shapes, there is no single universal way to implement these methods. The formulas for the area of a triangle, circle, and square are all quite different. What we would really like to do is include the methods `getArea()` and `getPerimeter()` in the superclass for shapes but not provide any implementation. This way we are guaranteed that all shapes will have the ability to determine their area and perimeter, but each shape must provide its own implementation of these methods.

In an **abstract class**, one or more methods are defined, but no implementation is provided. This gives us the ability to include methods in a superclass but forces the implementation of those methods on the appropriate subclasses. You can view an abstract class as a placeholder for declaring shared methods for use by subclasses.

Because it is missing some implementation, it is not possible to create an instance of an abstract class. An abstract class exists so other classes can extend it. An abstract class contains one or more methods that have been defined as abstract. An **abstract method** does not have a method body, and the declaration of the method ends with a semicolon instead of a compound statement. A class that contains one or more abstract methods must be declared as an abstract class. `private`, `final`, and `static` members cannot be abstract. The `Shape` class of Figure 3.53 has been modified to include the abstract methods `getArea()` and `getPerimeter()`.

Note the use of the keyword `abstract` in the `Shape` class of Figure 3.53. It appears in the class header, and it appears in the header of each of the two abstract methods. For the class to be accepted by the compiler, you need to include the keyword `abstract` in both the class and method headings. It is not enough to declare methods as abstract; you must also declare the class containing them as abstract.

With the concept of abstract classes, we are now coming close to achieving the **specification form** of inheritance first defined in Table 2.2. You will recall that in the specification form of inheritance, the superclass defines the behavior that is to be implemented by a subclass, but it does not provide an implementation for that behavior. That is exactly what is done in the `getArea()` and `getPerimeter()` methods in

```java
/**
 * The base class for shape objects.
 */

public abstract class Shape {
    private Point location;  // Location of the shape

    // public Shape()...
    // public Shape( Point center )...
    // public Point getLocation()...
    // public void setLocation( Point p )...

    /**
     * Return the area of this shape.
     *
     * @return the area of this shape.
     */

    public abstract double getArea();

    /**
     * Return the perimeter of this shape.
     *
     * @return the perimeter of this shape.
     */

    public abstract double getPerimeter();

} // Shape
```

FIGURE 3.53 Abstract base class for the Shape classes

Figure 3.53. The abstract `Shape` class is declaring that these two methods must be included in any subclass but does not provide an implementation. Compare that to the `getLocation()` and `setLocation()` methods. In this case, the abstract class specifies that these methods will be included, and it provides an implementation that all subclasses may use.

The syntax for writing a class definition that extends an abstract class is no different from the syntax used to extend a nonabstract class. You only need to ensure that in the subclass you include the implementation of all abstract methods in the abstract class. If you forget to implement one of these abstract methods, you will not be able to compile the subclass correctly.

◆ 3.3.3 Interfaces

The specification form of inheritance defines the behavior that must be provided by a subclass but not the implementation of that behavior. So far, the only way we have seen to use the specification form of inheritance in Java is to write an abstract class. Java provides another structure, an **interface**, that provides the ability to exploit the specification form of inheritance.

An interface is similar to a class in that it consists of a set of method headers and constant definitions. Unlike a class, however, an interface contains absolutely no executable code. An interface is a pure behavioral specification that does not provide any implementation.

The purpose of an interface is to specify the common behaviors that a group of classes are required to implement. In Chapter 2, we described the specification form of inheritance in terms of using a clock. In school, you were taught how to tell time in general, not how to read a Timex Model 921 travel series alarm clock. Your teacher explained that all analog clocks have hour, minute, and second hands. You were then taught how to read the hands on the dial to determine the current time.

An interface provides the same capability in a programming language. In an interface, you specify the behaviors that a class must implement in order to implement the interface. You do not care how the behavior is actually implemented; all you care about is that the behavior must be there. An interface is similar to an abstract class that has no state, and *every* method is abstract.

In an interface, all methods are public, even if the `public` modifier is omitted. An interface cannot define instance variables, but it can define constants that are declared both `static` and `final`. Since an interface is a behavioral specification, you cannot instantiate an interface. Interfaces, because they cannot be instantiated, do not have a constructor. To illustrate how to write an interface and a class that implements that interface, let's rewrite the `Shape` class of Figure 3.44 as an interface. The code that defines the interface `Shape` is given in Figure 3.54.

The `Shape` interface in Figure 3.54 should not look all that different to you. It has the same basic syntax as a class definition, but the word `interface` appears in the class declaration in place of the word `class`. Also notice that every method in the class is without an implementation. In fact, the methods look identical to the abstract methods discussed in the previous section.

An interface defines a set of behaviors that a class is required to exhibit. A class that provides all of the behaviors specified by the interface is said to **implement**

```
/**
 * An interface for shape objects.
 */

public interface Shape {

    /**
     * Determine the location of the center of the shape.
     *
     * @return a point that gives the location of the center of
     *         the shape.
     */

    public Point getLocation();

    /**
     * Set the location of the center of this shape to the
     * coordinates specified by the given point.
     *
     * @param p the location of the center of the shape.
     */

    public void setLocation( Point p );

    /**
     * Return the area of this shape.
     *
     * @return the area of this shape.
     */

    public double getArea();

    /**
     * Return the perimeter of this shape.
     *
     * @return the perimeter of this shape.
     */

    public double getPerimeter();

} // Shape
```

FIGURE 3.54 Shape interface

the interface. The Square class of Figure 3.55 implements the Shape interface of Figure 3.54.

Once again the Square class of Figure 3.55 should not look that different from the other classes in this chapter. The only difference is in the header of the class where the keyword implements declares that the class satisfies all behavioral requirements of

```
/**
 * A class that represents a square.  The state of a
 * square consists of the length of its side and a point
 * object.  The point object specifies the location of
 * the center of the square.
 */

public class Square implements Shape {

    private double side;      // Length of a side
    private Point location;   // Location of the square

    /**
     * Create a new square at location (0,0).
     *
     * @param length the length of one of the sides of the square.
     */

    public Square( double length ) {
        this( new Point( 0, 0 ), length );
    }

    /**
     * Create a square at the specified location with the given
     * length.
     *
     * @param center the location of the center of the square.
     * @param length the length of one of the sides of the square.
     */

    public Square( Point center, double length ) {
        side = length;
        location = new Point( center );
    }

    /**
     * Determine the length of one of the sides of the square.
     *
     * @return the length of one of the sides of the square.
     */

    public double getLength() {
        return side;
    }

    /**
     * Determine the location of the center of the square.
     *
     * @return a point that gives the location of the center of
     *         the square.
     */
```

(continued)

FIGURE 3.55 Square class that implements Shape

```java
    public Point getLocation() {
        return location;
    }

    /**
     * Determine the area of the square.
     *
     * @return the area of the square.
     */

    public double getArea() {
        return side * side;
    }

    /**
     * Determine the perimeter of the square.
     *
     * @return the perimeter of the square.
     */

    public double getPerimeter() {
        return 4 * side;
    }

    /**
     * Set the location of the center of this square to the
     * coordinates specified by the given point.
     *
     * @param p the location of the center of the square.
     */

    public void setLocation( Point p ) {
        location.setXY( p );
    }

} // Square
```

FIGURE 3.55 Square class that implements Shape *(continued)*

the Shape interface. Unlike the keyword extends, it is possible for a class to implement several different interfaces. It is also possible for a class to extend one class and implement one or more interfaces at the same time.

You might think it a little strange that Java supports multiple interfaces but does not support multiple inheritance. Recall that an interface uses the specification form of inheritance and specifies only the behaviors that a class must provide. In the specialization form of inheritance, the superclass provides the implementation of the method included in the subclass. Now consider what might happen if you were to extend multiple classes. If you inherited two methods from two different superclasses that had the same signature but different implementations, which one would you use? On the other hand, if you wrote a class that implemented two different interfaces and both interfaces specify the same method, there is no problem. As long as your class provides an implementation for the common method, it satisfies both interfaces.

Up to this point, we have only discussed the mechanics of how inheritance works in Java. We have not yet discussed how inheritance can be used in a program. In the next section, we will discuss polymorphism, which is one of the most common ways to use inheritance in an object-oriented program.

◆ 3.3.4 Polymorphism

Whether you are using the specialization or specification forms of inheritance, the end result is the same: The subclass will have the same public behavior as its super-class. It does not matter if the implementation of that behavior is the same as in the su-perclass or specializes the behavior of the superclass. What does matter is that we know that the behavior present in the superclass is present in the subclass. This means that since all instances of a subclass exhibit the same behavior as their superclass, an instance of a subclass can mimic the behavior of the superclass and should be indistin-guishable from an instance of the superclass. So it is possible to substitute instances of the subclass for the superclass in any situation with no observable effect. For example, if I were to give you a reference to a subclass but told you it was a reference to the su-perclass, you should be able to use the object without knowing exactly what type of object you were dealing with.

The observation in the previous paragraph should change the way you think about assignment. Previously, you were taught that the type of the expression on the right side of an assignment statement had to match the type of the variable on the left side. Consider the following statement:

```
Shape aShape = new Square( 10 );
```

Since Square is a subclass of Shape, an instance of the Square class can be substituted for an instance of the Shape class without any observable effect, and the assignment should be considered valid.

If the types in an assignment statement do not match, Java will automatically con-vert the type of the expression on the right side of the assignment to match the type of the variable on the left. For example, you are already aware that if you attempt to assign an int value to a double variable, Java will automatically promote the int value to a double and execute the assignment. In a similar way, Java will automati-cally convert the type of the expression on the right side of an assignment statement to the type of the variable on the left if the class of the expression on the right side is a subclass of the class of the variable on the left. The same holds true for interfaces and classes that implement the interface. In other words, it is perfectly valid to assign a subclass reference to a variable whose type is one of its superclasses. The reverse, however, is not true. The assignment of an object of a superclass to a subclass variable is an error. The following statement is not valid:

```
Square aSquare = new Shape();
```

Although a Square is a Shape and can stand in for a Shape, not all Shapes are Squares.

```java
public class PolyShapes {

    /**
     * Compute the total area of all the shapes in the
     * array.
     *
     * @param shapes array containing the shapes.
     *
     * @return the total area of all the shapes.
     */

    public static double totalArea( Shape shapes[] ) {
        double retVal = 0;

        for ( int i = 0; i < shapes.length; i++ ) {
            retVal = shapes[ i ].getArea();
        }

        return retVal;
    }

    public static void main( String args[] ) {
        Shape theShapes[] = new Shape[ 3 ];

        theShapes[ 0 ] = new Square( 10 );
        theShapes[ 1 ] = new Circle( 40 );
        theShapes[ 2 ] = new Triangle( 10, 30 );

        System.out.println( "Total area:  " +
                            totalArea( theShapes ) );
    }

} //PolyShapes
```

FIGURE 3.56 Using polymorphism

To see how this can be used in a program, assume that the classes Circle, Square, and Triangle all extend the Shape class of Figure 3.53. In other words, they are all subclasses of Shape. Now consider the program in Figure 3.56.

If you look at the totalArea() method of Figure 3.56, you will see that it takes as a parameter an array of shapes. Even though the method has no idea what specific shapes are referenced by this array, it can still compute the total area of all the shapes because each one has a getArea() method. For each of the shapes referenced by the area, the program invokes the same method (i.e., getArea()), but how the area is actually calculated will depend on the specific type of shape involved. If the shape is a square, the area is calculated by squaring the length, and if the shape is a circle, the radius of the circle will be squared and multiplied by the constant Math.PI. The fact that invoking the same method will have different effects based on the type of the object on which the method is invoked is an example of **polymorphism**.

The word *polymorphism* means "many forms," and in this case, the many forms refer to the fact that different types of calculations may take place and the correct calculation will be determined dynamically at run time. In an object-oriented program, polymorphism occurs when the method that is invoked can change depending on the type of object used in the program. Java supports polymorphism through inheritance and interfaces.

◆ 3.3.5 Class Object

In Java, every class is a subclass, either directly or indirectly, of the class Object. The class Object defines the basic state and behavior that all objects must exhibit. The methods that may be overridden by subclasses of class Object (i.e., the nonfinal methods of the class) are given in Table 3.3.

Each of the methods in Table 3.3 can play an important role in a Java program. The clone() method can be used to give a class the ability to create a deep copy of itself. The finalize() method is the closest thing that Java has to a destructor. The finalize() method for an object is guaranteed to be invoked before the object is garbage collected. If you have written a class that dynamically allocated system resources, you can use the finalize() method to return those resources before the object is removed from memory. We will discuss the hashCode() method in Chapter 8.

The toString() method in class Object is probably one of the most useful methods that you will ever write in a class. The toString() method is meant to return a String that provides a textual representation of the object. In situations where Java needs to convert an object to a string format, it will automatically invoke the toString() method on the object. In the Square class of Figure 3.57, the toString() method will return a string that contains the length of the side, the area, and the perimeter of the square.

TABLE 3.3 Nonfinal Method in Class Object

Method	Description
protected Object **clone**()	Performs a deep copy operation (i.e., creates a new copy of this object).
public boolean **equals**(Object obj)	Returns true if this object is equal to the object referred to by the parameter and false otherwise.
protected void **finalize**()	Invoked when there are no more references to the object and sometime before the object will be removed from memory by the garbage collector.
public int **hashCode**()	Returns a hash code value for the object.
public String **toString**()	Returns a string representation of this object. By default the method returns a string consisting of the name of the class and the hexadecimal representation of the hash code of the object.

```
public class Square extends Shape{

    private double side;        // Length of a side

    // public Square( double length )...
    // public Square( Point center, double length )...
    // public double getLength()...
    // public double getArea()...
    // public double getPerimeter()...

    /**
     * Return a textual representation of a square.
     *
     * @return a string representation of a square.
     */

    public String toString() {
        return ( "Square:  length=" + side +
                 " area=" + getArea() +
                 " perimeter=" + getPerimeter() );
    }

} // Square
```

FIGURE 3.57 Overriding `toString()` in the `Square` class

A class that has a `toString()` method can be "printed" using the method `System.out.println()`. The `println()` method takes a string as a parameter, but if you pass it an arbitrary object, the `toString()` method will be invoked to obtain a string that can be printed. Given the version of the `Square` class in Figure 3.57, the program in Figure 3.58 will create three squares of various sizes and then print them. A well-designed `toString()` method can be extremely useful when you are debugging your programs. A good coding habit is to write a `toString()` method for every class that you write. This will allow you to obtain a customized, printable version of every object that you create.

The `equals()` method can be used to perform a deep comparison on a class. To do a deep comparison, an object needs to know what to compare itself to. The parameter that is passed to the `equals()` method identifies the object with which you will be compared. Since the `equals()` method uses an object reference, it is possible to compare any two objects regardless of their class. The `Square` class in Figure 3.59 has been modified to override the `equals()` method.

The `equals()` method in Figure 3.59 uses the `instanceof` operator that will return true if the reference on the left side is either an instance of, a subclass of, or implements the class specified on the right side. So the `equals()` method first checks to determine if the argument refers to an instance of a `Square`. If it does, the method then compares the state of the two objects (i.e., the length of their sides) to determine whether or not they are equal.

```
public class SquareToString {

    /**
     * Illustrate the use of the toString method in the
     * Square class.
     *
     * When this program is run it will produce the following
     * output:
     *
     *     Square:  length=10.0 area=100.0 perimeter=40.0
     *     Square:  length=1.0 area=1.0 perimeter=4.0
     *     Square:  length=4.0 area=16.0 perimeter=16.0
     */

    public static void main( String args[] ) {

        Square s1 = new Square( 10 );
        Square s2 = new Square( 1 );
        Square s3 = new Square( 4 );

        System.out.println( s1 );
        System.out.println( s2 );
        System.out.println( s3 );
    }

}
```

FIGURE 3.58 Using the `toString()` method in the `Square` class

```
public class Square extends Shape{

    private double side;      // Length of a side

    // public Square( double length )...
    // public Square( Point center, double length )...
    // public double getLength()...
    // public double getArea()...
    // public double getPerimeter()...
    // public string toString()...

    /**
     * Compare this square to another object.
     *
     * @param o the object to compare myself with.
```

(continued)

FIGURE 3.59 Overriding `equals()` in the `Square` class

```
    *
    * @return true if the objects are equal and false otherwise.
    */

   public boolean equals( Object o ) {
       boolean retVal = false;

       if ( o instanceof Square ) {
           Square other = (Square)o;

           retVal = getLength() == other.getLength();
       }

       return retVal;
   }

} // Square
```

FIGURE 3.59 Overriding `equals()` in the `Square` class *(continued)*

3.4 COMPILING AND RUNNING A JAVA PROGRAM

◆ 3.4.1 Basic Concepts

Any program, regardless of language or the sophistication of the algorithms it uses, must ultimately be executed to be of any use. Processors are devices that understand a finite set of relatively simple instructions. Any program written in a high-level programming language must first be converted into an equivalent sequence of machine language instructions to be run on a computer.

The conversion of a program into machine language can happen either before the program is presented to the computer or as the program is running. A **compiled language** is converted to machine language before the program is run using a translator called a **compiler**. A compiler is a piece of software that checks the syntactical and semantic structure of a program. If it determines that the program is valid, it will generate the machine language equivalent of the high-level language program for a specific processor. If the program is to be run on a different processor, the program will need to be recompiled and converted into the machine language instructions understood by the new processor. Although the program itself may be run several times, the compilation process only has to occur once. Languages such as C or C++ are examples of compiled languages.

An **interpreted language**, on the other hand, delays the conversion of the program to machine language until the program is executed. An interpreted program is never actually converted into machine language form. Instead, a piece of software, referred to as an **interpreter**, is responsible for analyzing the program and causing the appropriate actions to take place. It is important to note that if a particular part of the program is executed repeatedly, that portion of the program is typically reinterpreted each time by the interpreter. Note that although the program is never really converted into machine language form, the interpreter must be expressed in machine language form to run on a specific processor.

To appreciate the differences between compiled and interpreted languages, imagine that you wanted to eat at a restaurant where the employees speak only German. Assuming that you cannot understand or speak German, there are two basic strategies that you could use to order food. The first approach is to determine, before you go to the restaurant, exactly what you want to order. Then you find someone who speaks German, and you ask him or her to translate your order into German. You can now go to the restaurant with your translation in hand. Of course, you can only order the food that is in your translation, and if you are asked any questions at the restaurant, you will not be able to answer them. Furthermore, should you instead decide to eat at a Chinese restaurant, you will need to start the process all over again.

A second approach would be to find a person who speaks both English and German and invite them to come to dinner with you. Your friend could then serve as an interpreter and help you order your food. Now if you were asked a question, you would be able to provide an answer since your friend would be with you to interpret. You would also be able to eat at a Chinese restaurant, assuming of course, that you can find someone to go to dinner with you who can speak Chinese. Probably, the biggest disadvantage to this approach is that it will take you longer to place your order since you must first tell your friend what you want to order and then wait for your friend to do the necessary translation.

The approach of translating your order to the target language (i.e., German) before going to the restaurant is equivalent to using a compiler. Here instead of translating from one natural language to another, the compiler converts the program written in the high-level language to machine language. Once the program has been converted, it can be presented to the processor to be run. The clear disadvantage to this approach is that if you need to run the program on a different processor, you need to recompile your program. The clear advantage to the compiled approach is speed. In a compiled language, the translation to machine language is done once, before the program is ever run.

Bringing a friend to act as a translator is similar to the way in which an interpreted program is run. Here the translation is being done as the order is being placed, or as the program is being run. The clear advantage to this approach is flexibility. You can order food in English at non-English-speaking restaurants provided there are translators at each restaurant. However, this approach is slower than the compiled approach. Here the translation occurs as you place the order, and every time you order the same thing, the translation has to take place again. But note that if you want to order the same food at a different restaurant, all you have to do is bring along a different friend.

In the next section, we will look at how Java uses both compiled and interpreted technologies to prepare and run programs on a variety of different platforms.

◆ 3.4.2 Compilation and Execution

After reading the previous section, you might be under the impression that languages are either compiled or interpreted. However, Java uses both interpreter and compiler technology to execute a program. What makes Java different from most programming languages is that the Java compiler does not produce code for an actual processor; instead, it produces code, called **bytecode**, for a hypothetical computer that is referred to as the Java Virtual Machine (JVM). The **Java Virtual Machine** is the cornerstone of the Java system. The JVM is the reason Java programs are platform and operating system independent. The JVM implements an abstract computer. Like a real computer, it has an instruction set and manipulates various memory areas at run time.

The power of using the JVM to execute programs is that when a program is compiled, it only needs to be compiled into bytecode. Any valid JVM is capable of interpreting the bytecodes and running the corresponding Java program. Thus, as long as you have a JVM that runs on your platform, you can run any compiled Java program on that platform as well.

So even though a Java program is interpreted by the JVM, you will first need to compile your programs to JVM bytecode before they can be run. If your program is syntactically correct, the compiler will place the bytecode to be interpreted by the JVM into a file known as a **class file**. The JVM will then interpret the bytecode in the class file to execute your program. This process is illustrated in Figure 3.60.

The bytecode associated with each class in a Java program is placed in a separate class file. For the JVM to run your program, it must be able to locate the class files that contain the bytecode for the classes it needs to use. This is one of the reasons you must place top-level classes into files that have the same name. For example, if your

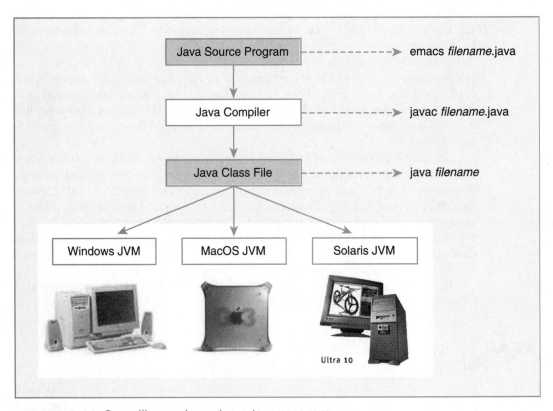

FIGURE 3.60 Compiling and running a Java program

program requires a `Square` class, then the JVM knows that the file that contains the bytecode version of this class will be in a file named `Square.class`.

The naming convention described in the previous paragraph does not necessarily provide enough information for the JVM to actually locate the file that contains the bytecode for a class. For example, what happens if the file that contains the bytecode is stored in a different directory? Every JVM uses an environment variable named `CLASSPATH` to help it locate the class files required to run a program. The `CLASSPATH` variable contains a list of directories that the JVM should look in when trying to locate a class file. The details regarding how you set the `CLASSPATH` environment variable and the directories that you should include depend on the particular operating system on which the JVM is running. We will not discuss the issue any further here and leave it to your instructor to provide the necessary details.

Now that you understand that you need both a Java compiler and a JVM to run your programs, the next question is: Where do I get them? The answer is that you can obtain all of the tools required to compile and run Java programs for free from Sun Microsystems. The Java tools that you need are bundled into a package called the Java Development Kit (JDK). The JDK includes the compiler, JVM, debugger, class libraries, and a number of demonstration programs. There are a variety of different JDKs for different types of computing platforms. If you download and install the Standard JDK, you will be able to do all the exercises in this text. You can obtain a copy of the Standard JDK at the Java home page, which can be found at the URL www.java.sun.com.

3.5 SUMMARY

This has been a long and detailed chapter, and it will surely keep you occupied for a good deal of time. It is also one of the book's most important chapters, and it is crucial that you have understood and mastered the concepts and techniques presented in the previous pages. Object-oriented programming is an enormously useful software development technique but only if you are able to realize and implement its ideas in a high-level programming language such as Java.

Chapter 1 overviewed the entire software development life cycle, which included the specification, design, and implementation phases. Chapter 2 discussed the fundamental concepts of object-oriented design in a high-level, language-independent manner. Finally, Chapter 3 presented a rather extensive catalog of how one particular language, Java, supports the object-oriented principles presented in Chapter 2. These concepts included classes, objects, inheritance, and polymorphism. However, the best way to appreciate the benefits that can accrue from the use of object-oriented design is to follow the solution of a single, interesting problem from start to finish. This would include (a) the development of the requirements and specifications documents in some formal notation such as UML, (b) the design of classes to solve that problem, including their state, behavior, and identity, and finally, (c) their translation into correct, elegant, and easy-to-read Java code.

That is exactly what we will be doing in the next chapter. Chapter 4 presents a detailed case study that ties together much of the material from the first three chapters. The problem that we will address is one that we frequently referred to at the very beginning of the text: the design and development of a home heating system.

EXERCISES

1. Explain why virtually all Java classes are declared to be `public` while instance variables are declared as either `protected` or `private`. What would be the effect of making an instance variable `public`?

2. Briefly explain why it is important to make mutable data members `private`. What consequences does this have, and how do we commonly get around them?

3. Explain the difference in how the compiler will handle these variable declarations if they appear inside class `Point`:

```
private int zCoordinate;
private static int zCoordinate;
private final int zCoordinate;
private static final int zCoordinate;
```

4. Create a class constant for the value π (which is 3.14159) and give it `public` scope in the class `Point`. What would be the effect of giving π `private` scope?

5. Is there any reason to make an instance method `private`? If so, give an example of a possible `private` method that might be useful in class `Point`.

6. Change the code in Figure 3.12 so that it handles a three-dimensional point. What are the signatures of the methods in the class?

7. Write a class method for class `Point` that, given a three-dimensional (x, y, z) coordinate, computes the distance of that point from the origin (0, 0, 0). The formula to compute the distance is $\sqrt{x^2 + y^2 + z^2}$. Rewrite the method so that it is an instance method instead of a class method. How does this change the signature of the method?

8. Write an instance method `flip()` for class `Point` that, given a three-dimensional (x, y, z) coordinate, will return the point that has the same (x, y) position but is on the opposite side of the z axis—that is, the point (x, y, −z).

9. Write a main program that uses your new three-dimensional `Point` class and does the following:

   Creates three different three-dimensional points.

   Computes and prints the distance of each of the points from the origin.

   Prints the "flip" of each point.

   Writes a copy constructor for the three-dimensional `Point` class.

10. Given the code:

```
public static int q10( int a, float b ) {
    int d;
    float e;
    a = (int)b;
    d = (int)b;
    b = 2 * b;
    e = b;
    return d;
}
```

If this method is invoked as follows

```
int x = 5;
float y = 6.0;
int z = q10( x, y );
```

what are the values of x, y, and z when these three lines of code are executed?

11. Given the method declaration for q10, is the following code valid? State why.

```
this.q10( x, y );
```

12. Write a subclass of the Polygon class in Figure 3.51 that will handle triangle objects. Your class should create a triangle, determine the perimeter, determine the area, and print the vertices.

13. Write an interface for polygon objects. Decide what behaviors you wish to include.

14. Write a class called Nagon that models a regular polygon with a given number N of sides. Nagon should extend Shape and provide a constructor Nagon(int numSides, int sideLength). Recall that such a figure will have perimeter (numSides * sideLength) and area (numSides * sideLength^2)/(4*tan(π/numSides). Java provides π and the tangent function in the Math class. Be sure to provide a toString() method which returns the string "3-agon" for a Nagon with three sides, the string "4-agon" for one with four sides, and so on.

15. Write a class that models the basic functionality of a duck. Ducks quack, eat, and fly around. Ducks have names, weights, and a best friend (which is also a duck). Be sure to provide accessors, mutators, and a toString() method for your Duck class. Draw a UML class diagram that describes your Duck class.

16. Give an example where two Duck objects satisfy (a) deep equality but not shallow equality, (b) shallow equality but not deep equality, (c) both shallow and deep equality, (d) neither shallow nor deep equality.

17. Write a subclass of Duck, ProgrammerDuck, which has a String variable containing the Duck's favorite programming language, suitable accessors and mutators, and a method evangelize() that prints a message proclaiming the duck's favorite programming language to be the best language ever.

18. Write a method called argue(ProgrammerDuck otherDuck) that asks the other ProgrammerDuck what its favorite language is. If the other duck likes a different language, the ProgrammerDuck should quack at the other duck repeatedly.

19. Write a simple program that prints its command-line arguments in "middle-out" order. For example, if given the arguments 1 2 3 4 5, your program should print 3 2 4 1 5. If an even number of arguments are provided, start with the element to the right of the middle. Thus, if given arguments 1 2 3 4 5 6, your program should print 4 3 5 2 6 1.

20. Given the following abstract class

```
abstract class Room {
    protected int size;
    protected int numberOfDoors;

    public Room ( int theSize, int theDoors ) {
        size = theSize;
        doors = theDoors;
    }

    public abstract String report();

    public int getSize() {
        return size;
    }
}
```

write the complete class BedRoom that inherits from the Room class. A BedRoom constructor accepts three arguments: the size, the number of doors, and the number of beds. Implement the method report() that returns a string containing the number of beds in the room: "The bedroom has XXXX beds." Note that XXXX represents the number of beds in the room.

21. Given the following interface

```
public interface Publication{
    public int getNumberOfPages();
    public boolean isPeriodical();
    public boolean isBook();
}
```

write a class TextBook that implements the Publication interface. Your class should include a constructor that takes a single parameter: the number of pages in the book.

22. An interface defines a collection of methods that any implementing class must define. This sounds like an abstract class in which all the methods are abstract and there are no instance variables inherited. What is the advantage of an interface?

23. Java allows a variable of type J to be assigned an instance of class C—that is, J = C—with certain conditions. What are those conditions?

24. What is the difference between overriding a method and overloading a method in a class?

25. Consider the following code:

```
 1| public class AnyClass {
 2|
 3|    public String toString() {
 4|       return "AnyClass object"";
 5|    }
 6|
 7|    public String whatAmI() {
 8|       return "AnyClass object";
 9|    }
10|
11|    public static void main( String[] args ) {
12|
13|       AnyClass anyObj = new AnyClass();
14|       List v = new ArrayList();
15|
16|       v.add( anyObj );
17|       System.out.println( v.get(0).toString() );
18|       System.out.println( v.get(0).whatAmI() );
19|    }
20| }
```

Use the numbers on the left as line number references. If line 17 is used, the program compiles and will print the text AnyClass object. If line 18 is used, it generates a compiler error from javac. Why does the compiler handle these two statements differently?

CHAPTER 4

Case Study in Object-Oriented Software Development

4.1 INTRODUCTION

The first three chapters described the sequence of steps involved in software development. Chapter 1 overviewed the software life cycle, and Chapters 2 and 3 went into greater detail on the design phase of this cycle—namely, object-oriented design in Java. Although this is important material, it is not possible to fully appreciate the complexities of modern software development by focusing on an individual phase any more than it is possible to appreciate all the intricacies of building a house by studying only mortgage financing or electrical contracting. Instead, it is necessary to observe the complete development of a program from initial specifications through design and implementation to final acceptance testing.

In this chapter, we design and implement a piece of software mentioned quite often in earlier chapters: a home heating system. We are not going to build the software that would actually be loaded into a real thermostat to control a real furnace. Instead, we will develop a *heating simulation program* that models the operational behavior of an arbitrary room/thermostat/furnace combination. Using this simulation program, we could perform a number of interesting experiments such as:

- estimating how well a specific furnace will work in a given climate
- approximating annual heating costs for a particular living space
- determining optimal parameter settings for a specific thermostat and furnace

Our software development process will parallel the life cycle steps discussed in Chapter 1 and diagrammed in Figure 1.2. A careful reading of this case study will help to clarify and integrate the many ideas presented in the preceding pages. At the end of the chapter, there are suggestions for similar projects that can be implemented using the software development techniques shown in the following sections.

4.2 THE PROBLEM REQUIREMENTS

Our first task is to create the problem requirements that describe exactly what the user wants the software to do. This will require the user (us, in this example) to make decisions about program behavior as well as choices regarding trade-offs between program efficiency, complexity, and cost.

Our home heating simulation program will simulate the operation of four components: a thermostat, a furnace, the living area (which we refer to as the "room" even though it may encompass more than a single room), and the environment (which represents the space outside the room). These four components are diagramed in Figure 4.1. Since our goal in this case study is to demonstrate software development, not to construct a production program, we model a house with only a single thermostat and single furnace, disregarding the issues of multizone heating systems.

The thermostat monitors the room temperature and turns the furnace on when the temperature falls below a user-specified setting. It turns the furnace off when the temperature reaches the correct level. Most thermostats do not turn the furnace off as soon as the desired temperature is reached. Instead, they overheat the room by a few degrees to prevent the furnace from cycling on and off too frequently.

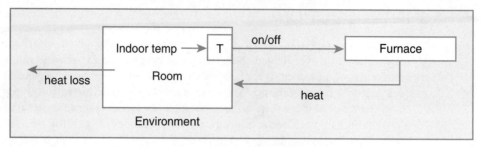

FIGURE 4.1 Four components in our simulation model

A furnace has two parameters of interest: its *capacity*, measured in BTUs per hour, and its *efficiency*. Capacity is the maximum amount of heat a furnace can produce, and efficiency is the percentage of capacity it is actually able to deliver. The capacity of a typical home furnace is about 20,000 to 100,000 BTU/hour. The U.S. government requires that all furnaces sold today have efficiency ratings of at least 78 percent. Modern furnaces are usually much higher, with efficiencies of 85 to 95 percent. The heat output of a furnace is determined by multiplying its capacity by its efficiency. The result is the number of BTUs generated in a 1-hour period.

Fluctuations in room temperature are caused by differences in the amount of heat pumped into a room by the furnace, which is 0 if the furnace is off, and the amount of room heat lost to the surrounding environment. The formula for the new temperature at time period $i + 1$ in a room with *FloorArea* square feet is:

$$RoomTemp_{i+1} = \frac{Q_{in} - Q_{loss}}{SHC \times FloorArea} + RoomTemp_i$$

Q_{in}, the *heat gain*, is the amount of heat coming in to the room from the furnace, and Q_{loss}, the *heat loss*, is the amount of heat lost to the outdoor environment. *SHC*, the *specific heat capacity* of the room, measures the amount of heat stored in the room itself—for example, in the walls, floors, and ceiling. The value of *SHC* for a typical house is 4.0 BTUs per square foot per degree Fahrenheit.

Q_{in}, the heat gain over a given period of time, is given by:

$Q_{in} = FurnaceOutput\ (in\ BTU/hour) \times time\ (in\ hours)$

In a more sophisticated simulator, the amount of heat entering a room would include other factors such as solar radiation, electrical devices, and people in the room, all of which generate heat. We will neglect these other factors and assume that the only heat produced comes from our furnace.

Q_{loss}, the heat loss to the surrounding environment over a given period of time, is given by:

$Q_{loss} = BLC \times FloorArea \times (InsideTemp - OutsideTemp) \times time\ (in\ hours)$

BLC, the *basic load constant*, measures resistance to heat loss. A large value of *BLC* is indicative of a room that loses heat quite easily. A small value of *BLC* represents a room that is more resistant to heat loss, such as one that is very well insulated. In our simulation, *BLC* is 1.0 BTU per square foot per degree Fahrenheit per hour, a typical value for a well-built house.

We are now in a position to describe the problem we want our software to solve. We begin with a room at some initial temperature at time $T = 0$. We now determine the room temperature at some future time $(T + \Delta)$ by computing how much heat has entered the room from the furnace and how much heat was lost to the environment during time increment Δ. We use this information to decide what action to take regarding the furnace. The possible operations are: (a) turning the furnace on if it is currently off and the temperature in the room has fallen below the thermostat setting, (b) turning the furnace off if it is currently on and the temperature in the room has risen above the thermostat setting plus some allowable amount of overheating, or (c) leaving the furnace in its current state and doing nothing. This process is repeated for the next time increment and continues until some maximum time limit is reached.

The next section will take this general problem statement and turn it into a complete, thorough, and unambiguous problem specification document that will provide all the information needed to design and implement the program that solves this problem.

4.3 PROGRAM SPECIFICATIONS

As was discussed in Chapter 1 and diagramed in Figure 1.3b, a specification is an input/output document that states exactly what outputs are produced by the program for every possible input. Thus, our goal now is to describe exactly what inputs are required by our simulation program and exactly what results should be displayed.

Our home heating simulation program will be started from the command line using the following command syntax:

```
java HeatingSimulation parameters ...
```

The user can provide a number of optional parameters that control the characteristics of the simulation. The arguments take the form `paramName=paramValue`, where `paramName` is one of the eight names listed in column 1 of Table 4.1 and `paramValue` is the initial numerical value assigned to this parameter. If a user does not explicitly specify a value for any of these eight parameters, the program should use the default value listed in column 3 of Table 4.1.

We selected this command-line format because it allows the program to be easily modified at some future date. To add another model parameter (e.g., to specify a different value for SHC, the specific heat capacity), we add a new parameter name and default value to the list in Table 4.1.

The program should ignore any invalid parameter names or out-of-range values. However, an invalid parameter value should terminate the program. For example, the following command line runs the simulation with a 1,000 square foot living area and an initial temperature of 65 degrees Fahrenheit. All other parameters are set to their default values:

```
java HeatingSimulation size=1000 in=65
```

Given the following command lines

```
java HeatingSimulation lenth=200
java HeatingSimulation eff=1.05
```

TABLE 4.1 Command-Line Parameters to the Simulation Program

Parameter Name	Description	Default Value
in	The initial temperature of the room in degrees Fahrenheit	72.0
out	The outside environment temperature in degrees Fahrenheit	50.0
set	The desired room temperature (the thermostat setting) in degrees Fahrenheit	72.0
cap	The capacity of the furnace in BTU/hour	8,500
eff	The efficiency of the furnace, given as a fraction of furnace capacity in the range 0.0 to 1.0, inclusive	0.95
size	The size of the living area in square feet	250.0
freq	The number of ticks of the clock between successive lines of output	5
length	The total number of seconds the simulation will run	7,200

the program will disregard the parameter `lenth` and instead use the default value of 7,200 for the parameter `length`. It will also disregard the parameter value assigned to `eff`, as it is out of range. However, the command

```
java HeatingSimulation eff = zero point eight
```

should terminate execution because the value provided for furnace efficiency has not been correctly expressed as a numerical value.

If all command line values are valid and the program begins execution, then the output is a printed report (on the standard output device) that first displays the objects in the simulation and their initial state. Then, as the simulation runs, a single line displaying the current room temperature and furnace status is displayed every `freq` ticks of simulated time. A sample run of the program and the desired output are given in Figure 4.2

One of the most important parameters in the program is the time increment Δ that is used to determine how often to recompute the room temperature. (Note: This is not the same as the parameter `freq` that determines how often to print a line of output. `freq` is expressed as a multiple of Δ.) We are constructing what is called a *discrete event simulator* that models the behavior of a system only at discrete points in time rather than continuously. In our simulation model, we determine the room temperature at time T and then again at time T + Δ. Any temperature change in the room between these two points in time is not part of the model. Thus, our clock will "tick" in units of Δ.

Obviously, we can achieve the highest level of accuracy by using a tiny value of Δ. However, the smaller the value of Δ, the greater the amount of computation re-

```
Created 4 Objects:
  [ GasFurnace: cap=8500.0 eff=0.95 pilot on=true heating=false ]
  [ Environment: temperature=50.0 ]
  [ Room: temp=72.0 area=250.0 SHC=4.0 BLC=1.0 ]
  [ Thermostat: setting=72.0 overheat=3.0]

Starting simulation: display frequency=5.0 length=7200.0

Time     Inside      Outside      Desired      Furnace
----     ------      -------      -------      -------
0        71.95       50.00        72.00        On
300      72.16       50.00        72.00        On
600      72.37       50.00        72.00        On
900      72.58       50.00        72.00        On
1200     72.78       50.00        72.00        On
1500     72.97       50.00        72.00        On
1800     73.17       50.00        72.00        On
2100     73.36       50.00        72.00        On
2400     73.54       50.00        72.00        On
2700     73.72       50.00        72.00        On
3000     73.90       50.00        72.00        On
3300     74.07       50.00        72.00        On
3600     74.24       50.00        72.00        On
3900     74.41       50.00        72.00        On
4200     74.57       50.00        72.00        On
4500     74.73       50.00        72.00        On
4800     74.89       50.00        72.00        On
5100     75.04       50.00        72.00
5400     74.52       50.00        72.00
5700     74.02       50.00        72.00
6000     73.52       50.00        72.00
6300     73.03       50.00        72.00
6600     72.56       50.00        72.00
6900     72.09       50.00        72.00
7200     71.90       50.00        72.00        On
```

FIGURE 4.2 Sample program output

quired to produce results because we must run the program from time T = 0 to T = length in steps of Δ. For example, to simulate 1 hour (3,600 seconds) with $\Delta = 0.001$ second, the program will need to carry out 3.6 million computations of the room temperature at times 0.001, 0.002, 0.003, . . . , 3,599.999, 3,600.0. That may require a prohibitively large amount of machine time and cause the program to run rather slowly. On the other hand, if Δ is large, the program does much less work, but it may not achieve a sufficient level of accuracy. For example, if $\Delta = 600$ seconds, or 10 minutes, we only need six iterations to simulate 1 hour, but the program will not model the activities of either the thermostat or the furnace for an entire 10-minute period.

There are two possible ways to select a value for Δ. One is to make Δ a user-specified parameter, exactly the same as the parameters listed in Table 4.1. This might result in a command line looking something like this:

```
java HeatingSimulation timeIncrement = 0.01
```

This is a reasonable approach. However, we have not chosen it because most of the users of our program will be totally unfamiliar with the technical concepts of discrete event simulation. Trying to explain how to set a time increment value may confuse them and leave them unable to make a reasonable and informed choice. Instead, we will set the value of this parameter (called SECS_BETWEEN_EVENTS in our model) to 60 seconds, or 1 minute. Thus, in our model, every clock tick will represent the passing of 1 minute of simulated time.

Figure 4.3 is a problem specification document describing the exact behavior of the software we wish to build. It is based on the many decisions, trade-offs, and assumptions that we have made in the previous pages. It is now the user's job to carefully read and review these specifications to ensure that this document completely and accurately describes the problem to be solved. If it does not, we can easily make changes to these specifications right now; later in the development process, it will be much more difficult.

Problem Specification Document

You are to build a home heating simulation program that models the behavior of four components: (a) a living area (or room) with `size` sq. ft. and an initial temperature of `in` at time 0, (b) a single thermostat with a setting of `set` that measures room temperature, (c) a single furnace of capacity `cap` and efficiency `eff` that can be turned on/off by the thermostat and which is initially off, and (d) the environment outside the room that has a fixed temperature of `out`. The values of `size`, `in`, `set`, `cap`, `eff`, and `out` can be provided by the user on the command line. If a parameter is not specified, then use the default values given in Table 4.1. If a parameter name is not valid, disregard it. If a parameter value is not valid, throw an exception and terminate execution.

Advance the simulation clock by a value of $\Delta = 60$ seconds and determine the new room temperature at this time using the heat gain and heat loss formulas given in Section 4.2, with the two constants SHC and BLC set to 4.0 and 1.0, respectively. Based on the new temperature `t`, the thermostat should take one of the following three actions: if `(t < set)` and the furnace is currently off, then turn it on; if `(t ≥ (set + 3))`, where 3 represents the allowable overheating, and the furnace is currently on, then turn it off; otherwise, do nothing. Produce one line of output, as shown in Figure 4.2, we have updated the simulation clock `freq` times, where `freq` is an input parameter that comes from the command line.

Continue this process until the simulation clock has reached or exceeded the value of `length`, which is also a command-line parameter. When that occurs, the program terminates.

FIGURE 4.3 Problem specification document

In the next section, we begin the process of designing the software that will correctly and efficiently implement the specifications given in Figure 4.3.

4.4 SOFTWARE DESIGN

◆ 4.4.1 Identifying Classes

We are now ready to begin designing a solution to the problem specified in Figure 4.3. The goals of the design phase are to (a) identify the essential classes that are needed, (b) describe the state information and behaviors associated with these classes, and (c) diagram the relationships that exist among these classes.

In Chapter 2, we showed that one of the best ways to identify the classes you need to solve a given problem is to look at the nouns that are found most often in the problem specification document. There are three nouns that appear repeatedly in the document of Figure 4.3, and they are excellent candidates to be made into classes:

Room. A class representing a living area object.

Thermostat. A class representing objects that monitor temperature and take actions based on that temperature.

Furnace. A class representing objects that generate heat.

Another noun that appears in the specification document is *environment,* which represents the world outside the room. Should that also be made into a class? It would certainly be possible to solve the problem without it. We could simply add an instance variable to our Room class that would keep track of the outside temperature. The problem with this approach is that the outside temperature is not really part of the state of a room. This is an example of a design that mixes state information from different sources into a single class, which can result in software that is both confusing and difficult to maintain. When designing classes, you want to keep the states and behaviors of unrelated entities in separate classes. Therefore, if you find yourself doing things like keeping employee salary information inside inventory objects or storing engine power data in driver objects, it is time to stop and rethink your entire design.

In this example, the room object should obtain the outside temperature from another source, which argues strongly for Environment to be its own separate class. This approach also provides increased program flexibility. For example, in our simulation model, the outside temperature is fixed. However, at some future time, we might want the outside temperature to fluctuate during the day—for example, start out cool in the morning, increase during the afternoon hours, and cool off at night. To add this feature, all we have to do is modify our Environment class. No other classes will be affected.

Thus, we will also include the following class in the design of our model:

Environment. A class representing the world outside the room.

Finally, there is a noun that appears rather frequently in Figure 4.3, but it is not as obvious a candidate for inclusion as the four classes identified so far. It is not as obvious because it is part of the simulator rather than the world being modeled. This is the "simulation clock." One of the most important responsibilities of the program is keeping track of time. This is necessary, for example, to determine when to compute a new temperature, produce output, or terminate the program. A `Clock` class would be responsible for keeping track of time and notifying other objects when certain events are to occur. Thus, the next class we will add to our design is:

> `Clock`. A class representing objects that can keep track of simulation time and inform other objects when certain events have occurred.

These then are the five classes that we will include in the design of our home heating simulator. The reader should carefully review the specification document in Figure 4.3 to see how its nouns have led to the selection of these five classes.

◆ 4.4.2 State and Behavior

There are many other nouns in the specification document of Figure 4.3, such as *capacity, efficiency, area,* and *temperature*. However, a little thought should convince you that these nouns do not represent individual classes but, rather, information about instances of the classes described in the previous section. For example, capacity and efficiency are not distinct entities or objects but part of the state of furnace objects. Area is certainly part of the state of a room object, and temperature is a state variable of both room objects (indoor temperature), environment objects (outdoor temperature), and thermostats (the desired temperature). Thus, we can see that the problem specification document is also essential in helping a designer identify state information.

Table 4.2 lists some of the important state information associated with the five classes we have chosen to include in our solution. We may discover others as we get further into the implementation.

Now that we have identified (at least initially) the five classes in our simulator as well as the state information maintained by instances of these classes, we can begin to describe the behaviors, or actions, of these classes. Three types of behavior are part of virtually every class, and they can be viewed as "standard boilerplate" to be included

TABLE 4.2 Classes and State Information

Class	State
Environment	◆ Temperature
Furnace	◆ Capacity ◆ Efficiency ◆ On/Off state
Room	◆ Temperature ◆ Area in square feet ◆ Reference to the furnace that heats the room ◆ Reference to the environment outside the room
Thermostat	◆ Desired temperature setting ◆ Amount of overheating ◆ Reference to the furnace that it controls ◆ Reference to the room in which it is located
Clock	◆ Current time ◆ Seconds between clock ticks

in every class you write. The first of these standard behaviors is the *constructors*. It is necessary to create instances of a class, so you always need one or more constructors. Exactly how many constructors will be needed depends on the characteristics of the class. For example, Room may require two constructors—one to create a room where the square footage and the initial temperature are provided by the user and a second that creates a new instance of a room using default values for both of these parameters.

The second of these standard behaviors is *accessor* and *mutator* functions that allow access to (and possibly modification of) the instance variables of a class. Since instance variables are almost always declared as private, it will be necessary to include methods of the form get*XXX*() that access and return the value of the private instance variable *XXX*, where *XXX* represents the name of this variable. If modifications of this variable are permitted, you should also include mutator methods of the form set*XXX*(newVal) that reset the value of the instance variable *XXX* to newVal.

For example, one of the state variables of Environment is temperature. A Room object needs this temperature to compute Q_{loss}, the heat lost to the environment. Room cannot access this value directly. Instead, it will invoke the accessor function getTemperature() in class Environment. Since our model does not allow changes to the outdoor temperature by the user, a public mutator method is not really needed. However, if this were possible, then Environment would include a method setTemperature(double t), which resets the outdoor temperature to t.

The third standard behavior is an overriding of the toString() method inherited by every object in Java from class Object. (This operation was highlighted in Figure 3.57 and Table 3.3.) The toString() method displays information about an object. However, this information is of a general nature because it must apply to every object in the system. It is often helpful to override this method with a new method that prints specific information about this particular object. This can be extremely helpful during debugging.

In addition to these three standard behaviors, objects also carry out actions appropriate only to them. How do we begin to identify these unique behaviors? The answer was again provided in Chapter 2, which said that we should look at the *verbs* contained in the problem specification document. These verbs can help us identify the actions that objects perform, and these actions frequently translate directly into methods contained in our classes.

For example, the problem specification states that we "determine the new room temperature . . ." Quite obviously, one of the behaviors of a room object is the ability to compute and store a new room temperature using the heat loss and heat gain formulas from Section 4.2. Using this method, the thermostat can query the room at selected time intervals asking for its current temperature.

```
// determine new room temperature t time units
// after last determination
public void determineTemperature(double t);
```

Similarly, the specification document contains statements that say the thermostat must "turn it [i.e., the furnace] on . . ." and "turn it off . . ." These actions translate into a Furnace class method that will look like this:

```
// set the furnace heating state to the value of onOff
public void setHeating(boolean onOff);
```

Using this method, the thermostat can send a message to the furnace to turn itself either on or off.

Finally, a statement in the specification document states "the thermostat should take one of the following actions: "if (`t < set`) and the furnace is currently off, then turn it on; if (`t` ≥ (`set + 3`)) . . . and the furnace is currently on, then turn it off; otherwise, do nothing." These actions translate into a thermostat method that determines whether or not we need to change the state of the furnace:

```
// Return true if we need to change the furnace state based on the
// thermostat setting, current room temperature, and amount of
// allowable overheating, which is currently 3 F. Otherwise,
// return false
public boolean determineStateChange();
```

If we do need to change the state of furnace `f`, then we invoke the `f.setHeating(b)` method, where `b` is the Boolean value returned by `determineStateChange`.

In a similar fashion, we go through the entire specification document identifying those verbs that correspond directly to desired behaviors in our objects. Table 4.3 is a listing of the five classes that are in our solution and some of the behaviors that we have identified for objects of that class. Of course, we may add behaviors as the development progresses.

TABLE 4.3 Classes and Their Behaviors

Class	Behavior

Environment	`// Create a new environment with the default temperature`
	`Environment();`
	
	`// Create a new environment with temperature t`
	`Environment(double t);`
	
	`// Return the current environmental temperature`
	`double getTemperature();`
	
	`// Set the environmental temperature to t`
	`void setTemperature(double t);`
	
	`// Return a string containing descriptive information about`
	`// the environment`
	`String toString();`

Furnace	`// Create a new furnace with capacity cap, efficiency eff,`
	`// and turned off`
	`Furnace(double cap, double eff);`
	
	`// Return the capacity of the furnace`
	`double getCapacity();`

(continued)

TABLE 4.3 Classes and Their Behaviors *(continued)*

Class	Behavior
| | ```
// Return the efficiency of the furnace
double getEfficiency();

// Return the on/off state of the furnace
boolean isHeating();

// Set the furnace state to the value onOff
void setHeating(boolean onOff);

// Determine the heat output of this furnace for the time
// period hours
double output(double hours);

// Return a string containing descriptive information about
// the furnace
String toString();
``` |
| Room | ```
// Create a room of size area and initial temperature
// initTemp. The room is heated by furnace f and is
// inside environment e
Room(Environment e, Furnace f, double area, double initTemp);

// Return the floor area of the room
double getFloorArea();

// Return the identity of the furnace heating this room
Furnace getFurnace();

// Return the identity of the environment outside the room
Environment getEnvironment();

// Determine the new temperature in the room after t
// units of time
void determineTemperatureChange(double t);

// Return a string containing descriptive information about
// the room
String toString();
``` |
| Thermostat | ```
// Create a new thermostat in room r connected to
// Furnace f
Thermostat(Room r, Furnace f);

// Return the identity of the room in which you are located
Room getRoom();
``` |

(continued)
```

TABLE 4.3 Classes and Their Behaviors *(continued)*

Class	Behavior

	```// Return the identity of the furnace that you control```
	```Furnace getFurnace();```
	
	```// Return the current temperature setting of this thermostat```
	```double getSetting();```
	
	```// Change the setting on this thermostat to the value```
	```// newSetting```
	```void setSetting(double newSetting);```
	
	```// Return the value of the constant overheat, which is how```
	```// much we will overheat a room before turning the```
	```// furnace off```
	```double getOverHeat();```
	
	```// Determine if we need to change the state of the```
	```// furnace based on the thermostat setting, the current```
	```// room temperature, and the amount of allowable overheating.```
	```void determineStateChange();```
	
	```// Return a string containing descriptive information about```
	```// the thermostat```
	```String toString();```

Clock	```// Create a new clock that moves ahead tickInterval seconds```
	```// on each advance```
	```Clock(int tickInterval);```
	
	```// Return a string containing descriptive information about```
	```// the clock```
	```String toString();```

◆ 4.4.3 Inheritance and Interfaces

Now that we have selected our classes and identified their states and behaviors, we should be ready to begin implementation. In fact, we could build a home heating simulator, and a good one at that, given the design work that has been done so far.

However, there are a couple of additional features that we wish to add to our design before jumping into implementation. These features will help to make the finished program more flexible and maintainable. They will also demonstrate the advantages that can accrue from the intelligent use of the concept of inheritance.

Specifically, we will utilize the specification and specialization forms of inheritance described in Section 2.2.3 and highlighted in Table 2.2.

Our first design change comes from recognizing that there are many types of furnaces in the marketplace with a range of operating characteristics. Although they all share certain properties, such as a given heating capacity, different models may have specialized features unique to themselves. This is an example of the *specialization* form of inheritance, in which the subclass is a more specialized form of its superclass.

For example, one popular furnace type is a gas furnace. We can confirm that this is a specialization form of inheritance by noting that these two entities satisfy the is-a relationship introduced in Section 2.2.3; that is, "a gas furnace is a furnace." A gas furnace and a furnace will share the same state information listed in Table 4.2, namely, heat capacity, efficiency, and on/off state. They also share the behaviors in Table 4.3—they can be turned on and off, and when on, they both generate heat. However, a gas furnace has one feature not found in general Furnace class objects, which is the idea of a *pilot light*. A gas furnace cannot generate heat unless its pilot light is on. (New homeowners often discover this fact on the first cold day of winter.) Thus, to implement the concept of a gas furnace, we can keep all the capabilities of our existing Furnace class. Then we only need to add new information about the state of the pilot light and new behaviors to check and set the pilot light's state.

Instead of creating a new class called GasFurnace, maybe we should simply add the following state variable

```
boolean pilotLight;
```

to the existing Furnace class, along with new instance methods that access and modify this variable. However, that would be a serious mistake. In effect, this approach is saying that every furnace has a pilot light, which of course is incorrect. At some later time, we might want to model the behavior of a furnace type that does not have a pilot light. Because of our design, making this small change could require modification of a good deal of code, increasing both maintenance costs and the likelihood of errors.

One of the important goals of software design is to *localize* changes that must be made to software. That is, if a change needs to be made to some portion of code X, then only the code that deals with X should have to be reviewed and modified. Those sections of code that have nothing to do with X should be unaffected by this change. In this example, if we change the furnace type, we should not have to worry about how to deal with a pilot light state variable, as the new furnace may not even have one.

We can achieve this type of localized behavior using inheritance. We let the superclass Furnace represent the shared state and behavior common to all furnaces. Then, whenever we want to model a new furnace type, we create a subclass that inherits these common states and behaviors and only adds or modifies those characteristics unique to this furnace type. That is, we only need to write new code to (a) implement specialized behaviors and (b) override existing behaviors that work differently on this new system. All other behaviors are inherited from its superclass and used as is. This approach will greatly simplify maintenance and minimize the chance for unexpected errors to creep into the code.

Thus, we will add the following new subclass to our design:

Subclass	Extends	New State	New or Changed Behaviors

GasFurnace	Furnace	pilotLight	// true if pilot on,
			// false otherwise
			boolean isPilotOn();
			
			// set pilot state to onOff
			void setPilot(onOff);
			
			// modify to produce heat only
			// if the pilot is on
			double output(**double** hours);

We would follow exactly the same steps described above to add other specialized furnace types to our simulation model.

Our second design change has to do with how the clock communicates with other objects in our software. As mentioned earlier, we are building a discrete event simulator. In this type of model, events happen only at discrete points in time. The clock is responsible for keeping track of simulation time and informing other objects when certain things must be done. It is not unlike having a single timekeeper in a sporting contest (the clock) that keeps track of the game time and informs the referees (the other objects) by a horn or a siren when certain events have occurred, such as the end of the game.

In our software, there are two classes that need to be informed of the current time: Room and Thermostat. The room object must compute the room temperature at explicit points in time (every 1 minute in our model), and the thermostat must access that new temperature and decide what, if anything, should be done regarding the state of the furnace. What is the best way for the clock to inform the room and thermostat objects of the current time?

One technique is for the room and thermostat objects to repeatedly send messages to the clock asking for the time. This is horribly inefficient and could lead to the type of behavior we see in small children going on a long car trip: "Are we there yet?" "Are we there yet?" "Are we there yet?" In a similar vein, the room and thermostat objects would be sending messages saying, in effect: "Is it time to recompute temperature?" "Is it time to recompute temperature?" "Is it time to recompute temperature?"

A much better way to handle this is to reverse the direction of the communications—that is, for the clock to send a message to the room and the thermostat when it is time for them to perform some operation, such as computing the new temperature in the room. The only question is how can we be sure that the room and thermostat objects are able to receive the messages sent from Clock? The solution is to create an interface that specifies all the messages that Clock can send. Then, any class that wishes to receive timing information can do so by implementing this interface. This is an example of the *specification form* of inheritance listed in Table 2.2, in which the superclass (the interface) defines behaviors that are implemented in the subclass (the classes implementing the interface) but not in the superclass.

Our design will include an interface called ClockListener that must be implemented by any class that wishes to receive timing information from the clock. The ClockListener interface will specify two behaviors:

```
// This method is invoked before an event is about to take place.
// It provides an object with the chance to update its state since the
// last event occurred, which was timeInterval ticks ago.
void preEvent(double timeInterval);


// This method indicates that the event has taken place.
void event();
```

For example, assume that `Room` implements the `ClockListener` interface just described. A room object needs to recompute its temperature based on what has happened since the last event. To do this, it must check the on/off status of the furnace, the outdoor temperature, and the time interval `t` since the last computation. It then solves the heat loss and heat gain formulas in Section 4.2. All these operations will be done when the room object receives a `preEvent(t)` message. However, the actual change to the room temperature state variable will not be made until the `event()` method is invoked.

Events are handled in this way to avoid any problems that could occur due to the order in which `event()` calls are made to specific objects. For example, in our model, we want to ensure that the thermostat checks the temperature in the room after the temperature has been updated, not before. If we send an `event()` message to both the room and thermostat telling them that it is time to carry out an event, we could not be sure in which order the operations will be done. The thermostat might access either the old temperature or the newly recomputed value. By sending the `preEvent()` message first, we ensure that all preparations for the upcoming event are done by every object receiving this message. Then, the assignment of these new values to the appropriate state variables is carried out when the `event()` operation is invoked.

Another feature is that, if we add new classes that also need timing information, it is easy for them to obtain. They just have to implement the `ClockListener` interface.

◆ **4.4.4** UML Diagrams

Our last task before beginning implementation is to diagram the relationships that exist among the various classes, subclasses, and interfaces in our solution. We have already identified some of these relationships during our preliminary specification and design work. For example, the following sentences, which describe important interactions between classes, come out of the discussions in the preceding sections:

"The room obtains the outside temperature from the environment . . ."

"The thermostat queries the room to learn the indoor temperature . . ."

"The thermostat turns the furnace on or off depending on its setting and the current indoor temperature . . ."

Because of the small size of this project—only five classes, one subclass, and one interface—it is probably not necessary to formally diagram the relationships between entities. There are so few we could probably keep them all in our head. (Note: The finished home heating simulation program is about 1,100 lines long, including comments. Looking back at Figure 1.1, this puts it in the Small category.) However, as we stressed in Chapter 1, real-world software packages are not small but quite large, incorporating tens or hundreds of thousands of lines of code and dozens or hundreds of packages, classes, subclasses, and interfaces. In this type of software development environment, UML diagrams are invaluable in helping the programmer write and maintain code. For that reason, we will present a few of the more important UML diagrams for this software project.

Figure 4.4 is a UML class diagram that includes the seven major components in our design. This figure contains five classes: Clock, Room, Thermostat, Furnace, and Environment. Room must know about the single Environment in which it is contained and the single Furnace that heats it. Thermostat must know about the Room it is in, and which Furnace it controls. Clock does not need to know directly about any other class. Instead, it sends messages to every class that implements the ClockListener interface. The dotted line in Figure 4.4 indicates that in our design the two classes Room and Thermostat implement this interface and will be able to communicate with Clock. Finally, Figure 4.4 specifies that GasFurnace is a subclass of Furnace.

This UML diagram captures all of the major relationships that exist among the classes, subclasses, and interfaces in our program. However, it does not specify the behaviors or states that exist within these classes. To capture that information, we create additional UML diagrams that deal only with segments of Figure 4.4, but contain additional information about the state and behavior of individual classes.

For example, Figure 4.5 is a UML diagram that focuses in on the heating component section of our solution: the Furnace, Thermostat, Room, and Environment

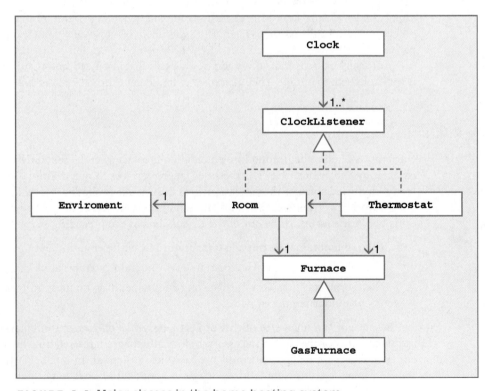

FIGURE 4.4 Major classes in the home heating system

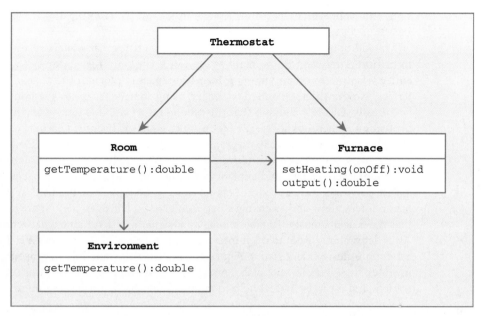

FIGURE 4.5 Simulation objects in the heating simulation

classes. This diagram identifies not only the relationships that exist between these components but also the methods that are used to communicate between these classes.

The Thermostat class uses the getTemperature() method of Room to access the current room temperature. If the state of the Furnace must be changed, then Thermostat uses the setHeating(onOff) method to turn the Furnace on or off. Room uses the output() method of Furnace to determine the amount of furnace heat entering the room, and the getTemperature() method of Environment to determine the outdoor temperature. From these two values, Room is able to compute the new room temperature.

Figure 4.6 is a UML diagram highlighting the timing section of our solution: the Clock class and the ClockListener interface. The diagram specifies that the two key timing operations of the clock are (a) creating a new Clock that ticks every tickInterval seconds (in our design, tickInterval is set to 60; in a different de-

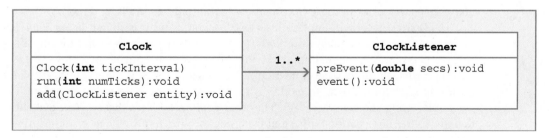

FIGURE 4.6 Clock and ClockListener

sign, this value might be input by the user) and (b) running the clock in steps of `tickInterval` from time 0 to time `numTicks`.

In addition, our `Clock` will keep a list of all entities that wish to receive timing information. There can be as many as we want, the only restriction being that every entity wishing to receive timing information must implement the `ClockListener` interface. New entities are added to the list using the `add(entity)` method of `Clock`.

Finally, Figure 4.6 shows that this timing information is sent to all entities on the list using the methods `preEvent(secs)` and `event()` discussed earlier.

These are the only UML diagrams we present in this case study. However, if this were a more complex software project, we would likely prepare additional diagrams that would help clarify and explain our design. One of the most important is the *sequence diagrams* introduced in Section 2.3.2.3. Sequence diagrams describe the dynamic interactions and exchanges between classes. For example, Figure 4.5 specified that `Thermostat` must query both `Room` and `Furnace` to determine what actions to take. After determining what to do, it interacts with `Furnace` to change its state. These interactions are clearly identified in Figure 4.5, but that diagram does not capture the order in which these actions take place. A sequence diagram provides just this type of information, and it can be a great help to the programmers implementing these classes.

4.5 IMPLEMENTATION DETAILS

Finally, after XX pages of requirements, specification, and design, we have arrived at implementation—the phase that many students mistakenly identify as the most creative and important part of software development. We hope that the discussions leading up to this section have helped to correct this mistaken view and have given you a better feeling for the amount of work that must be done, and done well, before even one line of code is written. The previous sections should also help you better understand the numbers that appear in Figure 1.10, which state that only 15 to 20 percent of the overall time on a software development project is spent on coding and debugging, while 30 to 40 percent is requirements, specifications, and design. Finally, we hope that these discussions have demonstrated that the truly creative and innovative part of software development is design, not implementation. Looking back at the many decisions already made—classes, subclasses, interfaces, states, behaviors, and interactions—it is obvious that much of the interesting work has already been done. Our task now is taking this work and translating it into correct and efficient Java code. Although that is not a trivial task, it is also not as creative as what has gone before. The job of the implementation phase is much like the responsibilities of a building contractor who must take the creative work of the architect and turn it into floors, walls, and roof.

The first class we will implement is `Environment`, and it is shown in Figure 4.7. There is not much to say about this class, as it is basically just a container for the outside temperature. Therefore, it might be viewed by some as unnecessary. However, as we said earlier, the advantage of making `Environment` a separate class is that, at some future time, it will be easier to modify it to allow the outdoor temperature to fluctuate in interesting and complex ways. The other point to notice is that we have overridden the `toString()` method inherited from class `Object` to provide more descriptive information about the `Environment`.

```java
/**
 * This class represents the external environment that a room
 * is contained in. The primary role of this class is to maintain
 * the outside temperature. We will be using a fixed outdoor
 * temperature, but it could be modified to vary according to
 * some environmental rules.
 */

public class Environment {

    // Initial temperature. Used by the default constructor.

    public static final double DEFAULT_TEMPERATURE = 72.;

    // The current temperature in this environment

    private double temperature;

    /**
     * Create a new environment using the default temperature.
     */

    public Environment() {
        this( DEFAULT_TEMPERATURE );
    }

    /**
     * Create a new environment with the specified temperature.
     *
     * @param initialTemp initial temperature of the environment.
     */

    public Environment( double initialTemp ) {
        temperature = initialTemp;
    }

    /**
     * Return the environment's current temperature.
     *
     * @return the current temperature.
     */

    public double getTemperature() {
        return temperature;
    }
```

(continued)

FIGURE 4.7 Environment.java

```
/**
 * Set the temperature of the environment.
 */

public void setTemperature( double newTemp ) {
    temperature = newTemp;
}

/**
 * Return a string representation of the environment.
 *
 * @return a string representation of the environment.
 */

public String toString() {
    return
        "[ Environment: " +
        " temperature=" + temperature +
        " ]";
    }
} // Environment
```

FIGURE 4.7 Environment.java *(continued)*

The next class we will implement is Furnace, and its code appears in Figure 4.8. This class contains three private instance variables: capacity, efficiency, and heating, a Boolean that specifies the on/off state of the furnace. There are accessor functions for each of these state variables as well as a mutator function, setHeating, which allows us to change the furnace's state. The other interesting method is output, which determines the total amount of heat generated by a furnace over a given time period using the formula from Section 4.2: heat output = (capacity * efficiency * time).

Our Furnace class represents an "idealized" furnace object. It includes only those characteristics that are common to all furnace types but no specialized characteristics unique to only one particular type.

```
/**
 * A furnace in the home heating simulation. When on a furnace
 * will produce a certain number of BTUs/hour of heat. The furnace
 * has a capacity which gives the maximum number of BTUs it can
 * generate and an efficiency which determines what percentage of the
 * furnace's capacity is actually generated as output.
 */
```
(continued)

FIGURE 4.8 Furnace.java

```java
public class Furnace {
    private double capacity;   // Capacity of the furnace in BTUs/hour
    private double efficiency; // The efficency of the furnace
    private boolean heating;   // Is the furnace producing heat?

    /**
     * Create a new furnace.
     *
     * @param cap the capacity of the furnace in BTUs/hr
     * @param eff the efficiency of the furnace
     */

    public Furnace( double cap, double eff ) {
        // Store the state of the furnace
        capacity = cap;
        efficiency = eff;

        // Make sure the furnace is off
        heating = false;
    }

    /**
     * Turn the furnace on (i.e., it will produce heat) or off.
     *
     * @param onOff if true the furnace will produce heat.
     */

    public void setHeating( boolean onOff ) {
        heating = onOff;
    }

    /**
     * Return the capacity of this furnace.
     *
     * @return the capacity of the furnace.
     */

    public double getCapacity() {
        return capacity;
    }

    /**
     * Return the efficiency of this furnace.
     *
     * @return the efficiency of this furnace.
     */

    public double getEfficiency() {
        return efficiency;
    }
```

(continued)

FIGURE 4.8 Furnace.java *(continued)*

```java
/**
 * Return the state of the furnace.
 *
 * @return true if the furnace is producing heat.
 */

public boolean isHeating() {
    return heating;
}

/**
 * Return the number of BTUs produced by the furnace during the
 * specified period of time.
 *
 * @param hours number of hours the furnace has been on.
 *
 * @return the number of BTUs produced by the furnace during
 * the specified time period.
 */

public double output( double hours ) {
    double btusGenerated = 0.0;

    if ( heating ) {
        btusGenerated = capacity * efficiency * hours;
    }

    return btusGenerated;
}

/**
 * Return a string representation of this furnace.
 *
 * @return a string representation of this furnace.
 */

public String toString() {
    return
        "[ Furnace:" +
        " cap=" + capacity +
        " eff=" + efficiency +
        " heating=" + heating +
        " ]";
}

} // Furnace
```

FIGURE 4.8 Furnace.java *(continued)*

We can handle the enormous range of furnace types by implementing them as subclasses of the Furnace class in Figure 4.8. The only type that we will include in this case study is GasFurnace, whose code is shown in Figure 4.9. However, it would be easy to add subclasses to implement the unique heating characteristics of such devices as solar panels and heat pumps. We would implement them as subclasses of Furnace exactly as is done in Figure 4.9.

The only state variable added to this subclass is pilotLight. In addition, we have included accessor and mutator functions called is PilotOn() and setPilot that allow us to check and set the value of this new state variable.

Note also how this new subclass overrides the output() method inherited from Furnace. This was necessary because a gas furnace will only generate heat if its pilot light is on. Also note that instead of rewriting the entire method, it uses super to invoke the output() method in the superclass once we are sure the pilot light is on.

```java
/**
 * A gas furnace. A gas furnace has a pilot light, which must be on
 * in order for the furnace to produce heat.
 */

public class GasFurnace extends Furnace {

   boolean pilotLight = false; // State of the pilot light

   /**
    * Create a new furnace.
    *
    * @param cap the capacity of the furnace in BTUs/hr
    * @param eff the efficiency of the furnace
    */

   public GasFurnace( double cap, double eff ) {
      super( cap, eff );

      // Pilot light is off
      pilotLight = false;
   }

   /**
    * Turn the pilot light on.
    *
    * @param onOff if true the pilot light is on.
    */

   public void setPilot( boolean onOff ) {
      pilotLight = onOff;
   }
```
(continued)

FIGURE 4.9 GasFurnace.java

```java
/**
 * Return the state of the pilot light.
 *
 * @return true if the pilot light is on.
 */

public boolean isPilotOn() {
    return pilotLight;
}


/**
 * Return the number of BTUs produced by the furnace during the
 * specified period of time.
 *
 * @param hours number of hours the furnace has been on.
 *
 * @return the number of BTUs produced by the furnace during
 * the specified time period.
 */

public double output( double hours ) {
    double btusGenerated = 0.0;

    if ( pilotLight ) {
        btusGenerated = super.output( hours );
    }

    return btusGenerated;
}


/**
 * Return a string representation of this furnace.
 *
 * @return a string representation of this furnace.
 */

public String toString() {
    return
        "[ GasFurnace:" +
        " cap=" + getCapacity() +
        " eff=" + getEfficiency() +
        " pilot on=" + pilotLight +
        " heating=" + isHeating() +
        " ]";
}

} // GasFurnace
```

FIGURE 4.9 GasFurnace.java *(continued)*

The next piece of code is the `ClockListener` interface. This is the interface that must be implemented by any object that wishes to receive timing information from the `Clock`. It includes the two methods described earlier: `preEvent` and `event()`. The `preEvent()` method is invoked prior to an event taking place. The idea is that when this method is called, an object is given the opportunity to perform whatever preliminary updates and computations are necessary. It is not until the `event()` method is invoked that the assignment of a new value to a state variable is actually done. The `ClockListener` interface is shown in Figure 4.10.

```java
/**
 * Simulation objects that implement this interface are interested
 * in being notified when the time recorded by a clock changes.
 *
 * There are two methods defined in this interface. The preEvent()
 * method will be invoked before an event is about to take place.
 * The purpose of this method is to provide a simulation object
 * with the opportunity to update its state before the next event
 * takes place. For example, a room may wish to calculate the change
 * in room temperature that occurred since the last event.
 *
 * The event() method indicates that an event has taken place.
 */

public interface ClockListener {

    /**
     * This method is called before the next event occurs so that
     * a simulation object can update its state based on what has
     * occurred since the last event. A simulation object will not
     * change its state when this method is called. It prepares itself
     * for the state change that will occur when the next event occurs.
     *
     * @param interval the number of seconds that have elapsed since
     *                 the last event (i.e., the length of the interval
     *                 between events).
     */
    public void preEvent( double interval );

    /**
     * Called when the next event occurs in the simulation.
     */

    public void event();

} // ClockListener
```

FIGURE 4.10 `ClockListener.java`

Now let's take a look at `Room.java`. The code for this class is given in Figure 4.11. First, notice that `Room` implements the `ClockListener` interface of Figure 4.10. This is necessary because `Room` must be sent information from `Clock` when it is time to update its internal room temperature.

The `Room` class includes constructors that use whatever input values are provided by the user and default values for quantities not provided. For example, the following constructor

```
public Room(Environment theWorld, Furnace heatSource, double area);
```

will set the `area` of the room to the user-specified value, but it sets the constants SHC, BLC, and the initial room temperature all to default values. Additional constructors exist for other combinations of defaults and user-provided inputs.

The implementation of Room includes accessor functions for the many state variables associated with objects of this class:

```
getEnvironment();        // access identity of the Environment outside
                         //    this room
getFurnace();            // access the identity of the Furnace that
                         //    heats this room
getSHC(); getBLC();      // access these two important heating constants
getFloorArea();          // access the size of the room
getTemperature();        // access the room temperature
```

The most interesting implementation issue is how to handle communications between `Room` and `Clock`, which specify when to compute a new temperature. Table 4.3 identified a method `determineTemperatureChange` that performs this computation. The interesting question is: What causes `Room` to execute this method? The answer is the two methods `preEvent()` and `event()` that are invoked by `Clock`. Since we have specified that `Room` implements `ClockListener`, we can be sure that the code for these two routines exists in `Room`.

Looking at the method `preEvent` inside `Room`, we see that here is where we implement the heat gain and heat loss formulas of Section 4.2. The invocation of this method by `Clock` causes the `Room` object to call `determineTemperatureChange()`. This method computes the heat gain (by querying `Furnace` to determine its output) and heat loss (by querying `Environment` as to its outdoor temperature) and uses these two values to determine `deltaTemp`, the change in room temperature since the last computation. However, the actual assignment of this change to the state variable temperature is not done until `Clock` invokes the second method, `event()`, which causes `Room` to actually update its temperature. As we mentioned in Section 4.4.3, this two-step process prevents errors caused by the order in which new values are computed and accessed.

The final point about `Room` is to notice that we have again overridden the `toString()` method to provide more descriptive information about the characteristics of `Room` objects. The code for `Room` is in Figure 4.11.

```
/**
 * A room in the heating simulation.
 */

public class Room implements ClockListener {

    // Constants

    /**
     * The specific heat capacity (SHC) gives the amount of heat
     * stored in the room. The SHC for a typical tract house in the
     * United States is 4 BTUs per square foot per degree Fahrenheit.
     */

    public static final double DEFAULT_SHC = 4.0;

    /**
     * The Basic Load constant (BLC) gives the resistance of heat flow
     * out of the room. A large BLC value is indicative of a room
     * that loses heat very easily.
     */

    public static final double DEFAULT_BLC = 1.0;
    public static final double MINIMUM_BLC = 1.0;
    public static final double MAXIMUM_BLC = 10.0;

    // State of the room

    private Environment outside;    // The outside world
    private Furnace myFurnace;      // The furnace heating this room
    private double shc;             // The SHC for this room
    private double blc;             // The BLC for this room
    private double floorArea;       // The floor area of this room
    private double temperature;     // The current temperature of the room

    private double deltaTemp;       // The change in room temperature during
                                    // the past time interval

    /**
     * Create a new room. The SHC and BLC for the room will be set
     * to the default values.
     *
     * @param theWorld the environment that the room will get the
     * outside temperature from.
     * @param heatSource the furnace providing heat to the room.
     * @param area the floor area of the room in square feet.
     * @param initialTemperature the initial temperature of the room in
     * degrees Fahrenheit.
     */
```

(continued)

FIGURE 4.11 Room.java

```java
public Room( Environment theWorld,
             Furnace heatSource,
             double area,
             double initialTemperature ) {

    this( theWorld,
          heatSource,
          DEFAULT_SHC, // default SHC
          DEFAULT_BLC, // default BLC
          area,
          initialTemperature );
}

/**
 * Create a new room. The SHC and BLC for the room will be set
 * to the default values. The initial temperature of the room will
 * be set to the current outside temperature.
 *
 * @param theWorld the environment that the room will get the
 *    outside temperature from.
 * @param heatSource the furnace providing heat to the room.
 * @param area the floor area of the room in square feet.
 */

public Room( Environment theWorld,
             Furnace heatSource,
             double area ) {

    this( theWorld,
          heatSource,
          DEFAULT_SHC,                    // default SHC
          DEFAULT_BLC,                    // default BLC
          area,
          theWorld.getTemperature() ); // outside temperature
}

/**
 * Create a new room.
 *
 * @param theWorld the environment that the room will get the
 *         outside temperature from.
 * @param heatSource the furnace providing heat to the room.
 * @param specificHeatCapacity the SHC for this room.
 * @param basicLoadConstant the BLC for this room. If the value of this
 *         parameter falls outside the valid range for the BLC, the
 *         default BLC value will be used.
 * @param area the floor area of the room in square feet.
 * @param initialTemperature the initial temperature of the room in
 *         degrees Fahrenheit.
 */
```

(continued)

FIGURE 4.11 Room.java *(continued)*

```java
public Room( Environment theWorld,
             Furnace heatSource,
             double specificHeatCapacity,
             double basicLoadConstant,
             double area,
             double initialTemperature ) {

    // Initialize the state of the room
    outside = theWorld;
    myFurnace = heatSource;
    shc = specificHeatCapacity;
    floorArea = area;
    temperature = initialTemperature;

    // Make sure the requested BLC is in range
    if ( basicLoadConstant < MINIMUM_BLC ||
         basicLoadConstant > MAXIMUM_BLC ) {
        blc = DEFAULT_BLC;
    }
    else {
        blc = basicLoadConstant;
    }

}

/**
 * Return the environment in which this room is located.
 *
 * @return the environment the room is located in.
 */

public Environment getEnvironment() {
    return outside;
}

/**
 * Return the primary heat source for this room.
 *
 * @return the furnace heating this room.
 */

public Furnace getFurnace() {
    return myFurnace;
}

/**
 * Return the specific heat capacity for this room.
 *
 * @return the SHC for this room.
 */
```

(continued)

FIGURE 4.11 Room.java *(continued)*

```
public double getSHC() {
    return shc;
}


/**
 * Return the basic load constant for this room.
 *
 * @return the BLC for this room.
 */

public double getBLC() {
    return blc;
}


/**
 * Return the floor area of this room.
 *
 * @return the floor area of this room.
 */

public double getFloorArea() {
    return floorArea;
}


/**
 * Return the current temperature of this room.
 *
 * @return the current temperature of the room.
 */

public double getTemperature(){
    return temperature;
}


/**
 * This method will compute the change in room temperature
 * since the last event.
 *
 * Heat into the room comes from the furnace:
 *
 *    Qin = FurnaceOutputBTUsPerHr * timeHours
 *
 * Heat loss is calculated as follows:
 *
 *    Qloss = BLC * FloorArea * ( InsideTemp - OutsideTemp ) * timeHours
 *
 * The Basic Load Constant (BLC) gives the resistance to heat flow
 * out of the room. The BLC can range from 1 to 10. A large BLC value
 * is indicative of a room that loses heat very quickly (like a car).
```

(continued)

FIGURE 4.11 Room.java *(continued)*

```
     *
     * The change in room temperature during the past interval is given
     * by the formula:
     *
     *   deltaTemp = ( Qin - Qloss ) / ( SHC * floorArea )
     *
     * SHC stands for specific heat capacity of the room and gives
     * the amount of heat that is stored in the room itself (i.e.,
     * in the walls, floors, etc.). The SHC for a typical tract house
     * in the US is 4 BTUs per square foot per degree Fahrenheit.
     *
     * @param interval the number of seconds of elapsed time.
     */

    public void determineTemperatureChange( double interval ) {
        // The number of hours that have passed since the last event
        double elapsedTimeInHours = interval / Clock.SECS_PER_HOUR;

        // Only heat into the room comes from the furnace
        double qIn = myFurnace.output( elapsedTimeInHours );

        // Compute the heat that has left the room
        double qLoss =
            blc *
            floorArea *
            ( temperature - outside.getTemperature() ) *
            elapsedTimeInHours;

        // Compute the change in temperature
        deltaTemp = ( qIn - qLoss ) / ( shc * floorArea );
    }


    /**
     * This method is called before the next event occurs so that it
     * can determine the temperature change that has occurred
     * since the last event. The room will not change its state when
     * this method is called. It prepares itself for the state change
     * that will occur when the next event occurs.
     *
     * @param interval the number of seconds that have elapsed since the
     *                 last event.
     */

    public void preEvent( double interval ) {
        // Determine the change in room temperature
        determineTemperatureChange( interval );
     */
    }
```

(continued)

FIGURE 4.11 Room.java *(continued)*

```
    /*
     * The room will update its current temperature when
     * this method is called.
     */

    public void event() {
        // Adjust the room temperature
        temperature = temperature + deltaTemp;
    }

    /**
     * Return a string representation of the room.
     *
     * @return a string representation of the room.
     */

    public String toString() {
        return
            "[ Room: " +
            " temp=" + temperature +
            " area=" + floorArea +
            " SHC=" + shc +
            " BLC=" + blc +
            " ]";
    }

} // Room
```

FIGURE 4.11 Room.java *(continued)*

The Thermostat class is similar in structure and layout to the Room class. It has a number of constructors that handle different combinations of user-specified and default parameter values. For example, the constructor

```
public Thermostat(Room theRoom, Furnace theFurnace);
```

will create a new Thermostat inside theRoom that controls a specified furnace called theFurnace. The initial thermostat setting and the amount of allowable overheating are both set to default values.

The Thermostat class contains accessor and mutator functions for all of its private instance variables:

```
getRoom();                    // access the identity of the room
                              //    monitored by this thermostat
getFurnace();                 // access the identity of the furnace
                              //    controlled by this thermostat
getSetting();                 // access the current thermostat
                              //    setting
```

```
setSetting(double newSetting);  // reset the current thermostat setting
getOverHeat();                  // access the allowable amount of
                                //    overheating
```

Finally, Thermostat, like Room, also implements the ClockListener interface. When its preEvent() method is invoked, it determines what, if any, changes need to be made in the state of the Furnace by calling determineStateChange(). This method queries Room to get the current room temperature and determines if the current temperature is either above (setting + overHeat) and the Furnace is on, or if it is below setting and the Furnace is off. It uses the Boolean variable activateFurnace to record the action to be taken. When event() is invoked, Thermostat invokes myFurnace.setHeating(activateFurnace) to set the state of myFurnace. The code for the Thermostat class is shown in Figure 4.12.

```java
/**
 * This class represents a thermostat in the home heating simulation
 * program. The thermostat monitors a single room and turns on the
 * furnace whenever the room temperature falls below the desired
 * setting. The thermostat will overheat the room slightly so that
 * the furnace will not cycle on and off too frequently.
 */

public class Thermostat implements ClockListener {

    // Default overheat setting
    public static final double DEFAULT_OVERHEAT = 3.0;

    // Default temperature setting
    public static final double DEFAULT_SETTING = 72.0;

    private Room myRoom;        // The room being monitored
    private Furnace myFurnace;  // The furnace that will heat the room

    private double setting;     // The desired room temperature
    private double overHeat;    // The amount the room will be overheated

    private boolean activateFurnace; // Used to determine if the furnace
                                     // should be turned on

    /**
     * Create a new thermostat with the default temperature setting and
     * overheat amount.
     *
     * @param theRoom the room that will be monitored by this thermostat.
     * @param theFurnace the furnace that will add heat to the room.
     */
```

(continued)

FIGURE 4.12 Thermostat.java

```java
public Thermostat( Room theRoom, Furnace theFurnace ) {
    this( theRoom, theFurnace, DEFAULT_SETTING, DEFAULT_OVERHEAT );
}

/**
 * Create a new thermostat with the default overheat amount.
 *
 * @param theRoom the room that will be monitored by this thermostat.
 * @param theFurnace the furnace that will add heat to the room.
 * @param desiredTemp the desired room temperature.
 */

public Thermostat( Room theRoom, Furnace theFurnace, double desiredTemp ) {
    this( theRoom, theFurnace, desiredTemp, DEFAULT_OVERHEAT );
}

/**
 * Create a new thermostat.
 *
 * @param theRoom the room that will be monitored by this thermostat.
 * @param theFurnace the furnace that will add heat to the room.
 * @param desiredTemp the desired room temperature.
 * @param overheatAmount the amount that the room will be overheated.
 */

public Thermostat( Room theRoom,
                   Furnace theFurnace,
                   double desiredTemp,
                   double overheatAmount ) {

    myRoom = theRoom;
    myFurnace = theFurnace;
    setting = desiredTemp;
    overHeat = overheatAmount;
}

/**
 * Return the room being monitored by this thermostat.
 *
 * @return the room monitored by this thermostat.
 */

public Room getRoom() {
    return myRoom;
}

/**
 * Return the furnace that will heat the room.
 *
```

(continued)

FIGURE 4.12 Thermostat.java *(continued)*

```
 * @return the furnace that the thermostat will use to add heat to
 * the room.
 */

public Furnace getFurnace() {
    return myFurnace;
}

/**
 * Return the setting of the thermostat.
 *
 * @return the current setting of the thermostat.
 */

public double getSetting() {
    return setting;
}

/**
 * Return the overheat setting for the thermostat.
 *
 * @return the overheat setting for the thermostat.
 */

public double getOverHeat() {
    return overHeat;
}

/**
 * Set the desired temperature setting for the thermostat.
 *
 * @param newSetting the new temperature setting for the thermostat.
 */

public void setSetting( double newSetting ) {
    setting = newSetting;
}

/**
 * Base the decision to turn on/off the furnace on the temperature
 * of the room during the past time period.
 *
 * @param interval the number of seconds that have elapsed since the
 *        last event.
 */

public void determineStateChange( double interval ) {
    double roomTemp = myRoom.getTemperature();
```

(continued)

FIGURE 4.12 Thermostat.java *(continued)*

```java
        if ( activateFurnace ) {
            // If the furnace is on, leave it on until the room temperature
            // is equal to or greater than the desired setting plus the
            // overheat amount
            activateFurnace = roomTemp < setting + overHeat;
    }
    else {
            // If the furnace is currently off, it should stay off until
            // the room temperature falls below the desired setting.
            activateFurnace = roomTemp < setting;
    }
  }


  /**
   * This method is called before the next event occurs so that
   * the thermostat can determine whether what it should do to the
   * furnace (i.e., turn it on, turn it off, or leave it alone) based
   * on what has happened since the last event. The thermostat
   * will not change its state when this method is called.
   * It prepares itself for the state change that will occur when the
   * next event occurs.
   *
   * @param interval the number of seconds that have elapsed since the
   *        last event.
   */

  public void preEvent( double interval ) {
      determineStateChange( interval );
  }


  /**
   * Turn on/off the furnace based on the temperature of the room.
   */

  public void event() {
      myFurnace.setHeating( activateFurnace );
  }


  /**
   * Return a string representation of the thermostat.
   *
   * @return a string representation of the thermostat.
   */

  public String toString() {
      return
          "[ Thermostat: " +
          " setting=" + setting +
          " overheat=" + overHeat +
          "]";
  }

} // Thermostat
```

FIGURE 4.12 Thermostat.java *(continued)*

Our final piece of code, except for `main()`, is the master clock of our simulation program, which is an instance of class `Clock`. Each increment of the clock represents the passing of `tickInterval` seconds, a constant that is set when the clock is created:

```
public Clock(int tickInterval); // num of seconds per tick
```

In our simulation, `tickInterval` is automatically set to 60 seconds. However, as discussed earlier, we may wish to allow users to set this parameter themselves, either to increase the accuracy of our model or to decrease the computational load placed on the computer.

The `run` method of `Clock` activates the simulation as it loops from $i = 0$ to $i = numTicks$, where each of these individual ticks represents the passing of `tickInterval` seconds. It is the `run()` method that truly starts the simulation process going.

The last interesting aspect of `Clock` is the `listeners[]` array. This is an array of objects that implements the `ClockListener` interface of Figure 4.10 and that are to be notified every time the clock ticks. Note that every time the clock ticks, it calls the method `listeners[j].preEvent` on every object in the `listeners[]` array. Following that operation, it calls `listeners[j].event()` on every object in the `listeners[]` array. The value `secsPerTick` is a state variable specifying how many seconds have passed since the last tick of the clock. (That is, it has the same value as `tickInterval`.)

We can see from the UML diagram in Figure 4.4 that the two methods that implement this interface in our model are `Room` and `Thermostat`. The question now is: How do we indicate that these two objects should be placed in the `listeners[]` array?

The answer is that we will **register** these two methods with the `Clock`. Registration is a common programming technique that means to invoke a method that will add a specific object name to a collection. This collection of objects will then be given certain privileges or will be treated in some special way. In our case, registration allows objects to receive timing information via the `preEvent` and `event` methods.

In this example, our registration method is `add(ClockListener entity)` which adds `entity` to our `listeners[]` array. Since `listeners[]` is an array structure, it has a fixed size, 10 elements in our case. If we tried to add an 11th object, there wouldn't be any room, and the array would overflow. Instead of generating a run-time error and terminating the program, we handle this problem by resizing the array. We dynamically create a new array whose size is twice its current size and then copy the elements of the current array into the newly created array. This allows the simulation to continue executing and produce the desired results.

In the next section of the text, you will learn about the linked list data structure, that can hold an arbitrarily large number of objects. In addition, you will see that this data structure is part of an existing package, called the Java Collection Framework, that is freely available to any Java programmer. Taking advantage of this feature would eliminate the need to do such mundane tasks as resizing arrays.

The code for `Clock` is given in Figure 4.13.

```java
/**
 * The master clock for the home heating simulation. Generates
 * events for ClockListeners that have been registered with the
 * clock. The interval between ticks is determined at the time the
 * clock is constructed.
 */

public class Clock {

    // Number of seconds in one minute
    public static final int SECS_PER_MINUTE = 60;

    // Number of seconds in one hour
    public static final int SECS_PER_HOUR = SECS_PER_MINUTE * 60;

    // Initial size of the array that holds the listeners
    private static final int INITIAL_SIZE = 10;

    // Objects to be notified when tick events occur
    private ClockListener listeners[];

    // The number of listeners registered with this clock
    private int numListeners;

    // The number of seconds that pass between ticks
    private int secsPerTick;

    /**
     * Create a new clock that will generate tick events at
     * the specified interval.
     *
     * @param tickInterval the number of seconds between ticks.
     */

    public Clock( int tickInterval ) {
        // Setup the array that will hold the listeners
        listeners = new ClockListener[ INITIAL_SIZE ];
        numListeners = 0;

        // The time interval for this clock
        secsPerTick = tickInterval;
    }

    /**
     * Run the clock for the specified number of ticks. The state of
     * the clock is valid between invocations of run(). This makes it
     * possible to call run multiple times within the simulation.
     *
```

(continued)

FIGURE 4.13 Clock.java

```java
     * @param numTicks the number of ticks to generate
     */
    public void run( int numTicks ) {
        for ( int i = 0; i < numTicks; i++ ) {

            // Notify the listeners that an event is about to happen
            for ( int j = 0; j < numListeners; j++ ) {
                listeners[ j ].preEvent( secsPerTick );
            }

            // The event occurs
            for ( int j = 0; j < numListeners; j++ ) {
                listeners[ j ].event();
            }
        }
    }

    /**
     * Add a listener to the collection of objects that are
     * notified when tick events occur.
     *
     * @param entity the listener to add to the collection
     */

    public void add( ClockListener entity ) {
        // Resize the array if it is full. A new array will be created
        // with twice the capacity and the contents of the old array
        // will be copied into the new array.
        if ( numListeners == listeners.length ) {

        // Create a new array that is twice as large
        ClockListener newListeners[] =
          new ClockListener[ listeners.length * 2 ];

        // Copy the old array into the new array
        for ( int i = 0; i < listeners.length; i++ ) {
          newListeners[ i ] = listeners[ i ];
        }

        // Make the class use the new array to keep track of the
        // listeners
        listeners = newListeners;
        }
        // Add the listener to the array
        listeners[ numListeners ] = entity;
        numListeners = numListeners + 1;
    }
} // Clock
```

FIGURE 4.13 Clock.java *(continued)*

The final class that we will develop is `HeatingSimulation`, which is the class that includes the `main()` method for the entire program. (Remember that the program is initiated via the command line `java HeatingSimulation`.) This class contains mostly initialization and "administrative" tasks. For example, this is where we process the command line, accessing the user-specified parameters, making sure that they are valid, and storing them into an array called `simParams`. This class is responsible for producing the output report shown in Figure 4.2. The program imports and uses the Java class `DecimalFormat` in the package `java.text` to assist it in printing the output in an elegant and appropriate format.

`HeatingSimulation` also creates the objects used in the simulation—in this example, one room, one furnace, one thermostat, one environment, and `masterClock`, the master simulation clock. It also registers the room and the thermostat with `masterClock` and turns on the pilot light of the furnace so that it can produce heat. Finally, it executes the statement that starts the simulation:

```
masterClock.run( (int)simParams[DISPLAY_FREQ] );
```

This statement does not run the entire simulation from beginning to end. Instead, it runs the simulation for one "output display" unit of time. Referring back to the sample output in Figure 4.2, this is 5 minutes, 300 seconds, the time interval between output lines. (Since the clock ticks in 1-minute intervals, this represents five ticks of the simulation clock.) When this amount of simulation time has been completed, the program prints a single line of output and invokes the run method again. This run/output loop continues until the master simulation clock has reached or exceeded the value of the parameter `length`, the value 7,200 seconds in Figure 4.2, which is the total time that the simulation is to run.

The code for `HeatingSimulation` is given in Figure 4.14, and this completes the implementation of our home heating simulation case study.

```java
import java.text.DecimalFormat;

/**
 * The program that runs the heating simulation. The heating
 * system modeled by this program consists of a single room heated
 * by one furnace which is controlled by a single thermostat.
 */

public class HeatingSimulation {

    // The simulation will always advance time in 60 second units

    private static final int SECS_BETWEEN_EVENTS = 60;
```

(continued)

FIGURE 4.14 `HeatingSimulation.java`

```java
// An array will be used to store the simulation parameters. This will
// make it easier to write the code that parses the command line and
// sets these parameters. The constants below identify the parameter
// that is stored in the corresponding position in the array

private static final int INSIDE_TEMP = 0;          // Inside temperature
private static final int OUTSIDE_TEMP = 1;          // Outside temperature
private static final int DESIRED_TEMP = 2;          // Desired temperature
private static final int FURNACE_CAPACITY = 3;      // Furnace capacity
private static final int FURNACE_EFFICIENCY = 4;    // Furnace efficiency
private static final int ROOM_SIZE = 5;             // Room size (sq ft)
private static final int DISPLAY_FREQ = 6;          // Display freq
private static final int SIM_LENGTH = 7;            // Time to run

// The array that holds the values of the parameters. The initializer
// is used to set the default value for each parameter.

private static double simParams[] = { 72.0,    // Inside temperature
                                      50.0,    // Outside temperature
                                      72.0,    // Desired temperature
                                      8500.0,  // Furance capacity
                                      .95,     // Furnace efficiency
                                      250.0,   // Room size
                                      5.0,     // Ticks between output
                                      7200.0   // Time to run (secs)
};

// This array holds the names of the parameters that will be used on
// the command line. Each name is stored in the same position as
// the corresponding value in the simParams[] array.

private static String simNames[] = { "in",    // Inside temperature
                                     "out",    // Outside temperature
                                     "set",    // Desired temperature
                                     "cap",    // Furnace capacity
                                     "eff",    // Furnace efficiency
                                     "size",   // Room size
                                     "freq",   // Display frequency
                                     "length"  // Time to run
};

public static void main( String args[] ) {
    // Format used to print report
    DecimalFormat fmt = new DecimalFormat( "###0.00" );

    // The references to the objects that make up the simulation.
    // In this simulation there is one room controlled by one
    // thermostat and heated by one furnace.
```

(continued)

FIGURE 4.14 HeatingSimulation.java *(continued)*

```
        GasFurnace theFurnace = null;
        Environment theWorld = null;
        Room theRoom = null;
        Thermostat theThermostat = null;

        // Process the command line arguments

        processCommandLine( args );

        // Create a furnace, a room, a thermostat, and an environment.

        theFurnace = new GasFurnace( simParams[ FURNACE_CAPACITY ],
                                     simParams[ FURNACE_EFFICIENCY ] );

        theWorld = new Environment( simParams[ OUTSIDE_TEMP ] );

        theRoom = new Room( theWorld,
                            theFurnace,
                            simParams[ ROOM_SIZE ],
                            simParams[ INSIDE_TEMP ] );

        theThermostat = new Thermostat( theRoom,
                                        theFurnace,
                                        simParams[ DESIRED_TEMP ] );

        // Create the clock that will drive the simulation and register
        // the room and the thermostat with the clock so that they
        // will be notified when events occur within the simulation

        Clock masterClock = new Clock( SECS_BETWEEN_EVENTS );
        masterClock.add( theRoom );
        masterClock.add( theThermostat );

        // Turn on the pilot light so the furnace will produce heat

        theFurnace.setPilot( true );

        // Print out the objects that were created

        System.out.println( "Created 4 Objects:" );
        System.out.println( " " + theFurnace );
        System.out.println( " " + theWorld );
        System.out.println( " " + theRoom );
        System.out.println( " " + theThermostat );
        System.out.println();
```

(continued)

FIGURE 4.14 HeatingSimulation.java *(continued)*

```
            // Run the simulation for the requested time period. When
            // displayFrequency ticks of simulated time have passed,
            // the current state of the objects within the simulation will be
            // displayed.

            System.out.println( "Starting simulation: " +
                            " display frequency=" + simParams[ DISPLAY_FREQ ] +
                            " simulated runtime= " + simParams[ SIM_LENGTH ] +
                            "\n" );

            System.out.println( "Time\tInside\tOutside\tDesired\tFurnace" );
            System.out.println( "—\t—\t—-\t—-\t—-" );

            for ( int simTime = 0;
                  simTime <= (int)simParams[ SIM_LENGTH ];
                  simTime = simTime +
                        (int)simParams[ DISPLAY_FREQ ] * SECS_BETWEEN_EVENTS) {

                // Run the simulation for display frequency ticks

                masterClock.run( (int)simParams[ DISPLAY_FREQ ] );

                // Print the statistics

                System.out.print( simTime + "\t" +
                            fmt.format( theRoom.getTemperature() ) + "\t" +
                            fmt.format( theWorld.getTemperature() ) + "\t" +
                            fmt.format( theThermostat.getSetting() ) );

                if ( theFurnace.isHeating() ) {
                    System.out.print( "\tOn" );
                }

                System.out.println();
            }
    }

/**
 * Scan the command line arguments and set any simulation parameters as
 * specified by the user. Invalid parameters settings will be ignored.
 * Note that if an invalid numeric value is specified on the command
 * line a runtime exception will be thrown and the program will
 * terminate.
 *
 * @param args the parameter settings to parse.
 */

private static void processCommandLine( String args[] ) {
```

(continued)

FIGURE 4.14 `HeatingSimulation.java` *(continued)*

```
        // Step through the settings...

    for ( int i = 0; i < args.length; i++ ) {

        // Parameter settings take the form: name=value

        int equals = args[ i ].indexOf( '=' );

        // If there is an equals sign in the setting it might be valid

        if ( equals != -1 ) {

            // Extract the name and the value

            String paramName = args[ i ].substring( 0, equals );
            String paramValue = args[ i ].substring( equals + 1 );

            // The index into the simParams array where the setting
            // is to be made. A value of -1 indicates that the name
            // is invalid

            int loc = -1;

            // Search for the name in the names array. Since the
            // name is stored in the same position as the corresponding
            // value, once the location of the name is determined we
            // know where the value is stored

            for ( int j = 0; loc == -1 && j < simNames.length; j++ ) {
                if ( paramName.equals( simNames[ j ] ) ) {
                    loc = j;
                }
            }

            // If the name is valid set the parameter. Note that
            // an invalid value entered on the command line will
            // cause a runtime exception and terminate the program.

            if ( loc != -1 && paramValue.length() > 0 ) {
                simParams[ loc ] = Double.parseDouble( paramValue );
            }
        }
    }
}

} // HeatingSimulation
```

FIGURE 4.14 HeatingSimulation.java *(continued)*

4.6 TESTING

The fact that this section on software testing appears at the very end of the chapter, following the discussion on implementation, does not imply that testing is delayed until all the code has been written. That is absolutely untrue, and postponing testing until the end of a software development project is a sure recipe for disaster—including budget overruns, missed delivery dates, and "buggy" code.

On the contrary, testing will be going on throughout implementation and, in some cases, even before. For example, selecting the test cases that will be used to determine the acceptability of the finished program is often done during specification and design, even before a single line of code has been written.

Thorough, complete, and "intense" testing of every single piece of code is an essential part of software development. The initial phase of testing is called **unit testing**, and it was first described in Section 1.2.5. During unit testing, you thoroughly test each and every individual unit of code (class, method, subclass) that you write as soon as you write it. You never place any source code into a library until it has been thoroughly checked using a carefully planned and well-designed set of test cases and it has successfully passed 100 percent of these unit tests.

For example, the first piece of code we developed was Environment (Figure 4.7). Following that, we went immediately into a discussion of the implementation of class Furnace. However, in a real-world project, we would thoroughly test all aspects of the Environment class to ensure they work correctly before starting to write the code for Furnace. Even though Environment is small and quite simple, there are still a number of cases that must be carefully checked. As we described in Section 1.2.5, unit testing involves testing every method in a class as well as every flow path in these methods. In the case of Environment, we must test each and every one of the following:

- the *default constructor* to ensure that it sets temperature to the correct default value
- the *one-parameter constructor* to ensure that it correctly sets temperature to the specified parameter
- the *accessor method* getTemperature()
- the *mutator method* setTemperature()
- the *overridden method* toString()

Figure 4.15 shows a main() method that tests each of these five cases. When this program is run, the expected output is the following (Note: Since we are using default formatting, the output might be slightly different from what is shown. However, right now, we are only concerned with the correctness of these values, not their exact layout.)

```
Temperature of e1 = 72.0
Temperature of e2 = 85.0
New temperature of e1 = 75.0
New temperature of e2 = 90.0
Object e1 = [ Environment: temperature=75.0 ]
Object e2 = [ Environment: temperature=90.0 ]
End of unit test of Environment
```

```
/**
 * A test program for the environment class.
 */

public class TestEnvironment {

    public static void main( String args[] ) {
        // First let's use both the default constructor
        // and the one-parameter constructor
        Environment e1 = new Environment();
        Environment e2 = new Environment( 85.0 );

        // Determine if the constructors and
        // the getTemperature method work
        System.out.println( "Temperature of e1 = " + e1.getTemperature() );
        System.out.println( "Temperature of e2 = " + e2.getTemperature() );

        // See if we can change the temperature
        e1.setTemperature( 75.0 );
        System.out.println( "New temperature of e1 = " + e1.getTemperature() );

        e2.setTemperature( 90.0 );
        System.out.println( "New temperature of e2 = " + e2.getTemperature() );

        // Determine if toString() works as expected
        System.out.println( "Object e1 = " + e1 );
        System.out.println( "Object e2 = " + e2 );

        System.out.println( "End of unit test of Environment" );
    }

} // TestEnvironment
```

FIGURE 4.15 Test program for the Environment class

If that is what is produced when the test program is executed, we can be confident that class Environment is working according to specifications. (Note: Because of its simplicity, we can probably stop after this one test suite. With more complex classes, we will probably want to run multiple test programs.) If this is not the output, we must immediately locate all of the bugs in this unit and correct them. However, this should be a relatively simple task, as we will only be examining a single class rather than the 1,100 lines of code in the entire software package.

When we feel confident about the correctness of this program unit, we can put it into our library and move on to write and test the next program unit, Furnace, assuming that these two classes are being developed by the same individual or team.

The Furnace class of Figure 4.8 would be tested in a similar way. We must test each of the following conditions:

◆ the two-parameter constructor

◆ the three accessor methods `getCapacity()`, `getEfficiency()`, and
  `isHeating()`

◆ the mutator method `setHeating()`

◆ the method `output()`, which computes heat output

◆ the overridden method `toString()`

Furthermore, the `output` method has two distinct cases that must be tested:

◆ computation of the heat output when the furnace is on

◆ computation of the heat output when the furnace is off

Figure 4.16 shows a possible test program for our `Furnace` class.

```
/**
 * Program to test the furnace class.
 */

public class TestFurnace {

    public static void main( String args[] ) {
        // First let's invoke the constructor
        Furnace f1 = new Furnace( 10000.0, 0.78 );
        Furnace f2 = new Furnace( 30000.0, 0.85 );
        Furnace f3 = new Furnace( 50000.0, 0.93 );

        // Determine if the constructors worked and if the
        // getCapacity and getEfficiency methods work
        System.out.println( "f1 Capacity = " + f1.getCapacity() +
                            " Efficiency = " + f1.getEfficiency() +
                            " Heating state = " + f1.isHeating() );

        System.out.println( "f2 Capacity = " + f2.getCapacity() +
                            " Efficiency = " + f2.getEfficiency() +
                            " Heating state = " + f2.isHeating() );

        System.out.println( "f3 Capacity = " + f3.getCapacity() +
                            " Efficiency = " + f3.getEfficiency() +
                            " Heating state = " + f3.isHeating() );

        // Now see if we can change the state of a Furnace
        f1.setHeating( true );
        System.out.println( "New heating state of f1 = " + f1.isHeating() );

        f2.setHeating( true );
        System.out.println( "New heating state of f2 = " + f2.isHeating() );
```

FIGURE 4.16 Test program for the `Furnace` class

```
            f3.setHeating( true );
            System.out.println( "New heating state of f3 = " + f3.isHeating() );

            // See if we can turn it off again
            f3.setHeating( false );
            System.out.println( "New heating state of f3 = " + f3.isHeating() );

            // Now let's compute the output of each of these
            // furnaces for 1 hour, 2 hours, and 3 hours. Since
            // furnace f3 is off, it won't produce any heat
            System.out.println( f1.output( 1.0 ) );
            System.out.println( f1.output( 2.0 ) );
            System.out.println( f1.output( 3.0 ) );

            System.out.println( f2.output( 1.0 ) );
            System.out.println( f2.output( 2.0 ) );
            System.out.println( f2.output( 3.0 ) );

            System.out.println( f3.output( 1.0 ) );
            System.out.println( f3.output( 2.0 ) );
            System.out.println( f3.output( 3.0 ) );

            // Determine if toString() works as we would expect
            System.out.println( "Object f1 = " + f1 );
            System.out.println( "Object f2 = " + f2 );
            System.out.println( "Object f3 = " + f3 );

            System.out.println("End of unit test of Furnace");
        }

} // TestFurnace
```

Figure 4.16 Test program for the Furnace class *(continued)*

When it is run, the output of the program in Figure 4.16 should be:

```
f1 Capacity = 10000.0 Efficiency = 0.78 Heating state = false
f2 Capacity = 30000.0 Efficiency = 0.85 Heating state = false
f3 Capacity = 50000.0 Efficiency = 0.93 Heating state = false
New heating state of f1 = true
New heating state of f2 = true
New heating state of f3 = true
New heating state of f3 = false
7800.0
15600.0
23400.0
25500.0
```

```
51000.0
76500.0
0.0
0.0
0.0
Object f1 = [ Furnace: cap=10000.0 eff=0.78 heating=true ]
Object f2 = [ Furnace: cap=30000.0 eff=0.85 heating=true ]
Object f3 = [ Furnace: cap=50000.0 eff=0.93 heating=false ]
End of unit test of Furnace
```

If this is the output produced by the test program, we can again feel confident about the correctness of our code. We put Furnace into our library and move on to the implementation and testing of the next class. We will leave the design of the remaining test programs as an exercise for the reader.

Looking back at the Furnace test program in Figure 4.16, it may seem like "overkill" to write a 45-line program to test a class that itself contains only about 100 lines. However, one of the most important rules of modern software development is:

Never skimp on testing!

If it requires a 50-line program to adequately test 50 lines of developed software, then that is what must be done. If your code is not correct, it doesn't matter how efficient, elegant, maintainable, and robust it may be. It won't be of use to anyone.

The second phase of testing is **acceptance testing**, and during this phase, the software is placed into the environment in which it will be regularly used. Rather than selecting data based on testing specific classes, methods, and flow paths, the program is tested with real-world data that reflect the typical operating conditions the program will experience when it is used on a daily basis. These test cases are usually selected by the user, and they are frequently included in the program specifications.

If the program operates in a successful manner on these acceptance cases, it is deemed to be "finished" and is delivered to the user. However, we all know that software is never truly finished, and it will likely be updated, modified, and adapted for many years to come. That is why maintenance is such a critically important part of the software development life cycle.

4.7 SUMMARY

We hope that this extended case study has helped to clarify the many important ideas presented in this part of the text. By observing the development of a program from initial problem statement to implementation and testing, you can better understand the many steps involved in the software development process. However, to truly appreciate this process, it is not enough to observe it; you must also *try* it. At the end of this chapter, there are suggestions for projects that you can work on either individually or as part of a development team. We strongly encourage you to design and implement one of these projects using the techniques presented in this chapter.

In Part II, we will investigate a completely new subject that is critical to the success of any significant software project: the topics of algorithms and data structures.

The case study just completed did not use any interesting data structures, except for a single one-dimensional array. However, virtually all real-world problems require more complex data structures, such as lists, stacks, priority queues, binary trees, hash tables, or graphs. The intelligent use of these structures will allow us to create faster and more efficient programs.

We will take an in-depth look at these data structures along with the algorithms required to manipulate them and the mathematical tools needed to analyze them. We will also introduce the Java Collection Framework, a set of classes and methods that makes many of these algorithms and data structures available to every Java programmer.

EXERCISES

For Questions 1–3, use the existing home heating simulator code in this chapter to run experiments that answer the following questions:

1. Set the outdoor temperature to 32°F, the initial and desired room temperature to 70°F, and the room size to 1,000 sq. ft. Test each of the following four furnaces and determine how much time the furnace is in the on state during a 5-hour time period. Print one line of output every 5 minutes and assume that if the output line states that the furnace is on, then it has been on for the entire 5-minute period.

   a. Capacity = 20,000   Efficiency = 0.90

   b. Capacity = 23,000   Efficiency = 0.88

   c. Capacity = 25,000   Efficiency = 0.82

   d. Capacity = 30,000   Efficiency = 0.78

   From the output produced by the simulator, answer the question: "Which of these furnaces is most cost efficient at keeping the house at 70°F, where efficient means that the furnace has been on for the least amount of time?

2. What percentage cost savings could we expect if we kept all the model parameters the same as in Exercise 1 but lowered the initial and desired room temperatures to:

   a. 68°F

   b. 65°F

   Assume that costs are directly proportional to how much time the furnace is on. You only need to test the one furnace from Exercise 1 that you determined to be most efficient.

3. In the chapter, we stated that a good choice for the time increment Δ is critical to the efficient behavior of our software. If it is too small, the program will do an excessive amount of computation to solve the problem. If it is too large, we may get highly inaccurate results. In our simulator, we set Δ to 60 seconds.

   Run the program using the default values in Table 4-1 and the parameters given in Table 4.1. Now make the following two changes and answer the questions given.

a. Set $\Delta = 0.0001$ seconds and run the simulation for 2 hours (7,200 seconds), keeping all other values unchanged. How much longer does it take to run the program and produce the same report shown in that figure? How much did the accuracy change? Did it seem worth it to use such a small value of Δ?

b. Set $\Delta = 600$ seconds (10 minutes) and run the simulation for 2 hours, keeping all other values unchanged. How accurate were the results? Did the model show any strange or unusual behavior? Was this value of Δ acceptable?

4. Modify the model so that the user can provide input values for the two constants SHC and BLC on the command line. Here are the specifications:

```
parameter name:        shc   Default value:       4.0
parameter name:        blc   Default value:       1.0
```

Your model should now be able to accept command lines that look like this:

```
java HeatingSimulation cap=10000 shc=5.5 blc=1.5
```

5. Carefully read and review the program specification document in Figure 4.4. Are there any important pieces of information you think are omitted from this document that could cause future errors or omissions? Are there any ambiguities or inconsistencies that you think could create problems during design and implementation? Critique the quality of the specifications in this document and discuss how you may have written them somewhat differently.

6. Modify the Environment class so that, instead of a fixed outdoor temperature, the temperature varies as a function of the Clock value. Assume that $\Delta = 60$ seconds and the outdoor temperature varies in the following way:

   ◆ For the first 480 clock ticks (8 hours), the temperature goes up 0.04°F at each tick.

   ◆ For the next 480 clock ticks, the temperature remains constant.

   ◆ For the next 480 clock ticks, the temperature goes down 0.04°F at each tick.

   If the run time of the model is more than 24 hours, simply repeat this cycle. If it is less than 24 hours, run as many ticks as the user specified, even if you don't get all the way through the cycle. Compare the behavior of the model with the output of the constant temperature Environment shown in Figure 4.3.

7. Assume that our model is going to be modified to use radiators to heat the living area. The main difference between radiators and the forced air furnaces described in this chapter is that a radiator stays warm for a while, even after the furnace has been turned off. Thus, there will be some continuing heat gain for a period of time.

   Write a new class, called RadiatorHeat, which is a subclass of Furnace. When this radiator-based furnace is on, the heat output is computed in exactly the same way as described in the chapter. However, when the furnace is turned off, rather than produce a heat output of 0, the heat output is computed as follows:

◆ One clock tick after the furnace was turned off, the heat output becomes two-thirds of what it was when the furnace was on.

◆ Two clock ticks after the furnace was turned off, the heat output becomes one-third of what it was when the furnace was on.

◆ Three clock ticks after the furnace was turned off and continuing until the furnace is turned back on, the heat output becomes 0.

8. a. Write a UML sequence diagram for the Thermostat class.

b. Discuss the benefits that such sequence diagrams can have for a programmer trying to implement code.

9. Explain why the values 1 .. * are on the arrow leading from class Clock to the ClockListener interface in the UML diagram shown in Figure 4.4. Why are all other values in that diagram set to 1?

10. Write test programs to thoroughly test the following classes in our simulator. Explain why you designed the test program as you did, and give the output that you would expect to see from your test program when it is run:

a. Room.java, as shown in Figure 4.11

b. Thermostat.java, as shown in Figure 4.12

Questions 11–13 describe simulation projects that can be implemented by either individuals or teams using the techniques described in this chapter. The descriptions that follow represent a preliminary user requirements document. This will need to be converted to a complete and unambiguous program specification document before design can begin.

11. You are to write a program to simulate the control tower for a local airport. Although our airport does not operate exactly like a normal airport, your experience with airports will help you to visualize the system operation.

The model is made up of an arbitrary number of independent runways; each runway has two waiting lines associated with it. One of the lines, the arrival queue, contains a list of all the airplanes waiting to land on this runway, and the other, the departure queue, contains a list of all the airplanes waiting to use the runway to leave the airport. Each of the runways is functionally equivalent. None are reserved for landings/departures or for particular planes, and so on. In addition, planes can land on different runways at the same time. The number of runways is determined at run time by having the program read a number from standard input.

When an airplane is generated to arrive/depart at this airport (i.e., enter a waiting line), the control tower looks at the queues for each of the runways and determines which has the shortest wait before access to the runway can be granted—that is, which one has the fewest planes waiting. Airplanes wishing to land at the airport have priority over airplanes wishing to depart from the airport.

The waiting time for an airplane wishing to land on a runway is the sum of:

1. the amount of time it will take for the plane currently using the runway to complete its arrival/departure.

2. the amount of time associated with each plane in the arrival queue ahead of us.

The wait for an airplane wishing to leave the airport is the sum of:

1. the amount of time it will take for the plane currently using the runway to complete its arrival/departure.

2. the amount of time associated with each plane currently in the arrival queue. (Note: This is an approximation, as new arrivals may enter the system while we are waiting, and this could increase the waiting time.)

3. the amount of time associated with each plane in the departure queue ahead of us.

Whenever a runway is not busy, the next airplane in the arrival queue is assigned to the runway; that is, the airplane is removed from the arrival queue and proceeds directly to the runway. If there are no airplanes in the arrival queue, the first airplane in the departure queue is removed from that queue and proceeds directly to the runway.

The first airplane requesting use of a runway in the simulation is assigned to runway 0. The system will remember that runway 0 was the last runway to have an airplane assigned to it. When assigning other airplanes to runways, the control tower will look first at the next runway numerically after the runway that last had an airplane assigned to it, in this case, runway 1. The search process is circular, which means that when the last runway is examined, the next runway that will be examined is runway 0.

The simulation is driven by five pieces of input:

- a seed to be used with the random number generator

- the average arrival rate of airplanes requesting arrival or departure

- the average amount of time for an airplane to arrive/depart

- the number of runways at this airport

- the amount of time that the simulation should run

After all input has been read, and all objects in the system have been created, the program will then enter the simulation loop. Each iteration through the simulation loop represents the passage of one unit of time. During each single time period, or tick, the following steps will be performed:

1. The airplane generator is asked for a possibly empty list of airplanes wishing to arrive/depart.

2. Each airplane is assigned to the runway that will allow it to arrive/land at the soonest available time. At the first tick, the control tower starts checking at runway 0.

3. Each runway determines if the current airplane requires any more time on the runway. If the current airplane has left the runway, then statistics information is updated, and if there is another airplane in either queue, the next airplane proceeds to the runway.

4. The clock used by the simulation is updated to indicate that one unit of time has passed.

After the simulation has been completed, the following is printed:

◆ Average time an airplane is on a runway.

◆ Average time an airplane must wait to use a runway (time it is in a queue).

◆ Average idle time of all of the runways.

◆ The final contents of both queues associated with each runway, starting with runway 0.

After this information is printed, the simulator can terminate.

12. You are to write a program that will simulate the running of a large central print shop. In this type of environment, users make print requests electronically, in the form of jobs. Each job is picked up and routed to a printer appropriate to the job's needs. We will refer to those needs as resources; they include such things as paper size and color, stapling or binding options, sorting options, and ink/toner color(s).

Some resources are basic capabilities of the printer and are not easily changed. Others, like paper and ink, can be changed as frequently as needed by an operator. This leads to some problems. What if

◆ a job request is made for paper that is not currently loaded into any printer?

◆ a job is queued up to print on a printer, and then the operator changes the printer so it no longer has what is needed for the job?

This is where the idea of print queues comes in. A print queue is created for every combination of resources that any job needs. If a printer currently offers that set of resources, then the print queue feeds jobs to that printer. If not, the print queue simply queues up jobs, waiting for some printer to be reconfigured to fit its needs. This is illustrated in the figure on the following page.

This diagram shows two printers; one is loaded with blue paper and the second has white paper. The queues that are holding requests for the blue and white paper are connected to printers. The third queue is not connected to a printer, because there is no printer that is currently loaded with yellow paper. For the job waiting for yellow paper to print, the paper in one of the printers must be changed.

Simulation

The simulation is driven by a data file that is logically divided into a printer and simulation section. The number of printers and their initial configuration are defined in the printer section. The simulation section contains information regarding print requests, in the form of jobs, made by users of the system. As job information is processed, the program assigns an expected duration time to the job, creates the job, and places it into the appropriate queue.

When the printer simulation begins, the program opens the data file and processes the printer section. After the printer section has been processed, all of the printers in the system will have been created and will be ready to accept jobs. The program will then enter the simulation loop.

Each iteration through the simulation loop represents the passage of one unit of time. During a single time period, or tick, the printers will be informed that one time unit has passed, and then lines from the simulation section of the

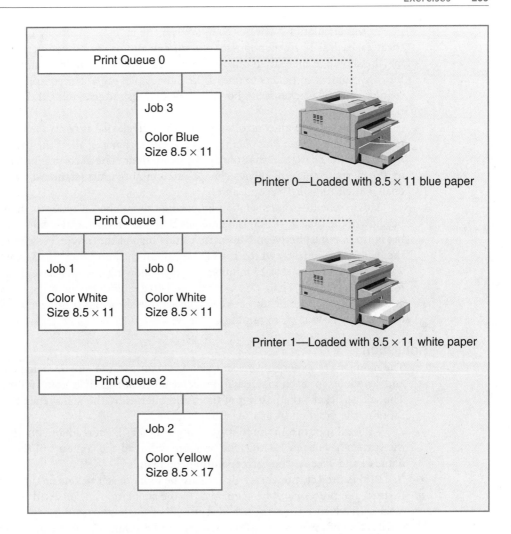

Printer 0—Loaded with 8.5 × 11 blue paper

Printer 1—Loaded with 8.5 × 11 white paper

data file will be processed. The loop repeats when all of the lines from the simulation section have been processed or a line indicating that all new jobs for this time period have been processed. The loop terminates when the entire simulation section has been processed and all the jobs have finished printing.

In this project, no actual printing will take place. Instead, the process will be simulated. In the simulation, a piece of software will receive the print request and claim to have printed it, even though nothing really came out. Since there is no real printing occurring, the program will produce diagnostic output to indicate what is going on. The main program will take care of changing the paper in the printers when it is necessary.

13. You are to write a program that will simulate the behavior of a theater complex. Although the theater complex is simplified from a typical movie theater complex, your experiences at movie complexes will help you visualize the system operation.

In this simulation a theater complex is made up of an arbitrary number of theaters, each with its own movie to be shown and its own schedule. A movie may be shown in more than one theater if it is popular enough. Customers may buy any number of tickets to one of the movies playing at the complex. The regular price of a ticket is $7; however, the price is reduced to $4 if the ticket is purchased before 4 P.M.

The theaters are all controlled by a master clock that is controlled by the manager of the theater complex. When the clock changes, all of the theaters are notified of the change so that they can update their state accordingly. The time on the master clock will always change in 15-minute units (standard clocks change their time in 1-second units).

Movie schedules are specified by giving the number of times the movie is to be shown, the time at which the movie is first shown during the day, and the break (in minutes) between consecutive showings of the movie. For example, the movie *Grumpy Cat,* which runs for 45 minutes, shows four times, starts at 7 P.M., and has a break of 15 minutes between showings, would have the following schedule: 7 P.M., 8 P.M., 9 P.M., and 10 P.M. Both the length of a movie and the length of the break between consecutive showings of the movie will each always be at least 15 minutes.

Simulation

The number of theaters in the complex, the names of the movies being shown, and schedules for each movie will be determined at run time from an input file. The sale of tickets, the passing of time, and queries by the management will be input to the program from a second input file.

After all input from the first data input file has been read and all objects in the system have been created, the program will read the contents of the second data file and execute the corresponding commands.

In this project, no work will actually be done to sell tickets or show movies. Instead, the process will be simulated. In the simulation, tickets will be sold, the clock will advance time, the schedule for all of the movies will be printed, the status of all of the movies will be printed, and a summary for the day will be printed.

ALGORITHMS AND DATA STRUCTURES

CHAPTER 5

The Analysis of Algorithms

5.1 INTRODUCTION

We have reached the point in the software development process where we have specified the problem to be solved and designed a solution in terms of classes, objects, and methods. We are now ready to implement these methods by selecting the *data structures* and coding the *algorithms* that manipulate the information stored in these structures. These are critically important decisions because our data structure and algorithm choices will have a profound impact on the run time of the finished code. Selecting the wrong data structures can reduce program efficiency by orders of magnitude.

The enormous increases in processor speed in the last few years may have lulled you into thinking that efficiency is no longer a major concern during software development. That is totally incorrect. What you are forgetting is that while processor speeds have increased dramatically, so has the size of the computational problems being addressed. We now run enormously large simulation models, search massive terabyte databases, and process extremely high-resolution visual images. Efficiency in the 21st century is just as important as it was when computing was in its infancy 50 to 60 years ago.

This chapter introduces the mathematical tools needed to formally analyze the performance of the algorithms and data structures discussed in the upcoming chapters. The data structures we will present (e.g., lists, stacks, queues, trees) are not introduced only because they are interesting but because we claim that they allow us to create more efficient algorithms for such common tasks as insertion, deletion, searching, and sorting. How can we demonstrate that this claim is valid? How do we show that algorithm X is truly superior to algorithm Y without relying on informal arguments or being unduly influenced by either the programming language used to code the algorithm or the hardware used to run it? Specifically, how can we demonstrate that one algorithm is superior to another without being misled by any of the following problems?

◆ *Special cases.* Every algorithm has certain inputs that allow it to perform far better than would be expected. For example, a sequential search algorithm works surprisingly well if the item you are looking for appears at the very front of the list (e.g., searching for AAA Auto Rental in the telephone book). However, this case is obviously special and not indicative of how the algorithm will perform for an arbitrary piece of data. We must not be misled by the performance of an algorithm on rare and unusual cases.

◆ *Small data sets.* An algorithm may not display its inefficiencies if the data set on which it is run is too small. For example, walking is a much slower way to travel than driving. However, that may not be true if the distance traveled is small, say, a few feet. In that case, the overhead of starting a car overwhelms any benefits from its increased speed. In general, a problem instance must be sufficiently large to demonstrate the benefits of one algorithm over another.

◆ *Hardware differences.* If an inefficient algorithm is running on a multimillion-dollar supercomputer while an efficient algorithm is running on a palmtop, the inefficient algorithm may appear to be superior because of the speed differences between the two machines.

◆ *Software differences.* If an inefficient algorithm was coded by a team of professionals in optimized assembly language while the efficient algorithm was written by a first-year computer science student in interpreted BASIC, then the inefficient algorithm may appear to be superior because of differences in the language used and the skill level of the programmers.

Are any of these concerns valid? Could any of them be used to argue a claim of superiority of one algorithm over another? If they are not valid, why not, and how can we formally refute them? This chapter presents the mathematical tools needed to answer these questions. It introduces a technique called the **asymptotic analysis** of algorithms, which is the fundamental tool for studying the run-time performance of algorithms. The results of this analysis are expressed using a representational technique called **big-O notation**. We then use these mathematical tools for analyzing the algorithms and data structures presented in succeeding chapters.

5.2 THE EFFICIENCY OF ALGORITHMS

The **efficiency** of an algorithm is a measure of the amount of resources consumed in solving a problem of size n. In general, the resource we are most interested in is *time*—how fast an algorithm can solve a given problem of size n. However, we can use the same techniques we will present to analyze the consumption of other resources, such as memory space.

It would seem that the most obvious way to measure the efficiency of an algorithm is to run it with some specific input and measure how much processor time is needed to produce the correct solution. This type of "wall clock" timing is called **benchmarking**. However, this produces a measure of efficiency for only one particular case, and it is inadequate for predicting how the algorithm would perform on a totally different data set. As mentioned in the previous section, the test data that we chose may be too small, or it may have special characteristics not present in other data sets. For example, an algorithm for finding a name in a telephone book by searching sequentially from A to Z will work quite well if we choose to test it on a book containing 500 entries, but it would be totally unacceptable for use with the New York City directory. Benchmarking is a technique for seeing if a finished program meets the timing specifications contained in the problem specification document described in Section 1.2.1. It is not an appropriate way to mathematically analyze the general properties of algorithms before we begin coding.

Instead, we need a way to formulate general guidelines that allow us to state that, for any arbitrary inputs, one particular method will likely be better than another. In the phone book example, a more helpful piece of information would be a statement that says something like, "Never use sequential lookup with a telephone book containing more than a few thousand entries as it will likely be too slow."

The time it takes to solve a problem is usually an increasing function of the size of the problem: The bigger the problem, the longer it will take to solve. We need a formula that associates n, the problem size, with t, the processing time required to obtain a solution. The value n is a measure of the size of the problem we are attempting to solve. For example, if we are searching or sorting a list, n would be the number of items in the list. If we are performing matrix operations on an $r \times r$ array, the problem size would be r, the dimensions of the array. If we are placing an object into a queue, the problem size might be the number of items currently in the queue.

The relationship between n and t can sometimes be expressed in terms of an explicit formula $t = f(n)$. If we had such a formula, we could plug in a value for n and determine exactly how many seconds it would take to solve a problem of that size. Given that information for a number of different techniques that solve the same problem, we could select the one algorithm that runs the quickest for problems of size n. However, such explicit formulas are rarely used. They are difficult to obtain since they rely on machine-dependent parameters that we may not know, such as instruction cycle time, memory access time, or the internal characteristics of our compiler. Furthermore, we usually do not want to use a formula $t = f(n)$ to compute exact timings for specific cases. Instead, as mentioned earlier, we want a general method that allows us to study the performance of an algorithm on data sets of arbitrary size.

We can get this type of information using a technique called asymptotic analysis. Using asymptotic analysis, we develop expressions of the form

$$t \approx O[f(n)]$$

which is read "t is on the order of $f(n)$." This representation is called big-O notation.

Formally, the expression $t \approx O[f(n)]$ states that there exist positive constants M and N_0 such that if $t \approx O[f(n)]$, then $t \leq Mf(n)$ for all $n > N_0$. This formidable looking definition is not as difficult as it may appear. It simply states that the rate of increase in the running time of an algorithm grows no faster than (i.e., is bounded by) a constant times a function of the form $f(n)$. If the order of the algorithm were, for example, $O(n^3)$, then the relationships between t and n would be given by a formula of the form $t = kn^3 + $ "lower order terms," although we generally do not know anything about the value of the constant k or the lower order terms. However, we can say that if the size of the problem doubles, the total time needed to solve the problem will increase about eightfold (2^3). If the problem size triples, the overall running time will be about 27 times greater (3^3).

For reasonably large problems, we always want to select an algorithm of the lowest order possible. If algorithm A is $O[f(n)]$ and algorithm B is $O[g(n)]$, then algorithm A is said to be of a **lower order** than B if $f(n) < g(n)$ for all n greater than some constant k. For example, $O(n^2)$ is a lower order algorithm than $O(n^3)$ because $n^2 < n^3$ for all $n > 1$. Similarly, $O(n^3)$ is a lower order than $O(2^n)$ because $n^3 < 2^n$ for all $n > 9$. Intuitively, this simply means that the expression n^2 grows more slowly than n^3, and the expression n^3 grows more slowly than the expression 2^n. Thus, we want to select an $O(n^2)$ algorithm to solve a problem rather than an $O(n^3)$ or $O(2^n)$ one if an $O(n^2)$ algorithm for this problem existed. When one algorithm is of a lower order than another algorithm, it is said to be **asymptotically superior**.

If we choose the lowest order algorithm to solve a problem, we will not know exactly how much time is required to obtain a solution, but we will know that as the problem size increases, there will always exist a point n^* beyond which the lower order method will take less time than a higher order algorithm. Figure 5.1 demonstrates this behavior for three algorithms whose running times are $t = n$, $t = \frac{1}{2}n^2$, and $t = n^3$, respectively. For small values of n, the choice of which algorithm to use is not critical, and in fact, the $O(n^2)$ or $O(n^3)$ may even be superior. However, when n becomes larger than 2.0, the $O(n)$ algorithm will always be superior to the other two algorithms, and it becomes better and better as n increases.

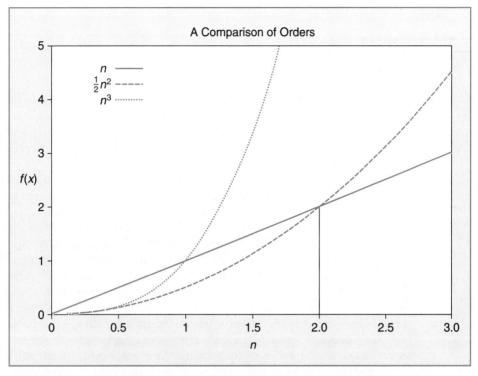

FIGURE 5.1 Graphical comparison of complexity measures O(n), O(n^2), and O(n^3)

Programmers are generally not concerned with efficiency for small data sets, and in these situations, any correct algorithm will usually run sufficiently fast. However, as the problem size increases, efficiency becomes a much more important concern. Big-O notation, which describes the asymptotic behavior of algorithms on large problems, provides exactly the type of information we need. That is why it is the fundamental technique for describing the efficiency properties of algorithms.

Figure 5.2 lists a number of common complexity classes ordered by increasing complexity function. In the next section, you will learn how to determine the complexity of some well-known algorithms in computer science.

Complexity	Name	Examples
O(1)	Constant time	Accessing an element in an array
O(log n)	Logarithmic time	Binary search of a sorted array
O(n)	Linear time	Sequential search of an unsorted array
O(n log n)	Optimal sorting time	Quicksort, merge sort
O(n^2)	Quadratic time	Selection sort, $n \times n$ matrix addition
O(n^3)	Cubic time	Matrix multiplication
O(2^n)	Exponential time	The traveling salesperson problem

FIGURE 5.2 Some common computational complexities

5.3 ASYMPTOTIC ANALYSIS

◆ 5.3.1 Average-Case versus Worst-Case Analysis

When analyzing an algorithm, there are three distinct behaviors we can investigate: the **best-case, average-case,** and **worst-case** behavior of the algorithm.

We rarely do a best-case analysis, which investigates the optimal behavior of an algorithm because an algorithm usually displays this optimal performance only under highly special or unusual conditions. Remember, we are trying to develop general guidelines that describe the overall behavior of an algorithm, not its performance in rare and exceptional circumstances.

Since we are trying to describe the general behavior of an algorithm under all possible circumstances, it would seem that the most important condition to investigate is average-case behavior, which attempts to categorize the performance of an algorithm over all possible inputs. This is true, and the average-case behavior of an algorithm is an important measure. However, in many situations, it is mathematically difficult to conduct an average-case analysis because it is difficult to determine what constitutes "average" input. Furthermore, software is often designed and implemented to meet strict user timing specifications. If we select algorithms on the basis of their average performance, we may not be able to assert that the finished program will always meet design specifications, but only that the program will perform within specifications most of the time. Under certain "pathological" conditions, the algorithm may display worse performance and fail to meet user requirements. An average-case analysis will not warn us about this; only a worst-case analysis can provide this type of information.

For example, both merge sort and quicksort take, on the average, $O(n \log n)$ time to sort a random list of length n. (We will show how to determine this in Section 5.5.) These two algorithms were implemented in Java, along with the $O(n^2)$ selection sort, and run with random arrays of length 10,000, and 100,000. The results are shown in Figure 5.3a.

Merge sort and quicksort are both $O(n \log n)$ in the average case. Figure 5.3a shows that in this example quicksort executes a tiny bit faster than merge sort be-

	List Size		
Method	*10,000*	*100,000*	
Merge Sort	0.6	6.7	
Quicksort	0.5	5.4	time (in seconds)
Selection Sort	11.2	105.6	

(a) Time for sorting a randomized list

Method	*10,000*	*100,000*	
Merge Sort	0.8	7.2	
Quicksort	3.4	89.5	time (in seconds)
Selection Sort	11.5	109.9	

(b) Time for sorting reverse ordered lists

FIGURE 5.3 Run times for three different sorting algorithms

cause of slightly lower constant factors in its complexity function. Because of this behavior, we would probably opt for quicksort when implementing any methods that require sorting. Also notice that, for larger data sets, both merge sort and quicksort are significantly faster than the inefficient $O(n^2)$ selection sort, as we would expect.

However, what if the problem specification document stated that "the finished program must sort any list of length 100,000 in 10 seconds or less." It seems there is no problem, because quicksort sorted the randomized list of 100,000 items in 5.4 seconds. However, if the list is either already sorted or in reverse order (i.e., exactly backward from what we want) then the performance of quicksort deteriorates badly. In this worst-case scenario, quicksort behaves more like an $O(n^2)$ than an $O(n \log n)$ algorithm.

We see this behavior in Figure 5.3b, where we reran the experiment with lists that were in exactly reverse order. The times for merge sort did not change markedly, as both its worst- and average-case behavior are $O(n \log n)$. However, quicksort "blew up," taking a minute and a half to solve the problem when N = 100,000, almost as much time as the inefficient selection sort. Given a firm performance requirement that all inputs of length 100,000 be sorted in under 10 seconds, we could not utilize quicksort in our software. However, if the performance requirements were changed to read "*most of the time* the program must sort a list of length 100,000 in under 10 seconds," then we would likely still choose quicksort. The backward data set of Figure 5.3b is extremely rare and would not be expected to occur with any great frequency. The superior performance of quicksort on the data sets we would encounter the overwhelming majority of the time would, in this case, be a more important factor. (Note: There are ways to modify quicksort so that its worst-case performance approaches $O(n \log n)$, independent of the distribution of the inputs. This "optimized quicksort" is the method of choice in most sorting libraries.)

This example clearly shows that a thorough and in-depth analysis of an algorithm involves a study of both its average-case behavior under expected conditions as well as its worst-case behavior under the least favorable of conditions.

◆ **5.3.2** The Critical Section of An Algorithm

When analyzing an algorithm, we do not care about the behavior of each statement. Such a detailed analysis is far too complicated and time-consuming. Besides, many parts of an algorithm are not executed very often, and an analysis of their individual behavior is not important in determining overall efficiency. For example, initialization is frequently done only once, and its behavior may not significantly affect the overall run time.

Instead, we focus our analysis on only one part of the algorithm, called a **critical section,** which is where the algorithm spends its greatest amount of time. (Note: There may be more than one critical section. If so, we may choose any one for the analysis.) The critical section, which may be either a single operation, a single statement, or a small group of statements, has the following two characteristics:

- It is an operation central to the functioning of the algorithm, and its behavior typifies the overall behavior of the algorithm.

- It is contained inside the most deeply nested loops of the algorithm and is executed as often as any other section of the algorithm.

The critical section can be said to be at the "heart" of the algorithm. Asymptotic analysis says that we can characterize the overall efficiency of an algorithm by counting how many times this critical section is executed as a function of the problem size. (If we are doing an average-case analysis, it is the average number of times executed; in a worst-case analysis, it is the maximum number of times.) The critical section of the algorithm dominates the completion time, and it is this property that allows us to disregard the contributions of the other sections of code. Another way to describe this characteristic is to say that if an algorithm is divided into two parts, the first that takes $O(f(n))$ followed by a second that takes $O(g(n))$, then the overall complexity of the algorithm is $O(\max[f(n), g(n)])$. The slowest and most time-consuming section determines the overall efficiency of the algorithm.

As an analogy, imagine that you have the job of delivering a gift to someone living in another city thousands of miles away. The job involves the following three steps:

1. wrapping the gift
2. driving 2,000 miles to the destination city
3. delivering the package to the proper person

The critical section of this algorithm is obviously step 2. The time it takes to perform this step characterizes the completion time of the entire task, and steps 1 and 3 can be ignored without any significant loss of accuracy. Changing step 2 to flying instead of driving would have a profound impact of the completion time of the task. However, taking a class to learn how to wrap packages more quickly will have no discernible effect.

Similarly, given the following fragment of code,

```
step 1;
for (int i = 0; i < 1000000; i++)
    step 2;
step 3;
```

steps 1 and 3 are executed only once. Their contribution to efficiency is negligible and may be disregarded without any loss of accuracy. It is step 2, the critical section, which is done 1 million times, that characterizes the overall run time of this code fragment.

To summarize, asymptotic analysis is a counting process that determines, for either the average case or the worst case, how many times the critical section of the algorithm is executed as a function of n, the problem size. This relationship, expressed in big-O notation, characterizes the inherent efficiency of the algorithm.

◆ 5.3.3 Examples of Algorithmic Analysis

In this section, we look at a few simple examples of the analysis of algorithms. We will do many more examples in succeeding chapters.

Figure 5.4 shows a simple **sequential search** algorithm. It looks at every item in an n-item list to locate the first occurrence of a specific key.

The critical operation in this algorithm is the comparison **if** (array[i] == target) . . . . This operation is the very heart of the search procedure and, being inside

```
/**
 * Searches the given array for the given integer. If found returns its
 * position, otherwise returns -1.
 *
 * @param array The array of integers to search
 * @param target The integer to search for
 *
 * @return target's position if found, -1 otherwise
 */

public static int search( int array[], int target ) {
    // Assume the target is not in the array
    int position = -1;

    // Step through the array until the target is found
    // or the entire array has been searched.
    for ( int i = 0; i < array.length && position == -1; i++) {
        // Is the current element what we are looking for?
        if ( array[ i ] == target ) {
            position = i;
        }
    }

    // Return the element's position
    return position;
}
```

FIGURE 5.4 Sequential search algorithm

the for loop, it is executed as often as any other operation in the algorithm. In the average case, the key will be located somewhere in the middle of the list, and the algorithm will do roughly $n/2$ comparisons, which is O(n). In the worst case, which occurs when the key is not in the list, this comparison must be performed n times. Therefore, the sequential search algorithm of Figure 5.4 has both an average- case and a worst-case behavior of O(n). This is called a **linear algorithm**. If the list were to double in size, the time required to search it using the algorithm in Figure 5.4 would also approximately double. (Note that we must say "approximately" rather than exactly because our computation does not account for the contributions of statements outside the critical section.) Linear time algorithms are common in computer science. For example, the time it takes to sum the elements in a one-dimensional array is a linear function of the array size.

In general, the structure of a linear time algorithm looks something like the following:

```
for (i = 0; i < n; i++) { // a loop executed n times, where n is the
                          //    problem size
    S;                    // S is the critical section
}
```

Linear algorithms are generally quite efficient because solution time grows at the same rate as the increase in problem size. However, remember there is a "hidden" constant in the big-O expression that may be quite large. For example, the actual relationship between t and n in an O(n) linear algorithm may be $t = 1,000,000,000\ n$. In this case, it would be faster for small n to use an algorithm whose run time is $t = 100\ n^2$ even though n is a lower order than n^2. All that asymptotic analysis tells us is that *eventually* there will exist a problem size, n^*, such that for all problems of size $n > n^*$, a linear algorithm to solve a specific problem will always run faster than a quadratic algorithm that solves the same problem. It does not say where the point n^* lies. (In this example, $n^* = 10^7$.)

If the list we are searching is sorted, we can do much better than O(n) by using the well-known **binary search** technique. Figure 5.5 shows an iterative version of the binary search algorithm.

The algorithm works by comparing the key we are searching for with the item located in the middle position of the array. If it matches, we have found the desired item, and we are finished. If not, we ignore the half of the array that cannot contain the desired key and repeat the process. Eventually, we find what we are looking for or have eliminated all the elements. With each iteration of the loop we (approximately) halve the size of the array being searched; that is, it becomes one-half, one-fourth, one-eighth, . . . its original size. In the worst case (when the key is not in the list), the process continues until the length of the list still under consideration is zero. If we consider the comparison **if** (target < array[middk]) . . . to be the critical operation, then in the worst case, the maximum number of comparisons required by the binary search method will be k, where k is the first integer such that

$2^k > n$ (the size of the list)

Another way to write this is

$k = \text{ceiling}(\log_2 n)$ where ceiling() is the smallest integer value larger than $\log_2 n$

and the efficiency of the binary search algorithm is O($\log n$). The time needed to find an element in a list using binary search is proportional to the logarithm of the list size rather than to the size of the list itself. This is a lower order algorithm than the O(n) sequential search because the function ($\log n$) grows more slowly than n. From Section 5.2, this means that we know there always exists a point n^* such that for all sorted lists of size $n > n^*$, the binary search algorithm will perform more efficiently than sequential search.

In general, the structure of an algorithm that displays logarithmic behavior is:

```
x = n;          // n is the problem size
while (x > 0) and "the problem is not solved" {
    S;          // the critical operation
    x = x / k   // reduce the problem to 1/kth its current size
}
```

We start with a problem of size n, and in each iteration of the loop, we reduce the problem to $1/k$th its current size until we either reach a size of 0 or the problem has been correctly solved. In the worst case, this requires a maximum of ($\log_k n$) iterations. (Note that $\log_k n = $ O($\log_2 n$) since $\log_k n$ and $\log_2 n$ only differ by a constant value.)

```
/**
 * Search the given array for the given integer using a binary
 * search. This method assumes that the elements in the array
 * are in sorted order. If the element is found, the method
 * returns the position of the element, otherwise it returns -1.
 *
 * @param array The array of integers to search
 * @param target The integer to search for
 *
 * @return target's position if found, -1 otherwise
 */

public static int search( int array[], int target ) {
    int start = 0;          // The start of the search region
    int end = array.length; // The end of the search region
    int position = -1;      // Position of the target

    // While there is still something list left to search and the element
    // has not been found
    while ( start <= end && position == -1 ) {
        int middle = (start + end) / 2; // Location of the middle

        // Determine whether the target is smaller than, greater than,
        // or equal to the middle element
        if ( target < array[ middle ] ) {
            // Target is smaller; must be in left half
            end = middle - 1;
        } else if ( target > array[ middle ] ) {
            // Target is larger; must be in right half
            start = middle + 1;
        } else {
            // Found it!!
            position = middle;
        }
    }

    // Return location of target
    return position;
}
```

FIGURE 5.5 Binary search algorithm

We can even improve on logarithmic behavior for performing a search operation. In Chapter 8, we will present a search technique called *hashing,* which can theoretically reduce the time needed to locate a key in a table of size N to O(1). This is called a **constant time algorithm**, and it means that the algorithm can locate any item in the list in a fixed amount of time, independent of the size of the list. Constant time algorithms are obviously the best possible class of algorithms because, regardless of how large a problem becomes, the time to solve it never increases.

Constant time algorithms may seem like an impossibility, but in fact, they are not uncommon in computer science. For example, the time it takes to retrieve an element from a two-dimensional array

value = X[i, j];

is independent of the size of the array X. This retrieval operation takes the same amount of time whether X is (3×3) or $(3,000 \times 3,000)$. The model for a constant time algorithm is extremely simple:

```
S; // S is the critical section, and it does not include a loop
```

Recall from our earlier discussion of binary search that the list we are searching must be sorted before we can apply the algorithm. One of the best known sorting algorithms (although as we shall soon see, one of the worst) is called **bubble sort**, and it is shown in Figure 5.6. This algorithm works by interchanging adjacent elements in

```java
/**
 * Sorts the given array using the bubblesort algorithm
 *
 * @param array The array of integers to sort
 */

public static void bubbleSort( int array[] ) {
    int i = 0;        // How many elements are sorted - initially none
    boolean swap;     // Was a swap made during this pass?
    int temp;         // Temporary storage for swap
    // Keep making passes through the array until it is sorted
    do {
        swap = false;

        // Make a pass through the array, swap adjacent elements that
        // are out of order
        for ( int j = 0; j < array.length - i - 1; j++ ) {
            // If the two elements are out of order - swap them
            if ( array[ j ] > array[ j + 1 ] ) {
                temp = array[ j ];
                array[ j ] = array[ j + 1 ];
                array[ j + 1 ] = temp;
                // Made a swap - array might not be sorted
                swap = true;
            }
        }

        // One more element is in the correct position
        i = i + 1;
    } while ( swap );
}
```

FIGURE 5.6 Bubble sort algorithm

the list if they are out of order. After one complete pass through the list, the largest item will be in its correct location (assuming we are sorting into ascending order). After making a pass through the list, the algorithm checks to see if any exchanges were made. If not, the list is sorted, and we are finished. If at least one exchange was made, we must make yet another pass through the list. We repeat this process until no exchanges occur.

Let the critical operation again be the comparison `array[j] > array[j + 1]`. In the worst case we have to make $(n - 1)$ complete passes through the list, each time comparing adjacent pairs of values from `array[1]` through `array[j]` where j = $n, n - 1, n - 2, \ldots , 2$. In the worst case, the total number of comparison operations needed to sort the list will be:

$$\sum_{j=2}^{n} j = [n (n + 1)/2] - 1 = (1/2) n^2 + (1/2) n - 1$$

As was mentioned earlier, when analyzing an algorithm, we can ignore the contributions of both constant factors and lower order terms. For example, if our analysis of an algorithm leads to a polynomial of the form

$$t = an^k + bn^{k-1} + cn^{k-2} + \ldots$$

then we would say that the algorithm is $O(n^k)$. The constant factor a only changes the location of the point n^* in Figure 5.1; it does not change the shape of the curve or our conclusions about the algorithm's inherent efficiency. An algorithm that is $3n^2$, $10n^2$, or even $1,000n^2$ is still of quadratic $O(n^2)$ complexity. In all cases, the function describing the relationship between problem size and run time grows quadratically. The shape of the curve does not change, just its specific location.

Similarly, since we only care about the behavior of the algorithm as n becomes large, we can disregard all lower order terms because, for large values of n, $n^k >> n^{k-1} >> n^{k-2} >> \ldots$ The following theorem proves that ignoring these values does not affect our determination of the correct complexity class of an algorithm.

Theorem: *If the run time of algorithm A is $t_A = a_0 n^m + a_1 n^{m-1} + a_2 n^{m-2} + \ldots + a_m$, where $n > 1$ is the problem size, then the complexity of algorithm A is $O(n^m)$.*
Proof:

$t_A = a_0 n^m + a_1 n^{m-1} + a_2 n^{m-2} + \ldots + a_m$ as specified in the theorem.

By the triangle inequality, which states that $|a + b| \leq |a| + |b|$, we can rewrite this equation as an inequality. Since the problem size n must be positive, we do not need to include the n^k terms inside the absolute value symbols as these values must be positive.

$$|t_A| \leq |a_0| \, n^m + |a_1| \, n^{m-1} + |a_2| \, n^{m-2} + \ldots + |a_m|$$

Next, we divide and multiply the right side of this inequality by n^m. This operation will not change the inequality.

$$|t_A| \leq (|a_0| + |a_1|/n + |a_2|/n^2 + \ldots + |a_m|/n^m) * n^m$$

Since $n > 1$, we can remove the n^k terms in the denominator, and the inequality will still remain valid:

$$|t_A| \leq (|a_0| + |a_1| + |a_2| + \ldots + |a_m|) * n^m \quad \text{for all n > 1}$$

The original definition of complexity given at the beginning of this chapter stated that for t to be order $O[f(n)]$, there must exist constants M and N_0 such that $t \le Mf(n)$ for all $n > N_0$. If we set $M = (|a_0| + |a_1| + |a_2| + \ldots + |a_m|)$ and set $N_0 = 1$, we have met all the requirements of this definition. Therefore, we have proved that algorithm A is $O(n^m)$.

However, remember that since we are disregarding both constant factors and lower order terms, we must be careful about any claims that we make concerning the efficiency of one algorithm over another. For example, if algorithm A is $O(n)$ and algorithm B is $O(n^2)$, we cannot say that algorithm A is always superior to algorithm B, but only that it will eventually be superior to algorithm B. The actual complexity of algorithm A may be $t = 1000n + 500$ while the actual complexity of B may be $t = 0.01n^2$. In this example, the quadratic algorithm will actually be faster than the linear one for all problems up to size $n^* = 100,000$. Beyond that point, however, the inherent efficiency of the linear method begins to dominate. At a problem size of $n = 10,000,000$, the linear algorithm has become 100 times faster than the quadratic one.

Using the preceding theorem, we can state that the bubble sort algorithm of Figure 5.6, which requires $(1/2)\, n^2 + (1/2)\, n - 1$ comparisons is $O(n^2)$, and it is an example of a **quadratic** algorithm. The typical structure of a quadratic algorithm has the critical section located inside two nested loops, each of which is executed $O(n)$ times, where n is the problem size:

```
for (i = 0; i < n; i++)   // n is the problem size
  for (j = 0; j < n; j++)
    S;                     // S is the critical section
```

Quadratic complexities are typical of a large class of sorting algorithms introduced in beginning programming courses as they are easy to understand and easy to implement. In addition to bubble sort, this group includes insertion sort, exchange sort, and selection sort.

However, we can do much better than $O(n^2)$ for sorting. There are a large group of algorithms, including quicksort, merge sort, and heap sort, whose running times are proportional not to n^2 but to the function $(n \log n)$. (We will determine the complexity of some of these recursive sorting algorithms in the following section.) This is a much better efficiency, and these algorithms typically run far faster than the $O(n^2)$ algorithms just mentioned. Figure 5.7 shows the number of operations needed to sort lists of different sizes using these two classes of sorting techniques. (This table ignores lower order terms and assumes that all the constant factors are 1.)

When n is small (e.g., $n < 100$) the difference between the two complexity classes in Figure 5.7 is small, and the choice of sorting method is relatively unimportant. (In fact, for problems this small, sorting by hand might actually be fastest!) As n gets large, however, the speed advantages of the $O(n \log n)$ algorithms become more apparent. When sorting a list of 1 million items, an $O(n \log n)$ algorithm requires almost five orders of magnitude fewer comparisons to sort the list than the simpler but slower class of $O(n^2)$ methods.

Let's do an example that clarifies this point even further. Assume that we run one program from each of the two classes of sorting algorithm listed in Figure 5.7 and a third "compromise" $O(n^{1.5})$ algorithm on three very different computers—a $1,000 laptop, a $100,000 mainframe, and a $10,000,000 supercomputer. The supercomputer

	Maximum Number of Comparisons to Sort a List of Size n	
Problem Size n	$O(n^2)$	$O(n \log_2 n)$
10	100	33
100	10,000	670
1,000	1,000,000	10,000
100,000	10^{10}	1,700,000
1,000,000	10^{12}	2×10^7

FIGURE 5.7 Comparison of $O(n^2)$ and $O(n \log n)$ complexity classes

will run the inefficient $O(n^2)$ method, the mainframe will execute the compromise $O(n^{1.5})$ algorithm, and the inexpensive laptop will be assigned the efficient $O(n \log n)$ technique. Furthermore, assume that we are able to develop exact formulas for the run time (in μsec) of the algorithms on each machine. Assume these formulas are:

$t_1 = n^2$ for the supercomputer

$t_2 = 1,000 \, n^{1.5}$ for the mainframe computer

$t_3 = 10,000 \, n \log n$ for the laptop

Notice how much larger the constant of proportionality is for the mainframe and the laptop to reflect the fact that they are three to four orders of magnitude slower than the high-end supercomputer. Figure 5.8 shows the hypothetical results of running these three different classes of sorting algorithm on the three different types of computer.

For small n, the supercomputer's immense speed allows it to overcome the limitations of its inefficient method, and it solves the problem 100 times faster than the mainframe and 700 times faster than the laptop. As the problem gets larger, this difference begins to disappear as the inefficiencies start to overwhelm the ability of the larger machine to keep up with the rapidly growing number of computations. At

	Approximate Run Times		
	Supercomputer	Mainframe	Laptop
Problem Size n	$t = n^2$	$t = 1,000 \, n^{1.5}$	$t = 10,000 \, n \log_2 n$
100	0.01 sec	1 sec	7 sec
1,000	1 sec	31 sec	100 sec
10,000	1.7 min	17 min	22 min
100,000	3 hr	9 hr	5 hr
1,000,000	12 days	12 days	2 days
10,000,000	3 yr	10 months	27 days

FIGURE 5.8 Comparison of run times of three classes of algorithms on three different types of computer

$n = 100,000$, all three computers take roughly the same amount of time to solve the problem—on the order of a few hours. At $n = 10,000,000$, the efficiency of the $O(n \log n)$ algorithm has become the dominant factor, and the laptop is completing the sorting task 40 times quicker than the supercomputer, a machine that costs 10,000 times more and runs thousands of times faster. Rewriting the $O(n^2)$ algorithm or buying a faster processor for the mainframe may postpone the problem, but it will not make the problem disappear. It is simply a fundamental property of a lower order algorithm that there will always exist a point (about $n^* = 100,000$ in this example) beyond which the lower order algorithm will always take less time to complete, regardless of the constants of proportionality.

As a final example, let us analyze the complexity of matrix multiplication, $C = A \times B$, defined as follows:

$$C_{ij} = \sum_{k=1}^{n} (A_{ik} * B_{kj}) \qquad i = 1, \ldots, n; j = 1, \ldots, n$$

The critical operations are the additions and multiplications needed to produce the result. If we assume that both A and B are $n \times n$ matrices, then this formula shows that the computation of each individual element of the product matrix C requires $2n - 1$ operations—n multiplications and $(n - 1)$ additions. These $2n - 1$ operations must be repeated for each of the $n \times n$ positions in the resulting matrix C. Thus, the total number of operations required to obtain C is $n^2(2n - 1) = 2n^3 - n^2$, and the complexity of matrix multiplication is $O(2n^3 - n^2)$. However, as mentioned earlier, all we are interested in is the limiting, or asymptotic, behavior of the function. When n gets large, the contributions of the n^2 term will be relatively insignificant compared to the value of n^3. Thus, we can say that the complexity of matrix multiplication as given by the previous formula is $O(n^3)$. This is a **cubic complexity** function. The general model of an algorithm with cubic complexity is:

```
for (i = 0; i < n; i++)          // outermost loop done n times, where
                                 //   n is the problem size
    for (j = 0; j < n; j++)      // middle loop done n times
        for (k = 0; k < n; k++)  // inner loop done n times
            S;                   // the critical operation
```

(It is interesting to note that there exists a faster algorithm, called *Strassen's method* for performing matrix multiplication. The number of operations required to solve the matrix multiplication problem using this technique has been reduced to $O(n^{2.81})$. The difference between n^3 and $n^{2.81}$ may not seem like much, but it is enormously important when multiplying large matrices.)

Most of the time complexities we have seen so far have been of the form $O(n)$, $O(n^2)$, and $O(n^3)$. Algorithms whose efficiencies are of the form $O(n^d)$ are called **polynomial time algorithms** because their complexity functions are polynomial functions of relatively small degrees. The computational demands of these algorithms are usually manageable, even for large problems, because their computational needs do not grow unreasonably fast. However, not all algorithms are of this type. A second and very distinct group of methods are the **exponential algorithms.** For these problems, no polynomial time algorithm has yet been discovered. The typical complexity displayed by this exponential class of algorithms is $O(2^n)$, $O(n^n)$, or $O(n!)$. The time demands of these algorithms grow extraordinarily fast and consume vast amounts of resources, even for very small problems. In most cases, it is not feasible to solve any realistically sized problem using an exponential algorithm, no matter how clever the programmer or how fast the computer.

This class of algorithms is not just of academic interest. They occur frequently in computer science, applied mathematics, and operations research. In fact, an important area of research has developed specifically to study this category of **computationally intractable** problems. One example of such an exponential algorithm is the *traveling salesperson problem*. In this problem, one of the most famous in computer science, a salesperson must travel to N other cities, visiting each one only once, ending up back home. This is called a *tour*. We want to determine if it is possible to make such a tour within a given mileage allowance, k. That is, the sum of all the distances traveled by the salesperson must be less than or equal to k. For example, here is a mileage chart showing the distance between four cities A, B, C, and D:

	A	B	C	D
A	—	500	100	800
B	500	—	900	150
C	100	900	—	600
D	800	150	600	—

Given a mileage allowance of 1,500 miles, a legal tour is possible starting at A: namely, $A \rightarrow B \rightarrow D \rightarrow C \rightarrow A$. The total length is $500 + 150 + 600 + 100 = 1{,}350$ miles. However, if the mileage allowance were 1,000 miles, no legal tour exists.

No algorithm has yet been discovered that allows us to solve this problem in a reasonable (i.e., polynomial) time. For example, an exhaustive search of all possible tours would begin by selecting any one of the N cities as its starting location. It would then select any one of the remaining $(N - 1)$ cities to visit next, then any of the remaining $(N - 2)$ cities, and so on. The total number of tours that need to be examined to see if they fall within our mileage allowance is

$$N \times (N - 1) \times (N - 2) \times \ldots \times 1 = N!$$

and the complexity of this type of **brute force** solution to the traveling salesperson problem is $O(N!)$. Better algorithms have been developed, but they still display this characteristic explosive exponential growth, which makes the problem unsolvable in the general case for anything but the tiniest values of N. For example, if $N = 50$, a computer that could evaluate 1 billion tours per second would need approximately 1 million centuries to enumerate all possible tours. Most salespeople would not be willing to wait that long!

As this example clearly demonstrates, exponential time methods may be theoretically describable, but they are computationally impractical. In those cases where no known polynomial algorithm exists, we are usually limited to achieving decent approximations, or "reasonable" rather than "optimal" solutions. These types of approximation algorithms are called **heuristics**.

5.4 OTHER COMPLEXITY MEASURES

When we write the expression $f(n) \approx O[g(n)]$, we are asserting that the function $f(n)$ is bounded above by (i.e., is less than or equal to) a function whose shape is of the form $g(n)$. Two other important types of notation express different complexity relationships.

The formula

$$f(n) \approx \Omega[g(n)]$$

read as "$f(n)$ is **big-omega** of $g(n)$," means that the function $f(n)$ is bounded below by (i.e., is greater than or equal to) a function of the form $g(n)$. Formally, it means that if $f(n) \approx \Omega[g(n)]$, then there exist positive constants M and N_0 such that $f(n) \geq Mg(n)$ for all $n > N_0$.

Big-omega notation is a way to put a lower bound on the growth rate of a function—that is, to state that the growth rate of an algorithm must be at least that value and cannot be any less. In a sense, it states that the solution to a particular problem will require at least this amount of time, and it cannot be done any faster. For example, it has been formally proved that all comparison-based sorting methods such as quicksort, merge sort, and bubble sort require at least ($n \log n$) operations to complete their task. Another way of saying this is that if algorithm A is a comparison-based sorting algorithm, then its run time $t \approx \Omega[n \log n]$. Big-omega is often used to put a lower bound constraint on the performance of a class of algorithms.

Finally, if $f(n) \approx O[g(n)]$ and $f(n) \approx \Omega[g(n)]$, then $f(n)$ is bounded both above and below by a function whose shape is of the form $g(n)$. This relationship is expressed using the notation

$$f(n) \approx \Theta[g(n)]$$

which is read "$f(n)$ is **big-theta** of $g(n)$." Big-theta notation allows us to state that the run-time efficiency characteristics of two algorithms are equal, at least to within a constant factor. If the run time of algorithm A is $t_1 \approx \Theta[g(n)]$ and the run time of algorithm B is $t_2 \approx \Theta[g(n)]$, then both A and B are bounded above and below by functions whose shape is $g(n)$, and A and B are said to be **asymptotically equal.**

5.5 THE ANALYSIS OF RECURSIVE ALGORITHMS

The asymptotic behavior of algorithms is used to study both iterative and recursive algorithms. However, the methods of analyzing these two different types of algorithms differ dramatically. With iterative methods, we focus on the loop structure of the program and count how many times a critical section of code within these loops is performed. However, this technique does not work for recursive algorithms because the fundamental control structure of a recursive program is not a loop but a recursive function call. For example, look at the code in Figure 5.9.

It is not at all obvious how to determine the number of times we will recursively call function `silly()` as a function of the value of its input parameter n. Determining the complexity of a recursive function is no longer a simple loop counting operation.

The technique to analyze recursive algorithms makes use of a mathematical construct called a **recurrence relation**. Recurrence relations typically are a pair of formulas of the following form:

```
public int silly(int n) {
    int a;
    int b;
    int retVal;

    if ( n <= 1 ) {
        retVal = 1;
    }
    else {
        a = silly( n / 2 );
        b = silly( n / 2 );
        retVal = a + b;
    }
}
```

FIGURE 5.9 Recursive function

$T(n) = f(T(m))$ $n > 0, m < n$ (the *recursive case*)
$T(1) = k$ where k is a constant not dependent on n (the *base case*)

These two formulas describe the value of a function T and its parameter n in terms of the same function T but with a simpler (i.e., smaller) value of its parameter. This is called the **recursive case**. We continue using this recursive case formula until we have reduced the value of the parameter to 1 (or some other small constant value). Then we use the second formula to directly determine the value of $T(1)$. This is called the **base case**.

When using recurrence relations to study the behavior of recursive functions, we relate the number of times the critical section of code is executed on a problem of size n with the number of times it is executed on the smaller subproblems generated by a recursive call. Let $T(n)$ represent the number of times the critical section is executed on a problem of size n. If we recursively call the procedure for a smaller problem of size m, we first determine the functional relationship between $T(n)$ and $T(m)$ and then we solve the recurrence relationship that we have developed. This will give us our answer.

For example, looking back at the function `silly()` in Figure 5.9 and assuming that the comparison **if** `(n <= 1)` . . . is the critical operation, we see that when n is less than or equal to 1, the comparison operation will be done only once. So $T(1) = 1$. If n is greater than 1, we must make that one comparison and, in addition, two recursive calls on function `silly()` using a parameter that is half the size of the current problem. The number of comparisons that will be done for each of these calls can be expressed as $T(n/2)$. Therefore, the total number of times the critical operation will be executed can be expressed as:

$T(n) = 2T(n/2) + 1$
$T(1) = 1$

This is a recurrence relation in the exact format that we described earlier. We solve this relation by using the technique called **repeated substitution**:

$$T(n) = 2T(n/2) + 1$$

To determine the value of $T(n/2)$, we substitute $n/2$ for n into the preceding formula and get

$$T(n/2) = 2T(n/4) + 1$$

Substituting this value back into the first equation for $T(n)$ gives

$$T(n) = 2(2T(n/4) + 1) + 1$$
$$= 4T(n/4) + 3$$

We can repeat this same operation, this time solving for the value of $T(n/4)$ and substituting it back into the preceding formula. These substitutions yield the following sequence of equations:

$$T(n) = 8T(n/8) + 7$$
$$= 16T(n/16) + 15$$
$$= 32T(n/32) + 31$$
$$= \ldots$$
$$= 2^k T(n/2^k) + (2^k - 1)$$

This last line represents a general formula that describes all the terms in the sequence in terms of a parameter called k. You can easily check this fact by letting $k = 1, 2, 3, \ldots$ generating all of the expressions that have been shown.

Now, let $n = 2^k$. That is, assume the original problem size is an integral power of 2. Then

$$T(n) = nT(1) + n - 1 \qquad \text{(remember, } T(1) = 1\text{)}$$
$$= n + n - 1$$
$$= 2n - 1$$

and the total number of operations carried out by the function `silly()` on a problem of size n is $2n - 1$, and therefore, its complexity is $O(n)$.

As a second example, Figure 5.10 shows a recursive implementation of the binary search algorithm first shown in Figure 5.5. Our analysis of that earlier iterative version led to a complexity of $O(\log n)$. We would expect the recursive algorithm to behave similarly.

If the list has length ≤ 1, then we will be done after a single comparison. Otherwise, we must do up to two more comparisons, for a total of three, and then call the binary search procedure with a new list whose length is approximately one-half the size of the current list. This leads to the following recurrence relationships:

$$T(n) = 3 + T(n/2)$$
$$T(1) = 1$$

Using the method of repeated substitution yields the following sequence:

$$T(n) = 3 + T(n/2)$$
$$= 6 + T(n/4)$$
$$= 9 + T(n/8)$$
$$= \ldots$$
$$= 3k + T(n/2^k) \qquad \text{(the general formula describing all terms)}$$

```
/**
 * Recursively searches the given array for the given integer. If found,
 * returns its position. If not, returns -1.
 *
 * @param array The array of integers to search
 * @param target The integer to search for
 * @param start First position included in the search range
 * @param end Last position included in the search range
 *
 * @return target's position if found, -1 otherwise
 */

public static int binarySearch( int array[],
                                int target,
                                int start,
                                int end ) {

    int position = -1;   // Assume the target is not here
    // Do the search only if there are elements in the array
    if ( start <= end ) {
        // Determine where the middle is
        int middle = ( start + end ) / 2;

        if ( target < array[ middle ] ) {
            // Target is smaller than middle. Search left half.
            position = binarySearch( array, target, start, middle - 1 );
        } else if ( target > array[ middle ] ) {
            // Target is larger than middle. Search right half.
            position = binarySearch( array, target, middle + 1, end );
        } else {
            // Target is equal to middle— we found it.
            position = middle;
        }
    }

    return position;
}
```

FIGURE 5.10 Recursive implementation of binary search

Let the problem size $n = 2^k$. Then $k = \log_2 n$, and the formula becomes:

$$T(n) = 3 \log_2 n + T(1)$$
$$= 3 \log_2 n + 1$$

Thus, the recursive implementation of binary search, like its iterative cousin, is also $O(\log n)$.

As our final example, we analyze the merge sort algorithm referred to in the discussion of Section 5.3.1. The algorithm is shown in Figure 5.11.

```
/**
 * Sort an array using merge sort.
 *
 * @param array the array that contains the values to be sorted
 * @param start the start of the sorting region
 * @param end the end of the sorting region
 */

public static void mergeSort( int array[], int start, int end ) {
    int middle;      // Middle of the array
    int left;        // First element in the left array
    int right;       // First element in the right array
    int temp;        // Temporary storage

    if ( start < end ) {
        // Split the array in half and sort each half
        middle = ( start + end ) /2;
        mergeSort( array, start, middle );
        mergeSort( array, middle + 1, end );

        // Merge the sorted arrays into one
        left = start;
        right = middle + 1;

        // While there are numbers in the array to be sorted
        while ( left <= middle && right <= end ) {
            // If the current number in the left array
            // is larger than the current number in the right
            // array the numbers need to be moved around
            if ( array[ left ] > array[ right ] ) {
                // Remember the first number in the right array
                temp = array[ right ];

                // Move the left array right one position to make
                // room for the smaller number
                for ( int i = right - 1; i >= left; i- ) {
                    array[ i + 1 ] = array[ i ];
                }

                // Put the smaller number where it belongs
                array[ left ] = temp;

                // The right array and the middle need to shift right
                right = right + 1;
                middle = middle + 1;
            }
            // No matter what the left array moves right
            left = left + 1;
        }
    }
}
```

FIGURE 5.11 Merge sort algorithm

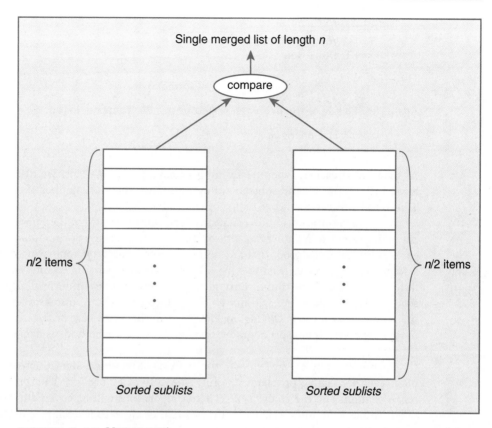

FIGURE 5.12 Merge sort

The algorithm splits the n-element list to be sorted into two parts of approximately equal size $n/2$ elements: One begins at start and goes up to middle, and the second begins at middle $+$ 1 and goes to end. These two parts are sorted (using merge sort) and then merged to produce the final result. This recursive process continues until we have a list containing only one item, which is returned directly.

If $T(n)$ is the number of comparisons done by merge sort on a list of length n, then the sorting phase of merge sort requires $2T(n/2)$ comparisons. Assume the merge phase takes some as yet unspecified number of comparisons called $f(n)$. Then the following recurrence relation gives the total number of comparisons required by merge sort:

$T(n) = 2T(n/2) + f(n)$ (where $f(n)$ is the number of operations required to do the merge)

$T(1) = 1$

The value of $f(n)$ can be determined by carefully analyzing Figure 5.12. To merge two sorted sublists into a single sorted list, we compare the top item of each sublist, select the larger of the two, and move that item into the next position in the final sorted list. Thus, a single comparison will determine a single value to be moved. Since there are a total of n items to be moved, the merge operation requires $O(n)$ comparisons, and $f(n) = an$, where a is some constant value. Putting this value into our recurrence relation and again using the technique of repeated substitution yields the following:

$$T(n) = 2T(n/2) + an$$
$$= 4T(n/4) + 2an$$
$$= 8T(n/8) + 3an$$
$$= \ldots$$
$$= 2^k T(n/2^k) + kan \qquad \text{(general formula)}$$

Again, let the size of the list being sorted be $n = 2^k$. Then $k = \log_2 n$.

$$= nT(1) + an \log_2 n$$
$$= n + an \log_2 n$$

As mentioned earlier, when performing an asymptotic analysis, we disregard both lower order terms (n) and constant values (a). Thus, the total number of comparisons T needed by merge sort to sort a list of length n is $O(n \log_2 n)$.

This is a significant improvement over the $O(n^2)$ behavior of the bubble sort algorithm diagrammed in Figure 5.6. One of the important results of computational mathematics has been the proof that any sorting method based on comparing elements of a sequence requires at least $O(n \log_2 n)$ comparisons—sorting cannot be done any faster. So, at least to within a constant factor, merge sort is an optimal algorithm for sorting lists of values. We will not go through the analysis of quicksort here, but in the average case it too is $O(n \log_2 n)$. However, in the worst case (a sorted list or a list in reverse order), quicksort degrades to a quadratic $O(n^2)$ method, as demonstrated in Figure 5.3.

As these examples have shown, the analysis of recursive algorithms can be complex, even for simple problems like function silly of Figure 5.9. The topic of recurrence relations and the analysis of recursive algorithms will be covered in greater detail in other computer science courses such as algorithm design, computational complexity, and discrete mathematics.

5.6 SUMMARY

This has been an introduction to the topic of the efficiency analysis of both iterative and recursive algorithms. The technique used to analyze these algorithms is not to time them with a clock and see how fast they run. This approach is too greatly influenced by the characteristics of the data set selected and the machine on which it is run. Instead, we characterize the asymptotic or limiting behavior of an algorithm as the problem size grows very large. This allows us to determine the complexity, or order, of the algorithm. Then we can choose the lowest order algorithm we can find. This guarantees that, to within a constant factor, we will achieve the highest possible level of efficiency.

The central point to remember about software efficiency is the critical importance of our choice of algorithm on the efficiency of the final solution. The selection of the best method is, ultimately, a much more important decision than the programming language, the hardware, or how well we wrote the code.

Looking back at Figure 5.8, we see that using an $O(n^2)$ algorithm to solve a problem of size 10^6 took almost 2 weeks on a large, expensive supercomputer. Nothing we can do in terms of clever coding or choosing a different language will bring that run time down to a reasonable value. It is simply an inherent problem of the technique that we selected:

Observation 1: You cannot make an inefficient algorithm efficient by how you choose to implement it or what machine you choose to run it on.

Similarly, if you select a highly efficient algorithm, almost nothing that you do regarding its implementation can destroy that inherent efficiency. As long as the algorithm is implemented correctly, there is not a whole lot to be gained spending hours poring over each line, each statement, and each procedure trying to squeeze out every wasted nanosecond. "Tweaking" the program code usually has only a small effect on its overall performance.

Observation 2: It is virtually impossible to ruin the efficiency of an efficient algorithm by how you implement it or what machine you run it on.

Putting these two observations together, we come up with the following fundamental rule that summarizes what we have been trying to stress throughout this chapter:

The "efficiency game" is won or lost once you have selected the algorithms and data structures to be used in your solution. This inherent level of efficiency is not significantly affected by how well or how poorly you implement the code.

This does not mean that we support or encourage sloppy code development. Sloppiness can detract from the legibility of your program and can affect the ability of other programmers to read, understand, and modify your code in the future. That can make it much more difficult, time-consuming, and expensive to locate and correct errors. However, your coding techniques will not greatly affect the efficiency of the program, which is an inherent characteristic of the methods that you choose. That is why this choice is so important.

In the following chapters, we will look at a number of interesting data structures as well as algorithms for manipulating the information stored in those structures. We will make extensive use of the mathematical tools presented in this chapter to select, for a given problem, the data structures that produce the highest possible level of efficiency.

EXERCISES

1. Time complexities generally have coefficients other than 1 and have lower order terms that are not considered. For example, the actual time or space complexity of an $O(n^3)$ algorithm might be:

$$(1/2)n^3 + 500n^2 - 1$$

However, this does not change the fact that if $f(n)$ is of a lower order than $g(n)$, there will always be a point n^* such that, for all $n > n^*$, $O[f(n)] < O[g(n)]$. Find the point n^* where the first complexity function is always less than the second.

  a. $(1/2)n^2 + (1/2)n - 1$ $(1/8)n^3$

   b. $\log_2 n$ $10,000n$

   c. $3n^3 + 50$ $(1/50)2^{n/2}$

   d. 5×10^6 $(1/10,000)n$

2. Looking at Figure 5.4, the sequential search, why would it be inappropriate to let the critical operation be the assignment statement

   int *position* $= -1$;

   on the first line of the program? If that were incorrectly called the critical operation, what would the time complexity of that method be?

3. In Figure 5.4, what other operations, aside from the comparison (`array[i] == target`), could properly be treated as the critical section and produce a correct time complexity of $O(n)$?

4. Given the following outline of a program

   ```
   S₁
   for (int i = 1; i < n; i++)   {
           S₂;
           for (int j = 1, j < n; j++)
                   S₃;
   }
   ```

   assume that n is the problem size. What would be the critical section of this program? Why? What is the time complexity of this program?

5. What is the complexity of the following algorithmic structures with respect to problem size n? Assume that S is the critical operation and a is a constant value greater than 1.

   ```
   a. for (i = 1; i <= n; i++)
           for (j = i; j <= i; j++)
                   S;
   ```

   ```
   b. for (i = 1; i <= n; i++)
           for (j = 1; j <= a; j++)
                   S;
   ```

   ```
   c. for (i = 1; i <= a; i++)
           for (j = i; j <= a; j++)
                   S;
   ```

   ```
   d. x = 1;
      do
            S;
            X = X * a;
      while X <= n
   ```

   ```
   e. for (i = 1; i <= n; i += a)
                   S;
   ```

6. The function e^x can be approximated using the following formula:

$$e^x = 1 + x + \frac{x^2}{2!} + \frac{x^3}{3!} + \cdots + \frac{x^k}{k!}$$

What is the complexity of this evaluation as a function of k, the number of terms in the expansion? For the critical operation, use the total number of arithmetic operations that are performed.

7. What starting conditions are necessary to produce the worst-case behavior in the bubble sort method shown in Figure 5.6?

8. Is the following argument valid?

   An O(1) algorithm, whose running time is independent of the problem size, will always be superior to an O(n³) algorithm, whose running time grows as the cube of the problem size.

   If valid, explain why. If invalid, give a counterexample.

9. The following is a description of a simple algorithm called *copy sort*, which sorts an array into ascending order. Copy sort searches an array A to find the smallest element, copies it to B[0], and "destroys" the original value in A by setting it to a very large value. The process of searching A, copying the value into the next cell of B, and destroying the value in A is repeated until the entire array has been copied, in ascending order, into array B. What is the time complexity of copy sort?

10. What is the time complexity of the matrix multiplication operation

    $C = A \times B$

    if A and B are no longer both $n \times n$, but A is $n \times p$ and B is $p \times m$?

11. What is the efficiency of matrix transposition for an $n \times n$ matrix? Transposition is defined as:

    $\text{Interchange}(A_{ij}, A_{ji})$ $i = 1, \ldots, n$ $j = 1, \ldots, i - 1$

    Sketch out the algorithm and analyze its complexity.

12. Assume that we have text containing n characters $T_1, \ldots, T_n$. We also have a pattern containing m characters $P_1, \ldots, P_m$ where $m \leq n$. We want to develop an algorithm to determine if the pattern $P_1, \ldots, P_m$ occurs as a substring anywhere within the text T. Our method is to line up P_1 with T_1 and compare up to the next m characters to see if they are all identical. If they all match, we have found our answer. If we ever encounter a mismatch, we stop the current comparison. We "slide" the pattern forward, line up P_1 with T_2, and compare the next m characters. We continue in this way until we either find a match or know that no such match exists.

    Sketch an algorithm for this generalized pattern-matching process and determine its time complexity.

13. a. A polynomial

      $P = a_n x^n + a_{n-1} x^{n-1} + \ldots + a_1 x + a_0$

      can be evaluated in many different ways. The straightforward way is to perform the multiplications and additions in exactly the order just specified:

      $P = (a_n {}^* x {}^* x {}^* \ldots {}^* x) + (a_{n-1} {}^* x {}^* \ldots {}^* x) + \ldots + a_0$

Write a procedure to evaluate a polynomial with coefficients $a_0, \ldots, a_n$ at the point x using this straightforward technique. Determine how many multiplications, additions, and assignments are required as a function of the degree, n, of the polynomial. What is the time complexity of this algorithm?

b. An alternative way to evaluate P is to factor the polynomial in the following manner (called **Horner's rule**):

$$P = (\ldots ((a_n{}^* x + a_{n-1})^* x + a_{n-2})^* x + \ldots + a_1)^* x + a_0$$

Write a procedure to evaluate a polynomial with coefficients $a_0 \ldots a_n$ at point x using Horner's rule. How many multiplications, additions, and assignments are required as a function of the degree n? What is the time complexity of this improved version of a polynomial evaluation algorithm?

14. Assume you are asked to develop an algorithm to determine, for a given set of cities and direct flights, whether or not there is a way to fly between any two arbitrary cities, i and j. This algorithm would be useful, for example, to travel agents for determining how to route someone from one city to another.

You are given a matrix M[i,j] that describes the direct connections between cities:

M[i,j] = 1 if there is a direct connection from city i to city j.
M[i,j] = 0 if there is no direct connection from city i to city j.

For example, if our connections are as follows:

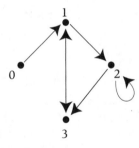

M would look like the following:

$$M = \begin{matrix} 0 & 1 & 0 & 0 \\ 0 & 0 & 1 & 1 \\ 0 & 0 & 1 & 1 \\ 0 & 1 & 0 & 0 \end{matrix}$$

There is a path from city 0 to city 2 ($0 \rightarrow 1 \rightarrow 2$), but there is no path from city 3 to city 0, and there is no path from city 2 to city 0. Develop an algorithm that will input a map M specifying the direct connections between n different cities. Next, your algorithm should input two indexes, i and j, and determine if there does or does not exist a path from city i to city j. What is the time complexity of your algorithm as a function of n, the number of cities?

15. In the example of Figure 5.8, the supercomputer was assigned the inefficient $O(n^2)$ algorithm whose actual relationship between time and size was $t = n^2$. If we changed that relationship to $t = 0.00001n^2$, would that change your

conclusion? At what point, if any, would the laptop and the supercomputer demonstrate identical performance?

16. Assume that we analyzed algorithm P and found that its time complexity was $O(\log_2(\log_2 n))$. Where would that complexity function fit within the ordered list of functions given in Figure 5.2?

17. Try to write the most efficient program you can to solve the following problem: You are given an array A of length n. The elements of A are all signed integers. Your program should find the subscript values i and j such that the sum of the contiguous values $A[i] + A[i + 1] + \ldots + A[j - 1] + A[j]$ is the largest possible value. For example, given the following seven-element array:

A:	10	−18	−2	40	21	−5	16
index:	0	1	2	3	4	5	6

your program would output the two values (3, 6) since the largest sum of values in contiguous elements of the array is contained in A[3] through A[6] (the sum is 72). After writing the program, evaluate it for efficiency in terms of its time complexity as a function of n, the size of the array.

Be careful with this problem, as there are many different ways to solve it with complexities running all the way from $O(n^3)$ down to $O(n)$.

18. A matrix is called *sparse* when it has very few nonzero elements. For example, the following 4×4 matrix would be considered sparse:

0	0	1.2	0
0	0	0	0
3.4	0	0	0
0	0	0	−5.9

Rather than storing these sparse matrices in their "regular" $n \times n$ representation, which requires n^2 array elements, we can use a more space-efficient representation in which we only store the information about the location of nonzero elements:

row	col	value
0	2	1.2
2	0	3.4
3	3	−5.9

a. What are the space requirements of this alternative representation?

b. Write a procedure called insert to add a new value X to position A[i,j], when A is stored in the sparse matrix representation shown. The calling sequence of the method is `public static void insert(A, i, j, X)`. Your procedure should look up the row and column indexes (i, j) in the sparse representation of array A. If it is there, the procedure should change the value field to X. If it is not there, the procedure should add it so that the table is still sorted by row and column index. What is the time complexity of the insert procedure?

19. Can you design an $O(1)$ algorithm to determine $n!$ for $1 \leq n \leq 25$?

20. An $n \times n$ *symmetric matrix* is one in which $A_{ij} = A_{ji}$ for $0 \leq i < n$, and $0 \leq j < n$. For example, the following is a 4×4 symmetric matrix.

$$
\begin{array}{rrrr}
1 & 8 & -13 & 4 \\
8 & 70 & 82 & 2 \\
-13 & 82 & 0 & -6 \\
4 & 2 & -6 & 99
\end{array}
$$

Develop a space-efficient representation for symmetric matrices that takes less than n^2 cells (assuming one integer value per cell). Now write a method to perform matrix addition in your new representation. Does it take longer than addition using the "regular" $n \times n$ representation? What is the time complexity of your addition method?

21. In Exercise 18, you developed a space-efficient representation for sparse matrices and then wrote an insert program to put new information into this structure. In Exercise 20, you developed a more space-efficient representation for symmetric matrices and then wrote a method to add two matrices that are in this representation. Compare the time complexities of these two routines with the time complexities of the methods for manipulating matrices in their regular format. What does this comparison say about what typically happens to run times of programs when you attempt to save memory space? (Note: This relationship is usually called the **time-space trade-off**.)

22. Solve the following recurrence relation:

$$
T(n) = \begin{array}{ll}
2T(n/2) + 2 & n > 2 \\
1 & n = 2 \\
0 & n = 1
\end{array}
$$

CHAPTER 6

Linear Data Structures

6.1 A TAXONOMY OF DATA STRUCTURES

This chapter begins our study of data structures. We will show, as was mentioned in Chapter 5, how the proper choice of data structures for a given problem can have a profound effect on the efficiency of the final solution.

A **data type** is a collection of values along with a set of operations defined on these values. For example, the *integer* data type is composed of the signed and unsigned whole numbers, up to some maximum value, along with the operations defined on these numbers, such as +, −, *, /, and abs(). A **simple data type**, also called a **primitive data type**, is one in which the elements belonging to the data type cannot be decomposed into simpler and more basic structures. Integer is a simple data type because its elements, such as the values 5 and −99, cannot be further decomposed.[1]

A **composite data type**, also called a **data structure**, is a data type in which its elements can be decomposed into either primitive types or other composite data types. Essentially, a data structure is a *collection* of elements rather than a single one. An example of a composite data type is the array. The following one-dimensional array *X*

X: | 21 | −4 | 302 |

is composed of three primitive integer values. The 3 × 3, two-dimensional array *Y*

Y:
21	−4	302
8	90	−1
0	12	13

can be initially subdivided into three one-dimensional arrays, and each of these one-dimensional arrays can be further subdivided into three integers.

---

[1]At a lower level of abstraction, simple types can be further decomposed. For example, the integer 5 might be stored in memory as the 16-bit sequence 0000000000000101. Thus, 5 can be decomposed into 16 separate binary digits. However, at this level of abstraction, we view simple types as nondecomposable.

The following three chapters will introduce many different data structures (e.g., lists, queues, binary trees, hash tables, weighted graphs), all with different characteristics and behaviors. However, these various structures should not be viewed as distinct and unrelated topics. On the contrary, there is a *taxonomy*, or classification scheme, that allows us to impose a logical structure on this rather huge and complex topic. It is based on categorizing the relationships that exist between individual elements of a data structure into one of four groupings.

The first grouping, the **linear data structures,** has a *one:one* relationship between elements in the collection. That is, if the data structure is nonempty, there exists a **first** element and a **last** element. Every element except the first has a unique **predecessor**, or element that comes immediately before, and every element except the last has a unique **successor**, or element that comes immediately after. The general model for all linear structures is diagrammed in Figure 6.1.

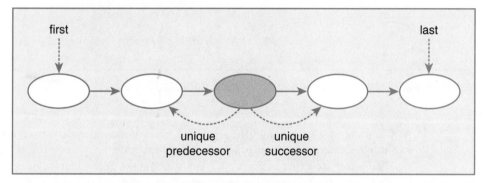

FIGURE 6.1 General model of a linear data structure

A linear structure has a unique ordering, so there is only a single way to begin at the first element and follow each element to its successor until you arrive at the last element. This unique ordering can be clearly seen in Figure 6.1. The process of sequencing through the nodes of a linear structure from beginning to end is called **iteration**.

There are many types of linear data structures, such as lists, stacks, queues, and priority queues. They do not differ in the fundamental organization shown in Figure 6.1. Instead, they differ in terms of restrictions they impose on exactly where we are allowed to perform such operations as insertions, deletions, and retrievals. Linear data structures will be discussed in detail in the remainder of this chapter.

The second grouping is the **hierarchical data structures** in which there exists a *one:many* relationship between elements in the collection. That is, if the data structure is nonempty, there exists a unique node called the **root** and zero, one, or more nodes called **leaves**. Every element except the root has a unique predecessor, and every node except the leaves will have zero, one, or more successors. If a node in a hierarchical data structure is neither the root nor a leaf, then it is an **internal node**. Internal nodes have exactly one predecessor and one or more successors. This general model for all hierarchical structures is shown in Figure 6.2.

As you move downward through the structure in Figure 6.2, you see that a node may point to many others; that is, it may have multiple successors. Thus, there does not exist only a single way to iterate through the elements of a hierarchical structure.

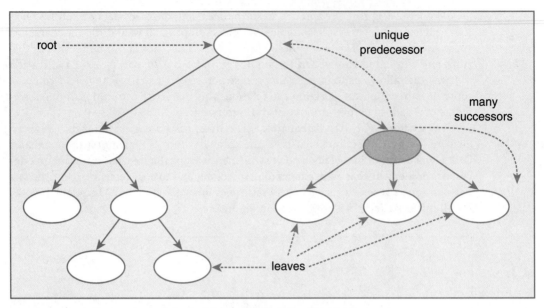

FIGURE 6.2 General model of a hierarchical data structure

As you move upward through the structure, every node, except the root, is connected to a single element; that is, it has a unique predecessor.

The linear structure of Figure 6.1 is a special case of the hierarchical structure of Figure 6.2 in which the number of successors of a node is limited to one. Thus, the hierarchical classification includes the linear structures, and mathematicians do not view linear and hierarchical data structures as distinct categories. However, in computer science, it is convenient to treat these groups as separate classes because, on certain types of problems, they display quite different performance characteristics.

Hierarchical structures are referred to as **trees**, and they are an extremely important form of data representation. There are many different types of tree structures, such as generalized trees, binary trees, and binary search trees, to name just a few. However, they all have the same basic structure shown in Figure 6.2. They differ only in such details as where in the tree we are permitted to do insertions, deletions, and retrievals and whether there are limits placed on the maximum number of successors of a node. Hierarchical data structures will be introduced in Chapter 7.

The third class of composite data type is the **graph**, and it represents the richest and most complex form of data representation. In a graph, there is a *many:many* relationship between elements in the collection. That is, there are no restrictions on the number of predecessors or successors of any element. Informally, we say that in a graph structure an element E can be connected to an arbitrary number of other elements, including itself, and an arbitrary number of other elements can connect to E. This general model for a graph is diagramed in Figure 6.3.

It is easy to see from Figure 6.3 that graphs subsume both the linear and hierarchical groupings, and from a mathematical point of view, it is really only necessary to identify and study this one classification. (The mathematics course that studies the

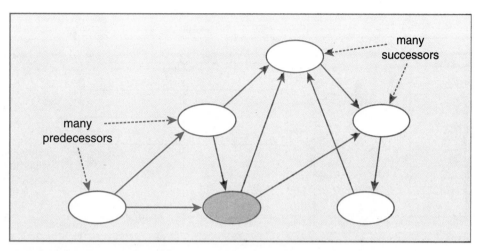

FIGURE 6.3 General model of a graph data structure

properties of these data structures is called *graph theory*.) However, as mentioned earlier, it is often useful to distinguish between these three composite structures because of their different uses and different performance characteristics. We will investigate the topic of graph structures in Chapter 8.

The fourth and final class of data structures is the **set**. In a set, there is no positional relationship between individual elements in the collection. There is no first element, no last element, no predecessor or successor, no root, and no leaves. Think of the elements of a set as having a *none:none* relationship with each other. Furthermore, duplicates are not allowed, so the set {1, 2, 2, 3, 3} should properly be written as {1, 2, 3}, which is identical to the sets {3, 2, 1} and {2, 1, 3}. If we were to reposition the elements in Figure 6.1, 6.2, or 6.3, we would end up with different linear, hierarchical, or graph structures. However, if we change the location of an element in a set, we would end up with the identical set. The only relationship shared by elements of a set structure is *membership*—they either do or do not belong to the same collection. The position of a given element is irrelevant.

Although sets are in widespread use, computer scientists more often use the closely related concept of a **table**, also called a **map**, to describe this type of position-independent data structure. In a table, the elements of the collection are usually expressed as pairs of values (K, V), where K is a unique **key field** and V is a **value field** associated with this key. The general model of a table structure is diagramed in Figure 6.4.

Access to elements in the table is done by providing a search key K* and determining if there is a (K, V) pair anywhere in the table in which the key field K matches the search key K*. If such a pair is found, then we return the value V associated with that key. If such a pair is not found, then the key K* is not a member of this table.

An example of this type of access would be a table containing student (ID, exam score) pairs. We do not care exactly where in the table any specific (ID, exam score) pair is located; we only want to input a specific student ID number and retrieve the exam score associated with this ID or find out that this ID number is not in the table. You will study tables and other forms of set structures in Chapter 8.

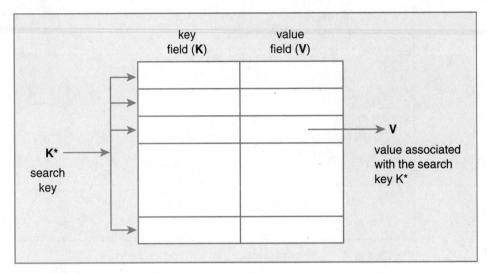

FIGURE 6.4 General model of a table data structure

These are the four classes of composite data types, or data structures, that we will be discussing. There is an enormous variety of data structures with very different characteristics, but they all fall into exactly one of the four groupings presented in this section.

6.2 LISTS

◆ 6.2.1 Introduction

This section introduces the **list** data structure. The list is the most general and most flexible of all linear structures. All other linear structures place restrictions on their usage, such as where you are permitted to do insertions, deletions, or retrievals. With a list, there are no such restrictions, and retrievals, insertions, and deletions may be done anywhere within the structure—beginning, middle, or end.

Formally, a list is an ordered collection of zero, one or more information units called **nodes**. Each node contains two fields: an **information field**, also called the **data field**, which we abbreviate I, and a **next field**, which represents an explicit way of identifying the unique successor of this node. (The type of the information field is not important and, for now, will be left unspecified.) A model of an n-element list L is shown in Figure 6.5. The symbol Λ (capital Greek lambda) is traditionally used to signify that there is no successor; that is, this is the last node in the list.

However, a word of caution is in order when looking at the model in Figure 6.5. This is a *logical,* or *conceptual,* view of a list, not an implementation model. The fact that this figure shows nodes connected to each other using arrows that point explicitly to their successor does not imply that the only way to implement a list is via pointers or references variables. Although references can be used to implement lists (and we will show many examples in later sections), they are not the only way. For

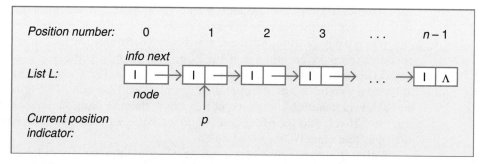

FIGURE 6.5 General model of a list structure

example, Section 6.2.3.1 will show an array-based implementation of a list. The key idea is that each node must explicitly identify its successor, but we are free to select how to implement that explicit identification.

◆ 6.2.2 Operations on Lists

Because lists are such general structures, there are an enormous number of possible operations we could choose to implement. Therefore, when selecting the methods to include in a list class, it is often necessary to have additional information about how client classes will use your list. That will allow you to select only the most useful and helpful operations. This section describes a fairly typical set of methods that operate on list objects; however, keep in mind that many others are possible.

When working with a list, we need to locate the node on which we wish to operate. For example, to delete a node, we must identify the specific node to be removed; to insert a new node, we must identify exactly where it will go—that is, between which two nodes it should be placed.

There are two ways to do this. The first is to use a **current position indicator**, also called a **cursor**. This is a variable that references, or points to, one of the nodes in the list, and its purpose is to identify the position in the list where the next operation will take place. This current position indicator is a part of the state information maintained for every list object. In Figure 6.5, the cursor p is referencing the second node in the list, and any method that operates on a single node will work on this element. For example, the call L.remove() might mean to delete the node in L currently referenced by the cursor p. When using a current position indicator, we must be sure that it points to the correct node. If not, we must reposition it before invoking the desired method.

The second way to implement list operations is by using the concept of **position numbers**, also called an **index**. Since every list has a first node and every node has a unique predecessor, there exists a well-defined numbering scheme for the nodes in a nonempty list L. Assign the first node in L the position number 0. Then, for every remaining node n in L, let position(n) = 1 + position(predecessor of n). This assigns the integer values 0, 1, 2, 3, . . . to the nodes, as shown in Figure 6.5. In a sense, this approach treats a list like a one-dimensional array, with position numbers serving the role of subscripts in an array. (However, unlike an array, we cannot directly access the list elements in O(1) time. We must iterate through the nodes in the list beginning with the first until we have reached the desired one, a linear time operation.)

When using position numbers, our list methods must include a parameter that specifies the position number of the node on which to work. For example, `L.re-move(3)` might mean to delete the fourth node in list L. (This assumes that L contains at least four nodes. If not, the operation is undefined.) `L.add(4, I)` might mean to insert a new node into L containing object I such that the position number of this new node is 4; that is, it is the fifth node. All nodes that come after this new node will have their position numbers increased by 1.

Both techniques—cursors and indexes—are used to implement list methods, and we will show examples of operations that use both approaches. The following examples assume that L is a list, I is an object of the type stored in the information field of the node, p is the current position indicator of L, and pos is an index value in the range $0 \leq pos <$ size of the list.

1. List methods based on the concept of a current position indicator p. To illustrate the behavior of these cursor-based methods, assume that list L and position indicator p currently have the following values:

For each method introduced, we describe the effect of this operation on this list L.

a. first(). Reset p so it refers to the first node in L. If L is empty, then reset p so that it is no longer pointing to any node in the list. When this happens, we say that p has been "moved off the list." The structure and content of L are unchanged. Executing the operation `L.first()` on the preceding list produces:

b. last(). Reset p so it refers to the last node in L. If L is empty, p is moved off the list. The structure and content of L are unchanged. Executing the operation `L.last()` on the list produces:

c. next(). Reset p so it refers to the successor of the node currently pointed at by p. If p points to the last node, this operation moves p off the list. The structure and content of the list are unchanged. After executing L.next(), the list will be in the following state:

```
L:     3 → 7 → 24 → 19
                ↑
                p
```

d. previous(). Reset p so it refers to the predecessor of the node currently pointed at by p. If p points to the first node, this operation moves p off the list. The structure and content of the list are unchanged. After executing L.previous(), the list will be in the following state:

```
L:     3 → 7 → 24 → 19
       ↑
       p
```

e. remove(). Delete the node referenced by the current position pointer p and reset p so it points to the successor of the node just deleted. If we delete the last node in the list, p is moved off the list. The size of the list is reduced by 1. After performing the operation L.remove(), we have:

```
L:     3 → 24 → 19
            ↑
            p
```

f. add(*I*). Create a new node containing object I in the information field. Add this new node as the predecessor of the node currently referenced by p and reset p to refer to the newly added node. The size of the list increases by 1. The call L.add(5) produces the following list:

```
L:     3 → 5 → 7 → 24 → 19
            ↑
            p
```

g. append(*I*). Create a new node containing object I in the information field. Add this new node to the end of the list. The size of the list is increased by 1, and p is reset to refer to the new node. The operation L.append(99) produces the following:

```
L:     3 → 7 → 24 → 19 → 99
                         ↑
                         p
```

h. get(). This method returns the information field of the node referenced by *p*. This method does not change the structure of the list or the position of *p*. If we perform the operation *L*.get(), the value returned by the function is 7.

i. set(*I*). This method changes the information field of the node referenced by *p* from its current value to the value *I*. This method does not change the position of *p*. The call *L*.set(35) produces the following new list:

$$L: \quad 3 \rightarrow 35 \rightarrow 24 \rightarrow 19$$
$$\uparrow$$
$$p$$

j. isOnList(). This Boolean function returns true if the current position indicator *p* is referencing one of the nodes in the list. If the indicator has been moved off the list, the method returns false. For example, the call *L*.isOnList() returns true.

2. List methods based on the concept of a position number.

To illustrate the behavior of our position number-based list methods, assume that this time we are starting with the following list *L*:

position number: 0   1   2   3   4

List L: 13 → 1 → 20 → 7 → 18
$$\uparrow$$
$$p$$

For each method introduced, we will describe its effect on this list *L*.

a. size(). This integer function returns the total number of nodes in the list *L*. Thus, the position numbers in the list will range from 0 to *L*.size()−1. The structure and content of the list are unchanged. In the preceding example, *L*.size() returns 5.

b. remove(*pos*). This method deletes the node whose position number is *pos*. The current position indicator *p* is reset to refer to the successor of the node just removed. If we removed the last node, *p* is moved off the list. The size of the list decreases by 1. Executing the method *L*.remove(3) produces:

position number: 0   1   2   3

L: 13 → 1 → 20 → 18
$$\uparrow$$
$$p$$

c. add(*pos, I*). This method creates a new node containing the object *I* in the information field. This new node is then inserted into the list so that its position number is *pos*. The current position indicator *p* is reset to point to this new node, and the size of the list increases by 1. Executing *L*.add(3, 30) produces the following:

```
         position number:   0    1    2    3    4    5

              L:    13 → 1 → 20 → 30 → 7 → 18
                                    ↑
                                    p
```

d. get(*pos*). This method returns the information field of the node whose position number is *pos*. The structure and content of the list as well as the current position pointer are unchanged. *L*.get(4) returns the value 18.

e. set(*pos, I*). This method changes the information field of the node whose position number is *pos* from its current value to the object *I*. The current position pointer *p* is unaffected. The call *L*.set(0, -44) produces the following structure:

```
         position number:   0    1    2    3    4

         List L:    -44 → 1 → 20 → 7 → 18
                            ↑
                            p
```

Figure 6.6 presents the specifications of a Java **interface** for a list data structure that includes the 15 operations just described. In the following section, we will develop two separate classes that both implement the interface of Figure 6.6.

```java
/**
 * This interface defines the operations that a List is expected to
 * provide. The operations that a list can support can be defined without
 * regard to the way in which the list is implemented.
 *
 * A list maintains an internal cursor that refers to the current
 * element in the list.
 */

public interface List {

    /**
     * Move the cursor to the first element in the list.
     *
```

(continued)

FIGURE 6.6 List interface

```
 * Preconditions:
 *     None.
 *
 * Postconditions:
 *     If the list is empty the cursor is moved off the list. Otherwise,
 *         the cursor is set to the first element in the list.
 *     The list's structure and content are unchanged.
 */

public void first();
/**
 * Move the cursor to the last element in the list.
 *
 * Preconditions:
 *     None.
 *
 * Postconditions:
 *     If the list is empty the cursor is moved off the list. Otherwise,
 *         the cursor is set to the last element in the list.
 *     The list's structure and content are unchanged.
 */

public void last();

/**
 * Move the cursor to the next element in the list.
 *
 * Preconditions:
 *     The cursor is on the list.
 *
 * Postconditions:
 *     If the cursor is at the end of the list the cursor is moved off
 *         the list. Otherwise the cursor is set to the next element.
 *     The list's structure and content are unchanged.
 */

public void next();

/**
 * Move the cursor to the previous node in the list.
 *
 * Preconditions:
 *     The cursor is on the list.
 *
 * Postconditions:
 *     If the cursor is at the front of the list the cursor is moved off
 *         the list. Otherwise the cursor is moved to the previous element.
 *     The list's structure and content are unchanged.
 */

public void previous();
```

FIGURE 6.6 List interface *(continued)*

```
/**
 * Remove the element the cursor is referring to.
 *
 * Preconditions:
 *    The cursor is on the list.
 *
 * Postconditions:
 *    The element the cursor is referring to is removed.
 *    The size of the list is decreased by 1.
 *    If the element that was removed was the last element in the list,
 *        the cursor is moved off the list. Otherwise the cursor is
 *        moved to the removed element's successor.
 */

public void remove();

/**
 * Remove the element at the specified position in the list.
 *
 * Preconditions:
 *    position >= 0 and position < size().
 *
 * Postconditions:
 *    The element at the specified position is removed from the list.
 *    Elements at positions greater than the specified position
 *        (if any) are shifted to the left by one position.
 *    The size of the list is decreased by 1.
 *    If the element that was removed was the last element in the list,
 *        the cursor is moved off the list. Otherwise the cursor is
 *        moved to the removed element's successor.
 *
 * @param position the position in the list where the element will
 *    be placed.
 */

public void remove( int position );

/**
 * Add a new element at the position indicated by the cursor.
 *
 * Preconditions:
 *    The list is empty or the cursor is on the list.
 *
 * Postconditions:
 *    If the list is empty, the element becomes the only element
 *        in the list. Otherwise the element is added at the
 *        position specified by the cursor.
 *    Elements at positions greater than or equal to the current
 *        position of the cursor (if any) are shifted to the right by
 *        one position.
 *    The size of the list has increased by 1.
```

(continued)

FIGURE 6.6 List interface *(continued)*

```
 *      The cursor refers to the element added to the list.
 *
 * @param element the element to be added to the list.
 */

public void add( Object element );

/**
 * Add a new element at the specified position in the list.
 *
 * Preconditions:
 *      position >= 0 and position <= size().
 *
 * Postconditions:
 *      The element is added at the specified position in the list.
 *      Elements at positions greater than or equal to the specified
 *         position (if any) are shifted to the right by one position.
 *      The size of the list is increased by 1.
 *      The cursor refers to the element added to the list.
 *
 * @param position the position in the list where the element will
 *      be placed.
 * @param element the element to be added to the list.
 */

public void add( int position, Object element );

/**
 * Add a new element to the end of the list.
 *
 * Preconditions:
 *      None.
 *
 * Postconditions:
 *      The specified element is the last element in the list.
 *      The size of the list is increased by 1.
 *      The cursor refers to the element added to the list.
 *      The other elements in the list (if any) are unchanged.
 */

public void append( Object element );

/**
 * Returns the element that the cursor is referring to.
 *
 * Preconditions:
 *      The cursor is on the list.
 *
```

FIGURE 6.6 List interface *(continued)*

```
 *  Postconditions:
 *      The list's structure, content, and cursor are unchanged.
 */

public Object get();

/**
 * Returns the element stored in the specified position in the list.
 *
 * Preconditions:
 *      position >= 0 and position < size().
 *
 * Postconditions:
 *      The list's structure, content, and cursor are unchanged.
 *
 * @param position the location of the element to be retrieved.
 */

public Object get( int position );

/**
 * Sets the element stored at the location identified by the cursor.
 *
 * Preconditions:
 *      The cursor is on the list.
 *
 * Postconditions:
 *      The element at the current cursor position is changed to the
 *          specified value.
 *      The list's structure and cursor are unchanged.
 *
 * @param element the element to place in the list.
 */

public void set( Object element );

/**
 * Sets the element stored in the specified position in the list.
 *
 * Preconditions:
 *      position >= 0 and position < size().
 *
 * Postconditions:
 *      The element at the specified position in the list is changed
 *          to the specified value.
 *      The list's structure and cursor are unchanged.
 *
 * @param position the location of the element to be changed.
```

(continued)

FIGURE 6.6 List interface *(continued)*

```
     * @param element the element to place in the specified location
     *     of the list.
     */

    public void set( int position, Object element );

    /**
     * Return the number of elements in the list.
     *
     * Preconditions:
     *     None.
     *
     * Postconditions:
     *     The list's structure, content, and cursor are unchanged.
     */

    public int size();

    /**
     * Determine if the cursor is on the list.
     *
     * Preconditions:
     *     None.
     *
     * Postconditions:
     *     The list's structure, content, and cursor are unchanged.
     */

    public boolean isOnList();

} // List
```

FIGURE 6.6 List interface *(continued)*

The methods included in Figure 6.6 are certainly not the only ones we could have selected. On the contrary, it is rather easy to think of additional possibilities—for example, *L*.swap(pos1, pos2), which interchanges the two nodes in *L* located at positions *pos1* and *pos2*, or *L*.printList(), which prints the contents of the information field of every node in *L* in order from first to last. Whether these or any other methods should be included in our interface depends on how our lists will be used.

However, the interface in Figure 6.6 does include most important list operations, and it will allow us to investigate some interesting implementations of lists.

◆ 6.2.3 Implementation of Lists

There are two quite different ways to implement the interface of Figure 6.6: the **array-based** and the **reference-based** methods. This section describes both techniques.

6.2.3.1 An Array-Based Implementation

To implement the interface in Figure 6.6, we can use two one-dimensional arrays. The first is an array of objects that stores the information field. The second is an array of integers to hold the next field. Thus, the elements stored in the same position of these two arrays, taken together, represent a single node in our list.

If we assume that the information field contains values of type `Object`, then the state information needed for the array representation of a list is shown in Figure 6.7.

```
// the initial size of the two arrays
private static final int INITIAL_SIZE = . . . ;

// a constant used to indicate a null value
private static final int OFF_LIST = -1;

// here are the two arrays that will implement the list
private Object data [];   // the information field
private int next[];       // the link field

// the state variables of the list object
private int head;         // reference to the first node in the list
private int tail;         // reference to the last node in the list
private int count;        // number of nodes in the list
private int cursor;       // the current position indicator
```

FIGURE 6.7 Declarations for the array representation of a list

The first array declared in Figure 6.7, called `data`, stores the information field, while the second array, `next`, holds the next field. This field is implemented as an integer value that identifies the row index of the successor of the current node. The constant −1 can be used to represent the quantity Λ because the row indexes of Java arrays always begin at 0. The variable `head` contains the row index of the first node in the list, and `cursor` represents the current position indicator p shown in Figure 6.5. To make our code more efficient, we added two additional state variables: `tail`, which points to the last node in the list, and `count`, which tells us how many nodes are in the list.

Thus, the four-node list of Figure 6.8a might be implemented in array form as shown in Figure 6.8b, assuming each array contains seven elements and the information field is integer objects.

In Figure 6.8b, the variable `head` contains a 1, indicating that the first node of the list is stored in row 1 of the `data` array. Row 1 contains the integer value 103, and row 1 of `next` contains a 4, indicating that the second node of the list is located in row 4, and so forth. The last node of the list has a −1 in the next field to indicate the end of the list. Therefore, the value of `tail` is 2, the row that contains the last node.

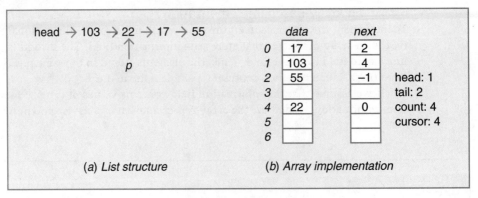

FIGURE 6.8 Array implementation of a list

To use this method properly, we also need a way to indicate that a specific row of the array is empty and available for use, such as rows 3, 5, and 6 in Figure 6.8b. Otherwise, when implementing an operation such as add, which creates a new node, we have no way of knowing if a row is or is not occupied and can hold this new node. Similarly, when deleting a node, we need a way to indicate that a row previously in use is now free and available for future allocation.

To keep track of the free rows in these two arrays, we will use the idea of an **available space list**. This is a linked list of nodes (i.e., rows of the array) that are empty and available for use. A reference to the first node of this available space list is stored in an instance variable called availHead. Thus, we must add the following declaration to the state information being maintained for our list object:

```
private int availHead;    // pointer to the head of a list of
                          //    available array slots
```

The available rows in our array are linked by the next fields of the empty nodes. Thus, in our array-based implementation, there are two "intertwined" lists: a linked list of data items beginning at the variable head and a linked list of available cells beginning at the variable availHead. Of course, the constructor must initialize the available space list whenever a new list is created. It must be initialized to the state shown in Figure 6.9 in which no data are stored in the array and every row of the array is marked as available. (The symbol — means that the value stored in that location is immaterial.)

	data	next	
0	–	1	
1	–	2	
2	–	3	availHead: 0
3	–	4	head: –1
4	–	5	tail: –1
5	–	6	count: 0
6	–	–1	cursor: –1

FIGURE 6.9 Initial state of the array-based implementation of a list

To add a new node to the empty list in Figure 6.9, we remove the first node from the available space list (the row referenced by availHead, 0 in this example), and we use that entry to hold the information field of this newly allocated node. We also re-set availHead to the successor of the node just removed, node 1 in this example. (Note: If availHead ever becomes −1, it means that we are "out of memory," and all rows of the array are in use. We will need to resize our arrays.) To delete a node, we remove the node from the list and add the row just recovered to the front of the available space list.

Figure 6.10 shows the list diagramed in Figure 6.8a, but this time including the links required to implement the available space list.

FIGURE 6.10 Array implementation of a list, including the available space list

Figure 6.11 is the code for the class ArrayList, an array-based implementation of the list interface of Figure 6.6. This implementation utilizes the declarations in Figure 6.7 along with the available space list management techniques described in the preceding paragraphs. If our arrays become full, they are dynamically expanded to double their current size, and all existing list elements are copied into this new structure.

```
/**
 * The following is an array-based implementation of the List interface.
 */

public class ArrayList implements List {

    // Used to mark an empty position in the array
    public static final int OFF_LIST = -1;

    // Initial size of the arrays
    private static final int INITIAL_SIZE = 20;

    private Object data[];   // Elements in the list
    private int next[];      // Links to the next element
```

(continued)

FIGURE 6.11 Array-based implementation of the List interface of Figure 6.7

```
    private int count;      // Number of elements in the list
    private int head;       // The start of the list
    private int tail;       // The end of the list
    private int cursor;     // Current node

    private int availHead;  // Head of the available list

    /**
     * Constructor for the list
     */

    public ArrayList() {
        // Initialize state
        data = new Object[ INITIAL_SIZE ];
        next = new int[ INITIAL_SIZE ];

        count = 0;
        head = OFF_LIST;
        tail = OFF_LIST;
        cursor = OFF_LIST;

        // Create the free list
        for ( int i = 0; i < next.length; i++ ) {
            next[ i ] = i + 1;
        }

        // "null" at the end of the list
        next[ next.length - 1 ] = OFF_LIST;
    }

    /**
     * Move the cursor to the first element in the list.
     *
     * Preconditions:
     *     None.
     *
     * Postconditions:
     *     If the list is empty the cursor is moved off the list. Otherwise,
     *         the cursor is set to the first element in the list.
     *     The list's structure and content are unchanged.
     */

    public void first() {
        cursor = head;
    }

    /**
     * Move the cursor to the last element in the list.
     *
```

FIGURE 6.11 Array-based implementation of the List interface of Figure 6.7 *(continued)*

```
    * Preconditions:
    *    None.
    *
    * Postconditions:
    *    If the list is empty the cursor is moved off the list. Otherwise,
    *        the cursor is set to the last element in the list.
    *    The list's structure and content are unchanged.
    */

public void last() {
   cursor = tail;
}

/**
 * Move the cursor to the next element in the list.
 *
 * Preconditions:
 *    The cursor is on the list.
 *
 * Postconditions:
 *    If the cursor is at the end of the list the cursor is moved off
 *        the list. Otherwise the cursor is set to the next element.
 *    The list's structure and content are unchanged.
 */

public void next() {
   cursor = next[ cursor ];
}

/**
 * Move the cursor to the previous node in the list.
 *
 * Preconditions:
 *    The cursor is on the list.
 *
 * Postconditions:
 *    If the cursor is at the front of the list the cursor is moved off
 *        the list. Otherwise the cursor is moved to the previous
 *        element.
 *    The list's structure and content are unchanged.
 */

public void previous() {
   cursor = findPrevious( cursor );
}

/**
 * Remove the element the cursor is referring to.
```

(continued)

FIGURE 6.11 Array-based implementation of the `List` interface of Figure 6.7 *(continued)*

```
 *
 * Preconditions:
 *    The cursor is on the list.
 *
 * Postconditions:
 *    The element the cursor is referring to is removed.
 *    The size of the list has decreased by 1.
 *    If the element that was removed was the last element in the list,
 *        the cursor is moved off the list. Otherwise the cursor is
 *        moved to the removed element's successor.
 */

public void remove() {
    removeElement( cursor, findPrevious( cursor ) );
}


/**
 * Remove the element at the specified position in the list.
 *
 * Preconditions:
 *   position >= 0 and position < size().
 *
 * Postconditions:
 *    The element at the specified position is removed from the list.
 *    Elements at positions greater than the specified position
 *        (if any) are shifted to the left by one position.
 *    The size of the list is decreased by 1.
 *    If the element that was removed was the last element in the list,
 *        the cursor is moved off the list. Otherwise the cursor is
 *        moved to the removed element's successor.
 *
 * @param position the position in the list where the element will
 *     be placed.
 */

public void remove( int position ) {
    int target = head;
    int before = OFF_LIST;

    // Find the node that contains the element we wish to
    // delete and the node immediately before it.
    while ( position > 0 ) {
        before = target;
        target = next[ target ];
        position = position - 1;
    }

    // Target is now pointing to the node we wish to remove
    removeElement( target, before );
}
```

FIGURE 6.11 Array-based implementation of the `List` interface of Figure 6.7 *(continued)*

```
/**
 * Add a new element at the position indicated by the cursor.
 *
 * Preconditions:
 *   The list is empty or the cursor is on the list.
 *
 * Postconditions:
 *    If the list is empty, the element becomes the only element
 *       in the list. Otherwise the element is added at the
 *       position specified by the cursor.
 *    Elements at positions greater than or equal to the current
 *       position of the cursor (if any) are shifted to the right by
 *       one position.
 *    The size of the list has increased by 1.
 *    The cursor refers to the element added to the list.
 *
 * @param element the element to be added to the list.
 */

public void add( Object element ) {
    int before = findPrevious( cursor );
    int after = cursor;

    // Add the node to the list
    addElement( element, before, after );
}

/**
 * Add a new element at the specified position in the list.
 *
 * Preconditions:
 *    position >= 0 and position <= size().
 *
 * Postconditions:
 *    The element is added at the specified position in the list.
 *    Elements at positions greater than or equal to the specified
 *       position (if any) are shifted to the right by one position.
 *    The size of the list is increased by 1.
 *    The cursor refers to the element added to the list.
 *
 * @param position the position in the list where the element will
 *    be placed.
 * @param element the element to be added to the list.
 */

public void add( int position, Object element ) {
    int after;
    int before;
```

(continued)

FIGURE 6.11 Array-based implementation of the `List` interface of Figure 6.7 *(continued)*

```
      // Set before and after to the appropriate values
      if ( position == 0 ) {
         before = OFF_LIST;
         after = head;
      }
      else {
         before = findPrevious( positionToIndex( position ) );
         after = next[ before ];
      }

      // Add the node to the list
      addElement( element, before, after );
   }

   /**
    * Add a new element to the end of the list.
    *
    * Preconditions:
    *    None.
    *
    * Postconditions:
    *    The specified element is the last element in the list.
    *    The size of the list is increased by 1.
    *    The cursor refers to the element added to the list.
    *    The other elements in the list (if any) are unchanged.
    */

   public void append( Object element ) {
      // Cursor is always set to the node that is added
      cursor = nextOpenIndex();

      // Store the data in the array
      data[ cursor ] = element;
      next[ cursor ] = OFF_LIST;

      if ( tail == OFF_LIST ) {
         // If the list is empty we need to set head
         head = cursor;
      }
      else {
         // There is a tail and it should refer to the element just added
         next[ tail ] = cursor;
      }

      // Tail always refers to the element added
      tail = cursor;

      // One more element in the list
      count = count + 1;
   }
```

FIGURE 6.11 Array-based implementation of the List interface of Figure 6.7 *(continued)*

```
/**
 * Returns the element that the cursor is referring to.
 *
 * Preconditions:
 *    The cursor is on the list.
 *
 * Postconditions:
 *    The list's structure, content, and cursor are unchanged.
 */

public Object get() {
   return data[ cursor ];
}


/**
 * Returns the element stored in the specified position in the list.
 *
 * Preconditions:
 *    position >= 0 and position < size().
 *
 * Postconditions:
 *    The list's structure, content, and cursor are unchanged.
 *
 * @param position the location of the element to be retrieved.
 */

public Object get( int position ) {
   return data[ positionToIndex( position ) ];
}


/**
 * Sets the element stored at the location identified by the cursor.
 *
 * Preconditions:
 *    The cursor is on the list.
 *
 * Postconditions:
 *    The element at the current cursor position is changed to the
 *       specified value.
 *    The list's structure and cursor are unchanged.
 *
 * @param element the element to place in the list.
 */

public void set( Object element ) {
   data[ cursor ] = element;
}


/**
 * Sets the element stored in the specified position in the list.
```
(continued)

FIGURE 6.11 Array-based implementation of the List interface of Figure 6.7 *(continued)*

```
 *
 * Preconditions:
 *     position >= 0 and position < size().
 *
 * Postconditions:
 *     The element at the specified position in the list is changed
 *         to the specified value.
 *     The list's structure and cursor are unchanged.
 *
 * @param position the location of the element to be changed.
 * @param element the element to place in the specified location
 *     of the list.
 */

public void set( int position, Object element ) {
    data[ positionToIndex( position ) ] = element;
}

/**
 * Return the number of elements in the list.
 *
 * Preconditions:
 *     None.
 *
 * Postconditions:
 *     The list's structure, content, and cursor are unchanged.
 */

public int size() {
    return count;
}

/**
 * Determine if the cursor is on the list.
 *
 * Preconditions:
 *     None.
 *
 * Postconditions:
 *     The list's structure, content and cursor are unchanged.
 */

public boolean isOnList() {
    return cursor != OFF_LIST;
}

/**
 * Return a string representation of this list.
 *
```

FIGURE 6.11 Array-based implementation of the List interface of Figure 6.7 *(continued)*

```
 * @return a string representation of this list.
 */

public String toString() {
    // Use a StringBuffer so we don't create a new
    // string each time we append
    StringBuffer retVal = new StringBuffer();

    retVal = retVal.append( "[ " );

    // Step through the list and use toString on the elements to
    // determine their string representation
    for ( int cur = head; cur != OFF_LIST; cur = next[ cur ] ) {
        retVal = retVal.append( data[ cur ] + " " );
    }

    retVal = retVal.append( "]" );

    // Convert the StringBuffer to a string
    return retVal.toString();
}

private void addElement( Object element, int before, int after ) {
    // Cursor is always set to the node that is added
    cursor = nextOpenIndex();

    // Store the data in the array
    data[ cursor ] = element;
    next[ cursor ] = after;

    // Is this a new head?
    if ( before == OFF_LIST ) {
        head = cursor;
    }
    else {
        next[ before ] = cursor;
    }

    // Is this a new tail?
    if ( after == OFF_LIST ) {
        tail = cursor;
    }

    // One more element in the list
    count = count + 1;
}

private int findPrevious( int index ) {
    int retVal = OFF_LIST;
```

(continued)

FIGURE 6.11 Array-based implementation of the List interface of Figure 6.7 *(continued)*

```
      for ( int cur = head;
            cur != OFF_LIST && index != cur;
            cur = next[ cur ] ) {
         retVal = cur;
      }
      return retVal;
   }


   /**
    * Return the index of the specified element in the list.
    *
    * @param position the position of the element.
    *
    * @return the index of the element in the list.
    */

   public int positionToIndex( int position ) {
      int retVal = head;
      while ( position > 0 ) {
         retVal = next[ retVal ];
         position = position - 1;
      }
      return retVal;
   }

   private void removeElement( int target, int before ) {
      // Cursor is always set to the next element
      cursor = next[ target ];

      // Write over the old data
      data[ target ] = null;

      if ( before == OFF_LIST ) {
         // We are deleting the head
         head = next[ target ];
      }
      else {
         // We are somewhere in the middle of the list
         next[ before ] = next[ target ];
      }

      // Did we just delete the tail?
      if ( target == tail ) {
         tail = before;
      }

      // One less item in the list
      count = count - 1;
      // Add the open space to the garbage list
      next[ target ] = availHead;
      availHead = target;
   }
```

FIGURE 6.11 Array-based implementation of the List interface of Figure 6.7 *(continued)*

```
/**
 * Return the index of the next free location in the array.
 *
 * @return the index of the next free location in the array.
 */

private int nextOpenIndex() {
    int retVal;

    // If the free space is gone - expand the arrays
    if ( availHead == OFF_LIST ) {
        expand();
    }

    // Take the location at the front of the list
    retVal = availHead;
    availHead = next[ availHead ];

    // Return the index
    return retVal;
}


/**
 * Double the capacity of the arrays that hold the data and the
 * links.
 */

private void expand() {
    // Make the new arrays twice the size of the old arrays
    Object newData[] = new Object[ data.length * 2 ];
    int newNext[] = new int[ next.length * 2 ];

    // Copy the contents of the old arrays to the new arrays
    for ( int i = 0; i < data.length; i = i + 1 ) {
        newData[ i ] = data[ i ];
        newNext[ i ] = next[ i ];
    }

    // Add the empty space to the available list
    for ( int i = data.length; i < newData.length; i++ ) {
        newNext[ i ] = availHead;
        availHead = i;
    }

    // Start using the new arrays
    data = newData;
    next = newNext;
}

} // ArrayList
```

FIGURE 6.11 Array-based implementation of the List interface of Figure 6.7 *(continued)*

It is easy to determine the complexity of the array-based methods in Figure 6.11. For example, the default constructor initializes the next field of each row of the array so that it points to its successor in the available space list, as shown in Figure 6.9. Thus, the complexity of the default constructor is O(M), where M = next.length, the number of rows in the next array. The method size() is O(1) because one of the state variables maintained for every list object is the number of nodes in the list. Thus, size() simply returns this value. Note that if count were not an instance variable of lists, then we would have to explicitly count the number of nodes in the list beginning from head, an O(N) operation, where N is the number of nodes in the list. Keeping this additional information allows us to significantly improve the efficiency of the size() method.

To locate the predecessor of a node n, we start at the head of the list and search until we come to a node whose successor is n. In the average case, the method will have to traverse N/2 nodes; in the worst case, N. Thus, any method that needs to locate the predecessor of a node, such as previous(), add(I), and add(pos, I), must be O(N).

The get() method, which returns the value of the node pointed at by the cursor, takes O(1) time, since we already have the reference to the desired node. However, implementing the position number-based equivalent, get(pos), requires us to locate the pos^{th} node in the list, beginning from head. This takes O(N) time in the worst case.

Figure 6.12 summarizes the time complexity of the methods in the ArrayList class in Figure 6.11.

Notice that moving forward through the list (next()) is much more efficient than moving backward (previous()), since we maintain pointers in only the forward direction. Also notice that retrieving or changing the current node (get(), set(I)) is faster than either inserting a node (add(I)) or deleting a node (remove()). Again, this

Method	Worst-Case Time Complexity
constructor	O(M), where M is the number of rows in the array
first()	O(1)
last()	O(1)
next()	O(1)
previous()	O(N), where N is the number of nodes in the list
remove()	O(N)
remove(pos)	O(N)
add(I)	O(N)
add(pos, I)	O(N)
append(I)	O(1)
get()	O(1)
get(pos)	O(N)
set(I)	O(1)
set(pos, I)	O(N)
size	O(1)
isOnList()	O(1)
toString()	O(N)

FIGURE 6.12 Time complexity of the list methods of Figure 6.11

is because additions and deletions require us to first locate the predecessor of a node, a linear time operation. Thus, the implementation in Figure 6.11 might be reasonable if our primary needs are moving forward through a list retrieving and/or changing the current node.

However, the array-based implementation of Figure 6.11 is not that widely used because it suffers from two problems. First, an array is a fixed-sized data structure whose size, once created, cannot be changed. Looking back at the implementation in Figure 6.11, we see the following constant declaration:

```
private static final int INITIAL_SIZE = 20;
```

The number of rows in our two one-dimensional arrays must be constant, 20 in this example. As long as there are fewer than 21 nodes, the methods of Figure 6.11 work just fine. However, if we attempt to add a 21st node, there is no room. We can choose to treat this condition as a fatal error. Alternatively, we can use the Java exception mechanism that will be introduced in Chapter 10. Another possibility, the one used in class ArrayList, is to resize our arrays dynamically. However, keep in mind that this can be time-consuming, as we must initialize the available space list of the new array and copy all existing nodes into the new structure. For each node copied, we must get space for it from the available space list and then call an insert method to properly place it into the new array. In total, these steps can consume a good deal of time. (With the 20-element arrays of Figure 6.11, time is obviously not a problem. However, our list could have tens or hundreds of thousands of nodes, and this resizing could cause a slowdown.)

An even less desirable solution is to make the original arrays so large that they never need to be resized. However, we may not always have a good idea of the maximum number of nodes that will be stored in the list, and creating huge arrays wastes a great deal of memory if it holds only a few nodes.

A second and more serious problem with ArrayList is the available space list. Specifically, the programmer is responsible for all aspects of maintaining and managing this structure. They must initialize this list. Every time an insertion is done, they must explicitly allocate space for the new node, and after every deletion, they must return the newly deleted node to the available space list. They must even detect and handle "out-of-memory" conditions. This is foolish and unnecessary because Java already includes a memory management system that provides these operations automatically via the new command (to allocate space) and the garbage collector (to return space). The methods in ArrayList duplicate work already done.

The next section presents a reference-based implementation of lists that solves these two problems.

6.2.3.2 A Reference-Based Implementation

This section shows how to use reference variables rather than arrays to implement the list interface of Figure 6.6, and it demonstrates the superiority of this approach over the array-based implementation just presented.

For our reference-based implementation, we will use a class, called LinkedNode, to specify the structure of a single node in our list. Each node will include the same two fields we have been using all along, namely, data and next. These are both implemented as private instance variables, so the class also includes two accessor methods, getData() and getNext(), and two mutator methods, setData() and setNext(). The LinkedNode class is shown in Figure 6.13.

```java
/**
 * This class represents the nodes in a singly linked list.
 */

public class LinkedNode {

    private Object data; // The data stored in this node
    private LinkedNode next; // The next node in the data structure

    /**
     * Default constructor for the LinkedNode
     */

    public LinkedNode() {
        this( null, null );
    }

    /**
     * Construct a node given the info and next references.
     *
     * @param newData the data to be associated with this node.
     * @param newNext a reference to the next node in the list.
     */

    public LinkedNode( Object newData, LinkedNode newNext ) {
        data = newData;
        next = newNext;
    }

    /**
     * Return the data stored in this node.
     *
     * Preconditions:
     *     None.
     *
     * Postconditions:
     *     The node is unchanged.
     *
     * @returns a reference to the data stored in this node.
     */

    public Object getData() {
        return data;
    }
```

FIGURE 6.13 LinkedNode class

```
    /**
     * Return a reference to the next node in the data structure.
     *
     * Preconditions:
     *     None.
     *
     * Postconditions:
     *     The node is unchanged.
     *
     * @return a reference to the next Node in the list, or null if this
     *     node has no successor.
     */

    public LinkedNode getNext() {
        return next;
    }

    /**
     * Set the data associated with this node.
     *
     * Preconditions:
     *     None.
     *
     * Postconditions:
     *     The data associated with this node has been changed.
     *
     * @param newData the data to be associated with this node.
     */

    public void setData( Object newData ) {
        data = newData;
    }

    /**
     * Set the reference to the next node.
     *
     * Preconditions:
     *     None.
     *
     * Postconditions:
     *     The reference to the next node has been changed.
     *
     * @param newNext the reference to the next node in the data structure.
     */

    public void setNext( LinkedNode newNext ) {
        next = newNext;
    }

} // LinkedNode
```

FIGURE 6.13 LinkedNode class *(continued)*

The state variables needed for our reference-based implementation are (a) a variable head that points to the first node in the list and (b) a current position indicator called cursor. The default constructor initializes both of these variables to null to create an empty list. In addition to these two variables, we can add any state information that will help improve the efficiency of our new implementation. For example, we might wish to keep a tail pointer that points to the node at the end of the list, as we did in Figure 6.7, and we can include a tally of the total number of nodes in the list. We have chosen to include both of these state variables in our implementation. The declarations for the reference-based implementation of our list interface, called LinkedList, are shown in Figure 6.14. They use the node structure defined by the LinkedNode class of Figure 6.13.

```
public class LinkedList implements List {

    private int count;          // The number of nodes in the list
    private LinkedNode head;     // The first node in the list
    private LinkedNode tail;     // The last node in the list
    private LinkedNode cursor;   // The current node in the list

    // The public methods go here
```

FIGURE 6.14 Declarations for a reference-based implementation of a list

Let's go through the reference-based implementation of some of the methods in the list interface of Figure 6.6. The first method we will discuss is add(I). It creates a new node containing I in the information field and inserts this new node into the list as the predecessor of the node pointed at by cursor. An obvious precondition is that the cursor is not off the list. Here are the starting conditions:

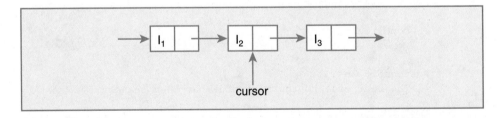

To insert the new node into its proper place, we must carry out the following algorithm. For each step in the algorithm, we give the Java code to accomplish it and provide a picture that shows the state of the list at this point in the addition process.

1. Locate the predecessor of the node referenced by cursor. This requires iterating through the list beginning at head. Set the reference variable before to point to the predecessor. (We will see exactly how to implement this operation shortly.)

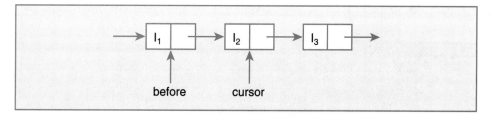

2. Allocate space for a new node containing I in the information field. This new node is referenced by the variable `temp`:

```
LinkedNode temp = new LinkedNode(I, null);
```

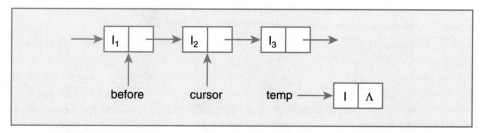

3. Set the next field of `temp` to refer to the node pointed at by `cursor`. If `before` is `null`, we are adding the new node at the beginning of the list. In this case, we must update the variable `head`.

```
temp.next = cursor;
if (before == null) head = temp;
```

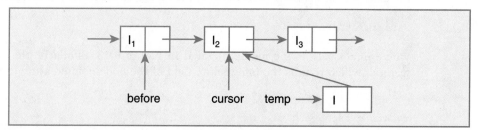

4. Reset the next field of the node referenced by `before` to point to `temp`.

```
before.next = temp;
```

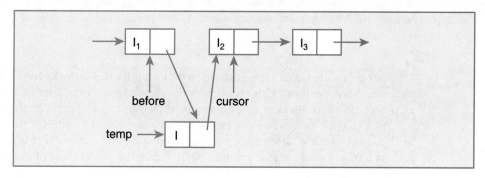

5. Finally, reset `cursor` to point to `temp` and update the node count by 1.

```
cursor = temp;
count++;
```

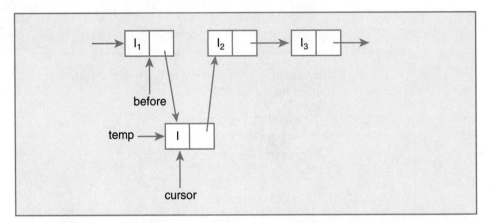

The `add()` method is now complete. We have added the new node in its proper spot, updated the current position indicator, and tallied that one more node has been inserted into the list. In addition, if the new node was added at the beginning of the list, we have reset `head`. The time complexity of this operation is O(N) because step 1 requires us to traverse the list to locate the predecessor of the node referenced by `cursor`.

The complexity of many of the methods in our reference-based implementation is O(1) because of the existence of the cursor. For example, `setData(I)`, which resets the data field of the node pointed at by the cursor, is implemented in a single line:

```
cursor.setData(I);
```

where `setData()` is the method shown in Figure 6.13. Similarly, the `getData()` method, which returns the information field of the node pointed at by the cursor, is O(1):

```
return cursor.getData();
```

Another reason for the O(1) behavior of many of the methods is the state information we added to our class. For example, in Figure 6.14, we included a state variable `tail` that references the last node of the list. Therefore, the method `last()`, which resets the cursor to point to the last element, also requires only one line of code:

```
cursor = tail;
```

Without this state variable, we would need to iterate through the list to locate the end—an O(N) operation. This shows how the clever selection of state information for an object can speed up the implementation of methods that operate on this object.

As a slightly more complex example, let's develop the code for the `remove()` method. This method deletes the node pointed at by the cursor. This is not quite as easy as it may sound because we must again locate the predecessor of the node referenced by cursor to reset its next field. This is identical to the operation that was carried out in step 1 of the add() method described earlier. Now we will show how it is done.

Unfortunately, the implementation of the LinkedNode class includes only a single pointer to the successor of a node. Thus, to locate the predecessor of cursor, we must traverse the entire list until we come to a node whose next field equals cursor. Only then will we be able to implement remove(). This operation is the method previous() included in the List interface of Figure 6.6. The code for previous() is given in Figure 6.15.

```
public void previous() {
    cursor = findPrevious();
}


private LinkedNode findPrevious() {
    LinkedNode prev = null; // Where we are in the list

    // If the cursor is off the list or the cursor is at the
    // head, there is no previous node.

    if ( cursor != null && cursor != head ) {
      prev = head;

        // Keep looking until we find the node whose next reference
        // is equal to the current node

        while ( prev.getNext() != cursor ) {
            prev = prev.getNext();
        }
    }

    // The variable prev is now referring to the previous node

    return prev;
}
```

FIGURE 6.15 Code for the method previous()

There are aspects of the code in Figure 6.15 that represent common programming pitfalls when working with lists. The first is to forget to consider the possibility of an **empty list**. If a list can be empty and you do not check for this condition, then you might attempt to dereference the null pointer—a fatal error. That is the reason we checked for the condition (cursor != **null**) in Figure 6.15.

Another common problem is an **off-by-one error**. With this error, you are iterating through a list but traverse one node too few or one node too many. In Figure 6.15, if the criterion to terminate the loop was improperly written as **while** (prev != cursor) rather than **while** (prev.getNext() != cursor), we would incorrectly go one step beyond the predecessor node. Whenever you iterate through a list, be sure to check that your loop terminates with the pointer in exactly the position you want.

One final pitfall is to forget to check for **special cases** that require unique handling. We have already mentioned one common special case: the empty list. Another example would be a code fragment that compares all pairs of adjacent list nodes to see if they are equal. This operation only makes sense if the list contains at least two nodes. So, we must explicitly check that the list length is greater than or equal to two. Other special cases that may need to be checked include:

◆ Operating on the **first node** in a list. This is special because the first node does not have a predecessor and because it is referenced by the special pointer value called `head`. Note that in Figure 6.15, we checked the special case of (`cursor !=` `head`) because the first node does not have a predecessor.

◆ Operating on the **last node** in a list. This is special because the last node does not have a successor and because it is referenced by the special pointer value called `tail`.

Thus, as you can see in the previous examples, there are a number of potential sources of error when working with references, and you must carefully handle each of the following conditions to ensure that your code works properly in all circumstances:

◆ Empty lists

◆ Off-by-one errors in list traversals

◆ Working on the first element of a list

◆ Working on the last element of a list

◆ Other special cases for this specific operation

Now that we have written and analyzed `previous()`, we can finish the implementation of `remove()`. Figure 6.16 shows the code for the `remove()` method. Its complexity is O(N) because it calls `findPrevious()`, which is O(N), to locate the predecessor of the node to be deleted.

Figure 6.17 shows a reference-based `LinkedList` class that implements the `List` interface of Figure 6.6. This implementation utilizes the declarations that were shown in Figures 6.13 and 6.14.

The time complexity of the methods in Figure 6.17 are the same as those of the array-based implementation in Figure 6.11 except for the constructor, which is O(1) rather than O(M). This is because our reference-based implementation does not have to create or initialize an available space list when the structure is created.

Although the efficiency of this new implementation has not changed significantly, the `LinkedList` class of Figure 6.17 is generally preferred to the array-based implementation of Section 6.2.3.1. This is because a linked list never needs to be resized as the list grows and because the programmer has been freed from the myriad responsibilities associated with memory management.

However, while we have gained some benefits from our new implementation, there are still problems. Specifically, some of the list operations of Figure 6.17 still require O(N) time, including such frequently used methods as `add()`, `remove()`, and `previous()`. The next section will present an improved implementation of lists that achieves a significantly higher level of efficiency.

```java
public void remove() {
    removeNode( cursor, findPrevious() );
}

private void removeNode( LinkedNode target, LinkedNode prev ) {
    // Cursor is always set to the target's successor
    cursor = target.getNext();

    if ( prev == null ) {
        // We are deleting the head
        head = target.getNext();
    }
    else {
        // We are somewhere in the middle of the list
        prev.setNext( target.getNext() );
    }

    // Did we just delete the tail?
    if ( target == tail ) {
        tail = prev;
    }

    // One less item in the list
    count = count - 1;
}
```

FIGURE 6.16 Code for the method `remove()`

```java
/**
 * An implementation of the List interface using references.
 *
 * This code assumes that the preconditions stated in the comments are
 * true when a method is invoked and therefore does not check the
 * preconditions.
 */

public class LinkedList implements List {

    protected int count;         // The number of nodes in the list
    protected LinkedNode head;    // The first node in the list
    protected LinkedNode tail;    // The last node in the list
    protected LinkedNode cursor;  // The current node in the list

    /**
     * Create a new list.
     */
```

(continued)

FIGURE 6.17 Reference-based implementation of the `List` interface of Figure 6.6

```
public LinkedList() {
    count = 0;
    head = null;
    tail = null;
    cursor = null;
}

/**
 * Moves the cursor to the first element in the list.
 *
 * Preconditions:
 *    None.
 *
 * Postconditions:
 *    If the list is empty the cursor is moved off the list. Otherwise,
 *       the cursor is set to the first element in the list.
 *    The list's structure and content are unchanged.
 */

public void first() {
    cursor = head;
}

/**
 * Moves the cursor to the last element in the list.
 *
 * Preconditions:
 *    None.
 *
 * Postconditions:
 *    If the list is empty the cursor is moved off the list. Otherwise,
 *       the cursor is set to the last element in the list.
 *    The list's structure and content are unchanged.
 */

public void last() {
    cursor = tail;
}

/**
 * Moves the cursor to the next element in the list.
 *
 * Preconditions:
 *    The cursor is on the list.
 *
 * Postconditions:
 *    If the cursor is at the end of the list the cursor is moved off
 *       the list. Otherwise the cursor is set to the next element.
 *    The list's structure and content are unchanged.
 */
```

FIGURE 6.17 Reference-based implementation of the List interface of Figure 6.6 *(continued)*

```
   public void next() {
      cursor = cursor.getNext();
   }


   /**
    * Moves the cursor to the previous node in the list.
    *
    * Since this list only has links in the forward direction, the only
    * way to find the previous node is to work from the front of the
    * list until we locate the previous node. This is an O(n)
    * operation.
    *
    * Preconditions:
    *     The cursor is on the list.
    *
    * Postconditions:
    *     If the cursor is at the front of the list the cursor is moved off
    *         the list. Otherwise the cursor is moved to the previous element.
    *     The list's structure and content are unchanged.
    */

   public void previous() {
      cursor = findPrevious();

   }
   /**
    * Deletes the element the cursor is referring to.
    *
    * Preconditions:
    *     The cursor is on the list.
    *
    * Postconditions:
    *     The element the cursor is referring to is removed.
    *     The size of the list has decreased by 1.
    *     If the element that was removed was the last element in the list,
    *         the cursor is moved off the list. Otherwise the cursor is
    *         moved to the removed element's successor.
    */

   public void remove() {
      removeNode( cursor, findPrevious() );
   }

   /**
    * Remove the element at the specified position in the list.
    *
    * Preconditions:
    *     position >= 0 and position < size().
```

(continued)

FIGURE 6.17 Reference-based implementation of the List interface of Figure 6.6
(continued)

```
 *
 * Postconditions:
 *     The element at the specified position is removed from the list.
 *     Elements at positions greater than the specified position
 *         (if any) are shifted to the left by one position.
 *     The size of the list is decreased by 1.
 *     If the element that was removed was the last element in the list,
 *         the cursor is moved off the list. Otherwise the cursor is
 *         moved to the removed element's successor.
 *
 * @param position the position in the list where the element will
 *     be placed.
 */

public void remove( int position ) {
   LinkedNode target = head;
   LinkedNode prev = null;

   // Find the node that contains the element we wish to
   // delete and the node immediately before it.
   while ( position > 0 ) {
      prev = target;
      target = target.getNext();
      position = position - 1;
   }

   // Target is now pointing to the node we wish to remove
   removeNode( target, prev );
}

/**
 * Add a new element at the position indicated by the cursor.
 *
 * Preconditions:
 *     The list is empty or the cursor is on the list.
 *
 * Postconditions:
 *     If the list is empty, the element becomes the only element
 *      in the list. Otherwise the element is added at the
 *      position specified by the cursor.
 *    Elements at positions greater than or equal to the current
 *      position of the cursor (if any) are shifted to the right by
 *      one position.
 *    The size of the list has increased by 1.
 *    The cursor refers to the element added to the list.
 *
 * @param element the element to be added to the list.
 */
```

FIGURE 6.17 Reference-based implementation of the List interface of Figure 6.6
(continued)

```
   public void add( Object element ) {
      LinkedNode before = findPrevious();
      LinkedNode after = cursor;

      // Add the node to the list
      addNode( element, before, after );
   }

   /**
    * Add a new element at the specified position in the list.
    *
    * Preconditions:
    *    position >= 0 and position <= size().
    *
    * Postconditions:
    *    The element is added at the specified position in the list.
    *    Elements at positions greater than or equal to the specified
    *       position (if any) are shifted to the right by one position.
    *    The size of the list is increased by 1.
    *    The cursor refers to the element added to the list.
    *
    * @param position the position in the list where the element will
    *    be placed.
    * @param element the element to be added to the list.
    */

   public void add( int position, Object element ) {
      LinkedNode after = null;
      LinkedNode before = null;

      // Set before and after to the appropriate values
      if ( position == 0 ) {
         before = null;
         after = head;
      }
      else {
         before = positionToReference( position - 1 );
         after = before.getNext();
      }
      // Add the node to the list
      addNode( element, before, after );
   }

   /**
    * Add a new element to the end of the list.
    *
```

(continued)

FIGURE 6.17 Reference-based implementation of the `List` interface of Figure 6.6
(continued)

```
 * Preconditions:
 *     None.
 *
 * Postconditions:
 *     The specified element is the last element in the list.
 *     The size of the list is increased by 1.
 *     The cursor refers to the element added to the list.
 *     The other elements in the list (if any) are unchanged.
 */

public void append( Object element ) {
   // Cursor is always set to the node that is added
   cursor = new LinkedNode( element, null );

   if ( tail == null ) {
      // If the list is empty we need to set head
      head = cursor;
   }
   else {
      // There is a tail and it should refer to the element just added
      tail.setNext( cursor );
   }

   // Tail always refers to the element added
   tail = cursor;
   // One more element in the list
   count = count + 1;
}

/**
 * Returns the element that the cursor is referring to.
 *
 * Preconditions:
 *     The cursor is on the list.
 *
 * Postconditions:
 *     The list's structure, content, and cursor are unchanged.
 */

public Object get() {
   return cursor.getData();
}

/**
 * Returns the element stored in the specified position in the list.
 *
 * Preconditions:
 *     position >= 0 and position < size().
 *
```

FIGURE 6.17 Reference-based implementation of the List interface of Figure 6.6 *(continued)*

```
 * Postconditions:
 *     The list's structure, content, and cursor are unchanged.
 *
 * @param position the location of the element to be retrieved.
 */

public Object get( int position ) {
   return positionToReference( position ).getData();
}


/**
 * Sets the element stored at the location identified by the cursor.
 *
 * Preconditions:
 *     The cursor is on the list.
 *
 * Postconditions:
 *     The element at the current cursor position is changed to the
 *         specified value.
 *     The list's structure and cursor are unchanged.
 *
 * @param element the element to place in the list.
 */

public void set( Object element ) {
   cursor.setData( element );
}


/**
 * Sets the element stored in the specified position in the list.
 *
 * Preconditions:
 *     position >= 0 and position < size().
 *
 * Postconditions:
 *     The element at the specified position in the list is changed
 *         to the specified value.
 *     The list's structure and cursor are unchanged.
 *
 * @param position the location of the element to be changed.
 * @param element the element to place in the specified location
 *     of the list.
 */

public void set( int position, Object element ) {
   LinkedNode target = positionToReference( position );
   target.setData( element );
}
```

(continued)

FIGURE 6.17 Reference-based implementation of the `List` interface of Figure 6.6 *(continued)*

```
/**
 * Return the number of elements in the list.
 *
 * Preconditions:
 *    None.
 *
 * Postconditions:
 *    The list's structure, content, and cursor are unchanged.
 */

public int size() {
    return count;
}

/**
 * Determine if the cursor is on the list.
 *
 * Preconditions:
 *    None.
 *
 * Postconditions:
 *    The list's structure, content and cursor are unchanged.
 */

public boolean isOnList() {
    return cursor != null;
}

/**
 * Return a string representation of this list.
 *
 * @return a string representation of this list.
 */

public String toString() {
    // Use a StringBuffer so we don't create a new
    // string each time we append
    StringBuffer retVal = new StringBuffer();

    retVal = retVal.append( "[ " );

    // Step through the list and use toString on the elements to
    // determine their string representation
    for ( LinkedNode cur = head; cur != null; cur = cur.getNext() ) {
        retVal = retVal.append( cur.getData() + " " );
    }

    retVal = retVal.append( "]" );
```

FIGURE 6.17 Reference-based implementation of the List interface of Figure 6.6 (continued)

```
        // Convert the StringBuffer to a string
        return retVal.toString();
    }

    /**
     * Return a reference to the previous node in the list.
     *
     * @return a reference to the node before the node referred to by
     *     the cursor.
     */

    private LinkedNode findPrevious() {
        LinkedNode prev = null; // Where we are in the list

        // If the cursor is off the list or the cursor is at the
        // head, there is no previous node.

        if ( cursor != null && cursor != head ) {
            prev = head;

            // Keep looking until we find the node whose next reference
            // is equal to the current node

            while ( prev.getNext() != cursor ) {
                prev = prev.getNext();
            }
        }

        // The variable prev is now referring to the previous node
        return prev;
    }

    /**
     * Remove the specified node from the list.
     *
     * @param target the node to remove.
     * @param prev the node before the node to be deleted.
     */

    private void removeNode( LinkedNode target, LinkedNode prev ) {
        // Cursor is always set to the target's successor
        cursor = target.getNext();

        if ( prev == null ) {
            // We are deleting the head
            head = target.getNext();
        }
        else {
```

(continued)

FIGURE 6.17 Reference-based implementation of the List interface of Figure 6.6 *(continued)*

```
            // We are somewhere in the middle of the list
            prev.setNext( target.getNext() );
      }

      // Did we just delete the tail?
      if ( target == tail ) {
         tail = prev;
      }

      // One less item in the list
      count = count - 1;
   }


   /**
    * Add the specified element to the list between the nodes
    *    identified by before and after.
    *
    * @param element the element to add.
    * @param before the node before the node to be added.
    * @param after the node after the node to be added.
    */

   private void addNode( Object element,
                         LinkedNode before,
                         LinkedNode after ) {

      // Create the node
      cursor = new LinkedNode( element, after );

      // Is this a new head?
      if ( before == null ) {
         head = cursor;
      }
      else {
         before.setNext( cursor );
      }

      // Is it a new tail?
      if ( after == null ) {
         tail = cursor;
      }

      // One more element in the list
      count = count + 1;
   }
```

FIGURE 6.17 Reference-based implementation of the `List` interface of Figure 6.6 *(continued)*

```
/**
 * Return a reference to the node with the specified position in the
 *    list.
 *
 * @param position the node to obtain the reference for.
 *
 * @return a reference to the node at the specified position.
 */

private LinkedNode positionToReference( int position ) {
    LinkedNode retVal = head;

    while ( position > 0 ) {
        retVal = retVal.getNext();
        position = position - 1;
    }
    return retVal;
}

} // LinkedList
```

FIGURE 6.17 Reference-based implementation of the `List` interface of Figure 6.6 *(continued)*

6.2.3.3 Doubly Linked Lists and Circular Lists

The operations of Figure 6.17 that require O(N) time are those that access the predecessor of the cursor, such as `previous()`, `remove()`, and `add()`, or those that must traverse the list from the beginning, such as `get()` or `set()`.

The `LinkedNode` class of Figure 6.13 contains a single reference field in each node—a pointer to its successor. Therefore, our physical implementation of a list is virtually identical to the logical model diagramed in Figure 6.5. This type of **singly linked list** allows us to iterate through the collection in a "forward" direction (i.e., from a node to its successor). However, if we ever need to access the node that precedes the current one, the only way is to traverse the list from the beginning. In the worst case, this requires O(N) time, where N is the list size. In a singly linked structure, any method that accesses the predecessor of the current node will always require at least linear time.

A solution to this problem comes from the realization that, just because the logical structure of a list (Figure 6.5) has pointers in only one direction, this does not imply that its physical realization must conform to that same structure. The state information we maintain for a list can include anything that will help us build a correct and efficient representation. (That is why, for example, we included `count` and `tail` as state variables in our singly linked implementation.) Therefore, we can create a node class that includes both forward and backward links, called `next` and `previous`, as shown in Figure 6.18. The `next` field points to the successor node and is identical to the `next` field of Figure 6.13. The new `previous` field points to its predecessor, and it is this field that will allow us to move in both directions through a list—from head to tail as well as from tail to head.

The `DoublyLinkedNode` class in Figure 6.18 produces a **doubly linked list**. Logically, this is still a linear structure but with state information (the previous field) added to the node to reduce the run time of some important list methods.

```java
/**
 * This is a doubly linked list node class suitable for building linked
 * data structures such as lists, stacks, and queues. It includes
 * a second, 'rear-facing' link that permits O(1) movement towards the
 * front of the list.
 */

public class DoublyLinkedNode {

    private Object data;             // The data stored in this node
    private DoublyLinkedNode next;    // The next node in the data structure
    private DoublyLinkedNode previous; // The rear-facing link

    /**
     * Create a new node.
     */

    public DoublyLinkedNode() {
        this( null, null, null );
    }

    /**
     * Construct a node given the info and next references.
     *
     * @param newData the data to be associated with this node.
     * @param newPrevious a reference to the previous node in the list.
     * @param newNext a reference to the next node in the list.
     */

    public DoublyLinkedNode( Object newData,
                             DoublyLinkedNode newPrevious,
                             DoublyLinkedNode newNext ) {

        data = newData;
        next = newNext;
        previous = newPrevious;
    }

    /**
     * Return the data stored in this node.
     *
```

FIGURE 6.18 Node class for a doubly linked implementation of a list

```
 * Preconditions:
 *    None.
 *
 * Postconditions:
 *    The node is unchanged.
 *
 * @returns a reference to the data stored in this node.
 */

public Object getData() {
   return data;
}


/**
 * Return a reference to the next node in the data structure.
 *
 * Preconditions:
 *    None.
 *
 * Postconditions:
 *    The node is unchanged.
 *
 * @return a reference to the next Node in the list, or null if this
 *    node has no successor.
 */

public DoublyLinkedNode getNext() {
   return next;
}

/**
 * Return a reference to the previous node in the data structure.
 *
 * Preconditions:
 *    None.
 *
 * Postconditions:
 *    The node is unchanged.
 *
 * @return a reference to the previous node in the data structure.
 */

public DoublyLinkedNode getPrevious() {
   return previous;
}

/**
 * Set the data associated with this node.
```

(continued)

FIGURE 6.18 Node class for a doubly linked implementation of a list *(continued)*

```
 *
 * Preconditions:
 *     None.
 *
 * Postconditions:
 *     The data associated with this node has been changed.
 *
 * @param newData the data to be associated with this node.
 */

public void setData( Object newData ) {
   data = newData;
}

/**
 * Set the reference to the next node.
 *
 * Preconditions:
 *     None.
 *
 * Postconditions:
 *     The reference to the next node has been changed.
 *
 * @param newNext the reference to the next node in the data structure.
 */

public void setNext( DoublyLinkedNode newNext ) {
   next = newNext;
}

/**
 * Set the reference to the previous node in the data structure.
 *
 * Preconditions:
 *     None.
 *
 * Postconditions:
 *     The reference to the previous node in the data structure is changed.
 */

public void setPrevious( DoublyLinkedNode newPrev ) {
   previous = newPrev;
}

} // DoublyLinkedNode
```

FIGURE 6.18 Node class for a doubly linked implementation of a list *(continued)*

Note that we are only changing the structure of the individual nodes, not the structure of a list built up from these nodes. The state information required by a DoublyLinkedList object is still the same: references to the first node (head) and last node (tail) in the list, a current position (cursor), and a count of the total number of nodes in the list (count).

Figure 6.19a shows the declarations required to implement the list interface using the doubly linked node structure of Figure 6.18. Figure 6.19b is a picture of what this doubly linked implementation would look like for a typical list.

```java
public class DoublyLinkedList implements List {
                                        // state variables to maintain for list
private DoublyLinkedNode head;          // pointer to the first node
private DoublyLinkedNode tail;          // pointer to the last node
private DoublyLinkedNode cursor;        // current position indicator
private int count;                      // number of nodes in the list
   . . .                                // public methods will go here
```

FIGURE 6.19a Declarations for a doubly linked implementation of a list

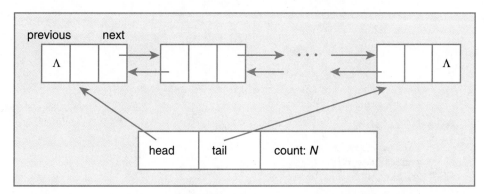

FIGURE 6.19b Picture of a doubly linked list structure created from declarations of Figures 6.18 and 6.19a

The time complexity of previous() using a singly linked list was O(N). Using our new doubly linked list structure, this operation can be completed in a single line:

```
cursor = cursor.getPrevious();
```

The existence of the previous field has made the implementation of this operation trivial and reduced run time from O(N) to O(1).

Figure 6.20 shows the doubly linked implementation of the add() method, one of the operations that motivated the need for both backward and forward pointers. As with previous(), the existence of backward pointer allows us to reduce the run time from O(N) in the singly linked structure of Figure 6.15 to O(1).

```
public void add( Object element ) {
   addNode( element, cursor );
}

private void addNode( Object element, DoublyLinkedNode after ) {
   DoublyLinkedNode before = null;

   // Determine what is before the new node
   if ( after == null ) {
      // Adding a new tail to the list
      before = tail;
   }
   else {
      // Adding somewhere in the middle of the list
      before = after.getPrevious();
   }

   // Create the node
   cursor = new DoublyLinkedNode( element, before, after );

   // Take care of the next reference of the node before the new node
   if ( before == null ) {
      // Adding a new head
      head = cursor;
   }
   else {
      // Somewhere in the middle of the list
      before.setNext( cursor );
   }

   // Take care of the previous reference of the node after the new node
   if ( after == null ) {
      // Adding a new tail
      tail = cursor;
   }
   else {
      after.setPrevious( cursor );
   }

   // One more node in the list
   count = count + 1;
}
```

FIGURE 6.20 Implementation of `add()` using a doubly linked data structure

However, as economists are fond of saying, there is no such thing as a "free lunch," and the price we must pay for this improved run time is twofold. First, the amount of memory required to hold our list has increased due to the second reference field in each node. If the list is large, this increased memory use may be significant.

Second, the programming complexity will increase because we must maintain and update two reference fields, not just one.

In the previous section, we discussed the pitfalls that lie in wait for a programmer writing a reference-based implementation of a list, pitfalls such as empty lists, special cases, and off-by-one errors. With a doubly linked list, the number of potential pitfalls is even greater. Looking at the add() code in Figure 6.20, we see that, even though it runs in constant time, it is rather complex. There are four pointer fields that must be correctly set: the next and previous links of the new node being added, the previous link of after, and the next link of before. In addition, there are two special cases that must be checked to ensure that the add code works correctly in all situations. These special cases are:

◆ If after is null, then we are adding this new node to the end of the list and must reset tail.

◆ If before is null, then we are adding this new node to the head of the list and must reset head.

When writing methods that use doubly linked list structures, great care must be taken to properly set all reference fields and to ensure that the code works correctly on both the expected cases as well as the special cases mentioned in the previous section.

The complete doubly linked implementation of the List interface of Figure 6.6 appears in Figure 6.21. It uses the declarations given in Figures 6.18 and 6.19a.

This is now our third complete implementation of the List interface, and these redesigns clearly demonstrate the power of the interface concept in Java. Each redesign provides either greater flexibility or better run-time efficiency. However, users will be totally unaffected by a change from any one of these classes to another because they all implement the List interface (except, perhaps, for slight differences in performance). This means they can be sure that the same methods with identical signatures will be provided by all three classes.

```
/**
 * An implementation of a list using forward and backward references.
 * This changes the order of moving backwards in the list from O(n)
 * to O(1) at the cost of adding one reference to each node in the list.
 *
 * This code assumes that the preconditions stated in the comments are
 * true when a method is invoked and therefore does not check the
 * preconditions.
 */

public class DoublyLinkedList implements List {

    private int count;                 // The number of nodes in the list
    private DoublyLinkedNode head;     // The first node in the list
    private DoublyLinkedNode tail;     // The last node in the list
    private DoublyLinkedNode cursor;   // The current node in the list
```
(continued)

FIGURE 6.21 Doubly linked implementation of the List interface

```
/**
 * Create a new list.
 */

public DoublyLinkedList() {
   count = 0;
   head = null;
   tail = null;
   cursor = null;
}

/**
 * Moves the cursor to the first element in the list.
 *
 * Preconditions:
 *    None.
 *
 * Postconditions:
 *    If the list is empty the cursor is moved off the list. Otherwise,
 *       the cursor is set to the first element in the list.
 *    The list's structure and content are unchanged.
 */

public void first() {
   cursor = head;
}

/**
 * Moves the cursor to the last element in the list.
 *
 * Preconditions:
 *    None.
 *
 * Postconditions:
 *    If the list is empty the cursor is moved off the list. Otherwise,
 *       the cursor is set to the last element in the list.
 *    The list's structure and content are unchanged.
 */

public void last() {
   cursor = tail;
}

/**
 * Moves the cursor to the next element in the list.
 *
 * Preconditions:
 *    The cursor is on the list.
 *
```

FIGURE 6.21 Doubly linked implementation of the List interface *(continued)*

```
 * Postconditions:
 *     If the cursor is at the end of the list the cursor is moved off
 *         the list. Otherwise the cursor is set to the next element.
 *     The list's structure and content are unchanged.
 */

public void next() {
    cursor = cursor.getNext();
}


/**
 * Moves the cursor to the previous node in the list.
 *
 * Since this list only has links in the forward direction, the only
 * way to find the previous node is to work from the front of the
 * the list until we locate the previous node. This is an O(n)
 * operation.
 *
 * Preconditions:
 *     The cursor is on the list.
 *
 * Postconditions:
 *     If the cursor is at the front of the list the cursor is moved off
 *         the list. Otherwise the cursor is moved to the previous element.
 *     The list's structure and content are unchanged.
 */

public void previous() {
    cursor = cursor.getPrevious();
}

/**
 * Deletes the element the cursor is referring to.
 *
 * Preconditions:
 *     The cursor is on the list.
 *
 * Postconditions:
 *     The element the cursor is referring to is removed.
 *     The size of the list has decreased by 1.
 *     If the element that was removed was the last element in the list,
 *         the cursor is moved off the list. Otherwise the cursor is
 *         moved to the removed element's successor.
 */

public void remove() {
    removeNode( cursor );
}
```

(continued)

FIGURE 6.21 Doubly linked implementation of the List interface *(continued)*

```
/**
 * Remove the element at the specified position in the list.
 *
 * Preconditions:
 *    position >= 0 and position < size().
 *
 * Postconditions:
 *    The element at the specified position is removed from the list.
 *    Elements at positions greater than the specified position
 *        (if any) are shifted to the left by one position.
 *    The size of the list is decreased by 1.
 *    If the element that was removed was the last element in the list,
 *        the cursor is moved off the list. Otherwise the cursor is
 *        moved to the removed element's successor.
 *
 * @param position the position in the list where the element will
 *    be placed.
 */

public void remove( int position ) {
    removeNode( positionToReference( position ) );
}


/**
 * Add a new element at the position indicated by the cursor.
 *
 * Preconditions:
 *    The list is empty or the cursor is on the list.
 *
 * Postconditions:
 *    If the list is empty, the element becomes the only element
 *        in the list. Otherwise the element is added at the
 *        position specified by the cursor.
 *    Elements at positions greater than or equal to the current
 *        position of the cursor (if any) are shifted to the right by
 *        one position.
 *    The size of the list has increased by 1.
 *    The cursor refers to the element added to the list.
 *
 * @param element the element to be added to the list.
 */

public void add( Object element ) {
    addNode( element, cursor );
}

/**
 * Add a new element at the specified position in the list.
 *
```

FIGURE 6.21 Doubly linked implementation of the List interface *(continued)*

```
 *  Preconditions:
 *      position >= 0 and position <= size().
 *
 *  Postconditions:
 *      The element is added at the specified position in the list.
 *      Elements at positions greater than or equal to the specified
 *          position (if any) are shifted to the right by one position.
 *      The size of the list is increased by 1.
 *      The cursor refers to the element added to the list.
 *
 *  @param position the position in the list where the element will
 *      be placed.
 *  @param element the element to be added to the list.
 */

public void add( int position, Object element ) {
    addNode( element, positionToReference( position ) );
}


/**
 *  Add a new element to the end of the list.
 *
 *  Preconditions:
 *      None.
 *
 *  Postconditions:
 *      The specified element is the last element in the list.
 *      The size of the list is increased by 1.
 *      The cursor refers to the element added to the list.
 *      The other elements in the list (if any) are unchanged.
 */

public void append( Object element ) {
    // Cursor is always set to the node that is added
    cursor = new DoublyLinkedNode( element, tail, null );

    if ( tail == null ) {
        // If the list is empty we need to set head
        head = cursor;
    }
    else {
        // There is a tail and it should refer to the element just added
        tail.setNext( cursor );
    }

    // Tail always refers to the element added
    tail = cursor;

    // One more element in the list
    count = count + 1;
}
```

(continued)

FIGURE 6.21 Doubly linked implementation of the List interface *(continued)*

```
/**
 * Returns the element that the cursor is referring to.
 *
 * Preconditions:
 *    The cursor is on the list.
 *
 * Postconditions:
 *    The list's structure, content, and cursor are unchanged.
 */

public Object get() {
    return cursor.getData();
}


/**
 * Returns the element stored in the specified position in the list.
 *
 * Preconditions:
 *    position >= 0 and position < size().
 *
 * Postconditions:
 *    The list's structure, content, and cursor are unchanged.
 *
 * @param position the location of the element to be retrieved.
 */

public Object get( int position ) {
    return positionToReference( position ).getData();
}

/**
 * Sets the element stored at the location identified by the cursor.
 *
 * Preconditions:
 *    The cursor is on the list.
 *
 * Postconditions:
 *    The element at the current cursor position is changed to the
 *       specified value.
 *    The list's structure and cursor are unchanged.
 *
 * @param element the element to place in the list.
 */

public void set( Object element ) {
    cursor.setData( element );
}
```

FIGURE 6.21 Doubly linked implementation of the `List` interface *(continued)*

```
    /**
     * Sets the element stored in the specified position in the list.
     *
     * Preconditions:
     *    position >= 0 and position < size().
     *
     * Postconditions:
     *    The element at the specified position in the list is changed
     *       to the specified value.
     *    The list's structure and cursor are unchanged.
     *
     * @param position the location of the element to be changed.
     * @param element the element to place in the specified location
     *    of the list.
     */

    public void set( int position, Object element ) {
       DoublyLinkedNode target = positionToReference( position );
       target.setData( element );
    }

    /**
     * Return the number of elements in the list.
     *
     * Preconditions:
     *    None.
     *
     * Postconditions:
     *    The list's structure, content, and cursor are unchanged.
     */

    public int size() {
       return count;
    }

    /**
     * Determine if the cursor is on the list.
     *
     * Preconditions:
     *    None.
     *
     * Postconditions:
     *    The list's structure, content and cursor are unchanged.
     */

    public boolean isOnList() {
       return cursor != null;
    }
```

(continued)

FIGURE 6.21 Doubly linked implementation of the `List` interface *(continued)*

```java
/**
 * Return a string representation of this list.
 *
 * @return a string representation of this list.
 */

public String toString() {
    // Use a StringBuffer so we don't create a new
    // string each time we append
    StringBuffer retVal = new StringBuffer();

    retVal = retVal.append( "[ " );

    // Step through the list and use toString on the elements to
    //   determine their string representation
    for ( DoublyLinkedNode cur = head; cur != null; cur = cur.getNext() ){
            retVal = retVal.append( cur.getData() + " " );
        }
    retVal = retVal.append( "]" );

        // Convert the StringBuffer to a string
    return retVal.toString();
}

/**
 * Remove the specified node from the list.
 *
 * @param target the node to remove.
 * @param prev the node before the node to be deleted.
 */

private void removeNode( DoublyLinkedNode target ) {
    DoublyLinkedNode before = target.getPrevious();
    DoublyLinkedNode after = target.getNext();

    // Cursor is always set to the target's successor
    cursor = after;

    // Set the next reference of the node before the target
    if ( before == null ) {
        // We are deleting the head
        head = after;
    }
    else {
        // We are somewhere in the middle of the list
        before.setNext( after );
    }
```

FIGURE 6.21 Doubly linked implementation of the `List` interface *(continued)*

```
            // Set the previous reference of the node after the target
         if ( after == null ) {
            // We are deleting the tail
            tail = before;
         }
         else {
            // We are somewhere in the middle of the list
            after.setPrevious( before );
         }
         // One less item in the list
         count = count - 1;
      }


   /**
    * Add the specified element to the list between the nodes
    * identified by before and after.
    *
    * @param element the element to add.
    * @param after the node after the node to be added.
    */

   private void addNode( Object element, DoublyLinkedNode after ) {
      DoublyLinkedNode before = null;

      // Determine what is before the new node
      if ( after == null ) {
         // Adding a new tail to the list
         before = tail;
      }
      else {
         // Adding somewhere in the middle of the list
         before = after.getPrevious();
      }

      // Create the node
      cursor = new DoublyLinkedNode( element, before, after );

      // Take care of the next reference of the node before the new node
      if ( before == null ) {
         // Adding a new head
         head = cursor;
         }
      else {
         // Somewhere in the middle of the list
         before.setNext( cursor );
         }

      // Take care of the previous reference of the node after the new node
      if ( after == null ) {
```

(continued)

FIGURE 6.21 Doubly linked implementation of the `List` interface *(continued)*

```
                // Adding a new tail
                tail = cursor;
            }
            else {
                after.setPrevious( cursor );
            }

            // One more node in the list
            count = count + 1;
    }


    /**
     * Return a reference to the node with the specified position in the
     * list.
     *
     * @param position the node to obtain the reference for.
     *
     * @return a reference to the node at the specified position.
     */

    private DoublyLinkedNode positionToReference( int position ) {
        DoublyLinkedNode retVal = head;

        while ( position > 0 ) {
            retVal = retVal.getNext();
            position = position - 1;
        }
        return retVal;
    }

} // DoublyLinkedList
```

FIGURE 6.21 Doubly linked implementation of the `List` interface *(continued)*

The last implementation we will present is the **circular list**. Assume that we have a "traditional" singly linked list structure and want to locate a specific data value, I_k, stored somewhere in the list. The only way is to begin at the head and iterate until we either find the value we are looking for or come to the end. In some situations, this O(N) approach is perfectly acceptable. However, there are applications where this can cause problems.

For example, imagine that our list contains the names and identifications of computational resources that can be allocated to programs, such as a list of networked printers. Each printer is either free or inuse, and when a request is made ("I need a printer."), our program searches this list until it finds a printer marked free. It marks it as now inuse and returns its name and identification to the requesting user, who is its sole owner and may use it for as long as he or she wants.

If we always begin our search for a free device at the head of the list, it is obvious that the printers whose names appear near the front will be allocated much more often than those whose names appear near the back. If these resources are printers, then the ones whose names are near the head of the list will have much greater wear and tear on their print head mechanisms. It would be fairer to allocate resources so that all devices are used for an equal amount of time.

A simple way to do that is to maintain a state variable called startSearch telling us where the last search in the list ended. When a request comes in, we do not begin our search from the node pointed at by head but from the node pointed at by startSearch. This way, the starting point for the search will move circularly through the list, and in the long run, all nodes will be allocated on a roughly equal basis. The state variable startSearch serves a role similar to the variable cursor in Figure 6.14 in the sense that it tells us where to begin this list operation.

To implement this circular search procedure, we must be able to quickly and easily iterate through the list, including going from the last node in the list back to the first. We could check for the occurrence of the special symbol Λ that marks the end of the list and, when we find it, reset startSearch to the value of head. However, there is an easier way. Instead of marking the end of the list with a next field value of Λ, we can have it point back to the first node in the list. This produces a structure called a **circular list**, which is diagramed in Figure 6.22.

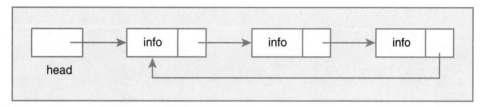

FIGURE 6.22 Logical model of a circular list

A circular list allows us to traverse the list beginning at any node without having to worry about the special case caused by reaching the end of the list. In a sense, a circular list eliminates the very idea of a first and last node. It is not really different from the singly linked list structure whose declarations were shown in Figure 6.14. The only real difference is that if we are at the last node in the list and do a next() operation, we go to the first node, and if we are at the first node in the list and do a previous() operation, we go to the last node. Otherwise, everything else behaves the same.

The fact that the circular list has only two specialized behaviors (next() and previous()) suggests that its implementation should use the specialization form of inheritance and extend the LinkedList class of Figure 6.17. This allows us to inherit all the methods that work the same on both lists and only write the new behaviors for next() and previous() that handle the automatic wrap-around feature. The implementation of CircularLinkedList is shown in Figure 6.23. Note that it includes only two methods, the two methods that implement the specialized behaviors of a circular list. Also note that in both methods, if we do not have one of these special situations (because we are not at the front or back of the list), then we invoke the corresponding method in the superclass via the commands **super**.next() and **super**.previous().

```
/**
 * This is a simple circular linked list class. We only need to implement
 * the two specialized methods next() and previous(). All other methods
 * will be inherited from LinkedList.
 */

public class CircularLinkedList extends LinkedList {

    /**
     * Move the cursor to the next element in the list.
     *
     * Preconditions:
     *     The cursor is on the list.
     *
     * Postconditions:
     *     If the cursor is at the end of the list the cursor is moved off
     *         the list. Otherwise the cursor is set to the next element.
     *     The list's structure and content are unchanged.
     */

    public void next() {
        // If the cursor is at the end of the list, wrap around to the
        // head of the list, otherwise advance the cursor as usual
        if ( cursor == tail ) {
            cursor = head;
        }
        else {
            super.next();
        }
    }

    /**
     * Move the cursor to the previous node in the list.
     *
     * Preconditions:
     *     The cursor is on the list.
     *
     * Postconditions:
     *     If the cursor is at the front of the list the cursor is moved off
     *         the list. Otherwise the cursor is moved to the previous element.
     *     The list's structure and content are unchanged.
     */

    public void previous() {
        // If the cursor is at the front of the list wrap around to the
        // end of the list, otherwise go backwards as usual
        if (cursor == head) {
            cursor = tail;
        }
        else {
            super.previous();
        }
    }

} // CircularLinkedList
```

FIGURE 6.23 Declarations to create a circular singly linked list

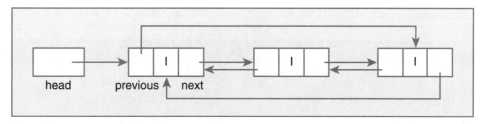

FIGURE 6.24 Circular doubly linked list

This is a beautiful example of the gains in software productivity that can be achieved through inheritance. A complex data structure, such as this circular linked list, has been implemented in about 12 lines of code. That is because all remaining behaviors are inherited directly from the base class LinkedList.

As our final example, let's combine the two ideas just presented—doubly linked lists and circular lists—to create a **circular doubly linked list** with the structure depicted in Figure 6.24.

The list structure in Figure 6.24 can be created using the same doubly linked list declarations as in Figures 6.18 and 6.19a. We only need to replace the Λ values located at the two ends of the list with references to the first and the last nodes. This circular doubly linked list structure allows us to efficiently iterate through the list in either the forward or backward direction, beginning at any arbitrary node. For some applications, these added capabilities could be very important. We leave it as an exercise to the reader to design a class that implements the List interface of Figure 6.6 using the structure in Figure 6.24. Your class should extend the DoublyLinkedList class of Figure 6.20.

◆ 6.2.4 Summary

This section has introduced an important taxonomic classification scheme for data structures: the linear, hierarchical, graph, and set structures. It also began our discussion of data structures by introducing the most flexible of all linear structures—the list. Even though a list is an elementary data structure with a simple *one:one* relationship between elements, there are a number of different techniques for implementing it. This section presented both array-based and reference-based approaches and, in the latter case, described both the singly linked as well as the more complex doubly linked, circular, and circular doubly linked variations.

Lists are not just a textbook curiosity but a fundamentally important data representation in computer science. For example, operating systems maintain lists of processes waiting to execute on a processor. They also maintain lists of available memory blocks that can be allocated to processes. Simulation models use lists to model the waiting lines found in many systems, such as email messages waiting in line to use a communications link. In functional programming languages, such as LISP and Scheme, the list is the only data structure available. These languages do not support such familiar and well-known structures as arrays. Instead, programmers must express their solutions only in terms of lists and the list operations of the type included in Figure 6.6.

Even though the list is the most general and flexible of all linear structures, it is not the only one. The next section will introduce a number of linear structures that place restrictions on where one is allowed to carry out certain operations, such as additions, removals, and retrievals. These restrictions produce linear structures with some very interesting and useful properties.

6.3 STACKS

The list structure described in the previous section is the most general of all linear structures because it allows insertions, deletions, and retrievals to be done any-where—at the beginning, middle, or end of the list. The following sections look at two important linear structures that place restrictions on where we are permitted to do insertion, deletion, and retrieval operations. These two structures are the stack and the queue, and they are widely used in computing applications.

◆ 6.3.1 Operations on Stacks

A **stack** is a last-in, first-out (LIFO) linear data structure in which the only object that can be accessed is the last one placed on the stack. This element is called the **top** of the stack. When a new value is inserted into the stack, it becomes the new top element. Thus, unlike the list in which we could retrieve, change, and delete any arbitrary node, in a stack we are limited to retrieving, changing, and deleting only this top node.

Figure 6.25a is a diagram of a stack containing three objects, X, Y, and Z, which were stored on the stack in just that order. Only the last item inserted, in this case Z, can currently be retrieved or deleted. Deleting the top item of a stack is called **popping** the stack, and executing the operation pop() produces the stack shown in Figure 6.25b. Note that the element Y has become the top item because it is now the last item inserted.

The process of adding a new element to the stack is called **pushing** a value on to the stack. Executing the operation push(W) on the stack of Figure 6.25b makes W the new top element and results in the situation shown in Figure 6.25c. No element, other than the one most recently pushed, can be accessed via a push or pop operation.

Because of these restrictions, the set of operations permitted on stacks is rather limited, and the typical Stack interface is smaller and much more standardized than the List interface of Figure 6.6.

top → Z		top → W
Y	top → Y	Y
X	X	X
(a) A three-element stack	(b) After a pop() operation	(c) After a push(W) operation

FIGURE 6.25 Last-in, first-out behavior of a stack

In addition to the two mutator operations push(V), which adds a new value V to the top of the stack, and pop(), which discards the top value of the stack, another essential operation is determining whether or not a stack is empty. Stack users do not know how the stack is built, so they cannot check for an empty condition by seeing if top == null, top == 0, or any other test that depends on a knowledge of the underlying implementation. If they did, then a change to the implementation would "break" the user's code. Instead, we provide an empty() method to test for this condition. The empty() operation returns a Boolean that is true if the stack is empty and false otherwise. It is typically used in the following manner:

```
if (S.empty())
        // do something for the case in which the stack S is empty
else
        // do something for the case in which the stack S is not empty
```

A similar method is full(). This operation determines whether attempting to push another value onto the stack would cause a fatal error. The full() operation returns a Boolean value that is true if the stack is full and false otherwise.

A method similar to the pop() operation is top(). top() returns the value of the top element of the stack without deleting it. Recall from Figure 6.25b that pop() is a mutator that deletes the top element. However, top() is an accessor that returns the element on top of the stack but does not alter the stack in any way. In particular, then, if you execute two successive top() operations on the same stack, you will get the same element.

An interface for a stack data structure is given in Figure 6.26. It includes the five operations described: push(), pop(), top(), empty(), and full(). Other stack operations are possible, but these are the most common and widely used operations on stack structures.

```
/**
 * An interface for a simple stack.
 */

public interface Stack {
    /**
     * Places its argument on the top of the stack.
     *
     * Preconditions:
     *     Stack is not full.
     *
     * Postconditions:
     *     Stack size has increased by 1.
     *     Data are on top of the stack.
     *     The rest of the stack is unchanged.
     *
     * @param data Object to place on the stack.
     */
    public void push( Object data );
```
(continued)

FIGURE 6.26 Stack interface

```
    /**
     * Removes the top of the stack.
     *
     * Preconditions:
     *    Stack is not empty.
     *
     * Postconditions:
     *    Stack size has decreased by 1.
     *    The top item of the stack has been removed.
     *    The rest of the stack is unchanged.
     */
    public void pop();

    /**
     * Returns the top element of the stack.
     *
     * Preconditions:
     *    The stack is not empty.
     *
     * Postconditions:
     *    The stack is unchanged.
     *
     * @return the top element of the stack.
     */
    public Object top();

    /**
     * Determines if the stack is empty.
     *
     * Preconditions:
     *    None.
     *
     * Postconditions:
     *    The stack is unchanged.
     *
     * @return true if the stack is empty, false otherwise.
     */
    public boolean empty();

    /**
     * Determines if the stack is full.
     *
     * Preconditions:
     *    None.
     *
     * Postconditions:
     *    The stack is unchanged.
     *
     * @return true if the stack is full and false otherwise.
     */
    public boolean full();

} // Stack
```

FIGURE 6.26 Stack interface *(continued)*

◆ **6.3.2** Applications of Stacks

Last-in, first-out data structures are widely used throughout computer science. For example, whenever a method is called, the computer saves the memory address of the instruction following the call to return to the correct statement when it is finished. Furthermore, all addresses must be saved regardless of how many nested calls are made, and we must return to each method in exactly the right order.

For example, in Figure 6.27a, we have a situation in which method A calls method B, which calls method C, which calls method D.

procedure A()	procedure B()	procedure C()	procedure D()	top $\rightarrow$ R_C
B();	C();	D();		R_B
R_A: . . .	R_B: . . .	R_C: . . .	**return;**	R_A

(a) Example of nested procedure calls   *(b) Run-time stack while in procedure D*

FIGURE 6.27 Using stacks to implement nested procedure calls

When D finishes execution, the program must return to the address immediately following the call to D in method C, the location labeled R_C in Figure 6.27a. A stack makes this task quite easy for one important reason: We return in exactly the reverse order in which the methods were invoked. This fits the LIFO model of a stack perfectly.

When a method is called, the return address is pushed onto a **run-time stack** S. That is, the compiler translates the call P; into the following sequence:

```
if (! S.full())
        S.push(address of the instruction following the call);
        jump to method P;
else
        "stack overflow error"
```

This situation is diagramed Figure 6.27b, which shows a simplified model of what the run-time stack looks like during execution of method D in Figure 6.27a. (It is simplified because the run-time stack holds more than just return address. It also holds information on parameters and local variables.)

When a method finishes execution, the return address is popped from the run-time stack, and program execution is transferred to that location. That is, the statement **return;** is translated by the compiler into:

```
return address = S.top();
S.pop();
continue execution with the instruction at the return address;
```

Our choice of a stack to hold return addresses allows us to return to each method in exactly the correct order. This technique also supports *recursive* methods, since this only means the run-time stack holds many invocations of the same method rather than different ones.

Stacks can be used to convert arithmetic expressions from **infix notation** to **postfix notation**. An infix expression is one in which operators are located between their operands. This is the way we are used to writing expressions in standard mathematical notation. In postfix notation, the operator immediately follows its operands. Examples of infix expressions are:

$$a * b \qquad f * g - b \qquad d / e * c + 2 \qquad d / e * (c + 2)$$

The corresponding postfix expressions (assuming Java precedence rules) are:

$$ab* \qquad fg*b- \qquad de/c*2+ \qquad de/c2+*$$

In a postfix expression, a binary operator is applied to the two immediately preceding operands. A unary operator is applied to the one immediately preceding operand. Notice that the operands in a postfix expression occur in the same order as the corresponding infix expression. Only the position of the operators is changed.

A feature of postfix is that the order in which operators are applied is always unambiguous. That is, there is only a single interpretation of any postfix expression. This is not true of infix. For example, the meaning of the infix expression

$$a + b * c$$

is unclear. Does it mean (a + b) * c or a + (b * c)? Without parentheses or additional rules, we cannot say. In Java, precedence rules dictate that multiplication is performed before addition, and we say that multiplication "takes precedence" over addition.

The corresponding postfix expression is a b c * +, and there is no ambiguity. It is explicit that the multiplication operator applies to the immediately two preceding operands b and c. The addition operation is then applied to the operand a and the result (b * c). If we had meant the expression (a + b) * c, we would have written it in postfix notation as a b + c *. Now the + operation is applied to the two operands a and b, while * is performed on the two operands c and the result (a + b).

Because of the existence of this unique interpretation, some compilers will first convert arithmetic expressions from the standard infix notation written by programmers to postfix to simplify code generation. To convert an infix expression to postfix, we must use a stack to hold operators that cannot be processed until their operands are available.

Assume that we are given as input the infix string a + b * c − d. This is equivalent to the parenthesized infix arithmetic expression (a + (b * c)) − d. To convert this to postfix format, we scan the input from left to right. If the next symbol in the input stream is an operand (e.g., a), it is placed directly into the output stream without further processing (Note: In the following diagrams, the symbol ^ indicates the current scan location.)

Input: a + b * c − d	Output: a	opStack: empty
^		

If the next symbol in the input string is an operator (e.g., +), then we compare the precedence of this operator to the operator on top of a stack called opStack, short for *operator stack*, which is initialized to empty at the start of the scan. If opStack is currently empty (as it now is) or if the precedence of the next operator in the input stream is greater than the precedence of the one on top of opStack, then we push the operator from the input string onto opStack and continue.

Let's explain what is happening a little more intuitively. We are trying to locate the highest precedence operation to determine what operation should be done next. As long as the operators being scanned are increasing in precedence, we cannot do anything with our infix expression. Instead, we stack them and continue scanning the input string.

```
Input: a + b * c – d          Output: a              opStack: +
       ^                                                      ^
                                                             top


Input: a + b * c – d          Output: a  b            opStack: +
       ^                                                      ^
                                                             top


(assume the precedence of * > precedence of +)

Input: a + b * c – d          Output: a  b            opStack: + *
           ^                                                    ^
                                                               top


Input: a + b * c – d          Output: a  b  c         opStack: + *
           ^                                                    ^
                                                               top
```

At this point, we encounter the – operator whose precedence is lower than *, the operator on top of the stack. We now pop operators from opStack until either (a) opStack is empty or (b) the precedence of the operator on top of opStack is strictly less than that of the current operator in the input string. In this example, we will pop both the * and + operators and place them into the output stream:

```
Input: a + b * c – d          Output: a  b  c  *  +    opStack: empty
           ^
```

This scanning process continues until we come to the end of the input. Then, any remaining operators on opStack are popped into the output and the algorithm terminates.

```
Input: a + b * c – d          Output: a  b  c  *  +    opStack: –
           ^                                                     ^
                                                                top
```
(continued)

Input: a + b * c − d
            ^
	Output: a b c * + d	opStack: −
		        ^
		       top

Input: a + b * c − d ^	Output: a b c * + d −	opStack: empty

The algorithm has produced the expression a b c * + d −, the correct postfix representation of our original input.

In this example, a stack was the right structure to hold operators from the input stream because of the nature of the algorithm. Operators must be saved until we determine their proper location, and then they are placed into the output stream in the reverse order of their occurrence in the input. Again, this is a perfect match with the LIFO model of a stack.

Figure 6.28 shows a program for converting an infix expression (without parentheses) into its equivalent postfix expression. It uses the resources of the class LinkedStack that implements the Stack interface of Figure 6.26. We will design and implement this (and another) class in the coming section.

```
/**
 * This is a simple demonstration program utilizing a stack to convert a
 * restricted class of infix expressions to their postfix equivalent. The
 * class is as follows:
 *
 * Expressions consist of single-letter variable names ('a' through 'z'),
 * separated by the mathematical operators '/', '*', '-', and '+'.
 * Expressions may not contain spaces.
 *
 * Precedence rules are:
 * High: '/', '*'
 * Low:  '+', '-'
 *
 * Example expressions:
 *
 * Valid:
 *     a+b
 *     a+b/c-d*e
 *
 * Invalid:
 *     a + b
 *     a^b
 *     (a+b)*c
 */
```

FIGURE 6.28 Using a stack for infix-to-postfix conversion

```java
public class Infix2Postfix {
    /**
     * Translate infix expressions to postfix expressions.
     *
     * @param args the expression to be converted.
     */

    public static void main( String args[] ) {
        // The stack that will hold the operators
        Stack opStack = new LinkedStack();

        // Make sure there is something to convert
        if ( args.length != 1 ) {
            System.err.println( "Usage: Infix2PostFix expr" );
        }
        else {
            // Convert the expression on the command line
            for ( int pos = 0; pos < args[ 0 ].length(); pos = pos + 1 ) {
                // Put the current character in a variable for convenience
                char ch = args[ 0 ].charAt( pos );
                // Handle this character
                if ( ch >= 'a' && ch <= 'z' ) {
                    // It's a variable - just print it
                    System.out.print( ch );
                }
                else {
                    // It is an operator. Pop any operators off the stack
                    // that have greater or equal precedence.
                    while ( !opStack.empty() &&
                        comparePrecedence( ch, opStack ) <= 0 ) {

                        System.out.print( opStack.top() );
                        opStack.pop();
                    }

                    // Push the current operator
                    opStack.push( new Character( ch ) );
                }
            }

            // Input exhausted - dump any remaining operators
            while( !opStack.empty() ) {
                System.out.print( opStack.top() );
                opStack.pop();
            }

            // End output with a newline
            System.out.println();
        }
    }
}
```

(continued)

FIGURE 6.28 Using a stack for infix-to-postfix conversion *(continued)*

```java
/**
 * Compare the precedence of the given operator with the
 * operator on top of the stack. Returns a positive number
 * if the precedence of the given operator is greater, 0 if
 * it is equal, and a negative number if it is less.
 *
 * Precondition:
 *    Stack is not empty.
 *
 * Postcondition:
 *    Stack is unchanged.
 *
 * @return returns a positive number if the precedence of
 *    the given operator is greater than the operator
 *    on top of the stack, 0 if the precedences are
 *    the same, and -1 if the precedence of the given
 *    operator is less.
 */

private static int comparePrecedence( char op, Stack stk ) {
    char top = ( (Character)stk.top() ).charValue();
    int opGroup = 0;
    int topGroup = 0;

    // Convert precedences into numbers to make this
    // easy. Multiplicative operators are assigned 1,
    // additive operators are assigned 0.

    if ( op == '*' || op == '/' ) {
        opGroup = 1;
    }

    if ( top == '*' || top == '/' ) {
        topGroup = 1;
    }

    // Simply return the difference

    return opGroup - topGroup;
}

} // Infix2Postfix
```

FIGURE 6.28 Using a stack for infix-to-postfix conversion *(continued)*

◆ 6.3.3 Implementation of a Stack

6.3.3.1 An Array-Based Implementation

A simple way to implement a stack is using a one-dimensional array of Objects. There must also be an instance variable `top` that points to the top element of the stack. A `top` value in the range [0 . . . STACKSIZE-1] will refer to a specific element in a nonempty stack, and a value of −1 represents the empty stack. The declarations for this array-based implementation are given in Figure 6.29.

```
public class ArrayStack implements Stack        {
                                         // declarations for an array-
                                         // based implementaton of a stack
        private final int STACKSIZE = 100; // the maximum stack size
        private Object theStack[];         // this is the actual stack
        private int top = -1;              // pointer to the top element
                                         //     in the stack
                                 // the value -1 means an empty stack
        . . .                    // the public methods will go here
```

FIGURE 6.29 Declarations for an array-based implementation of a stack

Implementation of the five operations in the `Stack` interface using the declarations of Figure 6.29 is simple. For example, to push a new value onto the stack, we increment `top` and store the new value in this slot of the array, assuming, of course, that the stack is not full. To pop a value, we decrement `top`, assuming that the stack is not empty. To retrieve the top value, we return `s[top]`. In fact, all five stack operations are executed in O(1) time. The restrictions placed on the location of insertions, retrievals, and deletions make the array an efficient implementation model for a stack. An array-based class that implements the `Stack` interface of Figure 6.26 is shown in Figure 6.30.

```
/**
 * An array-based implementation of a stack.
 */
public class ArrayStack implements Stack {

    private Object theStack[];                  // The stack itself
    private final static int STACK_SIZE = 100; // Most items we can have
    private int top;                            // Position of top element

    /**
     * Construct a new stack
     *
                                                                (continued)
```

FIGURE 6.30 Implementation of a stack using arrays

```
 *  Preconditions:
 *     None.
 *
 *  Postconditions:
 *     The ArrayStack is ready for use.
 */

public ArrayStack() {
    // Create storage for the stack
    theStack = new Object[ STACK_SIZE ];

    // Top will be -1 for an empty stack because it is incremented before
    // it is used to add a new element to the stack.
    top = -1;
}

/**
 * Removes the top of the stack.
 *
 * Preconditions:
 *    Stack is not empty.
 *
 * Postconditions:
 *    Stack size has decreased by 1.
 *    The top item of the stack has been removed.
 *    The rest of the stack is unchanged.
 */

public void pop() {
    theStack[ top ] = null; // Erase location so object can be garbage
                            // collected

    top = top - 1; // Lower the top of the stack
}

/**
 * Places its argument on the top of the stack.
 *
 * Preconditions:
 *    Stack is not full.
 *
 * Postconditions:
 *    Stack size has increased by 1.
 *    Data are on top of the stack.
 *    The rest of the stack is unchanged.
 *
 * @param data the object to place on the stack
 */
```

FIGURE 6.30 Implementation of a stack using arrays *(continued)*

```
public void push( Object data ) {
    top = top + 1;          // Increment the stack pointer
    theStack[ top ] = data; // Put the data in the stack
}

/**
 * Returns the top element of the stack
 *
 * Preconditions:
 *     The stack is not empty.
 *
 * Postconditions:
 *     The stack is unchanged.
 *
 * @return the element on top of the stack
 */

public Object top() {
    return theStack[ top ]; // Return the topmost element
}

/**
 * Returns true if the stack is empty
 *
 * Preconditions:
 *     None.
 *
 * Postconditions:
 *     The stack is unchanged.
 *
 * @return true if the stack is empty and false otherwise.
 */

public boolean empty() {
    return top == -1; // Empty if top is -1
}


/**
 * Determines whether the stack is full
 *
 * @return true if the stack can accept no more elements, false
 *     otherwise.
 * Preconditions:
 *     None.
 *
 * Postconditions:
 *     The stack is unchanged.
```

(continued)

FIGURE 6.30 Implementation of a stack using arrays *(continued)*

```
     *
     * @return true if the stack is full and false otherwise
     */

    public boolean full() {
        return top == theStack.length; // Full if the top is at the end of
                                       // the array

    }

} // ArrayStack
```

FIGURE 6.30 Implementation of a stack using arrays *(continued)*

The code in Figure 6.30 is simple, straightforward, and easy to understand, and that is why arrays are frequently used to implement stacks. However, there is still the same problem we have discussed previously; the fixed size restriction on arrays. Once our array is filled with STACK_SIZE elements, we cannot do any more push operations to it. Instead, we must either remove some existing elements or dynamically resize the array and copy the current values into this new structure. A better implementation would allow our stack to grow to whatever size we desire without the possibility of stack overflow, or at least not until all available memory has been exhausted. This can be achieved using a linked list-based implementation, introduced in the next section.

6.3.3.2 A Linked List-Based Implementation

The previous section showed how to use an array to implement a stack. However, it is sometimes better to implement a stack using a singly linked list. As mentioned earlier, the advantage of a list is that we do not need to declare a maximum stack size. Instead, the stack can grow as large as desired and will never be full.

In a linked list implementation, head points to the top element of the stack. Since we only ever access the top element, we will always access our stack via the head pointer. The next field of each node points to the element in the stack "underneath" this one. This approach is diagramed in Figure 6.31b, which shows the three-element stack of Figure 6.31a, containing the objects X, Y, and Z, implemented as a linked list.

The declarations to create this linked list implementation are similar to the declarations used to produce the singly linked list structure of Figures 6.13 and 6.14. The

(a) Logical view of the stack   *(b) Its linked list implementation*

FIGURE 6.31 List implementation of a stack

only differences are (a) there is no longer a need for a tail pointer because we can no longer access the node at the end of the list, and (b) there is no need for a current position indictor because we only ever work with the top node.

The linked list implementation of the five methods in the Stack interface is again quite simple. For example, to push an object e onto the stack, we add it as the first element in the stack so that it is referenced by the head pointer:

```
LinkedNode
temp = new LinkedNode();    // get space for the new node
temp.data = e;              // fill in the data field
temp.next = head;          // have its next field point to what was
                           //    previously the top element
head = temp;               // and have head now point to this one
```

Similarly, pop() removes the node currently pointed at by head, an operation identical to the remove(0) method in Figure 6.7.

```
head = head.next;
```

The top() operation is easily implemented by the following single line:

```
return(head.data);    // return data field of the first node
```

Figure 6.32 presents the code for a LinkedStack class that implements the Stack interface of Figure 6.26. The node structure in this implementation is specified by the class LinkedNode of Figure 6.13.

```
/**
 * A simple linked list implementation of the Stack interface.
 */

public class LinkedStack implements Stack {
    private LinkedNode top; // Reference to the top of the stack

    /**
     * Create a new stack.
     */

    public LinkedStack() {
        top = null; // Create an empty stack
    }

    /**
     * Places its argument on the top of the stack.
     *
```

(continued)

FIGURE 6.32 Linked list-based Stack class

```
 * Preconditions:
 *     Stack is not full.
 *
 * Postconditions:
 *     Stack size has increased by 1.
 *     V is on top of the stack.
 *     The rest of the stack is unchanged.
 *
 * @param data Object to place on the stack
 */

public void push( Object data ) {
   // Create a new node and make it point to the top of the stack
   LinkedNode newTop = new LinkedNode( data, top );
   // The top of the stack is the new node
   top = newTop;
}

/**
 * Remove element at the top of the stack.
 *
 * Preconditions:
 *     Stack is not empty.
 *
 * Postconditions:
 *     Stack size has decreased by 1.
 *     The top item of the stack has been removed.
 *     The rest of the stack is unchanged.
 */

public void pop() {
   // The new top is the node after the current top
   top = top.getNext();
}

/**
 * Return element currently on top of the stack
 *
 * Preconditions:
 *     The stack is not empty.
 *
 * Postconditions:
 *     The stack is unchanged.
 *
 * @return the element currently on top of the stack
 */

public Object top() {
   return top.getData();
}
```

FIGURE 6.32 Linked list-based `Stack` class *(continued)*

```
/**
 * Returns true if the stack is empty
 *
 * Preconditions:
 *      None.
 *
 * Postconditions:
 *      The stack is unchanged.
 *
 * @return returns true if the stack is empty and false otherwise
 */

public boolean empty() {
    // The stack is empty if top is null
    return top == null;
}


/**
 * Determines whether the stack is full
 *
 * Preconditions:
 *      None.
 *
 * Postconditions:
 *      The stack is unchanged.
 *
 * @return returns true if the stack is full and false otherwise.
 */

public boolean full() {
    // LinkedStacks are never full
    return false;
}

} // LinkedStack
```

FIGURE 6.32 Linked list-based `Stack` class *(continued)*

All five operations are completed in O(1) time, and this linked list implementation is equally as efficient as the array-based one shown earlier. However, we no longer need to worry about memory limitations imposed by the underlying implementation—note that `full()` always returns false. This implementation never runs out of memory as long as the memory manager is able to satisfy our requests. The small price we pay for this is the increased space required for the pointers in the `next` field of each node.

It is interesting to look back and review what we have done regarding the implementation of our `Stack` interface. We have taken the interface of Figure 6.26 and built two totally different implementations:

1. A one-dimensional array-based implementation (Figure 6.30)
2. A singly-linked list implementation (Figure 6.32)

Each of these approaches has certain advantages and disadvantages. However, the most important point is that, regardless of which technique is ultimately chosen, the user is blissfully unaware of the myriad technical details regarding pointers, declarations, efficiency, or memory space. All he or she cares about are the resources provided by these classes and how to access them. This is the beauty of object-oriented programming.

6.4 QUEUES

A **queue** is a first-in, first-out (FIFO) linear data structure in which all retrievals and deletions are made at one end, called the **front** or **head** of the queue, and all insertions are made at the other end, called the **back** or **tail** of the queue. Thus, while a stack uses only one end, the top, for all its operations, the queue uses both ends—the front for taking things out and the back for putting new things in.

This situation is diagramed in Figure 6.33a, which shows a queue containing the elements X, Y, and Z added in just that order; X is the element at the front of the queue, and Z is the element at the back. The only value we can access (i.e., retrieve, modify, or delete) is X, the object at the front. If we delete it, we have the situation in Figure 6.33b in which Y has moved to the front. If we add a new element, W, to the queue of Figure 6.33b, it is placed at the back of the queue, producing the situation shown in Figure 6.33c.

X Y Z	Y Z	Y Z W
^ ^	^ ^	^ ^
front back	front back	front back
(a) Three-element queue	*(b) After deletion of X*	*(c) After insertion of W*

FIGURE 6.33 Queue data structure

Like the stack, queues are an important and widely used data structure. Their first-in, first-out (FIFO) behavior models a waiting line, and a queue is often used to store information about objects waiting to access resources or to request services. Examples include processes waiting to obtain a processor or I/O requests queued up for service at a disk. (This last example will be discussed in more detail later in this chapter.)

◆ 6.4.1 Operations on Queues

The operation of inserting a new item at the back of a queue is called **enqueue**, and its behavior was shown in Figure 6.33c. The `enqueue(e)` method is a mutator that produces a new queue identical to the original except that the object `e` has been added at the back, and the queue length is 1 greater than its previous value. If the queue is full when this method is invoked, then its behavior is undefined. For example, assume we start with the following four-element queue

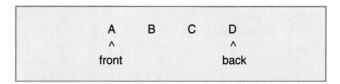

and execute the three operations `enqueue(X)`, `enqueue(Y)`, `enqueue(Z)`, in exactly that order. We end up with the following:

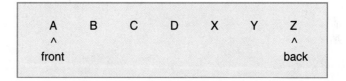

The process of removing the value at the front of the queue is termed **dequeue** (pronounced dee-Q), and its behavior was diagrammed in Figure 6.33b. `dequeue()` is a mutator that produces a new queue identical to the original except that the item at the front has been removed, and the queue length is 1 less than its previous value. If the queue is empty when this method is invoked, its behavior is undefined. If we start with the previous seven-element queue and perform the series of operations `dequeue()`, `dequeue()`, `enqueue(W)`, `dequeue()`, we end up with the following queue structure:

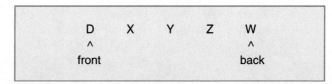

`enqueue()` and `dequeue()` are the most important mutator operations on queues.

There are two important accessor methods for queues. The method `front()` returns the element currently located at the front of the queue, but like the stack method `top()` discussed in the previous section, `front()` does not alter the queue. This method allows us to inspect the object at the front without removing it. Invoking `front()` on the queue of Figure 6.33c returns the value Y. Similarly `back()` allows us to inspect the last object in the queue without deleting it. Invoking `back()` on the queue of Figure 6.33c returns W.

The two predicates `full()` and `empty()` operate exactly as their counterparts in the stack classes of Figures 6.30 and 6.32. The method `full()` returns true if the queue is full—that is, an attempt to enqueue a new item would result in a fatal error—and false otherwise. `empty()` returns true if the queue is currently empty and false otherwise.

Figure 6.34 presents a `Queue` interface that contains the six methods that have been described. These six are standard and almost universally included in every queue class, but other operations are possible. For example, we might wish to include a method `size()`, which returns the number of elements in the queue. Whether this or other operations are worthwhile to include depends on how the queue will be used.

```
/**
 * An interface for Queue
 */

public interface Queue {

    /**
     * Places the given object at the back of the queue
     *
     * Preconditions:
     *     The queue is not full.
     *
     * Postconditions:
     *     The value V has been added to the back of queue
     *     The size of the queue has increased by one
     *     No other structure of the queue has changed.
     *
     * @param data the object to place in the queue.
     *
     */
    public void enqueue( Object data );

    /**
     *
     * Removes the element at the front of the queue.
     *
     * Preconditions:
     *     The queue is not empty.
     *
     * Postconditions:
     *     The size of the queue has decreased by one.
     *     The first item of the queue has been removed.
     *     No other structure of the queue has changed.
     */
    public void dequeue();

    /**
     * Return the element at the front of the queue
     *
     * @return the element at the front of the queue
     *
```

FIGURE 6.34 Queue interface

```
         * Preconditions:
         *    The queue is not empty.
         *
         * Postconditions:
         *    The queue is unchanged.
         *
         * @return the element currently at the front of the queue.
         */
       public Object front();

       /**
         * Return the element at the back of the queue
         *
         * Preconditions:
         *    The queue is not empty.
         *
         * Postconditions:
         *    The queue is unchanged.
         *
         * @return the element at the back of the queue.
         */
       public Object back();

       /**
         * Determine if the queue is empty.
         *
         * Preconditions:
         *    None.
         *
         * Postconditions:
         *    The queue is unchanged.
         *
         * @return true if the queue is empty and false otherwise.
         */
       public boolean empty();

       /**
         * Determine if the queue is full.
         *
         * Preconditions:
         *    None.
         *
         * Postconditions:
         *    The queue is unchanged.
         *
         * @return true if the queue is full and false otherwise.
         */
       public boolean full();

   } // Queue
```

FIGURE 6.34 Queue interface

◆ 6.4.2 Applications of Queues

The FIFO characteristic of a queue accurately models the behavior of a waiting line in which newly arriving objects are placed at the back of the line, and the object at the front of the line is the next to be served. Thus, a queue is useful whenever we have a time-ordered set of objects waiting for service and the service policy is first come, first served. This section looks at an example of this type of usage in computer science: **disk request queues**.

A disk drive, such as a floppy disk, DVD, or hard drive, is a **direct-access storage device** in which data are recorded magnetically in concentric circles, called **tracks**, on the surface of a thin metal disk rotating at high speed. Each track contains an identical number of **sectors** where the data are stored. Each sector has a unique address, so it is possible to go directly to a specific sector by providing its address. Most disks have a single read/write head, and this head is moved in and out to position itself over any track. We read a sector on that track by waiting for the sector to rotate under the read/write head. The physical layout of a typical disk is diagrammed in Figure 6.35.

The time needed to read the data contained in a sector is the sum of the following three components:

1. **Seek time**. The time to position the read/write head over the correct track.

2. **Rotation time**. The time for the start of the desired sector to rotate under the read/write head.

3. **Transfer time**. The time to read the data in that sector and transfer them into memory. This is the time for the entire sector to pass under the head.

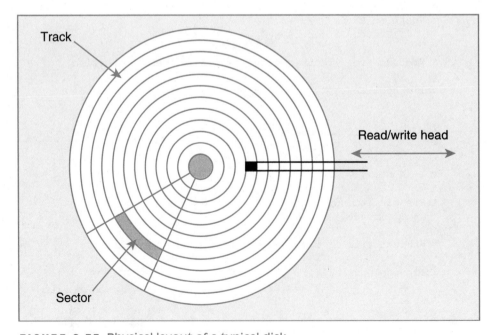

FIGURE 6.35 Physical layout of a typical disk

Of these three components, seek time usually contributes the most because it involves the relatively slow and cumbersome mechanical operation of moving the read/write arm from one track to another. Therefore, a great deal of effort has gone into the design of **disk scheduling algorithms** that attempt to minimize this time-consuming in and out arm movement to maximize disk throughput.

From the system's point of view, the worst possible scheduling policy is one that services user requests in the exact order they arrive. For example, assume that our disk has 500 tracks, and it receives the following four user requests in the order shown:

> *track number requested*
> *0, 499, 0, 499, . . .*
> → *time*

If we service requests in the exact order they arrive, then we will have a great deal of arm motion—from track 0 to 499, back to 0, and back to 499—and the disk will not be used very efficiently. The majority of its time will be spent moving the read/write arm, not reading data. However, if we were a little more clever, we would service both requests for track 0 before moving the arm to track 499, even though that is not the order in which the requests arrived. Only after servicing the two requests for track 0 would we handle the two requests for track 499. This scheduling policy is called **shortest seek time first (SSTF)** because the request serviced next is not necessarily the next one in line but the one closest to the current location of the read/write head (i.e., the one with the shortest seek time).

An easy way to implement an SSTF disk scheduling policy is to store the requests in an array of queues, one queue for each track on the disk. Assume that the tracks are numbered 0 to MAX − 1. Then we would declare our array as follows:

```
Request q[MAX];      // an array of request queues
```

When a request object R asks to read or write data from track i, $0 \leq i \leq \text{MAX} - 1$, we enqueue that request into q[i] by invoking q[i].enqueue(R). When the read/write head is positioned above track i, it services all of the requests in queue[i] from front to back by executing the following loop:

```
while (! q[i].empty()) {
    Request r = q[i].front();
    q[i].dequeue();
    service disk request r;
}
```

When it has finished with all requests for track i, it determines the track closest to i that contains at least one request. It moves the head to that track and continues.

However, there is still one problem. If our only criterion for selecting a request is shortest seek time, then it is possible for the read/write head to remain over one part of the disk forever and never service requests for information on distant tracks. For example, assume that the arm is positioned over track 5, and there are a large number of requests for data on tracks 3, 4, 5, 6, and 499. The arm will remain in the region [3 . . . 6] and never move to track 499. The seek time required to reach that distant track will always be much greater than the seek time to tracks 3 through 6. Thus, an SSTF policy could be unfair to some users.

To ensure that all user requests get a reasonable level of service, we will make one small change to our algorithm. We will move the arm in only one direction at a time, moving first from track 0 up to MAX − 1, and then sweeping back down from track MAX − 1 to track 0. This is a **one-directional SSTF policy**, also called the **sweep algorithm**, and it ensures that all disk requests will eventually get serviced. We select the next request by taking the one with the shortest seek time, but only in the direction we are moving. This sweep algorithm is widely used on modern computing systems.

Figure 6.36 outlines this one-directional SSTF disk scheduling algorithm. Note how it makes use of the queue operations just described to determine if a queue is empty and, if not, to access the next request on that track. This algorithm assumes that whenever a program reads or writes to a sector on track i, it does so by creating a request object r and enqueueing it into the correct queue by invoking q[i].enqueue(r).

```
// Create an array of request queues q[] whose length equals the number of
//    tracks
// Set current track to 0 and set the initial direction to Up

Loop
     // service every request on the current track
     while (! q[currentTrack].empty() ) {
          Request r = q[currentTrack].front();
          q[currentTrack].dequeue();
          Service request r
     }
     // now move to the next track, but only in the direction specified
     if (direction == Up) && (currentTrack < MAX-1)
           currentTrack++;
     else if (direction == Up) && (currentTrack == MAX-1)
           direction = Down;
     else if (direction == Down) && (currentTrack > 0)
           currentTrack--;
     else if (direction == Down) && (currentTrack == 0)
           direction = Up;

EndLoop
```

FIGURE 6.36 One-directional shortest seek time first disk scheduling algorithm

◆ 6.4.3 Implementation of a Queue

6.4.3.1 An Array-Based Implementation

We can use a one-dimensional array to implement a queue, but there is one small problem. If we start with the six-element array and the queue q shown in Figure 6.37a and carry out the following four operations

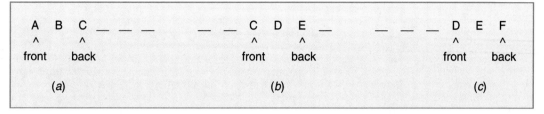

FIGURE 6.37 Example of queue operations

```
q.dequeue();
q.dequeue();
q.enqueue(D);
q.enqueue(E);
```

we will end up with the condition shown in Figure 6.37b. Note that the elements in the queue have "slid" to the right. This is called the *inchworm effect,* and it is due to the fact that we are removing elements from one end but adding them to the other. If we now perform the following two operations

```
q.dequeue();
q.enqueue(F);
```

we end up with the queue in Figure 6.37c, where we have reached the end of the array even though there are still three empty slots at the front.

How can we solve this problem? An easy and rather simple way is not to view the array as a structure indexed linearly from 0 to MAX − 1 but as a **circular array**, or **ring**, in which the first element of the array, q[0], immediately follows the last element of the array, q[MAX − 1], as shown in Figure 6.38. This is done by incrementing

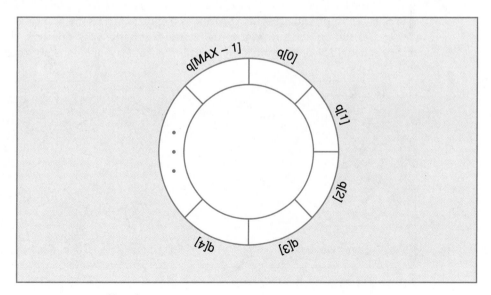

FIGURE 6.38 Circular array

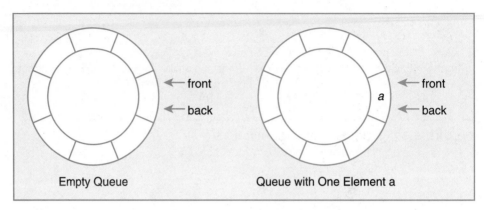

FIGURE 6.39a Trying to distinguish between an empty queue and a queue with one element

our array index modulo the array size MAX. Then the array element accessed after q[MAX − 1] is q[0], since [(MAX − 1) + 1] % MAX = 0.

However, this solution leads to yet another problem: detecting the difference between an empty queue and at least one other queue that is nonempty. For example, if we initialize the pointers of an empty queue so that both front and back are 0 (or any integer value between 0 and MAX − 1), we will not be able to distinguish between a queue with no elements and a queue with exactly one element. When there is a single element stored in location 0 of the array, both the front and back pointers will also be set to 0. This situation is shown in Figure 6.39a.

We might instead choose to initialize the queue so back = front − 1. However, in that case, we will not be able to tell the difference between an empty queue and a full queue. When the queue is full, the front pointer will have some value n, $0 \le n \le$ MAX − 1, and the back pointer will have the value $(n − 1)$ % MAX—exactly the same condition as the empty queue. This situation is diagramed in Figure 6.39b.

In fact, no matter how you initialize the front and back pointers, their initial empty state will always be indistinguishable from at least one nonempty state. This is

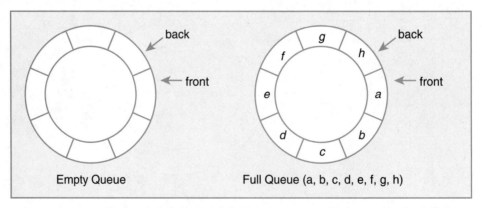

FIGURE 6.39b Trying to distinguish between an empty queue and a full queue

because there are $n + 1$ different number of elements that can be stored in a queue of size n, namely, 0, 1, 2, 3, . . . , n. However, once you have fixed the location of one of the pointers, say, front, there are only n possible positions for the other pointer. Thus, it is impossible to represent $(n + 1)$ distinct queue states with only n possible locations for front and back.

There are a number of solutions to this problem. The easiest is to use an auxiliary state variable called `size`, which counts the number of elements in the queue, and this is the solution used in Figure 6.40. By checking this variable, we can determine whether a queue is either empty or full. Of course, all methods that alter the number of elements in the queue must correctly reset this state variable.

An `ArrayQueue` class that implements the `Queue` interface of Figure 6.34 using a circular array is shown in Figure 6.40.

```
/**
 * An implementation of a queue using circular arrays
 */

public class ArrayQueue implements Queue {

    // The size of the array

    public static final int MAX_SIZE = 100;

    private Object theQueue[];   // The queue
    private int front, back;     // Front and back positions in the queue
    private int size;            // Number of elements in the queue

    /**
     * Create a new queue.
     */
    public ArrayQueue() {
        // Create the array that will be the queue
        theQueue = new Object[ MAX_SIZE ];

        // Initialize state

        size = 0;
        front = 0;
        back = -1;
    }

    /**
     * Places the given object at the back of the queue
     *
     * Preconditions:
     *     The queue is not full.
     *
```

(continued)

FIGURE 6.40 Queue class using a circular array implementation

```
 * Postconditions:
 *     The value V has been added to the back of queue
 *     The size of the queue has increased by one
 *     No other structure of the queue has changed.
 *
 * @param data the object to place in the queue.
 *
 */
public void enqueue( Object data ) {
   // Determine where the new element will be placed
   back = ( back + 1 ) % MAX_SIZE;
   // Add the element
   theQueue[ back ] = data;
   // One more thing in the queue
   size = size + 1;
}

/**
 *
 * Removes the element at the front of the queue.
 *
 * Preconditions:
 *     The queue is not empty.
 *
 * Postconditions:
 *     The size of the queue has decreased by one.
 *     The first item of the queue has been removed.
 *     No other structure of the queue has changed.
 */
public void dequeue() {
   // Eliminate reference for garbage collection
   theQueue[ front ] = null;

   // Remove the first element by incrementing the location
   // of the first element
   front = ( front + 1 ) % MAX_SIZE;

   // There is now one less element in the queue
   size = size - 1;
}

/**
 * Return the element at the front of the queue
 *
 * @return the element at the front of the queue
 *
 * Preconditions:
 *     The queue is not empty.
 *
 * Postconditions:
 *     The queue is unchanged.
 *
```

FIGURE 6.40 Queue class using a circular array implementation *(continued)*

```
    * @return the element currently at the front of the queue.
    */
  public Object front() {
     return theQueue[ front ];
  }


  /**
   * Return the element at the back of the queue
   *
   * Preconditions:
   *    The queue is not empty.
   *
   * Postconditions:
   *    The queue is unchanged.
   *
   * @return the element at the back of the queue.
   */
  public Object back() {
     return theQueue[ back ];
  }

  /**
   * Determine if the queue is empty.
   *
   * Preconditions:
   *    None.
   *
   * Postconditions:
   *     The queue is unchanged.
   *
   * @return true if the queue is empty and false otherwise.
   */
  public boolean empty() {
    return size == 0;
  }

  /**
   * Determine if the queue is full.
   *
   * Preconditions:
   *    None.
   *
   * Postconditions:
   *    The queue is unchanged.
   *
   * @return true if the queue is full and false otherwise.
   */
  public boolean full() {
    return size == MAX_SIZE;
  }

} // ArrayQueue
```

FIGURE 6.40 Queue class using a circular array implementation *(continued)*

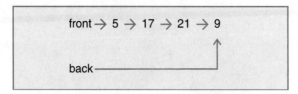

FIGURE 6.41 Linked list view of a queue

6.4.3.2 A Linked List-Based Implementation

Rather than using an array, we can implement our queue as a linked list (Figure 6.41). It may actually be easier to implement a queue using the representation of Figure 6.41 instead of the array representation discussed in the previous section. First, we do not have to worry about the inchworm effect diagramed in Figure 6.37. In addition, there is never a problem distinguishing between empty and full queues because with a linked list, a queue can never be full. Therefore, applications that use queues often prefer a linked list representation.

The linked list implementation of a queue is similar to the linked list implementation of a stack, and the declarations to create this structure are virtually identical. The only major difference is the inclusion of a `back` pointer that references the last element in the queue. This state variable was not needed by the stack.

The default constructor creates an empty queue by setting the `front` and `back` pointers to `null` and the queue size to 0.

The method `enqueue(I)`, which adds a new object I to the back of the queue, is very similar to the `append()` operation on lists shown in Figure 6.17. The existence of a back pointer allows the enqueue method to be completed in O(1) time. Without it, we would have to iterate through the queue to locate the end of the queue where the enqueue takes place, an O(N) operation.

The `dequeue()` method, which deletes the element at the front of the queue, is virtually identical to the `pop()` operation on stacks, which also removes the first element in the collection. The only difference is ensuring that the `back` pointer is correctly reset if we delete the last item. An attempt to dequeue from an empty queue is a fatal error. Later, you will learn how to use exceptions to handle these and similar unusual conditions.

A complete implementation of a `LinkedQueue` class that implements the `Queue` interface is shown in Figure 6.42.

```
/**
 * A linked list implementation of a queue.
 */

public class LinkedQueue implements Queue {

    private LinkedNode front;  // The first node in the queue
    private LinkedNode back;   // The last node in the queue
    private int size;          // The number of elements in the queue
```

FIGURE 6.42 Linked list implementation of the Queue interface

```
/**
 * Constructs a LinkedQueue
 */
public LinkedQueue() {
    // Initialize state
    size = 0;
    front = null;
    back = null;
}

/**
 * Places the given object at the back of the queue
 *
 * Preconditions:
 *     The queue is not full.
 *
 * Postconditions:
 *     The value V has been added to the back of the queue
 *     The size of the queue has increased by one
 *     No other structure of the queue has changed.
 *
 * @param data Object to put into the queue
 */
public void enqueue( Object data ) {
    // Initialize a new node
    LinkedNode newNode = new LinkedNode( data, null );

    // Is the queue empty?
    if ( back == null ) {
        // If the queue is empty the new node is
        // also the front of the queue
        front = newNode;
    }
    else {
        // Make the last thing in the queue refer
        // to the new element.
        back.setNext( newNode );
    }

    // Back should refer to the new node
    back = newNode;

    // One more element in the queue
    size = size + 1;
}

/**
 * Remove the item at the front of the queue.
 *
```

(continued)

FIGURE 6.42 Linked list implementation of the `Queue` interface *(continued)*

```
    * Preconditions:
    *     The queue is not empty.
    *
    * Postconditions:
    *     The size of the queue has decreased by one.
    *     The first item of the queue has been removed.
    *     No other structure of the queue has changed.
    */
public void dequeue() {
    // Remove the front element
    front = front.getNext();

    // Queue is empty - back should not refer to anything
    if (front == null) {
        back = null;
    }

    // One less item in the queue
    size = size - 1;
}


/**
 * Return the item at the front of the queue.
 *
 * Preconditions:
 *     The queue is not empty.
 *
 * Postconditions:
 *     The queue is unchanged.
 *
 * @return the item at the front of the queue.
 */
public Object front() {
    return front.getData();
}


/**
 * Return the item at the back of the queue.
 *
 * Preconditions:
 *     The queue is not empty.
 *
 * Postconditions:
 *     The queue is unchanged.
 *
 * @return the item at the back of the queue.
 */
public Object back() {
    return back.getData();
}
```

FIGURE 6.42 Linked list implementation of the Queue interface *(continued)*

```
/**
 * Determine if the queue is empty
 *
 * Preconditions:
 *    None.
 *
 * Postconditions:
 *    The queue is unchanged.
 *
 * @return true if the queue is empty and false otherwise.
 */
public boolean empty() {
   return size == 0;
}

/**
 * Determine if the queue is full.
 *
 * Preconditions:
 *    None.
 *
 * Postconditions:
 *    The queue is unchanged.
 *
 * @return true if the queue is full and false otherwise.
 */
public boolean full() {
   // Linked structures are never full
   return false;
}

} // LinkedQueue
```

FIGURE 6.42 Linked list implementation of the Queue interface *(continued)*

◆ 6.4.4 Queue Variations: The Deque and Priority Queue

We conclude this chapter by describing two interesting and useful variations on the queue structure just described. They are the deque and the priority queue.

The word **deque** (pronounced deck) stands for *d*ouble-ended *que*ue. With a deque, you can make insertions and deletions at either end of the queue—that is, at either the front or the back. So while we are still restricted to performing operations at only the two ends of the queue, we allow both of our mutator methods—enqueue() and dequeue()—to be done at either end. For example, given the following four-element deque

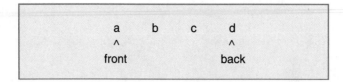

we can add a new item e either at the back as in a regular queue, producing a b c d e, or at the front, producing e a b c d. Similarly, we are permitted to dequeue either the front item, producing b c d, or the back item, producing a b c. Thus, the front and the back of a deque are functionally equivalent.

Another interesting variation is the **priority queue**. If a queue can be thought of as a data structure that models a waiting line, then a priority queue can be viewed as a data structure that models a waiting line with "cuts." That is, we allow objects to get into line anywhere based on a numerical value called a **priority**, which is a measure of this object's importance. However, we still are restricted to removing only the first object in line (i.e., the one at the front) because that will be the object with the highest priority.

The `dequeue()`, `first()`, `last()`, `full()`, and `empty()` methods on priority queues all behave identically to their counterpart in the regular queue described in Section 6.4.1. Only the `enqueue()` operation needs to be modified. It now must include a parameter that specifies the priority value, or importance, of this item:

```
public void enqueue(Object item, int priority);
```

Instead of adding this new item to the back of the queue, as was done previously, we add it to the queue in priority order. That is, we add it so that it is located behind all other items with equal or higher priority but ahead of all items with lower priority.

In a sense, a regular queue, which is ordered by time, can be thought of as a priority queue in which the priority of an item is the time of its insertion. With a priority queue, we are allowed to use values other than time to order elements in the collection. For example, assume you have the following priority queue in which the pairs represent an element and its associated priority (with higher numbers representing higher priority):

$$(a, 9) \rightarrow (b, 7) \rightarrow (c, 7) \rightarrow (d, 5) \rightarrow (e, 2) \rightarrow (f, 1)$$

  ^   ^

front   back

Invoking the method `enqueue(g, 6)` will insert the object g between the existing elements c and d, producing the following:

$$(a, 9) \rightarrow (b, 7) \rightarrow (c, 7) \rightarrow (g, 6) \rightarrow (d, 5) \rightarrow (e, 2) \rightarrow (f, 1)$$

  ^   ^

front   back

Since a new item may be inserted anywhere, depending on its priority level, the enqueue operation for priority queues behaves much like the insert operation on lists. However, the operation `dequeue()` still removes only the front element, the value *a* in the priority queue shown, because the object at the front has the highest priority. Similarly, `first()` and `back()` will still return *a* and *f*, and `empty()` and `full()` would still both return false. With the exception of `enqueue()`, all operations behave in an identical fashion when applied to a priority queue.

Priority queues are widely used. For example, when we insert processes into a waiting line for access to a processor, we may not want to treat them all equally. Instead, we may want to give operating system processes, like the garbage collector, memory manager, and disk scheduler, a higher priority than user processes. This would guarantee that important system routines would receive a higher level of service. Alternatively, we may want to give interactive jobs a higher priority than batch jobs because users are waiting for responses from their interactive jobs.

A complete linked list implementation of a priority queue is given in Figure 6.43. The `LinkedPriorityQueue` class uses `PrioritizedLinkedNodes` to implement the nodes that make up the queue. A `PrioritizedLinkedNode` is the same as the `LinkedNode` class of Figure 6.18 except that it includes an integer value that represents the priority of the item stored in the node. The `PrioritizedLinkedNode` class provides the methods `getPriority()` and `setPriority()` to obtain or change the priority associated with the node. Note that the enqueue operation now requires O(N) time since we must, in the worst case, search the entire queue to locate the proper insertion spot. This makes the complexity of the enqueue operation on priority queues significantly slower than the enqueue operation on queues, which is O(1). In the next chapter, we introduce a new data structure that will allow us to insert an object into a priority queue in O(log *n*), logarithmic time, rather than linear time, a significant improvement.

```
/**
 * A linkable-node class suitable for building prioritized linked data
 * structures such as lists, stacks, and queues.
 *
 */

public class PrioritizedLinkedNode {
    private int priority;                 // This node's priority
    private Object data;                  // The data stored in this node
    private PrioritizedLinkedNode next;   // The next node in the data structure

    /**
     * Construct a node given the info and next references.
     *
     * @param newData the data to be associated with this node.
     * @param newNext a reference to the next node in the list.
     */
```

(continued)

FIGURE 6.43 Implementation of a `LinkedPriorityQueue`

```
public PrioritizedLinkedNode( Object newData, int p ) {
   data = newData;
   priority = p;
   next = null;
}

/**
 * Return the data stored in this node.
 *
 * Preconditions:
 *    None.
 *
 * Postconditions:
 *    The node is unchanged.
 *
 * @return a reference to the data stored in this node.
 */

public Object getData() {
   return data;
}

/**
 * Return a reference to the next node in the data structure.
 *
 * Preconditions:
 *    None.
 *
 * Postconditions:
 *    The node is unchanged.
 *
 * @return a reference to the next Node in the list, or null if this
 *    node has no successor.
 */

public PrioritizedLinkedNode getNext() {
   return next;
}

/**
 * Set the data associated with this node.
 *
 * Preconditions:
 *    None.
 *
 * Postconditions:
 *    The data associated with this node has been changed.
 *
 * @param newData the data to be associated with this node.
 */
```

FIGURE 6.43 Implementation of a `LinkedPriorityQueue` *(continued)*

```
public void setData( Object newData ) {
   data = newData;
}

/**
 * Set the reference to the next node.
 *
 * Preconditions:
 *    None.
 *
 * Postconditions:
 *    The reference to the next node has been changed.
 *
 * @param newNext the reference to the next node in the data structure.
 */

public void setNext( PrioritizedLinkedNode newNext ) {
   next = newNext;
}

/**
 *
 * setPriority() changes the priority of this node.
 *
 * Preconditions:
 *    None.
 *
 * Postconditions:
 *    Node's priority has been updated.
 *
 * @param p this datum's priority
 *
 */

public void setPriority(int p) {
   priority = p;
}

/**
 *
 * getPriority() returns the priority of this node
 *
 * Preconditions:
 *    None.
 *
 * Postconditions:
 *    Node is unchanged.
 *
 * @return priority of this node
 *
 */
```

(continued)

FIGURE 6.43 Implementation of a `LinkedPriorityQueue` *(continued)*

```java
      public int getPriority() {
        return priority;
      }

} // PrioritizedLinkedNode

/**
 * A simple prioritized linked queue. This class assumes that priorities are
 * nonnegative integers, with 0 being the highest priority.
 */

public class LinkedPriorityQueue implements Queue {

    /**
     * Minimum priority.
     */
    public static final int MIN_PRIORITY = 0;

    private PrioritizedLinkedNode front;      // Front of the queue
    private PrioritizedLinkedNode back;       // Back of the queue
    private int size;                         // Number of elements in the queue

    /**
     * Create a new priority queue.
     */

    public LinkedPriorityQueue() {
        // Initialize state
        front = null;
        back = null;
        size = 0;
    }

    /**
     * Remove the item at the front of the queue.
     *
     * Preconditions:
     *     The queue is not empty.
     *
     * Postconditions:
     *     The size of the queue has decreased by one.
     *     The first item of the queue has been removed.
     *     No other structure of the queue has changed.
     */
    public void dequeue() {
        // Remove the front element
        front = front.getNext();
        // Queue is empty - back should not refer to anything
        if (front == null) {
            back = null;
        }
```

FIGURE 6.43 Implementation of a `LinkedPriorityQueue` *(continued)*

```
        // One less item in the queue
        size = size - 1;
    }

    /**
     * Return the item at the front of the queue.
     *
     * Preconditions:
     *     The queue is not empty.
     *
     * Postconditions:
     *     The queue is unchanged.
     *
     * @return the item at the front of the queue.
     */

    public Object front() {
        return front.getData();
    }

    /**
     * Return the item at the back of the queue.
     *
     * Preconditions:
     *     The queue is not empty.
     *
     * Postconditions:
     *     The queue is unchanged.
     *
     * @return the item at the back of the queue.
     */

    public Object back() {
        return back.getData();
    }

    /**
     * Determine if the queue is empty
     *
     * Preconditions:
     *     None.
     *
     * Postconditions:
     *     The queue is unchanged.
     *
     * @return true if the queue is empty and false otherwise.
     */

    public boolean empty() {
        return size == 0;
    }
```

(continued)

FIGURE 6.43 Implementation of a `LinkedPriorityQueue` *(continued)*

```
/**
 * Determine if the queue is full.
 *
 * Preconditions:
 *     None.
 *
 * Postconditions:
 *     The queue is unchanged.
 *
 * @return true if the queue is full and false otherwise.
 */

public boolean full() {
   // Linked structures are never full
   return false;
}


/**
 * Add an element to the queue. The item is added with
 * minimum priority. This method must be provided to
 * satisfy the Queue interface.
 *
 * Preconditions:
 *     The queue is not full.
 *
 * Postconditions:
 *     The value V has been added to the back of queue
 *     The size of the queue has increased by one
 *     No other structure of the queue has changed.
 *
 * @param data Object to put into the queue
 */

public void enqueue( Object data ) {
   // Let the other enqueue method do the work.
   enqueue( data, 0 );
}


/*
 * Add an element to the queue with the given priority.
 *
 * Preconditions:
 *     The queue is not full.
 *
 * Postconditions:
 *     The value V has been added to the back of queue
 *     The size of the queue has increased by one
 *     No other structure of the queue has changed.
 *
```

(continued)

FIGURE 6.43 Implementation of a LinkedPriorityQueue *(continued)*

```
    * @param data Object to put into the queue
    * @param priority the priority of this item.
    */

   public void enqueue( Object data, int priority ) {
      PrioritizedLinkedNode cur = front; // The current node
      PrioritizedLinkedNode prev = null; // The last node visited

      // The node this item will be placed in
      PrioritizedLinkedNode newNode =
      new PrioritizedLinkedNode( data, priority );

      // Adding to an empty queue is easy
      if ( back == null ) {
         front = newNode;
         back = newNode;
      }
      else {
         // Step through the queue looking for the first node with
         // a priority less than the priority of the new node.
         // When the loop has terminated cur will refer to the
         // node after the new node in the queue and prev will
         // refer to the node before the new node.
         while ( cur != null && cur.getPriority() >= priority ) {
            prev = cur;
            cur = cur.getNext();
         }

         if ( cur == null ) {
            // Item must be added at the end of the queue
            back.setNext( newNode );
            back = newNode;
         }
         else if ( prev == null ) {
            // Item must be added to the front of the queue
            newNode.setNext( front );
            front = newNode;
         }
         else {
            // Insert between prev and cur
            prev.setNext( newNode );
            newNode.setNext( cur );
         }
      }

      // One more item in the queue
      size = size + 1;
   }

} // LinkedPriorityQueue
```

FIGURE 6.43 Implementation of a `LinkedPriorityQueue` *(continued)*

6.5 SUMMARY

These last two sections continued our investigation of linear data structures, this time examining structures that place restrictions on where we may do insertions, deletions, and retrievals. Thus, they are less general and flexible than the list structures discussed at the beginning of the chapter.

The stack allows operations at only one end, the location called the top of the stack. The queue allows insertions at one end, called the back of the queue, while deletions and retrievals are permitted at the other end, called the front of the queue. These are the two most important restricted linear structures, and they are widely used throughout computer science. This chapter also introduced two queue variations called the deque and the priority queue.

Figure 6.44 summarizes the behavior of the five linear data structures presented in this chapter. The next chapter will begin our investigation of an important new class of data structures, which have a more complex (*1:many*) relationship between their elements. This classification is called the hierarchical data structures.

Structure	Insertions	Deletions, Retrievals
List	Anywhere	Anywhere
Priority Queue	Anywhere (by priority)	Front
Deque	Front or back	Front or back
Queue	Back	Front
Stack	Front (called the top)	Front

FIGURE 6.44 Summary of the behavior of linear data structures

EXERCISES

1. Using the taxonomy introduced in Section 6.1, explain which of the four data structure classifications best fits each of the following collections:

   a. A character string such as ABCDEF

   b. The organization chart of a corporation

   c. A line of people waiting to get into a theater

   d. A road map

   e. The names and identification numbers of students in a computer science class

2. Referring to the list interface in Figure 6.6, propose some additional positioning, insertion, deletion, or retrieval operations that you think might be useful to include in this interface. For each operation you propose, give its pre- and postconditions and its calling sequence.

3. Assume you are using the array-based implementation of a list given in Figure 6.11. Write the Boolean instance method `find` that attempts to locate a specific object in the list. The calling sequence for `find` is:

```
/* preconditions: none
     postconditions: find searches through a list looking for the
          first occurrence of item. If the item is found, the method
          returns the position number in the list where the item
          occurred, and resets cursor to point to this item. If item
          does not occur anywhere in List, the method returns a -1 and
          cursor is unaffected */
public int find(Object item)
```

4. Assume that you are using the array-based implementation of a list shown in Figure 6.11. Write the class method concatenate that merges two separate lists into a single list. The calling sequence for concatenate is:

```
/* precondition: L1 is a list of length m, m ≥ 0. L2 is a list of
     length n, n ≥ 0.
     postcondition: L1 is a list of length (m + n), with all the
         elements of L2 added after the elements of list L1. L2 is the
         empty list. */
public static void concatenate(List L1, List L2)
```

5. Here is the array implementation of a list. Diagram the logical structure of the list that is represented by this implementation.

	info	next	
0	0	−1	
1	−1	8	
2	9	0	
3	15	6	
4	12	2	head = 1
5	−8	4	availHead = 7
6	4	−1	tail = 6
7	10	3	cursor = 8
8	65	5	count = 5

6. Why did we include both add(I) and append(I) methods in the list interface of Figure 6.6? Explain the problems that we would encounter if we omitted the append method from the interface.

7. Assume that we have decided to implement a list using a one-dimensional array in which we simply store the elements of the list in order within the array. That is, we store the first element of the list in a[0], the second element of the list in a[1], and so on. We do not need a head pointer, since the head of the list is always in position 0 of the array. However, we do keep a tail pointer to help us locate the end of the list. We also have a cursor, which serves the same function as before—locating the current node on which we are working. This leads to the following structure:

```
head → 23 → 5 → 7 → 100        index        value
                                 0            23
                                 1             5      tail = 3
                                 2             7      cursor = 1
                                 3            100
                                              . . .
        (a) Logical view of the list      (b) One-dimensional array implementation
```

Discuss the ease and/or difficulty of implementing each of the following list operations:

a. first()   f. set(I)

b. previous()   g. isOnList()

c. remove()   h. remove(pos)

d. add(I)   i. add(pos, I)

e. append(I)   j. size()

Discuss the strengths and weaknesses of this new one-dimensional array representation and state under what conditions it might be a good alternative to the array representation shown in Figure 6.10.

8. a. Assume that you are using the referenced-based implementation of a list given in Figure 6.17. Would the following two operations be constant time O(1) or linear time O(N) operations?

   (1) swapNext().   Swap the contents of the data field of the node referenced by the cursor with the data field of the successor node.

   (2) swapPrev().   Swap the contents of the data field of the node referenced by the cursor with the data field of the predecessor node.

   b. Implement these two instance methods using the declarations in Figures 6.13 and 6.14. For each method, include the pre- and postconditions in the comments.

9. You are given a singly linked list L of n integer values I_k, $k = 0, \ldots, n - 1$

```
L → 12 → 15 → 35 → 42 → 51
```

The list is implemented using the declarations in Figures 6.13 and 6.14. Write the Boolean instance method inOrder() that compares adjacent values and ensures that the second value is always greater than or equal to the first. That is, $I_k \leq I_{k+1}$, $k = 0, 1, 2, \ldots, n - 2$. If all pairs of nodes in the list meet this condition, return true; otherwise, return false. Be careful that you correctly handle all special cases.

10. Using the declarations in Figures 6.13 and 6.14, write an instance method of the class LinkedList to reverse a list. That is, if L has the initial value

$$L \rightarrow 12 \rightarrow 15 \rightarrow 35 \rightarrow 42 \rightarrow 51$$

then a call on reverse should produce the new list

$$L \rightarrow 51 \rightarrow 42 \rightarrow 35 \rightarrow 15 \rightarrow 12$$

If the list is originally empty, then the method should do nothing and return. The calling sequence of this instance method is **public void** reverse().

11. A classic use of linked lists is for the representation and manipulation of polynomials. A polynomial is a mathematical formula of the following form:

$$a_n x^n + a_{n-1} x^{n-1} + \ldots + a_1 x^1 + a_0$$

This formula can be represented by a list using the following node structure. Each node in the linked list would store the information about one nonzero term of the polynomial.

Node:

coefficient
exponent
next

This would allow us to efficiently represent polynomials of arbitrarily large degree. For example, the polynomial

$$5x^{20} + 2x - 8$$

is a 20th degree polynomial, but it has only three nonzero terms. Therefore, its linked list representation will have only three nodes and would be represented as follows:

$$L \rightarrow (5, 20) \rightarrow (2, 1) \rightarrow (-8, 0)$$

Design and build a Polynomial class that implements polynomials using the LinkedList representation of Figure 6.17. Your Polynomial class should be able to read and write polynomials from the standard input file as well as add and subtract polynomials. Try out your Polynomial class on the following problems:

a. input the following polynomial: $A = x^5 + x^3 + x^2 - 5$

b. input the following polynomial: $B = 3x^4 + 2x^3 - x^2 + 6$

c. write out both A and B

d. compute and print the value of $A + B$

e. compute and print the value of $A - B$

12. Referring to the doubly linked list class of Figure 6.21, add an instance method called back(n), which moves you backward n nodes in the list beginning from the current position indicator. That is, move the cursor to the nth predecessor of the current node. If there are not n predecessors of the current node (i.e., you encounter a null pointer), then reset the cursor to null.

13. Repeat Exercise 12, but this time assume that the list is a circular doubly linked list of the type shown in Figure 6.24. Discuss how the use of a circular doubly linked list did or did not simplify the implementation of this instance method.

14. Given the following stack S

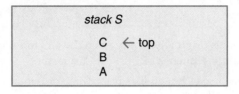

show exactly what the stack will look like after each of the following sequences of operations. (Assume each sequence begins from the preceding state.)

a. S.push(D)   c. S.pop()   d. S.pop()   e. S.push(D)

                     S.pop()   S.pop()   S.pop()

b. S.push(D)   S.push(D)   S.pop()   S.push(E)

   S.push(E)   S.pop()   S.pop()

                     S.push(E)   S.pop()

15. a. Use the infix-to-postfix conversion algorithm given in Section 6.3.2 to convert the following infix expression into postfix notation (assume Java precedence rules):

$$a + b * c - d / e$$

b. Explain how the infix-to-postfix conversion algorithm of Figure 6.28 could be modified to include expressions containing parentheses, assuming that an expression inside parentheses has the highest precedence of all. Thus, the expression (a + b) * c would be expressed as ab+c* in postfix. The final postfix representation would not include any parentheses.

c. Rewrite the code of Figure 6.28 so that it handles parentheses expressions and test it on the following:

   (1) $a * (b - c) * d$

   (2) $(a + b) * (c + d)$

   (3) $a / (b * (c - d))$

   (4) $(((a)))$

16. Add the following two instance methods to the `ArrayStack` class of Figure 6.30:

   a. `remove(n)`   Remove the top *n* elements from the stack. If the stack does not contain at least *n* elements, leave it empty.

   b. `size()`   Return the total number of elements contained in the stack. The contents of the stack are unchanged.

For each operation, provide the pre- and postconditions. Propose additional useful operations on the stack data structure.

17. Repeat Exercise 16, but this time use the `LinkedStack` class of Figure 6.32.

18. Change the behavior of the `pop()` method in Figure 6.32 so that it now combines the behaviors of both `pop()` and `top()`. That is, `pop()` removes the top element of the stack and returns it. Which of these two approaches do you think represents a better design?

19. Propose solutions other than the one in Section 6.4.3.1 to the problem of distinguishing between a full and empty queue. Discuss whether you think your solution is or is not better than the one proposed in the book—that is, using a size field that specifies how many nodes are contained in the queue.

20. Given the following six-element circular queue containing the three elements A, B, and C

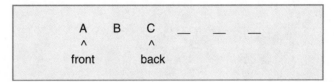

    show what state the queue would be in after each of the following series of operations. (Assume each one starts from the preceding conditions.)

    a. `dequeue()`   b. `enqueue(D)`   c. `enqueue(D)`
       `dequeue()`   `enqueue(E)`   `enqueue(E)`
       `enqueue(D)`   `dequeue()`   `enqueue(F)`
       `enqueue(E)`

21. Can you think of any situations in which the one-dimensional SSTF disk scheduling algorithm given in Figure 6.36 might not work correctly? (Tip: Think about the arrival rates of requests.) Propose a solution to any problem that you identify.

22. Add the following three instance methods to the circular array-based `ArrayQueue` class shown in Figure 6.40:

    a. `size()`   Returns the total number of elements in the queue.

    b. `remove(n)`   Removes the first *n* items from the front of the queue. If the queue does not contain at least *n* items, then leave it empty.

    c. `cutsInLine(I, n)`   Inserts item I into position *n* of the queue rather than at the end of the queue.

23. Repeat Exercise 22, but this time use the linked list implementation of a queue given in Figure 6.42.

24. Design a deque interface that includes all of the important methods carried out on the deque data structure described in Section 6.4.4. Then select an appropriate representation for a deque and build a class that implements this interface.

CHAPTER 7

Hierarchical Data Structures

7.1 INTRODUCTION

This chapter investigates some data structures that are quite different from the lists, stacks, and queues of Chapter 6. Those structures are linear, which means they have a first and last element, and every element, except the first and last, has a unique successor and a unique predecessor. Now we begin our look at **hierarchical data structures**, first diagramed in Figure 6.2. These structures are characterized by the fact that, although each element still has a single predecessor, it may have zero, one, or more successors. In computer science, hierarchical structures are usually referred to as **trees**.

Trees will be familiar to you from everyday life. For example, everyone has a family tree of the type shown in Figure 7.1. Sporting competitions, corporate structures, and term paper outlines are often displayed in a treelike manner as well. We can see from Figure 7.1 that every node in the tree, except Joe, has exactly one predecessor, but a node may have zero (Ruth), one (Tom), or many (Joe, Michael) successors.

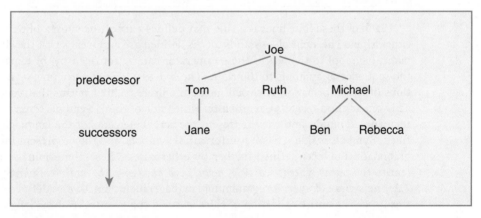

FIGURE 7.1 Family tree

Trees have many applications in computer science. One important use is in the construction of a parse tree as part of the compilation process. A **parse tree** is a hierarchical data structure that reflects the grammatical relationships between syntactic elements of a language. You probably first encountered parse trees in elementary school when you learned to diagram sentences. For example, Figure 7.2 is a parse tree for the sentence "The man bit the dog". When a compiler analyzes a computer program to determine if it is syntactically correct, it attempts to generate a parse tree like the one in Figure 7.2.

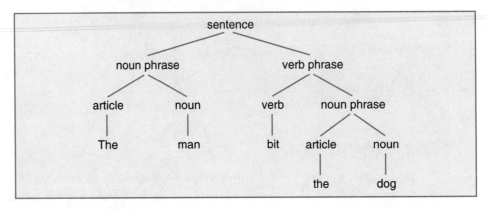

FIGURE 7.2 Sample parse tree

Let's illustrate this process by showing how a compiler might check the correctness of some simplified arithmetic expressions. A four-rule grammar for these expressions is:

rule 1:   <expression> → <term> { + | − <term> }
rule 2:   <term> → <factor> { * <factor> }
rule 3:   <factor> → <letter> | (<expression>)
rule 4:   <letter> → **a** | **b** | **c**

Each of these four lines is a rule that defines part of the syntax of our arithmetic expressions. The symbol → stands for "is defined as" and means that the single grammatical symbol to the left of the → operator can be replaced by, or expanded into, the sequence of symbols to the right. The braces { } mean zero, one, or more repetitions of the information enclosed inside the braces, and | means that you select exactly one of the alternative symbols on either side of the |. Symbols set in boldface are **terminal** symbols, and they represent the actual elements of the language being defined. Symbols inside < > are **nonterminal** symbols, and they represent intermediate grammatical objects defined further by other rules. These nonterminals are equivalent to the terms *sentence, article, noun, verb phrase, verb,* and *noun phrase* in Figure 7.2. The syntax of every programming language, including Java, is defined by rules of this type. The entire collection of rules is called the **grammar** of the language.

When you write an arithmetic expression in your program, such as a + b * c, the compiler uses this grammar to try to construct a valid parse tree for that expression. If a parse tree can be built, then the expression is syntactically valid in this language. If the compiler cannot build such a tree, the expression is not valid, and an appropriate error message would be displayed.

To construct this parse tree, the compiler starts with the nonterminal symbol that we have called <expression>, the top-level object it is trying to validate. It then applies a rule of the grammar to expand this symbol into a sequence of one or more terminal and nonterminal symbols. For example, we can expand <expression> by applying rule 1 and selecting the + alternative to produce the following:

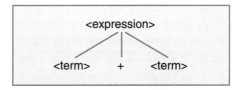

We repeat this process of using rules to expand the nonterminal symbols until we have either constructed the desired expression (i.e., we have generated all the terminal symbols in our expression) or we can go no further with the parse.

For example, given the expression a * b + c and the four-rule grammar given earlier, a compiler could construct the parse tree shown in Figure 7.3, thereby proving that the expression a * b + c is a valid <expression> in this simple language.

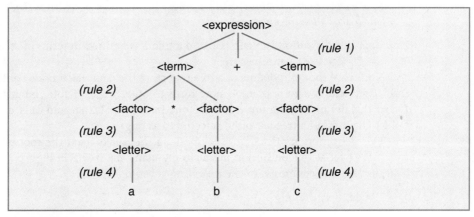

FIGURE 7.3 Parse tree for a * b + c

However, try as hard as we might, no valid parse tree will ever be found for the expression a +. For example:

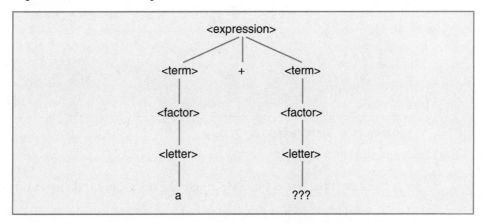

We are at a dead end. We have built a parse tree for the expression a + <letter>, where <letter> can be expanded into either a, b, or c, but we cannot construct one for the sequence a +. Therefore, the compiler rejects this expression with an error message that says something like ***Error: Missing term in expression***.

Parsing is just one of many examples of the use of hierarchical data structures in computer science. You will see many more examples later in this chapter.

7.2 TREES

A **general tree**, or more simply a **tree**, has the following definition:

> *Definition: A tree T is a finite set of one or more nodes such that there is a specially designated node t ∈ T, called the **root** of T, and T − {t} can be partitioned into zero, one, or more disjoint subsets $T_1, T_2, \ldots, T_n$, each of which is itself a tree and which are called the **subtrees** of T.*

Note that this definition is recursive, and a tree T is defined in terms of structures T_1, $T_2, \ldots, T_n$ that are themselves trees.

Nodes are the components of a tree that store the data. Each node contains an information field and zero, one, or more links to other nodes. (Note the difference between this definition of a node and the one in Chapter 6 that had only a single link field.) The links of a tree are often referred to as **edges**.

This definition implies that every node in the tree is itself the root of some subtree. Let's look at this definition more closely using the tree T in Figure 7.4. The tree T in the figure is composed of the following seven nodes:

$$T = \{a, b, c, d, e, f, g\}$$

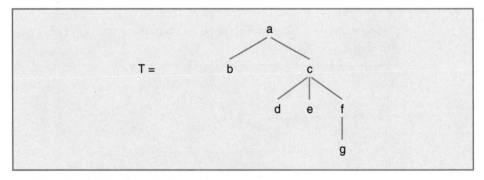

FIGURE 7.4 Sample tree structure

The root of the tree is the node containing the value *a*. It has two subtrees:

$$T_1 = \{b\} \quad T_2 = \{c, d, e, f, g\}$$

The root of T_1 is *b*, and it has no subtrees. The root of T_2 is *c*, and it has three subtrees {*d*}, {*e*}, and {*f, g*}.

In contrast, we cannot partition the following four-node structure

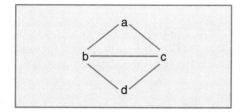

into a root and a collection of disjoint subtrees. If we call the node containing the value a the root, then the subtrees would be $\{b, c, d\}$ and $\{c, d, b\}$, which are not disjoint. This type of structure is a graph, not a tree, and it will be investigated at length in Chapter 8.

The number of subtrees of a node is called the node's **degree**. Hence, node a in Figure 7.4 has degree 2, node b has degree 0, and node c has degree 3. Nodes with degree = 0, such as b, d, e, and g in Figure 7.4, are **leaf nodes**, or **terminal nodes**. All other nodes are **nonterminal nodes**, and their degree is always greater than or equal to 1. In Figure 7.4, the nonterminal nodes are a, c, and f. They are also called **internal** or **branch nodes**.

When discussing trees, we often use familial terms to describe the relationships between elements in the collection (perhaps because family trees, like the one in Figure 7.1, were among the earliest uses of tree structures). For example, node a in Figure 7.4 is said to be the **parent** of nodes b and c rather than their predecessor, and nodes b and c are called the **children** of node a instead of its successors. Nodes that have the same parent are called **siblings**. In Figure 7.4, nodes b and c are siblings. So are d, e, and f.

A **path** is a sequence of nodes n_1, n_2, n_3, . . . , n_k such that either n_{i+1} is a child of n_i, or n_{i+1} is the parent of n_i, for i = 1, 2, . . . k − 1. Referring to the tree in Figure 7.4, bac is a path and so are dcfg and gfcace. A path in which all nodes are unique is called a **simple path**. Usually, when we use the term *path*, we will mean a simple path.

The **ancestors** of node N are all the nodes that lie on the path from node N to the root of the tree. For example, in Figure 7.4, the ancestors of node g are $\{f, c, a\}$. The **descendants** of node N are all the nodes in the subtree rooted at N. The descendants of node c are $\{d, e, f, g\}$. The **height** of a tree is defined as the length (in terms of the total number of nodes) of the longest path from any node N to the root of the tree. The height of the tree in Figure 7.4 is 4 because the longest simple path from any node to the root is $\{g, f, c, a\}$. Finally, the **level** of a node measures the distance of that node from the root. We assign the root a level number of 1. Then the level of any node N is defined recursively as 1 + (level of the parent of N). An equivalent definition is that the level of a node is the length of the path from that node to the root of the tree. The height of a tree would then be the maximum level number of any node.

Given these terms, we can state two important properties of tree structures that come from the previous definitions:

1. Every node N in a tree T has a unique simple path from N to the root of T.
2. Every node N, except for the root, has exactly one parent.

We can now understand why a structure like the four-node graph shown previously is not a tree. The node *d* has two parents, *b* and *c,* and there are multiple paths from *d* to the root: {*d, b, a*}, {*d, c, a*}, {*d, c, b, a*}, and {*d, b, c, a*}.

We have been describing a **general tree**. It is characterized by the fact that the nodes of the tree can have arbitrary degree; that is, they may have any number of children, as shown in the following diagram:

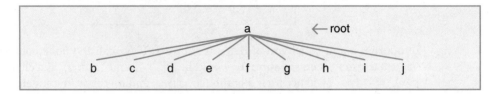

General trees are easy to describe, but they can be somewhat difficult to implement, so they are not widely used in computer science. (Although, in Section 7.5, we will show an example of a tree that can have up to 26 children.) To understand why general trees can be so difficult, let's look at how we might implement one. When we attempt to specify the structure of an individual node, we run into trouble.

```
/**
 * A linked node for use in describing generalized trees.
 */

public class GTreeNode {
    // Links to this node's children
    private GTreeNode child1; // child number 1
    private GTreeNode child2; // child number 2
    private GTreeNode child3; // child number 3
    private GTreeNode child4; // child number 4
    private GTreeNode child5; // child number 5

    // This node's data
    private Object data;

} // GtreeNode
```

FIGURE 7.5 Possible representation of a node in a generalized tree

The node implementation in Figure 7.5 is unsatisfactory because a general tree can have an arbitrary number of children, not just five. It does not do any good to add fields to Figure 7.5 because there are no restrictions on the maximum number of successors. For any number N of child references we allocate in our node, we might require N + 1. Similarly, it does no good to construct an array of child references

```
private GTreeNode child[];
```

because an array is a fixed size structure, and when it is initially created, we have to specify its size. (Although we could use the array resizing and recopying techniques found in Chapter 6, which will be used again later in this chapter.)

There are ways to internally represent general trees that do not have this problem. For example, we could create two parallel arrays called `info` and `childList`. Row i of the `info` array contains the information field, and row i of `childList` is the head of a linked list containing all the children of this node. Since the length of a list is unlimited, a node can have an arbitrary number of children. For example, to represent the following generalized tree

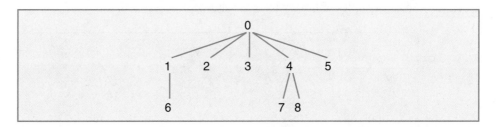

we could use the following array structure:

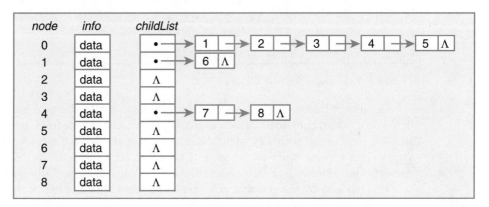

This approach allows a node to have an arbitrarily large number of children. However, we still have the problem first encountered in Chapter 6 when we described the array implementation of lists, stacks, and queues. The size of an array is static and fixed at compile time. So instead of being limited in the maximum number of children of a node, we are now limited in the total number of nodes that can be stored in the tree. That value cannot exceed the declared array size unless we are willing to dynamically resize the array and copy the existing elements into this new structure.

Fortunately, there is a simple solution to our problem of working with general trees. We simply restrict the degree of a node (i.e., place a limit on the maximum number of children). One of the most important and widely used of these restricted hierarchical structures is the binary tree, which places a limit of two on the degree of all nodes in the tree. As you will see in the next section, binary trees are easy to work with, and they have the useful property that any general tree can be represented as a binary tree.

7.3 BINARY TREES

◆ 7.3.1 Introduction

Binary trees are distinct from general trees in three ways: (a) all nodes in a binary tree have degree less than or equal to two, (b) binary trees can be empty, and (c) they explicitly identify a node as being either the left child or the right child of its parent.

> *Definition: A **binary tree** T is a finite set of nodes that is either empty or consists of a root and two disjoint binary trees called the left and right subtrees of T.*

Some examples of binary trees are shown in Figure 7.6.

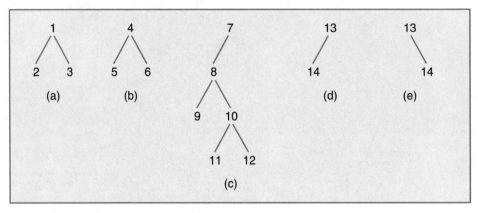

FIGURE 7.6 Examples of binary trees

The binary trees in Figures 7.6a and 7.6b are structurally identical and differ only in the data values contained in their nodes. However, the binary trees in Figures 7.6d and 7.6e are not structurally identical. The root of the binary tree in 7.6d has an empty right subtree, whereas the one in 7.6e has an empty left subtree. This is an important point. Binary trees are **ordered**. A tree is identified not only by the data it contains but also by the position of its nodes within either the left or right subtree. Therefore, when drawing a binary tree, be careful to indicate clearly whether a node is the right or left subtree of its parent. Diagrams such as

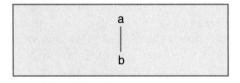

are ambiguous and can lead to confusion and error because it is not at all clear whether we meant to write:

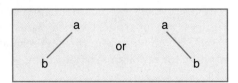

It is also important to observe that, technically, a binary tree is not a tree. Reread the definitions of a tree and a binary tree and notice that a general tree must have at least one node, whereas a binary tree can be empty.

◆ 7.3.2 Operations on Binary Trees

When designing a binary tree class, we first decide on the appropriate methods. That is, we determine the desired behaviors for binary tree objects.

One of the most common operations performed on binary trees is **tree traversal**. This operation starts at the root of the tree and visits every node in the tree exactly once. The phrase "visit a node" means to perform some processing operation on the data in that node. The exact nature of this operation depends on the application and could mean, for example, printing the contents of each node or summing all the node values in the entire tree. Tree traversal of a hierarchical structure is equivalent to iterating through the nodes of a linear structure from the first element to the last.

There are a number of different ways to traverse a tree. One method starts at the root and visits it. Then we have a choice: We can traverse the nodes in either the left subtree or the right subtree. If we choose the left subtree, we traverse it in exactly the same way as the original tree. That is, we visit the root of the subtree and then traverse all the nodes in its left subtree followed by all the nodes in its right subtree. This is a **preorder traversal**. Let's see how this algorithm behaves using the binary tree of Figure 7.7.

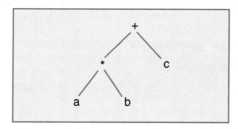

FIGURE 7.7 Sample tree used for tree traversal

The three-step algorithm for a preorder tree traversal is as follows:

1. Visit the root: +.
2. Traverse the left subtree: (* a b).
3. Traverse the right subtree: (c).

Steps 2 and 3 each involve traversing a subtree, which can be accomplished by recursively reapplying the same three steps:

1. Visit the root: +.
2. Traverse the left subtree: (* a b).
   2.1. Visit the root: *.
   2.2. Traverse the left subtree: (a).
   2.3. Traverse the right subtree: (b).

3. Traverse the right subtree: (c).

    3.1. Visit the root: c.

    3.2. Traverse the left subtree: (empty).

    3.3. Traverse the right subtree: (empty).

When a subtree is empty (steps 3.2 and 3.3), we have reached the base case, and we are finished. Therefore, the complete preorder traversal of the tree in Figure 7.7 is given by:

1. Visit the root: +.

2. Traverse the left subtree: (* a b).

    2.1. Visit the root: *.

    2.2. Traverse the left subtree: (a).

        2.2.1. Visit the root: a.

        2.2.2. Traverse the left subtree: (empty).

        2.2.3. Traverse the right subtree: (empty).

    2.3. Traverse the right subtree: (b).

        2.3.1. Visit the root: b.

        2.3.2. Traverse the left subtree: (empty).

        2.3.3. Traverse the right subtree: (empty).

3. Traverse the right subtree: (c).

    3.1. Visit the root: c.

    3.2. Traverse the left subtree: (empty).

    3.3. Traverse the right subtree: (empty).

If R is a reference to the root of a binary tree, the preorder traversal algorithm of this tree is shown in Figure 7.8.

```
// This is the preorder traversal algorithm for a
// binary tree whose root is referenced by R
preorderTraversal(R) {
        if (R refers to an empty tree)
                return;              // the base case
        else {                       // the recursive case
                visit the node referenced by R;
                preorderTraversal(left subtree of R)
                preorderTraversal(right subtree of R)
    }
}
```

FIGURE 7.8 Preorder tree traversal algorithm

In the list structures of Chapter 6, there was only a single way to iterate through a list—that is, from the first node to its unique successor, then to that node's unique successor, and so forth. However, with hierarchical structures like the binary tree in Figure 7.7, there are multiple ways to traverse the nodes. A preorder traversal method walks through the tree by visiting the root node before visiting the left and right subtrees. We can produce other traversal methods by permuting the order of these operations. Two permutations of interest are the **postorder traversal**

1. Traverse the left subtree.
2. Traverse the right subtree.
3. Visit the root.

and the **inorder traversal**

1. Traverse the left subtree.
2. Visit the root.
3. Traverse the right subtree.

There is a natural correspondence between the preorder, postorder, and inorder traversals of an expression tree and the prefix, postfix, and infix representations of an arithmetic expression introduced in Section 6.3.2. Using the expression tree given in Figure 7.7, and assuming that the phrase "visit the root" means to output the data field of the root, the three tree traversal methods just described produce the following:

```
Prefix representation of a * b + c:     +*abc
Preorder traversal of the tree:         +*abc

Postfix representation of a * b + c:    ab*c+
Postorder traversal of the tree:        ab*c+

Infix representation of a * b + c:      a*b+c
Inorder traversal of the tree:          a*b+c
```

The recursive algorithms for postorder and inorder traversals of a binary tree are given in Figure 7.9.

```
// This is the postorder traversal algorithm for a
// binary tree whose root is referenced by R
postorderTraversal(R) {
    if (R refers to an empty tree)
        return;          // the base case
    else {               // the recursive case
        postorderTraversal(left subtree of R);
        postorderTraversal(right subtree of R);
        visit the node referenced by R;
    }
}
```

(continued)

FIGURE 7.9 Postorder and inorder binary tree traversal algorithms

```
// This is the inorder traversal algorithm for a
// binary tree whose root is referenced by R
inorderTraversal(R) {
    if (R refers to an empty tree)
        return;        // the base case
    else{              // the recursive case
        inorderTraversal(left subtree of R);
            visit the node referenced by R;
            inorderTraversal(right subtree of R);
    }
}
```

FIGURE 7.9 Postorder and inorder binary tree traversal algorithms *(continued)*

An important question to ask is: What is the complexity of the traversal algorithms of Figures 7.8 and 7.9? We will answer that question using the recurrence relation technique for analyzing recursive algorithms first presented in Section 5.5.

Assume our binary tree contains N nodes and looks like this:

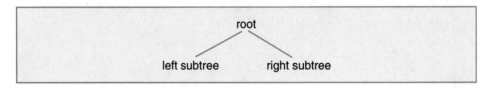

Furthermore, assume that the binary tree and all of its subtrees are roughly in balance, which means that every left and right subtree is approximately the same size. To traverse the tree, we first visit the root, which takes one step, and then visit both the left and right subtrees, each roughly of size N/2, since we assumed that the tree is balanced. If we use the notation T(N) to mean the time required to traverse a tree of size N, then the recurrence relations describing the time complexity of our traversal algorithms are given by:

$$
\begin{aligned}
T(1) &= 1 \\
T(N) &= \underset{\text{root}}{1} + \underset{\text{left subtree}}{T(N/2)} + \underset{\text{right subtree}}{T(N/2)} \\
&= 1 + 2\,T(N/2)
\end{aligned}
$$

To solve this recurrence relation, we use the method of repeated substitution:

$$T(N) = 1 + 2\,T(N/2)$$

We solve for T(N/2):

$$
\begin{aligned}
T(N/2) &= 1 + 2\,T(N/4), \text{ and now plug this into the preceding formula} \\
T(N) &= 1 + 2\,(1 + 2\,T(N/4)) \\
&= 3 + 4\,T(N/4)
\end{aligned}
$$

We repeat this substitution process, yielding the following sequence of equations:

$$T(N) = 7 + 8\ T(N/8)$$
$$= 15 + 16\ T(N/16)$$
$$= 31 + 32\ T(N/32)$$
$$= \ldots$$

The general formula for all the terms in the series is given by:

$$T(N) = (2^k - 1) + 2^k\ T(N/2^k) \quad k = 1, 2, 3, \ldots$$

We now let $N = 2^k$:

$$T(N) = (N - 1) + N\ T(1)$$

However, the original problem statement said that $T(1) = 1$. So this yields

$$T(N) = (N - 1) + N = 2\ N - 1$$
$$= O(N)$$

and we have shown that the traversal of a binary tree is a linear time $O(N)$ operation. Intuitively, this is exactly what is expected because the traversal methods of Figures 7.8 and 7.9 visit every one of the N nodes in the tree exactly once. (Note: Even if the binary tree is not evenly balanced between left and right subtrees, we still get the same result. See Exercise 5b at the end of the chapter.)

In addition to traversal, there are many other important operations that should be part of any binary tree interface. However, as was the case with the list structure in Chapter 6, because of the enormous flexibility of this data structure, there is no universal agreement on exactly what methods should be included. In general, we will need additional information about how this data structure is to be used to determine exactly what methods are best to include or omit. In this section, we present some typical and widely used operations on binary trees. We then suggest additional possibilities in the exercises at the end of the chapter (see Exercise 9).

To describe the behavior of our methods, we will use the idea, first presented in Chapter 6, of a **current position indicator**, also called a **cursor**. This is an instance variable of a binary tree object that references, or points to, one of the nodes in the tree, called the *current node*. Most of our methods will automatically operate on this current node.

We will need to include in our binary tree interface the following cursor positioning, checking, retrieval, mutator, and traversal methods:

Positioning:	`toRoot()`	reposition the cursor to the root of the tree
	`toParent()`	reposition the cursor to the parent of the current node
	`toLeftChild()`	reposition the cursor to the left child of the current node
	`toRightChild()`	reposition the cursor to the right child of the current node
	`find(Object o)`	reposition the cursor to the first node containing Object o in the data field when doing an inorder traversal

Checking:	hasParent()	true if current node has a parent, false otherwise
	hasLeftChild()	true if current node has a left child, false otherwise
	hasRightChild()	true if current node has a right child, false otherwise
	isValid()	true if cursor is pointing to a node in the tree, false otherwise
	equals(Object o)	true if Object o and this object are identical, false otherwise
	size()	return the number of nodes in the tree
	height()	return the height of the tree
Retrieval:	get()	return the information field of the current node
Mutator:	set(Object o)	reset the information field of current node to the Object o
	insertRight(Object o)	add a new node containing Object o as the right child of the current node
	insertLeft(Object o)	add a new node containing Object o as the left child of the current node
	prune()	delete the entire subtree rooted at the current node
Traversal:	preorder()	do a preorder traversal of the tree
	postorder()	do a postorder traversal of the tree
	inorder()	do an inorder traversal of the tree

Three important mutator methods on binary trees are insertLeft(), insertRight(), and prune. The two methods insertLeft() and insertRight() create a new node containing the specified object in the information field and then insert this new node into the tree as either the left child or right child of the current node. A necessary precondition of both these methods is that the place we are inserting the new node is unoccupied. So, for example, given the binary tree in Figure 7.7 and assuming that the cursor currently references the node containing a, the call insertLeft(d) would insert a new node containing the value d as the left child of node a, producing the following tree:

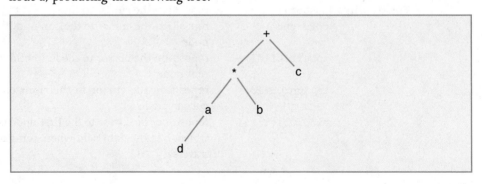

These two methods are the primary means of constructing binary trees. You start with an empty tree and insert new nodes, one at a time, into their proper location.

The `prune()` method is a mutator that removes nodes from a binary tree. However, we cannot simply delete an individual node N unless it is a leaf node. Instead, we must delete the entire subtree rooted at N. For example, given the six-node tree just shown, deleting the node labeled * also requires us to delete the entire subtree rooted at this node, the four nodes {*, a, b, d}. (Note: It is possible to describe a method that deletes a single node, but it involves not only the deletion of a single node but reconstruction of the tree as well.) In our interface, `prune()` will delete the entire subtree rooted at the node referenced by the cursor.

The `equals()` method determines if two binary trees are identical. This means that (a) the parameter provided to `equals` is a binary tree, (b) the shape of the two trees is identical, and (c) the data values in the information field of every node are the same. The operator returns a Boolean that is true if the trees are identical and false otherwise. This is called a **deep compare** and was introduced in Section 3.3.5.

Two methods that help us characterize the size and shape of a binary tree are `size()` and `height()`, which return the number of nodes in the tree and the height of the tree, respectively. Remember from Section 7.2 that the height of a tree is defined as the maximum level number of any individual node.

Finally, our interface includes the three traversal operations—`preorder()`, `inorder()`, and `postorder()`—described at the beginning of this section. However, we have chosen to implement them in a rather interesting way. If you remember from our earlier discussion, a traversal visits every node, where visit means to perform some as yet unspecified operation on the data field of every node. Now that we are actually implementing these traversals and not simply explaining them, how do we specify the operation that the visit method should carry? We could assume that visit does a specific operation, such as print the data value stored in a node. However, that is not a very flexible solution and does not permit the user to do something else.

Instead, we will use a Java language feature known as a **callback**. We will pass a callback object, `cb`, to each of our three traversal methods. The parameter `cb` refers to a user-created object that is guaranteed to contain an instance method called `visit()`. Now, instead of having `visit()` be an instance method of our binary tree class (and not knowing exactly what it should do), we invoke `cb.visit(data)`, which invokes the user-provided `visit()` method of the object named as a parameter, passing to it the data contained in the node being visited. Since `visit()` is free to do anything it wants, this makes the three traversal operations completely general.

Figure 7.10 is a `BinaryTree` interface specification that includes the 20 methods just described. This interface should not be viewed as either definitive or complete. On the contrary, there are many other methods that would be good candidates for inclusion in this interface. We would need additional information about how these classes will be used to know whether or not these other methods should be added to our interface.

```
/**
 * An interface for the binary tree data structure
 */
```
(continued)

FIGURE 7.10 Interface specifications for a binary tree

```
public interface BinaryTree {
   /**
    * Positions the cursor at the root of the tree.
    *
    * Preconditions:
    *    None.
    *
    * Postconditions:
    *    If the tree is empty, the cursor is invalid.
    *    Otherwise, the cursor refers to the root of the tree.
    *    The tree structure is unchanged.
    */
   public void toRoot();

   /**
    * Determine if the current node has a left child.
    *
    * Preconditions:
    * The cursor is valid.
    *
    * Postconditions:
    *    The tree structure is unchanged.
    *    The cursor is unchanged.
    *
    * @return true if the node identified by the cursor has a left
    *    child and false otherwise.
    */
   public boolean hasLeftChild();

   /**
    * Determine if the current node has a right child.
    *
    * Preconditions:
    *    The cursor is valid.
    *
    * Postconditions:
    *    The tree structure is unchanged.
    *    The cursor is unchanged.
    *
    * @return true if the node identified by the cursor has a right
    *    child and false otherwise.
    */
   public boolean hasRightChild();

   /**
    * Determine if the current node has a parent.
    *
    * Preconditions:
    *    The cursor is valid.
    *
```

FIGURE 7.10 Interface specifications for a binary tree *(continued)*

```
   *  Postconditions:
   *     The tree structure is unchanged.
   *     The cursor is unchanged.
   *
   *  @return true if the current node has a parent and false otherwise.
   */
  public boolean hasParent();

  /**
   *  Determine if the cursor is on the tree.
   *
   *  Preconditions:
   *     None.
   *
   *  Postconditions:
   *     The tree structure is unchanged.
   *     The cursor is unchanged.
   *
   *  @return true if the cursor is on the tree and false otherwise.
   */
  public boolean isValid();

  /**
   *  Positions the cursor at the current node's parent, if any.
   *
   *  Preconditions:
   *     The cursor is valid.
   *
   *  Postconditions:
   *     If the cursor has no parent (i.e. referred to the root node),
   *        the cursor is invalid. Otherwise, the cursor refers to its
   *        previous referent's parent.
   *     The structure of the tree is unchanged.
   */
  public void toParent();

  /**
   *  Positions the cursor at the left child of the current node.
   *
   *  Preconditions:
   *     The cursor is valid.
   *
   *  Postconditions:
   *     If the left child of the current node is invalid, the cursor
   *        is invalid. Otherwise, the cursor is changed to refer to
   *        the left child of the current node.
   *     The structure of the tree is unchanged.
   */
  public void toLeftChild();
```

(continued)

FIGURE 7.10 Interface specifications for a binary tree *(continued)*

```
/**
 * Positions the cursor at the right child of the current node.
 *
 * Preconditions:
 *    The cursor is valid.
 *
 * Postconditions:
 *    If the left child of the current node is invalid, the cursor
 *        is invalid. Otherwise, the cursor is changed to refer to
 *        the right child of the current node.
 *    The structure of the tree is unchanged.
 */
public void toRightChild();


/**
 * Inserts the given data in the left child of the current node.
 * If the cursor is null and the tree has no root, a new root
 * is created containing these data.
 *
 * Preconditions:
 *    The tree is empty, or the cursor is valid and the left child is
 *        not empty.
 *
 * Postconditions:
 *    The cursor has not changed.
 *    The size of the tree has increased by one.
 *    No other structure of the tree has changed.
 *
 * @param data the data to put in the left child.
 */
public void insertLeft( Object data );


/**
 * Inserts the given data in the right child of the currrent node.
 * If the cursor is null and the tree has no root, a new root
 * is created containing this data.
 *
 * Preconditions:
 *    The tree is empty, or the cursor is valid and the right child is
 *        not empty.
 *
 * Postconditions:
 *    The cursor has not changed.
 *    The size of the tree has increased by one.
 *    No other structure of the tree has changed.
 *
 * @param data the data to put in the right child.
 */
public void insertRight( Object data );
```

FIGURE 7.10 Interface specifications for a binary tree *(continued)*

```
/**
 * Return a reference to the data stored at the current node.
 *
 * Preconditions:
 *    The cursor is on the tree.
 *
 * Postconditions:
 *    The tree is unchanged.
 *
 * @return a reference to the data at the current node.
 */
public Object get();

/**
 * Set the data stored at the current node.
 *
 * Preconditions:
 *    The cursor is on the tree.
 *
 * Postconditions:
 *    The reference of the current node is changed.
 *    The rest of the tree is unchanged.
 *
 * @param data the reference to store in the current node.
 */
public void set( Object data );

/**
 * Removes the subtree rooted at (including) the cursor.
 *
 * Preconditions:
 *    The cursor is on the tree.
 *
 * Postconditions:
 *    The specified subtree has been removed. If the cursor
 *       referred to the root node, the tree is empty.
 *    The tree's size has decreased.
 *    No other structure of the tree has changed.
 *    If the resulting tree is empty, the cursor is invalid.
 *    Otherwise the cursor refers to the parent of the current
 *       node.
 */
public void prune();

/**
 * Determines if the given object is identical to this one.
 *
 *
 * Preconditions:
 *    None.
 *
```

(continued)

FIGURE 7.10 Interface specifications for a binary tree *(continued)*

```
 * Postconditions:
 *     The cursors of both trees refer to the root of their
 *         respective trees.
 *
 * @param t the Object to compare to
 *
 * @return true if and only if all of the following are true:
 *     The other object is a BinaryTree
 *     The structure of the two trees are identical
 *     The data contained in corresponding nodes of the
 *         two trees are identical.
 */
public boolean equals( Object o );

/**
 * Returns the number of nodes in this tree.
 *
 * Preconditions:
 *     None.
 *
 * Postconditions:
 *     The tree is unchanged.
 *
 * @return the number of nodes in the tree.
 */
public int size();

/**
 * Returns the height of the tree.
 *
 * Preconditions:
 *     None.
 *
 * Postconditions:
 *     The tree is unchanged.
 *
 * @return the height of the tree.
 */
public int height();

/**
 * Position the cursor on the first (as seen by an inorder traversal)
 * occurrence of the given data. Equality is determined by invoking
 * the equals method.
 *
 * Preconditions:
 *     Key is not null.
 *
 * Postconditions:
 *     The tree is unchanged.
```

FIGURE 7.10 Interface specifications for a binary tree *(continued)*

```
 *      If key is found, cursor refers to the first occurrence of
 *          the key. If key is not found, the cursor is off the tree
 *
 * @param target object containing the data to be searched for.
 */
public void find( Object target );

/**
 * Perform a preorder traversal on this tree with the specified
 * callback object.
 *
 * Preconditions:
 *    cb is not null.
 *
 * Postconditions:
 *    The tree is unchanged.
 *
 * @param cb the callback object used to process each node.
 */
public void preOrder( Callback cb );

/**
 * Perform an inorder traversal on this tree with the specified
 * callback object.
 *
 * Preconditions:
 *    cb is not null.
 *
 * Postconditions:
 *    The tree is unchanged.
 *
 * @param cb the callback object used to process each node.
 */
public void inOrder( Callback cb );

/**
 * Perform a postorder traversal on this tree with the specified
 * callback object.
 *
 * Preconditions:
 *    cb is not null.
 *
 * Postconditions:
 *    The tree is unchanged.
 *
 * @param cb the callback object used to process each node.
 */
public void postOrder( Callback cb );

} // BinaryTree
```

FIGURE 7.10 Interface specifications for a binary tree *(continued)*

◆ 7.3.3 The Binary Tree Representation of General Trees

We have covered the topic of binary trees in depth because of an important property of hierarchical data structures: Every general tree can be represented as a binary tree without any loss of information. Therefore, instead of working with the somewhat cumbersome general tree of Section 7.2, we first convert it into a binary tree and then work with this much simpler structure.

Recall that every node in a binary tree has at most two links: one that points to the left subtree and the other that points to the right subtree. We can use these two links to convert any general tree into a binary tree using the **oldest child/next sibling algorithm**. It uses the two links in the binary tree as follows:

1. The left pointer of a node points to the "oldest" (i.e., leftmost) child of that node in the general tree or `null` if a node has no children.

2. The right pointer of a node points to the "next" (i.e., the one immediately to the right) sibling of a node in the general tree or `null` if that node has no siblings to its right.

For example, given the following general tree

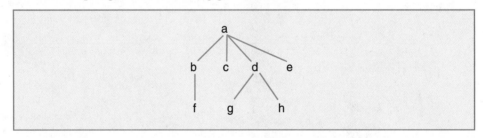

we convert it into a binary tree in the following manner. In the general tree, the oldest child of node *a* is node *b*. So we use the left pointer of *a* in the new binary tree to point to *b*. Since *a* has no siblings, its right pointer in the binary tree is set to `null`. The right pointers of *b, c,* and *d* in the binary tree point to their next (i.e., rightmost) sibling in the general tree, *c, d,* and *e,* respectively, while *e,* which has no right sibling, has its right pointer set to `null`. The left pointer of *b* points to *f,* its oldest (i.e., leftmost) child. The left pointers of *c* and *e* are `null` because they have no children. The left pointer of *d* points to *g,* its oldest child. Both the right and left pointers of node *f* are `null` since it has neither children nor siblings. The right pointer of *g* points to its next sibling *h,* while its left pointer is `null`. Finally, both the right and left pointers of *h* are `null` since it also has no siblings to its right and no children. The final binary tree representation of the eight-node general tree just described is shown in Figure 7.11.

This conversion algorithm allows us to represent a general tree of arbitrary degree as a binary tree without any loss of information. All relationships present in the original general tree are still present in the new binary tree. For example, to identify all the children of a given node in the general tree, we follow the left pointer of that node in the binary tree to its first child and then follow the right pointer of all nodes until we reach a `null` value. These are the children of the original node. Similar algorithms exist for determining all other important structural relationships.

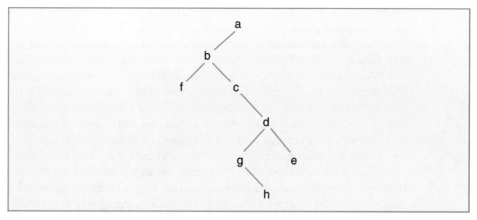

FIGURE 7.11 The binary tree representation of a general tree

◆ 7.3.4 The Linked List Implementation of Binary Trees

To build a class that implements the binary tree interface of Figure 7.10, we first select an internal representation for the tree nodes. As was the case with the data structures discussed previously, we can implement our binary tree nodes using either array-based or reference-based techniques. This section describes a reference-based method; the following section will describe how to implement a binary tree using an array. Figure 7.12 shows the declarations for a binary tree node using references that point to the left and right subtrees of the node.

Although the declarations in Figure 7.12 are a very common way to implement the nodes of a binary tree, they are by no means the only way. For example, using the declarations in Figure 7.12, it is easy to locate the children of a node—just follow the left and right pointers. However, moving up the tree is much more difficult because there is no pointer from a child to its parent. The only way to locate the parent of a node is to traverse the entire tree beginning from the root. If moving in an upward direction, from the leaves toward the root, is a common occurrence, then we may wish to consider adding a "parent" pointer field to each node.

The addition of this pointer is quite similar to our inclusion of a "previous" pointer to the doubly linked list of Section 6.2.3.3 that allowed us to quickly move to both the predecessor and successor of a node. However, as was the case with the

```
// This class defines the structure of a node in a binary tree
public class BinaryTreeNode {

    private BinaryTreeNode left;     // The left child
    private BinaryTreeNode right;    // The right child
    private Object data;             // The data in this node

    // public methods go here
```

FIGURE 7.12 BinaryTreeNode class

doubly-linked list, this increase in functionality is not free. The price you pay for adding a parent pointer is an increase of 50 percent in the number of reference fields in each node, from two to three. For large trees, this increased memory usage could be significant.

We have now specified the behavior of our binary tree class (the 20 operations in the interface of Figure 7.10), and we have selected a representation for the individual nodes. All that remains is to decide exactly what state information to maintain for a binary tree object. We certainly need a reference to the root of the tree. In addition, we need to have a current position indicator, or cursor, that is used by most of our tree methods. These are the only two state variables that are absolutely required, since once we have located the root of the tree, we can locate and access all other nodes. However, there is additional information that might be useful to include, such as the height of the tree or the total number of nodes. Keeping this as state information inside our object could, for example, simplify the implementation of the instance methods `height()` and `size()` as they would only need to return these values. Of course, every time we add or remove either a node or a subtree, we must recompute both the height and size of the new tree. Thus, keeping this information may not produce as much of a time savings as we would hope for.

A complete reference-based implementation of the binary tree interface of Figure 7.10 is given in Figure 7.13. It includes the class `BinaryTreeNode`, which provides the state and behaviors for the individual nodes in the tree.

```
/**
 * A node for use in binary trees.
 */

public class BinaryTreeNode {
    private BinaryTreeNode left;   // The left child
    private BinaryTreeNode right;  // The right child
    private Object data;           // The data in this node

    /**
     * Create a new node.
     */
    public BinaryTreeNode() {
        this( null, null, null );
    }


    /**
     * Create a new node containing the specified data.
     *
     * @param theData the data to place in this node.
     */
    public BinaryTreeNode( Object theData ) {
        this( theData, null, null );
    }
```

FIGURE 7.13 Reference-based binary tree class

```
/**
 * Create a new node with the specified data and children.
 *
 * @param theData the data to place in this node.
 * @param leftChild the left child.
 * @param rightChild the right child.
 */
public BinaryTreeNode( Object theData,
                       BinaryTreeNode leftChild,
                       BinaryTreeNode rightChild ) {
   data = theData;
   left = leftChild;
   right = rightChild;
}


/**
 * Returns the data stored in this node.
 *
 * Preconditions:
 *    None.
 *
 * Postconditions:
 *    This node is unchanged.
 *
 * @return the data stored in this node.
 */
public Object getData() {
   return data;
}


/**
 * Returns a reference to the left child.
 *
 * Preconditions:
 *    None.
 *
 * Postconditions:
 *    This node is unchanged.
 *
 * @return a reference to this node's left child.
 */
public BinaryTreeNode getLeft() {
   return left;
}


/**
 * Returns a reference to the right child.
 *
```

(continued)

FIGURE 7.13 Reference-based binary tree class *(continued)*

```
 * Preconditions:
 *    None.
 *
 * Postconditions:
 *    This node is unchanged.
 *
 * @return a reference to this node's right child.
 */
public BinaryTreeNode getRight() {
   return right;
}


/**
 * Sets this node's left child to the given node.
 *
 * Preconditions:
 *    None.
 *
 * Postconditions:
 *    This node's left subchild has been changed to the given node.
 *
 * @param newLeft the node to become this node's left child.
 */
public void setLeft( BinaryTreeNode newLeft ) {
   left = newLeft;
}

/**
 * Sets this node's right child to the given node.
 *
 * Preconditions:
 *    None.
 *
 * Postconditions:
 *    This node's right subchild has been changed to the given node.
 *
 * @param newRight the node to become this node's right child.
 */
public void setRight( BinaryTreeNode newRight ) {
   right = newRight;
}

/**
 * Sets the data field of the current node
 *
 * Preconditions:
 *    None.
 *
```

FIGURE 7.13 Reference-based binary tree class *(continued)*

```
 *  Postconditions:
 *      This node's data field has been updated.
 *
 *  @param newData Node to become this node's right child.
 */
public void setData( Object newData ) {
    data = newData;
}


/**
 * Performs an inorder traversal of the BinaryTree rooted at this node.
 * Each visited node is visited with the given callback.
 *
 * Preconditions:
 *     cb is not null.
 *
 * Postconditions:
 *     All nodes in the tree have been visited by the given
 *         callback in the specified order.
 *
 * @param cb the callback object used to process nodes.
 */

public void inOrder( Callback cb ) {
    // First we visit the left subtree, if any
    if ( left != null ) {
        left.inOrder( cb );
    }

    // Then we visit this node
    cb.visit(data);

    // Last we visit the right subtree, if any
    if ( right != null ) {
        right.inOrder( cb );
    }
}

/**
 * Performs an preorder traversal of the BinaryTree rooted at this node.
 * Each visited node is visited with the given callback.
 *
 * Preconditions:
 *     cb is not null.
 *
 * Postconditions:
 *   All nodes in the tree have been visited by the given
 *       callback in the specified order.
```

(continued)

FIGURE 7.13 Reference-based binary tree class *(continued)*

```
 *
 * @param cb the callback object used to process nodes.
 */
public void preOrder( Callback cb ) {
   // First we visit the current node
   cb.visit( data );

   // Then we visit our left subtree, if any
   if ( left != null ) {
      left.preOrder( cb );
   }

   // Last we visit our right subtree, if any
   if ( right != null ) {
      right.preOrder( cb );
   }
}


/**
 * Performs a preorder traversal of the BinaryTree rooted at this node.
 * Each visited node is visited with the given callback.
 *
 * Preconditions:
 *    cb is not null.
 *
 * Postconditions:
 *    All nodes in the tree have been visited by the given
 *       callback in the specified order.
 *
 * @param cb the callback object used to process nodes.
 */
public void postOrder( Callback cb ) {
   // First we visit our left subtree, if any
   if ( left != null ) {
      left.postOrder( cb );
   }

   // Then we visit our right subtree, if any
   if ( right != null ) {
      right.postOrder( cb );
   }

   // Last we visit this node
   cb.visit( data );
}

/**
 * Returns the height of the tree rooted at this node.
 *
```

FIGURE 7.13 Reference-based binary tree class *(continued)*

```
 * Preconditions:
 *    None.
 *
 * Postconditions:
 *    The tree rooted at this node is unchanged.
 *
 * @return the height of this tree.
 */
public int height() {
    int leftHeight = 0;    // Height of the left subtree
    int rightHeight = 0;   // Height of the right subtree
    int height = 0;        // The height of this subtree

    // If we have a left subtree, determine its height
    if ( left != null ) {
        leftHeight = left.height();
    }

    // If we have a right subtree, determine its height
    if ( right != null ) {
        rightHeight = right.height();
    }

    // The height of the tree rooted at this node is one more than the
    // height of the 'taller' of its children.
    if (leftHeight > rightHeight) {
        height = 1 + leftHeight;
    } else {
        height = 1 + rightHeight;
    }

    // Return the answer
    return height;
}

/**
 * Returns the number of nodes in this tree.
 *
 * Preconditions:
 *    None.
 *
 * Postconditions:
 *    The tree rooted at this node is unchanged.
 *
 * @return the number of nodes in this tree.
 */
public int size() {
    int size = 0; // The size of the tree
```

(continued)

FIGURE 7.13 Reference-based binary tree class *(continued)*

```
      // The size of the tree rooted at this node is one more than the
      // sum of the sizes of its children.
      if ( left != null ) {
         size = size + left.size();
      }

      if ( right != null ) {
         size = size + right.size();
      }

      return size + 1;
   }

   /**
    * Position the cursor on the first (as seen by an inorder traversal)
    * occurrence of the given data. Equality is determined by invoking
    * the equals method.
    *
    * Preconditions:
    *    Key is not null.
    *
    * Postconditions:
    *    The tree is unchanged.
    *    If key is found, cursor refers to the first occurrence of
    *       the key. If key is not found, the cursor is off the tree
    *
    * @param target object containing the data to be searched for.
    */
   public BinaryTreeNode find( Object target ) {
      BinaryTreeNode location = null; // The node that contains the target

      // Is the target in the left subtree?
      if ( left != null ) {
         location = left.find( target );
      }

      // If we haven't found it, is it in this node?
      if (location == null && target.equals( data ) ) {
         location = this;
      }

      // If we haven't found it, and we have a right child, check there
      if ( location == null && right != null ){
         location = right.find( target );
      }

      // Return the location of the target
      return location;
   }
```

FIGURE 7.13 Reference-based binary tree class *(continued)*

```
    /**
     * Locate the parent of the given node looking in the tree whose
     * root is this node.
     *
     * Preconditions:
     *     target is not null.
     *
     * Postconditions:
     *     The tree rooted at this node is unchanged.
     *
     * @param target the node whose parent is to be located.
     *
     * @return the parent of the given node.
     */
    public BinaryTreeNode findParent( BinaryTreeNode target ) {
        BinaryTreeNode parent = null;

        // Are we parent to the target node?
        if ( left == target || right == target ) {
            parent = this;
        }

        // If we have not found the parent, check the left subtree
        if ( parent == null && left != null ) {
            parent = left.findParent( target );
        }

        // If we have not found the parent, check the right subtree
        if ( parent == null && right != null ) {
            parent = right.findParent( target );
        }

        // Return the parent
        return parent;
    }

    /**
     * Return a string representation of this node.
     *
     * @return a string representation of this node.
     */
    public String toString() {
        return data.toString();
    }

} // BinaryTreeNode

/**
 * A link based implementation of a binary tree.
 */

public class LinkedBinaryTree implements BinaryTree {
```

(continued)

FIGURE 7.13 Reference-based binary tree class *(continued)*

```
private BinaryTreeNode root;    // The root of the tree
private BinaryTreeNode cursor; // The current node

/**
 * Positions the cursor at the root of the tree.
 *
 * Preconditions:
 *     None.
 *
 * Postconditions:
 *     If the tree is empty, the cursor is invalid.
 *        Otherwise, the cursor refers to the root of the tree.
 *     The tree structure is unchanged.
 */
public void toRoot() {
   cursor = root;
}


/**
 * Determine if the current node has a left child.
 *
 * Preconditions:
 *     The cursor is valid.
 *
 * Postconditions:
 *     The tree structure is unchanged.
 *     The cursor is unchanged.
 *
 * @return true if the node identified by the cursor has a left
 *     child and false otherwise.
 */
public boolean hasLeftChild() {
   return cursor.getLeft() != null;
}


/**
 * Determine if the current node has a right child.
 *
 * Preconditions:
 *     The cursor is valid.
 *
 * Postconditions:
 *     The tree structure is unchanged.
 *     The cursor is unchanged.
 *
 * @return true if the node identified by the cursor has a right
 *     child and false otherwise.
 */
public boolean hasRightChild() {
   return cursor.getRight() != null;
}
```

FIGURE 7.13 Reference-based binary tree class *(continued)*

```
    /**
     * Determines if the current node has a parent.
     *
     * Preconditions:
     *    The cursor is valid.
     *
     * Postconditions:
     *    The tree structure is unchanged.
     *    The cursor is unchanged.
     *
     * @return true if the current node has a parent and false otherwise.
     */
    public boolean hasParent() {
        return root.findParent( cursor ) != null;
    }


    /**
     * Determines if the cursor is on the tree.
     *
     * Preconditions:
     *    None.
     *
     * Postconditions:
     *    The tree structure is unchanged.
     *    The cursor is unchanged.
     *
     * @return true if the cursor is on the tree and false otherwise.
     */
    public boolean isValid() {
        return cursor != null;
    }


    /**
     * Positions the cursor at the current node's parent, if any.
     *
     * Preconditions:
     *    The cursor is valid.
     *
     * Postconditions:
     *    If the cursor has no parent (i.e. referred to the root node),
     *        the cursor is invalid. Otherwise, the cursor refers to its
     *        previous referent's parent.
     *    The structure of the tree is unchanged.
     */
    public void toParent() {
        cursor = root.findParent( cursor );
    }
```

(continued)

FIGURE 7.13 Reference-based binary tree class *(continued)*

```
/**
 * Positions the cursor at the left child of the current node.
 *
 * Preconditions:
 *    The cursor is valid.
 *
 * Postconditions:
 *    If the left child of the current node is invalid, the cursor
 *        is invalid. Otherwise, the cursor is changed to refer to
 *        the left child of the current node.
 *    The structure of the tree is unchanged.
 */
public void toLeftChild() {
    cursor = cursor.getLeft();
}


/**
 * Positions the cursor at the right child of the current node.
 *
 * Preconditions:
 *    The cursor is valid.
 *
 * Postconditions:
 *    If the right child of the current node is invalid, the cursor
 *        is invalid. Otherwise, the cursor is changed to refer to
 *        the right child of the current node.
 *    The structure of the tree is unchanged.
 */
public void toRightChild() {
    cursor = cursor.getRight();
}


/**
 * Inserts the given data in the left child of the current node.
 * If the cursor is null and the tree has no root, a new root
 * node for the tree is created.
 *
 * Preconditions:
 *    The tree is empty, or the cursor is valid and the left child is
 *        empty.
 *
 * Postconditions:
 *    The cursor has not changed.
 *    The size of the tree has increased by one.
 *    No other structure of the tree has changed.
 *
 * @param data the data to put in the left child.
 */
public void insertLeft( Object data ) {
```

FIGURE 7.13 Reference-based binary tree class *(continued)*

```
      // Create the node that will hold the data
      BinaryTreeNode newNode = new BinaryTreeNode( data );

      // If the tree is empty this becomes the only node in the
      // tree, otherwise make the new node the right child of the
      // cursor
      if ( root == null ) {
         root = newNode;
      }
      else {
         cursor.setLeft( newNode );
      }
   }


   /**
    * Inserts the given data in the right child of the currrent node.
    * If the cursor is null and the tree has no root, a new root
    * node for the tree is created.
    *
    * Preconditions:
    *    The tree is empty, or the cursor is valid and the right child is
    *       empty.
    *
    * Postconditions:
    *    The cursor has not changed.
    *    The size of the tree has increased by one.
    *    No other structure of the tree has changed.
    *
    * @param data the data to put in the right child.
    */
   public void insertRight( Object data ) {
      // Create the node that will hold the data
      BinaryTreeNode newNode = new BinaryTreeNode( data );

      // If the tree is empty this becomes the only node in the
      // tree, otherwise make the new node the left child of the
      // cursor
      if ( root == null ) {
         root = newNode;
      }
      else {
         cursor.setRight( newNode );
      }
   }


   /**
    * Return a reference to the data stored at the current node.
    *
```

(continued)

FIGURE 7.13 Reference-based binary tree class *(continued)*

```
 * Preconditions:
 *     The cursor is on the tree.
 *
 * Postconditions:
 *     The tree is unchanged.
 *
 * @return a reference to the data at the current node.
 */
public Object get() {
   return cursor.getData();
}


/**
 * Set the data stored at the current node.
 *
 * Preconditions:
 *     The cursor is on the tree.
 *
 * Postconditions:
 *     The reference of the current node is changed.
 *     The rest of the tree is unchanged.
 *
 * @param data the reference to store in the current node.
 */
public void set( Object data ) {
    cursor.setData( data );
}


/**
 * Removes the subtree rooted at (including) the cursor.
 *
 * Preconditions:
 *    The cursor is on the tree
 *
 * Postconditions:
 *     The specified subtree has been removed. If the cursor
 *        referred to the root node, the tree is empty.
 *     The tree's size has decreased.
 *     No other structure of the tree has changed.
 *     If the resulting tree is empty, the cursor is invalid.
 *     Otherwise the cursor refers to the parent of the current
 *        node.
 */
public void prune() {
   // Are we trying to delete the root node?
   if ( cursor == root ) {
      // Delete the root and invalidate the cursor
      root = null;
      cursor = null;
   } else {
      // Find the parent of the node to delete
      BinaryTreeNode parent = root.findParent( cursor );
```

FIGURE 7.13 Reference-based binary tree class *(continued)*

```
        // Is it the parent's left child?
        if ( parent.getLeft() == cursor ) {
          // Delete left child
          parent.setLeft( null );
        } else {
          // Delete right child
          parent.setRight( null );
        }
          // Update the cursor
          cursor = parent;
    }
}

/**
  * Determines if the given object is identical to this one.
  *
  * Preconditions:
  *     None.
  *
  * Postconditions:
  *     The cursors of both trees refer to the root of their
  *         respective trees.
  *
  * @param o the Object to compare to
  *
  * @return true if and only if all of the following are true:
  *     The other object is a BinaryTree
  *     The structure of the two trees are identical
  *     The data contained in corresponding nodes of the
  *         two trees are identical.
  */
public boolean equals( Object o ) {
    boolean retVal = false;

    // We can only do the comparison if the other object is a tree
    if ( o instanceof BinaryTree ) {
        BinaryTree other = (BinaryTree)o;

        // Start at the top of both trees
        toRoot();
        other.toRoot();

        // Use the recursive helper method to do the actual work
        retVal = equalHelper( other );

        // Reset the iterators
        toRoot();
        other.toRoot();
    }

    return retVal;
}
```

(continued)

FIGURE 7.13 Reference-based binary tree class *(continued)*

```
/**
 * Compare the content and structure of this tree to a second
 * binary tree.
 *
 * @param tree the tree to compare this tree with
 *
 * @return true if the content and structure of a given tree is
 *     identical to this tree and false otherwise.
 */

private boolean equalHelper( BinaryTree tree ) {
    // Handle the case where both trees are empty. If both
    // trees are empty, they are equal.
    boolean retVal = ( cursor == null && !tree.isValid() );

    // If both trees have something in them – compare them
    if ( cursor != null && tree.isValid() ) {

        // Both nodes should have the same data and both
        // should have the same type of children
        retVal =
            cursor.getData().equals( tree.get() ) &&
            hasLeftChild() == tree.hasLeftChild() &&
            hasRightChild() == tree.hasRightChild();

        // If they are equal and have left children - compare them
        if ( retVal && hasLeftChild() ) {
            toLeftChild();
            tree.toLeftChild();
            retVal = equalHelper( tree );
            // Back up the cursors
            toParent();
            tree.toParent();
        }

        // If they are equal and have right children - compare them
        if ( retVal && hasRightChild() ) {
            toRightChild();
            tree.toRightChild();
            retVal = retVal && equalHelper( tree );
            // Back up the cursors
            toParent();
            tree.toParent();
        }
    }

    return retVal;
}
```

FIGURE 7.13 Reference-based binary tree class *(continued)*

```
/**
 * Returns the number of nodes in this tree.
 *
 * Preconditions:
 *    None.
 *
 * Postconditions:
 *    The tree is unchanged.
 *
 * @return the number of nodes in the tree.
 */
public int size() {
   int size = 0;

   // If the root is null, the size of the tree is zero. Otherwise, the
   // size of the tree is the size of the root node.
   if ( root != null ) {
      size = root.size();
   }

   return size;
}


/**
 * Returns the height of the tree.
 *
 * Preconditions:
 *    None.
 *
 * Postconditions:
 *    The tree is unchanged.
 *
 * @return the height of the tree.
 */
public int height() {
   int height = 0;
   // If the root is null, the height of the tree is zero. Otherwise, the
   // height of the tree is the height of the root node.
   if ( root != null ) {
      height = root.height();
   }
   return height;
}


/**
 * Position the cursor on the first (as seen by an inorder traversal)
 * occurrence of the given data. Equality is determined by invoking
 * the equals method.
 *
```

(continued)

FIGURE 7.13 Reference-based binary tree class *(continued)*

```
 * Preconditions:
 *    Key is not null.
 *
 * Postconditions:
 *    The tree is unchanged.
 *    If key is found, cursor refers to the first occurrence of
 *       the key. If key is not found, the cursor has moved off the tree
 *       from the last node, as seen by an inorder traversal.
 *
 * @param target object containing the data to be searched for.
 */
public void find(Object key) {
   // If the root is null, there is no node containing the given key.
   // Otherwise, check the tree rooted at the root node.
   if (root != null) {
      cursor = root.find(key);
   } else {
      cursor = null;
   }
}


/**
 * Perform a preorder traversal on this tree with the specified
 * callback object.
 *
 * Preconditions:
 *    cb is not null.
 *
 * Postconditions:
 *    The tree is unchanged.
 *
 * @param cb the callback object used to process each node.
 */
public void preOrder( Callback cb ) {
   // Start the traversal at the root node
   if ( root != null ) {
      root.preOrder( cb );
   }
}

/**
 * Perform an inorder traversal on this tree with the specified
 * callback object.
 *
 * Preconditions:
 *    cb is not null.
 *
 * Postconditions:
 *    The tree is unchanged.
```

FIGURE 7.13 Reference-based binary tree class *(continued)*

```
     *
     * @param cb the callback object used to process each node.
     */
    public void inOrder( Callback cb ) {
        // Start the traversal at the root node
        if ( root != null ) {
            root.inOrder( cb );
        }
    }


    /**
     * Perform a postorder traversal on this tree with the specified
     * callback object.
     *
     * Preconditions:
     *     cb is not null.
     *
     * Postconditions:
     *     The tree is unchanged.
     *
     * @param cb the callback object used to process each node.
     */
    public void postOrder( Callback cb ) {
        // Start the traversal at the root node
        if ( root != null ) {
            root.postOrder( cb );
        }
    }

    /**
     * Return a string representation of this tree. The string
     * returned by this method will show the structure of the
     * tree if the string is rotated 90 degrees to the right.
     *
     * @return a string representation of this tree.
     */
    public String toString() {
        StringBuffer retVal = new StringBuffer();

        // Get the string
        treeToString( root, retVal, "" );

        // Convert the string buffer to a string
        return retVal.toString();
    }

    /**
     * A recursive method that does an RVL traversal of the tree
     * to create a string that shows the contents and structure of
     * the tree.
```

(continued)

FIGURE 7.13 Reference-based binary tree class *(continued)*

```
*
* For a tree that has the following structure:
*
*
*                          A
*                  B            C
*              D       E
*
* This method will return the following string
*
*              C
* A
*                  E
*      B
*              D
*/

private void treeToString( BinaryTreeNode cur,
                           StringBuffer str,
                           String indent ) {
   if ( cur != null ) {
       // Get the string representation of the right child. Indent
       // is increased by 4 since this subtree is one level deeper in
       // the tree
       treeToString( cur.getRight(), str, indent + "  " );

       // Convert the information in the current node
       str.append( indent );
       str.append( cur.getData().toString() );
       str.append( "\n" );

       // Get the string representation of the left child.
       treeToString( cur.getLeft(), str, indent + "  " );
   }
}

} // LinkedBinaryTree
```

FIGURE 7.13 Reference-based binary tree class *(continued)*

♦ 7.3.5 An Array-Based Implementation of Binary Trees

Although the reference-based implementation of binary trees presented in Section 7.3.4 and shown in Figure 7.13 is a highly efficient technique, it is not the only one. For example, we could implement a binary tree using an array. (We used exactly this technique in Section 6.2.3.1 to implement a list.) We create a one-dimensional array of objects, called data, to hold the information field of a node, and a two-dimensional $k \times 2$ array, called children, in which the first column holds a pointer to the left subtree and the second column holds a pointer to the right subtree. Thus, the following six-node tree

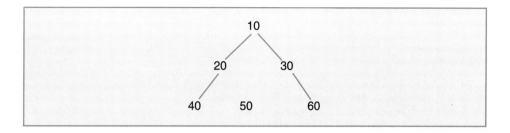

could be represented using 10-element arrays (Figure 7.14).

The root of the tree, the integer 10, is stored in row 3 of the `data` array as indicated by the state variable `root`. The root of the left subtree is stored in row 1, as specified by the value in the column labeled left in row 3, and the root of the right subtree is in row 5. The rest of the tree is stored in similar fashion. If a node does not have either a left child or a right child, the value −1, equivalent to the value `null`, is entered into the appropriate column of the `children` array.

To indicate that a row is empty and not being used, Figure 7.14 uses the character value —. To implement that concept, we need to utilize the same available space list management techniques introduced in Chapter 6 and diagramed in Figure 6.10. We maintain a state variable called `availHead` that is the head of a linked list of unused rows—rows 4, 7, 8, and 9 in Figure 7.14. The elements of this list are linked together using either the left or right pointer fields of the children array. The class constructor initializes the available space list to an empty state similar to what is shown in Figure 6.9.

	data	children (left)	(right)
0	60	−1	−1
1	20	6	2
2	50	−1	−1
3	10	1	5
4	—	—	—
5	30	−1	0
6	40	−1	−1
7	—	—	—
8	—	—	—
9	—	—	—

root = 3

FIGURE 7.14 Implementation of a binary tree using arrays

Figure 7.15 is the code for an array-based `BinaryTree` class that implements the `BinaryTree` interface of Figure 7.10.

```
/**
 * A array-based binary tree implementation.
 */

public class ArrayBasedBinaryTree implements BinaryTree {
    // Constants for selecting children
    public static final int LEFT = 0;
    public static final int RIGHT = 1;

    // Constants for selecting traversals
    public static final int IN_ORDER = 0;
    public static final int PRE_ORDER = 1;
    public static final int POST_ORDER = 2;

    // Marks an empty position in the array
    public static final int OFF_TREE = -1;

    // Initial size of the arrays
    public static final int INITIAL_SIZE = 2;

    private Object data[];      // Array containing node data
    private int leftChild[];    // The left children
    private int rightChild[];   // The right children

    private int root;           // The root node
    private int cursor;         // Current node
    private int count;          // Number of nodes in the tree

    private int availHead;      // Start of free list (maintained in rightChild)

    /**
     * Create a new tree.
     */
    public ArrayBasedBinaryTree() {
        // Initialize storage arrays
        data = new Object[ INITIAL_SIZE ];
        leftChild = new int[ INITIAL_SIZE ];
        rightChild = new int[ INITIAL_SIZE ];

        // Tree is empty
        root = OFF_TREE;
        cursor = OFF_TREE;
        count = 0;

        // Initialize children arrays. Free list is in the right child array.
        availHead = 0;
        for ( int i = 0; i < INITIAL_SIZE - 1; i++ ) {
```

FIGURE 7.15 An array-based binary tree class

```
            // Add this node to our 'free' list.
            rightChild[ i ] = i+1;

            // Ensure other nodes don't link anywhere
            leftChild[ i ] = OFF_TREE;
        }

        leftChild[ INITIAL_SIZE-1 ] = OFF_TREE;
        rightChild[ INITIAL_SIZE-1 ] = OFF_TREE;
    }

    /**
     * Positions the cursor at the root of the tree.
     *
     * Preconditions:
     *     None.
     *
     * Postconditions:
     *     If the tree is empty, the cursor is invalid.
     *     Otherwise, the cursor refers to the root of the tree.
     *     The tree structure is unchanged.
     */
    public void toRoot() {
        cursor = root;
    }

    /**
     * Determine if the current node has a left child.
     *
     * Preconditions:
     *     The cursor is valid.
     *
     * Postconditions:
     *     The tree structure is unchanged.
     *     The cursor is unchanged.
     *
     * @return true if the node identified by the cursor has a left
     *     child and false otherwise.
     */
    public boolean hasLeftChild() {
        return leftChild[ cursor ] != OFF_TREE;
    }

    /**
     * Determine if the current node has a right child.
     *
```

(continued)

FIGURE 7.15 An array-based binary tree class *(continued)*

```
 * Preconditions:
 *     The cursor is valid.
 *
 * Postconditions:
 *     The tree structure is unchanged.
 *     The cursor is unchanged.
 *
 * @return true if the node identified by the cursor has a right
 *     child and false otherwise.
 */
public boolean hasRightChild() {
   return rightChild[ cursor ] != OFF_TREE;
}


/**
 * Determines if the current node has a parent.
 *
 * Preconditions:
 *     The cursor is valid.
 *
 * Postconditions:
 *     The tree structure is unchanged.
 *     The cursor is unchanged.
 *
 * @return true if the current node has a parent and false otherwise.
 */
public boolean hasParent() {
   int parent = OFF_TREE;

   // If there is a tree to search - look for the parent
   if ( root != OFF_TREE ) {
      parent = findParent( root, cursor );
   }

   // If we found a parent return true
   return parent != OFF_TREE;
}

/**
 * Determines if the cursor is on the tree.
 *
 * Preconditions:
 *     None.
 *
 * Postconditions:
 * The tree structure is unchanged.
 *     The cursor is unchanged.
 *
 * @return true if the cursor is on the tree and false otherwise.
 */
```

FIGURE 7.15 An array-based binary tree class *(continued)*

```
      public boolean isValid() {
         return cursor != OFF_TREE;
      }


      /**
       * Positions the cursor at the current node's parent, if any.
       *
       * Preconditions:
       *    The cursor is valid.
       *
       * Postconditions:
       *    If the cursor has no parent (i.e. referred to the root node),
       *       the cursor is invalid. Otherwise, the cursor refers to its
       *       previous referent's parent.
       *    The structure of the tree is unchanged.
       */
      public void toParent() {
         // If there is no tree to search - invalidate the cursor
         if ( root == OFF_TREE ) {
            cursor = OFF_TREE;
         }
         else {
            // Set the cursor to the parent
            cursor = findParent( root, cursor );
         }
      }


      /**
       * Positions the cursor at the left child of the current node.
       *
       * Preconditions:
       *    The cursor is valid.
       *
       * Postconditions:
       *    If the left child of the current node is invalid, the cursor
       *       is invalid. Otherwise, the cursor is changed to refer to
       *       the left child of the current node.
       *    The structure of the tree is unchanged.
       */
      public void toLeftChild() {
         cursor = leftChild[ cursor ];
      }


      /**
       * Positions the cursor at the right child of the current node.
       *
       * Preconditions:
       *    The cursor is valid.
       *
```

(continued)

FIGURE 7.15 An array-based binary tree class *(continued)*

```
 * Postconditions:
 *     If the left child of the current node is invalid, the cursor
 *         is invalid. Otherwise, the cursor is changed to refer to
 *         the right child of the current node.
 *     The structure of the tree is unchanged.
 */
public void toRightChild() {
   cursor = rightChild[ cursor ];
}


/**
 * Inserts the given data in the left child of the currrent node.
 * If the cursor is null and the tree has no root, a new root
 * node for the tree is created.
 *
 * Preconditions:
 *     The tree is empty, or the cursor is valid and the left child is
 *         empty.
 *
 * Postconditions:
 *     The cursor has not changed.
 *     The size of the tree has increased by one.
 *     No other structure of the tree has changed.
 *
 * @param element the data to put in the left child.
 */
public void insertLeft( Object element ) {
   // Find the place in the arrays where the new node will
   // be placed
   int pos = nextIndex( );
   data[ pos ] = element;

   // If the tree is empty this becomes the only node in the
   // tree, otherwise make the new node the left child of the
   // cursor
   if ( root == OFF_TREE ) {
      root = pos;
   }
   else {
      leftChild[ cursor ] = pos;
   }
}


/**
 * Inserts the given data in the right child of the currrent node.
 * If the cursor is null and the tree has no root, a new root
 * node for the tree is created.
 *
```

FIGURE 7.15 An array-based binary tree class *(continued)*

```
   * Preconditions:
   *    The tree is empty, or the cursor is valid and the right child is
   *        empty.
   *
   * Postconditions:
   *    The cursor has not changed.
   *    The size of the tree has increased by one.
   *    No other structure of the tree has changed.
   *
   * @param element the data to put in the right child.
   */
  public void insertRight( Object element ) {
     // Find the place in the arrays where the new node will
     // be placed
     int pos = nextIndex( );
     data[ pos ] = element;

     // If the tree is empty this becomes the only node in the
     // tree, otherwise make the new node the right child of the
     // cursor
     if ( root == OFF_TREE ) {
        root = pos;
     }
     else {
        rightChild[ cursor ] = pos;
     }
  }


  /**
   * Return a reference to the data stored at the current node.
   *
   * Preconditions:
   *    The cursor is on the tree.
   *
   * Postconditions:
   *    The tree is unchanged.
   *
   * @return a reference to the data at the current node.
   */
  public Object get() {
     return data[ cursor ];
  }


  /**
   * Set the data stored at the current node.
   *
   * Preconditions:
   *    The cursor is on the tree.
```

(continued)

FIGURE 7.15 An array-based binary tree class *(continued)*

```
 *
 * Postconditions:
 *     The reference of the current node is changed.
 *     The rest of the tree is unchanged.
 *
 * @param element the reference to store in the current node.
 */
public void set( Object element ) {
   data[ cursor ] = element;
}


/**
 * Removes the subtree rooted at (including) the cursor.
 *
 * Preconditions:
 *     The cursor is on the tree.
 *
 * Postconditions:
 *     The specified subtree has been removed. If the cursor
 *         referred to the root node, the tree is empty.
 *     The tree's size has decreased.
 *     No other structure of the tree has changed.
 *     If the resulting tree is empty, the cursor is invalid.
 *     Otherwise the cursor refers to the parent of the current
 *         node.
 */
public void prune() {
   int parent = findParent( root, cursor );

   // Add the nodes in the tree being deleted to the free list
   freeIndex( cursor );

   // Did we delete the entire tree?
   if ( parent == OFF_TREE ) {
      // Invalidate the root and the cursor
      root = OFF_TREE;
      cursor = OFF_TREE;
   } else {
      // Is it the parent's left child?
      if ( leftChild[ parent ] == cursor ) {
         // Deleted the left child
         leftChild[ parent ] = OFF_TREE;
      } else {
         // Deleted the right child
         rightChild[ parent ] = OFF_TREE;
      }
```

FIGURE 7.15 An array-based binary tree class *(continued)*

```
              // Update the cursor
              cursor = parent;
          }
      }


      /**
       * Determines if the given object is identical to this one.
       *
       * Preconditions:
       *    None.
       *
       * Postconditions:
       *    The cursors of both trees refer to the root of their
       *        respective trees.
       *
       * @param o the Object to compare to
       *
       * @return true if and only if all of the following are true:
       *    The other object is a BinaryTree
       *    The structure of the two trees are identical
       *    The data contained in corresponding nodes of the
       *        two trees are identical.
       */
      public boolean equals( Object o ) {
          boolean retVal = false;

          // We can only do the comparison if the other object is a tree
          if ( o instanceof BinaryTree ) {
              BinaryTree other = (BinaryTree)o;

              // Start at the top of both trees
              toRoot();
              other.toRoot();

              // Use the recursive helper method to do the actual work
              retVal = equalHelper( other );

              // Reset the iterators
              toRoot();
              other.toRoot();
          }

          return retVal;
      }
```

(continued)

FIGURE 7.15 An array-based binary tree class *(continued)*

```
public boolean equalHelper( BinaryTree tree ) {
    // Handle the case where both trees are empty. If both
    // trees are empty, they are equal.
    boolean retVal = ( cursor == OFF_TREE && !tree.isValid() );

    // If both trees have something in them — compare them
    if ( cursor != OFF_TREE && tree.isValid() ) {

        // Both nodes should have the same data and both
        // should have the same type of children
        retVal =
            data[ cursor ].equals( tree.get() ) &&
            hasLeftChild() == tree.hasLeftChild() &&
            hasRightChild() == tree.hasRightChild();

        // If they are equal and have left children - compare them
        if ( retVal && hasLeftChild() ) {
            toLeftChild();
            tree.toLeftChild();
            retVal = equalHelper( tree );

            // Back up the cursors
            toParent();
            tree.toParent();
        }

        // If they are equal and have right children - compare them
        if ( retVal && hasRightChild() ) {
            toRightChild();
            tree.toRightChild();
            retVal = retVal && equalHelper( tree );

            // Back up the cursors
            toParent();
            tree.toParent();
        }
    }

    return retVal;
}

/**
 * Returns the number of nodes in this tree.
 *
 * Preconditions:
 *    None.
 *
```

(continued)

FIGURE 7.15 An array-based binary tree class *(continued)*

```
 *  Postconditions:
 *     The tree is unchanged.
 *
 *  @return the number of nodes in the tree.
 */
public int size() {
   return count;
}


/**
 *  Returns the height of the tree.
 *
 *  Preconditions:
 *     None.
 *
 *  Postconditions:
 *     The tree is unchanged.
 *
 *  @return the height of the tree.
 */
public int height() {
   int height = 0;

   // If there is a tree determine its height
   if ( root != OFF_TREE ) {
      height = height( root );
   }

   return height;
}

/**
 *  Determine the height of the tree with the specified root.
 *
 *  @param the root of the tree.
 *
 *  @return the height of the tree.
 */

private int height( int root ) {
   int leftHeight = 0;
   int rightHeight = 0;
   int height = 0;

   // Determine the height of the left subtree
   if ( leftChild[ root ] != OFF_TREE ) {
      leftHeight = height( leftChild[ root ] );
   }
```

(continued)

FIGURE 7.15 An array-based binary tree class *(continued)*

```
      // Determine the height of the right subtree
      if ( rightChild[ root ] != OFF_TREE ) {
         rightHeight = height( rightChild[ root ] );
      }

      // The height of the tree rooted at this node is one more than the
      // height of the 'taller' of its children.
      if (leftHeight > rightHeight) {
         height = 1 + leftHeight;
      } else {
         height = 1 + rightHeight;
      }

      // Return the answer
      return height;
   }

   /**
    * Position the cursor on the first (as seen by an inorder traversal)
    * occurrence of the given data. Equality is determined by invoking
    * the equals method.
    *
    * Preconditions:
    *    Key is not null.
    *
    * Postconditions:
    *    The tree is unchanged.
    *    If key is found, cursor refers to the first occurrence of
    *       the key. If key is not found, the cursor is off the tree
    *
    * @param target object containing the data to be searched for.
    */

   public void find( Object target ) {
      // If there is no tree - cursor should be off the tree
      if ( root == OFF_TREE ) {
         cursor = OFF_TREE;
      } else {
         // Find the target and set cursor
         cursor = search( root, target );
      }
   }

   /**
    * Search the tree at the specified root for the given target.
    *
    * @param root the root of the tree to search.
    * @param target the element being looked for.
```

FIGURE 7.15 An array-based binary tree class *(continued)*

```
 *
 * @return the location of the node that contains the target,
 *    or OFF_TREE if the target cannot be found.
 */

private int search( int root, Object target ) {
   int location = OFF_TREE;

   // Is the target in the left subtree?
   if ( leftChild[ root ] != OFF_TREE ) {
      location = search( leftChild[ root ], target );
   }

   // If we haven't found it, is it in this node?
   if (location == OFF_TREE && target.equals( data[ root ] ) ) {
      location = root;
   }

   // If we haven't found it, and we have a right child, check there
   if ( location == OFF_TREE && rightChild[ root ] != OFF_TREE ){
      location = search( rightChild[ root ], target );
   }

   // Return the location of the target
   return location;
}

/**
 * Return a string representation of this tree. The string
 * returned by this method will show the structure of the
 * tree if the string is rotated 90 degrees to the right.
 *
 * @return a string representation of this tree.
 */
public String toString() {
   StringBuffer retVal = new StringBuffer();

   // Get the string
   treeToString( root, retVal, "" );

   // Convert the string buffer to a string
   return retVal.toString();
}

/**
 * A recursive method that does a RVL traversal of the tree
 * to create a string that shows the contents and structure of
 * the tree.
```

(continued)

FIGURE 7.15 An array-based binary tree class *(continued)*

```
 *
 * For a tree that has the following structure:
 *
 *
 *                          A
 *                    B           C
 *                 D       E
 *
 * This method will return the following string
 *
 *           C
 *  A
 *             E
 *       B
 *             D
 */

private void treeToString( int cur, StringBuffer str, String indent ) {
    if ( cur != OFF_TREE ) {
        // Get the string representation of the right child. Indent
        // is increased by 4 since this subtree is one level deeper in
        // the tree
        treeToString( rightChild[ cur ], str, indent + "    " );

        // Convert the information in the current node
        str.append( indent );
        str.append( data[ cur ].toString() );
        str.append( "\n" );

        // Get the string representation of the left child.
        treeToString( leftChild[ cur ], str, indent + "    " );
    }
}


/**
 * Perform a preorder traversal on this tree with the specified
 * callback object.
 *
 * Preconditions:
 *     cb is not null.
 *
 * Postconditions:
 *     The tree is unchanged.
 *
 * @param cb the callback object used to process each node.
 */
public void preOrder( Callback cb ) {
    // Start the traversal at the root node
```

FIGURE 7.15 An array-based binary tree class *(continued)*

```
            if ( root != OFF_TREE ) {
                preOrder( root, cb );
            }
        }


        /**
         * Do a preorder traversal of the tree with the given root.
         *
         * @param root the root of the tree to traverse.
         * @param cb the callback object used to process each node.
         */
        private void preOrder( int root, Callback cb ) {
            // Process the data in the current node
            cb.visit( data[ root ] );

            // Process the left child - if there is one
            if ( leftChild[ root ] != OFF_TREE ) {
                preOrder( leftChild[ root ], cb );
            }

            // Process the right child - if there is one
            if ( rightChild[ root ] != OFF_TREE ) {
                preOrder( rightChild[ root ], cb );
            }
        }


        /**
         * Perform an inorder traversal on this tree with the specified
         * callback object.
         *
         * Preconditions:
         *     cb is not null.
         *
         * Postconditions:
         *     The tree is unchanged.
         *
         * @param cb the callback object used to process each node.
         */
        public void inOrder( Callback cb ) {
            // Start the traversal at the root node
            if ( root != OFF_TREE ) {
                inOrder( root, cb );
            }
        }


        /**
         * Do an inorder traversal of the tree with the given root.
         *
```

(continued)

FIGURE 7.15 An array-based binary tree class *(continued)*

```
  * @param root the root of the tree to traverse.
  * @param cb the callback object used to process each node.
  */
private void inOrder( int root, Callback cb ) {
    // Process the left child - if there is one
    if ( leftChild[ root ] != OFF_TREE ) {
        inOrder( leftChild[ root ], cb );
    }

    // Process the current node
    cb.visit( data[ root ] );

    // Process the right child - if there is one
    if ( rightChild[ root ] != OFF_TREE ) {
        inOrder( rightChild[ root ], cb );
    }
}

/**
 * Perform a postorder traversal on this tree with the specified
 * callback object.
 *
 * Preconditions:
 *     cb is not null.
 *
 * Postconditions:
 *     The tree is unchanged.
 *
 * @param cb the callback object used to process each node.
 */
public void postOrder(Callback cb) {
    // Start the traversal at the root node
    if (root != OFF_TREE) {
        postOrder( root, cb );
    }
}

private void postOrder( int root, Callback cb ) {
    // Process the left child - if there is one
    if ( leftChild[ root ] != OFF_TREE ) {
        postOrder( leftChild[ root ], cb );
    }

    // Process the right child - if there is one
    if ( rightChild[ root ] != OFF_TREE ) {
        postOrder( rightChild[ root ], cb );
    }
```

FIGURE 7.15 An array-based binary tree class *(continued)*

```
            // Process the current node
            cb.visit( data[ root ] );
   }


   /**
    * Return the position of the parent given a root of the tree
    * and the child.
    *
    * @param root the root of the tree to search.
    * @param child the child whose parent we are looking for.
    *
    * @return the location of the parent in the tree or OFF_TREE
    *     if the parent cannot be found.
    */

   protected int findParent( int root, int child ) {
      int parent = OFF_TREE;

      // Is the root the parent?
      if ( leftChild[ root ] == child || rightChild[ root ] == child ) {
         parent = root;
      } else {
         // Check left child - if there is one
         if ( leftChild[ root ] != OFF_TREE) {
            parent = findParent( leftChild[ root ], child );
         }
         // If it has not been found - check the right child
         if (parent == OFF_TREE && rightChild[ root ] != OFF_TREE ) {
            parent = findParent( rightChild[ root ], child );
         }
      }

      return parent;
   }


   /**
    * Locate the next open index in the arrays holding the tree nodes.
    * If there is not enough room in the arrays for the new node,
    * the arrays will be expanded.
    *
    * @return the next open index in the node arrays.
    */

   private int nextIndex() {
      int retVal;

      // If the free space is gone - expand the arrays
      if ( availHead == OFF_TREE ) {
         expand();
      }
```

(continued)

FIGURE 7.15 An array-based binary tree class *(continued)*

```
      // Take the location at the front of the list
      retVal = availHead;
      availHead = rightChild[ availHead ];

      // Ensure the location doesn't link to the available list any more
      rightChild[ retVal ] = OFF_TREE;

      // One more node in the tree
      count = count + 1;

      // Return the index
      return retVal;
   }

   /**
    * Double the capacity of the arrays that hold the data and the
    * links.
    */

   private void expand() {
      // Make the new arrays twice the size of the old arrays
      Object newData[] = new Object[ data.length * 2 ];
      int newLeftChild[] = new int[ newData.length ];
      int newRightChild[] = new int[ newData.length ];

      // Copy the contents of the old arrays to the new arrays
      for ( int i = 0; i < data.length; i = i + 1 ) {
         newData[ i ] = data[ i ];
         newLeftChild[ i ] = leftChild[ i ];
         newRightChild[ i ] = rightChild[ i ];
      }

      // Add the empty space to the available list
      for ( int i = data.length; i < newData.length; i++ ) {
         newRightChild[ i ] = availHead;
         newLeftChild[ i ] = OFF_TREE;
         availHead = i;
      }

      // Start using the new arrays
      data = newData;
      leftChild = newLeftChild;
      rightChild = newRightChild;
   }

   /**
    * Add the array locations occupied by the specified tree to the
    * free list.
    *
```

FIGURE 7.15 An array-based binary tree class *(continued)*

```
     * @param root the root of the tree to delete.
     */

    private void freeIndex( int root ) {
       // Add the nodes in the left tree to the free list
       if ( leftChild[ root ] != OFF_TREE ) {
          freeIndex( leftChild[ root ] );
          leftChild[ root ] = OFF_TREE;
       }

       // Add the nodes in the right tree to the free list
       if ( rightChild[ root ] != OFF_TREE ) {
          freeIndex( rightChild[ root ] );
          rightChild[ root ] = OFF_TREE;
       }

       // Add this node to the free list
       rightChild[ root ] = availHead;
       availHead = root;

       // One less node in the tree
       count = count - 1;
    }

} // ArrayBasedBinaryTree
```

FIGURE 7.15 An array-based binary tree class *(continued)*

Although useful for languages that do not support reference variables, this array implementation suffers from some of the same problems first mentioned in Section 6.2.3.1 with respect to linked lists. Specifically, the programmer must know in advance exactly how much space to allocate for array storage, the declaration INITIAL_SIZE = 100 in Figure 7.15. If we attempt to insert 101 nodes into our binary tree, we overflow the array and must resize it using the method called expand(), which doubles the current size. In addition, if there are only a few nodes in the tree, there is a good deal of wasted space. Finally, the programmer is again responsible for maintenance of the available space list, including allocating nodes (i.e., rows), reclaiming deleted nodes, and handling out-of-memory conditions. Because of these problems, the reference-based implementation in Figure 7.13 is preferred.

We have now looked at tree structures with few, if any, restrictions on the location where operations can be performed or on the type of data that can be stored in a node. In a general tree, you may insert, delete, or access any node. In a binary tree, you are also free to insert, delete, or access any value, with the one restriction that no node in the tree may have more than two children.

The next three sections look at some special-purpose tree structures that place restrictions on either the type of data that may be stored in a node or the location where new data can be inserted. These trees can be used to efficiently solve problems in such areas as searching, sorting, and finding maxima or minima.

7.4 BINARY SEARCH TREES

◆ 7.4.1 Definition

One variation of the binary tree discussed in the previous section is particularly useful for carrying out search operations. It is called the **binary search tree,** often abbreviated BST.

> *Definition: A* **binary search tree (BST)** *is a binary tree in which one of the data values stored in the node is a special value called the key. Every key value stored in the left subtree of a node is less than the key value stored in that node, and every key value stored in the right subtree of a node is greater than the key value stored in that node. This ordering is called the* **binary search tree property**.

Exactly one of the data fields in the node is designated the **key**, and it must be possible to compare keys—that is, determine if one key is less than, equal to, or greater than another. It is usually assumed (but not required) that the keys in a BST are unique, and duplicates are not allowed. We make that assumption in all of our examples, so two keys should never test equal. Figure 7.16 shows an example of a binary search tree.

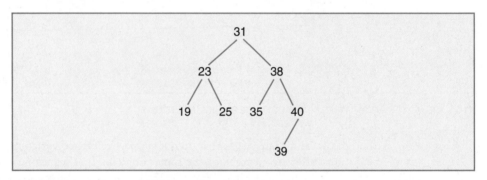

FIGURE 7.16 Example binary search tree

Every key in the left subtree of the root of Figure 7.16, {19, 23, 25}, is less than the root value 31, and every key in the right subtree of the root, {35, 38, 39, 40}, is greater than the root value 31. Similarly, looking at the subtrees, we see that this ordering property holds not just for the root but for every node in the tree. For example, every key in the left subtree of the tree rooted at 23 {19} is less than 23. Similarly, every key in the right subtree {25} is greater than 23. Every key in the left subtree of the tree rooted at 38 {35} is less than 38, and every key in the right subtree {39, 40} is greater than 38.

◆ 7.4.2 Using Binary Search Trees in Searching Operations

There are two important differences between the binary search tree just introduced and the binary tree presented in Section 7.3. First, the insertion of a node into a binary tree can be done anywhere, but insertion into a binary search tree must guarantee that the insert() method maintains the binary search tree property. Second, the

contains() method can exploit the binary search tree property to speed up the
process of locating a value in the tree. A BinarySearchTree interface that includes
both of these two methods—insert() and contains()—is shown in Figure 7.17. It
also includes the two utility methods size(), which returns the number of nodes in
the tree, and height(), which returns the height of the tree.

```
/**
 * An interface for the Binary Search Tree
 *
 * This interface assumes that duplicate entries are forbidden in the tree.
 */

public interface BinarySearchTree {
    /**
     * Inserts the given data into the correct position within the tree.
     *
     * Preconditions:
     *    The data to be added does not equal any data currently in the
     *    tree.
     *
     * Postconditions:
     *    The size of the tree has increased by one.
     *    The element added is in the correct position within the tree.
     *
     * @param data the data to insert into the tree.
     */
    public void insert( Comparable data );

    /**
     * Determine the size of the tree.
     *
     * Preconditions:
     *    None.
     *
     * Postconditions:
     *    The tree is unchanged.
     *
     * @return the number of elements in the tree.
     */
    public int size();

    /**
     * Determine the height of the tree.
     *
     * Preconditions:
     *    None.
     *
```

(continued)

FIGURE 7.17 Interface for a binary search tree

```
 *  Postconditions:
 *      The tree is unchanged.
 *
 *  @return the height of the tree.
 */
public int height();

/**
 *  Determine if the given element is in the tree.
 *
 *  Preconditions:
 *      Target is not null.
 *
 *  Postconditions:
 *      The tree is unchanged.
 *
 *  @param target the element being searched for.
 *
 *  @return true if the element is found and false otherwise.
 */
public boolean contains( Comparable target );

} // BinarySearchTree
```

FIGURE 7.17 Interface for a binary search tree *(continued)*

When inserting a node into the binary tree of Section 7.3, we used its state variable `cursor` to identify where it should be attached. However, when inserting a node into a binary search tree, we do not specify the location of the insertion. Instead, we provide the data to be inserted and a reference to the root of the tree. The `insert()` method itself will determine where to insert this new value so that the binary search tree property is maintained. This is done by comparing the value to be inserted, V, to the data value contained in the current node, N. If V < N, then we follow the left branch of the node and repeat the process. If V > N, then we follow the right branch of the node and repeat the process. This continues until one of two things happens:

1. V = N. This means the data to be inserted are already in the tree. However, we assumed that we would not store duplicates, so the method returns without modifying the tree. In some circumstances, this may be treated as an error.

2. child pointer = `null`. This is the correct location to insert the new node.

Figure 7.18 shows the sequence of four comparisons required to locate the correct place to insert the value 26 into the binary search tree. We initially compare 26 to the value in the root of the tree, 30. Since it is less, we must go to the left. We repeat this process, now comparing 26 to the value in the current node, which this time is a 20. Since 26 is greater, we must move to the right. This process continues as we arrive at the nodes containing a 25 and then a 27. This time when we compare our data value 26 to the node value 27 and see that it is less, we will attempt to move to the left.

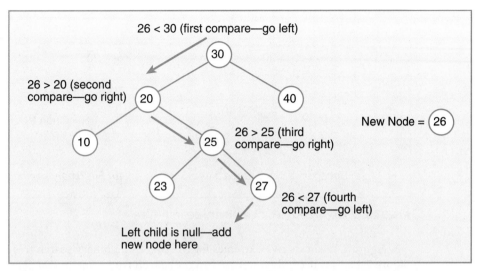

FIGURE 7.18 Placement of a new node in a binary search tree

However, the left pointer of this node is `null`. This means that we have found the correct place to insert this new node—as the left child of the node whose key value is 27. An examination should convince you that the binary search tree property still holds for this new tree after the insertion is completed.

The questions we must now answer are: What is the advantage of using a binary search tree? What gains justify the price of maintaining the binary search tree property whenever we insert a new node? After all, both the `insertLeft` and `insertRight()` methods for regular binary trees, given on pages 386–387, are efficient O(1) operations. Now, we must search through the tree to locate the correct insertion point.

The answer lies in the speed and efficiency of the `contains()` method. Searching through a collection of elements to locate a specific value is one of the most common and widely performed operations in computer science. When we search an unordered list of N values looking for a special key, we will, on the average, have to look at N/2 items until we find what we want. In the worst case, we will have to look at all N items, and the time complexity of this search process on unordered lists is O(N). For large values of N, this can be somewhat slow. This condition also holds for binary trees, such as those in Figure 7.6. If we do not know exactly where a value is located within a binary tree, the best we can do is search the entire tree using the traversal algorithms of Figures 7.8 or 7.9, and as shown earlier, these are also O(N).

However, with a binary search tree, we do not have to examine all the nodes in the tree to locate a given key, but only those nodes that lie on the path followed by the `insert()` operation when that key value was initially stored. Thus, we never need to look at more than H items, where H is the height of the binary search tree, the distance required to reach the leaf node furthest from the root. We saw this in Figure 7.18 where we traveled from the root node to a leaf node looking for the correct place to insert the value 26. The distance traveled was H, the height of the tree.

The next questions we must ask are: What is the value of H, and is it always the case that H < N? More specifically, can we perform the `contains()` operation on a binary search tree with a lower order complexity than O(N)?

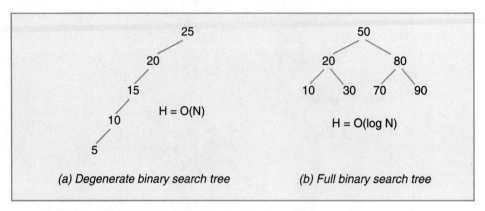

FIGURE 7.19 Depth, H, of a binary search tree

Figure 7.19 shows two extremes for the shape of a binary search tree. The tree in Figure 7.19a is called a **degenerate binary search tree**—one in which every nonterminal node has exactly one child. In a degenerate BST, H = N, where N is the number of nodes in the tree, and we have gained nothing since the BST has effectively become a linked list. (In fact, it is even worse because we have to allocate a good deal of memory space for unused pointers.) The time to locate a node is still O(N).

The tree in Figure 7.19b represents the other extreme, a structure called a **full binary search tree**. A full binary search tree is one in which all leaf nodes are on the same level and all nonleaf nodes have degree = 2. Let's determine how many nodes N are contained in a full binary search tree of height H:

	Level	Number of nodes on this level
(root)	1	1
	2	2
	3	4
	4	8
	. . .	. . .
(H)	i	2^{i-1}

The number of nodes on level i in a full binary search tree is 2^{i-1}, so the total number of nodes N in the tree of Figure 7.19b is the sum of the number of nodes on all levels from 1 to H, the height of the tree:

$$N = \sum_{i=1}^{H} 2^{i-1} = 2^0 + 2^1 + 2^2 + \ldots + 2^{H-1}$$
$$N = 2^H - 1$$

Solving for H, the height of the tree, we get

$H = \log_2(N+1)$ or
$H = O(\log N)$

Thus, the maximum distance from the root to the leaves is a logarithmic function of N, the number of nodes in the tree, rather than a linear function of N. If our binary search tree looks more like the one in Figure 7.19b than the one in Figure 7.19a, we have gained a great deal. We will be able to locate any item in the tree with at most O(log N) compares rather than the O(N) compares required by either the sequential search of an unordered list or the traversal of an unordered binary tree.

For large N, log(N) << N. For example, if N = 100,000, we can locate any node in the tree with approximately $\log_2 100,000 = 17$ compares, an improvement of almost four orders of magnitude. As was stated in Chapter 5, the "efficiency game" in software development is most strongly affected by your choice of data representations, not by the details of coding or the speed of the machine on which you run the final program. This example clearly illustrates that point.

Figure 7.20 shows the code for LinkedBinarySearchTree, a linked list implementation of the BinarySearchTree interface in Figure 7.17. The only instance variable needed by this implementation is root, a pointer to the root of the tree. We no longer need the current position indicator, cursor, because the insert() method itself determines the proper location for the insertion operation. Note that insert() first checks to see if root == null. This is because a binary search tree, like a binary tree, can be empty. Also note that the parameters to both insert() and contains() are of type Comparable. This is to ensure that it is meaningful to compare two keys to see if they are less than, equal to, or greater than each other. Any class that implements the Comparable interface is guaranteed to support the compareTo() method that compares one object to another and determines their relative ordering.

```
/**
 * Specifications for a node in a binary search tree.
 *
 */
public class BinarySearchTreeNode {
   Comparable data;              // Data stored in this node
   BinarySearchTreeNode left;    // Left child
   BinarySearchTreeNode right;   // Right child

   /**
    * Create a new node.
    */
   public BinarySearchTreeNode() {
      this( null );
   }

   /**
    * Create a new node that contains the specified element.
    *
    * @param element the element to place in the node.
    */
   public BinarySearchTreeNode( Comparable element ) {
      data = element;
      left = null;
      right = null;
   }
```

(continued)

FIGURE 7.20 Linked list implementation of a binary search tree

```
/**
 * Get the data stored in this node.
 *
 * @return the data stored in this node.
 */
public Comparable getData() {
   return data;
}

/**
 * Get a reference to the left child of this node.
 *
 * @return a reference to the left child of this node.
 */
public BinarySearchTreeNode getLeft() {
   return left;
}

/**
 * Get a reference to the right child of this node.
 *
 * @return a reference to the right child of this node.
 */
public BinarySearchTreeNode getRight() {
   return right;
}

/**
 * Set the data to the specified value.
 *
 * @param newData a reference to the data to place in this node.
 */
public void setData( Comparable newData ) {
   data = newData;
}

/**
 * Set the left child of this node.
 *
 * @param newLeft a reference to the left child of this node.
 */
public void setLeft( BinarySearchTreeNode newLeft ) {
   left = newLeft;
}

/**
 * Set the right child of this node.
 *
```

FIGURE 7.20 Linked list implementation of a binary search tree *(continued)*

```
      * @param newRight a reference to the right child of this node.
      */
     public void setRight( BinarySearchTreeNode newRight ) {
        right = newRight;
     }

} // BinarySearchTreeNode

/**
 * A linked list-based implementation of binary search tree.
 */

public class LinkedBinarySearchTree implements BinarySearchTree {

     private BinarySearchTreeNode root; // the root of the tree

     /**
      * Inserts the given data into the correct position within the tree.
      *
      * Preconditions:
      *     The data to be added are not equal to any
      *        data currently in the tree.
      *
      * Postconditions:
      *     The size of the tree has increased by one.
      *     The element added is in the correct position within the tree.
      *
      * @param data the data to insert into the tree.
      */

     public void insert( Comparable data ) {
        BinarySearchTreeNode cur = root;
        BinarySearchTreeNode newNode = new BinarySearchTreeNode( data );
        if ( root == null ) {
           root = newNode;
        }
        else {
           while ( cur != null ) {
              int compare = data.compareTo( cur.getData() );

              if ( compare < 0 ) {
                 // The new element is less than the current element
              if ( cur.getLeft() == null ) {
                 // There is no left child so insert data here
                 cur.setLeft( newNode );
                 cur = null;
              }
              else {
```

(continued)

FIGURE 7.20 Linked list implementation of a binary search tree *(continued)*

```
            // There is a left child - insert into it
            cur = cur.getLeft();
        }
    }
    else if ( compare > 0 ) {
        // The new element is greater than the current element
        if ( cur.getRight() == null ) {
            // There is no right child so insert data here
            cur.setRight( newNode );
            cur = null;
        }
        else {
            // There is a right child - insert into it
            cur = cur.getRight();
        }
    }
        else {
            // The new element is already in the tree - do not add
            cur = null;
        }
    }
}

/**
 * Determine the size of the tree.
 *
 * Preconditions:
 *     None.
 *
 * Postconditions:
 *     The tree is unchanged.
 *
 * @return the number of elements in the tree.
 */
public int size() {
    int size = 0;

    // If there is a tree determine the size of it
    if (root != null) {
        size = size( root );
    }

    return size;
}

/**
 * Determine the size of the tree with the specified root.
```

FIGURE 7.20 Linked list implementation of a binary search tree *(continued)*

```
 *
 * @param root the root of the tree.
 *
 * @return the size of the tree.
 */
private int size( BinarySearchTreeNode root ) {
   int size = 0; // The size of the tree

   // The size of the tree is one more than the sum of
   // the sizes of its children.
   if ( root.getLeft() != null ) {
      size = size( root.getLeft() );
   }
   if ( root.getRight() != null ) {
      size = size + size( root.getRight() );
   }
   return size + 1;
}

/**
 * Determine the height of the tree.
 *
 * Preconditions:
 *    None.
 *
 * Postconditions:
 *    The tree is unchanged.
 *
 * @return the height of the tree.
 */
public int height() {
   int height = 0;

   // If there is a tree determine the height
   if ( root != null ) {
      height = height( root );
   }

   return height;
}

/**
 * Determine the height of the tree with the specified root.
 *
 * @param root the root of the tree.
 *
 * @return the height of this tree.
 */
```

(continued)

FIGURE 7.20 Linked list implementation of a binary search tree *(continued)*

```
private int height( BinarySearchTreeNode root ) {
   int leftHeight = 0;       // Height of the left subtree
   int rightHeight = 0;      // Height of the right subtree
   int height = 0;           // The height of this subtree

   // If we have a left subtree, determine its height
   if ( root.getLeft() != null ) {
      leftHeight = height( root.getLeft() );
   }

   // If we have a right subtree, determine its height
   if ( root.getRight() != null ) {
      rightHeight = height( root.getRight() );
   }

   // The height of the tree is one more than the
   // height of the 'taller' of its children.
   if (leftHeight > rightHeight) {
      height = 1 + leftHeight;
   } else {
      height = 1 + rightHeight;
   }

   // Return the answer
   return height;
}

/**
 * Determine if the given element is in the tree.
 *
 * Preconditions:
 *    Target is not null.
 *
 * Postconditions:
 *    The tree is unchanged.
 *
 * @param target the element being searched for.
 *
 * @return true if the element is found and false otherwise.
 */
public boolean contains( Comparable target ) {
   boolean found = false;
   BinarySearchTreeNode cur = root;

   // Keep looking until we find the element or fall off the tree
   while ( !found && cur != null ) {
      int compare = target.compareTo( cur.getData() );
```

FIGURE 7.20 Linked list implementation of a binary search tree *(continued)*

```
            if ( compare < 0 ) {
                // The target is smaller - look left
                cur = cur.getLeft();
            }
            else if ( compare > 0 ) {
                // The target is greater - look right
                cur = cur.getRight();
            }
            else {
                // Found it!!
                found = true;
            }
        }

        return found;
    }


    /**
     * Return a string representation of this tree. The string
     * contains the elements in the tree listed in the
     * order they were found during an inorder traversal of the tree.
     *
     * @return a string representation of this tree.
     */
    public String toString() {
        // Use a string buffer to avoid creating many temporary strings
        StringBuffer result = new StringBuffer();

        // If there is a tree traverse it
        if ( root != null ) {
            inorder( root, result );
        }

        // Return the result
        return result.toString();
    }


    /**
     * Perform an inorder traversal of the tree. When a node is
     * processed, the contents of the node are converted to a string
     * and appended to the specified string buffer.
     *
     * @param root the root of the tree to traverse.
     * @param result the string buffer that will contain the string
     *        representations of the strings in the tree.
     */
    private void inorder( BinarySearchTreeNode root,
                          StringBuffer result ) {
```

(continued)

FIGURE 7.20 Linked list implementation of a binary search tree *(continued)*

```
        // If there is a left child - traverse it
        if ( root.getLeft() != null ) {
            inorder( root.getLeft(), result );
        }

        // Process the current node by converting the data to a string
        // and appending the result to the string buffer. A space is
        // placed between consecutive elements in the string
        result.append( root.getData() );
        result.append( " " );

        // If there is a right child - traverse it
        if ( root.getRight() != null ) {
            inorder( root.getRight(), result );
        }
    }

} // LinkedBinarySearchTree
```

FIGURE 7.20 Linked list implementation of a binary search tree *(continued)*

The final question we must address is this: Assume we are given a random sequence of N data values. If we construct a binary search tree from this sequence, will the final height H of the tree be closer to N (Figure 7.19a) or $\log_2 N$ (Figure 7.19b)? That is, will its final shape tend toward the unbalanced degenerate form or the more balanced full structure? For example, given the sequence {20, 17, 25, 22, 13, 30}, the insert method of Figure 7.20 will produce the following binary tree structure:

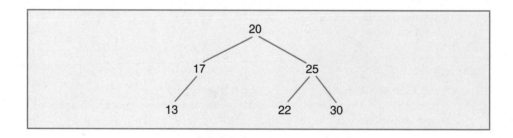

This is a balanced structure that has the minimum possible height for a binary tree of six nodes, H = 3, which is $O(\log_2 N)$.

However, if the same seven input values are used, but this time in the order {30, 13, 17, 20, 25, 22}, we end up with:

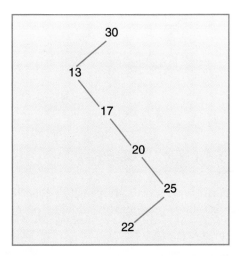

This is a degenerate tree whose height is H = 6, which is O(N). Are these two cases equally likely? If not, which type of structure can we expect to observe?

This is a difficult and complex mathematical problem and one that we will not solve here. Instead, we simply state the result. A binary search tree constructed from a random sequence of values will be roughly balanced. The likelihood is that it will look more like the tree in Figure 7.19b than the one in Figure 7.19a, and its height H will satisfy the relationship H = O(log N). While a binary search tree built from a random input sequence will almost certainly not be of minimum height, it will be within a constant factor k of that minimum, H = k * $\log_2$N, which makes it O(log N). Exercise 13 at the end of this chapter asks you to demonstrate this behavior empirically by analyzing the height of a number of binary search trees constructed from random input sequences. This experiment will also allow you to approximate the value of k, the factor by which a randomly constructed binary search tree will exceed the minimum $\log_2$N height of a perfectly balanced binary search tree containing N nodes.

Thus, for searching arbitrary lists of values, the binary search tree is an efficient data structure that allows you to locate any item in approximately logarithmic time. However, remember that there do exist certain input sequences that generate a degenerate tree and produce a worst-case linear time behavior. The Java libraries make extensive use of a variation of a binary search tree called a **red-black tree**, which is a binary search tree that is always maintained in a balanced state. It will be introduced and discussed in Chapter 9.

◆ 7.4.3 Tree Sort

Another use of binary search trees is to sort a list of random values into ascending or descending order. Assume that we have constructed a BST such as the following:

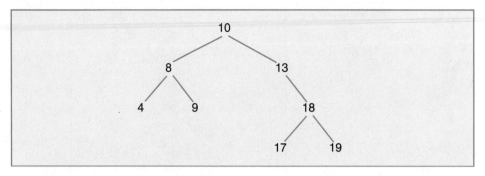

If we now perform an inorder traversal of this tree, as in Figure 7.9, printing each node as we visit it, we produce the following output:

  4, 8, 9, 10, 13, 17, 18, 19

which are the original input values in ascending order.

An algorithm to sort N numbers, called **tree sort**, is shown in Figure 7.21. It uses instance methods drawn from the binary search tree class in Figure 7.20.

```
// The tree sort algorithm. Assume that you start with an empty tree t.
// Phase I. Construct a binary search tree t from the N input values
for (int i = 1; i <= N; i++) {
    Input the next value, num
    t.insert(num)
}
// Phase II. Traverse the binary search tree using an inOrder
// traversal, printing each node's data value as you visit it.
    t.inorder()
```

FIGURE 7.21 The tree sort algorithm

Let's determine the time complexity of the algorithm in Figure 7.21. The insert() method in Phase I is called N times, once for each input value. To do this insert operation, we must travel from the root of the tree to the leaf node where we will perform the actual insertion, exactly as pictured in Figure 7.18. We have already shown that this distance H is $O(\log_2 N)$ for the average case. Therefore, the time complexity of Phase I, building the N-node binary search tree, is N times the complexity of a single insertion operation, or $O(N \log_2 N)$. The inorder traversal of this tree in Phase II involves visiting every node in the tree exactly once. Since there are N nodes in the tree, the inorder traversal is $O(N)$. This analysis was done previously in Section 7.3.2.

In Section 5.3.2, we stated that if an algorithm is in two sections, the first of which is $O(f(n))$ and the second $O(g(n))$, then the complexity of the entire algorithm is $\max(O(f(n)), O(g(n)))$. That is, the overall complexity of the algorithm is determined by its most time-consuming section. Using this result, we can say that the complexity of the tree sort algorithm of Figure 7.21 is $\max (O(N \log_2 N), O(N)) = O(N \log_2 N)$. This is the same complexity as the merge sort and quicksort algorithms presented in Section 5.3.1.

However, remember that this analysis applies only to the average case behavior. In the worst case, a binary search tree degenerates into a linear structure, and the insert procedure becomes O(N) rather than O(log N). Since we must repeat this process N times, the time required by the insertion becomes O(N²), and the complexity of tree sort is max (O(N²), O(N)) = O(N²), an inefficient quadratic algorithm.

Figure 7.22 shows the performance of the tree sort algorithm on input sequences of length N = 100,000 in random and reverse order. This is exactly the same performance test we applied to merge sort and quicksort in Figure 5.3, and those data are repeated here for ease of comparison. (We have also included the timing of a sorting method called heap sort, which will be introduced later.)

N = 100,000 (all times in seconds)		
Algorithm	Random order	Reverse order
Merge Sort	6.7	7.2
Quicksort	5.4	89.5
Tree Sort	9.6	101.7
Heap Sort	7.5	6.8

FIGURE 7.22 Performance of the tree sort algorithm

Notice that for numbers in random order, the performance of tree sort is roughly comparable to the other two O(N log N) algorithms that we looked at—merge sort and quicksort. However, when the lists are in reverse sorted order, the insert method produces a degenerate tree, and the performance of the algorithm degrades dramatically and runs more slowly by a factor of about 10. This worst-case behavior is one of the reasons that tree sort is not as widely used as other sorting algorithms. Tree sort also suffers from memory space problems because it requires storage for two pointers per node.

In Section 7.6, we will introduce one more tree-based sorting method called heap sort, which does not suffer from either worst-case time problems or excessive memory demands. Thus, this algorithm is a popular sorting algorithm in computer science.

7.5 INDEXED SEARCH TREES (TRIES)

Another search tree with some very interesting behavior is the **indexed search tree**, also called a **trie** (pronounced "try").

In a binary search tree, we treat the key located in the node as a single indivisible object when determining in which direction to move. For example:

If the value we are searching for is 58, then we compare 58 to the node value 63 and move left. If the value we are looking for is 102, we compare 102 to 63, and in this case, we would move right.

However, sometimes the value we are searching for is not a single indivisible object, like the value 63, but rather a composite object made up of a sequence of individual components c_i drawn from the set $V = \{v_1, v_2, \ldots, v_m\}$, as in

$$\text{key} = c_1c_2c_3 \ldots c_n \qquad \text{where } c_i \, \varepsilon \, V \qquad i = 1, \ldots, n$$

In a trie, the individual components c_i, rather than the entire key, are used to build the nodes and to traverse the tree. The data field of a particular node, if it exists, represents the concatenation of all the individual components along the path from the root to that given node.

Assume that the set V of possible values for the component elements of the keys, c_i, has m members; that is, $V = \{v_1, v_2, \ldots v_m\}$. Then each node in the trie will have $m + 1$ fields—one information field and m pointer fields (Figure 7.23).

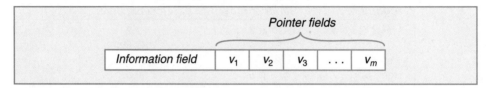

FIGURE 7.23 Trie node structure

The basic idea behind a trie is that if we reach a node by following a specific sequence of k pointers $v_1 \, v_2 \, v_3 \ldots v_k$, then this node represents the key value $c_1c_2c_3 \ldots$ c_k, where $c_1 = v_1, c_2 = v_2, \ldots, c_k = v_k$. If the sequence $c_1c_2c_3 \ldots c_k$ is a valid key, then we indicate that by storing a value in the information field. If this sequence is not a valid key, then the information field is set to `null`.

The trie search algorithm for locating the key $c_1c_2c_3 \ldots c_n$ in a trie structure is outlined in Figure 7.24

```
// This algorithm attempts to locate the information field value associated
// with the key c₁c₂c₃...cₙ in a trie structure
set P to point to the root of the trie structure
for (int i = 1; i <= n; i++)        {    // n is the number of components in the key
          remove component cᵢ from the key
          cᵢ = vⱼ for some j = 1, ..., m
          if the vⱼ pointer field of the node referenced by P is null then
                    this key is not in the tree. Terminate the algorithm and report that
                    the key was not found
          else set P = vⱼ
}
// we are now positioned at the correct node in the trie
if the information field of the node referenced by P is null
          the key c₁c₂c₃...cₙ is not in the trie so report that the key was not found.
else
          the key is in the trie and the information field contains the desired value.
          return the information field of the node referenced by P
```

FIGURE 7.24 Trie search algorithm

Looking at this algorithm, we see that every node in a trie corresponds to some prefix value $c_1c_2c_3 \ldots c_i$. If that prefix itself is a valid key, then the data field of that node will hold a nonnull value corresponding to that key. Furthermore, if $c_1c_2c_3 \ldots c_ic_{i+1}$ is also a valid prefix for $c_{i+1} = v_j$, then the v_j pointer in the node will be nonnull, and it will point to the node in the tree corresponding to the prefix $c_1c_2c_3 \ldots c_ic_{i+1}$. If $c_1c_2c_3 \ldots c_ic_{i+1}$ is not a valid prefix for $c_{i+1} = v_j$, then the v_j pointer is set to null.

Let's illustrate this idea using a simple example—Morse code. The keys are a finite sequence of dots and dashes, so the set of values for the component elements of the keys is $V = \{\bullet, \text{-}\}$. We will use the data field of a node to store either the letter corresponding to the sequence of dots and dashes used to reach this node or null if the sequence is not a valid part of the Morse code set. In addition to the data field, each node has two pointers corresponding to the two values • and -. Since a trie for the entire set of Morse code symbols would be rather large and bulky, we will work with a limited trie containing only the nine letters E, I, S, A, T, N, D, M, and O (Figure 7.25).

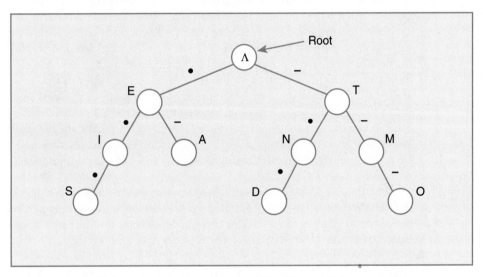

FIGURE 7.25 Trie structure for representing Morse code (partial)

Searching the trie of Figure 7.25 is quite easy. Given a key containing a sequence of dots and dashes and beginning at the root, we strip off each component of the key, one at a time, and follow the dot or dash pointer from the node where we are currently located. If at any time during this process we encounter a **null**, then the key c_1 $c_2 \ldots c_n$ is not a valid Morse code sequence (at least in terms of our partial trie), and the search process ends. If we do not encounter a **null** pointer, then after we have completed this operation for all n elements of the key, we will have reached the node that represents this key. Whether or not it is a valid key depends on the value stored in the information field. If the information field is **null**, then this sequence of dots and dashes is not a valid Morse code sequence. If the information field is nonnull, it is a valid Morse code sequence, and the data field contains the letter that corresponds to this sequence of symbols.

Let's illustrate each of these possible cases using the trie structure of Figure 7.25. Starting from the root, the three-element sequence ••• brings us to a trie node whose information field contains the letter S, the English character equivalent of the Morse code sequence •••. The empty sequence " " leaves us at the root of the trie, but its information field is `null` (indicated by the symbol Λ). Thus, the empty sequence is not a valid key in Morse code. Finally, the sequence •-• will cause us to encounter a `null` pointer when we try to follow the second • pointer, so •-• is also not a valid key in our limited example.

Insertion into a trie is similar to the search procedure just described. We must examine each individual element of the key that we wish to insert into the trie structure. There are three cases that can occur during insertion, and we again illustrate them using the trie in Figure 7.25.

Case 1 occurs when the node corresponding to the key to be inserted already exists in the structure. All that needs to be done to finish the insertion is to set the information field to the desired value. This would be the case if we wished, for example, to reassign the sequence - - from its current value M to another letter. We would simply change the value in that node from M to its new value. This would also be the case if we wanted to assign a value to a node whose data field is currently `null`.

Case 2 occurs when the prefix for the new key already exists within the trie structure. That is, we wish to insert a new key $c_1 c_2 \ldots c_n$, and the node corresponding to the prefix $c_1 c_2 \ldots c_{n-1}$ already exists. In that case, we create a new trie node, set its information field to the desired value, set all m pointer values in this new node to Λ, and finally, set the v_k pointer of the prefix node to point to this new node, where v_k is the value of the last element of the key c_n. This would occur, for example, if we want to add the symbol -•- (K) to Figure 7.25, since the prefix node -• is already there. We only need to create a new node corresponding to -•-, set its information field to K and all its pointers to Λ, and finally, set the - pointer of the prefix node to refer to this new node.

The final case, Case 3, occurs when we wish to add the key $c_1 c_2 \ldots c_n$ to the trie and the prefix $c_1 c_2 \ldots c_{n-1}$ is not in the trie. Now we must not only add the final data node, but we must also add one or more intermediate, or "dummy," nodes to create a path to this new node. If the new key is $c_1 c_2 \ldots c_n$ and the longest prefix of that key currently in the trie is $c_1 c_2 \ldots c_i$, $i < (n-1)$, then we need to add $(n-i-1)$ dummy nodes representing the elements $c_{i+1}, c_{i+2}, \ldots, c_{n-1}$. Each of these nodes will have a `null` information field and a single nonnull pointer value referencing the next dummy node in the prefix. This case would occur, for example, if we wanted to add the key ---•• which is Morse code for the digit 8. The prefix value ---• is not in the tree, only ---. Therefore, in addition to the final data node, we also need to insert one intermediate node corresponding to the prefix value ---• that is not in the tree. This situation is diagrammed in Figure 7.26.

The deletion process for a trie also has three cases: deleting an interior node (e.g., E), deleting a leaf node (e.g., S), and deleting a leaf node connected to the trie by only dummy nodes (e.g., 8).

When deleting an interior node, we cannot delete the node itself and reclaim the space. This is because the node represents not only a data value (e.g., E in Figure 7.26) but also a valid prefix for other nodes in the trie (e.g., I, S, and A). Instead, we reset the information field to `null` to indicate that the symbol E is no longer valid.

When deleting a leaf node such as S, A, D, or 8, we can delete the entire node. This is because the node is not being used as a prefix for any other node. We must also

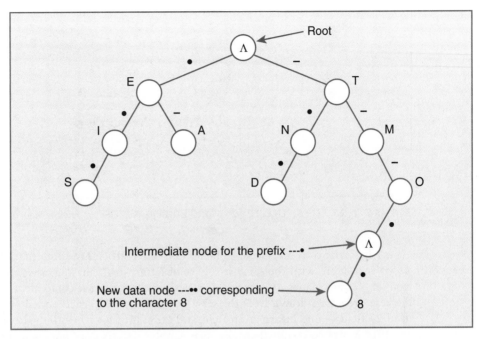

FIGURE 7.26 Adding an intermediate node to a trie

remember to reset the appropriate pointer of the parent node to **null**. For example, if we delete the D node of Figure 7.26, we must also reset the • pointer of its parent N to null.

Finally, when deleting a node such as the 8, we not only can delete the node itself but also all the intermediate, or dummy, nodes as well because they no longer serve as prefixes for any valid data items in the trie. Therefore, when deleting the node representing the symbol 8, we can also delete the node that we reach via the prefix ---•. We can determine if a dummy node is a candidate for deletion by seeing if both its information field and all its pointer fields are null. If so, it may be deleted.

The major advantage of a trie is that the number of operations needed to find a key is proportional to the length of the key being searched, not the number of nodes in the trie. For example, if we want to know what symbol is represented by the Morse code string -•, we can find the answer in two steps because the key is two symbols long— one dash and one dot. That is a highly efficient search. As a second example, assume we have a dictionary of 100,000 English words stored in a binary search tree. As you learned in Section 7.4.2, the number of comparisons needed to find a key is approximately $O(\log_2 100{,}000) \approx 17$. However, if the dictionary were represented using a trie, then the number of comparisons needed to locate a key would be equal to the average length of an English word, which is about five characters. This is a reduction in average search time of about 70 percent. For this reason, trie structures could be quite popular in textual applications, such as editors, thesauruses, and spelling checkers.

However, the price for this time reduction can be enormously high in terms of memory. Figure 7.27 is a trie for the five English words a, an, at, and, and any.

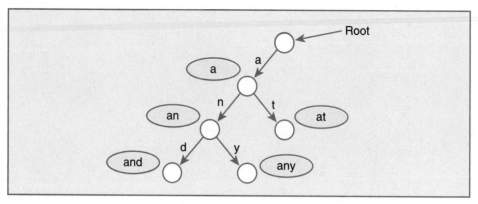

FIGURE 7.27 Trie structure for some English words

At first glance it may seem to be an extremely efficient representation because words that begin with the same sequence of letters (e.g., an, and, any) share a common set of prefix nodes. However, this is not correct. Since the component elements of the keys are letters drawn from the set V = {A, B, . . . , Z}, each node in the trie will need 27 fields—one information field and 26 pointers, rather than the 2 pointers, {•, -}, of Morse code. (Furthermore, this simple analysis does not even consider the problem of upper- and lowercase letters and special symbols.) The nodes for the trie structure of Figure 7.27 would look like this:

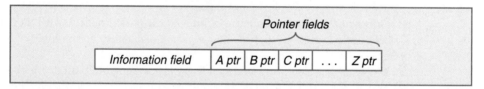

If we want to store 50,000 English words in our trie, we will have 50,000 data nodes and a much larger number of intermediate nodes, which are there not because they are valid words but because they are valid prefixes of other English words (e.g., C, CO, COM, COMP, . . . to store the word COMPUTER). Each of these nodes will have 26 pointers, as shown earlier. When we add the memory space needed for the words themselves with the memory demands caused by these intermediate nodes, we find that we will need enormous amounts of memory, far beyond the available capacity. Because of this, it is usually infeasible to store a complete trie data structure—that is, one which includes all n components of a key. However, a **partial trie**, when used in conjunction with other data structures, may be helpful in representing and managing collections of textual data.

In a partial trie, we only store the first k components of the key rather than the entire key. Then, the leaf nodes of the partial trie will point to some type of a collection (e.g., a list, an array) of all keys that share this common prefix. For example, we might use a trie structure for the first $k = 2$ letters of words, as shown in Figure 7.28

The data field of the nodes corresponding to AA, AB, AC, . . . ZY, ZZ might point to a linked list of strings containing the remaining $(k - 2)$ characters of all valid words that begin with this two-character sequence. This is illustrated by the linked list node

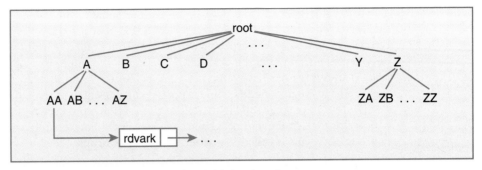

FIGURE 7.28 Example of a partial trie structure

in Figure 7.28 containing the string rdvark. It is in the linked list pointed at by the data field in the AA node and which represents the word *aardvark*.

To locate a word such as COMPUTER in the partial trie of Figure 7.28, we would strip off the first element, C, and follow it to the C node. Then we pick off the second letter O, and follow the O pointer from the C node to the CO node. That is the end of the trie structure. The data field of this CO node is a pointer to a list (or possibly an array) of all English words that begin with the prefix CO. Now we must search this collection for a node whose data field contains the string MPUTER.

Since there are $26 \times 26 = 676$ different two-letter combinations, after two operations on the trie we will have theoretically reduced the number of elements that must be searched by a factor of 676. (But it does not work this well in practice. The distribution of letter usage in English is very uneven, and there are many more words beginning with SH than with AA.) In addition, we will have saved some memory by not having to repeatedly store the first two letters of words that start with the same symbols, such as computer, color, constant, consider, and comb. Instead, the symbols co will appear only once in the trie, while the list stores the remaining $k - 2$ letters of the word. Exercise 17 at the end of the chapter asks you to determine if the amount of memory saved is greater than or less than the amount of memory needed to construct the two-level trie shown in Figure 7.28.

7.6 HEAPS

◆ 7.6.1 Definition

A heap is another example of a restricted binary tree. It is particularly useful in solving three types of problems:

1. Finding a minimum or maximum value within a collection of scalar values.
2. Sorting numerical values into either ascending or descending order.
3. Implementing another important data structure called a priority queue, which was introduced in Section 6.4.4.

This section shows examples of all three of these important applications.

A **heap** is a binary tree that satisfies the following two conditions:

1. The data value stored in any node is less than or equal to the value of all that node's descendants. Unlike the binary search tree of Section 7.4, there are no restrictions placed on the ordering of values within the left or right subtrees, only between a parent and its children. Therefore, the value stored in the root node is always the smallest value in the heap. (Note: We could just as easily define a heap where a node's value is greater than or equal to the value stored in its children. In that case all algorithms in this section would simply change the < operator to >, and every occurrence of the word *smallest* is replaced by the word *largest*.) This is called the **order property** of heaps.

2. A heap is a complete binary tree. A **complete binary tree** has *i* levels, and all leaf nodes are located only on level *i* or level *i* − 1. In addition, all of the leaves on level *i* are located as far to the left as possible. This is called the **structure property** of heaps.

Figure 7.29 shows examples of complete binary trees as well as those that violate the foregoing constraints.

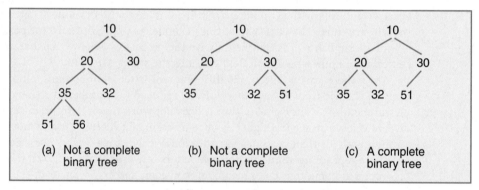

FIGURE 7.29 Examples of valid and invalid complete binary trees

The tree in Figure 7.29a is not a complete binary tree because the leaves occur on levels 2, 3, and 4 rather than just on levels 3 and 4. Figure 7.29b is also not a complete binary tree because the leaves on level 3 have not been placed as far to the left as possible. (Notice that the right child of the node containing 20 is empty.) However, the tree in Figure 7.29c is a valid heap, as it satisfies both the order and the structure properties. Informally, we can say that you will produce a valid heap structure if you insert new nodes by moving across level *i* in a strictly left-to-right fashion until it is full and only then begin to insert new nodes on level *i* + 1, again in a strictly left-to-right fashion.

The most important mutator methods for heaps are (a) inserting a new value into the heap, and (b) retrieving the smallest value stored in the heap (i.e., removing the root).

The insertHeapNode() method adds a new node to the heap. It must ensure that the insertion maintains both the order and structure properties of heaps. The heap retrieval method, getSmallest(), removes and returns the smallest value in the heap, which is the value stored in the root. This method must also rebuild the heap since it removes the root, and all nonempty trees must, by definition, have a root. You will learn how to carry out these operations in the next section. The other important operation on heaps is the Boolean function `empty()` that returns true if the heap is empty and false otherwise.

An interface for a heap data structure is shown in Figure 7.30. It includes the three basic operations just described: `insertHeapNode()`, `getSmallest()`, and `empty()`. The input parameter to `insertHeapNode()` and the return value for `getSmallest()` are both of type `Comparable`. This is to guarantee that it is always meaningful to determine if a value stored in a node is or is not smaller than all other nodes in the heap structure.

```
/**
 * An interface for a heap data structure
 */

public interface Heap {
   /**
    * Adds the given information to the heap.
    *
    * Preconditions:
    *     data is not null.
    *     data is of the same data type as the other nodes in the heap.
    *
    * Postconditions:
    *     data has been added to the heap.
    *     The heap property has been preserved.
    *
    * @param info the information to be added
    */
   public void insertHeapNode( Comparable info );

   /**
    * Remove and return the smallest element in the heap
    *
    * Preconditions:
    *     The heap is not empty.
    *
    * Postconditions:
    *     The element has been removed.
    *
    * @return the smallest value in the heap
    */
   public Comparable getSmallest();
```

(continued)

FIGURE 7.30 Interface for a heap data structure

```
/**
 * Determine whether the heap is empty.
 *
 * @return true if the heap is empty, false otherwise
 *
 * Preconditions:
 *    None.
 *
 * Postconditions:
 *    The heap is unchanged.
 *
 * @return true if the heap is empty and false otherwise
 */
public boolean empty();

} // Heap
```

FIGURE 7.30 Interface for a heap data structure *(continued)*

◆ 7.6.2 Implementation of Heaps Using Arrays

One of the problems faced by all the tree structures described in this chapter is the amount of memory space required for pointers. This problem was demonstrated most vividly when we discussed trie structures for English words and saw that it required 26 reference fields per node. A reference is a memory address, and it typically requires 4 bytes of memory, sometimes more. So the total amount of memory required by a tree node can become rather large.

However, it is possible to take advantage of the restricted structure of a heap to produce an extremely space-efficient one-dimensional array representation that requires no reference values at all. To do this, we store the elements of our heap in a one-dimensional array in strict left-to-right, level order. That is, we store all of the nodes on level i in left-to-right order before we store the nodes on level $i + 1$. This type of array representation of a heap, called a **heapform**, is diagrammed in Figure 7.31b.

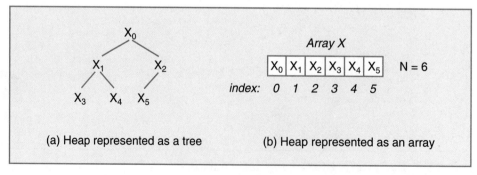

(a) Heap represented as a tree   (b) Heap represented as an array

FIGURE 7.31 Tree and one-dimensional array representations of a heap

The reason we do not need pointers in this array-based representation of a heap is that the parent, children, and siblings of a given node are all in fixed and known locations within the array that can be determined using some very simple calculations.

Assume that the root of the heap is in location 0 of the array, as shown in Figure 7.31b. Now, for any node stored in array location i, $0 \leq i < N$, where N is the total number of nodes in the heap, the locations in the array of the parent, left child, right child, and sibling of that node are given by the following expressions:

Parent$(i) = $ **int** $((i - 1)/ 2)$ if $(i > 0)$, else i has no parent
LeftChild$(i) = 2i + 1$ if $(2i + 1) < N$ else i has no left child
RightChild $(i) = 2i + 2$ if $(2i + 2) < N$ else i has no right child
Sibling $(i) =$
  if odd(i) then $i + 1$ if $i < N$ else i has no sibling
  if even (i) then $i - 1$ if $i > 0$ else i has no sibling

Using these formulas, we can recover all the hierarchical relationships that were present in the original tree representation of a heap shown in Figure 7.31a.

For example, look at the node labeled X_2 in Figure 7.31a. It is stored in slot 2 of the array. We can reconstruct all of the original tree-based relationships visible in Figure 7.31a using the formulas just given:

Parent $= $ **int** $(((2 - 1) / 2)) = 0$ The node in location 0 is the parent of X_2
LeftChild $= 2 * 2 + 1 = 5$ The node in location 5 is the left child of X_2
RightChild $= 2 * 2 + 2 = 6$ Since 6 is not less than N, X_2 has no right child
Sibling $= 2 - 1 = 1$ The node in location 1 is the sibling of X_2

As a second example, take a look at the node X_5. It is stored in slot 5 of the array. We can locate its parent, children, and siblings as follows:

Parent $= $ **int** $(((5 - 1) / 2)) = 2$ The node is X_2 is the parent of X_5
LeftChild $= 2 * 5 + 1 = 11$ Since $11 > 6$, we know that node X_5 has no left child
RightChild $= 2 * 5 + 1 = 12$ Since $12 > 6$, we know that node X_5 has no right child
Sibling $= 5 + 1 = 6$ Since 6 is not less than N, node X_5 has no sibling

Assume that we use the following declarations to create our heapform array `heapForm`:

```
private static final int INITIAL_SIZE = . . . ;
                                // the initial array size
private Comparable heapForm[] = new Comparable[INITIAL_SIZE];
private int size = 0;
```

We now can describe the implementation of the two basic mutator operations on heaps: `insertHeapNode()` and `getSmallest()`.

To insert a new value into the heap `heapForm`, we initially place that value in the unique location that maintains the structure property of heaps. This is either the leftmost unoccupied slot on level i or the leftmost slot on level $(i + 1)$ if level i is full. In

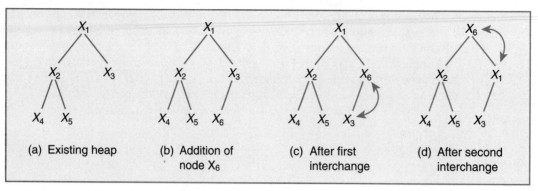

FIGURE 7.32 The insert operation on heaps

either case, this location corresponds to element `heapForm[size]` in the heapform array, where size is the number of nodes stored in the heap prior to the insertion operation. This situation is shown in Figures 7.32a and 7.32b which starts with a five-element heap (i.e., size = 5) and adds a new sixth item.

However, referring to Figure 7.32b, it may be true that $X_6 < X_3$, in which case the placement of this node violates the order property of heaps. If this is true, then we interchange the child and parent nodes that are out of order (Figure 7.32c). We now know that X_3 and X_6 are in the proper order, but X_1 and X_6 may not be. If not, then we repeat the interchange of child and parent nodes one more time (Figure 7.32d). We continue this interchange process until we have either found the correct location for the new value or, as was the case here, we reach the root of the heap. Referring to Figure 7.32d, we know that X_6 and X_1 are in the correct order because they were explicitly compared, but what about X_6 and its left child X_2? Are they in the proper order? We know that $X_1 < X_2$ because we assumed that Figure 7.32a was a valid heap and X_1 was the root, which means that X_1 was less than any other node. We also know that $X_6 < X_1$, as we just mentioned. Therefore, $X_6 < X_2$, and this node has been placed into the correct location within the heap. This proves that the swapping operation just described correctly restores the order property of heaps. Figure 7.33 shows a specific numerical example of this insertion operation. Here we are inserting the new value 8 into the heap structure. After two exchanges, we have restored the order property, and the tree in Figure 7.33d is a valid heap.

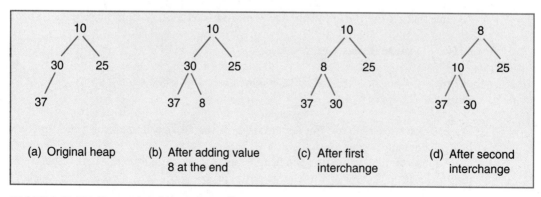

FIGURE 7.33 Example of heap insertion

The code for the insertHeapNode() method is given in Figure 7.34. Note that if we attempt to insert a new node and the heap is full, then we dynamically enlarge the heapform array via a call to the method expandHeap().

```
/**
 * Adds the given information to the heap.
 *
 * Preconditions:
 *    data is not null.
 *    data is of the same data type as the other nodes in the heap.
 *
 * Postconditions:
 *    data has been added to the heap.
 *    The heap property has been preserved.
 *
 * @param data the information to be added
 */
public void insertHeapNode( Comparable data ) {
    // Is there room in the heap for another element?
    if ( size == heapForm.length ) {
        // No - resize the heap
        expandHeap();
    }

    heapForm[ size ] = data;    // Put new data into the heap
    size = size + 1;            // One more element in the heap

    interchangeUp();            // Ensure that the ordering property
                               // of the heap holds after the item
                               // has been inserted
}

/**
 * Ensure that the ordering property of the heap holds after
 * the insertion of a new element into the heap.
 */
private void interchangeUp() {
    int cur = size - 1;      // Location of last item added
    int parent = cur / 2;    // Parent is always child / 2

    // We only need to check heaps with more than 1 element
    if ( size > 1 ) {

        // Walk up the heap until you reach the top or stop finding
        // values that are out of place
        while ( parent >= 0 &&
               heapForm[ cur ].compareTo( heapForm[ parent ] ) == -1 ) {
```

(continued)

FIGURE 7.34 insertHeapNode() method

```
            // Swap the parent and child values
            Comparable temp = heapForm[ parent ];
            heapForm[ parent ] = heapForm[ cur ];
            heapForm[ cur ] = temp;

            // Move up one level in the heap
            cur = parent;
            parent = cur / 2;
        }
    }
}
```

FIGURE 7.34 `insertHeapNode()` method *(continued)*

Looking at the code in Figure 7.34, we see that, in the worst case, we may need to exchange node pairs starting at a leaf and traveling all the way up to the root. A heap is, by definition, a balanced tree since we always maintain the structure property that keeps the leaf nodes on at most two levels. Therefore, its height will be O(log N), where N is the number of nodes, and the maximum number of times we will ever need to do the interchange operation is O(log N). Since the time for a single interchange is constant, the time complexity of the `insertHeapNode()` method in Figure 7.34 is O(log N).

The `getSmallest()` operation works in a similar fashion. We first remove the smallest element from the heap, which, by definition, is the value located in the root node. To reconstruct the tree, we need to move a new node into the root position, and the only node that can be moved and still maintain the structure property of the heap is the "last" one (i.e., the rightmost node on the lowest level *i*). The heap will now contain (size − 1) elements rather than size. This process is diagramed in Figures 7.35a and 7.35b, which show the removal of the smallest element in a five-element heap.

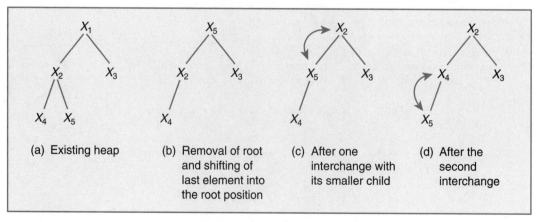

(a) Existing heap

(b) Removal of root and shifting of last element into the root position

(c) After one interchange with its smaller child

(d) After the second interchange

FIGURE 7.35 `getSmallest()` operation on heaps

As was the case with insertion, we must now determine the correct location for the value that was moved into the root, namely, X_5. If $(X_5 < X_2)$ and $(X_5 < X_3)$, then this node is in the correct location. If not, we interchange X_5 with the smaller of its one or two children, as shown in Figure 7.35c. (This diagram assumes that $X_2 < X_3$.) We repeat this downward interchange process until we have either found the correct location for X_5, or we have reached a leaf node. This algorithm restores the order property of the heap.

The maximum number of times we must interchange a node with its smallest child is equal to the height of the heap. We have already shown that the height of a heap is O(log N), where N is the number of elements. Since the time for a single interchange is constant, the time complexity of the getSmallest() operation of Figure 7.35 is O(log N).

Figure 7.36 shows a specific example of the behavior of the getSmallest() method. It diagrams the removal of the smallest value from the heap in Figure 7.33d and the rebuilding of the heap structure. In this example, the rebuilding process requires only a single interchange. The code for the getSmallest() method is shown in Figure 7.37.

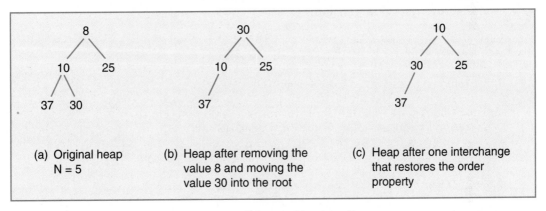

(a) Original heap
N = 5

(b) Heap after removing the value 8 and moving the value 30 into the root

(c) Heap after one interchange that restores the order property

FIGURE 7.36 Example of the getSmallest() operation

```
/**
 * Remove and return the smallest element in the heap
 *
 * Preconditions:
 *     The heap is not empty.
 *
 * Postconditions:
 *     The element has been removed.
 *
 * @return the smallest value in the heap
 */
                                                    (continued)
```

FIGURE 7.37 getSmallest() method

```
public Comparable getSmallest() {
    // The smallest element is always the root
    Comparable smallest = heapForm[ 0 ];

    // One less time in the heap
    size = size - 1;

    // Replace the smallest (root) node with the largest (last) node
    heapForm[ 0 ] = heapForm[ size ];
    heapForm[ size ] = null;

    // Ensure that the ordering property holds
    interchangeDown();

    return smallest;
}

/**
 * Make sure the ordering property holds after removing the
 * smallest element from the heap.
 */
private void interchangeDown() {
    int parent = 0;          // Parent position
    int left;                // Left child
    int right;               // Right child

    int minPos;              // Position of the smallest child
    Comparable minValue;     // Value of the smallest child

    boolean continueScan;    // When true heap is ordered

    // Only need to look if the heap size is greater than 1
    if ( size > 1 ) {
        do {
            left = parent * 2 + 1;
            right = parent * 2 + 2;

            continueScan = false;

            if ( left < size ) {
                // I have at least one child
                if ( right < size ) {
                    // I have two children - figure out which is
                    // the minimum
                    if ( heapForm[left].compareTo(heapForm[right]) < 0 ) {
                        // Left is the smallest
                        minValue = heapForm[ left ];
                        minPos = left;
                    }
```

FIGURE 7.37 getSmallest() method *(continued)*

```
                    else {
                        // Right is the smallest
                        minValue = heapForm[ right ];
                        minPos = right;
                    }

                    // If the parent is larger than the smallest child
                    // swap them and continue scan
                    if ( heapForm[ parent ].compareTo( minValue ) > 0 ) {
                        swap( parent, minPos );
                        parent = minPos;
                        continueScan = true;
                    }
                }
                else {
                    // Only one child (must be the left) - is the
                    // parent larger than the left child?
                    if (heapForm[parent].compareTo(heapForm[left] ) > 0) {
                        // Yes - swap them
                        swap( parent, left );
                        parent = left;
                        continueScan = true;
                    }
                }
            }
        } while ( continueScan );
    }
}

/**
 * Swap two elements in the heap.
 *
 * @param pos1 the position of the first element.
 * @param pos2 the position of the second element.
 */
private void swap( int pos1, int pos2 ) {
    Comparable temp = heapForm[ pos1 ];
    heapForm[ pos1 ] = heapForm[ pos2 ];
    heapForm[ pos2 ] = temp;
}
```

FIGURE 7.37 getSmallest() method *(continued)*

◆ 7.6.3 Application of Heaps

One of the most important uses of the heap data structure is as the foundation for a popular sorting algorithm known as **heap sort**. Assume a random sequence of *n* values $\{i_1, i_2, \ldots, i_n\}$ that we wish to sort into ascending order. Heap sort performs this task in two phases called the *building phase* and the *removing phase*. During the building phase, we construct a heap structure containing the *n* elements to be sorted. We do this by creating an empty heap and then inserting the elements from the sequence into the heap, one number at a time, using the `insertHeapNode()` method in Figure 7.34. This phase can be summarized as follows:

// Phase I. The building phase of heap sort in which
// we create a heap h from the N numbers to be sorted
for (int k = 0; k < N; k++) {   *// assume we are going to sort N numbers*
        Input(num);   *// input the next number from the sequence*
        h.insertHeapNode(num);   *// and insert it into the heap h*
}

This heap building phase is illustrated in Figure 7.38 for the set {11, 5, 13, 6, 1}. (Although we are showing the heap as a tree for clarity, the values are stored internally as a one-dimensional heapform array as described in the previous section.)

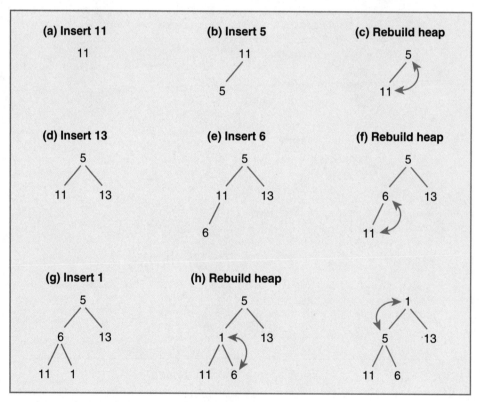

FIGURE 7.38 Building phase of heap sort

Once we have built the heap, it becomes a rather simple matter to obtain the elements in sorted order. We remove the root, which by definition is the smallest value, print it, and rebuild the heap, which now contains one less item. This is simply the `getSmallest()` method in Figure 7.37. The removing phase of heap sort can be summarized as follows:

// Phase II. The removing phase of heap sort. We remove the elements in the
// heap one number at a time. This will produce the values in ascending order

```
for (int k = N; k > 0; k—) {
    smallest = h.getSmallest ();
    Output (smallest);
}
```

This process of removing the smallest item and rebuilding the heap is shown in Figure 7.39. It uses the heap built in Figure 7.38.

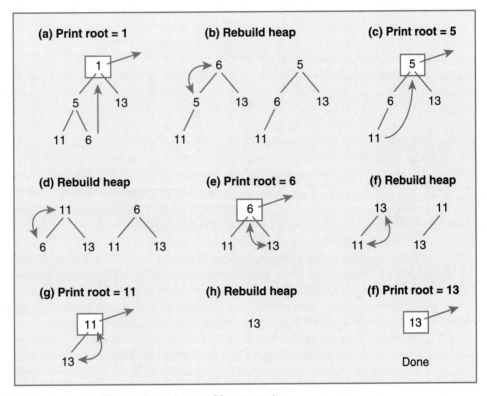

FIGURE 7.39 Removing phase of heap sort

Both `insertHeapNode()` and `getSmallest()` are O(log N). Both of these operations are encased inside loops that are executed N times, where N is the number of elements to be sorted. Therefore, both phases of this algorithm—building and removing—are O(N log N), and the time complexity of heap sort is O(N log N). This behavior is achieved in both the average and the worst case, so heap sort, like merge sort, is an excellent sorting algorithm for applications where we must guarantee efficient performance under all conditions.

We measured the run time of heap sort using lists of 100.000 values in both random and reverse order, exactly the same tests run on our other O(N log N) sorting techniques—merge sort, quicksort, and tree sort. The results for all four algorithms are summarized in Figure 7.22. Note how the performance of both tree sort and quicksort degrades when presented with ordered data, but the performance of merge sort and heap sort stays approximately the same.

The final application we will discuss is the use of a heap to implement the priority queue data structure introduced in Section 6.4.4. Remember that in a traditional queue structure, all objects are kept in time-ordered sequence, and in a sense, time can be thought of as its priority mechanism—the earlier you arrive, the higher your priority, and the closer you are to the front. However, in a priority queue, we are no longer restricted to using time as the only priority. Instead, we allow the user to specify the numerical value of the priority field explicitly. This is done by modifying the behavior of the enqueue, front, and dequeue methods as follows (assume that PQ is a priority queue object):

```
PQ.enqueue(obj, p);        // Put object obj into priority queue PQ with
                           // priority p

obj = PQ.front();          // Return the item with the highest priority
                           // in the priority queue PQ

PQ.dequeue();              // Delete the item in priority queue PQ that
                           // has the highest priority
```

Priority queues are an important data structure in computer science because they model situations that occur quite frequently in computer systems. In many designs, time alone is insufficient to obtain optimal behavior for a system. Instead, we need the ability to prioritize requests and indicate that some are more important and must be serviced before others, regardless of the order in which they arrived. (We discussed exactly this problem when designing disk scheduling algorithms in Section 6.4.2.)

For example, a process controlling the setting of the wing flaps on a commercial airliner cannot be delayed for any significant length of time. It must be given a processor as soon as one becomes available. It is obviously a lot more important than processes controlling the showing of in-flight movies or regulating the air-conditioning level in the cabin. A simple way to implement this is to assign priority values to these different types of processes. For example:

Process Type	Priority Level
In-flight movies	4 (lowest)
Oxygen/pressurization software	3
Engine/wing/tail control software	2
Crash avoidance software	1 (highest)

All incoming requests from the plane's sensors are kept in a priority queue rather than a regular queue. When we retrieve the next item, we are not simply given the next arrival in line, as in a regular queue. Instead, we are given a priority 1 process before any others, if one exists. If there are no priority 1 processes, then we are given a priority 2 process. If there are none of those, then we move to a priority 3 process. Only when all of these higher priority jobs have been serviced will we get a priority 4 process and begin showing our in-flight movies.

We now need to select a data structure that will allow us to efficiently implement the `enqueue()`, `front()`, and `dequeue()` operations on priority queues. If we select a linked list, as described in Chapters 6, we have two possibilities:

1. Keep the list in sorted order by priority as we carry out the enqueue. Then the `front()` and `dequeue()` operations simply return the first element in the queue. To find out where to enqueue this new object, we must search the entire list, an O(N) operation. Thus, if we keep the elements in sorted order, we have the following complexities:

    enqueue = O(N)   *front, dequeue = O(1)*

2. Instead, we could enqueue each new request at the end of the list, regardless of its priority. However, when we wish to locate the highest priority element, we must search the entire list looking for the largest priority value. Thus, if we keep the elements in unsorted order, we have the following complexities:

    enqueue = O(1)   *front, dequeue = O(N)*

In both cases, we obtain efficient O(1) constant time behavior for one operation at the expense of spending O(N) linear time on another.

However, there is a third possibility: implementing our priority queue as a heap. We implement the `enqueue()` operation as the heap insertion operation `insertHeapNode()` using the priority field p as the key field of the heap. (Assume that a smaller value of p represents a higher priority.) As shown in the previous section, this takes only O(log N) time. Our `front()` and `dequeue()` methods become the heap operation `getSmallest()`, which removes and returns the object with the smallest value of p (i.e., the highest priority) and rebuilds the heap. This takes O(log N) time.

The result is that we have traded an implementation (sorted/unsorted lists) that demonstrates one excellent, O(1), and one poor, O(N), behavior for an implementation (heap) that demonstrates very good, O(log N), behavior for both. This is a worthwhile trade-off, and it is why heaps are frequently used to store collections of objects ordered by priority field and retrieved in order of the smallest (or largest) value in that field.

7.7 THE IMPORTANCE OF GOOD APPROXIMATIONS

This chapter has demonstrated how important good data structure design is to the success of your software development project. Different choices for the algorithms and data structures in your program can produce enormous differences in run time. For example, assume that you want to keep 1 million objects in a priority queue. Using a list will require you to perform about 500,000 compares, either when you originally store the object or when you attempt to locate the highest priority object in the collection. If you are a little cleverer in your choice of data structure and store those 1 million items in a heap, you can both store and locate the highest priority item with only $(\log_2 1,000,000) = 20$ compares—a reduction of almost 5 orders of magnitude. When designing and building programs, be sure to spend adequate time on both the structure of the program as well as the selection of all key data structures. This latter decision can be instrumental to the success or failure of your project.

Sometimes we forget that computer science is both a theoretical and an applied discipline. While a theoretical mathematician is concerned primarily with formally proving that a certain solution is correct, the computer scientist is concerned with both the existence of a correct solution as well as the implementation of a program that produces those correct results in a reasonable amount of time. A method that can be formally proven to produce correct results in 100 years is of no interest whatsoever.

Therefore, the ability to do good approximations (sometimes jokingly referred to as **back-of-the-envelope calculations**) is an important skill for the computer scientist. When deciding on an algorithm or data structure, you should first try to approximate how long it will take to solve this problem using your proposed solution. If your approximation shows that the program will produce the answer 10 to 20 times faster than the specifications require, you can be reasonably confident that this approach will meet the user's needs, even if you are off by a little bit. On the other hand, if the approximation shows that the finished program will run about 10 to 20 times slower than required, you should probably not waste your time implementing this technique and start looking for something better.

Let's do a simple example to illustrate this point. Assume that we are asked to build a spelling checker for a company that develops word processing software. Our program inputs a word from a text file and looks it up in a dictionary. If it is there, we assume it is spelled correctly; otherwise, the program states that it is incorrect. Our dictionary contains about 100,000 words, and the performance specifications for the project state that the finished program must be able to spell check one entire page of error-free text (500 words) in under 1 second. To store the dictionary entries, should we use an unordered array? A sorted list? A binary search tree? A partial trie? It is hard to say without first doing some rough approximations. We would hate to waste our time designing and building a program that has no chance of meeting the user's requirements.

If we store our dictionary as a simple unordered list of words, then we will not have to re-sort the list whenever a user adds a new word. That is a feature that could possibly make the unordered list an attractive choice. However, each time we attempt to locate a word to see if it is correctly spelled, we have to search through about half the dictionary, roughly 50,000 words. Let's say that we did a rough measurement and found that it takes about 1.0 μsec (10^{-6} seconds) to compare, character by character, one word from the text with one word in the dictionary. Then for each word in the text, we need to spend, in the average case, $50,000 \times 1.0 \times 10^{-6}$ second, or about 0.05 seconds, to check the spelling. Since we assumed that there are 500 words per page, the total time to spell check one page of text is $500 \times 0.05 = 25$ seconds. This is 25 times larger than what is stated in the specification document, and it is a good indication that the use of a simple unordered list will probably not work. Even if our back-of-the-envelope calculations are off by an order of magnitude, we would still be unable to meet the design goals. This simple approximation has potentially saved us many hours of wasted work designing and building a program that would almost certainly not meet our needs.

What if we instead choose to store our dictionary using the binary search tree structure described in Section 7.4? Now, instead of examining 50,000 words of text, as we needed to do with the unordered list, we only have to examine ($\log_2 100{,}000$) or about 17 dictionary entries to determine if a word is correctly spelled. Now the time needed to spell check one page of text is about:

500 words/page $\times$ 17 compares/word $\times 1.0 \times 10^{-6}$ sec/compare $= 0.009$ sec

This is more than 100 times faster than the specifications call for, so even if our approximation is off by as much as two orders of magnitude, we should still be able to meet the user's needs. This approach seems to fit the bill, and we can continue with our design and implementation. (Note: Exercises 17 and 18 at the end of the chapter ask you to do the same back-of-the-envelope calculation for the partial trie of Section 7.5 and compare it with the results obtained for the other two methods.)

The point of this example is to convince you that, before investing a good deal of time and effort in implementing a solution, spend a little bit of time trying to determine whether the proposed solution will or will not solve the problem in a timely and adequate manner.

7.8 SUMMARY

This has been only a brief introduction into the interesting topic of hierarchical data structures. This chapter has looked at both general trees as well as trees that place restrictions on the maximum number of successors (binary trees) or the location in the tree where you are permitted to add new nodes (binary search trees, heaps, tries). It also has demonstrated a number of interesting applications of trees in computer science, such as program compilations (parse trees), sorting (tree sort, heap sort), searching (tries, binary search trees), and accessing elements in priority order (heaps/priority queues). There are many other tree structures, and the interested reader is encouraged to read further about this important topic.

But it is time now to move on and look at the final two classifications presented in the data structure taxonomy of Section 6.1. The next chapter will investigate two interesting ways to organize data using collections called sets and graphs.

EXERCISES

1. a. Using the four-rule grammar given on page 354, show a parse tree for the following expression:

   a + (b + c * d)

   b. Using that same grammar, show how a compiler could determine that the expression

   a + b +

   is not a valid statement of the language.

2. Given the following general tree

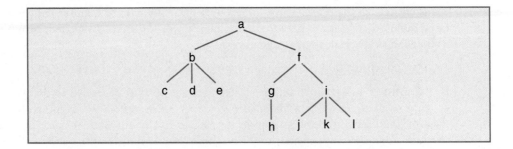

answer the following questions:

a. What are the terminal nodes?

b. What are the nonterminal nodes?

c. What is the root of the tree?

d. What is the degree of node a, node b, node c?

e. Who are the siblings of node c, node i?

f. Who are the ancestors of node h, node l, node a?

g. Who are the descendants of node f, node d?

h. What is the level of node b, node c?

i. What is the height of the tree?

3. Which of the following are trees? If a structure is not a tree, explain why.

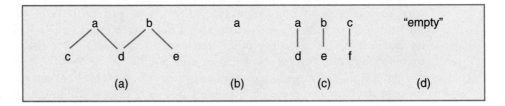

4. Convert the general tree shown in Exercise 2 to a binary tree using the oldest child/next sibling algorithm presented in Section 7.3.3.

5. a. Given the following binary tree T

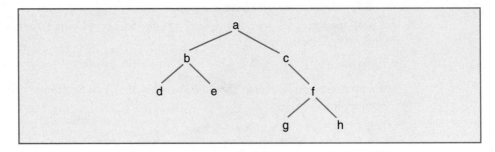

what is the order of visitation of nodes in a:

• preorder traversal

- postorder traversal
- inorder traversal

b. Prove that, even if a binary tree T is unbalanced, the time complexity of these three traversal algorithms is still O(N).

6. Given the binary tree

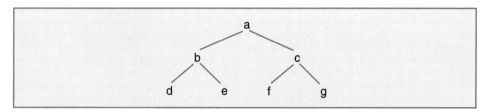

sketch out an algorithm that visits the node of a tree in *level order*—that is, visits all nodes on level i before visiting nodes at level $i + 1$, $i = 1, 2, 3, \dots$. In the above tree, a level order traversal would visit the nodes in the order abcdefg. Assume that you start with R, a reference to the root of the tree.

7. A binary tree is said to be **full** if all of its internal nodes have two children and all its leaf nodes occur on the same level. For example, the binary tree in Exercise 6 is full because all the internal nodes (a, b, c) have two children and all the leaf nodes (d, e, f, g) occur on level 3. Design an algorithm that takes a pointer to the root of a binary tree and determines whether or not that tree is full. It returns true if the tree is full and false otherwise.

8. In Exercise 6, there are $n = 7$ nodes in a full binary tree of height 3. Develop a formula for the relationship between n, the total number of nodes in a full binary tree, and i, the level number on which the terminal nodes occur.

9. a. Specify the pre- and postconditions for the following operations on binary trees and add them to the binary tree interface of Figure 7.10.

   (1) A method that makes an identical copy of a binary tree and returns a reference to the root of the copy.

   (2) A method that prints the information field of every node in the tree.

   (3) A method that is true if the tree is empty and false otherwise.

   b. Now implement these three methods using the linked list representation of a binary tree presented in Section 7.3.4.

10. Show what the following binary tree might look like when stored in the array representation discussed in Section 7.3.5 and diagramed in Figure 7.14.

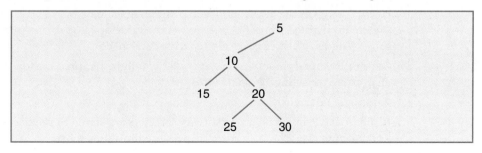

11. Show the binary search tree that would result from inserting the following values in exactly the order shown, beginning with an empty tree:

a. 38, 65, 27, 29, 81, 70, 14, 53, 12, 20

b. 81, 73, 70, 52, 51, 40, 42, 38, 35, 20

What do these two cases say about the structure of the binary search tree as a function of the order of the input data?

12. Write a method that uses the resources of the `LinkedBinaryTree` class to identify the node furthest from the root. The specifications for this method are:

```
/*    Precondition: none
      Postcondition: the method returns the identity of the node
         that is furthest from the root. If there is more than one
         node the same distance from the root, this method can return
         the identity of any one of them.          */
   public BinaryTreeNode distantNode ()
```

13. In a binary search tree with 1,023 nodes, the minimum height would be 10 if the tree were full as shown in Figure 7.19b. The maximum height would be 1,023 if the tree were degenerate as shown in Figure 7.19a. Generate 100 distinct sequences of exactly 1,023 random integers, build a binary search tree from each sequence, and determine the height, H, of each binary search tree using the `height()` method in the `LinkedBinarySearchTree` class. Use your data to show empirically that the expected height of a BST built from a random sequence of values is closer to $(\log_2 N)$ than to N. How close to $(\log_2 N)$ was your average?

14. Show that if we delete a node in a binary search tree and replace it by its successor in an inorder traversal, then the resulting tree is still a binary search tree. Does this also hold true for either the preorder or postorder traversal successor?

15. Show the trie structure that would be produced if we store the following 10 English words using the trie structure of Section 7.5.

ten   the

tent   them

pen   then

penny   thin

pin   think

16. Figure 7.24 gives the algorithm for locating a key value $c_1 c_2 \ldots c_n$ in a trie. Sketch out the algorithms for *inserting* a new value $d_1 d_2 \ldots d_m$ into a trie. Be sure to address all three cases discussed in Section 7.5.

17. Compute the total amount of memory that would be required to store a dictionary containing 100,000 words using:

a. a singly linked list.

b. a partial trie in which the first two characters are stored in the trie and the remaining characters of the word are stored in a linked list.

In doing the computations, assume the following:

- a reference variable requires 4 bytes.
- a character requires 1 byte.
- each English word is 5 bytes in length.

18. Estimate roughly how long it would take to locate a specific word in the partial trie of Exercise 17. Then determine whether or not we could meet the user specifications for the spelling checker application discussed in Section 7.7. Assume that it takes 1 μsec to access both an individual node in the partial trie and a node in the linked list. Also assume that the linked lists are all about the same length, admittedly a very weak assumption. Look over your answers to Exercise 17 and this exercise and state whether or not you think a two-level partial trie would be a good data structure for storing a 100,000-word dictionary when compared with the other methods analyzed in Section 7.7.

19. For each of the following shapes, state whether or not that shape represents a *complete* binary tree. If not, explain why.

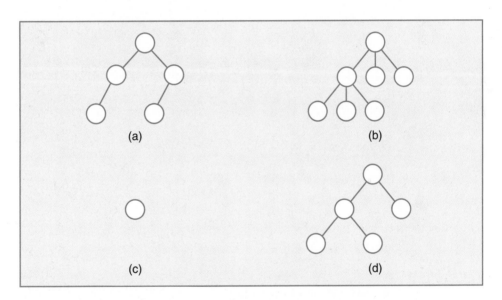

(a)

(b)

(c)

(d)

20. a. Show the final structure that results from constructing a heap from the following seven integers in exactly the order shown:

$$S = \{20, 19, 17, 23, 18, 22, 15\}$$

b. Show how the final heap would be stored internally as a heapform.

21. Develop the formula that determines whether a heap node, stored as a heapform, does or does not have *first cousins*. Two nodes are said to be first cousins if they have the same grandparent but different parents. Looking at Figure 7.31a, nodes (X_3, X_5) and (X_4, X_5) are first cousins. None of the other nodes stand in this relationship. Develop a formula firstCousin(i) that returns all of the first cousins of i that exist in the heapform.

22. Starting from the following heap, what would the heap look like after completing each of the following three operations in sequence (i.e., do operation b on the heap produced by operation a etc.)?

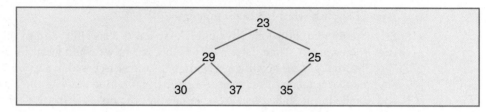

a. Insert a 26.

b. Insert a 22.

c. Delete the smallest value.

d. Delete the smallest value.

CHAPTER 8

Set and Graph Data Structures

8.1 SETS

We have now looked at two of the four groups of data structures introduced in Section 6.1 and diagramed in Figures 6.1 and 6.2: the linear (Chapter 6) and the hierarchical (Chapter 7). In this chapter, we investigate the two remaining groupings in that taxonomy—sets and graphs. Sets are introduced in Sections 8.1 and 8.2; graphs are discussed in Section 8.3.

◆ 8.1.1 Operations on Sets

In the data structures studied so far, the position of elements within a collection is an essential characteristic. For example, the following binary trees

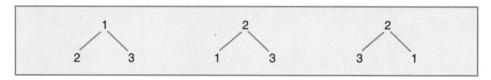

are all different not because of differences in the elements—they all hold the same three integer values 1, 2, and 3—but because of differences in the location of these values within the collection (i.e., root vs. leaf, right child vs. left child). In the set structure introduced in this section, we will no longer care about an element's position within the collection.

Formally, a **set** is a collection of objects with the following two properties:

◆   There are no duplicates.

◆   The order of objects within the collection is immaterial.

Because of this location-independent property, the following two sets S′ and S″

S′ = {1, 7, 13, −8, 105, 99}

S″ = {7, 99, 13, −8, 105, 1}

are identical, even though their elements appear in a different order.

This is the fundamental difference between sets and the linear and hierarchical structures studied previously. In these latter two groups, there was an explicit ordering imposed on the elements. In the linear structures of Chapter 6, these ordering relationships were called first, last, successor, and predecessor. So, for example, if the two previous sets S′ and S″ were linear structures, then the successor of 7 would be 13 in S′ and 99 in S″. The same applies to the hierarchical structures of Chapter 7 whose ordering relationships were termed parent, sibling, and children. In a set structure, none of these mappings exist. Asking about the successor of 7 in S′ or the first element of S″ makes no sense because order is immaterial. The entries in a set are unrelated to each other except by their common membership within the overall collection.

The operations performed on sets are quite well known, and it is rather easy to describe a standard Set interface. This differs markedly from some of the data structures looked at in earlier chapters, such as the list and binary tree. In these structures, there was an enormous range of operations, and the appropriate ones to include were application dependent. The specifications for a Set interface are given in Figure 8.1.

```
/**
 * An interface for a set. A collection of objects that
 * contains no duplicates and has no order.
 */

public interface Set {
    /**
     * Add the given element to this set.
     *
     * Preconditions:
     *     This set is not full.
     *     e is not null.
     *
     * Postconditions:
     *     e is contained in this set.
     *
     * @param e The element to add.
     *
     * @return false if e was already in the set, true otherwise
     */
    public boolean add( Object e );

    /**
     * Removes the given element from this set.
     *
     * Preconditions:
     *     This set is not empty.
     *     e is not null.
     *
     * Postconditions:
     *     e is not contained in this set.
     *
     * @param e The element to remove from this set.
     *
     * @return true if the object was present, false otherwise.
     */
    public boolean remove( Object e );
```

(continued)

FIGURE 8.1 A Set interface

```
/**
 * Adds to this set all elements of the given set.
 *
 * Preconditions:
 *     s is not null.
 *
 * Postconditions:
 *     All elements of s are contained in this set.
 *
 * @param s the Set whose elements are to be added
 */
public void union( Set s );

/**
 * Removes from this set all elements not in the given set.
 *
 * Preconditions:
 *     s is not null.
 *
 * Postconditions:
 *     This set contains no elements not found in s.
 *
 * @param s The set to intersect with.
 */
public void intersection( Set s );

/**
 * Removes all elements in this set which are members of
 * the given set (i.e., retains those elements not in the
 * given set).
 *
 * Preconditions:
 *     s is not null.
 *
 * Postconditions:
 *     This set contains no elements in the given set.
 *
 * @param s The set to 'subtract' from this set.
 */
public void difference( Set s );

/**
 * Determines whether this set is empty.
 *
 * Preconditions:
 *     None
 *
```

FIGURE 8.1 A Set interface *(continued)*

```
 *  Postconditions:
 *      The set is unchanged.
 *
 *  @return true if this set is empty, and false otherwise.
 */
public boolean isEmpty();

/**
 *  Determine if an object is a member of this set.
 *
 *  Preconditions:
 *      e is not null.
 *
 *  Postconditions:
 *      The set is unchanged.
 *
 *  @param e Object to check for set membership.
 *
 *  @return true if the given element is a member of this set,
 *      and false otherwise.
 */
public boolean contains( Object e );

/**
 *  Determine if set s is a subset of this set.
 *
 *  Preconditions:
 *      s is not null.
 *
 *  Postconditions:
 *      The set is unchanged.
 *
 *  @param s the set to test if it is a subset.
 *
 *  @return true if set s is a subset of the given set, and
 *      false otherwise.
 */
public boolean subset(Set s);

/**
 *  Return an array that contains references to the elements in
 *  this set.
 *
 *
 *  Preconditions:
 *      None
 *
```

(continued)

FIGURE 8.1 A Set interface *(continued)*

```
    * Postconditions:
    *     The set is unchanged.
    *
    * @return an array representation of this set.
    */
   public Object[] toArray();

   /**
    * Determine the size of this set.
    *
    * Preconditions:
    *     None
    *
    * Postconditions:
    *     The set is unchanged.
    *
    * @return the number of elements in this set.
    */
   public int size();

} // Set
```

FIGURE 8.1 A Set interface *(continued)*

There are five mutator operations in the interface of Figure 8.1. The add() method places a new element into an existing set and returns true. Since duplicates are not stored, nothing is done if this element is already a member of the set, and add() returns false. This is not an error but rather a fundamental characteristic of sets. The remove() method removes an element from a set if it is there and returns true. If the element is not a member of the set, then nothing is done, and the method returns false. This is also not considered an error.

There are three mutator methods that combine elements of two sets to produce a new set. The **union** operator, written S1 ∪ S2, produces a set whose members include all objects that are members of either set S1 or set S2 or both, eliminating duplicates. The **intersection** operator, written S1 ∩ S2, builds a set whose members are all those objects that belong to both set S1 and set S2, again eliminating duplicates. Finally, the **difference** operator, written S1 − S2, constructs a set whose members include only those objects that are members of set S1 but not members of set S2.

The behavior of these last three mutator operations appears in Figure 8.2 using a notation called a **Venn diagram**. The shaded areas of each diagram represent the elements included in the newly constructed set.

The three observer methods included in the interface of Figure 8.1 are isEmpty(), contains(), and subset(). The isEmpty() method returns true if this set is the **empty set** (i.e., it has no members) and false otherwise. (The empty set is written {}.) The method contains(e) returns true if e is a member of this set and false otherwise. Finally, subset(S) returns true if every element in S is also a member of this set;

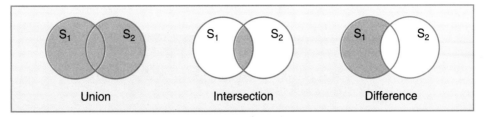

FIGURE 8.2 Venn diagrams of three basic set operations

otherwise it returns false. This method can be used to determine if the two sets S1 and S2 are identical. Simply evaluate S1.subset(S2) and S2.subset(S1). If both return true, then S1 == S2.

The following are examples of the behavior of the methods included in the set interface of Figure 8.1. Each example assumes the following starting values:

$S = \{1, 2, 3, 4\}$ $T = \{3, 4, 5, 6\}$ $U = \{\}$ $V = \{2, 3\}$

Operation	Result	Return Value
S.add(6)	$S = \{1, 2, 3, 4, 6\}$	true
S.add(4)	$S = \{1, 2, 3, 4\}$	false
T.remove(3)	$T = \{4, 5, 6\}$	true
T.remove(2)	$T = \{3, 4, 5, 6\}$	false
S.union(T)	$S = \{1, 2, 3, 4, 5, 6\}$	void
S.intersection(T)	$S = \{3, 4\}$	void
S.difference(T)	$S = \{1, 2\}$	void
T.difference(S)	$T = \{5, 6\}$	void
T.isEmpty()	no change in T	false
U.isEmpty()	no change in U	true
T.contains(2)	no change in T	false
T.contains(3)	no change in T	true
S.subset(V)	no change in S	true
S.subset(T)	no change in S	false

Finally, there are two helpful utility routines included in our interface. The method toArray() takes the n elements contained in our set and stores them linearly into an n-element array. (Since order is immaterial in a set, the order of placement of the elements into the array is also immaterial.) The size() method returns the number of elements in the set.

◆ 8.1.2 Implementation of Sets

There are two widely used techniques for implementing sets: arrays and linked lists. (This is identical to our discussions on the implementation of lists in Section 6.2.3 and binary trees in Section 7.3.)

We can store the elements of our set S in an unordered one-dimensional array structure s declared as follows:

```
private final int MAX = . . . ;   // the maximum number of elements
private Object s[MAX];    // elements are stored in s in arbitrary order
private int size;         // the number of elements in s, 0 ≤ size ≤ MAX
```

Using these declarations, the six-element set S = {10, 13, 41, −8, 22, 17} might be stored into array s as follows

S:	13	10	−8	22	17	41
	s[0]	s[1]	s[2]	s[3]	s[4]	s[5]

size = 6

The order of elements within the array need not match the order that elements were inserted into the set because order is immaterial.

When using an array implementation, the set operations in the interface of Figure 8.1 will generally translate into sequential searches of the array. For example, to determine if element e is contained in set S, we must search array s from beginning to end until either e is found or we come to the end of the array. Similarly, to add an element e to the set S, we first search the array to see if e is or is not present. If it is not present, we place it at the end of the array. The remove() method determines if e is present and, if so, removes it by moving up one position all elements in the array that follow e. Thus, the three methods add(), remove(), and contains() are all O(N) operations, where N is the number of elements in S.

Figure 8.3 shows the array-based implementation of the intersection operation S1.intersection(S2). For each element e in S1, we search set S2 to see if e is contained in S2. If so, we keep the element in S1; if not, we remove it. If S1 and S2 are both unordered and each has O(N) members, then the intersection method of Figure 8.3 is O(N^2). (We can do a little better if both S1 and S2 are sorted. This problem is left as an exercise.) Using techniques similar to Figure 8.3, it is rather easy to determine that union, difference, and subset can also be completed in O(N^2) time.

```
public void intersection(Set S2) {
    for (int i = 0; i < size; i++ ) {
        if ( !S2.contains( s[i] ) ) {
            remove( s[i] );
            i--; // Don't skip the next element
        }
    }
}
```

FIGURE 8.3 Array implementation of set intersection

The second approach to implementing a set is to represent it as an unordered singly linked list of the type originally presented in Section 6.2. Using this representation, the set S = {1, 5, 4} might look like the following:

Because order is immaterial, we must search the entire linked list to carry out the operations in the Set interface of Figure 8.1. For this reason, the methods subset(), intersection(), union(), and difference() are still O(N²), where N is the number of elements in each set, while the contains() and remove() functions remain O(N).

At first, it may seem that the add() method should be completed in O(1) time because it only attaches a new element e to the head of a linked list, which takes constant time. However, remember that duplicates are not allowed in a set, so before the insertion, we must first search the entire list to ensure that element e is not already there—making this an O(N) operation as well. The following list summarizes the time complexities of the 10 methods in Figure 8.1. These complexities hold whether the implementation uses an array or a linked list.

Operation	Complexity
add	O(N)
remove	O(N)
union	O(N²)
intersection	O(N²)
difference	O(N²)
isEmpty	O(1)
contains	O(N)
subset	O(N²)
toArray	O(N)
size	O(1)

There is an alternative way to implement a set that can, under very specialized conditions, produce a significant performance improvement over both arrays and linked lists. If we make two assumptions about the nature of the **base type** of our set—that is, the data type of the objects in the set—we can use an extremely efficient representation called a **bit vector**. These two assumptions are that (a) the total number, N, of values that belong to this base type (called its **cardinality**) is relatively small, and (b) there exists a 1:1 function f that maps the N elements of the base type onto the integer values $[0 \ldots N - 1]$:

---

f: e ➝ I   where: e is an element of the base type of a set with cardinality N
              I is an integer in the range $[0 \ldots N - 1]$

such that if e_1 e_2, $f(e_1)$ $f(e_2)$.

A good example of a base type that meets these criteria would be the Java primitive types character, Boolean, or a small subrange of the integers.

To implement a set S of cardinality N, we create a Boolean array of length N. Each array element—true or false—specifies whether the unique element e that maps to location $i = f(e)$ is or is not a member of S. For example, given the following

```
// The cardinality of the base type of set S
private static final int N = . . . ;
```

```
// Bit vector implementation of set S
private boolean s[] = new boolean[N];
```

there exists a highly efficient way to implement the set operations described in the previous section. To insert a new element e into set S, we set array element s[f(e)] to true. (If it was true to begin with, it will remain true, so there are no duplicate elements.) To remove element e from set S, we set s[f(e)] to false. To determine if e is or is not contained within S, we examine array location s[f(e)]. If that location is true, e is a member of the set S; if it is false, it is not a member. These are all O(1) operations.

As a more concrete example of this bit vector implementation, assume we are creating a set S2 whose base type is the days of the week "monday", "tuesday", . . . , "sunday". Since there are seven days in a week, the declaration for the bit vector implementation of S2 would be

```
private boolean s2[] = new boolean[7];
```

and the function *f* would do the following mappings:

f("monday") = 0
f("tuesday") = 1
. . .
f("sunday") = 6

The bit vector representation of set S2 = {"monday", "wednesday", "friday"} would be:

S2	true	false	true	false	true	false	false
	s2[0]	s2[1]	s2[2]	s2[3]	s2[4]	s2[5]	s2[6]

To determine if "tuesday" is a member of set S2, examine array element s2[f("tuesday")] = s2[1], which currently is false, indicating that "tuesday" is not a member. To delete "friday" from set S2, set s2[f("friday")] = s2[4] to false.

As a final example, assume the base type for set S3 is the lowercase alphabetical values ['a'. . . 'z'], which have the Unicode values [97 . . . 122]. The declaration for the bit vector implementation of S3, which has a maximum of 26 elements, is

```
private boolean s3[] = new boolean[26];
```

and the mapping function *f* is

```
f(e) = Character.getNumericValue(e) - 97;
```

where getNumericValue(e) is the Java library function that returns the integer value of the Unicode character e.

Using this bit vector approach, the four set operations of intersection, union, subset, and difference can all be implemented in O(N) time, where N is the cardinality of the two sets. For example, the set intersection operation shown in Figure 8.3 was $O(N^2)$. However, with bit vectors, we only need to do a logical AND operation between the corresponding elements of the two bit vector arrays. If both locations are true, then the result will be true; otherwise, the result will be false.

```
// assume we are computing the intersection between set S2 and this set,
// where both sets are implemented as bit vector arrays s of size N
```

```
for (int i = 0; i < N; i++)
        s[i] = (s[i] && S2.s[i]);
return;
```

This is a more efficient O(N) implementation of intersection than the array or linked list techniques described earlier, both of which required O(N²) comparisons. Figure 8.4 compares the efficiency of the array and linked list methods with the bit vector implementation just presented. In every case, the bit vector method produces more efficient behavior.

Operation	Array/List Complexity	Bit Vector Complexity
add	O(N)	O(1)
remove	O(N)	O(1)
union	O(N²)	O(N)
intersection	O(N²)	O(N)
difference	O(N²)	O(N)
isEmpty	O(1)	O(1)
contains	O(N)	O(1)
subset	O(N²)	O(N)
toArray	O(N)	O(N)
size	O(1)	O(1)

FIGURE 8.4 Complexities of different set implementation techniques

However, although highly efficient, bit vectors have limited usage because of their unrealistic assumptions—namely, that the cardinality of the base type of the set is very small. Most sets draw their components from extremely large base types, which makes the use of bit vectors highly problematic.

The bit vector implementation of the Set interface shown in Figure 8.1 is left as an exercise for the reader.

8.2 MAPS

◆ 8.2.1 Definition and Operations

Sets are an important concept in formal mathematics, and they are studied extensively in the branch of mathematics called *set theory*. However, the set structure described in Section 8.1 is not widely used, and operations such as union, intersection, subset, and difference do not occur very often in computer science. (But we will show an interesting use of sets when developing the minimum spanning tree algorithm in Section 8.3.2.3.) That does not mean, however, that sets have little or no role to play in software development. On the contrary, with a few small changes to the definitions in Section 8.1, we can produce an extremely important variation of the set data structure that is widely used in computer science. This new structure is called a **key-access table**, also commonly referred to as a **table** or a **map**.

Let's make the following modifications to our original definition of a set:

1. Assume that the elements of our set are 2-tuples of the form (k_i, v_i), where k_i is the **key field** and v_i is the **value field**. There is no limit to the number of tuples that can be in a set, although it must, of course, be finite. Thus, our new view of a set S, now called a map, is:

$$S = \{ (k_0, v_0), (k_1, v_1), \ldots, (k_n, v_n) \} \qquad n < \infty$$

2. The k_i are of type `keyType`, and the v_i are of type `valueType`. Neither `keyType` nor `valueType` is limited to primitive types; indeed, they can be any objects. The k_i must be unique within the set; the v_i need not be. In addition, the k_i are generally considered immutable objects, and their values should not change once they are added to the map. The v_i may change as often as desired.

3. We are no longer interested in the traditional set operations of union, intersection, difference, and subset described in the previous section and included in the interface of Figure 8.1. Instead, the operations we will focus most closely on are called `put()`, `remove()`, and `get()`. These operations place new tuples into the map (put), remove tuples from the map (remove), and locate a specific tuple within the map (get).

The `put()` method takes a map S, a key k, and a value v. It adds the tuple (k, v) to S if k is not the key field of any tuple currently contained in S; otherwise, the table is unchanged. Essentially, `put()` performs the following set operation:

$$S = S \cup \{(k, v)\}$$

`remove()` takes a map S and a key k. If there exists a tuple in S of the form (k, *), where * represents any value field, then this tuple is removed from S. If there is no tuple of the form (k, *), then the table is unchanged. `remove()` is equivalent to the following set operation:

$$S = S - \{(k, *)\} \quad \text{where * matches any value field}$$

Finally, `get()` takes a map S and a key value k. If there exists a tuple anywhere in S of the form (k, v), then this method returns the corresponding value field v; otherwise, it returns `null` indicating that there was no tuple of the form (k, *) in S.

The structure just described represents a collection in which all data values are associated with a unique identifier, called a **key**, and are stored as a 2-tuple (key, value). All retrievals of data values are done via the associated key rather than by the tuple's location within the structure. Since the key is stored within the tuple itself, the position of the tuple within the map is immaterial. In addition, since all keys are unique, every tuple is unique, and there are no duplicates. Together, these characteristics demonstrate that the map data structure does satisfy the definition of a set given in the previous section.

However, instead of having limited use, a map is an extremely useful data structure. This type of "key access" models a number of problems encountered quite frequently in computer science. For example:

Key Field	*Value Fields*
Student ID No.	(Name, Major, GPA, Year)
Social Sec. No.	(Name, Address, Occupation)

Key Field	Value Fields
Part No.	(Part Name, Supplier, Amount in Hand)
Confirmation No.	(Flight No., Seat No., Departure Time)
License Plate No.	(Owner, Make, Year, Color, Fees Paid)
Process ID	(Process Name, Process State, Owner, Resources Used)

In all these examples, the typical way that the map would be used is to have the user provide a key, and we either retrieve the value fields associated with that key or discover that the key is not present in the table. This is exactly what happens when someone retrieves your student data, tax records, or flight booking information based on a unique identification number that you provide.

Figure 8.5 is an interface for the key-access table structure we have defined. It includes the three routines put(), remove(), and get(). There are two utility routines, isEmpty() and size(), whose function is identical to the routines of the same name in Figure 8.1. Finally, the interface includes the methods getKeys() and getValues(), which copy all the key fields and value fields, respectively, from the table into an array data structure.

In the next section, you will learn how to efficiently implement this structure and see some examples of its use.

```
/**
 * An interface describing the Table data structure, also called a Map
 */

public interface Table {
    /**
     * Puts the given value into the table, indexed by the given key.
     *
     * Preconditions:
     *    Key is not null.
     *    Key's hashCode() method returns an element in this
     *       Table's domain.
     *    Value is not null;
     *
     * Postconditions:
     *    The given value has been associated with the given key.
     *
     * @param key the key to refer to the given value by.
     * @param value the data to associate with the given key.
     */
    public void put( Object key, Object value );

    /**
     * Removes the object associated with the given key, if any.
     *
     * Preconditions:
     *    Key is not null.
```
(continued)

FIGURE 8.5 Interface specification for a Table data structure

```
 *
 * Postconditions:
 *     The element (if any) associated with the given key has
 *         been removed.
 *
 * @param key the key to remove.
 */
public void remove( Object key );

/**
 * Returns the object associated with the given key.
 *
 * Preconditions:
 *     Key is not null
 *
 * Postconditions:
 *     The Table is unchanged.
 *
 * @param key the key to look up in the table.
 */
public Object get( Object key );

/**
 * Determine whether the Table is empty.
 *
 * Preconditions:
 *     None
 *
 * Postconditions:
 *     The Table is unchanged.
 *
 * @return true if the table is empty and false otherwise.
 */
public boolean isEmpty();

/**
 * Determine the size of the Table.
 *
 * Preconditions:
 *     None
 *
 * Postconditions:
 *     The Table is unchanged.
 *
 * @return the number of elements in the table.
 */
public int size();
```

FIGURE 8.5 Interface specification for a `Table` data structure *(continued)*

```
/**
 * Determine the cardinality of the Table.
 *
 * Preconditions:
 *     None
 *
 * Postconditions:
 *     The Table is unchanged.
 *
 * @return a number one greater than the maximum domain element.
 */
public int cardinality();

/**
 * Get all the keys in this Table.
 *
 * Preconditions:
 *     None
 *
 * Postconditions:
 *     The Table is unchanged.
 *
 * @return an array containing all of the keys in the table.
 */
public Object[] getKeys();

/**
 * Get all values stored in this Table. There is no correlation
 * between the order of the elements returned by this method and
 * the getKeys() method.
 *
 * Preconditions:
 *     None
 *
 * Postconditions:
 *     The Table is unchanged.
 *
 * @return an array containing all of the values in the table.
 */
public Object[] getValues();

} // Table
```

FIGURE 8.5 Interface specification for a `Table` data structure *(continued)*

◆ 8.2.2 Implementation Using Arrays and Linked Lists

There are a number of rather simple and straightforward ways to implement the `Table` interface in Figure 8.5. However, as you will see, these simple approaches often produce inefficient and unacceptable performance.

The most obvious approach is to implement our map using two parallel one-dimensional arrays called `key` and `value`. Each row of the `key` array holds a key value, and the corresponding row of the `value` array holds its associated value field. Thus, the two elements `key[i]` and `value[i]` together represent a single tuple.

One possible set of declarations to create this array-based implementation is:

```
private final int MAX = . . . ;   // the maximum size of the two arrays
private KeyType key[];             // the key array
private ValueType value[];         // the value array
```

Pictorially, the map $S = \{(k_1, v_1), (k_2, v_2), (k_3, v_3)\}$ might look something like Figure 8.6.

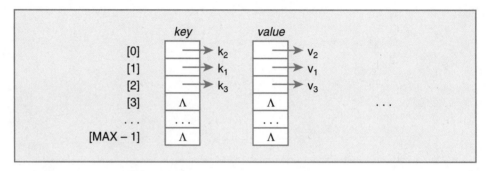

FIGURE 8.6 A map implemented using two parallel arrays

We have two choices about how to maintain the information stored in these two arrays. We can keep the tuples sorted in order by key field k_i. (Note: This assumes that objects of type `KeyType` implement the `Comparable` interface and can be compared to each other and put into a natural ordering.) For example, if we are storing tuples in ascending order, then the key values in Figure 8.6 would satisfy the relationship $k_2 < k_1 < k_3$. If we do choose to keep the keys in sorted order, then we may need to move elements around when we add or remove a tuple. This would be necessary, for example, if we were inserting the tuple (k_4, v_4) into the two arrays where $k_2 < k_4 < k_1$. This insertion requires us to move both (k_1, v_1) and (k_3, v_3) down one slot to make room for the new tuple, which requires O(N) time. However, keeping the arrays sorted by key allows us to use the efficient O($\log_2$ N) binary search whenever we attempt to locate a key and retrieve its value field.

Alternatively, we could keep our tuples in unsorted order and place new tuples at the end of the arrays. This will take only O(1) time, not counting the time required to check for duplicate entries. However, if the keys are in no particular order, both `remove()` and `get()` will require a sequential search to locate a specific tuple, which takes O(N) time. A linked list implementation does not fare any better. Insertions can be done in O(1) time by linking new items to the head of the list, again not counting the time spent checking for duplicates. However, both `remove()` and `get()` now require O(N) time because they must search the list to locate the correct tuple. A linked list also requires additional memory space for the reference fields in each node.

The performance of the three basic table operations using sorted arrays, unsorted arrays, and linked lists is summarized in Figure 8.7. It appears we have the same prob-

	Run-Time Performance		
Operation	Unsorted Array	Sorted Array	Linked List
put()	O(1)*	O(N)	O(1)*
remove()	O(N)	O(N)	O(N)
get()	O(N)	O(log N)	O(N)

*Does not include the time required to check for duplicates.

FIGURE 8.7 Performance of array and linked list implementations of a table

lem first encountered during the implementation of array-based list structures. Either we spend time during the insertion phase to keep the table in sorted order, and thus have fast retrievals, or we spend virtually no time at all during insertions but pay for it dearly with slower retrievals and deletions.

Another possibility is to use the binary search tree described in Section 7.4. We could use the key field of the (key, value) tuples to order the tree. If the tree is well balanced, insertions, deletion, and removals of the tuples can all be completed in $O(\log_2 N)$ time, far better than the behavior summarized in Figure 8.7 (see Figure 7.19b). However, the problem here is that the worst-case performance of a binary search tree is O(N), so we cannot be guaranteed of achieving this logarithmic performance (see Figure 7.19a).

Which approach should we choose? The correct answer is none of the above. There is an alternative implementation of maps that demonstrates superior performance when compared with the behaviors of all the previous methods. The performance of the three fundamental operations on maps using this new method (at least theoretically) is:

Operation	Performance
put()	O(1)
remove()	O(1)
get()	O(1)

You can't do any better than that! This method, called *hashing*, is the most popular method of building and maintaining map data structures, and we discuss this technique in detail in the next section.

◆ 8.2.3 Hashing

The technique called **hashing** works by transforming the key field k into a number, called a **hash value,** in the range [0 . . . N − 1]. It then uses this hash value as an array index to determine where in an N-element array h[], called a **hash table,** we should store the value field. That is, given a (k, v) tuple, we apply a function f, called a **hash function,** to the key k to obtain an index $i = f(k)$ and then store the value v into array location h[i].

To retrieve the value associated with key k from h[], we compute $i = f(k)$ and examine the contents of location h[i]. If entry i contains a nonnull value, then the tuple is in the table, and we return the contents of h[i], which must be the value field associated with the key. If entry *i* is empty, then the tuple (k, v) is not in the table, and we return `null` to indicate its absence. (Note: This assumes that every element of the hash table array h[] has been initialized to an "empty" state.) The logical structure of a hash table is diagramed in Figure 8.8.

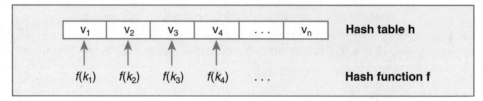

FIGURE 8.8 Logical structure of a hash table

One of the most important aspects of hashing is the design of the **hashing function** *f* that maps keys to array locations. As an example, assume that we are using people's names as key values. We can associate a number with each letter; for example, a and A are assigned the value 1, b and B are assigned the value 2, and so on. If the *k* letters in a name are designated $c_1, c_2, \ldots, c_k$, and the function `intValue(letter)` maps a, . . . , z and A, . . . , Z to their associated integer value 1, 2, . . . , 26, then a possible hashing function *f* is given by the following:

$$f = \left[\sum_{i=1}^{k} \text{intValue}(c_i) \right] \% N \qquad \begin{array}{l} \text{where N = the hash table size} \\ \text{and \% is the modulo function} \end{array}$$

To see how this hashing function operates, assume a hash table size of N = 50, key values that are names, and value fields that contain information about that person. Each (name, information) tuple stored in the table must hash to a value in the range 0 to 49, corresponding to the location where the data about that person will be stored. Figure 8.9a shows the application of the above hash function *f* to the name "Smith."

letter		value
'S'	=	19
'm'	=	13
'i'	=	9
't'	=	20
'h'	=	8
Total	=	69

Hash value = (69 % 50) = 19

FIGURE 8.9a Computation of the hash value for the key "Smith"

The name "Smith" hashes to location 19, so the information about the individual named "Smith" is stored in location h[19] of hash table h. To retrieve the information associated with the key "Smith," we again hash on the key, obtain the integer value 19, and go directly to entry h[19]. This either contains the desired information or is marked as "empty," and we know that the information about "Smith" is not in the table.

If hashing always worked as described, inserting a (k, v) tuple into hash table h, the map operation called put() would be an O(1) operation:

```
put(k, v) :    i = f(k);     // hash on the key field to get an index
               h[i] = v;     // store the value field in that position
                             //   of the array
               return;
```

Retrieval from a hash table, the map operation called get(), would also be O(1):

```
v = get(k) :   i = f(k);              // hash on key field to get an index
               if h[i] is empty
                       return null;  // the tuple is not in the table
               else
                       return h[i];  // the tuple is in the table,
                             //    return v.
```

Comparing the performance of these two algorithms with the values in Figure 8.7 shows quite clearly that a hash-based implementation of a map is far superior to either the array or linked list implementation presented in Section 8.2.2. Unfortunately, the analysis is not that simple, and hashing does not always work as described.

A **perfect hashing function** f is one with the property that if x and y are two distinct keys, then $f(x) \neq f(y)$. Unfortunately, perfect hash functions are rare, and even very good hash functions produce the condition that for some $x \neq y$, $f(x) = f(y)$. When two distinct keys hash to the same location, it is called a **collision**. For example, using the hash function described earlier, the name "Posen" would hash to the same location as the key "Smith," as shown in Figure 8.9b.

letter		value
'P'	=	16
'o'	=	15
's'	=	19
'e'	=	5
'n'	=	14
Total	=	69

Hash value = (69 % 50) = 19, the same value as "Smith"

FIGURE 8.9b Computation of the hash value for the key "Posen"

If we go to the hash table and see that row 19 contains some information, how do we tell if it is the information associated with Mr. Smith or Ms. Posen? The answer is that, since we now have a situation where two or more tuples can hash to the same location, we must store not only the value field but the key field as well. Then we are able to determine if the value stored in a particular slot of the hash table is or is not associated with a particular key.

Collisions are generally unavoidable because the number of keys is very large, typically much larger than the hash table size. For example, if the keys are people's names and we assume that last names can contain up to 12 letters, then the total number of possible keys is 26^{12}—a monstrously large value (1 followed by 17 zeros). It is impossible to create a table large enough to guarantee that there will never be any collisions. Besides, it would be wasteful of space because the overwhelming majority of slots would be unused.

How do we address this problem and make hashing a reasonably efficient technique? We must do two things. First, even though collisions are unavoidable, we must minimize the number of collisions, and second, we must develop procedures to deal with the inevitable collisions that will occur.

To minimize the number of collisions, we need to select the best possible hashing function, where "best possible" is defined as a function that scatters the keys uniformly over the N rows, $[0 \ldots N-1]$, of the hash table. That is, if we randomly select a large number, M, of keys, then an approximately equal number, M/N, will hash to each of the N rows in the hash table. A uniform scattering minimizes the number of keys that hash to a given location i, reducing the number of collisions. (This is why hashing functions are also called **scatter functions**.) An example of a poor hashing function is:

f(key) = [2 * **int**(key)] % N   (where the table size N is an even number)

This function will map the set of keys to only the even numbered locations 0, 2, 4, 6, . . . of the table, completely ignoring the odd numbered slots. This will effectively double the total number of collisions and seriously impair performance.

The study of the mathematical properties of hashing functions is rather complex and well beyond the scope of this text. We leave it to courses in function theory and numerical analysis to discuss this subject in greater detail. Here, we simply state that one type of hashing function that often works well for typical table sizes and keys is the **multiplicative congruency method**. This method first casts the key to an integer value, regardless of its original type, and then computes the following value for a hash table with array indexes in the range $[0 \ldots N-1]$.

f(key) = [(a * **int**(key)) % N]   where N, the hash table size, and the parameter a are both large prime numbers

The function f will, for many choices of a and N, produce reasonably well-scattered integer values in the range $[0 \ldots N-1]$.

However, the designers of Java realized early on the importance of hashing and the difficulty of designing and validating good hashing functions. Therefore, they included the following method in class `Object`:

```
public int hashCode(); // converts an object into a random integer that
                       // can be used to store values into a hash table
```

Since `Object` is the root class of Java, every object in your program inherits this method, and it can be used to implement the hashing techniques described in this chapter. So, for example, given our earlier example of people's names and a 50-element hash table, another way to implement our hashing function is:

```
String name;    // a person's name
. . .
// hash on name using the inherited function hashCode()
// reduce the result to the range [0 . . . 49] using the % operator
int i = (name.hashCode()) % 50;
```

Even with a well-designed hashing function, we are still going to encounter the condition of two or more distinct keys hashing to the same location. How can we handle these inevitable collisions? We investigate two methods in this section: open addressing and chaining.

With **open addressing**, the (k, v) tuples are stored in the N-element array structure itself. Each row of the array holds a single tuple, where a tuple is an object containing the two state variables `key` and `value`. We first initialize all hash table entries to `null`, representing the state empty, or not in use:

Now assume we want to implement the `put()` operation that inserts the new tuple (k, v) into this hash table. As always, we first compute the value $i = f(k)$. If location h[i] is not empty, then this slot is already occupied, and we have a collision. The open addressing algorithm says to search sequentially through the hash table looking for an empty location. That is, if row i is occupied, then search in locations i + 1, i + 2, i + 3, . . . looking for an empty slot to store (k, v). This search is done modulo the table size N so that after looking at the last item in the table, h[N − 1], we wrap around and continue our search from the entry h[0]. The `put()` operaton terminates when we either find an empty location and have successfully stored this new tuple, or we return to location i. In this latter case, the table is full, and the insertion fails.

For example, assume our hash table contains six slots, numbered 0 to 5, and the keys of our tuple map to the following locations:

$$f(k_1) \rightarrow 3$$
$$f(k_2) \rightarrow 5$$
$$f(k_3) \rightarrow 3$$
$$f(k_4) \rightarrow 4$$

Then the final contents of the hash table will be the following, assuming that the tuples are added to the table in the order just shown:

	Hash table h
h[0]	(k_4, v_4)
h[1]	Λ
h[2]	Λ
h[3]	(k_1, v_1)
h[4]	(k_3, v_3)
h[5]	(k_2, v_2)

The get() operation works in a similar fashion. To retrieve the value field of the tuple whose key field is k, we again compute $i = f(k)$. If location $h[i] = \Lambda$, then the tuple is not in the table, and we are finished. If h[i] is nonnull, then we examine the key field of the tuple referenced by h[i] to see if it equals the desired key k. If it does not, then this slot is occupied by a different tuple. We now search sequentially through the rows of h until we either find the desired key k and return its associated value field, v, or we cycle through the entire table and return to location i. This means the table is full and the key field k is not present. The other possibility is that we encounter a null entry during our search. This means that the key k is not in the table because, if it were, it would have been stored in this location.

Figure 8.10 shows a class that implements the hashing and open addressing algorithms just described. It uses the resources of another class called Tuple that describes the structure of an individual tuple in the hash table.

```
/**
 * A class describing a (key,value) pair, or 2-tuple.
 */

public class Tuple {
    private Object key; // The Key
    private Object value; // The value

    /**
     * Construct a new Tuple containing the given data.
     *
     * @param key the key of the pair
     * @param value the value to associate with the key
     *
     * Preconditions:
     *     Key is not null
     *     Value is not null
     *
```

FIGURE 8.10 Implementation of hashing using open addressing

```
 * Postconditions:
 *    The Tuple is ready for use.
 *
 * @param newKey the key.
 * @param newValue the value.
 */
public Tuple( Object newKey, Object newValue ) {
   key = newKey;
   value = newValue;
}

/**
 * Get this Tuple's key.
 *
 * Preconditions:
 *    None
 *
 * Postconditions:
 *    The Tuple is unchanged.
 *
 * @return the key associated with this tuple.
 */
public Object getKey() {
   return key;
}

/**
 * Get this Tuple's value.
 *
 * Preconditions:
 *    None
 *
 * Postconditions:
 *    The Tuple is unchanged.
 *
 * @return the value associated with this tuple.
 */

public Object getValue() {
   return value;
}

/*
 * Set Tuple's key field. Caution: The key should really not be changed
 * while the tuple is in a table. The tuple should be removed, the
 * key changed, and then the tuple should be placed back into the
 * table. Keys are generally immutable
 *
```

(continued)

FIGURE 8.10 Implementation of hashing using open addressing *(continued)*

```
   * Preconditions:
   *     None
   *
   * Postconditions:
   *     The Tuple has the specified key.
   *
   * @param newKey the new key to associated with this tuple.
   */
  public void setKey( Object newKey ) {
     key = newKey;
  }

  /**
   * Set this Tuple's value.
   *
   * Preconditions:
   *     None
   *
   * Postconditions:
   *     The Tuple has the specified value.
   *
   * @param newValue the value to associated with this tuple.
   */
  public void setValue( Object newValue ) {
     this.value = value;
  }

  /**
   * Return a string representation of this tuple.
   *
   * Preconditions:
   *     None
   *
   * Postconditions:
   *     The Tuple is unchanged.
   *
   * @return a string representation of this tuple.
   */
  public String toString() {
     return "(" + key + "," + value + ")";
  }

} // Tuple


/**
 * Implementation of a hash table that uses open addressing.
 */
```

FIGURE 8.10 Implementation of hashing using open addressing *(continued)*

```
public class OpenAddressingHashTable implements Table {
   // Safety constants for the domain
   public static int CARDINALITY = 27;
   public static int ADDR_STEP = 17;

   // The hashTable
   private Tuple table[];
   private int size;

   /**
    * Create a new hash table.
    */
   public OpenAddressingHashTable() {
      table = new Tuple[ CARDINALITY ];
      size = 0;
   }

   /**
    * Puts the given value into the table, indexed by the given key.
    *
    * Preconditions:
    *    Key is not null
    *    Key's hashCode() method returns an element in this
    *       Table's domain
    *    Value is not null
    *    The table is not full
    *
    * Postconditions:
    *    The given value has been associated with the given key.
    *
    * @param key the key to refer to the given value by.
    * @param value the data to associate with the given key.
    */
   public void put( Object key, Object value ) {
      int pos = key.hashCode();

      // Find an open position
      while ( table[ pos ] != null ) {
         pos = ( pos + ADDR_STEP ) % table.length;
      }

      table[ pos ] = new Tuple( key, value );
      size = size + 1;
   }

   /**
    * Removes the object associated with the given key, if any.
    *
```

(continued)

FIGURE 8.10 Implementation of hashing using open addressing *(continued)*

```
 * Preconditions:
 *    Key is not null
 *
 * Postconditions:
 *    The element (if any) associated with the given key has
 *       been removed.
 *
 * @param key the key to remove.
 */
public void remove( Object key ) {
   int loc = find( key );

   if ( loc != -1 ) {
      table[ loc ] = null;
      size = size - 1;
   }
}


/**
 * Return the location in the table where the tuple with the
 * specified key is found. A -1 is returned if the key cannot
 * be found in the table.
 *
 * @param key the key to search the table for.
 *
 * @return the location of the key in the table or -1 if the key
 *    cannot be found.
 */
private int find( Object key ) {
   int probe = key.hashCode();
   int loc = -1;

   // Check the 'next' open address until we find the key or we have
   // checked the entire array
   for ( int i = 0; i < table.length && loc == -1; i = i + 1) {
      Tuple curTuple = table[ probe ];

      // Is this the tuple we are looking for?
      if ( curTuple != null && curTuple.getKey().equals( key ) ) {
         loc = i;
      } else {
         // Calculate the next table location to probe
         probe = ( probe + ADDR_STEP ) % table.length;
      }
   }

   return loc;
}
```

FIGURE 8.10 Implementation of hashing using open addressing *(continued)*

```
/**
 * Returns the object associated with the given key.
 *
 * Preconditions:
 *     Key is not null
 *
 * Postconditions:
 *     The Table is unchanged.
 *
 * @param key the key to look up in the table.
 */
public Object get( Object key ) {
    int loc = find( key );
    Object retVal = null;

    if ( loc != -1 ) {
        retVal = table[ loc ];
    }

    return retVal;
}

/**
 * Determine whether the Table is empty.
 *
 * Preconditions:
 *     None
 *
 * Postconditions:
 *     The Table is unchanged.
 *
 * @return true if the table is empty and false otherwise.
 */
public boolean isEmpty() {
    return size == 0;
}

/**
 * Determine the size of the Table.
 *
 * Preconditions:
 *     None
 *
 * Postconditions:
 *     The Table is unchanged.
 *
 * @return the number of elements in the table.
 */
```

(continued)

FIGURE 8.10 Implementation of hashing using open addressing *(continued)*

```
public int size() {
   return size;
}


/**
 * Determine the cardinality of the Table.
 *
 * Preconditions:
 *    None
 *
 * Postconditions:
 *    The Table is unchanged.
 *
 * @return a number one greater than the maximum domain element.
 */
public int cardinality() {
   return CARDINALITY;
}


/**
 * Get all the keys in this Table.
 *
 * Preconditions:
 *    None
 *
 * Postconditions:
 *    The Table is unchanged.
 *
 * @return an array containing all of the keys in the table.
 */
public Object[] getKeys() {
   Object retVal[] = new Object[ size ];
   int pos = 0;

   for ( int i = 0; i < table.length; i = i + 1 ) {
      if ( table[ i ] != null ) {
         retVal[ pos ] = table[ i ].getKey();
         pos = pos + 1;
      }
   }

   return retVal;
}


/**
 * Get all values stored in this Table. There is no correlation
 * between the order of the elements returned by this method and
```

FIGURE 8.10 Implementation of hashing using open addressing *(continued)*

```
     * the getKeys() method.
     *
     * Preconditions:
     *    None
     *
     * Postconditions:
     *    The Table is unchanged.
     *
     * @return an array containing all of the values in the table.
     */
   public Object[] getValues() {
      Object retVal[] = new Object[ size ];
      int pos = 0;

      for ( int i = 0; i < table.length; i = i + 1 ) {
         if ( table[ i ] != null ) {
            retVal[ pos ] = table[ i ].getValue();
            pos = pos + 1;
         }
      }

      return retVal;
   }


   /**
    * Return a string representation of the hash table.
    *
    * @return a string representation of the hash table.
    */
   public String toString() {
      StringBuffer hashAsString = new StringBuffer( "" );

      for ( int i = 0; i < table.length; i = i + 1 ) {
         hashAsString.append( "h[" + i + "]==" );

         if ( table[ i ] != null ) {
            hashAsString.append( table[ i ] );
         }

         hashAsString.append( "\n" );
      }

      return hashAsString.toString();
   }

} // OpenAddressingHashTable
```

FIGURE 8.10 Implementation of hashing using open addressing (continued)

One problem with open addressing is that it frequently produces long chains of occupied cells followed by long chains of empty cells. This is because when a collision occurs, we search sequentially for an available slot. If location i is occupied, the new value is inserted into location $i + 1$, assuming it is empty. Now, if a key hashes to either location i or $i + 1$, it is placed in position $i + 2$, assuming it is empty. Therefore, the probability of a value being stored in location $i + 2$ is greater than the probability of it being stored in some other cell, and we begin to build chains of occupied slots. These chains degrade performance as we need to make longer and longer searches to find a location. If the empty slots were more evenly distributed throughout the table, searches would be shorter since an empty slot is what terminates the retrieval operation.

Thus, a small but important modification to open addressing is that when a collision occurs, do not search the table in increments of 1 but rather in increments of c, where $c > 1$ and is relatively prime with (i.e., shares no common factor with) the hash table size N. This is what was done in Figure 8.10, in which the increment size is the constant labeled ADDR_STEP. For example, assume N = 10 and ADDR_STEP = 3 (actually, it was set to 17 in Figure 8.10). If our key originally hashes to location 5 and that position is occupied, then the rows of the hash table are searched in the order 5, 8, 1, 4, 7, 0, 3, 6, 9, 2 rather than 5, 6, 7, 8, 9, 0, 1, . . . as in a traditional sequential search. This technique does a better job of scattering tuples throughout the hash table and distributing empty slots more evenly. This in turn helps improve the performance of open addressing.

You can analyze the time to do a retrieval from a hash table using open addressing. Looking at the get() operation in Figure 8.10, we see that in the best case (no collisions), retrieval requires only a single comparison to locate the desired key, and it is an O(1) algorithm. This is the theoretically optimum performance described at the beginning of the chapter. However, in the worst case, we may have to search the entire N-element hash table to discover whether or not the key is present. In this case, hashing degenerates to O(N).

In the average case, the number of comparisons required for a successful retrieval using open addressing depends on how many tuples are stored in the hash table. For example, in a sparsely occupied table, there are few collisions, and we usually go directly to the desired key or to an empty slot, which tells us the key is not present. As the table becomes fuller, the chances of a collision increase. Therefore, the efficiency of retrieval from a hash table using open addressing will depend on a value α, the **load factor**, defined as follows:

α = *number of entries in the hash table / hash table size*   *($0 \le \alpha \le 1$)*

The computation of the average number of comparisons required for a hash table retrieval is quite complex. (The derivation of these formulas can be found in the classic computer science text by Donald Knuth.[1]) Knuth's approximation for the average number of comparisons C needed for a successful search of a hash table with load factor α using open addressing is:

$$C \approx 1/2\,[\,1 + 1\,/\,(1 - \alpha)]$$

[1]Donald E. Knuth, *The Art of Computer Programming, Vol. 3: Sorting and Searching* (Reading, Mass.: Addison-Wesley, 1998).

For example, if our hash table is half full ($\alpha = 0.5$), the formula says that, on average, it will require about $1/2 * (1 + 2) = 1.5$ comparisons to locate a specific key and retrieve the associated data. Compare this result to either a sequential or binary search of a table with 100,000 entries. They will require, on average, about 50,000 (N/2) or 17 ($\log_2 N$) searches, respectively. Even if our table is 80 percent full ($\alpha = 0.8$), hashing and open addressing require only about $[0.5 * (1 + 5)] = 3$ searches, still a vast improvement. However, be aware that this performance increase is coming at the expense of a good deal of extra memory. If our hash table size is N = 100,000, then at 50 percent occupancy, we are leaving 50,000 slots unused. At 80 percent occupancy, 20,000 slots must be left empty. Hashing and open addressing are a reasonable strategy only if there are adequate memory resources, and we are willing to leave a portion of our hash table vacant.

We can observe this behavior more clearly by determining exactly how many comparisons are required to retrieve a value from a hash table of size N = 100 with load factors ranging from $\alpha = 0.1$ to $\alpha = 0.99$. The results are summarized in Figure 8.11.

Figure 8.11 shows that in a table whose load factor is in the range $0.0 \leq \alpha \leq 0.7$, the number of searches needed to retrieve a value grows slowly as a function of α, and hashing displays a roughly O(1) constant time performance. In the range $\alpha = [0.7 \ldots 0.95]$, the rate of growth in the number of comparisons increases markedly. The performance of hashing becomes more comparable to the O($\log_2 N$) binary search technique that needs an average of $\log_2 100 \approx 7$ comparisons to successfully locate a specific key. For α in the range $[0.95 \ldots 0.99]$, performance degrades significantly, and retrieval requires roughly 50 comparisons, the same number as a sequential search. Thus, to get good behavior from hashing and open addressing, it is best to keep the value of the load factor $\alpha < 0.8$. This means that at least 20 percent of the table should remain empty.

Aside from the extra memory required to obtain reasonable performance, open addressing also suffers from another problem: deletions. Assume we have inserted the

α	Number of Comparisons	Approximate Behavior	(Table Size N = 100)
0.1	1.06		
0.2	1.13		
0.3	1.21		
0.4	1.33	O(1)	
0.5	1.50		
0.6	1.75		
0.7	2.17		
0.8	3.00		
0.9	5.50	O(log N)	
0.95	10.5		
0.98	26.5	O(N)	
0.99	50.5		

FIGURE 8.11 Performance of hashing using open addressing with N = 100

key values 10, 15, and 20, in that order, into our hash table, and they all originally hashed to location 1. Also assume that our increment size is 1 so that we search sequentially for an empty slot if the original slot is full. Here is what will result. (Note: we are not showing the value field.)

Location	Key
0	Λ
1	10
2	15
3	20
4	Λ
. . .	

(where Λ represents "empty")

If we delete the value 15 stored in table slot 2, we end up with the following:

Location	Key
0	Λ
1	10
2	Λ
3	20
4	Λ
. . .	

If we now attempt to retrieve the key 20, we encounter a problem. We hash to location 1, see that it is occupied by another key (10), and begin the sequential search of the table from that point. However, slot 2 is empty, and we will incorrectly conclude that 20 is not in the table because, if it were, it would have been stored in slot 2. The error is caused by the fact that slot 2 was occupied when we did the original insertion of the key.

With open addressing, deletions are problematic. If we do a delete operation, we must indicate that, although this space is now empty, it was previously occupied. We can do this using a different type of empty marker such as "*". Then, when doing a retrieval, we can terminate the operation when we encounter a true empty marker (Λ), but we continue searching if we encounter the empty but previously occupied symbol (*). If our hash table is highly dynamic and there are a large number of deletions, the table soon fills with * markers rather than Λ, and performance suffers as the average search length increases. For this reason, as well as the space required to keep a portion of the table empty, an alternative method of handling collisions is far more popular.

The second approach to collision resolution, called **chaining**, is quite different from the open addressing method just described. The N elements of the hash table h[ ] are no longer used to store the actual (k, v) tuples themselves, but only a reference to a linked list of all tuples that hash to this location. That is, element h[i] is the head of a linked list containing all tuples (k, v) such that $i = f(k)$.

For example, assume that our hash table has length 5. If the keys a and b hash to 2, c hashes to 4, and d, e, and f hash to 1, then the table might look like the diagram shown in Figure 8.12, disregarding the value field:

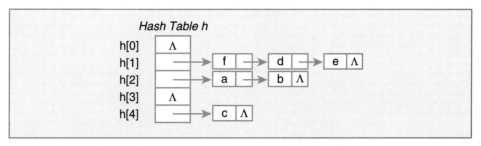

FIGURE 8.12 Example of using chaining to handle collisions

The use of chaining simplifies the insertion of new tuples into the table after collisions. We no longer need to search the entire table to locate where a tuple should be stored. Instead, we add the new (k, v) tuple to the head of the linked list pointed at by the value in the corresponding hash table location, assuming it is not already there. (If it is there, then we do nothing and return.) To retrieve a value, we do a sequential search of the linked list pointed at by h[i], where $i = f(k)$.

A class that implements these chaining-based hashing algorithms is shown in Figure 8.13. It uses the `hashCode()` method inherited by all Java objects.

```
/**
 * The implementation of a Hash Table using chaining for
 * collision resolution.
 */

public class ChainingHashTable implements Table {
    // The table itself
    private List hashTable[];
    int size;

    /**
     * Create a new hash table.
     *
     * Preconditions:
     *     None
     *
     * Postconditions:
     *     The Table is ready for use.
     *
     * @param cardinality the number of elements in the domain.
     */
```

(continued)

FIGURE 8.13 Implementation of hashing using chaining

```
public ChainingHashTable(int cardinality) {
    hashTable = new LinkedList[ cardinality ];
    size = 0;
}

/**
 * Puts the given value into the table, indexed by the given key.
 *
 * Preconditions:
 *    Key is not null
 *    Key's hashCode() method returns an element in this
 *        Table's domain
 *    Value is not null;
 *
 * Postconditions:
 *    The given value has been associated with the given key.
 *
 * @param key the key to refer to the given value by.
 * @param value the data to associate with the given key.
 */
public void put( Object key, Object value ) {
    int bucket = key.hashCode();

    // Do we need to create a new list for this bucket?
    if ( hashTable[ bucket ] == null ) {
        hashTable[ bucket ] = new LinkedList();
    }

    hashTable[ bucket ].append( new Tuple( key, value ) );
    size = size + 1;
}

/**
 * Removes the object associated with the given key, if any.
 *
 * Preconditions:
 *    Key is not null
 *
 * Postconditions:
 *    The element (if any) associated with the given key has
 *        been removed.
 *
 * @param key the key to remove.
 */
public void remove( Object key ) {
    int bucket = key.hashCode();
    List chain = hashTable[ bucket ];
    boolean found = false;
```

FIGURE 8.13 Implementation of hashing using chaining *(continued)*

```
      // Is there a chain to search?
      if ( chain != null ) {
         // Step through the chain until we fall off the end or
         // find the tuple to delete
         for ( chain.first();
               !found && chain.isOnList();
               chain.next() ) {

            // If this tuple has the key we are looking for
            // delete it and stop the loop
            if ( ( (Tuple)chain.get() ).getKey().equals( key ) ) {
               chain.remove();
               found = true;
            }
         }
      }
   }


   /**
    * Returns the object associated with the given key.
    *
    * Preconditions:
    *    Key is not null
    *
    * Postconditions:
    *    The Table is unchanged.
    *
    * @param key the key to look up in the table.
    */
   public Object get(Object key) {
      int bucket = key.hashCode();
      List chain = hashTable[ bucket ];
      Object retVal = null;

      // Is there a chain to search?
      if ( chain != null ) {
         // Step through the chain until we find the element or
         // run out of list.
         for ( chain.first();
               retVal == null && chain.isOnList();
               chain.next() ) {

            // If this tuple has the key we are looking for,
            // extract the value
            if ( ( (Tuple)chain.get() ).getKey().equals( key ) ) {
               retVal = ( (Tuple)chain.get() ).getValue();
            }
         }
      }
```

(continued)

FIGURE 8.13 Implementation of hashing using chaining *(continued)*

```
        return retVal;
    }

    /**
     * Determine whether the Table is empty.
     *
     * Preconditions:
     *     None
     *
     * Postconditions:
     *     The Table is unchanged.
     *
     * @return true if the table is empty and false otherwise.
     */
    public boolean isEmpty() {
        return size == 0;
    }

    /**
     * Determine the size of the Table.
     *
     * Preconditions:
     *     None
     *
     * Postconditions:
     *     The Table is unchanged.
     *
     * @return the number of elements in the table.
     */
    public int size() {
        return size;
    }

    /**
     * Determine the cardinality of the Table.
     *
     * Preconditions:
     *     None
     *
     * Postconditions:
     *     The Table is unchanged.
     *
     * @return a number one greater than the maximum domain element.
     */
    public int cardinality() {
        return hashTable.length;
    }
```

FIGURE 8.13 Implementation of hashing using chaining *(continued)*

```
/**
 * Get all the keys in this Table.
 *
 * Preconditions:
 *    None
 *
 * Postconditions:
 *    The Table is unchanged.
 *
 * @return an array containing all of the keys in the table.
 */
public Object[] getKeys() {
   List chain;
   List keys = new LinkedList();

   // Go through each chain and create a list that contains all
   // of the keys in the table
   for ( int i = 0; i < hashTable.length; i++ ) {
      if ( hashTable[ i ] != null) {
         chain = hashTable[ i ];

         for ( chain.first(); chain.isOnList(); chain.next() ) {
            keys.append( ( (Tuple)chain.get() ).getKey() );
         }
      }
   }

   // Convert the list of keys to an array
   return listToArray( keys );
}


/**
 * Return an array that contains all the elements of the specified
 * list.
 *
 * @param theList the list to convert.
 *
 * @return an array that contains the elements in the list.
 */

private Object[] listToArray( List theList ) {
   // Create an array of the right size
   Object retVal[] = new Object[ theList.size() ];

   // Step through the list and put the elements in the array
   theList.first();
   for ( int i = 0;
      theList.isOnList();
      theList.next(), i = i + 1 ) {
```

(continued)

FIGURE 8.13 Implementation of hashing using chaining *(continued)*

```
            retVal[ i ] = theList.get();
        }

        // Return the result
        return retVal;
    }

    /**
     * Get all values stored in this Table. There is no correlation
     * between the order of the elements returned by this method and
     * the getKeys() method.
     *
     * Preconditions:
     *     None
     *
     * Postconditions:
     *     The Table is unchanged.
     *
     * @return an array containing all of the values in the table.
     */
    public Object[] getValues() {
        List chain;
        List values = new LinkedList();

        // Go through each chain and create a list that contains all
        // of the keys in the table
        for ( int i = 0; i < hashTable.length; i++ ) {
            if ( hashTable[ i ] != null) {
                chain = hashTable[ i ];

                for ( chain.first(); chain.isOnList(); chain.next() ) {
                    values.append( ( (Tuple)chain.get() ).getValue() );
                }
            }
        }

        // Convert the list to an array and return the result
        return listToArray( values );
    }

    /**
     * Return a string representation of this hash table.
     *
     * @return a string representation of this hash table.
     */
    public String toString() {
        StringBuffer hashAsString = new StringBuffer( "" );
        List chain = null;
```

FIGURE 8.13 Implementation of hashing using chaining *(continued)*

```
        for ( int i = 0; i < hashTable.length; i = i + 1 ) {
           hashAsString.append( "h[" + i + "]==" );

           if ( hashTable[ i ] != null ) {
              chain = hashTable[ i ];

              for ( chain.first(); chain.isOnList(); chain.next() ) {
                 hashAsString.append( " " + chain.get() );
              }
           }

           hashAsString.append( "\n" );
        }

        return hashAsString.toString();
     }

} // ChainingHashTable
```

FIGURE 8.13 Implementation of hashing using chaining *(continued)*

One noteworthy characteristic of chaining is that it is possible to store more than N keys in the hash table, where N is the table size. (We saw exactly this in Figure 8.12 where we stored the six keys, a, . . . , f in a hash table of size N = 5.) With open addressing, we were limited to a maximum of N entries, at which time the table became full, and no further insertions were possible.

On average, each linked list in a hash table will be of length $\alpha = k/N$, where k is the total number of tuples stored in the table and N is the hash table size. The time needed to insert a new (k, v) tuple into our table using chaining is the sum of the following three steps:

Step 1. Accessing the reference value stored in location h[i], where $i = f(k)$.

Step 2. Searching the entire list pointed at by the head pointer to see if the key being inserted is already there (remember, no duplicates allowed).

Step 3. If it is not there, inserting the new tuple at the head of the list.

Steps 1 and 3 take O(1) constant time, while step 2 takes time proportional to $\alpha = k/N$, the average length of each linked list, assuming the key is not already there. Thus, insertion into a chained hash table takes $(2 + \alpha)$ steps if the key is not in the table.

Similarly, retrieval takes one access to the head of the linked list followed by an average search of half the linked list before we find the desired key. So retrieval from a chained hash table requires an average of $(1 + \alpha/2)$ operations. Knowing an approximate value for the number of tuples that we will be storing, we can adjust the hash table size N to give an acceptable level of performance with a minimum of wasted space. For example, if we plan to store about 1,000 tuples into our hash table using chaining, then a table size of N = 10 will produce linked lists with an average length of 100, requiring about $(1 + 100/2) = 51$ comparisons per retrieval, which is rather poor. A table size of N = 50 will produce linked lists of length 20 and an average of 11 operations per retrieval, comparable to binary search ($\log_2 1000 \approx 10$). Finally, a table size of N = 500 produces an average of 2 comparisons per retrieval, which as shown in Figure 8.11 is roughly comparable to open addressing with a load factor $\alpha = 0.65$.

Again, it is interesting to note that these performance improvements are achieved at the expense of extra memory. This time the space is needed for the reference values contained in both the hash table and the nodes in the linked lists. For example, assume that the number of keys is 1,000 (disregard the value field for now), N, the table size, is 500, and each integer and each reference value occupy 4 bytes. The chaining technique requires 500 reference values in the table plus 1,000 linked list nodes, each containing a single key and a single reference. This is a total of (500 * 4 + 1000 * 8) = 10,000 bytes of storage. By way of comparison, open addressing with $\alpha = 0.65$ produces about the same level of performance but requires only 6,150 bytes, about 38 percent less space. (We need 4,000 bytes to hold the 1,000 4-byte keys plus 2,150 additional bytes to keep the table 35 percent empty.) However, both of these hashing methods require much more space than either a sequential or a binary search, which is just the 4,000 bytes needed to store the key values themselves. This is a good example of what computer scientists like to call the **time-space trade-off**, in which the use of extra memory can potentially reduce the execution time needed to obtain a solution.

To conclude our discussion of hashing, let's analyze what happens when we use a hash table to implement a 60,000 word English language dictionary. These dictionaries are part of virtually every modern word processing package to provide users with spell checking services. A dictionary is an excellent candidate for hashing. The two operations typically carried out by a dictionary object are:

◆ Adding new words (so users can customize the dictionary to their needs).

◆ Checking to see if a given word is or is not in the dictionary to determine if it is spelled correctly.

These are identical to the operations put() and get() in the Table interface of Figure 8.5. Furthermore, the word-lookup operation must be completed very quickly as it must be carried out once for every word in the document. For large text files (like this book), that could mean tens or hundreds of thousands of words. Users will not be happy if they have to wait minutes, or even tens of seconds, for their spelling checker to complete its operations. Thus, the speed-up that can be achieved via hashing could be very important to the success of our software package.

If we use the open addressing method to store our dictionary, we know that performance is highly dependent on the load factor α. For $\alpha > 0.9$, performance can degrade significantly. For $\alpha > 0.98$, hashing will begin to approximate linear behavior, which will almost certainly be unacceptable for meeting performance specifications.

Assume that we allocate 12 bytes of space for each word in our dictionary, allowing for a maximum of 12 characters/word. Keeping 10 percent of the table empty ($\alpha = 0.9$) means that our 60,000-entry hash table will need to include 6,000 unused slots, which will require $6,000 \times 12 = 72$ KB of extra storage beyond what is needed for the 60,000 words themselves. If we keep the table 5 percent empty ($\alpha = 0.95$), it will only require an extra 36 KB of memory. Another potential problem with open addressing is that deletions must be handled in a special way. As mentioned earlier, if the user removes a word from the dictionary, we must mark that slot with an entry to indicate that, although currently empty, it once was occupied. If there were a large number of deletions, this could slow down the retrieval operation. However, words are rarely removed from a dictionary, so this should not be a problem.

Instead of open addressing, we could use a chaining scheme with an array of N references and about 60,000/N words per linked list. Now our word lookup will consist of one access to the N-element hash table, followed by a search of about one-half of the (60,000/N) words that hash to this location. For example, if we want to locate words in an average of six comparisons, then we want the following relationship to hold:

$$1 + \alpha/2 = 6, \text{ or}$$
$$\alpha = 10$$

Since $\alpha = k \, / \, N$ and we know that k = 60,000, we can solve for N

$$\alpha = k \, / \, N$$
$$10 = 60,000 \, / \, N$$
$$N = 6,000$$

and we must set N, our hash table size, to approximately 6,000.

Now, in addition to the node storage required for the 60,000 words themselves, we need to allocate space for 66,000 references—the 6,000 references in the hash table, plus the 60,000 references contained in the nodes of the linked lists. If we assume that a reference occupies 4 bytes, then chaining will require an extra 66,000 × 4 = 264 KB of memory, significantly more than was required by open addressing and α = 0.9 or 0.95. If we want better performance, we can increase the size of the hash table, thus decreasing the average length of the linked lists. For example, setting N = 30,000 reduces the average number of comparisons to two—one look into the hash table and a search of about half of a linked list of length 2. However, this requires storage for 90,000 reference values (30,000 in the hash table + 60,000 in the list nodes), which requires 90,000 × 4 = 360 KB of additional memory.

If, instead, we had kept the 60,000 words in sorted order in an array, we could do a binary search of the dictionary. This does not require any extra space for either pointers or empty locations. However, the average number of comparisons required to locate a word is now about $\log_2 60,000 = 16$, significantly more than either hashing method.

Figure 8.14 summarizes the memory demands and performance characteristics of all the dictionary implementation methods that were discussed.

Technique	Extra Memory Space Required	Approximate Number of Comparisons
Binary Search	0	16
Open Addressing, α = 0.95	36 KB	10.5
Open Addressing, α = 0.9	72 KB	5.5
Chaining, N = 6,000	264 KB	6
Chaining, N = 30,000	360 KB	2

FIGURE 8.14 Comparison of different dictionary implementation techniques

This extended example clearly demonstrates the potential advantages of hashing. By utilizing additional memory, either for empty table slots or reference values, we were able to reduce the average number of comparisons needed to locate a word in the dictionary from 16 to between 2 and 10.5, up to an eightfold improvement. This speed-up may represent the difference between a highly profitable software package and a program that is rarely, if ever, used. That agonizingly long 15-second delay required to spell check a document using binary search could be reduced to a quite acceptable 2 seconds using hashing and the appropriate parameters. This shows quite dramatically how important the selection of good data structures and algorithms are to the success of a modern software development project.

8.3 GRAPHS

◆ 8.3.1 Introduction and Definitions

A graph is the most general and most powerful of all data representations. Both the linear structures of Chapter 6 and the hierarchical structures of Chapter 7 are specialized forms of graphs in which the connections between nodes have been restricted in some way. In formal mathematics, the study of lists, trees, and graphs are lumped together into one course called *graph theory*.

Formally, a **graph** is a data structure in which the elements of the collection can be related to an arbitrary number of other elements. That is, a graph is a *many:many* data structure in which each element can have an arbitrary number of successors and an arbitrary number of predecessors.

A graph consists of a set of information units called **nodes** or **vertices**. We will refer to this set of nodes as N = $\{n_1, n_2, \ldots, n_k\}$. For example, in Figures 8.15a and 8.15b, the six nodes are labeled A, B, C, D, E, and F. We are allowed to store any type of object in the information field of a node in our graph. However, for simplicity and to focus on the algorithms themselves, in this section we limit the information contained in a node to either a single character or single digit. There are two distinct types of graphs, and they are diagramed in Figure 8.15.

The nodes of a graph are connected to each other by a set of links called **edges**. An edge connecting node n_i to node n_j is usually written as $<n_i, n_j>$, and the set of all edges is referred to as E = $\{<n_i, n_j>, <n_k, n_l>, \ldots\}$. If the edges have a direction,

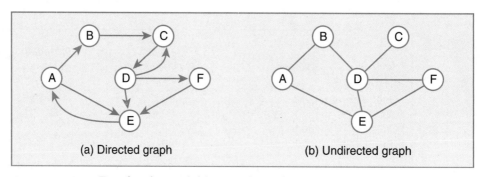

(a) Directed graph   (b) Undirected graph

FIGURE 8.15 Two fundamental types of graphs

then the graph is termed a **directed graph** (Figure 8.15a). If $<n_i, n_j>$ is an edge in a directed graph, then n_i is the **tail**, and n_j is the **head** of the edge. We also say that node n_i is **adjacent to** or **incident to** node n_j.

If there is no direction associated with an edge, then the structure is an **undirected graph**, and the presence of an edge implies the existence of an link in both directions (Figure 8.15b). The following two graphs are equivalent and represent the set of edges E = {<A, B>, <B, A>}.

However, the following two graphs are not equivalent. The one on the left is an undirected graph containing an edge connecting A to B and B to A. The one on the right is a directed graph containing an edge connecting A to B but not B to A.

There can only be a single edge connecting one node to another. That is, the set of edges E cannot have the same entry <A, B> more than once. (If it did, then E would no longer be a set, as duplicates are not allowed.) The following structure, in which there are three distinct edges connecting the same two nodes, is called a **multigraph**

and in traditional graph structures, they are not permitted. They will not be discussed any further in this chapter.

In addition to being directed or undirected, edges can be either **weighted** or **unweighted**. A weighted edge <A, B> has associated with it a scalar value W, and it is written <A, B, W>. W represents a numerical measure of the cost of using this edge to go from A to B. For example,

The meaning of this notation is that traveling from A to B along this edge costs 8 units. These could represent dollars, time, distance, effort, or any other measure of the consumption of resources. If the edges are unweighted, the cost of traversing an edge is identical for all edges. (In an unweighted graph, we assume the cost associated with each edge is some constant value, usually 0 or 1.)

Figure 8.16 shows the definitions for the two classes `Edge` and `Vertex` that define these two basic components of a graph. The `Edge` class includes state variables for the starting and ending vertices of this edge and its cost. (For an unweighted graph, this cost variable is set to 0.) The `Vertex` class includes instance variables containing the information stored in the vertex (called `name`) as well as a table of all edges that start at this vertex.

```
/**
 * An edge in a graph.
 */

public class Edge implements Comparable {
   private Vertex source; // Where the edge begins
   private Vertex dest;   // Where the edge ends
   private int cost;      // The cost to traverse this edge

   /**
    * Create an Edge.
    *
    * @param theSource starting Vertex.
    * @param theDest ending Vertex.
    * @param theCost cost to traverse this Vertex.
    */
   public Edge( Vertex theSource, Vertex theDest, int theCost ) {
      source = theSource;
      dest = theDest;
      cost = theCost;
   }

   /**
    * Create an Edge with no cost.
    *
    * @param theSource starting Vertex.
    * @param theDest ending Vertex.
    */
   public Edge( Vertex theSource, Vertex theDest ) {
      this( theSource, theDest, 0 );
   }

   /**
    * Get the source vertex.
    *
    * @return the source vertex.
    */
   public Vertex getSource() {
      return source;
   }

   /**
    * Get the destination vertex.
    *
    * @return the destination vertex.
    */
   public Vertex getDest() {
      return dest;
   }
```

FIGURE 8.16 Edge and Vertex classes

```
/**
 * Get the cost associated with this edge.
 *
 * @return the cost associated with this edge.
 */
public int getCost() {
    return cost;
}


/**
 * Return a String representation of this Edge.
 *
 * @return a String of the form "(startVertex->endVertex:cost)"
 */
public String toString() {
    return
        "(" + source.getName() + "->" +
        dest.getName() + ":" + cost + ")";
}


/**
 * Determine if this edge is equal to another object.
 *
 * @param other the object to compare this edge to.
 *
 * @return true if this edge is equal to the given object and
 *         false otherwise.
 */
public boolean equals( Object other ) {
    boolean retVal = false;

    if ( other instanceof Edge ) {
        Edge otherEdge = (Edge)other;

        retVal =
            source.getName().equals( otherEdge.source.getName() ) &&
            dest.getName().equals( otherEdge.dest.getName() ) &&
            cost == otherEdge.cost;
    }

    return retVal;
}


/*
 * Compare this edge to another edge. Edges are compared based on
 * their cost. If the costs are the same the edges will be ordered
 * based on the names of the vertices they connect.
 *
 * @param other the edge to compare this edge to.
```

(continued)

FIGURE 8.16 Edge and Vertex classes *(continued)*

```
         *
         * @return 0 if the edges are equal, a positive number if this edge
         *    is greater than the given edge, and a negative number if
         *    this edge is less than the given edge.
         */
      public int compareTo( Object other ) {
         Edge otherEdge = (Edge)other;

         // Compare costs by computing their difference. If positive
         // the cost of this edge is greater, if 0 the costs are the same,
         // if negative the cost of this edge is less.
         int retVal = cost - otherEdge.cost;

         // If the costs are the same - break the tie by looking
         // at the alphabetical ordering of the names of the vertices.
         // This way compareTo() will be consistent with equals().
         if ( retVal == 0 ) {
            // Costs are the same - compare the sources
            retVal =
               source.getName().compareTo( otherEdge.source.getName() );

            if ( retVal == 0 ) {
               // Sources are the same - compare the destinations
               retVal =
                  dest.getName().compareTo( otherEdge.dest.getName() );
            }
         }

         return retVal;
      }

} // Edge


/**
 * A class representing a named vertex in a graph.
 */

public class Vertex {
   private String name; // The name of this vertex (the information field)
   private boolean tag; // A flag that can be set by the user
   private Table edges; // The edges that start at this vertex

   /**
    * Create a new vertex.
    *
    * @param newName the name of this vertex.
    */
```

FIGURE 8.16 Edge and Vertex classes *(continued)*

```
      public Vertex( String newName ) {
         name = newName;
         tag = false;
         edges = new ChainingHashTable( 31 );
      }

      /**
       * Get the name of this vertex.
       *
       * Preconditions:
       *    None
       *
       * Postconditions:
       *    The vertex is unchanged.
       *
       * @return the name of this vertex.
       */
      public String getName() {
         return name;
      }

      /**
       * Get the flag associated with this vertex.
       *
       * Preconditions:
       *    None
       *
       * Postconditions:
       *    The vertex is unchanged.
       *
       * @return the state of the tag associated with this vertex.
       */
      public boolean getTag() {
         return tag;
      }

      /**
       * Set the tag associated with this vertex.
       *
       * Preconditions:
       *    None
       *
       * Postconditions:
       *    The flag has the given value.
       *
       * @param newTag the tag's new value.
       */
      public void setTag( boolean newTag ) {
         tag = newTag;
      }
```

(continued)

FIGURE 8.16 Edge and Vertex classes *(continued)*

```
/**
 * Add an edge to this vertex. If the edge already exists,
 * it will be replaced by the new edge.
 *
 * Preconditions:
 *     The edge is not null.
 *     The source of the edge is this vertex.
 *
 * Postconditions:
 *     This Vertex has the specified edge.
 *
 * @param theEdge the edge to add to this vertex.
 */

public void addEdge( Edge theEdge ) {
    edges.put( theEdge.getDest().getName(), theEdge );
}

/**
 * Get the edge that starts at this vertex and ends at the
 * vertex with the given name.
 *
 * Preconditions:
 *     The name is not null.
 *
 * Postcondtions:
 *     The vertex is not changed.
 *
 * @param name the name of the destination vertex.
 *
 * @return a reference to the edge that leads from this vertex
 *     to the specified vertex or null if the edge does not
 *     exist.
 */
public Edge getEdge( String name ) {
    return (Edge)edges.get( name );
}

/**
 * Determine if the vertex with the given name is a neighbor of
 * this vertex.
 *
 * Preconditions:
 *     The name is not null.
 *
 * Postconditions:
 *     The vertex is not changed.
 *
 * @param name the name of the vertex.
```

FIGURE 8.16 Edge and Vertex classes *(continued)*

```
      *
      * @return true if one of the neighbors of this vertex has
      *     the specified name and false otherwise.
      */
     public boolean isNeighbor( String name ) {
        return edges.get( name ) != null;
     }


     /**
      * Get the neighbors of this vertex.
      *
      * Preconditions:
      *     None.
      *
      * Postconditions:
      *     The vertex is unchanged.
      *
      * @return an array containing all of the vertices that
      *     are neighbors of this vertex.
      */
     public Vertex[] getNeighbors() {
        Object values[] = edges.getKeys();
        Vertex retVal[] = new Vertex[ values.length ];

        for ( int i = 0; i < values.length; i = i + 1 ) {
           Edge cur = (Edge)values[ i ];
           retVal[ i ] = cur.getDest();
        }

        return retVal;
     }


     /**
      * Get the edges that start from this vertex.
      *
      * Preconditions:
      *     None.
      *
      * Postconditions:
      *     The vertex is unchanged.
      *
      * @return an array containing all of the edges that start from
      *     this vertex.
      */
     public Edge[] getEdges() {
        Object values[] = edges.getValues();
        Edge retVal[] = new Edge[ values.length ];
```

(continued)

FIGURE 8.16 Edge and Vertex classes *(continued)*

```
      for ( int i = 0; i < values.length; i = i + 1 ) {
         retVal[ i ] = (Edge)values[ i ];
      }


      return retVal;
   }


   /**
    * Returns a String representation of this vertex.
    *
    * @return a String representation of this vertex.
    */
   public String toString() {
      StringBuffer vertexAsString = new StringBuffer( "" );
      Object values[] = edges.getValues();

      vertexAsString.append( name + " (tag=" + tag +")\n" );

      for ( int i = 0; i < values.length; i = i + 1 ) {
         vertexAsString.append( " " + values[ i ] + "\n" );
      }

      return vertexAsString.toString();
   }

} // Vertex
```

FIGURE 8.16 Edge and Vertex classes *(continued)*

A **path** through a graph is a finite sequence of nodes $n_1 n_2 n_3 \ldots n_k$ such that each pair of nodes n_i, n_{i+1}, $i = 1, \ldots k - 1$ is connected by an edge $< n_i, n_{i+1} >$. For example, in Figure 8.15a, the sequence ABCD is a path, but ABE is not because there is no edge connecting nodes B and E. The sequence BCDCD is a path that contains repeated nodes. Usually we are only interested in paths in which all of the nodes n_i are distinct. As you first learned in Chapter 7, this is called a **simple path**. When we use the word *path* by itself, we will usually mean a simple path.

A very important type of path is the **cycle**. This is a simple path $n_1 n_2 n_3 \ldots n_k$ exactly as defined earlier, but with the added requirement that $n_1 = n_k$. Informally, a cycle is a path that begins at a node, visits any number of other nodes in the graph at most once, and then ends up back at the originating node. Referring to Figure 8.15b, BCDB is a cycle. So are CDC and ABCDFEA. This latter example has a special name. A cycle that visits every node in the graph exactly once is a **Hamiltonian cycle**.

A graph is **connected** if, for every pair of nodes n_i and n_j, there exists a path from n_i to n_j. Both graphs in Figure 8.15 are connected. Neither of the structures in Figure 8.17 are connected. The directed graph in Figure 8.17a does not contain paths from B to A, from C to B, or from C to A. The undirected graph in Figure 8.17b contains three sets of nodes {A,B,C}, {D,E,F}, and {G} that are connected among themselves but that are disconnected from each other. These sets are called **connected subgraphs**.

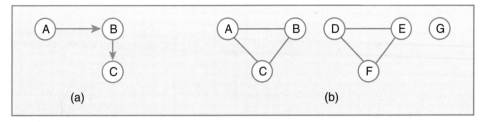

FIGURE 8.17 Examples of unconnected graphs

Graphs occur often in real life, and we encounter them in a number of situations. For example, a road map showing the interstate highway connections between various cities is an excellent example of an undirected graph because all interstate highways are two-way. We could also add weights to each edge to indicate the distance in miles, or driving time in hours, between the two cities, producing a weighted undirected graph:

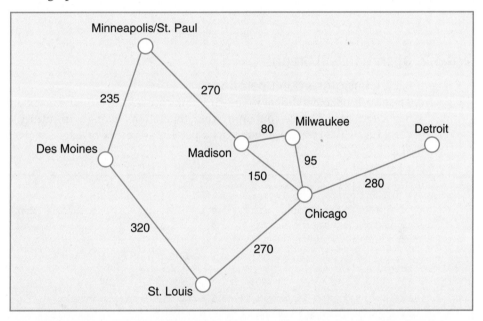

The sequence of courses that one must take to complete a degree in computer science can also be represented as a graph. This time, it is a directed graph, with the direction of the edge implying the specific order in which courses must be completed. The computer course graph shown at the top of page 508 is interesting in that it contains no cycles. This structure is called a **directed acyclic graph**, usually abbreviated DAG.

An example more closely related to computer science is a wide-area computer network such as the Internet. In this type of network, computers are interconnected via high-speed point-to-point communication channels such as phone lines and fiber optic cables. We can use a graph-based representation of a network to determine how to optimally route messages from one node to another as well as to find backup routes in case of node or line outages.

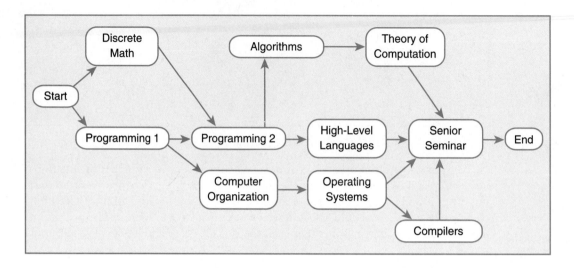

◆ 8.3.2 Operations on Graphs

8.3.2.1 Basic Insertion Operations

The two fundamental operations on graphs are adding a new vertex and adding a new edge. An interface containing these operations, along with utility routines for checking whether a graph contains a particular vertex or edge, is given in Figure 8.18.

```
/**
 * An interface for a Graph data structure. Every Vertex in the Graph is
 * identified by a unique name.
 */

public interface Graph {
    /**
     * Add a vertex to the graph if the graph does not contain a
     * vertex with the same name.
     *
     * Preconditions:
     *     The name is not null.
     *
     * Postconditions:
     *     The Graph contains a Vertex with the given name.
     *
     * @param name the name of the vertex.
     */
    public void addVertex( String name );
```

FIGURE 8.18 Specifications for a Graph interface

```
/**
 * Add an edge to the graph if the graph does not contain an edge
 * whose source and destination vertices are the same as those
 * specified.
 *
 * Preconditions:
 *     The source vertex is in the graph.
 *     The destination vertex is in the graph.
 *
 * Postconditions:
 *     The specified edge is in the Graph.
 *
 * @param source the name of the source vertex.
 * @param dest the name of the destination vertex.
 * @param cost the cost to traverse this edge.
 */
public void addEdge( String source, String dest, int cost );

/**
 * Add an edge to the Graph. If the Graph already contains this edge,
 * the old data will be replaced by the new data.
 *
 * Preconditions:
 *     The source vertex is in the graph.
 *     The destination vertex is in the graph.
 *
 * Postconditions:
 *     The specified edge is in the Graph.
 *
 * @param source the name of the source vertex.
 * @param dest the name of the destination vertex.
 */
public void addEdge( String source, String dest );

/**
 * Determine whether the Graph contains a Vertex with the given name.
 *
 * Preconditions:
 *     The name is not null.
 *
 * Postconditions:
 *     The Graph is unchanged.
 *
 * @param name the name of the vertex.
 *
 * @return true if the graph contains a vertex with the given name
 *     and false otherwise.
 */
public boolean hasVertex( String name );
```

(continued)

FIGURE 8.18 Specifications for a Graph interface *(continued)*

```
/**
 * Determine whether there is an edge between the given Vertices.
 *
 * Preconditions:
 *     Source is not null.
 *     Dest is not null.
 *
 * Postconditions:
 *     The Graph is unchanged.
 *
 * @return true if there is an edge between the vertices and false
 *     otherwise.
 */
public boolean hasEdge( String source, String dest );

/**
 * Get the vertex with the specified name.
 *
 * Preconditions:
 *     None
 *
 * Postconditions:
 *     The graph is unchanged.
 *
 * @param name the name of the vertex.
 *
 * @return a reference to the vertex with the specified name and
 *     null if no such vertex exists.
 */
public Vertex getVertex( String name );

/**
 * Get the edge that connects the specified vertices.
 *
 * Preconditions:
 *     None
 *
 * Postconditions:
 *     The graph is unchanged.
 *
 * @param source the name of the source vertex.
 * @param dest the name of the destination vertex.
 *
 * @return a reference to the edge that connects the specified
 *     vertices and null if the edge does not exist.
 */
public Edge getEdge( String source, String dest );
```

FIGURE 8.18 Specifications for a Graph interface *(continued)*

```
    /**
     * Get all of the vertices in the graph.
     *
     * Preconditions:
     *     None.
     *
     * Postconditions:
     *     The graph is unchanged.
     */
    public Vertex[] getVertices();

    /**
     * Get all of the edges in the graph.
     *
     * Preconditions:
     *     None.
     *
     * Postconditions:
     *     The graph is unchanged.
     */
    public Edge[] getEdges();

} // Graph
```

FIGURE 8.18 Specifications for a Graph interface *(continued)*

Using these building block operations, we can construct any arbitrary graph structure. For example, assuming that G is a graph object that is currently empty and A, B, C, and D are the names of our vertices, then the following sequence of eight operations

```
G.addVertex(A);          // add a new node A
G.addVertex(B);          // add a new node B
G.addVertex(C);          // add a new node C
G.addEdge(B, C, 5);      // connect nodes B and C by an edge of weight 5
G.addEdge(A, B, 2);      // connect nodes A and B by an edge of weight 2
G.addVertex(D);          // now add a new node D
G.addEdge(A, D, 6);      // and link A to it with an edge of weight 6
G.addEdge(B, D, 7);      // and link B to it with an edge of weight 7
```

will produce the following sequence of graphs structures:

1. empty

2. (A)

(continued)

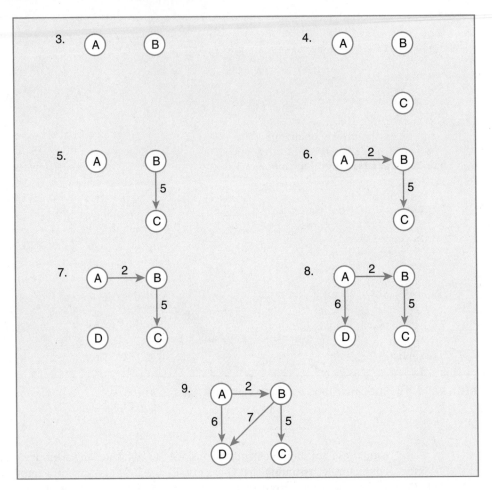

Furthermore, the operations included in the interface of Figure 8.18 can be used to construct both undirected and unweighted graphs. To create an undirected graph, whenever you add an edge from A to B in the graph, you also add an edge from B to A with the same weight:

```
G.addEdge(A, B, 5);     // here is how to create an undirected graph
G.addEdge(B, A, 5);
```

To create an unweighted graph, just omit the cost parameter:

```
G.addEdge(A, B);        // this will create an unweighted edge
```

The cost of the edge from A to B will be set to 0.

The methods contained in the interface of Figure 8.18 are the basic building blocks of graphs. However, the really interesting operations on graphs are not these low-level edge and vertex insertions but the higher level operations that can be carried out using these building blocks. We look at some of these operations in the next three sections.

8.3.2.2 Graph Traversal

One of the most important high-level operations on graphs is a **traversal**, in which we visit every node in the graph exactly once and where *visit* means to carry out some local processing operation on that node. Graph traversals form the underlying basis of many other graph operations. For example, to print the contents of the information field of every node, we traverse the graph and output the value stored in each node as it is visited. To locate a specific key in a graph, we again traverse it, this time comparing the data value stored in the node being visited to our desired key.

The two basic techniques for traversing a graph are the **breadth-first** and the **depth-first** methods. Informally, a breadth-first search means that we visit all the neighbors of a given node before visiting nodes that are not neighbors. Node B is defined as a neighbor of node A if there is an edge connecting A to B. A breadth-first traversal can be viewed as a series of expanding concentric circles in which we visit the closer nodes in circle i before moving on to visit more distant nodes in circle $i + 1$. This view is diagramed in Figure 8.19a. We first visit the three neighbors of the shaded node N—A, B, and C—before moving on to the nonneighbor nodes such as D, E, F, G, H, I, and J.

A depth-first search behaves quite differently. It follows a specific path in the graph as far as it leads. Only when that path has been exhausted (i.e., it dead-ends or cycles back to an earlier node) do we back up and begin to search another path. For example, in Figure 8.19b, we would continue to follow the path ABCD . . . as far as it led, even though there are closer nodes, such as E or F.

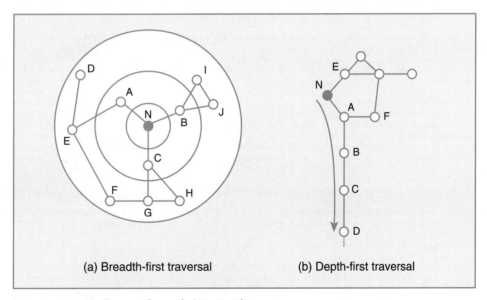

(a) Breadth-first traversal   (b) Depth-first traversal

FIGURE 8.19 Types of graph traversals

There are two issues we must address before we can flesh out the breadth-first traversal algorithm diagrammed in Figure 8.19a more completely. First, a node N may be the neighbor of two or more nodes as in the following:

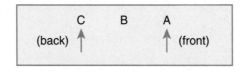

Node N may first have been visited as a neighbor of A. Later, when we visit node B, we do not want to visit its neighbor N again. We solve this problem by **marking** a node. Each vertex N will keep a **status value**, also called a **tag**, that can have one of the following three values:

Tag Value	Meaning
visited	This node has been visited, and its processing has been completed.
waiting	A neighbor of this node has been visited, and this node is currently in line waiting to be visited.
not visited	Neither this node nor any of its neighbors has yet been visited.

All nodes in the graph start in the not visited state. When one of its neighbors is visited, a node goes into the waiting state, and it is placed in a waiting line. When its turn finally comes, it is processed and marked as being in the visited state. By checking the current value of the tag field, we prevent a node from being visited more than once.

Our second concern is the selection of the proper data structure for the collection of nodes that are in the waiting state. A little thought should convince you that this collection is a first-in, first-out queue data structure of the type described in Section 6.4. When traversing the graph of Figure 8.19a, we first visit the shaded node N. We then queue up N's three neighbors A, B, and C and mark them as being in the waiting state. The line of waiting nodes would look like this, assuming we add nodes to the queue in alphabetical order:

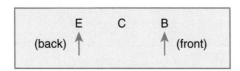

After finishing with node N and marking it as visited, we remove the front node A, visit it, and queue up its neighbors (only E because N has already been visited). The waiting line now holds:

Notice that the new node E has been placed at the end of the line since we must visit all three neighbors of node N before moving on to their neighbors. We now remove node B, visit it, and queue up its two neighbors I and J, producing:

Each time we visit a node, we queue only those neighbors whose status is not visited. If their status is visited, then they have already been processed. If their status is waiting, the node is currently in line, and there is no need to add it to the queue a second time.

A breadth-first graph traversal method called BFSTraverse that utilizes the marking scheme just described is shown in Figure 8.20. The marking of vertices is done using the instance variable tag contained in every Vertex object (see Figure 8.16). The queue of waiting nodes is called waiting, and it is implemented using the LinkedQueue class in Figure 6.42. The actual processing of each individual Vertex object is carried out by the visit() method of the callback object cb that is passed to this method as a parameter.

```
/**
 * Perform a breadth first traversal of the vertices in
 * the given graph starting at the specified node. The
 * call back object is used to process each node as it
 * appears in the traversal.
 *
 * @param g the graph to traverse
 * @param start the vertex where the traversal will start
 * @param cb the object that processes vertices.
 */
public void BFSTraverse( Graph g, Vertex start, Callback cb ) {
    Queue waiting = new LinkedQueue(); // Queue of waiting vertices

    // Ensure the graph has no marked vertices
    Vertex vertices[] = g.getVertices();
    for ( int i = 0; i < vertices.length; i = i + 1 ) {
        vertices[ i ].setTag( false );
    }

    // Put the start vertex in the work queue
    waiting.enqueue( start );

    // While there are waiting vertices
    while ( !waiting.empty() ) {
        // Get the next Vertex
        Vertex curVertex = (Vertex)waiting.front();
        waiting.dequeue();
```
(continued)

FIGURE 8.20 Breadth-first graph traversal method

```
                // If this Vertex hasn't been processed yet
            if ( !curVertex.getTag() ) {
                cb.visit( curVertex ); // Process the vertex
                curVertex.setTag(true); // Mark it as visited

                // Put its unmarked neighbors into the work queue
                Vertex neighbors[] = curVertex.getNeighbors();
                for ( int i = 0; i < neighbors.length; i = i + 1 ) {
                    if ( !neighbors[ i ].getTag() ) {
                        waiting.enqueue( neighbors[ i ] );
                    }
                }
            }
        }
    }
}
```

FIGURE 8.20 Breadth-first graph traversal method *(continued)*

When the algorithm of Figure 8.20 is applied to the following graph G

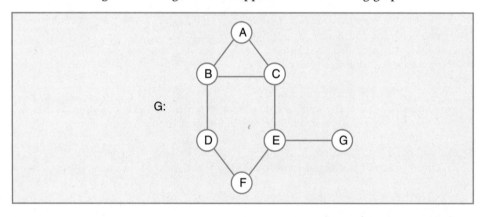

one possible traversal of G, beginning from node A, would be the order ABCDEFG. The actual order in which nodes at the same level in the graph would be processed is dependent on the order in which the vertices are returned by the `getNeighbors()` method.

One of the uses of this breadth-first traversal algorithm is to determine if an undirected graph G is or is not connected; that is, determining if there exists a path from node *i* to node *j* for all *i* and *j*. If the breadth-first search of Figure 8.20 is applied to a connected undirected graph G, then the traversal algorithm will ultimately mark every node in the graph as visited, and G will have been shown to be connected. However, if one or more vertices remain marked as not visited, then the graph is disconnected, and there exist nodes that are unreachable from our starting node.

We could do a second traversal operation starting at any of the unmarked nodes to produce a set of **connected subgraphs**. For example, a traversal of the following six-node graph G beginning at node A

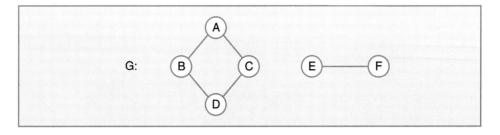

would mark nodes {A, B, C, D} as visited, while leaving E and F marked as not visited. A second breadth-first traversal beginning at either of the unmarked nodes produces the set {E, F}. These are the two connected subgraphs of the graph G.

A depth-first graph traversal is very similar, except that our collection of nodes in the waiting state now must be a last-in, first-out structure (i.e., a stack). Referring to Figure 8.19b, we can see how a depth-first traversal would work, beginning with the solid node N. We would first visit node N and then stack up its two neighbors A and E (again, we are assuming that nodes appear on the stack in alphabetical order):

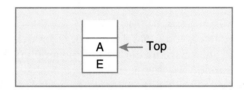

We now pop the stack returning node A, visit that node, and then stack the two neighbors of that node, B and F. The stack now holds:

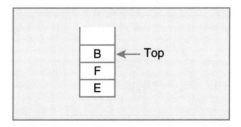

Notice that the most recently added nodes are on top of the stack, and they will be the ones visited next. We pop node B, visit it, and then stack its neighbor C.

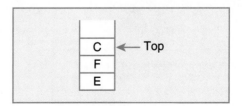

Because we are using a stack instead of a queue, we next visit those nodes that were added most recently, which causes us to continue to follow the current path wherever it may lead. In this case, we keep following the path ABCD . . . in a depth-first fashion until there are no more unmarked nodes on that path. At that point, we pop the stack and start following another path in a depth-first fashion. The new path that we will follow begins at the last node visited in the current path. Given the following graph

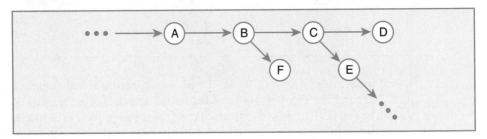

after following path ABCD to its end at D, we will back up to the previous node, C, and begin following the path ABCE. . . .

We leave the implementation of the depth-first graph traversal algorithm just described as an exercise for the reader.

8.3.2.3 Minimum Spanning Trees

Every connected graph G has a subset of edges that connects all its nodes and forms a tree. This is called a **spanning tree** of the graph G. Spanning trees are important because they contain the minimum number of edges, $n - 1$, that leave the n-node graph in a connected state. Think of the process of creating a spanning tree as one of discarding extraneous edges from a graph, extraneous only in the sense that a path between these nodes already exists using other edges.

Figure 8.21b shows a spanning tree T of the connected graph G in Figure 8.21a. Notice that G contains six nodes and eight edges. The spanning tree T contains the same six nodes but only five edges, and it is still connected.

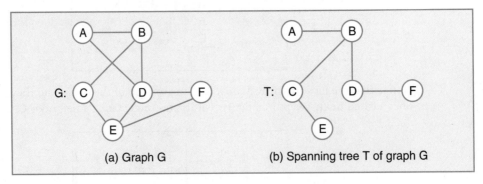

(a) Graph G   (b) Spanning tree T of graph G

FIGURE 8.21 Sample spanning tree

If a graph is unweighted, as in Figure 8.21a, there is a simple way to generate a spanning tree. The traversal algorithms of Section 8.3.2.2 visit every node in a graph exactly once. If there is a cycle and we return to a node via a different edge, we disregard it and do not visit it a second time. Thus, if we save the edges that were used to traverse the graph in either a breadth-first or a depth-first traversal, this set of edges will form a spanning tree of G. For example, given the graph

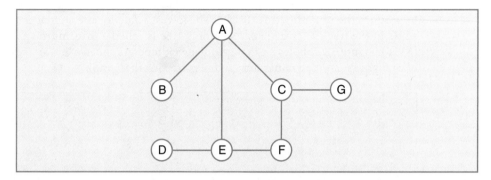

a breadth-first search, beginning at node A and queuing nodes in strict alphabetical order, would visit nodes in the order ABCEFGD, and it would use the six edges <A, B>, <A, C>, <A, E>, <C, F>, <C, G>, and <D, E>. The spanning tree that results, called a **breadth-first spanning tree,** is the following:

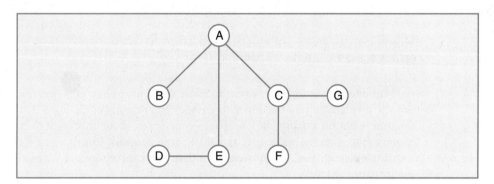

A spanning tree generated by a depth-first traversal is called, appropriately enough, a **depth-first spanning tree**. For the same seven-node graph just shown, a depth-first traversal of G beginning at A would produce the following spanning tree:

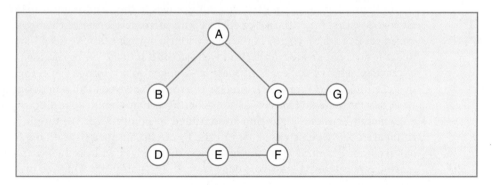

The previous two diagrams show only two of the many different spanning trees that can be constructed from a single graph. The problem becomes more interesting when the edges of the graph are weighted. In an unweighted graph, we do not care which particular spanning tree we produce because they will all have *n* nodes and $(n-1)$ edges of equal weight. This is not the case in a weighted graph. Now we want to produce the spanning tree that has the lowest value for the sum of the costs of all edges in the tree. This particular spanning tree is called a **minimum spanning tree (MST)**. Figure 8.22 shows an example of a weighted graph, an arbitrary spanning tree of that graph, and the minimum spanning tree for that graph.

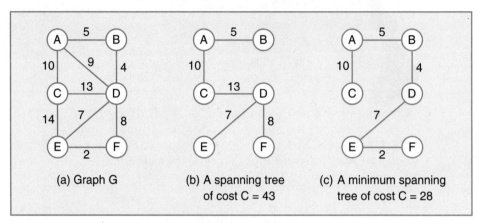

(a) Graph G

(b) A spanning tree of cost C = 43

(c) A minimum spanning tree of cost C = 28

FIGURE 8.22 Minimum spanning trees

Minimum spanning trees occur in many real-life applications because they represent the least costly way to connect the nodes in a graph. For example, how can we interconnect N cities using the cheapest set of roads or airline flights? Given N telephones, how can we make sure that everyone can talk to everyone else using the fewest telephone lines? The answer to both of these questions is to construct the minimum spanning tree.

The best-known technique for building an MST is **Kruskal's algorithm**. It is a **greedy algorithm**, which always selects the locally optimal choice at each step, regardless of whether it may or may not be a globally optimal choice. Essentially, a greedy algorithm always grabs the biggest or best thing currently available.

In Kruskal's algorithm, we keep adding edges to the spanning tree in order of lowest cost. We first order the set of edges E into increasing order of their cost. From this sorted set E of edges, we select the edge with the lowest cost. We keep that edge in the tree if it does not create a cycle, and we reject it if it does. We repeat the process until we have selected $(n-1)$ edges. If these $n-1$ edges do not form a cycle, then they must by definition form a tree that connects the root of the tree to all *n* nodes in the graph.

The seven steps involved in constructing the minimum spanning tree of Figure 8.22c using Kruskal's algorithm are outlined in Figure 8.23. We terminate the algorithm after the seven steps shown in the figure because we have added five edges to our six-node graph. If there are no cycles, these edges will produce a spanning tree. Since we selected the least-cost edge at each decision point, the tree produced must have minimal cost.

The real trick to implementing Kruskal's algorithm is determining whether the addition of an edge to the spanning tree would or would not create a cycle. There is a

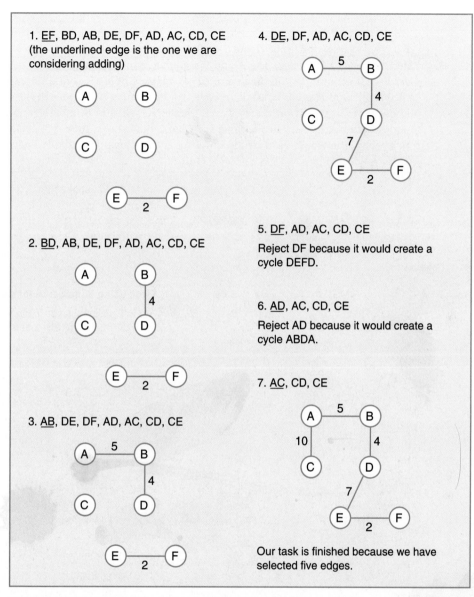

1. EF, BD, AB, DE, DF, AD, AC, CD, CE
(the underlined edge is the one we are
considering adding)

2. BD, AB, DE, DF, AD, AC, CD, CE

3. AB, DE, DF, AD, AC, CD, CE

4. DE, DF, AD, AC, CD, CE

5. DF, AD, AC, CD, CE

Reject DF because it would create a
cycle DEFD.

6. AD, AC, CD, CE

Reject AD because it would create a
cycle ABDA.

7. AC, CD, CE

Our task is finished because we have
selected five edges.

FIGURE 8.23 Using Kruskal's algorithm to produce a minimum spanning tree

very elegant way to implement this step using the set data structure discussed in
Section 8.1. We simply maintain sets of connected subgraphs—that is, sets of nodes
that are connected to each other but not to nodes in other sets.

For example, given the two sets A = {n_1, n_2, . . . } and B = {n_3, n_4, . . . }, all nodes
in set A are connected to each other, and all nodes in set B are connected to each
other, but no node in set A is connected to a node in set B, and no node in set B is
connected to a node in set A. When the algorithm begins, every node is in its own set
because there are no edges in the spanning tree. If we maintain these sets of connected

subgraphs as we insert edges, it is easy to determine if adding an edge to the tree would or would not create a cycle. If an edge connects a node in set A to a node in set B (or vice versa), it cannot create a cycle because these nodes were previously unconnected. Since all nodes in sets A and B are now connected, we reset A to (A ∪ B), discard set B, and repeat the process until we have a single set containing all *n* nodes in the graph. On the other hand, if an edge would connect two nodes in the same set, we know that this would produce a cycle. There must already be a path connecting these nodes because they are in the same set. Figure 8.24 shows how this cycle determination technique would work when building an MST using Kruskal's algorithm.

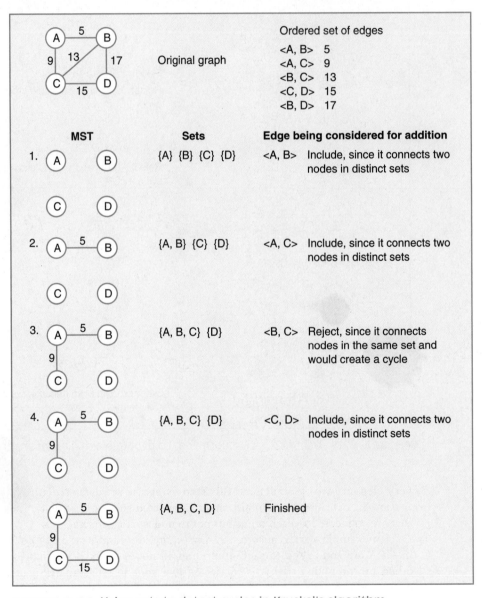

FIGURE 8.24 Using sets to detect cycles in Kruskal's algorithm

A program to implement Kruskal's algorithm, including the use of sets to detect cycles, is shown in Figure 8.25. It uses a number of the data structures discussed in this and previous chapters. For example, it uses the set called curSet to hold the names of vertices that are contained within a single connected subgraph. It then creates a linked list named vertexSets to store all connected subgraphs. Finally, it uses a heap structure called edges to hold our collection of edge objects so that we can quickly access (via getSmallest) the one edge with the lowest cost. This is a beautiful example of how important it is to have a solid familiarity with a range of data structures to create elegant and efficient solutions to important problems.

```
/**
 * Use Kruskal's algorithm to create a minimum spanning tree
 * for the given graph. The MST is returned in the form of a
 * graph.
 *
 * @param g the graph from which to generate the MST
 *
 * @return a graph containing the vertices of g and the
 *     edges necessary to form a minimum spanning tree.
 */
public Graph kruskalMST( Graph g ) {
    Graph mst = new LinkedGraph();        // The graph will have the MST
    Vertex vertices[] = g.getVertices(); // All the vertices
    List vertexSets = new LinkedList();   // List of vertex sets

    // Add the vertices in the original graph to mst
    // and create the vertex sets at the same time
    for ( int i = 0; i < vertices.length; i = i + 1 ) {
        String curName = vertices[ i ].getName();
        Set curSet = new ArrayBasedSet();

        // Add the name of the current vertex to its set and then
        // add the set to the list that contains the vertex sets
        curSet.add( curName );
        vertexSets.add( curSet );

        // Add the current vertex to the MST graph
        mst.addVertex( curName );
    }

    // Put the edges into a heap which effectively sorts them
    Heap edges = new ArrayBasedHeap();
    Edge allEdges[] = g.getEdges();
    for ( int i = 0; i < allEdges.length; i = i + 1 ) {
        edges.insertHeapNode( allEdges[ i ] );
    }
```

(continued)

FIGURE 8.25 Kruskal's algorithm

```
    // Setup is complete - run the algorithm

    // There is more than one set left in the list vertex sets

    while ( vertexSets.size() > 1 ) {
       // Get the smallest edge
       Edge cur = (Edge)edges.getSmallest();

       // Find the sets where these vertices are located
       int sourcePos = findSet( vertexSets, cur.getSource().getName() );
       int destPos = findSet( vertexSets, cur.getDest().getName() );

       // If the vertices are in different sets - add the edge to
       // the MST
       if ( sourcePos != destPos ) {
          Set sourceSet = (Set)vertexSets.get( sourcePos );
          Set destSet = (Set)vertexSets.get( destPos );

          // Add the edge to the MST
          mst.addEdge( cur.getSource().getName(),
                       cur.getDest().getName(),
                       cur.getCost() );

          // Merge the sets
          sourceSet.union( destSet );
          vertexSets.remove( destPos );
       }
    }

    // The MST can be read from this graph
    return mst;
}

/**
 * Return the position of the first set in the list that
 * contains the specified name.
 *
 * @param vertexSets a list of sets to search.
 * @param name the name being searched for.
 *
 * @return the position of the first set in the list that contains
 *     the name or -1 if the name cannot be found.
 */

private int findSet( List vertexSets, String name ) {
    int retVal = -1;
```

FIGURE 8.25 Kruskal's algorithm *(continued)*

```
   // Step through the list and examine each set. Stop when you
   // find a set with the name or we fall off the list
   for ( int i = 0; retVal == -1 && i < vertexSets.size(); i = i + 1 ) {
      Set curSet = (Set)vertexSets.get( i );

      // Does the current set contain the name we are looking for?
      if ( curSet.contains( name ) ) {
         retVal = i;
      }
   }

   // Return the position of the set
   return retVal;
}
```

FIGURE 8.25 Kruskal's algorithm *(continued)*

8.3.2.4 Shortest Paths

The final high-level graph operation we will investigate is the **shortest path** problem. We are given a weighted graph G and any two nodes in G: n_i, the **source**, and n_j, the **destination**. We want to identify the path from n_i to n_j with the minimal value for the sum of the weights of all edges in the path. That is, we want to determine the path $P = (n_i\, n_{i+1}\, n_{i+2} \ldots n_{j-1}n_j)$ having the following property:

$$P = \min \left[\sum_{k=i}^{j-1} \text{getCost}(< n_k, n_{k+1} >) \right] \qquad \text{where getCost(e) returns the cost of edge e}$$

Note that we are explicitly concerned about finding the shortest path, not simply any path. To determine the latter, we could build a spanning tree rooted at the source node. If the source and destination nodes are connected, then the destination will be a node in the spanning tree, and there will be a unique path from the root to that node. However, we cannot guarantee that this path will have minimal weight. Looking at Figure 8.22a, the shortest path from C to F is CEF with a cost of 16 units (14 + 2). However, the minimum spanning tree of Figure 8.22c produces the path CABDEF with a total cost of 28 units, almost double the least-cost path.

Determining shortest paths is an important real-world problem when managing large-scale computer networks such as the Internet. When an email message or a Web page is transmitted from one machine to another, the network must determine the path that this message will take. Ideally, it should be as close as possible to the optimal (i.e., shortest) path possible. Thus, Internet routing is nothing more than determining shortest paths between two computers in a connected network, and it uses techniques very similar to those we will be describing. (In fact, the Internet routing algorithm currently in use around the world is called OSPF, for Open Shortest Path First.)

The algorithm we will use to determine the shortest path was developed by Edsgar Dijkstra, and it is called, appropriately, **Dijkstra's algorithm**. Instead of determining the shortest path from a single source node n_i to a single destination node n_j, Dijkstra's algorithm determines the cost of the shortest path from a source node n_i to all other nodes in the graph.

The algorithm operates by dividing the N nodes of the graph G into two disjoint sets: a set S, which contains those nodes for which we have determined the shortest path, and a set U, which contains those nodes for which we have not yet determined the shortest path. These two sets are initialized to the values S = $\{n_i\}$, the source node (since the shortest path to yourself always has cost 0), and U = {all nodes in G except the source node n_i}. We also maintain a data structure called the **cost list**, written as C[j], which represents the cost of reaching node j, $j \in$ U, only going through nodes currently in S. Informally, C[j] represents the cost of reaching out from the current set of shortest path nodes and visiting a node for which we have not yet determined the shortest path. Figure 8.26 shows the relationship among S, U, and C[j]. At the point in the algorithm diagramed in Figure 8.26, we have determined the shortest path from source node 1 to nodes 1 and 2, but we have not yet determined the shortest path from source node 1 to node 3, 4, or 5. The cost to reach node 3, 4, or 5 from source node 1, traversing only nodes 1 and/or 2, is C[3], C[4], and C[5], respectively.

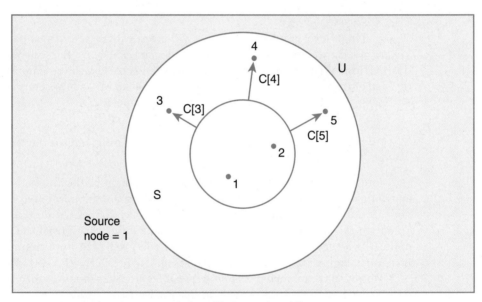

FIGURE 8.26 Basic concepts in Dijkstra's algorithm

The basic idea behind Dijkstra's algorithm is to use a greedy technique similar to Kruskal's algorithm. At each step, we select a single node n_i from set U, determine the shortest path to it, and place it in S. We repeat this operation until all nodes are in set S and set U is empty. The algorithm then terminates.

The node we select at each step is the one that will cost us the least to reach from the current set S. This is the node k, $k \in$ U with the minimum value of C[k].

Step 1: Determine the minimal value C[k], for $k \in$ U.
  Remove node k from the set U.
  Place node k in set S.

After finishing step 1, we update the cost list C, since we have added a new node k to S.

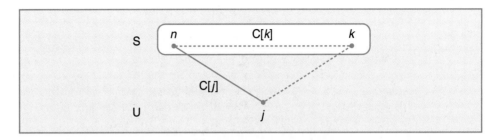

Previously, the cost of reaching node j, $j \in U$, from only nodes in S was $C[j]$—the solid line. Now that we added node k to S, it may be cheaper to go from node n to our new node k and then directly out to j—the dotted line. The cost of this new path will be $[C[k] + \text{EdgeCost}(k, j)]$, where $\text{EdgeCost}(k, j)$ is the cost of the edge connecting nodes k and j or infinity if no such edge exists. We are essentially determining whether the addition of node k to the set S has created a new shortest path to other nodes outside S.

Step 2: set $C[j] = \min(C[j], C[k] + \text{EdgeCost}(k, j))$ for all $j \in U$

This two-step process iterates until all nodes are in S and U is empty.

Figure 8.27 shows the application of this updating process to a five-node graph G using node 1 as the source node.

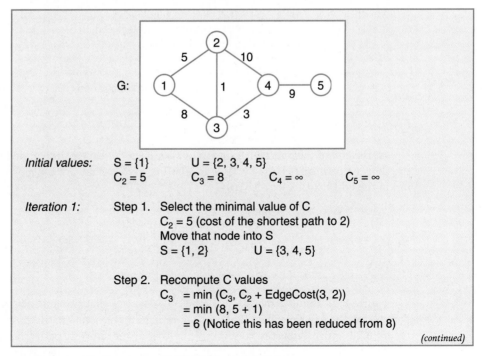

Initial values: $S = \{1\}$ $U = \{2, 3, 4, 5\}$
                      $C_2 = 5$ $C_3 = 8$ $C_4 = \infty$ $C_5 = \infty$

Iteration 1:   Step 1. Select the minimal value of C
                              $C_2 = 5$ (cost of the shortest path to 2)
                              Move that node into S
                              $S = \{1, 2\}$ $U = \{3, 4, 5\}$

                Step 2. Recompute C values
                              C_3 $= \min(C_3, C_2 + \text{EdgeCost}(3, 2))$
                                    $= \min(8, 5 + 1)$
                                    $= 6$ (Notice this has been reduced from 8)

(continued)

FIGURE 8.27 Example of Dijkstra's algorithm

$$C_4 = \min (\infty, 5 + 10)$$
$$= 15 \text{ (Notice this has been reduced from } \infty\text{)}$$

$$C_5 = \min (\infty, 5 + \infty)$$
$$= \infty \text{ (No change here)}$$

Iteration 2:   Step 1. Select the minimal value of C
$$C_3 = 6 \text{ (cost of the shortest path to 3)}$$
Move that node into S
$$S = \{1, 2, 3\} \qquad U = \{4, 5\}$$

Step 2. Recompute C values
$$C_4 = \min (15, 6 + 3)$$
$$= 9 \text{ (We have lowered it a second time)}$$

$$C_5 = \min (\infty, 6 + \infty)$$
$$= \infty$$

Iteration 3:   Step 1. Select the minimal value of C
$$C_4 = 9 \text{ (cost of the shortest path to 4)}$$
Move that node into S
$$S = \{1, 2, 3, 4\} \qquad U = \{5\}$$

Step 2. Recompute C values
$$C_5 = \min (\infty, 9 + 9)$$
$$= 18 \text{ (We have reduced it from infinity)}$$

Iteration 4:   Step 1. Select minimal value of C
$$C_5 = 18 \text{ (cost of the shortest path to 5)}$$
Move that node into S
$$S = \{1, 2, 3, 4, 5\} \qquad U = \{ \}$$

Step 2. U is now empty, and we are finished

FIGURE 8.27 Example of Dijkstra's algorithm *(continued)*

At the end of the operations shown in Figure 8.27, we have determined the cost of the shortest path from source node 1 to all other nodes. They are the most recent values in the cost list C.

Node	Shortest Path Cost C[j]
2	5
3	6
4	9
5	18

Figure 8.28 shows a method called `dijkstraSP()` that implements the shortest path technique just described. Rather than returning the actual path, the algorithm in Figure 8.28 returns an array containing the cost of the shortest path from the source node to all other nodes. We leave it as an exercise to make the necessary changes so the algorithm returns a list of the actual nodes contained in the shortest path.

```
/**
 * Perform Dijkstra's Shortest Path algorithm on the given graph,
 * starting at the given vertex.
 *
 * @param g the Graph to traverse.
 * @param name the name of the vertex where the traversal starts.
 *
 * @return an array containing vertex path costs.
 */
public int[] dijkstraSP( Graph g, String name ) {
    Set u = new ArrayBasedSet();      // Names for which best path is not known
    Set s = new ArrayBasedSet();      // Names for which best path is known
    Vertex v[] = g.getVertices();     // All of the vertices in the graph
    Vertex start = g.getVertex( name ); // The starting vertex
    int c[] = new int[ v.length ];       // Lowest costs so far
    Edge curEdge = null;                  // Temporary edge used in loops
    Heap names = new ArrayBasedHeap();   // Used to sort vertices by name

    // Sort the vertices by name so that the costs will
    // appear in order by name
    for ( int i = 0; i < v.length; i = i + 1 ) { // Building phase
        names.insertHeapNode( v[ i ].getName() );
    }
    for ( int i = 0; !names.empty(); i = i + 1 ) { // Removing phase
        v[ i ] = g.getVertex( (String)names.getSmallest() );
    }

    // We "know" the shortest path to the source
    s.add( name );

    // For each vertex, compute the starting cost
    for ( int i = 0; i < v.length; i = i + 1 ) {
        // If this isn't the start node
        if ( !v[ i ].getName().equals( name ) ) {
            // Put it in the unknown set
            u.add( v[ i ].getName() );

            // Compute the initial cost to reach this Vertex
            curEdge = start.getEdge( v[ i ].getName() );

            if ( curEdge != null ) {
                c[ i ] = curEdge.getCost();
            } else {
                // This Vertex is currently unreachable
                c[ i ] = Integer.MAX_VALUE;
            }
        } else {
            // It costs 0 to get to the start vertex
            c[ i ] = 0;
        }
    }
```

(continued)

FIGURE 8.28 Dijkstra's shortest path algorithm

```
// Set is complete - run the algorithm until all of
// the paths are known

while ( !u.isEmpty() ) {
    // Find the position of the lowest-cost unknown node
    int min = Integer.MAX_VALUE;
    int minPos = -1;
    for ( int i = 0; minPos == -1 && i < c.length; i = i + 1 ) {
        if ( c[ i ] < min && u.contains( v[ i ].getName() ) ) {
            min = c[ i ];
            minPos = i;
        }
    }

    // We know the shortest path to the vertex
    s.add( v[ minPos ].getName() );
    u.remove( v[ minPos ].getName() );

    // Update the costs based
    for ( int i = 0; i < c.length; i = i + 1 ) {
        // Get the edge between the new shortest and the
        // current node in the array
        curEdge = v[ minPos ].getEdge( v[ i ].getName() );

        // If there is an edge
        if ( curEdge != null ) {
            // If going through the new node is better than
            // what has been seen update the cost
            if ( c[ i ] > c[ minPos ] + curEdge.getCost() ) {
                c[ i ] = c[ minPos ] + curEdge.getCost();
            }
        }
    }
}

return c;
}
```

FIGURE 8.28 Dijkstra's shortest path algorithm *(continued)*

It is not always the case that a greedy algorithm produces an optimal solution. To prove that Dijkstra's algorithm does indeed produce the shortest path, we must examine the following diagram:

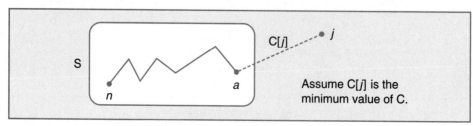

Assume that C[*j*] is the minimal value contained in cost list C. Assume that the shortest path to node *j* from the source node *n* wanders around nodes inside S, eventually reaching some node *a*. The cost of this wandering is C[*a*]. From there, the path goes out from S directly to node *j*. We claim that this path, which we will write *n* . . . *a* . . . *j*, is the lowest cost path.

By definition, this path is the lowest cost path containing only nodes in S, as this is the definition of C, and we selected the minimum entry C[*j*]. If it is not the overall shortest path to *j*, then there must be at least one node *b* ∉ S on that other path:

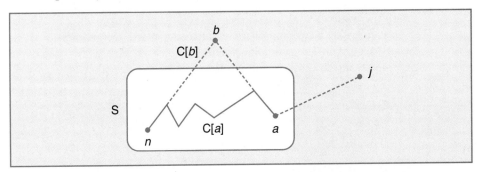

Now the proposed shortest path from *n* to *j* will wander around nodes in S, but eventually, it will go outside S to some node *b* ∈ U. The cost of going from *n* to *b* via nodes within S is C[*b*]. However, since node *a* ∈ S and node *b* ∉ S, we know that C[*a*] < C[*b*] because nodes are being added to S in strict increasing order of their cost in the cost list C. Therefore, the cost of path *n* . . . *a* must be less than the cost of the path *n* . . . *b* . . . *a*, and the path *n* . . . *a* . . . *j* must be lower in cost than the path *n* . . . *b* . . . *a* . . . *j*. Thus, Dijkstra's algorithm does indeed produce the shortest path.

It is easy to show that Dijkstra's algorithm is $O(N^2)$, where N is the number of nodes in the graph. In each iteration of the algorithm, we move one node from the set U to the set S. Originally, there are (N − 1) nodes in U, so repeating the algorithm until U is empty requires O(N) steps. During each iteration, we must locate the minimum value in the cost list C and recompute all values in C. The length of C is originally (N − 1) and decreases by 1 after each iteration. The number of steps required to find a minimum of N elements and to recompute a new value for N elements is obviously O(N), resulting in an $O(N^2)$ algorithm.

◆ 8.3.3 Implementation

8.3.3.1 The Adjacency Matrix Representation

There are two popular techniques for representing graph structures: the **adjacency matrix** and the **adjacency list**. This section looks at the first of these two approaches.

Assume that the N nodes in graph G are uniquely numbered 0, . . . , N − 1. An adjacency matrix represents the graph using an N × N two-dimensional array M of Boolean values, as shown in the following:

```
private static final int MAX = . . . ;   // the maximum size of the
                                          //    matrix

private boolean M[MAX] [MAX];             // the adjacency matrix itself
```

```
private int N;                    // the actual number of nodes
                                  //    in M. 0 ≤ N ≤ MAX
```

If M(x, y) = true, there is a directed edge from node x to node y, $0 \le x, y \le N$. If M(x, y) = false, there is no edge. The amount of space needed to represent G is $O(MAX^2)$.

If the graph is undirected, then M(x, y) = M(y, x) for all x, y, and we need to store only the upper or lower triangular portion of the adjacency matrix. If the edges are weighted, we can implement the graph as a two-dimensional array of real numbers, with the value M[i, j] representing the weight of the edge <i, j>.

Figure 8.29 is an example of an adjacency matrix representation of an undirected weighted graph. The symbol ∞ stands for some extremely large positive number, and represents infinite cost. It is used to encode the absence of an edge between two nodes.

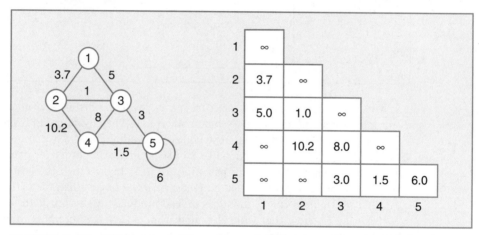

FIGURE 8.29 Adjacency matrix representation of an undirected weighted graph

An adjacency matrix representation makes sense only if a graph is **dense**—that is, if it contains a large percentage of the N^2 edges that can theoretically exist in a graph with N vertices. However, if a graph is **sparse** and contains something closer to the minimum number of edges in a connected graph, namely, (N − 1), the adjacency matrix will be quite empty, with only about 1/Nth of its cells having values other than ∞. For example, in a directed graph with 30 nodes, the 30 × 30 adjacency matrix representation would require 900 cells; however, the graph could be connected with as few as 29 edges, leaving 871 cells unused.

The basic operations of inserting and deleting an edge are particularly easy to implement using the adjacency matrix representation because of the random access property of arrays. To add an edge from node *i* to node *j*, we simply say

　　`M[i, j]` = true (or `M[i, j]` = r for some real value *r* if the graph is weighted)

which takes O(1) time. Deletion of an edge is virtually identical

　　`M[i, j]` = false (or `M[i, j]` = ∞ if it is a weighted graph)

which is also O(1).

Adding a new node to a graph involves incrementing the value of N, the number of nodes in G, and setting all the entries in both row N and column N of the matrix to false or ∞. Because of the fixed size restriction on arrays, this operation can fail if N = MAX − 1. In that case, there is no room for another node, and we must resize and copy the entire array into a newer, larger structure.

When deleting a node, we must not only mark node *i* as deleted, but we must also locate all edges connected to node *i* and remove them from the matrix This involves traversing both row *i* and column *i* of M, looking for any edge that either begins or ends at node *i* and setting it to false (or to ∞ if the graph is weighted).

```
// deleting node i
for (k = 0; k < N; k++) {
        M(i, k) = false;
        M(k, i) = false;
}
```

This is an O(N) operation.

8.3.3.2 The Adjacency List Representation

A potentially more space-efficient method for representing graphs is the **adjacency list**. With this technique, we first create an N-element, one-dimensional array A[MAX], where MAX is the maximum number of nodes in the graph. This is called the **node list**. Each element A[*i*] in the node list is the head of a linked list of all the neighbors of node *i*—that is, all nodes connected to node *i* by an edge in the graph. This is called a **neighbor list**, and each entry in a neighbor list is a **neighbor node**. For example, if the neighbor list beginning at the entry A[3] includes the value 5, there is a directed edge from node 3 to node 5. If the edge is undirected, then there will be a separate entry in the neighbor list pointed at by A[5] that includes the value 3.

Referring back to the five-node graph G in Figure 8.29, the adjacency list representation of G, excluding the weight field, would be:

Node	Neighbor List
1	2 → 3
2	1 → 3 → 4
3	1 → 2 → 4 → 5
4	2 → 3 → 5
5	3 → 4 → 5

It is easy to include the concept of weighting in an adjacency list. We make the elements in the neighbor list 2-tuples of the form (node number, weight). Now the weighted graph G of Figure 8.29 would be represented as follows:

Node	Neighbor List
1	(2, 3.7) → (3, 5.0)
2	(1, 3.7) → (3, 1.0) → (4, 10.2)

(continued)

Node	Neighbor List
3	(1, 5.0) → (2, 1.0) → (4, 8.0) → (5, 3.0)
4	(2, 10.2) → (3, 8.0) → (5, 1.5)
5	(3, 3.0) → (4, 1.5) → (5, 6.0)

An adjacency list can be implemented using an array of references to objects of type `Neighbor`. Each `Neighbor` object contains a node identifier, a weight field (optional), and a reference to another node.

```
private static final int MAX = . . . ;   // Maximum number of nodes
public class Neighbor {
        private int nodeID;               // The node number
        private float edgeWeight;         // Weight associated with this
                                          //    edge
        private Neighbor next;            // Next node in the neighbor
                                          //    list
                                          // Public accessors and
        . . .                             //    mutators here
}

private Neighbor A[MAX];                  // The node list
```

Using these declarations, the directed graph of Figure 8.29 would be represented as shown in Figure 8.30. (This figure does not show the edge weights.)

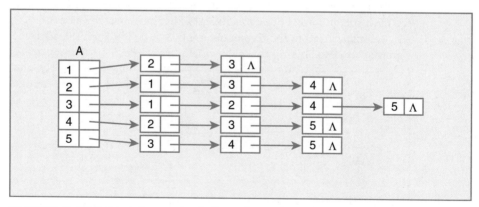

FIGURE 8.30 Internal representation of graphs using adjacency lists

In a directed unweighted graph containing N nodes and E edges, there is one integer and one reference for each of the entries in the node list and one integer (the node ID) and one reference (next) for each edge E—two if the edges are undirected. If both an `int` and a reference require 4 bytes, then the amount of space needed for the adjacency list representation of a directed unweighted graph G is:

total space = space for the node list + space for the neighbor list nodes
$$= (4 + 4) * N + (4 + 4) * E = 8N + 8E$$
$$= O(N + E)$$

This compares with the $O(N^2)$ cells required by the adjacency matrix technique.

Figure 8.31 compares the memory space needed by these two techniques to represent a directed unweighted graph G with N = 50 nodes, as the number of edges E varies from 49 to 2,500, the minimum and maximum for a connected graph. It does not include any space required by a weight field, and it assumes that the number of bytes needed to store both a node identifier and a reference variable is 4.

	Space Required (in Bytes) for a Graph with N = 50 Nodes		
	Edges	Adjacency Matrix	Adjacency List
(minimum)	49	10,000	792
	100	10,000	1,200
	250	10,000	2,400
	500	10,000	4,400
	1,000	10,000	8,400
	1,200	10,000	10,000
	1,500	10,000	12,400
	2,000	10,000	16,400
(maximum)	2,500	10,000	20,400

FIGURE 8.31 Comparison of the space needs of two graph representation techniques

For graphs with fewer than 1,200 edges, the adjacency list is a more compact representation. For the smallest connected graph, E = 49, there is a space savings of 92 percent, an enormous reduction. As the graph becomes denser, the adjacency matrix technique eventually becomes superior as we no longer need to allocate space for the large number of references required by the adjacency list representation. Although the cutoff points will change for different graph sizes and graph types, the basic conclusions about the space efficiency of these two techniques remain the same.

Assume that our node list is an array that can be accessed in O(1) time. The operations of adding and removing an edge both need to search the linked list of neighbor nodes referenced by that element in the node list. (When adding, we need to search the list to make sure that the edge is not already there.) On average, each neighbor list will contain E/N nodes, and the insert and delete edge operations will be O(E/N) using the adjacency list method.

To delete a node i, we first set A[i] to Λ. This will eliminate every edge for which node i is the head node of the edge. However, we must also delete every edge for which node i is the tail. This involves a search of every neighbor list in the table, which requires O(E) time, where E is the total number of edges in the graph. For example, referring to Figure 8.30, to delete node 1, we not only must set A[1] to Λ, but we must also remove the entries for (2, 1) and (3, 1) contained in the neighbor lists of nodes 2 and 3, respectively.

Finally, to delete edge <m, n> from a graph, we must search the neighbor list referenced by A[m] looking for an entry in the neighbor list containing the node identifier n. This will require O(E/N) time.

Figure 8.32 summarizes the time complexities of the basic insertion and deletion operations using the adjacency matrix and adjacency list representations. In a sparse graph, where $E \approx N$, the two methods are generally comparable in run time. Given the space savings that can accrue from the adjacency list method, this becomes the technique of choice. However, as the graph gets denser, $E \approx N^2$, and the adjacency list implementation performs more poorly than the adjacency matrix method as well as using more space. In this situation, the adjacency matrix method is definitely the technique of choice.

Operation	Adjacency Matrix	Adjacency List
insert node	O(1)	O(E/N)
insert edge	O(1)	O(E/N)
delete node	O(N)	O(E)
delete edge	O(1)	O(E/N)

FIGURE 8.32 Time complexities of insertions and deletions

An analysis of the run times of graph algorithms often depends on which implementation technique represents the graph internally. For example, the breadth-first traversal algorithm in Figure 8.20 has an outer while loop that is executed N times, since we must visit all N vertices in the graph before we are finished. Within this outer loop, the critical operation is an inner loop that locates all the neighbors of a given vertex and checks their status. If we are using adjacency matrices to represent a graph, this will require us to examine all N elements in row y of the adjacency matrix looking for every occurrence of the value true. This takes O(N) time. Coupled with the N repetitions of the outer loop, the complexity of a breadth-first graph traversal algorithm implemented with adjacency matrices is $O(N^2)$.

Using adjacency lists, the number of edges contained in each of the N linked lists is approximately E/N. Since we must search this list each time we execute the outer loop of the algorithm in Figure 8.19, the complexity of a breadth-first traversal using adjacency lists is N * (E/N) = O(E). If the graph is dense, then $E \approx N^2$, and the two methods take roughly the same time. In sparse graphs, $E \approx N$, and the complexity is closer to O(N), a significant improvement.

8.4 SUMMARY

This completes our discussion of the four types of data structures: linear, hierarchical, sets, and graphs. Of course, the subject of data structures is enormous, and there are a large number of advanced topics that were not covered: frequency-ordered lists, indexed lists, AVL trees, red-black trees, B-trees, bags, and multigraphs, to name just a few. Many of these structures will be studied in future computer science courses.

One of the most important trends in modern software development is the rapid growth of "data structure libraries." For many of the data structures we have looked at, it is completely unnecessary to develop your own code from scratch. Instead, you import and reuse existing code from a standard library. In Java, this library of standard data structures is called the Java Collection Framework, and the next chapter will introduce you to this important set of packages and classes. It will show that many of the data structures discussed in Chapters 6 through 8 already exist and are available to the Java programmer. It will also show how to extend the Java Collection Framework using inheritance and polymorphism to construct new data structures not yet included. This type of code reuse and class extensions are fundamental characteristics of modern software development.

EXERCISES

1. Given the following four sets

   $A = \{5, 10, 15, 20\}$ $\quad$ $C = \{6, 8, 10\}$

   $B = \{1, 2, 3, 4, 5\}$ $\quad$ $D = \{\}$

   what is the result of performing each of the following set operations?

   a. $A \cup B$

   b. $A \cup C$

   c. $A \cup D$

   d. $A \cap B$

   e. $A \cap D$

   f. $B \cap C$

   g. $A - B$

   h. $B - A$

   i. `D.isEmpty()`

   j. `C.contains (6)`

   k. `D.contains (0)`

   l. `A.subset (B)`

2. Define the calling sequence and pre- and postconditions for a new set operation called `nIntersection()`, for nonintersection. This operation produces a new set containing only those elements that are either in set S_1 or in set S_2 but not in both. Using the Venn diagrams of Section 8.1.1, this operation produces a new set containing only the values in the shaded area shown:

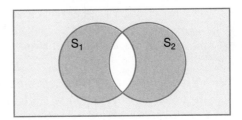

Was this operation really necessary? That is, could the operation have been defined in terms of the methods contained in the `Set` interface of Figure 8.1?

3. How would you revise the intersection method in Figure 8.3 if the elements of the two sets S_1 and S_2 were integer objects sorted into ascending order? What is the time complexity of this newly revised method?

4. Assume our set is implemented as a linked list using the following declarations:

```
public class SetNode { // the class representing the nodes in the
                       // linked list
private Object info;
private SetNode next;
}
private SetNode head;   // pointer to the first element of this set
```

In addition, assume that the class includes the standard accessor and mutator methods getInfo(), getNext(), setInfo(), and setNext(). Implement the union and difference operations contained in the Set interface of Figure 8.1.

5. Assume that we used a bit vector implementation for sets over the base type [0 . . . 10]. Given the declaration for the bit vector array, show the internal representation of each of the following sets using this array.

   a. {2, 4, 6, 8}   c. {}
   b. {0, 1, 2, 3, 4, 6, 7, 8, 9, 10}   d. {1, 2}

6. Write the bit vector implementation of the Set interface in Figure 8.1. Include the implementation of all 10 methods in this interface.

7. Using the same hashing function shown in Figures 8.9a and 8.9b, where would the information on Tymann be stored in the hash table? What about Schneider?

8. The keys that you want to store in a 50-element hash table are words exactly five characters in length: $c_1c_2c_3c_4c_5$. Assume you are using the following hashing function:

$$f = \left[\sum_{i=1}^{5}(a * \mathrm{intValue}(c_i))\right] \% \, 50 \qquad \text{where intValue(ci) returns the integer Unicode value of the character } c_i$$

Select a large prime value for a and test how well your hashing function works on a selection of 1,000 random five-letter sequences. Does it scatter reasonably well over the 50 slots in your hash table? If not, choose another value for a and see if it works better. What happens when you choose a = 2? (Note: If you have had an elementary course in statistics, you can use a chi-square goodness of fit test to formally test the scattering ability of function f. If you do not know this test, then just eyeball the results.)

9. a. Given a hash table of size N = 8, with indexes running from 0 to 7, show where the following keys would be stored using hashing, open addressing, and a step size of c = 1. That is, if there is a collision, search sequentially for the next available slot. Assume that the hash function is just the ordinal position of the letter in the alphabet modulo 8—that is, f(a) = 0, f(b) = 1, . . . , f(h) = 7, f(i) = 0).

   d, e, l, t, g, h, q

b. Repeat the same operations, but this time using a step size of c = 3.

c. Why must the step size c be relatively prime with the table size N? Show what would happen in part b if we had selected a step size of c = 4.

10. Assume a hash table size of N = 50,000. After approximately how many insertion operations (with no deletions) will retrieval using hashing and open addressing display about the same performance, in terms of the worst-case number of comparisons, as binary search? How about sequential search?

11. One of the major problems with open addressing is the issue of deletions. We cannot simply delete entries in a hash table that uses open addressing for collision resolution.

a. Show exactly what happens with a 10-element integer hash table h, open addressing, and the following hash function

f(key) = (key % 10)

when we execute the following five operations, one right after the other:

(1) insert the value 10

(2) insert the value 20

(3) insert the value 30

(4) delete the value 20

(5) retrieve the value 30

Explain exactly what happened.

b. Is there any way that we can solve the problem? If so, describe your solution and implement the modified delete operation that you have designed.

12. Using the data and hash function from Exercise 9a and a table size of N = 8, show what the hash table will look like after insertion of those same seven letters if we are using the collision resolution technique called chaining.

13. Assume we are using chaining and want to store approximately 1,000 keys into our hash table. About how large should we make the hash table so that the average number of comparisons needed to retrieve any given key is approximately four? How much extra space is required for the table as well as the 1,000 keys compared to keeping the 1,000 keys in an array? Disregard the value field and assume that each object requires 4 bytes.

14. Given the dictionary analysis of Figure 8.14, what would be the average number of comparisons to perform a retrieval if we were using chaining and could increase the size of our hash table to N = 60,000? How much extra memory is required? Do you think this is a beneficial thing to do? Explain why or why not.

15. Implement a variation on the chaining method in which each entry in the hash table is a reference to the root of a binary search tree like those discussed in Section 7.4. This binary search tree contains all of the (key, value) entries that hashed to this location. The structure of a hash table H would resemble the following:

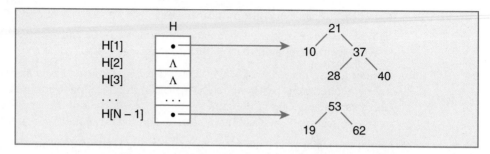

Design and implement a Java class that implements the `Table` interface of Figure 8.5 using this variation of the chaining method.

16. Given the following unweighted directed graph

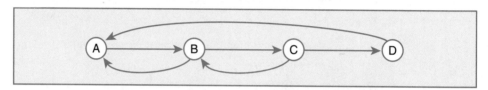

list its nodes, edges, and cycles. Why is the weighted directed graph considered the most general of all the different graph types?

17. Given the following weighted, undirected graph

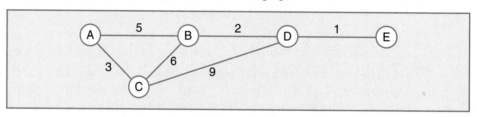

identify all the simple paths from A to E. What is the shortest path?

18. Is the following graph connected or disconnected? Explain your answer.

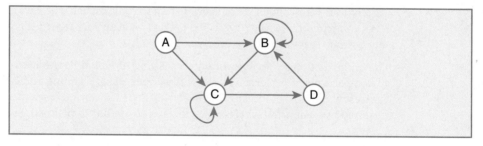

19. What graph structure results from the following sequence of basic operations, assuming that G is initially empty?

```
G.addVertex(A)
G.addVertex(B)
G.addVertex(C)
```

```
G.addVertex(D)
G.addEdge(A, B, 1)
G.addEdge(B, C, 1)
G.addEdge(C, D, 2)
```

20. What is wrong with the following pair of graph operations?

```
G.addEdge(A, B, 1)
G.addEdge(A, B, 5)
```

21. a. In exactly what order would the nodes in the following graph

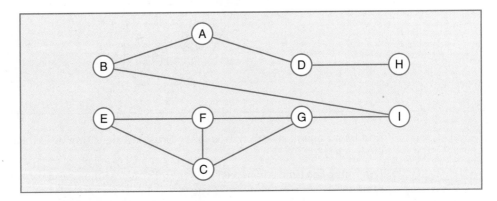

be visited using a breadth-first traversal beginning at node C? What if we began from node I? (Assume that nodes are queued in strict alphabetical order.)

b. Repeat the same questions from part a but this time using a depth-first traversal.

22. Design and implement an instance method that determines, for a given graph G, the total number of connected subgraphs within G. For example, given the following three graphs

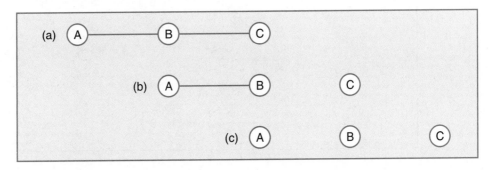

your method would output the values 1, 2, and 3, respectively. You may use the breadth-first traversal method of Figure 8.20 in your solution.

23. Design and implement an instance method that, for a given graph G, performs a depth-first traversal of the nodes of G.

24. Using the nine-node graph diagramed in Exercise 21, determine the following:

    a. a breadth-first spanning tree rooted at node B

    b a depth-first spanning tree rooted at node C

25. a. Given the following weighted undirected graph

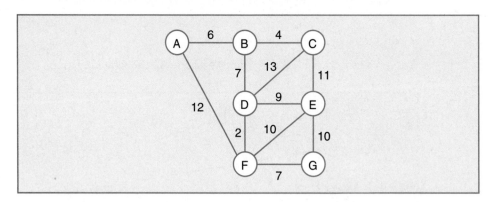

    find its minimum spanning tree using Kruskal's algorithm described in Section 8.3.2.3.

    b. Determine the time complexity of Kruskal's algorithm in terms of the number of nodes, N, and the number of edges, E.

26. Using the weighted graph of Exercise 25, what is the shortest path from node A to node E? From node B to node G? Determine the cost of the shortest path from node A to all other nodes using Dijkstra's algorithm.

27. Modify Dijkstra's algorithm in Figure 8.28 so that it prints the edges contained in the shortest path as well as the cost of that path.

28. Given the following directed acyclic graph (DAG)

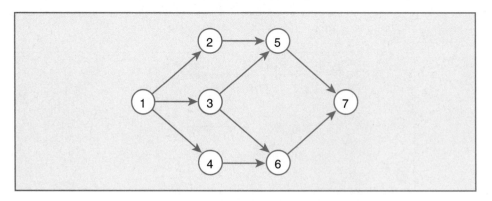

    show its representation using:

    a. an adjacency matrix

    b. an adjacency list

Determine how much space is required for each method and state for this example which of the two is more space efficient. Assume that all stored values (integers and references) require 4 bytes.

29. Write the method `addEdge(i, j, W)`, which inserts the edge <i, j, W> into a graph G. Assume that G is represented using the adjacency list technique described in Section 8.3.3.2.

The Java Collection Framework

9.1 INTRODUCTION

In the early days of software development, when programmers wanted to produce a sequence of random numbers, perhaps for a model such as the heating simulator of Chapter 4, they had to do all of the work themselves. They had to study the algorithms for generating random values, write and debug the code, and finally, test the statistical properties of the random numbers they produced. Today, that approach would be seen as utterly antiquated. Now, software developers go to a program library, locate the routines they need, import them into their code, and use them. (In Java, the code to produce random numbers is in the class `Random` in the package `java.util`.) Similarly, if it were necessary to sort an array of numerical values, it would be highly unusual for programmers to write their own quicksort, merge sort, or heap sort method. Instead, they would use one of the many sorting routines provided by the language. (The `Arrays` class in the `java.util` package includes an implementation of merge sort that sorts information stored in an array.)

The creators of these routines realized early on that one of the best ways to increase software productivity is to provide libraries of carefully tested, highly optimized routines for common everyday tasks. By using these libraries, programmers would not have to write every single function themselves but, instead, could think and work at a higher level of abstraction. Rather than building the program from scratch, they can utilize components available from a class library. This reduces the time required to develop the software and produces programs that are more likely to be bug-free. This idea applies not only to random numbers and sorting but to data structures as well.

One of the most important and powerful features of Java is the *Java Collection Framework*. This is a set of resources that provides many of the data structures introduced and discussed in the last three chapters (e.g., lists, stacks, sets, and maps), so it is no longer necessary for programmers to build these structures from scratch. Using the Java Collection Framework, software developers can obtain enormous increases in productivity and can significantly reduce both implementation time and costs.

The existence of these data structure libraries does not mean that the concepts and ideas presented in the previous three chapters are no longer relevant. On the contrary, software designers must have a solid grounding in the fundamental characteristics of data structures, and they must be able to determine which data structures would work best in a given situation. It is no longer as important to be able to build these structures. Instead, what is vitally important is the ability to select the best data structure to solve a particular task. For example, how would you know whether an array or a linked list implementation of a queue is best for a given situation? How do you evaluate the time-space trade-offs between an adjacency matrix and an adjacency list representation of a graph? What are the efficiency implications of using a binary search tree in place of an unsorted array? It is only possible to answer these questions if you have a thorough understanding of the basic characteristics of data structures and their associated algorithms. However, because of the existence of libraries like the Java Collection Framework, the primary focus of the topic of data structures is changing from learning how to *implement* and *build* them to learning how to *understand, analyze,* and *use* them. This knowledge allows software designers to make intelligent, well-informed decisions about which classes in the framework are most appropriate for a given application.

This chapter describes the services and capabilities of the Java Collection Framework. It relies on the data structure concepts and ideas presented in Chapters 6, 7, and 8. It also makes extensive use of the algorithm analysis concepts initially described in Chapter 5.

9.2 THE JAVA COLLECTION FRAMEWORK

◆ 9.2.1 Overview

A **framework** is a unified architecture for providing a set of related services. That is, it is a collection of routines designed to work together in a seamless fashion and to provide a common external face to its users (i.e., a similar "look and feel"). The **Java Collection Framework**, which is found in the package `java.util`, represents a unified architecture for creating and manipulating important and widely used data structures.

Java is not the only programming language to provide this type of data structure package. For example, in 1994 both the American National Standards Institute (ANSI) and the International Organization for Standardization (ISO) voted to make the **Standard Template Library (STL)** an official part of the C++ language. STL is a library that, like the Java Collection Framework, provides such common data structures as lists, stacks, queues, and sets, as well as the algorithms required to manipulate them. However, many of these earlier collection frameworks were extremely complex and difficult to learn. Because of this complexity, programmers often found it quicker to design and build their own code from scratch rather than spend the time learning how to make effective use of these existing collection classes. To rectify this problem, the Java Collection Framework was carefully designed to be extremely simple and straightforward, which makes it rather easy to learn and use. By the end of this chapter, you should be able to exploit this enormous package of data structure and algorithmic services.

In addition to increasing programmer productivity, the Java Collection Framework can enhance and improve software development in a number of other ways:

◆   *Better run-time efficiency.* The routines in the collection framework have been carefully optimized to provide the highest possible run-time performance. It would be quite time consuming, not to mention technically demanding, for individual programmers to duplicate these optimizations every time they designed and built their own methods.

♦ *Increased program generality.* Programmers can use standardized interfaces to represent a collection and are free to change the underlying implementation at will. For example, we can create a List and choose to implement it using either an ArrayList or a LinkedList, depending on the nature of the problem. We can even choose to change that implementation without affecting the correctness of the program.

♦ *Interoperability.* Unrelated programs can more easily exchange collections with each other using the standardized services of the Java Collection Framework. This would facilitate, for example, sharing information across a network.

The following sections explain the structure and design of the Java Collection Framework so that you can begin to take advantage of its many capabilities.

◆ 9.2.2 Collections

The Java Collection Framework is organized around the concept of a collection. A **collection** is an object that groups together multiple elements into a single entity. In Chapter 6, we referred to this idea as a *composite data type* or a *data structure*. These terms all mean generally the same thing. Collections store information, retrieve information, manipulate information, and transmit information from one application to another (e.g., sending a list of items from a client process to a server). Collections typically represent data items that form a naturally related groups of entities, such as a telephone directory, a deck of cards, a list of products purchased by a user, or the set of integers in the range [0 . . . 10].

The Java Collection Framework is made up of three components: interfaces, implementations, and algorithms. **Interfaces** provide the specifications (i.e., behaviors) for a particular type of collection. It lists the set of services that this collection can provide, independent of the implementation that will ultimately be used to provide these services. **Implementations** represent the specific way that we choose to construct the methods in an interface. With some interfaces, we may choose to provide multiple implementations because of differences in their performance characteristics for certain types of operations. We did just this in the previous chapters where we often described multiple implementations (e.g., array-based and linked list) of a single structure. One implementation might, for example, perform well with retrievals, whereas the other does poorly on retrievals but is much faster with insertions and deletions. Finally, **algorithms** are methods that manipulate the data stored in a collection. For example, the Java Collection Framework includes algorithms that can sort a collection, search a collection, or randomize the order in which elements appear in a collection. These algorithms are chosen to provide their services in the most efficient method possible.

We describe each of these three components in the following sections.

9.3 INTERFACES

The six interfaces included in the Java Collection Framework are shown in the UML class diagram of Figure 9.1.

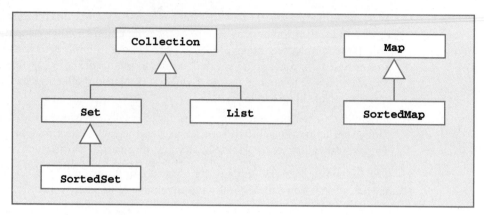

FIGURE 9.1 Interfaces in the Java Collection Framework

◆ 9.3.1 The Collection Interface

The Collection interface is the root of the collection hierarchy, and it represents the most general and flexible of all collection types. For example, some types of collections allow duplicates, but others do not; some collections represent a position-dependent sequence of elements, but others are unordered. Basically, the Collection interface represents a group of elements with virtually any characteristics.

The Java Collection Framework does not provide an implementation for the Collection interface. The idea is that we will take this highly general interface and create a number of lower level "subinterfaces" that impose specific characteristics on a collection. The main use of the Collection interface is to describe a general set of methods that are applicable to all collection types, since every subinterface of Collection will inherit all these methods. Another use of the Collection interface is to pass collections of objects between applications with the maximum amount of generality. The Collection interface, found in the Java package java.util, is shown in Figure 9.2.

The interface in Figure 9.2 includes 13 methods, but 6 of these are denoted as optional. If a class that implements Collection chooses not to provide an implementation for one of these optional methods, it will throw an UnsupportedOperationException. (You will learn how to deal with exceptions in Chapter 10. For now, you can view an exception as an error.) The decision by the designers of the Java Collection Framework to include optional methods in interfaces was controversial. It is controversial because a user of a class called C that implements the Collection interface cannot be sure that a call to one of these optional methods will not "break" the program. For example, this harmless looking sequence

```
C coll;                            // coll is a collection
Object e;                          // and e is an Object

boolean success = coll.add(e);     // add e to coll
```

could actually cause this program to terminate with an exception because add() is an optional method, and it may not have been implemented by class C.

```
public interface Collection {
    // Basic Operations
    int size();
    boolean isEmpty();
    boolean contains(Object element);
    boolean add(Object element);                    // Optional
    boolean remove(Object element);                 // Optional
    Iterator iterator();

    // Bulk Operations
    boolean containsAll(Collection c);
    boolean addAll(Collection c);                   // Optional
    boolean removeAll(Collection c);                // Optional
    boolean retainAll(Collection c);                // Optional
    void clear();                                   // Optional

    // Array Operations
    Object[] toArray();
    Object[] toArray(Object a[]);
}
```

FIGURE 9.2 Collection interface

This approach was taken to reduce the number of interfaces that needed to be included in the framework. For example, the Java Collection Framework supports the idea of a read-only collection—a collection whose contents can be accessed but cannot be changed. Clearly, this type of collection should not contain methods that change the contents of the collection, such as add() or remove(). This would mean that the top-level interface could not include these methods, resulting in an inheritance hierarchy that might resemble the one in Figure 9.3.

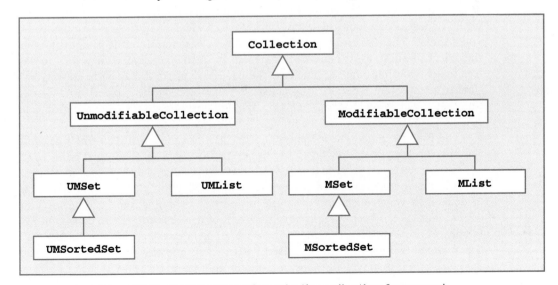

FIGURE 9.3 The effect of adding interfaces to the collection framework

By adding a separate interface for read-only collections, called Unmodifiable-Collection, we have approximately doubled the total number of interfaces in the framework. Now consider the fact that the framework also provides support for synchronized collections. This means that the number of interfaces in the framework would more than triple in size, as it would now include UnModifiableSynchronized-Set, UnmodifiableSet, ModifiableSynchronizedSet, and so on. So a design decision was made to reduce the number of interfaces in the collection by marking some methods as optional. Note that, even though a method such as add() might be optional, it must still be included in any class that implements the interface. In the sense of the collection framework, optional means that a method may throw an exception if it is invoked. For example, a read-only collection must still provide an add() method, but that method will not actually add an element to the collection. Instead, it will throw an exception whenever it is invoked. In our examples, we will assume that all optional methods have been fully implemented.

The methods size() and isEmpty() in Figure 9.2 allow us to determine the number of elements in the collection. Most of the other methods in the Collection interface should be familiar to you from our discussions in the previous three chapters, although the generality of the Collection interface means that the semantics of its methods are defined in the most general way possible. For example, the rules describing the behavior of the add() method say that the object is added to the collection in the "proper way." This means do not add the object to the collection if it is there and duplicates are not allowed. If duplicates are permitted, the method does add it to the collection. The add() method returns true if the collection was changed in any way and false otherwise. The rules for the behavior of remove() are specified in a similar fashion in that it is guaranteed to work in a manner consistent with the characteristics of the specific collection. For example, if duplicates are allowed, then remove() takes out a *single* instance of the object. It returns true if the collection was changed in any way and false otherwise.

The contains() method allows you to determine if a given object is a member of a collection or not. The contains() method uses the equals() method to determine if two objects are equivalent. The code that implements the contains() method consists of a loop that steps through each element in the collection and invokes the equals() method on the current object to determine if it is equivalent to the object in question. Whenever it is necessary in the collection framework to determine if two objects are equivalent, the equals() method makes the determination. It is important when writing classes whose objects will be placed in a collection that the class includes an equals() method appropriate for comparing objects belonging to this class.

The four methods whose names end in All are called **bulk operations**, and they perform an operation on the entire collection in a single step. The method s1.containsAll(s2) returns true if every element in collection s2 is also in s1. The operation s1.addAll(s2) adds every element in collection s2 to s1. This addition is done in a way consistent with the properties of collection s1. The method s1.retainAll(s2) keeps an element in s1 only if it is also present in collection s2. Finally, s1.removeAll(s2) removes from s1 all elements that are in collection s2. The removal is done in a way consistent with the properties of collection s1. The method clear() removes all elements from the collection.

The `toArray()` methods allow the elements in a `Collection` to be stored as an array. The order of placement of elements in the array must be consistent with the specific characteristics of the collection.

The method called `iterator()` requires some special discussion. An **iterator** is an object that allows us to move in order through a collection from one element to another. The order in which we sequence through a collection obviously depends on the particular type of collection with which we are working. For example, in a linear structure such as a list, we would move from a node to its unique successor. In a tree or a graph, we have more flexibility about how to iterate through the collection (e.g., preorder, postorder, breadth-first, depth-first). In a set, it does not matter how we do the iteration because the elements in a set are position independent.

In the previous three chapters, the data structures we described all used what is termed an **internal iterator**. This means that, rather than being an object separate from the collection itself, the iterator is a state variable of the collection, and it is a part of the collection. For example, the `LinkedList` class in Figure 6.17 included a state variable called `cursor`, which identified a position within the list. We iterate through a list using the instance methods `first()`, `next()`, and `isOnList()`:

```
LinkedList aList = new LinkedList();

// Set the cursor to the beginning of the list
aList.first();

while ( aList.isOnList() ) {
    // Perform some operation on the current node
    aList.next();         // Move cursor to the next node
}
```

In this example, `cursor` is an internal iterator because it is part of the state of the `LinkedList` object `aList`. However, the problem with this technique is that we are limited to using only the number of iterators directly provided by the collection. For example, since the `List` class of Chapter 6 contains only a single cursor, it would not be possible to perform two iterations over the list at the same time.

To eliminate this restriction, the Java Collection Framework uses **external iterators**. An external iterator is an object that references an element in a collection but is separate from the collection object itself. The `Iterator` interface is shown in Figure 9.4.

```
public interface Iterator {
    boolean hasNext();
    Object next();
    void remove();        // Optional
}
```

FIGURE 9.4 `Iterator` interface

An object that implements the `Iterator` interface generates a sequence of elements from the collection, one at a time. The method `next()` returns the "next" object in this collection using ordering rules that are appropriate for the particular type of collection with which it is working. In addition to returning a reference to the current object in the iteration, invoking `next()` also causes the cursor to be advanced to the next element in the iteration. The method `hasNext()` returns true if the iteration contains more elements and false otherwise.

One of the most common uses of an iterator is to examine every element in a collection. For example, if `aCollection` is an instance of a class that implements the `Collection` interface, then we can use an `Iterator` to print the elements in the collection as follows:

```
// Create an iterator over the collection
Iterator i = aCollection.iterator();

// Iterate through the collection, one element at a time
while ( i.hasNext() ) {
        // Print the next element in the iteration and
        //      advance the cursor
        System.out.println( i.next() );
}
```

The `Iterator` interface also includes an optional `remove()` method that removes from the collection the last element returned by a call to `next()`. Since `remove()` operates on the element that was already returned by the last call to `next()`, the removal of an object from the collection does not affect the state of the iteration as the cursor has already advanced past the element that was removed. The `remove()` method can only be called once per call to `next()`.

A helpful feature of external iterators is that we can create and use as many iterators over a collection as we want. We are no longer limited to the number of internal iterators provided by the collection object itself. Note that since the state of the iterator is separate from the state of the collection over which it is iterating, changes made to the collection may result in unpredictable behavior by the iterator. Using the `remove()` method in the iterator class is the only safe way to modify a collection while an iteration is in process.

We have spent a good deal of time describing the `Collection` interface, but as mentioned earlier, the Java Collection Framework does not provide any direct implementation of this interface, as it is too general for most applications. We need to create subinterfaces that have the characteristics of the different types of data structures described in Chapters 6 through 8. The first two we will discuss are the `Set` and `List` interfaces of Figure 9.1.

◆ 9.3.2 The `Set` and `List` Interfaces

As you learned in Chapter 8, a **set** is collection of unique elements that is position independent. To implement this idea in the Java Collection Framework, the `Set` interface extends `Collection` but explicitly forbids duplicates. Two `Set` objects are considered equal if they contain exactly the same elements, regardless of where those elements may appear within the collection.

The `Set` interface contains only the methods inherited from `Collection`. Therefore, it looks exactly the same as the interface in Figure 9.2 but with more specific semantics regarding the allowable behavior of the methods in the interface. These set-related behaviors are described in Figure 9.5.

Method	Behavior in the `Set` Interface
`add(e)`	Adds `e` to the collection only if it is not currently there.
`remove(e)`	Removes `e` from the collection if it is there.
`contains(e)`	True if element `e` appears anywhere in the collection.
`containsAll(c)`	The subset operation defined in Section 8.1.1.
`addAll(c)`	The set union operation diagramed in Figure 8.2.
`retainAll(c)`	The set intersection operation diagramed in Figure 8.2.
`removeAll(c)`	The set difference operation diagramed in Figure 8.2.
`toArray()`	Places the elements of the set into an array in arbitrary order.

FIGURE 9.5 Behavior of the methods in the `Set` interface

To illustrate how to use a set, consider the problem of trying to remove duplicate items from a collection. One way would be to remove the elements from the collection and put them into a set. Since a set does not allow duplicates, the duplicate elements in the collection would not be added. The set would then contain all of the unique items from the collection with the duplicates automatically removed. Now we would simply copy the items in the set back into the original collection.

The method `removeDuplicates()` in Figure 9.6 uses this technique to remove duplicates from an arbitrary collection. (The method uses an implementation of sets called a `HashSet`, which will be discussed at length in Section 9.4.1.1.)

```
public void removeDuplicates( Collection aCollection ) {
    // The set that will be used to remove the duplicates
    Set noDups = new HashSet();

    // Step through the elements in the collection using an
    // iterator. Add each element to the set. If the element is
    // already in the set it will not be added a second time since
    // sets do not allow duplicates.
    Iterator i = aCollection.iterator();
    while ( i.hasNext() ) {
        noDups.add( i.next() );
    }
```
(continued)

FIGURE 9.6 Removing duplicates from a collection

```
      // Remove all elements from the collection
      aCollection.clear();

      // Now step through the elements in the set and add them
      // to the empty collection. The result will be the original
      // collection without duplicates.
      i = noDups.iterator();
      while ( i.hasNext() ) {
         aCollection.add( i.next() );
      }
   }
```

FIGURE 9.6 Removing duplicates from a collection *(continued)*

Fortunately, the collection classes also provide bulk operators, which eliminate the need to place the elements from the collection into the set, one at a time, and then step through the set a second time putting elements back into the collection. Using these bulk methods, it is possible to rewrite the `removeDuplicates()` method using only three statements (Figure 9.7).

```
public void removeDuplicates( Collection aCollection ) {
   // Create a set that contains all of the unique elements
   // from the collection
   Set noDups = new HashSet( aCollection );

   // Remove all elements from the collection
   aCollection.clear();

   // Put all of the elements in the set back into the collection
   aCollection.addAll( noDups );
}
```

FIGURE 9.7 Removing duplicates from a collection using the bulk operations

As a second example of the usefulness of sets, let's consider the method `numUnique()` in Figure 9.8 that returns the number of unique elements in an arbitrary collection called `aCollection`. The method creates a new set from the collection and then uses the `size()` method to return the number of elements contained in the newly constructed set. This can all be accomplished in a single line of code. It is a good demonstration of the power and capabilities of the Java Collection Framework.

```
public int numUnique( Collection aCollection ) {
   return new HashSet( aCollection ).size();
}
```

FIGURE 9.8 Determining the number of unique items in a collection

As you saw in Chapter 6, a **list** is a data structure that differs from a set in two fundamental ways: It is an ordered collection, and it can contain duplicates. The List interface in the Java Collection Framework inherits all of the methods in the Collection interface of Figure 9.2, but it adds additional methods to support these two specific behaviors of lists. Specifically, these new methods allow us to do the following operations:

- *Positional access.* As we described in Section 6.2.2 and diagrammed in Figure 6.5, we can access an element in a list using either a current position indicator (now termed an iterator) or by its position number within the list. The List interface includes methods for implementing this latter type of positional access.

- *Positional search.* We can search for a specific object in a list and return the position number in the list where that object was found.

- *Extended iteration.* The List interface includes iteration methods that explicitly take advantage of the inherent linear ordering of lists.

- *Subrange operations.* These methods allow us to perform operations on any subrange of the list—that is, on elements in the list in positions [$m \ldots n$], for any legal values of m, n.

The List interface of the Java Collections Framework is shown in Figure 9.9.

```
public interface List extends Collection {
    // Positional Access
    Object get(int index);
    Object set(int index, Object element);           // Optional
    void add(int index, Object element);             // Optional
    Object remove(int index);                        // Optional
    abstract boolean addAll(int index, Collection c);  // Optional

    // Positional Search
    int indexOf(Object o);
    int lastIndexOf(Object o);

    // Extended Iteration
    ListIterator listIterator();
    ListIterator listIterator(int index);

    // List subranges
    List subList(int from, int to);
}
```

FIGURE 9.9 List interface

The get(), set(), add(), and remove() methods in Figure 9.9 work virtually identically to their counterparts described in Chapter 6 and included in the List interface of Figure 6.6. (Note that the methods listed in Figure 9.9 are in addition to the 13 methods that List inherits from the Collection interface. For example, the add(o) method inherited from Collection adds its element to the end of the list, and the `remove(o)` method inherited from `Collection` deletes the first occurrence of its element from the list.) The abstract method `addAll()` of Figure 9.9 adds all the elements of a collection to the list beginning at the specified position. The `indexOf()` and `lastIndexOf()` methods locate an occurrence of an object within the list. The `indexOf()` method returns the index of its first occurrence in the list; `lastIndexOf()` returns the index of the last occurrence.

Lists provide an additional type of iterator object called `ListIterator`. `ListIterator` is a subclass of the `Iterator` interface in Figure 9.4, and it provides a much richer set of positioning and movement operations appropriate for `List` data structures. The specifications for the `ListIterator` interface are given in Figure 9.10.

```
public interface ListIterator extends Iterator {
      boolean hasNext();
      Object next();

      boolean hasPrevious();
      Object previous();

      int nextIndex();
      int previousIndex();

      void remove();          // Optional
      void set(Object o);      // Optional
      void add(Object o);      // Optional
}
```

FIGURE 9.10 `ListIterator` interface

The `ListIterator` methods defined in the `List` class of Figure 9.9 provide the ability to obtain a `ListIterator` object that is either positioned at the first element in the list (no parameters) or at the element whose position number is specified by the integer parameter. A `ListIterator` can iterate in the forward and reverse directions through a list, and it provides the ability to obtain the current position of the iterator in the list. From the users' point of view, a `ListIterator` behaves like the doubly linked list structure that we presented in Section 6.2.3.3. The `next()` and `hasNext()` methods allow you to traverse a list from the first element to the last, whereas the `previous()` and `hasPrevious()` methods provide the ability to traverse from last to first.

When dealing with a `ListIterator`, it can be useful to think of the cursor as not directly referring to one of the nodes in the list but as lying between two nodes in the list (Figure 9.11).

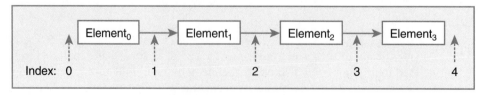

FIGURE 9.11 Cursor locations in a `ListIterator`

Invoking `next()` on a `ListIterator` object will return the element to the right of the current cursor and advance the cursor forward one position. Invoking `previous()` will return the element to the left of the cursor and move the cursor back one position. Note that invoking `next()` immediately after an invocation of `previous()` will return the same element. The `nextIndex()` method returns the index of the list element that will be returned by the next invocation of `next()`, and correspondingly, the `previousIndex()` method returns the index of the list element that will be returned by the next invocation of `previous()`. Figure 9.12 illustrates example invocations of these iterator methods on a list and the values that they return.

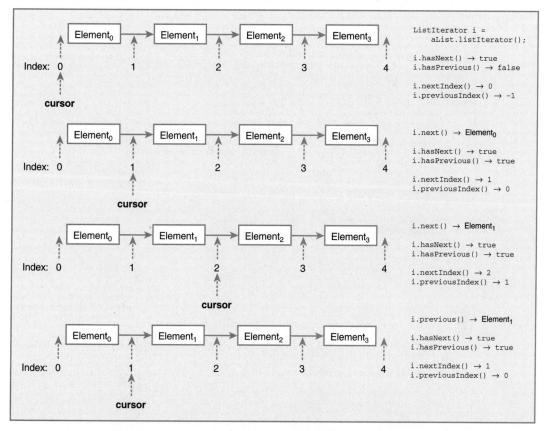

FIGURE 9.12 Using the `ListIterator` methods

The `ListIterator` interface includes methods that modify the list over which it is iterating. The `remove()` method for a `ListIterator` will remove the element just returned by either `next()` or `previous()`, similar to the behavior of the `remove()` method in the `Iterator` interface. The `add()` method in the `ListIterator` class behaves in exactly the same way as the `add()` method in the `Iterator` class. It will insert the new element into the list before the element that would be returned by `next()` and after the element that would be returned by `previous()`. If the list is empty, the new element becomes the only element in the list. The element is inserted before the cursor, which means that `next()` will not be affected, while a call to `previous()` would return the element just added to the list. The `set()` method is used to replace the last element returned by `next()` or `previous()` in the list.

To illustrate the use of a `ListIterator`, consider the problem of removing duplicate elements from a list. The technique in Figure 9.7 to remove duplicates from an arbitrary collection will not work for a list because we cannot guarantee anything about the order in which the elements will be copied from the set back into the list. However, the program must preserve the ordering of the elements in the list if it is to work correctly. The method in Figure 9.13 removes duplicates from a list using a `Set` and the `remove()` method in the `ListIterator` class. The program uses a `ListIterator` to step through the elements in the list. As the iterator examines each element, the element is added to a set. If the element cannot be added to the set, then it has been seen already, and it is removed from the list.

```
public void removeDuplicates( List aList ) {
    Set unique = new HashSet();
    ListIterator i = aList.listIterator();

    while( i.hasNext() ) {
        if ( !unique.add( i.next() ) ) {
            i.remove();
        }
    }
}
```

FIGURE 9.13 Removing duplicates from a list

The last `List` method we will look in this section is the method `subList()`. The `List` returned by the method `subList(int m, int n)` includes all elements contained in the original `List` from position m to position n, inclusive. Note that the value returned does not represent a new list object but simply a new "view" of the original list that includes the specified elements. Therefore, any changes to the `List` returned by the sublist method are, in effect, changes to the original `List` itself. For example, assuming that l1 and l2 are objects that implement the `List` interface of Figure 9.9, the following two operations

```
l2 = l1.sublist( 3, 5 );
l2.clear();
```

will remove the items in positions 3, 4, 5 from the list l1.

The `ListPriorityQueue` class of Figure 9.14 illustrates how a `List` can be used to implement the priority queue data structure introduced in Section 6.4.4. The list stores the elements in priority order—the element with the highest priority is stored in position 0 of the list, and the item with the lowest priority is stored at the end of the list. The `enqueue()` method uses a `ListIterator` to determine the location in the list where the new item is to be placed.

```
import java.util.List;
import java.util.LinkedList;
import java.util.ListIterator;

/**
 * A priority queue that is implemented using a list.
 * This queue holds strings and bases the priority on the
 * alphabetical order of the strings. Strings at the beginning
 * of the dictionary have priority over those at the end.
 */
public class ListPriorityQueue {

    private List queue; // The actual queue

    /**
     * Create a new priority queue.
     */
    public ListPriorityQueue() {
        queue = new LinkedList();
    }

    /**
     * Add an element to the queue.
     *
     * @param val the element to add to the queue.
     */
    public void enqueue( String val ) {
        // Will iterate over the list and find the index where the
        // new value should go
        ListIterator i = queue.listIterator();

        // The location of the new element
        int loc = 0;

        // While there is something left to iterate over and
        // the value is not greater than the current element
        // keep looking
        while( i.hasNext() && val.compareTo( (String)i.next() ) > 0 ) {
            // Remember the index of the next element we will examine.
            // If the element is smaller this is where the new one should
            // go.
            loc = i.nextIndex();
        }

        // Add the element to the queue.
        queue.add( loc, val );
    }
```

(continued)

FIGURE 9.14 A list-based priority queue

```
/**
 * Return an item with the highest priority.
 *
 * @return an element with the highest priority.
 */
public String dequeue() {
    // Highest priority element is always at the front of the
    // queue
    return (String)queue.remove( 0 );
}

/**
 * Determine if the queue is empty.
 *
 * @return true if the queue is empty and false otherwise.
 */
public boolean isEmpty() {
    // If the list is empty the queue is empty
    return queue.isEmpty();
}

} // ListPriorityQueue
```

FIGURE 9.14 A list-based priority queue *(continued)*

To summarize the characteristics of the interfaces that we have introduced so far, we can say that the `Collection` interface represents an arbitrary group of objects. The `Set` interface extends `Collection` by forbidding duplicate elements in the collection. Finally, the `List` interface extends `Collection` by allowing both duplicates and positional indexing and accessing of elements.

◆ 9.3.3 The `Map` Interface

In Section 8.2, we introduced the **map** data structure, also called a **key-access table**. We showed that a map is a special type of set in which the members of the collection are not individual elements but 2-tuples of the form (key, value), where every key is unique. This pair represents a mapping from key objects to value objects in the sense that, given a unique key, we can use that key to locate its associated value object. Some examples of mappings might be:

◆   A map of student ID numbers to student database records.

◆   A dictionary in which words are mapped to their meanings.

◆   A mapping from values in base-2 to their value in base-10.

The primary difference between a `Collection` and a `Map` is that in a `Collection` you add, remove, and look up individual items, whereas in a `Map` you add, remove, and look up items using a key-value pair. The typical use of a `Map` data structure is to provide direct access to values stored by key.

Because maps access elements in a way quite different from the techniques used in `Collection` , the `Map` interface does not extend the `Collection` interface but, instead, stands on its own. The `Map` interface of the Java Collection Framework is listed in Figure 9.15.

```
public interface Map {
    // Basic Map Operations
    Object put(Object key, Object value);
    Object get(Object key);
    Object remove(Object key);
    boolean containsKey(Object key);
    boolean containsValue(Object value);
    int size();
    boolean isEmpty();

    // Bulk Operations
    void putAll(Map t);
    void clear();

    // Collection Views
    Set keySet();
    Collection values();
    Set entrySet();

    // Interface for entrySet elements
    public interface Entry {
        Object getKey();
        Object getValue();
        Object setValue(Object value);
    }
}
```

FIGURE 9.15 Map interface

The behavior of the five map operations `put()`, `get()`, `remove()`, `isEmpty()`, and `size()` shown in Figure 9.15 is virtually identical to the methods described in Section 8.2 and included in the `Table` interface of Figure 8.5. The `put()` method adds a (key, value) tuple to the map, `remove()` deletes the tuple with the given key field if it is present in the map, and `get()` returns the value field associated with a given key field if such a key field exists. The primary difference between the `Table` interface of Chapter 8 and the `Map` interface of Figure 9.15 is that the `put()` and `remove()` methods in the `Map` interface return a reference to the value that was previously associated with this key. For `put()`, a return value of `null` indicates that the key was not in the map and had no previous value field associated with it. A nonnull value indicates that a new value has been associated with an existing key, and the value that was returned was the previous value field. A `null` return value from `remove()` indicates that the key was not in the table.

The Map interface in Figure 9.15 is also much richer than the interface shown in Figure 8.5, and it includes a number of additional helpful methods. For example, it allows you to check if either a specific key or value is present in the map using the containsKey() and containsValue() methods, respectively. The containsKey() method is quite efficient because there is a direct mapping between a key and its location within a map. (This mapping is specified by the hashing function.) However, the containsValue() method is significantly slower since there is no quick way to locate a value field except from its mapping via key. Therefore, this method must iterate through the entire map looking for this value, an O(N) linear time operation, where N is the number of tuples in the map. The putAll() method is the equivalent of the addAll() method in the Set interface. It adds all of the mappings in one map into another, ensuring that all key values remain unique. The clear() method does the obvious—it removes all the (key, value) tuples from the map.

An interesting group of methods in the Map interface of Figure 9.15 are the three "collection views." Since a Map is a set of tuples rather than individual elements, it does not make much sense to talk about "iterating" through a Map. Would we iterate through the key fields? The value fields? Both? To give meaning to the concept of iterating through a Map, the interface allows you to restructure the map so that it can be viewed as different types of collections. For example, the keySet method allows you to view your Map as a Set that contains all the keys present in the original Map structure. Thus, if our map contained the four tuples (1, 2), (8, 14), (5, 2), and (17, 33), then the set returned from a call to keySet would be S = {1, 8, 5, 17}, although the exact ordering is immaterial. We could now obtain an iterator over the Set S to an array, using the iterator() method, and then iterate sequentially through the keys in the map.

The method values() in the interface of Figure 9.15 takes a Map and returns a collection that includes all the value fields present in the original Map. Using the same four tuples given earlier, the Collection object returned by a call to values() would be (2, 14, 2, 33). Note that this object is not a Set, since different keys, in our case, 1 and 5, can map to the same value, in our case, 2. Finally, the method entrySet returns a Set object whose elements are the (key, value) pairs contained in the Map. The Map interface includes an inner interface, called Map.Entry, that represents the data type of the elements in the Set returned by the entrySet method.

The BookShelf class of Figure 9.16 illustrates the use of a Map. The BookShelf class allows a user to store book titles by their unique ISBN code—an acronym for International Standard Book Number. A Map, called theShelf, holds the ISBNs (keys) and the titles (values). Most of the methods in the BookShelf class are simple wrappers around the corresponding Map methods. The toString() method makes use of an iterator to iterate through the keys stored in the map. These keys then retrieve the titles with which they are associated.

```
import java.util.Iterator;
import java.util.List;
import java.util.ArrayList;
import java.util.Map;
import java.util.HashMap;
```

FIGURE 9.16 BookShelf class

```java
/**
 * A class that represents a bookshelf. Books on the shelf
 * are stored and retrieved by ISBN.
 */
public class BookShelf {

    private Map theShelf; // The books

    /**
     * Create a new book shelf.
     */
    public BookShelf() {
        theShelf = new HashMap();
    }


    /**
     * Add a book to the bookshelf. The book is added only if a book
     * with the same ISBN is not already on the shelf. The return
     * value indicates whether or not the book was added to the shelf.
     *
     * @param isbn the ISBN of the book to be added.
     * @param title the title of the book.
     *
     * @return true if the book was added to the shelf and false
     * otherwise.
     */
    public boolean addTitle( String isbn, String title ) {
        // If the ISBN is a key in the map - the book is already on the shelf
        boolean onShelf = theShelf.containsKey( isbn );

        // If the book is not already there - add it
        if ( !onShelf ) {
            theShelf.put( isbn, title );
        }

        return onShelf;
    }


    /**
     * Return the title associated with the given ISBN.
     *
     * @param isbn the ISBN of the title to be retrieved.
     *
     * @return the title of the book or null if the ISBN
     *    is not on the shelf.
     */
    public String getTitle( String isbn ) {
        return (String)theShelf.get( isbn );
    }
```

(continued)

FIGURE 9.16 BookShelf class *(continued)*

```
/**
 * Remove the title with the specified title from the
 * shelf. The return value indicates whether the title
 * was removed from the shelf or not.
 *
 * @param isbn the ISBN of the title to remove.
 *
 * @return true if the title was removed from the shelf
 *    and false otherwise.
 */
public boolean removeTitle( String isbn ) {
    // Remove returns null if the key is not in the
    // map so if the return value was not null - the
    // title was there
    return theShelf.remove( isbn ) != null;
}


/**
 * Return a list that contains all of the titles on the
 * shelf.
 *
 * @return a list that contains all of the titles on the shelf.
 */
public List getAllTitles() {
    // Values returns a collection - convert it to a list
    return new ArrayList( theShelf.values() );
}


/**
 * Return a string that contains the ISBN and the titles
 * on the shelf.
 *
 * @return a string representation of the books on the shelf.
 */
public String toString() {
    // Use a string buffer for efficiency
    StringBuffer books = new StringBuffer( "The books:\n" );

    // Iterate over the ISBNs
    Iterator i = theShelf.keySet().iterator();

    while ( i.hasNext() ) {
        String isbn = (String)i.next();

        // Use the ISBN to get the corresponding title
        books.append( " " +
            isbn +
            " " +
```

FIGURE 9.16 BookShelf class *(continued)*

```
                theShelf.get( isbn ) +
                "\n" );
        }

      return books.toString();
    }

} // BookShelf
```

FIGURE 9.16 BookShelf class *(continued)*

◆ 9.3.4 Sorted Interfaces

9.3.4.1 The Natural Ordering of Objects

Looking back at Figure 9.1, we see that the Java Collection Framework includes two sorted interfaces: SortedSet and SortedMap. These sorted interfaces provide the ability to retrieve objects stored in their collections in sorted order. The question that we need to answer before we can discuss the behavior of these interfaces is: How does a collection know how to sort its objects? Clearly, for objects like numbers or strings, the answer is easy—sort them numerically or alphabetically. However, what about a collection of objects that represents something like first and last names or breeds of dogs? Now the natural order of these objects is not so obvious.

Just as the equals() method in class Object provides a way to determine if two objects are equal, we need to provide a method that defines the relative ordering of two objects. The Java API defines the interface Comparable for this exact purpose. The Comparable interface specifies only a single method, compareTo(), which can be used to determine if an object is less than, equal to, or greater than another object. The Comparable interface is given in Figure 9.17.

```
public interface Comparable {
    int compareTo( Object o );
}
```

FIGURE 9.17 Comparable interface

The compareTo() method returns an integer value that indicates the relative ordering of the objects being compared. For example, the method invocation

```
aString.compareTo( anotherString );
```

will return a negative value if aString is strictly less than anotherString, zero if aString is equal to anotherString, and a positive number if aString is strictly greater than anotherString. Note that the specification of compareTo() does not specify the magnitude of the return value, only its sign. Thus, the following if statement

```
if ( aString.compareTo( anotherString ) == -1 ) {
    // . . .
}
```

might not correctly detect all of the situations when aString is less than anotherString. The correct way to do the comparison is to consider only the sign of the return value and not its magnitude:

```
if ( aString.compareTo( anotherString ) < 0 ) {
    // . . .
}
```

The compareTo() method is referred to as a class's **natural comparison method**, and the ordering it imposes on the objects of the class is referred to as the **natural ordering** of the class.

Writing a compareTo() method for a class is very easy. Consider the Name class of Figure 9.18 that consists of a first and last name. The class defines both the methods equals() and compareTo(). Two names are considered equal if their first and last names are the same. The compareTo() method in Figure 9.18 defines a natural ordering where names are ordered by their last name and, in cases where the last names are the same, by their first name. Note that the Name class implements the Comparable interface.

```
/**
 * A class that represents a name consisting of a first and
 * last name.
 */
public class Name implements Comparable {
    // The name
    String first;
    String last;

    /**
     * Create a new name.
     *
     * @param firstName the first name.
     * @param lastName the last name.
     */
    public Name( String firstName, String lastName ) {
        first = firstName;
        last = lastName;
    }

    /**
     * Get the first name.
```

FIGURE 9.18 Defining a compareTo() method

```
    *
    * @return the first name.
    */
   public String getFirst() {
      return first;
   }

   /**
    * Get the last name.
    *
    * @return the last name.
    */
   public String getLast() {
      return last;
   }

   /**
    * Compare two names and determine their relative order. This
    * method will first compare the last names. If they are different
    * then alphabetical order will determine the order of the names.
    * If the last names are the same, the first names will be used to
    * determine the order.
    *
    * @param o the name to compare this name to.
    *
    * @return a negative number if this name is less than the given name,
    *     zero if the names are equal, and a positive number if this
    *     name is greater than the specified string.
    */
   public int compareTo( Object o ) {
      // Unlike method equals we assume we are being passed a
      // name. If we are not given a name we cannot make the
      // comparison and a ClassCastException will be thrown.
      Name anotherName = (Name)o;

      // Compare the last names using the compareTo() method
      // defined in the string class.
      int retVal = last.compareTo( anotherName.getLast() );

      // If the last names are equal, compare the first names.
      if ( retVal == 0 ) {
         retVal = first.compareTo( anotherName.getFirst() );
      }

      return retVal;
   }
```

(continued)

FIGURE 9.18 Defining a `compareTo()` method *(continued)*

```
    /**
     * Determine if this name is equal to the specified object.
     *
     * @param o the object to compare this name to.
     *
     * @return true if this name is equal to the specified object
     *      and false otherwise.
     */
    public boolean equals( Object o ) {
        boolean retVal = false;

        // Unlike compareTo() we can deal with objects that are not
        // names. If this method is passed a reference to something
        // other than a name the objects are not equal.
        if ( o instanceof Name ) {
            Name anotherName = (Name)o;

            // Two names are equal if their first and last names
            // are the same.
            retVal =
                last.equals( anotherName.getLast() ) &&
                first.equals( anotherName.getFirst() );
        }

        return retVal;
    }

} // Name
```

FIGURE 9.18 Defining a `compareTo()` method *(continued)*

The first thing that must be done when writing a `compareTo()` method is to cast the `Object` passed in as an argument into an object belonging to the class for which the method is being defined. In Figure 9.18, this means that the `Object` parameter o is cast into a reference to a `Name`. Unlike the `equals()` method, the `compareTo()` method does not check to make sure that it has been passed a reference to a `Name` before making the cast. Instead, if a reference to something other than a `Name` is passed to the method, it throws a `ClassCastException`. Unlike `equals()`, the `compareTo()` method can only compare objects from the same class.

There are several rules that must be followed when writing a `compareTo()` method. First, the method must be written so that the sign of the result returned by an invocation of x.`compareTo(y)` is the opposite of the sign returned by an invocation of y.`compareTo(x)`. Second, the `compareTo()` method must be transitive. In other words, if x.`compareTo(y) > 0` and y.`compareTo(z) > 0`, then x.`compareTo(z) > 0`. Finally, if x is equal to y, then the results returned by the invocation of x.`compareTo(y)` and y.`compareTo(x)` must both be 0.

Notice that, for a class that implements the `Comparable` interface, there are two ways to determine if objects are equal. You could invoke either `equals()` or compareTo(). It is important to write the equals() method and the compareTo() method so that they are consistent. In order words, if equals() returns true for two objects, then compareTo() should return 0 for the same two objects. Writing a class in which the compareTo() method is inconsistent with the equals() method can result in strange and unpredictable behavior.

There are some classes that have no natural ordering or that may have multiple orderings. Consider, for example, the Dog class of Figure 9.19. The state of a Dog consists of its name, breed, and gender. The equals() method for this class does exactly what you would expect: It compares the name, breed, and gender of the dogs and returns true if all three values are identical.

```java
/**
 * A class that represents a dog. The state of a dog consists of its
 * name, breed, and gender. Note that this class is not comparable.
 */

public class Dog {

    // State for the dog
    private String breed;
    private String name;
    private String gender;

    /**
     * Create a new dog object.
     *
     * @param theBreed the breed of the dog
     * @param theName the name of this dog
     * @param theGender the gender of this dog
     */
    public Dog( String theBreed, String theName, String theGender ) {
        breed = theBreed;
        name = theName;
        gender = theGender;
    }

    /**
     * Return the breed of this dog
     *
     * @return the breed of this dog
     */
    public String getBreed() {
        return breed;
    }

    /**
     * Return the name of this dog
```

(continued)

FIGURE 9.19 Dog class

```
        *
        * @return the name of this dog
        */
       public String getName() {
          return name;
       }

       /**
        * Return the gender of this dog
        *
        * @return the gender of this dog
        */
       public String getGender() {
          return gender;
       }

       /**
        * Indicates whether some other object is equal to this one.
        *
        * @param o the object to be compared with
        *
        * @return true if this object is the same as the argument; false
        *      otherwise
        */
       public boolean equals( Object o ) {
          boolean retVal = false;

          if ( o instanceof Dog ) {
             Dog other = (Dog)o;
             retVal =
                breed.equals( other.getBreed() ) &&
                name.equals( other.getName() ) &&
                gender.equals( other.getGender() );
          }

          return retVal;
       }

    } // Dog
```

FIGURE 9.19 Dog class *(continued)*

However, there are many possible ways to compare two dog objects to see which one is greater. We could compare the dogs simply by their name. Alternatively, we might want to use some combination of their name and breed. The problem with these approaches is that it will be difficult to write a compareTo() method that is fully consistent with the equals() method. In situations such as this, it is probably best to design our class so that it does not implement the Comparable interface.

A **comparator** can be used to provide a natural ordering for classes that do not implement the `Comparable` interface or for classes in which there is more than one way to order the objects. A `Comparator` is an object that encapsulates an ordering in the same way that an external iterator is an object that encapsulates an iteration over a collection. The `Comparator` interface, like the `Comparable` interface, defines a single `compare()` method, except that the `compare()` method of the `Comparator` interface requires two object references when it is invoked instead of one. The `Comparator` interface is shown in Figure 9.20.

```
public interface Comparator {
    int compare( Object o1, Object o2 );
}
```

FIGURE 9.20 Comparator interface

Figure 9.21 shows two comparators that could be used with the `Dog` class. The first comparator provides an ordering based on the name of the `Dog`. The second comparator implements an ordering based first on the breed of the dog and then by the dog's name.

```
public class DogByName implements Comparator {
    public int compare( Object o1, Object o2 ) {
        Dog d1 = (Dog)o1;
        Dog d2 = (Dog)o2;

        return d1.getName().compareTo( d2.getName() );
    }
}

public class DogByBreedAndName implements Comparator {
    public int compare( Object o1, Object o2 ) {
        Dog d1 = (Dog)o1;
        Dog d2 = (Dog)o2;

        int retVal = d1.getBreed().compareTo( d2.getBreed() );

        if ( retVal == 0 ) {
            retVal = d1.getName().compareTo( d2.getName() );
        }

        return retVal;
    }
}
```

FIGURE 9.21 Comparators for the Dog class

Both of the comparators in Figure 9.21 have the same look and feel as the compareTo() method of the Comparable interface. The major difference is that two references are required to identify the objects being compared instead of one. In the next section, we will discuss how to use Comparable objects and Comparator objects with the sorted collections of the Java Collection Framework.

9.3.4.2 Sorted Sets and Sorted Maps

A SortedSet is a Set that maintains its elements in ascending order according to either (a) the natural ordering of its elements or (b) a Comparator that is provided when the set is created. The methods provided by a SortedSet behave in exactly the same way as the methods provided by a Set except that the SortedSet guarantees two things: First, its iterator will traverse the elements of the set in ascending order, and second, the array returned by the toArray() method will contain the set's elements stored in ascending order. The elements in a SortedSet must implement the Comparable interface, or a Comparator must be provided to the set at creation time that specifies how to order the elements.

The SortedSet interface provides additional operators that take advantage of the ordering of its elements. The SortedSet interface is given in Figure 9.22.

```
public interface SortedSet extends Set {
    // Range View
    SortedSet subSet(Object from, Object to);
    SortedSet headSet(Object to);
    SortedSet tailSet(Object from);

    // Endpoints
    Object first();
    Object last();

    // Comparator
    Comparator comparator();
}
```

FIGURE 9.22 SortedSet interface

The three range-view operations provided by the SortedSet interface return a subset of the set that contains the elements of the original set that fall within the specified boundaries. The subSet() method takes two endpoints and returns a subset that contains all of the elements that are greater than or equal to the from endpoint and are strictly less than the to endpoint. The methods headSet and tailSet work in a similar fashion, but one of their endpoints is the first or last element, respectively. A range view of a sorted set is a window into whatever portion of the set lies in the designated range. Changes made to the range view change the original SortedSet, and changes made to the SortedSet change the range view. The first() and last() methods of the SortedSet interface return the first (smallest) and last (largest) elements in the set, respectively.

To see what can be done using the range-view operators, imagine a set that contains the serial numbers of the computing equipment at a university. The serial numbers consist of five characters. The first character is a letter that identifies the vendor, and the remaining four characters are digits that uniquely identify a specific piece of equipment from that vendor. Assume that the variable serialNumbers refers to a SortedSet that contains all of the serial numbers at the university. You could determine the number of machines manufactured by the vendor identified by the character A using the following line of code:

```
int num = serialNumbers.subset( "A0000", "B0000" ).size();
```

The subset returned by the subset() method is a SortedSet that contains all serial numbers that start at "A0000" and run up to, but do not include, serial number "B0000". The size of this subset is the number of machines manufactured by vendor A.

As a second example, you could remove all of vendor A's equipment from the set by executing the following line of code:

```
serialNumbers.subset( "A0000", "B0000" ).clear();
```

Again the subset() method returns all of the serial numbers that correspond to vendor A in a SortedSet. The clear() method removes these elements from the subset, but since the subset is simply a window onto the original SortedSet, the elements are removed from the sorted set as well.

A SortedMap is similar to a SortedSet. A SortedMap is a Map whose keys are stored in ascending order based on the natural ordering of its keys. Like the SortedSet, a Comparator can be used to determine order if the keys do not implement the Comparable interface or if you wish to use an ordering that is different from the natural order of the keys. The SortedMap interface is given in Figure 9.23.

The methods in the SortedMap interface behave in the same fashion as the SortedSet.

```
public interface SortedMap extends Map {
    // Range View
    SortedSet subMap(Object from, Object to);
    SortedSet headMap(Object to);
    SortedSet tailMap(Object from);

    // Endpoints
    Object first();
    Object last();

    // Comparator
    Comparator comparator();
}
```

FIGURE 9.23 SortedMap interface

9.4 IMPLEMENTATIONS

The implementations reflect how the Java Collection Framework chooses to build classes that implement the interfaces presented in Section 9.3. That is, what types of structures—arrays, linked lists, trees, hash tables—are used to construct the sets, lists, and map collections contained in the framework?

It is important to keep clear in your mind the difference between an interface and its implementation. For example, in Section 9.3.2, we described a `List` interface that included such methods as `add()`, `remove()`, and `indexOf()`. We can choose to implement that `List` interface using either an array, as we did in Section 6.2.3.1, entitled An Array-Based Implementation, or we might opt for the linked list described in Section 6.2.3.2, A Reference-Based Implementation. This would represent a single interface with two distinct and separate implementations. When designing software, you should always think in terms of interfaces, not implementations. This way, your program is not dependent on idiosyncratic methods found in only one particular type of implementation, leaving you free to change implementations at a later time if desired.

When designing a piece of software, the most important question to ask yourself is: What type of collection is the best choice to hold my data elements? Once you have answered that question, you can instantiate a variable of the proper interface type and place the elements into this object. For example, if you have determined that you will use a linear data structure to hold the elements in your collection, then you would do the following:

```
List L = . . . ;    // Create a object that implements the List
                    // interface and place a reference to the object
                    // in the variable L
```

You now design your program in terms of list objects and the standard list methods contained in the interface of Figure 9.9. In terms of correctness, it does not matter how you choose to actually implement list L, and you can develop your software without worrying about that issue. The only effect that your choice of implementations will have (although it can be an important one) is the performance that you are able to obtain.

In this section, we focus on what are termed the **general-purpose implementations** of the Java Collection Framework. These are public classes that represent the most general and the most flexible implementations used the overwhelming majority of time. The general-purpose implementations are summarized in Figure 9.24. The naming convention used for all these implementations is *<implementation><interface>*, where *<implementation>* is the name of the data structure used in the implementation, and *<interface>* is the name of one of the standard interfaces included in Figure 9.1. So, for example, the class name `HashMap` means that this class does a `Hash` table implementation of the `Map` interface shown in Figure 9.15.

Note from Figure 9.24 that the Java Collection Framework provides two different implementations for each of the interfaces presented in Section 9.3, except for `Collection`, which as mentioned earlier does not have any implementations. The two implementations of each interface will typically exhibit different performance charac-

Interface	Implementation				Historical
Set	HashSet		TreeSet		
List		ArrayList		LinkedList	Vector Stack
Map	HashMap		TreeMap		HashTable Properties

FIGURE 9.24 Implementation classes

teristics on certain operations within the interface. One implementation may work well for operation a() but fare quite poorly with b(), whereas the other implementation behaves in exactly the opposite manner. It is up to the software developer to decide which of the two implementations provided by the Java Collection Framework is most appropriate for a specific problem. Alternatively, we may decide to design and implement a totally new implementation. This decision will require a thorough understanding of the data structure ideas and concepts presented in Chapters 6, 7, and 8.

In addition to the default constructor, all collection implementations provide, by convention, a one-parameter constructor that takes a Collection as its argument. The constructor initializes the object to contain all of the elements in the specified Collection. The sorted collections, SortedSet and SortedMap, provide two other standard constructors: one constructor that takes a Comparator and one that takes a sorted collection. The constructor that takes a Comparator creates a new sorted collection whose elements are sorted according to the specified Comparator. The constructor that takes a sorted collection will create a new sorted collection containing the elements in the given collection and sorted by the same Comparator.

◆ 9.4.1 Sets

9.4.1.1 HashSet

Our first implementation of sets is HashSet, which as its name implies uses the hash table techniques presented in Section 8.2.3 to implement a set data structure. In Chapter 8, we described how to use hashing to implement a map containing 2-tuples of the form (key, value). However, the identical techniques described there can be used to implement a Set simply by ignoring the value field. Since all the keys are unique, they will, by definition, form a set.

The most important decision made by the designers of the Java Collection Framework regarding hashing was whether to use the open addressing (Figure 8.10) or chaining (Figures 8.12 and 8.13) method to handle collisions. They decided to use chaining, probably because it allows more than N values to be stored in a hash table of size N (although we would have to ask them to confirm this).

Using a HashSet implementation, the four-element set S = {24, 88, 1, 9} would be stored in a 10-element chained hash table h as shown in Figure 9.25, assuming the following values were produced by our hash function f: f(24) = 7, f(88) = 3, f(1) = 7, f(9) = 2.

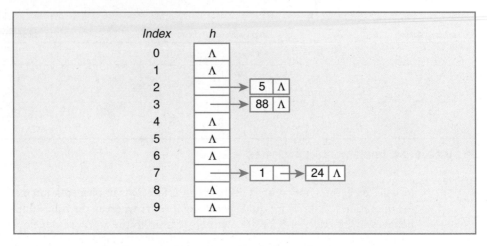

FIGURE 9.25 Implementation of a set using `HashSet`

As mentioned in Section 8.2.3, under best-case conditions, adding, retrieving, and removing elements from a `HashSet` are all O(1), the most efficient implementation possible. If the hash table h is quite sparse, there will be very few elements in each of the linked lists referenced by h[i], typically 0 or 1. To add a new element e to the set, we first search the linked list whose head pointer is stored in $i = f(e)$ to see if this element is already there. If the table is very sparsely occupied, this takes only a single step. If it is not there, we add it to the head of the linked list, which takes a constant number of steps. Overall, then, the operation is O(1). The same analysis holds for deletions and retrievals. However, if E, the total number of elements stored in the hash table, is significantly larger than the size of the hash table N, typically referred to as the number of **buckets**, then the linked lists average E/N elements in length rather than 0 or 1, and the time to add, retrieve, and delete is O(E/N).

Therefore, to make a `HashSet` implementation work reasonably well, it is important to *parameterize* it well. The two parameters that are most important to a successful implementation are (a) the **initial capacity** of the hash table, the value N = 10 in Figure 9.25, and (b) the **load factor** α. In Section 8.2.3, we defined the load factor as:

α = number of elements/size of the hash table

Referring to Figure 9.25 and using this definition, the load factor for this table would be:

$\alpha = 4/10 = 0.40$

However, the Java Collection Framework defines α in a slightly different way. In the framework, the load factor is defined as the *maximum* allowable ratio of the number of elements to the size of the hash table before we must resize and rebuild the hash table. That is, if $\alpha = 0.8$, it means that whenever α exceeds 0.8, we must enlarge the table (typically it is doubled) and then rehash all entries in the existing table to find their proper location in the newly enlarged table.

You can set both of these hash table parameters using the following two-parameter `HashSet` constructor:

```
HashSet(int initialCapacity, float loadFactor);
```

There also are `HashSet` constructors that allow you to use one or both of the default values for these numbers, namely, initialCapacity = 101, loadFactor = 0.75.

Higher values for `loadFactor` can save space and reduce the number of times that the hash table must be enlarged and rebuilt, a potentially time-consuming operation. However, you pay for this in terms of slower accesses and slower insertions, as the average length of the linked lists increases. Similarly, a larger `initialCapacity` helps to keep the load factor down, but it requires additional space for the larger table. In addition, iterating through the elements of a set requires time proportional to O(N + E), since we must not only visit every element of the set, but we must also check every one of the N entries in the hash table to determine if it is or is not empty. Thus, keeping the `initialCapacity` parameter of the hash table small can help to improve the efficiency of iteration operations.

If you have a good estimate for MAX, the maximum number of elements that can be placed into the set, and this value is not too large, then a good rule of thumb is: Make `initialCapacity` double the value of MAX and use the default value for `loadFactor`. Since you have about twice as many slots as set elements, the load factor will be about 0.5, which is well below its default value of 0.75. Therefore, no rebuilding or rehashing operations should ever be required. In addition, the length of each linked list will typically be 0 or 1 (assuming the hash function scatters elements reasonably well), so you should observe O(1) behavior for all accesses and insertions.

Notice how important it was to have a solid knowledge of both algorithm analysis and the basic properties of hashing, such as collisions, load factors, and chaining. Even though the Java Collection Framework provides a `HashSet` implementation, we still must understand how to use it wisely by configuring it in the proper way. This is an example of why an understanding of data structures, such as our discussions in Chapters 6 through 8, is so important to a modern software developer.

The last issue regarding the `HashSet` implementation is the hashing function f. As you know, the performance of a hash table is highly dependent on a good quality hashing function f that scatters keys evenly over the table. The root class of Java, `Object`, includes the following hashing function:

public int hashCode(); // return a hash code for this object

Since every object in Java inherits from `Object`, every object has a `hashCode()` method that can be used by one of the hash implementations. The default `hashCode()` method defined in class `Object` returns distinct integers for distinct objects. This is usually accomplished by converting the internal address of the object into an integer.

There is a relationship between the `hashCode()` and `equals()` methods that must be adhered to for the hash implementations to work correctly. Specifically, if two objects are equal according to the `equals()` method, then calling the `hashCode()` method on each of the objects must produce the same value. It is not required that, if two objects are unequal according to the `equals()` method, the `hashCode()` methods for the two objects return distinct values.

If you think about the way hashing works, you realize that these rules make perfect sense. Consider what might happen if two objects were equal according to the `equals()` method but had different hash code values. The `hashCode()` method would be used to find the bucket in which you would expect to find the object, but as you searched through the bucket, you would not find the object and incorrectly report that it was missing. On the other hand, the fact that hashCode() does not have to return distinct values for two objects that are not equal is precisely what causes a collision to occur in a hash table.

Essentially, what these rules mean is that whenever you override the equals() method, you must override hashCode() as well. The Dog class in Figure 9.26 illustrates the proper way to override the equals() and hashCode() methods in a class.

```java
/**
 * A class that represents a dog. The state of a dog consists of its
 * name, breed, and gender. Note that this class is not comparable.
 */

public class Dog {

    // code omitted . . .

    /**
     * Indicates whether some other object is equal to this one.
     *
     * @param o the object to be compared with
     *
     * @return true if this object is the same as the argument; false
     *     otherwise
     */
    public boolean equals( Object o ) {
        boolean retVal = false;

        if ( o instanceof Dog ) {
            Dog other = (Dog)o;
            retVal =
                breed.equals( other.getBreed() ) &&
                name.equals( other.getName() ) &&
                gender.equals( other.getGender() );
        }

        return retVal;
    }

    /**
     * Return a hash value for this object. The hash value for a dog
     * object is equal to the sum of the hash codes for the name, breed,
     * and gender of the dog.
     */
    public int hashCode() {
        return name.hashCode() + breed.hashCode() + gender.hashCode();
    }

} // Dog
```

FIGURE 9.26 Dog class

9.4.1.2 `TreeSet`

The second implementation of sets provided by the Java Collection Framework is `TreeSet`, and it uses a red-black tree to store the set elements. A **red-black tree** is a hierarchical data structure similar to those presented in Chapter 7. Although we did not discuss this particular tree structure, its characteristics will be quite familiar. It is a special form of the binary search tree discussed at length in Section 7.4.

In that discussion, the primary problem with the binary search tree was its worst-case performance. Referring to Figure 7.19, you can see the two extremes that are possible regarding the shape of a binary search tree. If it is well balanced, as in Figure 7.19b, then its height is $O(\log_2 N)$, and the worst-case time to insert or retrieve an element is logarithmic. However, if it is degenerate, as in Figure 7.19a, then its height is $O(N)$, and the worst-case insertion and retrieval times become linear in the number of elements. A red-black tree is a **balanced binary search tree** that does not permit the shape of the tree to look like the one in Figure 7.19a. It constantly maintains a balanced shape by performing a **rotation**, a restructuring of the tree around an individual element while maintaining the overall binary search tree property.[1] This guarantees that inserting and retrieving elements can be completed in $O(\log_2 N)$ time.

However, that doesn't seem very impressive since, as we showed in the previous section, if you choose your parameters well, insertion and retrieval using a `HashSet` are both $O(1)$. That is true, and if speed is the single most important consideration, then you should definitely choose a `HashSet` implementation over the `TreeSet`, as is done the great majority of the time.

So, what is the purpose of having this second `TreeSet` implementation? The answer lies in looking at Figure 7.21, the tree sort algorithm. If `T` is a binary search tree, then an inorder traversal of `T` visits the elements of `T` in sorted order. Thus, if it is important to be able to iterate through the elements of a set in ascending or descending order, then choose the `TreeSet`. Otherwise, go with the `HashSet` for its superior speed and performance. Since it is extremely important to iterate in order thorough a `SortedSet`, the `TreeSet` implementation is the only one provided by the framework for this type of interface.

◆ 9.4.2 Lists

9.4.2.1 `ArrayList`

The `ArrayList` implementation of `List` uses a one-dimensional array structure to store the elements in the list. This implementation is a bit different from the one discussed in Section 6.2.3.1 and diagrammed in Figure 6.8. In that implementation, even though we were using an array, we still maintained an explicit `next` field that identified the row number in the array where the next element is located. In the Java Collection Framework, the `ArrayList` implementation works like the array structure described in Exercise 7 at the end of Chapter 6.

In this approach, there is no explicit `next` field. We simply store the elements of list `L` in order in the array. That is, the first element of `L` is placed in position `a[0]`, the second element of `L` is in `a[1]`, and so on. The layout of the `ArrayList` implementation is shown in Figure 9.27, which comes from Exercise 7 in Chapter 6.

---

[1]To learn more about red-black trees and the rotation operation, the interested reader should check R. Sedgewick and M. Schidlowski, *Algorithms in Java*, 3rd ed. (Reading, Mass: Addison-Wesley, 2002).

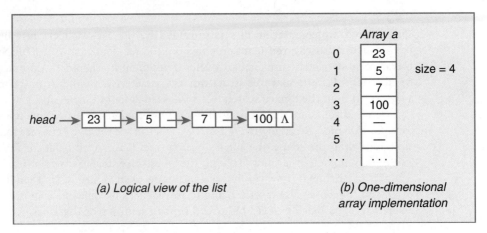

FIGURE 9.27 One-dimensional array implementation of a list

If we examine the structure shown in Figure 9.27b, we can quickly begin to appreciate the strengths and weaknesses of this array-based implementation. Positional access to an element in the list, the operation get(), is extremely fast due to the random access nature of arrays. For example, retrieving the third element of the list using the linked structure of Figure 9.27a would require us to traverse the list beginning from head, an O(N) operation. However, in the array implementation, we simply return the contents of a[2], a constant time O(1) operation. Similarly, changing the information field of an individual node, the operation set(), is also O(1). Adding a new element e to the end of the list is usually O(1) as well because we can write:

```
a[size] = e;
size++;
```

(Remember that in a List duplicates are allowed, so there is no need to first search the array to see if the element is there.) However, it is possible that the array has reached maximum capacity before we attempt to add this new element, and in that case, the array must be resized. When this occurs, the ArrayList implementation creates a new, larger array and copies all N elements from the old array into the new one. This requires O(N) time. Therefore, add() is O(1) if the array is not full and O(N) otherwise. (Although linear in time, the resizing operation is actually quite fast because of the method System.arraycopy(), which efficiently copies an entire array.) If accessing or modifying elements by position and adding new elements to the end of the list are common operations, then an ArrayList implementation works well, and it would be the implementation of choice.

When creating the ArrayList representation, there is a constructor that allows us to specify the initial capacity of the array:

```
ArrayList(int initialCapacity); // initial array size
```

If you have a good estimate of the maximum number of elements in the list, then create your array with an initialCapacity slightly larger than this maximum. Then you should never need a resizing and recopying operation.

The program in Figure 9.28 can measure the performance of random accesses within an array and linked list. The program creates two lists and fills them with random numbers. It then measures the amount of time required to perform 10,000 random accesses of each list. Not surprisingly, the time required for the linked list is approximately three times that of the array-based list.

```java
import java.util.ArrayList;
import java.util.LinkedList;
import java.util.List;

import java.util.Random;

/**
 * A program to test the efficiency of random access in an ArrayList
 * versus a LinkedList.
 */
public class RandomAccess {

    /**
     * This method will perform num random accesses of the given
     * list. The return value gives the number of milliseconds
     * required to perform the lookups.
     *
     * @param theList the list to access.
     * @param num the number of times to access the list.
     *
     * @return the number of milliseconds required to perform num
     *     accesses of the list.
     */
    public static int access( List theList, int num ) {
        Random rng = new Random();

        // Record the starting time
        long start = System.currentTimeMillis();

        // Access random locations within the list
        for ( int i = 0; i < num; i++ ) {
            Object x = theList.get( rng.nextInt( theList.size() ) );
        }

        // Return the time required to perform the loop
        return (int)( System.currentTimeMillis() - start );
    }

    /**
     * Fill a list with num random values.
     *
     * @param theList the list to fill.
```

(continued)

FIGURE 9.28 Timing random access of the `ArrayList` and `LinkedList` implementations

```
 * @param num the number of numbers to place in the list.
 * @param max the maximum value to place in the list.
 */
public static void fill( List theList, int num, int max ) {
   Random rng = new Random();

   for ( int i = 0; i < num; i++ ) {
       theList.add( new Integer( rng.nextInt( max ) ) );
   }
}

public static void main( String args[] ) {
   List aList = new ArrayList();
   List lList = new LinkedList();

   // Fill the lists
   fill( aList, 1000, 100 );
   fill( lList, 1000, 100 );

   // Report the time required to do 10,000 random accesses
   System.out.println( access( aList, 10000 ) );
   System.out.println( access( lList, 10000 ) );
}

} // RandomAccess
```

FIGURE 9.28 Timing random access of the `ArrayList` and `LinkedList` implementations *(continued)*

Looking back at Figure 9.27b, we can also begin to identify some of the `List` operations that might not work as well as those just discussed—that is, operations that make insertions or deletions somewhere in the middle of the array. For example,

```
add(int index, Object element);    // add element at position index
remove (int index);                // remove the element at index
```

In both cases, we will have to move elements down to make space for the new element to be added or move elements up to eliminate the space created by the remove. Depending on the exact value of `index`, both of the operations could take up to O(N) time in the worst case. Thus, operations such as adding a new element to the front of a list or iterating through a list removing items as you go may work slowly in an `ArrayList` implementation. If these operations are common, you may want to consider another implementation, called `LinkedList`, which is described in the next section. Exercise 9 at the end of the chapter asks you to use the program in Figure 9.28 to determine the performance implications of selecting an `ArrayList` versus a `LinkedList` implementation of a list.

9.4.2.2 `LinkedList`

The `LinkedList` implementation of the `List` interface is easy to describe as it is virtually identical to the doubly linked list structure discussed in Section 6.2.3.3 and diagramed in Figure 6.19b. This implementation maintains a forward and backward pointer in each node as well as references to both the first and the last element of the list. This implementation is diagramed in Figure 9.29.

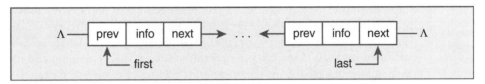

FIGURE 9.29 Doubly linked implementation of a list

Looking at Figure 9.29, we can quickly begin to understand the strengths and weaknesses of this implementation. The operations that were most efficient with the `ArrayList` implementation—accessing and modifying by position—become much slower in a `LinkedList` implementation. For example, to retrieve the eighth item in a linked list, we either have to start at first and move forward seven positions or start at last and move backward the correct number of positions, depending on which of the two indexes are closer to the target node. In either case, this requires in the worst case N/2 steps, making it O(N). This compares to O(1) in the `ArrayList`. Thus, if the most frequent operation performed on a list is accessing and/or modifying nodes scattered throughout the list, then `ArrayList`, with its ability to go directly to any node in constant time, is the better choice.

However, instead of accessing random nodes throughout the array, what if we want to iterate through the list, adding or deleting nodes as we traverse the structure? It is easy to traverse the linked list of Figure 9.12 in either the forward direction using the methods `first()` and `next()` or in the backward direction using `last()` and `previous()`. It is also easy to delete a node or add a node to a list in O(1) time once we have determined exactly where it is to go. (We showed this in Section 6.2.3.2.) Thus, if the most common operation on a list is traversing it and performing an addition or deletion operation on the nodes as we go, the `LinkedList` implementation will work very well.

Another noteworthy feature of `LinkedList` is that, like any reference-based implementation, it can grow as large as needed without ever having to be resized. There are no "tuning parameters" in the `LinkedList` constructors that require you to specify an initial capacity, and you do not have to make any estimates about the number of elements that will be added to the list. If your lists can be of widely varying sizes, from just a few to many thousands, this may be an important consideration.

In addition to the methods included in the `Collection` and `List` interfaces, the `LinkedList` implementation includes six methods not found in `ArrayList`. They are `addFirst()`, `addLast()`, `getFirst()`, `getLast()`, `removeFirst()`, and `removeLast()`. Their functions are obvious from the names, and given the existence of the `first` and `last` pointers in Figure 9.29, they can all be completed in O(1) time.

Interestingly enough, none of these routines are absolutely necessary because the operations they perform can all be done in other ways using existing routines. For example, `addFirst(Object e)` is identical to the method call `add(0, Object e)`. The method `getFirst()` behaves in an identical fashion to the call `get(0)`. The operation `removeLast()` is the same as `remove(size()-1)`. These six new methods were not added to the `LinkedList` implementation to extend its functionality but as a convenience to make it easier to construct the stack and queue data structures discussed in Sections 6.3 and 6.4.

If you remember from those earlier discussions, both a stack and a queue can be implemented using a linked list. These reference-based implementations were shown in Figure 6.31 (the stack) and Figure 6.41 (the queue). In these two data structures, we can only insert and delete items at the two ends of the list, what are called first and last in Figure 9.29. Therefore, the operations of adding, removing, and retrieving the first and last nodes in a list are identical to adding or removing elements from a stack and a queue. These equivalencies are summarized in Figure 9.30.

`LinkedList` Routine	Equivalent Stack Operation	Equivalent Queue Operation
`addFirst(Object e)`	`push(e)`	
`addLast(Object e)`		`enqueue(e)`
`e = getFirst()`	`e = top()`	`e = front()`
`e = getLast()`		`e = back()`
`e = removeFirst()`	`e = top(); pop()`	`e = front(); dequeue()`

FIGURE 9.30 `LinkedList` methods to implement a stack and a queue

For example, when you implement a stack, these additional routines allow you to think of the push operation as adding an element as the first item in the stack, `addFirst()`, rather than thinking of it as adding it to index position 0. Similarly, you can think of accessing the person at the back of a queue, `getLast()`, not the person at position `size()` - 1. It is a small difference, but the designers felt that allowing developers to work at a higher level of abstraction was sufficiently important to include these six additional routines in the `LinkedList` interface.

There is a special type of bidirectional iterator for `LinkedList` objects called `ListIterator`. The class that defines this object is a private class inside the `LinkedList` implementation. Therefore, users cannot explicitly declare these types of iterators themselves. Instead, they must use the following routine located in `LinkedList`:

`ListIterator listIterator(int index);`

This method creates an iterator that can sequence through the nodes of the list in either the forward or backward direction. The operations on `ListIterator` objects are summarized in Figure 9.31. (Note: There are also three optional methods in the `ListIterator` class—`add()`, `remove()`, and `set()`. However, since they are optional and their functions can be accomplished other ways, we do not describe them here.)

The only tricky thing when using list iterators is remembering the difference in behavior between the `next()` and `previous()` methods. Assume that a list `L` and a list iterator `p` are in the state shown below Figure 9.31:

Method	Description
`boolean hasNext()`	Returns true if there are more elements in the forward direction (i.e., the iterator is not null) and false otherwise.
`boolean hasPrevious()`	Returns true if there are more elements in the backward direction (i.e., we are not positioned at the first node) and false otherwise.
`Object next()`	Returns the next element in the list in the forward direction.
`Object previous()`	Returns the previous element in the list in the backward direction.
`int nextIndex()`	Returns the index of the element that would be returned by a subsequent call to next.
`int previousIndex()`	Returns the index of the element that would be returned by a subsequent call to previous.

FIGURE 9.31 `ListIterator` operations

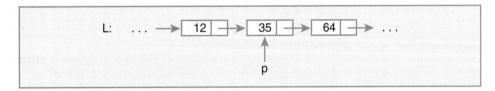

The `next()` method first returns the value of the object to which it is pointing, in this case 35, and then advances to the next node, the one containing the 64. The `previous()` method first retreats to the predecessor of the node it is currently referencing and then returns the value of that object, the integer 12. These differences in the behavior of `next()` and `previous()` mean that we must write our code somewhat differently when traversing the list in the forward and the backward directions. In the forward direction, we initialize our list iterator to the first item (the one with index 0) and continue until there are no more nodes (Figure 9.32a).

```
ListIterator p = L.listIterator(0);
while (p.hasNext()) {
        Object e = p.next();
        // and now do something with object e
}
```

FIGURE 9.32a Traversing a `LinkedList` in the forward direction

However, when moving in the reverse direction, we must initialize the list iterator one position beyond the end of the list. If we were to incorrectly initialize it to the last position, then when we made our first call to `previous()`, we would move to the second-to-last item, return it, and ignore the last item, producing an off-by-one error.

The size of the list is given by `size()`, and the indexes of the nodes go from 0 to `size() − 1`. Therefore, if we initialize our list iterator to the value of `size()`, it will be correctly positioned to do the traversal. This code is shown in Figure 9.32b.

```
ListIterator p = L.listIterator(size());
while (p.hasPrevious())    {
      Object e = p.previous();
      // and now do something with object e
}
```

FIGURE 9.32b Traversing a `LinkedList` in the reverse direction

◆ 9.4.3 Maps

The `HashMap` implementation of the `Map` interface is virtually identical to the `HashSet` implementation of the `Set` interface described in Section 9.4.1.1. In fact, a `HashSet` object is an instance of a `HashMap` object in which the value field of the (key, value) tuple is ignored. Otherwise, all of our discussions regarding `HashSet` apply in exactly the same fashion to a `HashMap` implementation. This includes making sure that you properly parameterize `HashMap` using appropriate values for both of the tuning parameters, `initialCapacity` and `loadFactor`.

Similarly, the `TreeMap` implementation of the `Map` interface is identical to the `TreeSet` implementation of `Set` described in Section 9.4.1.2. Again, all that differs is the fact that now we use the value field, whereas it was previously ignored. The `TreeMap` implementation uses the same red-black balanced tree structure described earlier. This produces O(log N) logarithmic behavior for insertion, deletion, and retrieval of elements to/from the map data structure.

Since the `HashMap` implementation, if properly parameterized, produces O(1) behavior for insertion and retrieval, we have the same question that we asked earlier: Why would we ever want to use a `TreeMap`? The answer is the same one given earlier: A `TreeMap` implementation guarantees that the map can be efficiently traversed in sorted sequence according to the "natural order" of the class of the key field. (See Section 9.3.4.1 for a discussion of natural ordering of elements and the behavior of the two methods `compareTo()` and `equals()`.) This ability to do a sorted traversal of keys is critical for the `SortedMap` (and `SortedSet`) interface discussed in Section 9.3.4. This is because the `Iterator` returned by the `iterator()` method in `Collection` must traverse a `SortedMap` (as well as a `SortedSet`) in key order. This can be done efficiently when using a `TreeMap` (and `TreeSet`) implementation, but it is extremely slow with the `HashMap` and the `HashSet`. In addition, when applied to a sorted collection (either `SortedSet` or `SortedMap`), the arrays returned by the `toArray()` methods must store the keys, values, or entries in key order.

Because of this need to provide ordered traversals and ordered array storage to the set of keys or the map of (key, value) tuples, the only implementations of `SortedMap` and `SortedSet` provided by the Java Collection Framework are `TreeMap` and `TreeSet`, respectively.

9.5 ALGORITHMS

The final part of the Java Collection Framework to be discussed in this chapter is the **algorithms** that operate on the different types of collections in the framework. The algorithms take the form of **static** class methods, and they are found in the `Collections` and `Arrays` classes. The `Collections` class provides algorithms designed to operate on arbitrary collections, whereas the algorithms in the `Arrays` class are designed to operate on standard Java arrays. We begin with the algorithms provided by the `Collections` class.

The majority of the methods in the `Collections` class work on `Lists`. However, there are a few methods that operate on arbitrary collections. If you look at the description of the algorithmic methods listed in Figure 9.33, you will realize that many of them require the collection on which they work to be an ordered collection. For example, you can only swap elements in an ordered collection because elements do not have a position in an unordered collection, and the concept of swapping would be meaningless.

The `Collections` class uses the binary search algorithm (discussed in Section 5.3.3) to search for a specific elements in a list. Thus, the list must be sorted before the

Signature	Description
`int binarySearch(List l, Object key);` `int binarySearch(List l, Object k, Comparator c);`	Searches the list for the specified value.
`void sort(List list);` `void sort(List list, Comparator c);`	Sorts the list.
`void reverse(List list);`	Reverses the contents of the list.
`void fill(List list, Object value);`	Fills the list with the specified value.
`void copy(List dest, List src);`	Copies the specified list.
`void shuffle(List list);` `void shuffle(List list, Random rng);`	Randomly shuffles the contents of the given list.
`Object max(Collection coll);` `Object max(Collection coll, Comparator c);`	Returns the maximum value in the collection.
`Object min(Collection coll);` `Object min(Collection coll, Comparator c);`	Returns the minimal value in the collection.
`boolean replaceAll( List l, Object old, Object new);`	Replaces all occurrences of old with new.
`void rotate(List list, int distance);`	Rotates the elements of the list the specified distance.
`void swap(List list, int i, int j);`	Swaps the specified elements in the list.

FIGURE 9.33 Some algorithms in the Java Collection Framework

binarySearch() method can be invoked. There are two forms of the binarySearch() method. The first, which takes only a list and a key as parameters, assumes that the elements in the list are sorted into ascending order according to their natural order. In other words, it assumes that the elements in the list implement the Comparable interface. The second form also includes a Comparator parameter c, and it can be used for lists whose elements do not have a natural order or if some other ordering is desired for the purposes of the search. A positive return value from binarySearch() indicates that the target was found in the list, and the return value gives the index position where the element was found. A negative return value indicates that the target was not found in the list.

The sort() method, like the binarySearch() method, has two forms: one that uses the natural order of the elements in the list and a second that specifies a Comparator that is used to impose an ordering on the elements in the list. The sort method repositions the elements in a list so that they appear in ascending order according to either the natural order of the elements in the list or according to the Comparator. The sort method uses the O(N $\log_2$ N) merge sort algorithm that was discussed and analyzed in Section 5.5.

An important feature of merge sort is that it is **stable**. This means that it does not reorder equal elements. If two elements in the list are equal, they will appear in the same order in the sorted list. This fact is useful when you have to sort a list by two different criteria. Consider, for example, the Dog class in Figure 9.19. If we wished to sort a list of dogs so that they were ordered by breed and then by name, we could sort the list once by name and then sort it a second time by breed. All dogs whose breeds are the same will appear in alphabetical order by name.

The following code shows how to use the sort() and binarySearch() methods to find a value in a List. Note that it is necessary to sort the list before calling binary search because the list itself is not ordered.

```
Collections.sort( dogs );
if ( binarySearch( dogs, target ) ) < 0 ) {
    System.out.println( target + " is not in the list" );
}
```

The max() and min() methods can be used to find the maximum and minimum values in an arbitrary Collection. These are the only methods in the Collections class that work on a Collection. All they require is the ability to iterate over the collection, which is something that all collections provide. By now, you should have a good feel for the methods in the Collections class, and it should come as no surprise there are two forms of max() and min(). One form assumes that the elements in the list are Comparable, and the second takes a Comparator that is used to order the elements.

You might wonder at this point what would happen if you invoked a form of a Collections method that expected its elements to be Comparable, but they were not. The answer is that it will cause an error. The code that implements the first form of the max() method uses an Iterator to individually examine each of the elements in the collection. The next() method of the iterator returns an Object that will, in this situation, be cast to Comparable. However, if the object does not implement the

Comparable interface, then a ClassCastException will be thrown. This holds true for the binarySearch() and sort() methods as well.

The remaining methods in Figure 9.33 provide algorithms to manipulate the data stored in a List in a variety of different ways. The shuffle algorithm does the opposite of what sort does: It randomizes the position of elements within a List. The following code shows how to create a list called aList that contains the integer values from 0 to 99 in some random order:

```
List aList = new ArrayList();

for ( int i = 0; i < 100; i++ ) {
    AList.add( new Integer( i ) );
}


Collections.shuffle( aList );
```

The Collections class also provides a number of **wrapper methods** that can be used to change the functionality of a collection in some interesting and useful ways. The only wrapper methods we present here are called **unmodifiable wrappers**, which are more commonly termed **read-only wrappers**.

These methods are extremely easy to explain—they basically allow a user to access and traverse a collection, but they cannot change it in any way. Thus, operations like get(), next(), previous(), size(), and isEmpty(), which do not alter the elements of the collection, will all function in exactly the same way that we have described. However, operations like add(), remove(), and set() are explicitly prohibited. If you have declared a collection to be read-only, then any attempt to modify the collection will be intercepted by the system, which will throw an UnsupportedOperationException and terminate your program. (You will see how to deal with exception objects in the following chapter.)

You create a read-only collection in two steps. The first step is to create a regular collection in exactly the way that we have been discussing throughout this chapter. This could be a Collection, Set, Map, List, SortedSet, or SortedMap. Then you "wrap" that collection inside a read-only collection using one of the following six **static** methods that correspond to each of the regular collection types:

```
public static Collection unmodifiableCollection(Collection c);
public static Set unmodifiableSet(Set s);
public static List unmodifiableList(List list);
public static Map unmodifiableMap(Map m);
public static SortedSet unmodifiableSortedSet(SortedSet s);
public static SortedMap unmodifiableSortedMap(SortedMap m);
```

The collection returned by these methods contains exactly the same elements in the initial collection but is a read-only object that cannot be modified.

One of the advantages of these read-only collections is that you can create two distinct classes of users. For example, given the following declaration

```
Set s;                         // The original set collection
Set ums;                       // The unmodifiable set
...                            // Build the set s (code omitted)
ums = unmodifiableSet( s );    // Create a read-only set ums
```

there will be "first-class" users who are allowed to do anything they want. For these users, you pass a reference to s, the original collection. They can look at s as well as change s. However, there will also be second-class users who are allowed to "look but don't touch." For these users, you will pass a reference to ums. Any attempt by these users to modify ums will be trapped and recognized as an error.

Another interesting application of these read-only collections is in the software development process. Assume that your code initially builds a collection. Then for the rest of the program, all you do is work with those elements, but you never change them. One example of this might be a dictionary of words. Once you build it, you only want to look up words; you don't want to remove words or modify definitions. One way to ensure that your program behaves in this fashion is to take your dictionary and make it a read-only structure as follows:

```
List d = new ArrayList();           // The dictionary
...                                 // Build the dictionary
dictionary = unmodifiableList(d);   // The contents of this
                                    // object cannot be changed
```

Now we discard the reference to the original dictionary, d, and keep only the read-only reference, called dictionary. All coding is done in terms of the read-only object dictionary, and the program is unable to change this collection. You can be sure of avoiding bugs in your software that would be caused by unexpected and incorrect changes to your dictionary data structure.

The Arrays class provides methods that allow you to convert an array to a list, search the array, sort the array, determine if two arrays are equal, and fill the array with a specific value. The methods in the Arrays class behave in the same way as those that we just described in the Collections class. The biggest difference you will notice when you look at the Arrays class is that it provides overloaded methods that work with arrays of any type.

9.6 SUMMARY

Virtually all assignments in a first computer science course ask students (either individually or as part of a team) to build a program from scratch. All code, with the exception of such minor library routines as abs() or sqrt(), is original and designed, written, and tested by the students themselves. This is viewed as necessary because the focus of these courses is on teaching the fundamental concepts of programming languages and implementation.

However, this approach does not at all model how programming is done in the real world. Building an entire application from scratch is horribly slow, extremely expensive, and highly prone to errors. Instead, programmers will try to reuse as much existing code as they can, either from the standard libraries provided by the language, existing software in the public domain, or from their own private collection of helpful routines. The operational policy for software development in the real world is not "how do I build it" but rather "where can I find it."

We hope that the discussions on the Java Collection Framework in this chapter have made this point quite clear. Chapters 6, 7, and 8 discussed a number of different data structures and provided implementations for many of them. There was a massive amount of original code presented so that we could demonstrate the concepts and ideas being discussed. These chapters represent the section of the text that focuses on teaching fundamental concepts in algorithms, complexity, and data structures. Although it is absolutely essential to understand these concepts (we emphasized that point a number of times), Chapter 9 reflects in a much more realistic way how a modern software developer actually works with these data structures.

The Java Collection Framework provides interfaces and implementations for virtually all of the structures that we have discussed, and you should be familiar with and comfortable with the ideas reflected in this framework. Then, when you have a problem to solve and a program to write, you won't have to start at the very beginning. Instead, you scan the available libraries and select the most appropriate and most efficient structures to solve your problem. Not only does this keep costs down, but it also goes a long way toward ensuring the correctness of the completed software package that is delivered to the user.

EXERCISES

1. Using the methods in the Java Collection Framework, write the method:

   public int countKey(List L, Object key);

   The method iterates through the list L, using a ListIterator, and returns the total number of times that the object named key occurs in the list.

2. Using the methods in the Java Collection Framework, write the method:

   public void deleteKey(List L, Object key);

   The method iterates through the list L, using a ListIterator, and deletes every occurrence of the object key in the list.

3. Referring to the BookShelf class in Figure 9.16, write the method

   public Collection getAllISBN();

   that returns a Collection that contains the ISBN of every book in the BookShelf.

4. Assume that the Name class of Figure 9.18 includes a first name, last name, and middle name. In addition, there is an accessor method, getMiddle(), that will return the middle name. Rewrite the compareTo() method of Name such that the rules for comparing two names are as follows:

a. A name is greater than another name if its last name is greater (in an alphabetical sense).

b. If the last names are the same, then a name is greater than another name if its first name is greater.

c. If both the first and last names are the same, then a name is greater than another name if its middle name is greater.

5. Write a Comparator for the Dog class of Figure 9.19 that implements comparisons in the following way:

a. Female dogs are greater than male dogs.

b. For two dogs of the same gender, order the dogs by their name.

c. For dogs of the same gender and name, order the dogs by their breed.

6. Assume that we have a SortedSet, called serialNumbers, that contains an ordered list of five-character serial numbers exactly as described in Section 9.3.4.2. The first character of the serial number is a letter A, B, . . . that identifies a particular vendor. The last four digits 0000, 0001, . . . identify a particular piece of equipment from that vendor. Assume that our 13 current vendors are assigned the letters A to M. Write a method that produces a table giving the number of pieces of equipment provided by each of our 13 vendors.

7. Using the built-in hashCode() method inherited by all objects from Object, perform the following computations:

```
int a[50];
for (int k = 0; k < 10000; k++)        {
        // generate a random integer n and convert n
        // to an Integer object nObj using the Integer class
        // this code is not shown
        i = (nObj.hashCode()) % 50;
        a[i]++;
}
```

Your function will generate 10,000 values, each in the range 0–49. If the hashing function hashCode() is working well, it should scatter these 10,000 values evenly, producing about 200 hits to each of the 50 buckets in the array a. Run this test program and look at how many values hashed to each of the 50 locations. Use these data to determine if the built-in hashing function does or does not seem to be working well. (If you know a little statistics, you can do this analysis formally using a chi-square goodness of fit test. If you don't know how to do this, then do an eyeball analysis.)

8. Construct a HashSet implementation of a Set using a range of different values for the initialCapacity and loadFactor parameters. Now measure exactly how long it takes to add 10,000 elements to the set and delete 10,000 from the set. Collect these times and graph them as a function of the different values of these two parameters. Discuss the effect that the values of these parameters have on the time that it takes to insert and delete elements using a HashSet implementation.

9. Build a `List` data structure using both an `ArrayList` and a `LinkedList` implementation. Store 10,000 elements into the `List` (the type of the elements does not matter) and time how long it takes to do each of these three operations:

a. Do 1,000 retrievals of a randomly selected position in the `List`.

b. Insert 1,000 new elements into the `List` in a random location.

c. Delete 1,000 randomly selected elements from the `List`.

Use the data you collected to discuss the performance implications of these two different implementations of a `List` data structure.

10. Write a program that reads the contents of a text file and produces a report that lists the 10 most common and the 10 least common words. The program should be written so that the name of the file to process is found on the command line. To have some fun with your program after it is written, look on the Web for Project Gutenberg (promo.net/pg/), which is a project to convert many classic pieces of literature to electronic form.

11. List two reasons you might want to use a `Comparator` in a Java program.

12. What output will be generated when the following program is executed?

```
import java.util.*;

public class Program1 {
    public static void main( String args[] ) {
        List lib = new ArrayList();

        lib.add( new Book( "Core Java", "Horstmann", 630 ) );
        lib.add( new Book( "Unix Power Tools", "Peek", 1127 ) );
        lib.add( new Book( "Java", "Buster", 1995 ) );
        lib.add( new Book( "Java", "Grumpy", 423 ) );

        list( lib );

        System.out.println();

        Collections.sort( lib, new ByTitleAndAuthor() );
        list( lib );
    }

    public static void list( List l ) {
        Iterator i = l.iterator();

        while ( i.hasNext() ) {
            System.out.println( i.next() );
        }
    }
}
```

13. The following program compiles but generates a `ClassCastException` when it runs. What is wrong with the program?

```
import java.util.*;

public class Program3 {
    public static void main( String args[] ) {
        List lib = new ArrayList();

        lib.add( new Book( "Core Java", "Horstmann", 630 ) );
        lib.add( new Book( "Unix Power Tools", "Peek", 1127 ) );
        lib.add( new Book( "Java", "Buster", 1995 ) );
        lib.add( new Book( "Java", "Grumpy", 423 ) );

        Collections.sort( lib );
        list( lib );
    }

    public static void list( List l ) {
        for ( Iterator i = l.iterator(); i.hasNext(); ) {
            System.out.println( i.next() );
        }
    }
}
```

14. The `TreeSet` class uses a red-black tree to avoid building unbalanced trees. An AVL tree is similar to a red-black tree in that it reorganizes itself from time to time to maintain balance. Find a description of AVL trees and write a class named `AVLTreeSet` that implements the `Set` interface using AVL trees.

15. Using classes from the Java Collection Framework, write an implementation of the `Graph` interface given in Figure 8.18.

16. You are designing an application that requires elements in a collection to be maintained in the sequence in which they are added to the collection. In addition, you know that elements will often be added and removed from the middle of the collection. Select the most appropriate implementation class and justify your selection.

17. In creating an object such as a `Set` or a `Map`, we choose an actual implementation, such as a `HashSet` or a `HashMap`. In declaring this object, we prefer to use an interface, such as `Set` or `Map`. Explain why and list the benefits of doing this.

18. The `LinkedList` class provides several methods that are not defined in the `List` interface. Why is it not a good idea to use these "special" linked list methods in a program?

19. Which sequence of digits will the following program print?

```
public class Lists {
    public static void main( String args[] ) {
```

```
        List list = new ArrayList();
        list.add( "1" );
        list.add( "2" );
        list.add( 1, "3" );
        List list2 = new LinkedList( list );
        list.addAll( list2 );
        list2 = list.subList( 2, 5 );
        list2.clear();
        System.out.println( list );
    }
}
```

20. Java iterators are described as being "fail-fast." Look on the Java home page java.sun.com to see what this means and then describe why it is important.

21. Design a SortedList interface for the Java Collection Framework. A SortedList should implement list and provide methods similar to those found in SortedSet and SortedMap that take advantage of the fact that the list is sorted. Write two classes that implement your SortedList interface using an array-based list and a linked list.

22. Write a program that measures the performance of the sorted list implementations that you wrote for Exercise 21. Does it make sense to implement a sorted list using an array?

23. Normally, a telephone book lists telephone numbers alphabetically by the name of the person who owns the number. This makes it almost impossible, given a telephone number only, to find the name of the person who owns the number. Write a PhoneBook class that manages a phone directory (i.e., you should be able to add, change, and delete directory entries). The class must provide two search methods, getByName() and getByNumber(), that retrieve the directory information for an individual given the name or number of the person in question. Both search methods must perform their searches in O(1) time.

24. Design and implement a class that simulates the operation of a cash register. Your class must include the following methods:

   ◆ purchase() that takes as parameters the UPC, description, and cost of an item that is being purchased.

   ◆ coupon() that takes the UPC number of the item the coupon applies to and the amount of money the coupon is worth.

   ◆ printReceipt() that prints a receipt for the items purchased and coupons that were redeemed. The items purchased by the customer must be listed in the same order as they were purchased, and the coupons must be listed in order based on the UPC of the item they apply to. The receipt must show the total cost of all the items purchased, the sum of the amounts of all of the coupons, and the total owed by the customer.

   The register should handle coupons as follows:

   ◆ Duplicate coupons (i.e., two coupons with the same UPC code) are not accepted. The cash register will accept only the first coupon.

◆ A coupon will not be accepted unless the corresponding item (an item with the same UPC code) has been purchased.

◆ If the value of the coupon is more than the price of the item it applies to, the value of the coupon will be reduced to match the price of the item.

25. Write a class that implements a dictionary. The class should provide methods to add words to the dictionary. The dictionary must include a method named `spellCheck()` that takes a string as an argument and returns a list that determines if the word is in the dictionary. If the word is in the dictionary, the list will be empty. If the word is not in the dictionary, the list will contain a sorted list of possible spellings for the word. You should write your class so that the `spellCheck()` method runs as quickly as possible.

PART III

MODERN PROGRAMMING TECHNIQUES

CHAPTER 10

Exceptions and Streams

10.1 INTRODUCTION

After a long, hard day at the office, it is time to head home. You find your car in the parking lot, start it, and begin to drive. About half way home you hear a thumping noise. You pull off the road, take a look, and discover that one of the front tires has gone flat. Fortunately, you know how to change a flat tire, so you quickly put on the spare, get back in the car, and resume the drive with only a minor delay. Flat tires are rare events that happen to an individual only once every few years, but you were prepared for it. Even though a spare tire and jack are seldom used, they must be there when you need them. Having this equipment in your car and knowing how to use it can help to prevent a small problem from becoming a major catastrophe.

Software systems, like human beings, also must deal with rare and unexpected events. In the area of software design, an unplanned event that lies outside the normal behavior of an algorithm is called an **exception**. For example, consider what might happen when a user instructs a spreadsheet program to save the current worksheet on a floppy disk. About 99.99 percent of the time, the user will have placed a usable and correctly formatted floppy disk into the appropriate drive before executing this command. However, a well-designed program must also deal with the possibility that the disk is not present, is not usable, or does not have enough room to store the information. All of these situations represent events that are not part of the normal concerns of the algorithm.

An exception is not simply a special case of the algorithm that should be handled by the program as part of its regular flow of control. Consider a program that locates the largest number in an array segment of size M within a larger array of length N. The fact that two or more entries might have the same largest value would not be considered an exception. It would be one of the cases that needs to be checked and handled within the program. However, if M, the size of the segment, is greater than N, this may need to be handled as an `ArrayIndexOutOfBoundsException`. Similarly, if we are reading data values into an integer array and we encounter a string, such as "three," this may be considered a `NumberFormatException`.

The idea of writing a program to deal with unexpected events is nothing new. In fact, programmers have been writing code to deal with these types of errors for years. Consider the task of writing the `pop()` method for the `Stack` interface defined in Figure 10.1. (Note: This version of `pop()` is slightly different from the one shown in

```
public interface Stack {
    public void push( Object element );
    public Object pop();

    public boolean isEmpty();
    public boolean isFull();
}
```

FIGURE 10.1 Simple `Stack` interface

Figure 6.26.) This `pop()` method, which removes the top value from the stack and returns it, must deal with the possibility that the stack is empty. Clearly, it is not difficult to determine if the stack is empty. The difficulty lies in deciding what to do should this case arise. One possibility, shown in Figure 10.2, is to print an error message and terminate the program.

```java
public Object pop() {
    Object returnVal = null;

    if ( isEmpty() ) {
        System.err.println( "Empty Stack" );
        System.exit( 1 );
    }

    // Set returnVal to the value currently on
    // top of the stack. Then remove that element
    // from the stack. This code is omitted to focus
    // on the issues of exception handling.

    return returnVal;
}
```

FIGURE 10.2 Handling exceptions using `System.exit()`

Although the version of `pop()` in Figure 10.2 will work if the stack is empty, how can the programmer be certain that, when this situation arises, the appropriate action is to terminate the program? Think about the possible consequences if automobiles were designed to turn the engine off whenever a flat tire was detected! It is often the case that there is not enough information available at the point in the program where an exception occurs to make a reasoned and informed decision about the best course of action. The fact that an exception has occurred may need to be passed to a higher level of the program where enough information is available to make a decision about how to handle the problem.

There are several ways in which `pop()` can be modified to pass information about the exception to the calling method. For example, the code in Figure 10.3 returns a `null` reference to indicate that an exception has occurred.

Although this code passes information about the exception back to the caller of the `pop()` method, there are still some serious drawbacks with this technique. To use a return value to indicate whether or not an exception occurred, it must be the case that this value cannot validly be returned by the method as a possible answer. In the code of Figure 10.3, if it were the case that `null` references could be stored in the stack, the code could not use the value `null` to unambiguously signal that an exception took place. There are ways around this limitation. One possibility, illustrated in Figure 10.4, is to define an instance variable within the `Stack` class that is set to indicate if the last operation was successful. The calling program would check the value of this instance variable after every call to `pop()` to determine if an error occurred.

```
public Object pop() {
   Object returnVal = null;

   if ( !isEmpty() ) {
      // set returnVal to the value
      // currently on the top of the stack,
      // and remove that element from the
      // stack. This code is not shown.
   }

   return returnVal;
}
```

FIGURE 10.3 Handling exceptions by returning `null`

```
public class Stack {
   // Instance variable used to indicate
   // if pop() worked properly

   private boolean success;

   public Object pop() {
      Object returnVal = null;

      if ( !isEmpty() ) {
         // set returnVal to the value currently
         // on the top of the stack, and remove
         // that element from the stack. This
         // code has been omitted.
         success = true;
      }
      else {
         success = false;
      }

      return returnVal;
   }

   public boolean getSuccess() {
      return success;
   }
}
```

FIGURE 10.4 Handling exceptions using state variables

The major drawback of the technique in Figure 10.4 is that the calling method is not required to check if an exception has occurred. The pop() method can provide information to the caller that an exception occurred, but there is no guarantee that the caller will do anything about it. The coding techniques in Figures 10.3 and 10.4 both depend on the calling program to actually check to see if an exception has taken place. The compiler itself does not enforce exception checking and handling.

Many programmers find it tedious to continually check return values or instance variables to determine if a method call was successful. Instead of writing the code shown in Figure 10.5a, programmers often get lazy and assume that the method invocation will work correctly, as shown in Figure 10.5b:

```
val = aStack.pop();                    // Assume an exception does not
                                       // occur (i.e. be lazy).
if ( aStack.getSuccess() ) {
   // Handle the successful case       // Assume val is correct
   // (code omitted)
} else {                               val = aStack.pop();
   // Handle the error case
   // (code omitted)
}

(a) The "correct" way                  (b) The "lazy" way
```

FIGURE 10.5 Handling exceptions

A second problem with the approach in Figure 10.5 is that error handling is intermixed with the code that implements the logic of the method itself, resulting in programs that can be harder to read and understand. For trivial programs, this may not be an issue, but for large-scale programs, this coding style can result in programs that are difficult to work with and, more important, difficult to maintain. Thus, as the last few paragraphs have shown, all the exception handling approaches described so far have serious and fundamental flaws.

Interestingly enough, it was not until 1975[1] that language designers began to think about creating formal control structures that would provide greater support for exceptions. The basic idea is to provide programmers with an **exception class** (or type in a traditional programming language) that can be used to describe unusual or erroneous events. Whenever a method wishes to inform a caller that an unusual event has occurred, it creates an **exception object** to describe the event and generates an exception. An **exception handler** in the calling method is invoked to analyze the exception object and take the appropriate actions. The set of possible actions may include passing the information to higher levels of the program.

To incorporate exceptions into your programs, you must understand three basic concepts. First, you need to know how exceptions are represented and created. In an object-oriented language, exceptions are usually represented as objects, and they are created in the same way as other objects in the language. Second, you must know how to define an exception handler that will process the exceptions that occur

---

[1]John B. Goodenough, *Exception Handling: Issues and a Proposed Notation, Programming Languages,* Vol. 18, December 1975.

within your program. When an exception handler is activated, you need to under-stand what variables are in scope and what restrictions, if any, are imposed by the language on the code contained in the handler. Finally, you must understand how control is passed from the program to an exception handler and what happens to the flow of control after the exception has completed. We address all of these issues in the following sections.

10.2 EXCEPTIONS IN JAVA

◆ 10.2.1 Representing Exceptions

Exceptions are represented as objects derived from the class `Throwable` or one of its subclasses. The state maintained by a `Throwable` object includes a record of the method calls leading up to the event that caused the exception object to be created and a string that provides textual information about the exception that occurred. This state can determine where in the program the problem occurred and produce an error message describing the nature of the problem. Some of the methods defined in the `Throwable` class are listed in Table 10.1.

Java divides the exceptions it recognizes into two broad categories called **checked** and **unchecked**. Unchecked exceptions, instances of the `Error` and `RunTime-Exception` classes, represent serious system errors that a typical program should not try to handle. Examples of unchecked exceptions include running out of memory, stack overflow in the Java Virtual Machine, or an attempt to load an invalid class file. All these problems are beyond the user's ability to recover from and continue. Checked exceptions, subclasses of the `Exception` class, represent errors that a typical program can handle. An overview of the exception hierarchy is shown in Figure 10.6.

TABLE 10.1 Methods Defined in Class `Throwable`

Method Signature	Description
`Throwable()`	Creates a new `Throwable` object with no message.
`Throwable( String message )`	Creates a new `Throwable` object with the specified error message.
`String getMessage()`	Returns the error message associated with this object.
`void printStackTrace()`	Prints a stack trace for this `Throwable` object on the error output stream. A stack trace is a record of the methods that were called and where they may be found in the source code leading up to the event that caused this object to be created. Typical output produced by this method is:
| | ```
java.lang.NullPointerException
        at Stack.pop(Stack.java:20)
        at Stack.main(Stack.java:33)
Exception in thread "main"
``` |
```

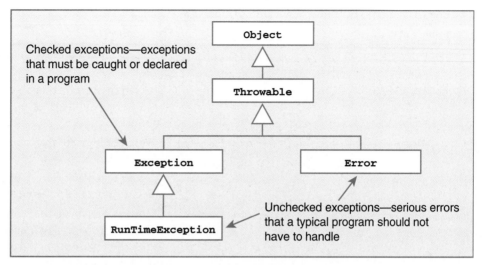

FIGURE 10.6 Java Exception class hierarchy

The Java language specification requires that a program either handle or declare any checked exceptions that might be generated either by providing a handler for that exception (catching it) or informing the calling program that you may generate this type of exception but will not personally handle it (declaring it). This policy, enforced by the Java compiler, is referred to as Java's **catch or declare** policy. This means that the programmer must account for any checked exception that might be generated in a program. Almost all of the exceptions that you will deal with in a Java program will be checked exceptions.

You might wonder why the designers of the Java programming language decided to split the exception classes into unchecked and checked categories. If you think about the types of serious run-time errors that unchecked exceptions represent, it is easy to see that the cost of handling unchecked exceptions often exceeds the benefit of catching or specifying them because the user generally cannot recover from them. Thus, the compiler does not require that you deal with unchecked exceptions, although you can if you wish. However, checked exceptions represent errors that a program should be able to deal with, and the compiler ensures that these types of exceptions are either caught or declared.

As you might expect, a large number of exception and error classes have already been defined in Java. These exception classes are usually defined within the package that contains the classes that generate the exceptions. For example, all of the exceptions that deal with input and output are found in the java.io package, and all of the exceptions that deal with networking errors are in the java.net package. Table 10.2 lists some of the most common Java exceptions along with the name of the package in which the exception is defined. By convention, each exception class provides two constructors: a no argument constructor and a one-parameter constructor that takes a string that provides an error message describing the nature of the exception.

Clearly, the software engineers at Sun could not anticipate every possible exception condition that may occur within a program, so from time to time, you may find it necessary to write your own exception classes to deal with a situation specific to your

TABLE 10.2 Some Common Java Exceptions

Exception	Package	Description
FileNotFoundException	java.io	Thrown when a request to open a file fails.
IllegalArgumentException	java.lang	Thrown to indicate that a method has been passed an illegal or inappropriate argument.
IOException	java.io	Thrown to indicate that some sort of I/O error has occurred.
NullPointerException	java.lang	Thrown when attempting to access an object using a null reference.
NumberFormatException	java.lang	Thrown when an application attempts to convert a string to a numeric type, but the string does not have the appropriate format.
UnsupportedOperationException	java.lang	Thrown when the object does not provide the requested operation.

application. Figure 10.7 shows the specification of a StackException class that could be used to indicate that an error occurred either when attempting to push an item on to a full stack or popping an element off of an empty stack. StackException is an error condition that we expect a program to handle, and that is why it extends the Exception class of Figure 10.6 rather than the Error class.

```
public class StackException extends Exception {
    public StackException() {}

    public StackException( String msg ) {
        super( msg );
    }
}
```

FIGURE 10.7 StackException class

Although the StackException class in Figure 10.7 is sufficient for describing the two exceptions that may occur when working with a Stack, the only way to determine the exact cause (i.e., whether we attempted to improperly add or remove an item) is to examine the string contained within the exception object.

Consider the two exception classes defined in Figure 10.8. The classes StackUnderflow and StackOverflow are still StackExceptions, but they more accurately define the nature of the problem that was encountered. We have created a separate exception class for each of the two distinct types of stack exceptions that can oc-

```
public class StackUnderflow extends StackException {
   public StackUnderflow() {}

   public StackUnderflow( String msg ) {
      super( msg );
}

public class StackOverflow extends StackException {
   public StackOverflow() {}

   public StackOverflow( String msg ) {
      super( msg );
}
```

FIGURE 10.8 Exception classes for use with the `Stack` class

cur. Adding these two classes gives a programmer writing code that uses the `Stack` class the flexibility to look for the more general `StackException` or the more specific `StackOverflow` and `StackUnderflow` exceptions. When designing classes that contain methods that generate exceptions, the designer needs to give careful attention to the amount of information that the exceptions can provide to the user.

◆ 10.2.2 Generating Exceptions

Now that you know how exceptions are represented in Java and how to create them, the next question is what to do with them. Instantiating an exception object is not enough to set the exception handling mechanism into action. After a program detects that an exceptional event has occurred and has created an exception object to represent that condition, it must trigger the exception handling code contained within the program. The process of invoking an exception handler is called **throwing** an exception. In Java, the `throw` statement is used to raise an exception and to trigger execution of the exception handling mechanism. The syntax of the `throw` statement is:

throw exceptionObject;

The `throw` statement takes as an argument a reference to an object from the class `Throwable` or one its subclasses as diagramed in Figure 10.6. The code in Figure 10.9 illustrates the proper use of the throw statement.

When a `throw` statement is executed, normal execution of the program is terminated, and the exception handling mechanism is put into action. Exceptions that are thrown must be handled, or the program will be terminated. Up to this point, you probably have not placed any code in your Java programs to handle exceptions, even though some of the code you wrote might have caused exceptions to be thrown. Consider, for example, the code in Figure 10.10 that implements a stack using a linked list (refer to Section 6.3.3.2 for more details).

```
public Object pop() throws StackUnderflowException {
   Object returnVal = null;

   if ( isEmpty() ) {
      throw new StackUnderflowException( "Empty Stack" );
   }

   // Set retval to the item at the top of the stack,
   // and remove the element from the stack.
   // This code has been omitted.

   return returnVal;
}
```

FIGURE 10.9 Correct use of the `throw` statement

```
// A linked list implementation of a stack. The element at the
// front of the list is the element currently at the top of the
// stack. An item is pushed on the stack by adding it to the
// front of the list. An element is removed from the stack
// by removing the first element in the list.

public class Stack {

   // An inner class used to create the nodes that make up the
   // linked list.

   private static class StackNode {
      public Object data;     // Data held by this node
      public StackNode next; // The next node in the list

       // Create a new stack node.

      public StackNode( Object theData, StackNode curTos ) {
         data = theData;
         next = curTos;
      }
   }

   // Reference to the node at the top of the stack

   private StackNode tos = null;

   // Push an item on the stack by adding it to the beginning
   // of the list
```

FIGURE 10.10 Linked list implementation of a `Stack`

```
public void push( Object o ) {
    tos = new StackNode( o, tos ); // Add the new stack node to the
                                   // front of the list.
}


// Pop an element from the stack by removing the first element
// in the list.

public Object pop() {
    Object retval = tos.data; // Get a reference to the data
    tos = tos.next;           // Make tos point to the next node
                              // (i.e. remove the first element).
    return retval;
}


// The stack is empty if the list is empty.

public boolean isEmpty() {
    return tos == null; // List is empty if tos is null
}


// Create a stack and attempt to remove an element from it.

public static void main( String args[] ) {
    Stack myStack = new Stack();

    //Attempt to pop an empty stack
    System.out.println( myStack.pop() );
}
}
```

FIGURE 10.10 Linked list implementation of a Stack *(continued)*

Although the program in Figure 10.10 will compile, when it is executed, the message shown in Figure 10.11 is displayed, and the program terminates.

```
java.lang.NullPointerException
    at Stack.pop(Stack.java:20)
    at Stack.main(Stack.java:33)
Exception in thread "main"
```

FIGURE 10.11 Stack class termination message

The output shown in Figure 10.11 is an example of a **stack trace** and is the result of calling the method printStackTrace() on the exception that was thrown. The first line of the stack trace gives the name of the exception (see Table 10.2) followed by the contents of the call stack at the time the exception occurred. The **call stack** is a record of all the methods that were called up to the point in the program when the exception was thrown. In this example, the method `main()` called the method `pop()`, which caused the `NullReferenceException` to be thrown.

An examination of the code in Figure 10.10 reveals the cause of the problem: an attempt to remove an item from an empty stack. Specifically, when the stack was empty, the method `pop()` attempted to execute the statement

```
Object retval = tos.data
```

when the instance variable `tos` had the value `null`. Since this was an attempt to access an object using a null reference, the Java run-time system threw a `NullPointerException`.

You will note that nowhere in Figure 10.10 did we specify how to deal with a `NullPointerException` or that when it occurs the program should print a stack trace and terminate the program. The reason we did not have to specify how this exception was to be handled is because the `NullPointerException` is an unchecked exception. In this case, the Java Virtual Machine handled it by printing a stack trace and terminating the program. However, if we wanted to, we could have handled it ourselves, perhaps to implement an alternative response to the specific error.

When an exception is thrown, normal execution of the program stops, and the Java run-time system searches for an exception handler to handle the exception. This search starts at the bottom of the call stack and works its way to the top of the call stack. The search terminates when either an appropriate handler for the exception is found or the search goes beyond the top of the call stack. An appropriate handler catches either the specific exception that was thrown or any one of its superclasses. For example, a handler that catches a `StackOverflowException`, `StackException`, or an `Exception` of Figure 10.8 could handle the `StackOverflowException`. If a handler is found, the code specified by the handler is executed, and the program continues execution from that point. If a handler is not found, as in the code shown in Figure 10.11, then when the call stack is exhausted (i.e., all of the active methods have been searched), the Java Virtual Machine prints a stack trace and terminates the thread in which the exception occurred.

The reason you have not had to worry about exceptions in your program up to this point is that the exceptions that might have been thrown were all unchecked exceptions. If any other type of exception is thrown in your program, then you must account for the exception by either providing a handler for this exception or declaring that this method may throw the exception. The syntax for writing handlers for exceptions and declaring them is discussed in the next section.

◆ **10.2.3** Handling Exceptions

The first step in writing an exception handler is to enclose all statements that might throw an exception within a **try block**. The general syntax of the `try` statement, which is used to define a try block, is shown in Figure 10.12.

You can think of the `try` statement as an "observer" whose job is to monitor the execution of the statements within its try block. As long as no exceptions are thrown inside the try block, the `try` statement does nothing out of the ordinary, and all of its

```
try {
    // This is a try statement
}
catch ( ExceptionType e ) {
    // This is a catch block
}
catch ( ExceptionType2 e ) {
    // You can have a catch block for every exception
    // that might occur in the try statement.
}
finally {
    // Executed regardless of what happens in the try
    // block
}
```

FIGURE 10.12 try statement

statements are executed exactly as they would be in a regular Java program. However, if any one of the statements inside the try block throws an exception, the try statement immediately stops execution of the remaining statements in its block. It then examines each of the **catch blocks** that follow the try block, searching for the first exception type parameter that matches the type of exception that was thrown. If a match is found, the code specified inside the catch block is executed, and program execution continues with the first executable statement that follows the try statement. If a matching catch block is not found, the method is terminated, and the exception is passed up the call chain to the program that invoked this method, and the search process begins all over again at this level. The code in Figure 10.13 illustrates the use of a try statement.

```
try {
    Stack myStack = new Stack();

    mystack.push( new Integer( 5 ) );
    System.out.println( myStack.pop() );
}
catch ( StackUnderflowException e ) {
    System.err.println( "Attempt to pop an empty stack" );
}
catch ( StackOverflowException e ) {
    System.out.println( "Attempt to push an item on a full stack" );
}
```

FIGURE 10.13 Using a try block to handle exceptions

For example, if the statement mystack.push(new Integer(5)) were executed when myStack is full, a StackOverflowException is generated. The try statement halts execution of the statements within the try block and searches for a catch block whose parameter matches the `StackOverflowException` or one of its subclasses. There is a `catch` block that matches the exception that was thrown, so the code within that `catch` block is executed, causing the message *Attempt to push an item on a full stack* to be printed to standard output. Similarly, if the `System.out.println(myStack.pop())` is executed on an empty stack, the message *Attempt to pop an empty stack* is printed. The `catch` block contains the code that is to be executed when an exception occurs. Essentially, it is the exception handler for the exception, or any of its subclasses, specified as a parameter to the `catch` block.

Some simple rules must be followed when associating `catch` blocks with a `try` block. First, the `catch` blocks associated with the `try` statement can only specify exceptions that might be thrown by one of the statements in the `try` block. For example, the `try` statement in Figure 10.13 could not include a `catch` block that specified a `FileNotFoundException` because this exception cannot be thrown by any of the statements in the `try` block. Second, the `catch` blocks must be placed in order from the most specific to the most general exception type. Using the `Stack` class examples, this means that a `StackOverflowException` must be caught before the more general `StackException`, which itself must be caught before the most general `Exception`.

The last aspect of handling exceptions in Java is called a **finally block**. A finally block may optionally be associated with a `try` block. The `finally` block is listed after all of the `catch` blocks and contains code that is guaranteed to be executed whether or not an exception occurs within the `try` block. The code contained within the `finally` block will be executed after the code in the `try` and `catch` blocks is executed. The code within a `finally` block is executed even if no exception is thrown and no `catch` blocks are executed. `finally` blocks are used to include code that must be executed whether or not an exception occurred. Probably the most common example of the use of a `finally` block is for properly closing a file. Imagine writing a loop that is reading a series of characters from a file. Whether all of the reads are successful or not, the file should be closed. This could be done in a `finally` block as shown in Figure 10.14.

```
public class FileCopy {
    public static void main( String args[] ) {
        BufferedInputStream in = null;    // Source file - file to copy
        BufferedOutputStream out = null; // Destination - file to copy to
        int data;                         // Data read from file

        try {
            // Open the input file. After the code is executed the reference
            // variable in will refer to the input file and can be used to
            // read characters from the file

            // Code omitted

            // Open the output file. After the code is executed the reference
            // variable out will refer to the output file and can be used to
            // write characters to the file.
```

FIGURE 10.14 Using `finally` to close files

```
         // All of this is done in a try block because a
         // FileNotFoundException will be thrown if the files cannot be
         // opened.
      }
      catch ( FileNotFoundException e ) {
         System.err.println( "FileCopy: " + e.getMessage() );
         System.exit( 1 );
      }


      // Now copy the files one byte at a time (note both in and
      // out are open at this point in the program)

      try {
         // Copy the files a byte at a time

         while ( ( data = in.read() ) != -1 ) {
            out.write( data );
         }
      }
      catch ( IOException e ) {

         // Something went wrong during the copy

         System.err.println( "FileCopy: " + e.getMessage() );
      }
      finally {
         // Whether the copy succeeded or not the input and output files
         // must be closed. This is done in the finally block which will
         // always be executed.

         // Note that the statements that close the files must be placed in
         // a try block since they may throw an exception. In this case the
         // exception is ignored.

         try {
            out.close();
            in.close();
         }
         catch ( IOException e ) {}
      }
   }

} // FileCopy
```

FIGURE 10.14 Using `finally` to close files *(continued)*

A `try` block defines lexical scope like any other block in Java. Thus, it is possible to declare variables that are local to the `try` block. These variables are not known outside the block, and therefore, they cannot be used outside the `try` block or any of the `catch` blocks associated with the `try` block. You must also be careful when initializing local variables inside of a `try` block as shown in the code in Figure 10.15.

```
public static void main( String args[] ) {
   int value;

   try {

       // The method parseInt() will throw a NumberFormatException
       // if it is given a string that cannot be interpreted as a
       // number (i.e. "one").

       value = Integer.parseInt( args[ 0 ] );
   }
   catch ( NumberFormatException e ) {
       System.out.println( "Bad argument" );
   }

   System.out.println( value );
}
```

FIGURE 10.15 Using local variables in a `try` block

Since the Java compiler enforces the rule that variables must be initialized before they are used, the code in Figure 10.15 will not compile because the Java compiler cannot guarantee that value will be initialized. If the `parseInt()` method throws a `NumberFormatException`, the assignment to value will never be completed, and the output operation will not be meaningful. The correct procedure in this situation is to initialize value when it is declared so that it contains a value before the `try` block is executed, as in the following:

```
int value = 0;
```

It is entirely possible that the method throwing the exception may not have sufficient information to know the correct action to take. In this case, both the `try` statement and the `catch` block should be placed in the calling method rather than in the method where the exception may be thrown, because the calling method may have a better idea of the proper action to take.

In all of the examples in this chapter, we have used `try` statements to "account" for the exceptions that might be generated in a program. It is also possible to account for exceptions not by actually catching them but by declaring that a method may throw an exception. Listing the exception that can be thrown in a method's **throws clause**, which immediately follows the method's declaration, does this. Consider the definition of the `pop()` method in Figure 10.16.

In Figure 10.16, an attempt to access an element from an empty stack will cause a `StackUnderflowException` to be thrown. There is no `try` statement in this method to account for the exception because the `pop()` method has chosen not to handle it. Instead, the programmer placed a `throws StackUnderflowException` clause in the method header that instructed the compiler to look for the `try` statement in the method that called `pop()`.

```
public Object pop() throws StackUnderflowException {
    Object retval = null;

    if ( tos == null ) {
        throw new StackUnderflowException();
    }

    retval = tos.data;
    tos = tos.next;

    return retval;
}
```

FIGURE 10.16 Declaring exceptions in a method header

10.3 DESIGN GUIDELINES AND EXAMPLES

◆ 10.3.1 Exceptions

This chapter has discussed the syntax and semantics of exceptions and exception handling in Java. Once you understand the basic rules incorporated into the Java language, it is not difficult to write code that can successfully deal with exceptions. You now know that if you invoke a method that throws a checked exception, you must either handle that exception via a try statement and a catch block or declare the exception using a throws clause. The basic mechanisms that define, throw, and handle exceptions in Java are not difficult to understand. However, there are several difficult design questions that are yet to be answered. For example, when writing a method, how do you decide under what conditions to throw an exception? If you do decide to throw an exception, what type of exception should you throw? Which exception should you throw and when? What is the appropriate action to take when an exception occurs?

The basic guideline for deciding whether or not to throw an exception is first to distinguish between special cases or conditions that are part of the normal logic of the algorithm and exceptional cases that are best handled using the exception mechanisms of Java. Special cases of the algorithm are usually dealt with by the program itself so execution can continue. Exceptional cases represent situations where continued program execution is often not possible, and the situation may be best handled via the Java exception mechanism.

For example, consider a method that reads a single byte from a file each time it is invoked. What action should this method take if a hardware error makes it impossible to read the current byte from the file? Clearly, this is something that the method cannot fix, and the normal flow of program execution would not be expected to continue. This condition would best be handled by an exception. Now consider what action to take if an attempt is made to read past the end of the file. Clearly, there are no more bytes that can be read from the file, but is this really a fatal program error in which normal program flow should be terminated? Probably not, so a reasonable way to handle this case might be to return a special value, such as −1, to indicate that the end of the file has been encountered but allow the program to continue execution. Generating an exception in this situation is probably not necessary.

Unfortunately, things are rarely this clear cut. Consider reading bytes from a file, but now assume that the file consists of N records each containing exactly 256 bytes, making the file size an even multiple of 256. Should this method throw an exception when an end of file is encountered? Based on what we have said so far, the answer seems to be no, an exception would not be required. Instead, we could return −1 to indicate that end of file has been reached. However, since this method is dealing with blocks instead of single bytes, we have to consider where the end of file condition occurred. If the end of file occurs in the middle of a block, this means that the size of the file being read was not a multiple of 256 bytes, and therefore was not in the proper format. This is something beyond the control of the algorithm and should probably be dealt with by throwing the appropriate exception. However, encountering the end of file before reading a new block or after reading an entire block means the file did have the proper format and thus should not cause an exception to be thrown. Deciding when to use the Java exception handling mechanism and when to incorporate the code to handle the situation into your program can be a difficult decision. It must be based on the specifications and the requirements for the program that you are writing, and a determination of whether this is part of the logical flow of the algorithm or an exceptional condition that is separate from the problem being solved.

Once you have decided to throw an exception, the next design question that must be answered is: What type of exception should be thrown? Java provides two general categories of exceptions, checked and unchecked, the difference being whether or not the compiler forces the programmer to handle the exceptions that are generated. Remember that one of the motivations behind building exception handling into a programming language is to provide a means by which the compiler can ensure that the programmer is properly handling the exceptional cases that arise. This is why the Java language enforces a catch or declare policy. Thus, the answer to the second question is that you should throw a checked exception when the condition that gave rise to the exception is something that can, and should, be handled by the program. This will ensure that the users of your code do not get lazy and simply assume everything will work out okay. If you throw a checked exception, someone (you or the users of your class) must deal with it. Probably 99.9 percent of all the exceptions that you throw will be checked exceptions.

The last question that needs to be answered is: Which exception should be thrown? When deciding on what type of exception to throw, you want to avoid forcing the programmer to examine the internal state of the exception to determine exactly what error condition caused the exception to be thrown. The `catch` blocks that follow a `try` statement are designed to allow the programmer to specify exactly what actions to take based on exactly which exception was generated. Thus, in most cases, you should design narrower and error-specific exception classes that can be used to precisely identify the problem that occurred.

For example, take a second look at the exception classes defined in Figure 10.8. The `StackUnderflowException` class clearly indicates that an underflow condition in the `Stack` class caused the exception to be thrown. We could also have used the more general `StackException` object containing the message *"Stack underflow"* to indicate what happened. However, this would require the programmer to examine the message within the StackException object to determine the cause of the problem. Using multiple exception types, each designed to identify a specific error, gives the programmer much more flexibility. Using catch blocks specific to each exception type, a programmer can choose to (a) individually handle each kind of exception, (b) catch an entire group of related exceptions with a single catch block, or (c) ignore some exceptions altogether.

◆ 10.3.2 Handling Exceptions

It is difficult to give software design guidance regarding the best way to handle exceptions, as what needs to be done in a given situation is often application specific. In some cases, it might be appropriate to handle the exception by terminating the program, whereas in other cases, it may be appropriate to execute a modified form of the algorithm or ignore the exception altogether and continue processing. In this section, we provide some examples of different ways in which exceptions might be handled.

Although it seems contrary to the philosophy of exceptions, there are situations where it is appropriate to ignore exceptions entirely. However, remember that Java will not allow you to ignore the exception; you must "handle" the exception by specifying an empty catch block that does nothing. Consider the code in Figure 10.17 that prints the sum of its command-line arguments.

```
public class SumArgs {
    public static void main( String args[] ) {
        int total = 0;

        for ( int i =0; i < args.length; i++ ) {
            try {
                total = total + Integer.parseInt( args[ i ] );
            }
            catch ( NumberFormatException e ) {
                // Ignore non-integer command line args
            }
        }

        System.out.println( "The sum is : " + total );
    }
}
```

FIGURE 10.17 Example of ignoring an exception

In this program, the parseInt() method converts the strings from the command line to integer values so that they can be added to the total. The problem here is what to do if the string that parseInt() is trying to convert does not contain a properly formatted integer value, (e.g., three), and a NumberFormatException is thrown. We may choose to terminate processing altogether, which in some cases may be the most appropriate response. However, it would not be unreasonable to say that if we encounter a string on the command line that cannot be converted into an integer, then that string is ignored and processing continues with the next command-line argument. That is what happens with the program in Figure 10.17. In that program, the output from the call

```
java SumArgs 1 two 3 4
```

would be 8, the sum of the three valid arguments 1, 3, and 4.

In some situations, the best way to handle an exception may be to throw yet another, and different, exception as shown in Figure 10.18.

```
public Object pop() throws StackUnderflowException {
    Object retval = null;

    try {
        retval = tos.data;
        tos = tos.next;
    }
    catch ( NullReferenceException e ) {
        throw new StackUnderflowException();
    }

    return retval;
}
```

FIGURE 10.18 Example of rethrowing an exception

As discussed earlier, if `Stack` is empty, `tos` will be `null` and any attempt to use `tos` to refer to an `Object` will result in a `NullReferenceException` being thrown. If the caller of the `pop()` method were to see the `NullReferenceException`, the only reasonable assumption would be that there is a serious problem with the implementation of the method, when in fact it simply means that an attempt was made to remove an element from an empty `Stack`. The proper procedure in this case is to notify the caller of the error by throwing a `StackUnderflowException`, which is exactly what the `catch` block will do if it is activated.

Thus, it is difficult to produce hard-and-fast rules about the best way to handle an exception condition. It depends on the specific problem being solved and the specific event that occurred. Some of the design options that should be considered include:

1. Writing a specific `catch` block to handle the error condition in a way that is appropriate for the application.
2. Declaring the exception in a `throws` block and letting the calling program decide what to do with that condition.
3. Ignoring the exception by writing an empty `catch` block (i.e., {}) and letting normal processing continue with the code after the `try` block.
4. Catching the exception and handling it by throwing another exception that will be handled by the calling program.

Although this section has discussed the fundamental concepts concerning exceptions, the best way to really learn how to use them is to carefully study programs that contain them. In the next section, we will introduce the classes provided by Java that allow a programmer to create methods that input and output data from external sources. These methods make a good deal of use of the exception handling concepts just presented. After reading this section, you should have a better understanding of how Java programs deal with external devices as well as a better understanding of exceptions in Java.

10.4 STREAMS

◆ 10.4.1 Overview

Up to this point in this text, all the Java programs we have discussed have worked with data from internal sources. Most modern software applications, however, process information that resides on external sources, such as a local file, a network connection, a serial connection, or even another program. For example, a word processor reads text as a series of keystrokes from a file and either writes it back to disk for long-term storage or prints it on standard output.

Although a keyboard, disk, and printer are dramatically different types of devices, a program deals with all these devices in the same way. When reading from a disk, for example, the program inputs one piece of data at a time from the device in a serial fashion. When reading from a keyboard, the characters typed by the user are sent to the program one character at a time and are processed by the program in the order they were typed. You can think of the input as a stream of data that flows from the keyboard to the program in the same way that water flows from one point to another in a stream.

Many modern object-oriented languages use a programming abstraction called a **stream** to deal with external devices in a generalized way. A stream carries an ordered sequence of data of undetermined length. You can think of a stream as a pipe that connects a source of data to a user of those data. The data flow through the stream, just like water flows through the pipes in your house. The stream model is commonly used in class libraries that provide access to external devices such as disks, keyboards, or printers. Figure 10.19 illustrates two of the streams that might be associated with a word processing program.

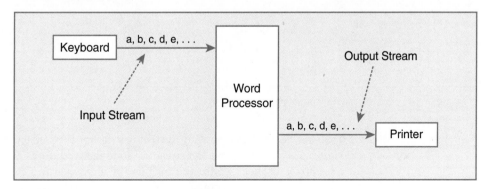

FIGURE 10.19 Examples of streams

A stream connects an entity that generates data, referred to as the **source**, to an entity that reads the data, called a **sink**. The data in the stream flow in one direction, from the source to the sink. The source places data into the stream one element at a time, and the sink reads the data one element at a time in the exact same order they were generated by the source. A program can serve as either a source or a sink of data. The difference lies in whether the program is generating information to be placed into a stream or is reading information from a stream. It is quite common for a single program to be working with more than one stream, and it may be acting as a source for some of the streams and a sink for others.

Before a program can use a stream, the identity of the entities that reside at the two endpoints must be established. For example, before the input stream in Figure 10.19 can be used, one end of the stream must be associated with the keyboard and the other end associated with the word processing program. The phrase **open a stream** describes the process of establishing the entities that lie at the ends of the stream. In most libraries, one end of the stream is associated with the program that created the stream. The program then specifies the device that will be associated with the other end of the stream, either when the stream is created or when it is opened. For example, in Figure 10.19, the word processing application may have created the input stream and specified that the keyboard is the other end of the stream. Once a stream has been opened, data can flow from the source to the sink. The transfer of data from the source to the sink continues until there are no more data to transfer.

Since the length of the data carried on the stream is not specified, the source must have a way of signaling the sink when there are no more data to be sent. The source will **close** the stream to indicate that it has no more data to send. In a typical application, the sink will enter a loop and continue to read characters from the stream until it detects that the stream has been closed. It then exits the loop and closes the stream on its end. The general algorithms to read information from or write information to a stream are given in Figure 10.20.

```
Source                              Sink

Open the stream                     Open the stream
While there is data to write {      While there is data on the stream
    Prepare the next piece of data          to read {
    Write the data to the stream        Read the next piece of data
}                                               from the stream
Close the stream                            Process the data
                                    }
                                    Close the stream
```

FIGURE 10.20 Algorithms for using streams

When a stream is closed, the operating system managing the transfer of information between devices is informed that the stream is no longer required. This allows it to release any resources it allocated for the purpose of implementing the stream. A common mistake made by many programs is forgetting to close streams when they are no longer needed. Failing to close a stream can result in an incomplete transfer of information across the stream or, worst yet, can cause the resources of an operating system to be allocated to streams that are no longer in use.

The Java API defines classes that provide a variety of different types of streams that programmers can use to deal with external devices. The classes that implement streams are contained in the `java.io` package. Each of the stream classes provides methods that allow you to open, read from, write to, and close a stream, making it possible to write programs that implement the algorithmic style of Figure 10.20. The next section will describe some of the more common stream classes in the `java.io` package.

◆ 10.4.2 The `java.io` Package

The `java.io` package contains classes that provide a variety of ways to access stream-oriented data. The stream classes in the `java.io` package can be divided into two categories based on whether they deal with character-based or byte-based data. Although the data being read by either type of stream always consist of byte data, the character-based streams convert these bytes into the character encoding used on the platform on which the program is running. Table 10.3 lists some of the important character- and byte-oriented streams in the `java.io` package.

All of the stream classes in the `java.io` package are subclasses of one of the following four abstract classes: `Reader`, `Writer`, `InputStream`, or `OutputStream`. Classes

TABLE 10.3 `java.io` Classes

Character Streams	Byte Streams	Description
Reader Writer	InputStream OutputStream	Base classes for all streams.
BufferedReader BufferedWriter	BufferedInputStream BufferedOutputStream	Implements buffering to provide efficient access.
CharArrayReader CharArrayWriter	ByteArrayInputStream ByteArrayOutputStream	Streams that can read/write from/to memory.
	DataInputStream DataOutputStream	Allows a program to read/write primitive Java types directly.
FileReader FileWriter	FileInputStream FileOutputStream	Streams to read/write from/to files.
InputStreamReader InputStreamWriter		Converts byte-based data to character-based data.
LineNumberReader		A buffered stream that keeps track of line numbers.
PipedReader PipedWriter	PipedInputStream PipedOutputStream	Channels the output from one thread into the input of another.
PrintWriter	PrintStream	Provides the ability to print different types of primitive data.
StringReader StringWriter		Reads from or writes to standard Java String objects.

that inherit from `Reader` or `Writer` are character-based streams, whereas the classes that extend `InputStream` or `OutputStream` are byte-based streams. You should note from Table 10.3 that the names of all the character-based stream classes end in either `Reader` or `Writer` and that the names of the byte-oriented, with the exception of `PrintStream`, streams end with either `InputStream` or `OutputStream`. This naming convention makes it easy to determine the type of data with which a particular stream class works.

Through the proper use of inheritance, it is possible to write a program that does not depend on the actual type of stream with which it will work. For example, if you wrote a method that took as a parameter a reference to a `Reader`, you could pass it any subclass of `Reader`, and it would still function correctly. Thus, the same method could be used to read information from a file, network connection, or a serial line without having to be modified in any way. This is possible because each of the subclasses overrides the methods in the superclass that actually read the data. This makes it possible for the class to work correctly on the specific device it was designed to work with.

The stream classes can be further subdivided based on whether they serve as source/sink streams or processing streams. **Source/sink streams** are connected directly to an external source, and they read/write directly to or from that source. An example of a source/sink stream is the `FileReader` class. A `FileReader` can be used to read character-based data from a file. Source/sink streams are used in Java to read data from a variety of different devices including files, keyboards, printers, and network connections. Some of the more common source/sink streams are listed in Table 10.4.

Table 10.4 identifies three different types of external sources: file, memory, and pipe. The file type identifies streams that can read data from and write data to a file. The file streams are probably the ones that you will use most often in your Java programs, and they will be discussed at length later in this chapter. Memory streams read and write data to and from memory using stream-based semantics. This type of stream is useful when dealing with certain types of network data, and they are discussed in Chapter 13. Finally, pipe streams direct the output of one thread into the input of another thread.

In contrast to the source/sink stream, a **processing stream** usually is placed between a stream and its source or sink. A processing stream performs some transformation operation on the data as they are flowing through the stream. For example, in Figure 10.21, a `BufferedReader` has been placed between a program and a `FileReader`

TABLE 10.4 Java Source/Sink Streams

Source/Sink Type	Character Streams	Byte Streams
File	FileReader	FileInputStream
	FileWriter	FileOutputStream
Memory	CharArrayReader	ByteArrayInputStream
	CharArrayWriter	ByteArrayOutputStream
	StringReader	
	StringWriter	
Pipe	PipedReader	PipedInputStream
	PipedWriter	PipedOutputStream

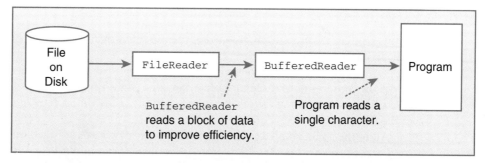

FIGURE 10.21 Using a processing stream

stream that is used to read character data from a disk file. The purpose of the `BufferedReader` is to buffer the read requests made by the program so that the information can be read from the disk as efficiently as possible.

Streams are often linked together, as shown in Figure 10.21, to perform a variety of operations on the data as they flow through the stream. This process of linking streams together in a pipeline fashion is often called **wrapping streams** around each other. In Figure 10.21, a `BufferedReader` has been wrapped around a `FileReader` to provide buffering in the data pipeline. Wrapping streams allows you to combine the beneficial features of several different streams.

Table 10.5 lists some of the more common processing stream classes. Given this description of the stream classes in the `java.io` package, you should be able to determine the correct class for a given situation. You first need to determine the type of data your program will be dealing with and then the type of the source or sink that you wish to use. Given those two pieces of information, it is relatively easy to determine the name of the class that provides the functionality you require. For example, a program that needs to read character information from a file would use a `FileReader`, whereas a program that writes byte data to memory would use a `ByteArrayOutputStream`.

Identifying the name of the class that you will use to implement a stream is only the first step in writing your program. After selecting the appropriate class, you have to write the code to actually create the stream and read or write the information. In the next section, we explain how to use the Java stream classes by presenting a number of sample programs that read or write information using these stream classes.

TABLE 10.5 Processing Streams

Process	Character Stream	Byte Stream
Buffering	BufferedReader	BufferedInputStream
	BufferedWriter	BufferedOutputStream
Byte/Character Conversion	InputStreamReader	
	InputStreamWriter	
Data Conversion		DataInputStream
		DataOutputStream
Printing	PrintWriter	PrintStream
Counting	LineNumberReader	

◆ **10.4.3** Using Streams

In this section, we present programs that use the Java stream classes to read data from a file, read information from the keyboard, and write data to a file. The first program that we discuss, `FileEcho`, takes the name of a text file from the command line and prints the contents of that file to standard output. Since the program is working with a text file made up of characters, it will use a `FileReader` object to read the contents of the file.

All of the `Reader` and `InputStream` classes provide a `read()` method that can be used to read the next piece of data from the stream. What might be surprising is that the signatures for the `read()` method are the same in both classes even though a `Reader` works with character-based streams and an `InputStream` works with byte-based streams. The `read()` method returns an integer value that contains the data read from the stream. The method will not return until either the data are available, the end of the stream is detected, or an exception is thrown.

The results returned by the `read()` method are interpreted differently depending on whether you are using an `InputStream` or a `Reader`. An `InputStream` always reads the next byte (8 bits) of data from the stream. This 8-bit value is returned as an integer and is in the range from 0 to 255. The number of bytes read by a `Reader` depends on the character encoding being used by the platform on which the program is running. If the characters are encoded using 8-bit ASCII, 1 byte will be read. If the characters are encoded using 16-bit Unicode, 2 bytes are read. The `Reader` automatically determines which character code to use when it is created. The method `read()`, when invoked on a `Reader`, will return the character code of the next character read from the stream as a 16-bit integer value in the range from 0 to 65,535.

The program `FileEcho`, shown in Figure 10.22, illustrates how to use a `FileReader` to read characters from a file. Recall from Figure 10.20 that a stream must be opened before any data can be read. The process of instantiating a new `FileReader` object opens the stream and associates it with a file. The `FileReader` class provides three constructors. The one-parameter form in Figure 10.22 takes a string, which is the name of the file to open. If the file cannot be opened (i.e., it does not exist or you do not have permission to read it), the constructor will throw a `FileNotFoundException`.

Once the file is opened, the program uses the `read()` method to obtain characters, one at a time, from the file. Since the `read()` method returns an integer value instead of a character, the program must read the character into an integer variable and then cast the value to a character before printing it. If you fail to do this, the program will print the numerical value of the character code instead of the characters that they represent (i.e., instead of printing an 'a' the program will output the integer 97).

The loop that reads characters from the file will execute until `read()` returns −1. When `read()` is invoked on a stream that has been closed by the source (i.e., there are no more data), it will return −1. Note that since −1 is outside the range of valid values returned by `read()` (0–255 for `InputStream`s and 0–65535 for `Reader`s), you do not have to worry about confusing the value representing that the stream has been closed with a valid data value.

```
/**
 * A program that opens a character based file, specified on the command
 * line, for reading and echoes its contents to standard output.
 */

import java.io.FileReader;
import java.io.FileNotFoundException;
import java.io.IOException;

public class FileEcho {
    public static void main( String args[] ) {
        FileReader in = null;
        int ch;

        // Make sure the number of arguments is correct

        if ( args.length != 1 ) {
            System.err.println( "Usage: FileEcho sourceFile" );
        }
        else {
            try {
                // Attempt to open the file for reading
                in = new FileReader( args[ 0 ] );

                // While there are characters left in the file, read one
                // and echo it to the screen. Note the cast on the invocation
                // of the method print(). Without it this program will print
                // the numeric values of the character codes instead of the
                // corresponding characters.

                while ( ( ch = in.read() ) != -1 ) {
                    System.out.print( (char)ch );
                }
            }
            catch ( IOException e ) {
                // Either an I/O error occured or the file could not be opened
                System.err.println( "FileEcho: " + e.getMessage() );
            }
            finally {
                // Close the file in a finally block. This way whether
                // an IOException is thrown or not, the file will be closed.
                // Note that the file must be closed in a try block since
                // close() throws an IOException.
```

(continued)

FIGURE 10.22 FileEcho.java

```
        try {
           if ( in != null ) {
              in.close();
           }
        }
        catch( IOException e ) {
           System.err.println( "FileEcho: " + e.getMessage() );
        }
      }
    }
  }

} // FileEcho
```

FIGURE 10.22 `FileEcho.java` *(continued)*

The stream used by the program to read the file is closed in the `finally` block of the `try` block. Recall that you are guaranteed that the `finally` block will always be executed. By writing the program in this way, you can be confident that whether the program succeeds or an exception occurs during execution, the stream will always be properly closed. The check to determine if the stream variable `in` is `null` is required because when the `finally` block is activated, we do not know exactly what has happened in the program. If an exception occurred during invocation of the constructor, `in` will be `null`. If the file was successfully opened and the program either terminates successfully or an exception occurs while reading the file, the variable `in` will refer to the stream object being used to access the file. If we attempt to invoke the `close()` method using a `null` reference, a `NullPointerException` will be thrown.

Note how the exceptions were handled in Figure 10.22. There is only one `try` block, and the only `catch` block associated with the block handles an `IOException`. Recall that the constructor, which opens the file and associates it with a stream, may throw a `FileNotFoundException`. Since a `FileNotFoundException` is a subclass of `IOException`, the single `catch` block for `IOException` will match either exception. The only consequence of writing the code in this manner is that it is not possible to determine, based only on the `catch` block that is activated, which type of exception occurred. However, in this program, it does not matter because all that is done if an exception occurs is to print an error message and terminate the program. If it were necessary to handle each exception type differently, then two separate `catch` blocks would have been used.

Reading data from a file character by character is inefficient. When working with a disk file, it is much more efficient to read a block of information at a time, that is, one complete disk sector. Essentially, it takes the same amount of time to read an entire block of data from a disk file as it does to read a single character. Therefore, most programs that work with data stored on a disk, buffer the reads and writes. The buffer allows you to save up, or **buffer**, several read requests and then execute a single read operation to obtain all of the data from the disk. Thus, although the program in Figure 10.22 works, it is not very efficient.

Changing the program in Figure 10.22 so that it uses buffering is quite trivial in Java. Recall that one of the processing streams provided in the `java.io` package is the `BufferedReader` class. A `BufferedReader` can be placed between a `FileReader` and a program, and it will automatically buffer the read requests so that the program executes more efficiently. The program in Figure 10.23, `BufferedFileEcho`, uses a `BufferedReader` to read data from the file. The streams in this program are connected as shown in Figure 10.21.

```java
/**
 * A program that opens a character based file, and uses a BufferedReader
 * to read the contents of the file by lines. The contents of the file
 * are echoed to standard output.
 */

import java.io.BufferedReader;
import java.io.FileReader;
import java.io.FileNotFoundException;
import java.io.IOException;

public class BufferedFileEcho {
    public static void main( String args[] ) {
        BufferedReader in = null;
        String line = null;

        // Make sure the number of arguments is correct

        if ( args.length != 1 ) {
            System.err.println( "Usage: BufferedFileEcho sourceFile" );
        }
        else {
            // Attempt to open the file for reading. It creates
            // the FileReader and then wraps a BufferedReader around
            // it. The program will read from the BufferedReader which
            // in turn will read from the FileReader.

            try {
                in = new BufferedReader( new FileReader( args[ 0 ] ) );

                // While there are lines left in the file, read a line and
                // print it on the screen. Note that readLine() strips the
                // line termination character(s) from the input which is why
                // the lines are printed using println()

                while ( ( line = in.readLine() ) != null ) {
                    System.out.println( line );
                }
            }
        }
```

(continued)

FIGURE 10.23 `BufferedFileEcho.java`

```
          catch ( IOException e ) {
             // Either an I/O error occurred or the file could not be opened
             System.err.println( "BufferedFileEcho: " + e.getMessage() );
          }
          finally {
             // Close the file in a finally block. This way whether
             // an IOException is thrown or not, the file will be closed.
             // Note that the file must be closed in a try block since
             // close() throws an IOException.
             try {
                if ( in != null ) {
                   in.close();
                }
             }
             catch( IOException e ) {
                System.err.println( "BufferedFileEcho: " + e.getMessage() );
             }
          }
       }
    }

} // BufferedFileEcho
```

FIGURE 10.23 BufferedFileEcho.java *(continued)*

Only two major changes have been made in the program of Figure 10.23. The first change involves the statement that invokes the constructor that creates the streams. In Figure 10.23, the streams are created by the following statement:

```
in = new BufferedReader( new FileReader( args[ 0 ] ) );
```

This is an example of the stream wrapping concept mentioned in the previous section. Notice how the constructor for the BufferedReader is wrapped around the constructor for FileReader. This declaration creates two streams: a FileReader and a BufferedReader. The FileReader is created as before. Its constructor takes as its only parameter a string containing the name of the file to read from. However, the reference to the FileReader object that is created is not assigned to the stream variable in but is passed as a parameter to the constructor for BufferedReader. This will cause the BufferedReader object to read information from the FileReader. Now when the program reads from the stream referred to by in, the request will be passed to BufferedReader, which will immediately return the information if it is in the buffer. Otherwise, it will read the next block of data from FileReader and pass the next character on to the program.

The second change to the program in Figure 10.23 is in the way the data are read from the file. In the FileEcho program, the data were read one character at a time using the read() method. In this program, the data are read using readLine(). The readLine() method reads an entire line of characters from the file. A text file can be viewed as consisting of lines of characters separated by a line termination character. The actual character that marks the end of a line may vary from platform to platform. The BufferedReader class will automatically determine and use the correct line termination characters for the platform on which it is running. These line termination characters are not read by readLine() because they only function to mark the end of a line. Therefore, it is necessary to print the lines in the file using the println() method instead of the print() method. Finally, note that the readLine() method returns a null reference when it reaches the end of the stream.

It is important to note that the program in Figure 10.23 could have been written to use the read() method instead of the readLine() method. In either case, the BufferedReader would still perform the buffering necessary to improve the efficiency of the program. The readLine() method makes printing the content of the file slightly easier and reduces the number of times the while loop has to execute.

The last observation to make on the program in Figure 10.23 involves the way the streams are closed. The close() method in the finally block is invoked only on the BufferedReader and not on both streams. The BufferedReader will invoke close() on the stream to which it is connected, namely, FileReader. So, in general, when you have wrapped streams around each other to read data, it is necessary only to close the "outermost" stream, BufferedReader in this example. This stream will in turn invoke close() on the streams around which it is wrapped.

For our third example, we will show how to make a copy of a file stored on disk. The FileCopy program of Figure 10.24 takes the name of two files entered on the command line. It will copy the entire contents of the first file named to the second file. If the second file already exists, its contents will be overwritten.

```
/**
 * Copy files from the command line. The contents of the first file on
 * the command line is copied into the second file on the command line.
 */

import java.io.BufferedInputStream;
import java.io.BufferedOutputStream;
import java.io.FileInputStream;
import java.io.FileOutputStream;
import java.io.FileNotFoundException;
import java.io.IOException;

public class FileCopy {
    public static void main( String args[] ) {
        BufferedInputStream in = null;
        BufferedOutputStream out = null;
        int data;

        // Check command line arguments
```
(continued)

FIGURE 10.24 FileCopy.java

```
        if ( args.length != 2 ) {
            System.out.println( "Usage: FileCopy sourceFile destFile" );
        }
        else {
            try {
                // Open the input file. A BufferedReader is used here to make
                // the copy more efficient. The copy could have been done
                // using the FileInputStream only.

                // The FileInputStream was used instead of a FileReader since
                // the program is interested in copying bytes and not
                // necessarily characters/strings.

                in = new BufferedInputStream(
                    new FileInputStream( args[ 0 ] ) );

                // Take care of the output side. If the output file exists, it
                // will be overwritten.

                out = new BufferedOutputStream(
                    new FileOutputStream( args[ 1 ] ) );

                // Copy the files a byte at a time
                while ( ( data = in.read() ) != -1 ) {
                    out.write( data );
                }
            }
            catch ( IOException e ) {
                System.err.println( "FileCopy: " + e.getMessage() );
            }
            finally {
                // The files are closed in the finally block so that no
                // matter what happens the files will be closed. Note that
                // two try blocks are used in case the first close fails.
                try {
                    if ( in != null ) {
                        in.close();
                    }
                }
                catch ( IOException e ) {
                    System.err.println( "FileCopy: " + e.getMessage() );
                }

                try {
                    if ( out != null ) {
                        out.close();
                    }
                }
```

FIGURE 10.24 FileCopy.java *(continued)*

```
            catch ( IOException e ) {
                System.err.println( "FileCopy: " + e.getMessage() );
            }
        }
    }
}

} // FileCopy
```

FIGURE 10.24 FileCopy.java *(continued)*

Note that the FileCopy program in Figure 10.24 is quite similar to the other programs discussed so far. The most significant difference is that it writes the contents of the first file to another file instead of to standard output. This significantly changes the behavior of the program, but in terms of its effect on coding, it only means that instead of writing to the screen we are writing to a FileWriter output stream. The basic structure of the program does not change. The program uses an InputStream instead of a FileReader so that it is capable of copying either text files or data files. Notice that the program uses buffered streams so that it reads and write the files as efficiently as possible.

The finally block in Figure 10.24 closes the two streams—the stream that reads the file and the stream that writes the file—in two separate try blocks. The reason is that an exception may be thrown when we attempt to close a stream. If both close statements were in the same try block and the first close statement threw an exception, then the second close() statement would never be executed, leaving the second file open and wasting system resources.

The examples discussed thus far have not processed the data in the file in any meaningful way, except to print them or copy them to another file. The program in Figure 10.25, ReadNums, illustrates how easy it is to modify a program that reads from a file so that it does some type of transformation upon the data it reads. In this program, the file being read is assumed to consist of lines containing a single integer value. The program reads the file one line at a time, converts the string representation of the number to an integer, and computes the sum of the numbers. When all the numbers in the file have been read, the program prints the sum, closes the file, and terminates.

```
/**
 * A program that opens a text file consisting of lines that
 * have one integer each. The numbers are read, summed, and the
 * total is printed.
 */

import java.io.BufferedReader;
import java.io.FileReader;
import java.io.IOException;
```

(continued)

FIGURE 10.25 ReadNums.java

```java
public class ReadNums {
    public static void main( String args[] ) {
        BufferedReader in = null;
        String line = null;
        int sum = 0;

        // Make sure the number of arguments is correct

        if ( args.length != 1 ) {
            System.err.println( "Usage: ReadNums sourceFile" );
        }
        else {
            try {
                // Attempt to open the file for reading
                in = new BufferedReader( new FileReader( args[ 0 ] ) );

                // Read the numbers a line at a time from the source file
                while ( ( line = in.readLine() ) != null ) {

                    // Attempt to convert the string to an int. If it
                    // can't be done ignore the line

                    try {
                        sum = sum + Integer.parseInt( line );
                    }
                    catch ( NumberFormatException e ) {}
                }

                // Numbers are read and summed, print out the results

                System.out.println( "The sum is " + sum );
            }
            catch ( IOException e ) {
                System.err.println( "ReadNums: " + e.getMessage() );
            }
            finally {
                try {
                    if ( in != null ) {
                        in.close();
                    }
                }
                catch ( IOException e ) {
                    System.err.println( "ReadNums: " + e.getMessage() );
                }
            }
        }
    }
} // ReadNums
```

FIGURE 10.25 ReadNums.java *(continued)*

At this point, you should realize that when you execute `System.out.print()` or `System.out.println()` to print something from your program, you are using a stream. If you look at the class `System` that is defined in the `java.lang` package, you will find that the class defines three class variables: `out`, `in`, and `err`. These variables refer to streams that can print information to the screen, read information from the keyboard, or print information to the error stream.

The class variables `out` and `err` refer to two different `PrintStreams` that are connected to the standard output device and the standard error device, respectively. The term **standard output** refers to the device that normally displays information, which for most computing systems is the screen. The **standard error** stream prints diagnostic messages. The idea behind having two streams is so the "normal" output from a program can, if desired, be separated from the diagnostic warning and error messages that may be printed while the program is executing. However, in most cases, the standard output and standard error devices are one and the same. You will notice that all error messages in the `catch` blocks in this section were printed using the standard error stream.

You should now understand that the `System.out` in `System.out.println()` refers to the `PrintStream` object connected to the standard output device, and you are invoking the `println()` method on that object. If you take a few minutes to look at the Javadoc pages for the `PrintStream` class, you will see that the class provides many different versions of the `print()` and `println()` methods. The primary difference between these methods is the type of data that each will print. For example, invoking `System.out.println(10)` in a program will execute the version of `println()` that takes an integer argument. This version of the `println()` method will convert the value 10 to the appropriate sequence of characters and send the result to the screen.

The class variable `in` refers to an `InputStream` object that is connected to the standard input device. On most computers, **standard input** refers to the keyboard. However, it really does not matter what the standard input stream is connected to because, regardless of the device type, your program will still read it as a stream. You might be surprised to find that `in` refers to an `InputStream` as opposed to a `Reader` since we typically think of the keyboard as a character-oriented device. A consequence of this decision by the designers of the Java class libraries is that, to read character-based data from the keyboard, you must first convert the byte data coming in from `System.in` to character data. If you wrap an `InputStreamReader` around `System.in`, then you can read the keyboard data as characters.

The `InputNums` program of Figure 10.26 illustrates how to read character data from the keyboard. This program is very similar to the `ReadNums` program of Figure 10.25. The only difference is the stream type used to obtain the input. In this example, `in` refers to a `BufferedReader` that has been wrapped around an `InputStreamReader` that in turn has been wrapped around `System.in`.

```
/**
 * A program reads integers from standard input,
 * sums them and prints out the result.
 */
```

(continued)

FIGURE 10.26 `InputNums.java`

```java
import java.io.BufferedReader;
import java.io.InputStreamReader;
import java.io.IOException;

public class InputNums {
   public static void main( String args[] ) {
      BufferedReader in = null;
      String line;
      int sum = 0;

      // Attempt to open the file for reading

      try {
         // Connect System.in to a BufferedReader

         in= new BufferedReader( new InputStreamReader ( System.in ) );

         while ( ( line = in.readLine() ) != null ) {

            // Attempt to convert the string to an int. If it
            // can't be done ignore the line

            try {
            }
            catch ( NumberFormatException e ) {}
         }
            sum = sum + Integer.parseInt( line );

         // Numbers are read and summed, print out the results

         System.out.println( "The sum is " + sum );
      }
      catch ( IOException e ) {
         System.err.println( "InputNums: " + e.getMessage() );
         System.exit(1);
      }
      finally {
         try {
            if ( in != null ) {
               in.close();
            }
         }
         catch ( IOException e ) {
            System.err.println( "InputNums: " + e.getMessage() );
         }
      }
   }

} // InputNums
```

FIGURE 10.26 InputNums.java *(continued)*

If you compare the codes in Figures 10.25 and 10.26, you will see that they are identical except for the fact that the input is coming from different streams. In Figure 10.25, in refers to a `BufferedReader` object that is wrapped around a `FileReader`. This means the program's input is coming from a character-based file. In Figure 10.26, the stream variable in again refers to a `BufferedReader` object. The difference is that in Figure 10.26, the `BufferedReader` object ultimately takes its input from `System.in`. In both programs, in refers to the same type of stream, a `BufferedReader`; thus, it is possible to combine these two programs into one.

The program in Figure 10.27 shows a method called `sumInput` that takes as a parameter a reference to a `BufferedReader` that contains the lines to be summed. The method does not care what type of stream `BufferedReader` is connected to. It may involve files, keyboards, or a network. Regardless of the actual type of device in use, polymorphism makes it possible for `sumInput` to read the lines on the device and compute the sum.

The `main` method in Figure 10.27 uses the command line to determine where the input to the program will come from. If an argument is found on the command line, the program attempts to create a `BufferedReader` that is wrapped around a `FileReader` connected to the file specified on the command line. If there are no arguments on the command line, then the program will wrap a `BufferedReader` around an `InputStreamReader` that is wrapped around `System.in`. Regardless of how it is actually created, the resulting `BufferedReader` object is passed to the `sumInput()` method to calculate the sum. Due to the polymorphic behavior of the stream classes, the appropriate code is executed when reading the information from the streams.

```
/**
 * This program will either sum numbers from standard input or from a
 * file, depending on whether or not the user specifies a file name on
 * the command line. The sum will be printed once the input has been
 * exhausted.
 */

import java.io.BufferedReader;
import java.io.FileReader;
import java.io.InputStreamReader;
import java.io.IOException;

public class SumNums {
    public static void main( String args[] ) {
        BufferedReader in = null;

        // Hook up in to System.in or a FileReader depending on
        // the command line argument

        try {
            if ( args.length > 0 ) {
```
(continued)

FIGURE 10.27 SumNums.java

```
                // Try to hook up to the first thing on the command line
                in = new BufferedReader( new FileReader( args[ 0 ] ) );
            }
            else {
                // Hook up to System.in
                in = new BufferedReader( new InputStreamReader( System.in ) );
            }

            // Sum the input and print the result
            System.out.println( "The sum is " + sumInput( in ) );
        }
        catch ( IOException e ) {
            System.err.println( "SumNums: " + e.getMessage() );
        }
        finally {
            try {
                if ( in != null ) {
                    in.close();
                }
            }
            catch ( IOException e ) {
                System.err.println( "SumNums: " + e.getMessage() );
            }
        }
    }

    /**
     * Read lines from the buffered reader and convert the integer values
     * on those lines to numbers. The sum of the numbers is returned.
     * Note that this method takes a buffered reader as parameter and it
     * does not care if the buffered reader is connected to a file or the
     * standard input stream.
     *
     * @param in the buffered reader to process.
     *
     * @return the sum of the numbers in the stream.
     */

    public static int sumInput( BufferedReader in ) throws IOException {
        String line = null;
        int sum = 0;

        // Read the BufferedReader one line at a time
        while ( ( line = in.readLine() ) != null ) {
            // Attempt to convert the string to an int. If it
            // can't be done ignore the line
            try {
                sum = sum + Integer.parseInt( line );
```

FIGURE 10.27 SumNums.java *(continued)*

```
        }
        catch ( NumberFormatException e ) {}
    }

    // Numbers are read and summed, return the results
    return sum;
    }

} // SumNums
```

FIGURE 10.27 SumNums.java *(continued)*

10.5 SUMMARY

Software systems, like human beings, need to deal with rare and unexpected events. In the area of software design, an unexpected event that lies outside the normal behavior of the algorithm being implemented is called an **exception**. Exception handling can be used to develop robust and fault-tolerant software. It does not allow errors to be ignored or overlooked. Instead, it forces the programmer to be aware of and deal with exceptional circumstances in the appropriate manner.

In Java, exceptions are objects that inherit from the class Throwable. The throw statement activates the exception handling mechanism. Java divides exceptions into two broad categories: checked and unchecked. Any checked exception that is thrown during the execution of a program must either be handled via a try statement or declared in a method header using the throws block. The actual code for handling the exception is contained in the catch block, which is specific to each exception type.

Streams are a common abstraction used in many object-oriented programs to describe how programs interact with external devices. Once a stream is opened, it is connected to a source that generates data and a sink that consumes the data. The sink typically enters a while loop that reads information until the source has closed its end of the stream. At this point, the loop terminates and the sink closes its end of the stream.

The stream classes in java.io are categorized by (a) the type of data they work with, either character or byte, and (b) whether or not the class is a source/sink stream or processing stream. Source/sink streams are used to read or write information to external devices, whereas processing streams are typically wrapped around other streams to process the data as they flow down the stream. The use of streams allows the programmer to write software that can accept and process data independent of where that data is coming from—a file, an I/O device, or a network.

EXERCISES

1. The following is a list of events that might occur as you make your way through a typical day. Which of these events would you handle as exceptions and which would you handle as a normal part of your day? Be sure to explain your rationale to classify the event.

- ◆ Your alarm clock going off in the morning.
- ◆ A power failure that causes your alarm clock to stop working.
- ◆ Taking a shower and running out of hot water.
- ◆ Burning your toast.
- ◆ Dropping your books on the ground on the way to class.
- ◆ Missing lunch.
- ◆ School is closed because of a health department emergency.
- ◆ Running out of quarters at the Laundromat.

2. Find other computer languages that support exceptions. How are exceptions implemented in these languages? How is the implementation different from Java? Give two advantages and two disadvantages of the way exceptions are implemented in each of the languages when compared to Java.

3. Read the paper cited in footnote 1 of Section 10.1. How closely does Java follow the ideas described in the paper?

4. Which digits, and in which order, will be printed when the following program is run?

```java
public class MyClass {
    public static void main( String args[] ) {
        int k = 0;
        try {
            int i = 5 / k;
        } catch ( ArithmeticException e ) {
            System.out.println( "1" );
        } catch ( RuntimeException e ) {
            System.out.println( "2" );
            return;
        } catch ( Exception e ) {
            System.out.println( "3" );
        } finally {
            System.out.println( "4" );
        }
        System.out.println( "5" );
    }
}
```

5. Java provides two general categories of exceptions: checked and unchecked. Give two reasons you should throw a checked exception. Give two reasons you might throw an unchecked exception.

6. What would be the programming consequences of making all exceptions in Java checked exceptions?

7. What happens if you do not have a catch block for an exception that might be thrown in a method?

8. Consider the following method:

```
public void increaseSize( double factor )
   throws SizeException {

      double increase = size * factor;
      size = size + increase;

      if (factor < 0) {
         throw
            new SizeException ( "Invalid factor" );
      }
}
```

Write the `SizeException` class.

Assume that `size` is a properly defined data member of the class. This method computes an object's size increase and applies the increase to the current size. It should throw an exception if the factor is negative (as this method increases size) and leave the size of the object unchanged. Assuming that the `SizeException` is properly defined, does this code work? Does this code properly protect against an invalid factor? If not, rewrite the code so that it works properly.

9. Describe the catch or declare policy that is enforced by the Java compiler.

10. Why does the following method defined within a Java class generate a compile-time error?

```
public void fileOperation() {
   try {
      FileReader in;

      in = new FileReader( "xxx.yyy" );

      // code omitted . . .
   }
   catch( Exception e ) {
      System.out.println( e.getMessage() );
   }
   catch(FileNotFoundException e) {
      System.out.println( "fileOperation: " + e.getMessage() );
   }
}
```

11. Design a `Queue` class that uses exceptions to handle the situations of trying to put things into a full queue or trying to access things from an empty queue. Your queue class should provide `enqueue()`, `dequeue()`, `front()`, `back()`, and `size()` methods.

12. The home heating case study presented in Chapter 4 was written without exceptions. This was necessary because exceptions had not yet been covered in the text. Look at the code that was written in Chapter 4 and identify places where exceptions should be used. Rewrite the code so that it uses the exceptions you identified.

13. Write a program that takes the name of a file on the command line and prints the length of the file in bytes.

14. Draw a UML class diagram that shows the inheritance relationships that exist among the following classes:

    ```
    ClassCastException
    Exception
    FileNotFoundException
    IOException
    NullPointerException
    RuntimeException
    ```

15. If you have the following declaration in your program, what is the program trying to do? Be sure to clearly specify what kind of data is coming into the program, where it is coming from, any conversions made to it, and what it looks like to the program itself.

    ```
    BufferedReader in =
        new BufferedReader( new InputStreamReader( System.in ) );
    ```

16. The `StreamTokenizer` class in the `java.io` package provides the ability to break a stream of data into a series of tokens. Write a program that uses a `StreamTokenizer` and the appropriate source stream to read a Java program and print all of the declarations that appear in the program.

17. Write a Java program that works like the `FileEcho` program in Figure 10.22 except that it prints the line number in addition to the contents of the line.

18. Write a program called `Replace.java` that takes three command-line arguments: a file name, a search string, and a replace string. The program will open the input file and replace all occurrences of the search string with the replace string. The resulting output is printed to standard output. This type of "find and replace" operation is a common feature of most word processing programs.

19. Write a processing stream class named `ReplaceStream` that replaces all occurrences of a specified string with a replacement string. The constructor for your stream class should take three arguments: the search string, the replace string, and a `Reader` that contains the text to be changed. Rewrite the program in Exercise 18 so that it uses the `ReplaceStream` class to do the work.

20. `wc` is a UNIX utility that reads one or more input files and, by default, writes the number of newline characters, words, and bytes contained in each input file to the standard output. The utility also writes a total count for all named files if more than one input file is specified. `wc` considers a word to be a nonzero length string of characters delimited by white space (e.g., Space, Tab, etc.).

On your favorite UNIX system, look at the man page for wc and then write a Java program that implements "your" version of wc.

21. Write a program that reads the contents of a text file and produces a report giving the 10 most common and the 10 least common words. The program should be written so that the name of the file to process is taken from the command line. To have some fun with your program after it is written, look on the Web for Project Gutenberg, promo.net/pg/, which is a project to convert some classic books to electronic form. Run your program using some of these book files.

CHAPTER 11

Threads

11.1 Introduction

It is quite easy, and natural, for human beings to do more than one thing at a time. Right now, you are reading the words in this book, and even though this material is captivating, reading is not the only thing your brain is doing at this instant. While your eyes are scanning these words, your brain is simultaneously causing your heart to beat, your lungs to fill with air, and your stomach to rumble when your ears hear the call, "Dinner is ready." The ability to perform several tasks at the same time is **multitasking**. Multitasking is becoming a vital part of modern life. Most people find it necessary to balance three or four tasks several times each day. For example, when I come home at night, I often have to prepare a meal, feed the cat, and answer the phone all at the same time.

Modern computing systems, like human beings, also have the ability to multitask. Multitasking is a powerful design technique that is common in the implementation of modern software systems. A chat program, for example, not only needs to communicate with the user sitting in front of the computer, but it also has to monitor the network for incoming connections and detect when new users have logged on to the system. All of this could be done by a single task, but the ability to implement these functions as multiple independent tasks makes the software development process easier and the underlying implementation more efficient.

At first glance, you might think that restricting a computer to performing one task at a time would be an efficient way to utilize computing resources, since the entire system would be focused on one thing. As it turns out, however, computing resources are actually being wasted because the processor may be idle for significant periods of time during the execution of a single program. A typical program does not spend 100 percent of its time computing. At various points during its execution, a program may need to wait for some event to take place. For example, the program may be waiting for the user to enter data or waiting for the next block of data to be read off the disk.

While a program is waiting for an event to take place, the processor is idle. If there is only one program in memory, there is nothing else that the processor can do but wait. To make matters worse, a typical program, as shown in Figure 11.1, often has to wait several times during its lifetime for different events to take place. The program in Figure 11.1 takes a total of 7 seconds to execute; however, during those 7 seconds, the program waits three times for a total of 3 seconds. This means that if this is

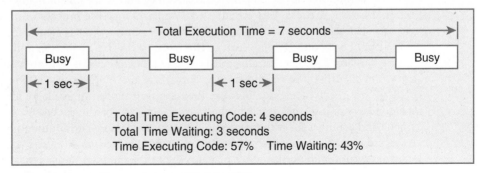

FIGURE 11.1 Process execution profile

the only program in the computing system, the processor is idle about 43 percent of the time. Clearly, to use a computing system to it fullest potential, the goal should be to utilize the processor 100 percent of the time for productive work.

One of the primary goals of operating systems research is to improve the efficiency of computing systems by reducing the idle time of the processor. Much of the early work in this field focused on ways to utilize the processor during periods of program inactivity. Researchers realized that if multiple programs were loaded into memory, it would be possible to interleave program execution, resulting in an improvement in processor usage. Figure 11.2 illustrates how the execution of two programs, P1 and P2, can be interleaved so that when one program is inactive, the other program utilizes the processor. In this case, the result is dramatic. Instead of being idle 43 percent of the time, the processor efficiency is nearly 100 percent.

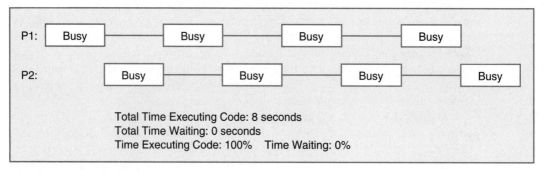

P1: Busy — Busy — Busy — Busy

P2: Busy — Busy — Busy — Busy

Total Time Executing Code: 8 seconds
Total Time Waiting: 0 seconds
Time Executing Code: 100%   Time Waiting: 0%

FIGURE 11.2 Interleaving process execution

Typically, the operating system is responsible for deciding how to interleave program execution so that the processor is never idle. In a **time-sharing**, or **multitasking**, operating system, the processor executes several programs by switching between them. The process of switching between programs is done so quickly and so frequently that the users of the system are often not even aware that this process is taking place. The **scheduler** is the part of the operating system that selects which program to run and determines when the currently running program should be stopped and a new one started. One of the primary goals of the scheduler is to increase the utilization of the processor.

A program that has been loaded into memory and is capable of being executed is referred to as a **process**. The scheduler attempts to increase processor utilization by executing processes in such a way that the processor always has some useful work to do. Although it sounds complicated, the basic operation of the scheduler is rather easy to understand. It maintains a list, or queue, of processes that are ready to execute. This is called the **ready queue.** There is also a queue that contains processes that are not ready to execute because they are waiting for an event to occur. This is called the **waiting queue.** The scheduler selects one of the processes in the ready queue and arranges for it to be executed by the processor. The running process is allowed to execute until it either terminates, is pre-empted, or it blocks (i.e., it has to stop and wait for an event to take place). When the scheduler detects that the current process is waiting, it will move it to the waiting queue and select one of the processes in the ready queue for execution.

Not only does scheduling improve the utilization of computing systems, but it also provides programmers with the ability to utilize concurrency in their programs. **Concurrent programming** is a technique whereby a program is divided into several independent tasks that are executed concurrently by the scheduler—that is, interleaved in time. Concurrency creates the illusion that more than one thing is happening at the same time. A computer with a single processor can obviously execute only one instruction and thus be executing only one process at any instant; however, it can switch between processes very quickly and create the illusion that multiple processes are running simultaneously.

Concurrent programming is a tool that can help programmers develop sophisticated software. However, it also increases system overhead. Part of the problem lies in the fact that during the time the scheduler is switching processes, no useful work is being done. During a **context switch**, when the scheduler removes the current process and brings in a new one, all of the information associated with the running process must be saved, and the state of the new process must be restored. In most operating systems, the amount of time required to perform a context switch is extremely small, which means that the advantages of using concurrency in a program far outweigh the small amount of overhead required by the operating system for process management.

In a modern operating system, there is a considerable amount of information associated with the state of a process, which in turn increases the amount of time required to perform a context switch. The processor is doing work during a context switch, but it is not useful work. During a context switch, only the scheduler is using the processor, so there can be no user process running. Context switches occur so frequently that even the slightest amount of wasted time can drastically affect overall system efficiency.

If the amount of information saved and restored during a context switch is reduced, the amount of time required to perform the switch is reduced as well. This idea led to development of the concept of a **thread**, also called a **lightweight process**. A thread is a single flow of execution through a program. The amount of state information associated with a thread is significantly less than that of a process, so it is possible to save and restore the state of a thread quickly. This leads to reduced context switching time, which results in an increase in overall system efficiency. To reduce the information associated with a process, threads must often share resources. For example, all of the threads in a single Java program utilize the same memory space and the same set of system resources.

Prior to Java, scheduling was performed by the operating system. If you were lucky enough to be developing software that would run on a platform that provided multitasking, you could utilize concurrency in your programs. Since most conventional operating systems do support multitasking, this was not a big problem. However, the world is changing and software is now being developed for diverse computing environments, including cell phones, personal data assistants (PDAs), and even washing machines. The operating systems managing these devices may not provide support for concurrent programming.

One of the big advantages of Java is that not only will your software run on any platform for which there is a Java Virtual Machine (JVM), but your software can also utilize concurrency regardless of the capabilities of the computing platform on which it is running. This is possible because the JVM itself provides the support required for scheduling threads in a Java program rather than relying on the underlying computing services provided by the operating system. This means that Java programmers can use concurrency in programs whenever they deem it necessary, whether the program is running on a supercomputer, a PDA, or a washing machine.

Concurrency has become one of the standard tools used in developing modern software. With very few exceptions, the programs that you run on a regular basis utilize concurrency. For example, browsers use separate threads to load the images that are on a Web page. Word processors perform spelling checks in a separate thread so that as you type your document the spelling can be checked simultaneously. It used to be the case that "newly minted" programmers required only a thorough understanding of programming language concepts, data structures, and algorithms to begin their work. However, given the widespread use of concurrency in modern software systems, today it is essential that every programmer can work with and understand programs that utilize multiple threads.

This chapter discusses how to use threads in a Java program. It starts with a discussion of how to create a thread and specify the code that it will execute. It then looks at the inner workings of the JVM scheduler to help you understand how threads interact with each other. The chapter concludes by looking at the tools that Java provides to synchronize threads so that the actions of one thread do not inadvertently affect the actions of a second thread.

11.2 THREADS

◆ 11.2.1 Creating Threads

A thread in a Java program is represented by an instance of the `Thread` class. The `Thread` class provides methods to create, access, modify, control, and synchronize a thread. An instance of the `Thread` class contains the information required to manage the execution of a thread. The key methods from the `Thread` class that will be discussed in this chapter are listed in Table 11.1.

To create a new thread in a Java program, you must instantiate an object from the `Thread` class. The thread represented by this object will remain inactive until its `start()` method is invoked. The `start()` method informs the scheduler that the thread is ready to run and that it should be put in the ready queue and scheduled for execution. Invoking the `start()` method does not cause the thread to begin executing; it only informs the scheduler that it is ready to run. The scheduler may be managing many other threads that are either waiting for some event or utilizing the processor. In this situation, the newly activated thread might have to wait before it can start executing. It is likely that a bit of time will pass between the moment that the `start()` method is invoked and the time when the new thread actually begins execution. All that can be said about the status of the new thread after `start()` has been called is that the thread is in the state labeled *Alive* in Figure 11.3.

A thread is considered alive if the scheduler is aware of it and is managing its execution. However, remember that even though the scheduler is managing the execution of a particular thread, it does not mean it is actually running on the processor. The thread may be blocked waiting for the processor, it may be waiting for some event to occur, or it may be in the process of terminating. The method `isAlive()`, de-

TABLE 11.1 Class Thread Methods

Method	Description
static Thread **currentThread()**	Returns a reference to the thread that is currently executing.
String **getName()**	Returns the name of the thread.
int **getPriority()**	Returns the priority of the thread.
void **interrupt()**	Interrupts the thread.
boolean **isAlive()**	Returns true if this thread has been started and has not yet died.
void **join()**	Returns when the thread has died.
void **run()**	If this thread was constructed using a separate Runnable run object, then that Runnable object's run method is called; otherwise, this method does nothing and returns.
void **setDaemon( )**	Marks the thread as a daemon thread.
void **setName()**	Changes the name of the thread.
void **setPriority()**	Changes the priority of the thread.
static void **sleep()**	Causes the currently executing thread to temporarily cease execution for the specified number of milliseconds.
void **start()**	Causes this thread to be scheduled. When the thread is activated for the first time, the JVM will invoke the run() method of the thread.
static void **yield()**	Causes the currently executing thread object to temporarily pause and allows other threads to execute.

fined in the Thread class, returns true if a thread has been started but has not yet died. If the isAlive() method returns true, you know that the scheduler is managing the thread, but you can't say for certain what it is actually doing.

The run() method of a thread contains the code that will be executed by the thread. The scheduler invokes run() when the thread executes for the first time. There is nothing special about run(). You can invoke the run() method of a Thread

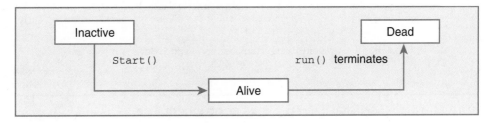

FIGURE 11.3 Stages in thread activation

object in the same way that you invoke a method on any other object, and it will be executed just like any other method we have seen. What makes run() special is that it is invoked automatically by the JVM when the thread starts to execute code. The role that the run() method plays for a thread is similar to the role that the main() method plays in a Java program. The main() method is invoked by the JVM when the program first starts, just as run() is invoked by the JVM when the thread obtains control of the processor for the first time.

A thread remains alive until the run() method terminates. The run() method terminates like any other method in Java by either returning or throwing an exception. In either case, once the run() method returns the thread is no longer alive and it enters the state labeled *Dead* in Figure 11.3. When a thread dies, the Thread object that represents the thread is still valid and can be used to access the state of the thread; however, it cannot be restarted or rerun.

To be useful, a programmer must be able to specify the code that a thread will execute when it is started. There are two ways to define the run() method for a thread. The first is to use inheritance to override the default behavior of the run() method defined in the Thread class. This is done by writing a class that extends Thread and provides its own run() method. The program in Figure 11.4 that creates and starts a thread that prints the message "I am a Thread" illustrates this technique.

```
/**
 * Create an additional thread in a Java program by extending
 * the Thread class.
 */

public class ExtendThread extends Thread {

    /**
     * This code will be executed after the thread has been
     * started. This method prints the message "I am a Thread"
     * on standard output and then terminates.
     */

    public void run() {
        System.out.println( "I am a Thread" );
    }

    /**
     * Create an instance of this class and schedule it for
     * execution.
     *
     * @param args command line arguments (ignored)
     */
```

FIGURE 11.4 Specifying Thread code using inheritance

```
    public static void main( String args[] ) {

        // Create the thread

        Thread theThread = new ExtendThread();

        // Start the thread. Note this method returns
        // immediately. The new thread may, or may not,
        // be executing code when it returns.

        theThread.start();
    }

} // ExtendThread
```

FIGURE 11.4 Specifying `Thread` code using inheritance *(continued)*

The second way to specify the code executed by a thread is to create a new class that implements the `Runnable` interface. The `Runnable` interface specifies exactly one method, `run()`, which is used to identify the code that is executed when a thread becomes active. When using the `Runnable` interface, you must create two objects: an object that implements `Runnable` and a `Thread` object that represents the thread. When the `Thread` object is created, it is passed a reference to the `Runnable` object as a parameter to its constructor. When `start()` is invoked on the `Thread` object, it will in turn invoke the `run()` method in the `Runnable` object. The code in Figure 11.5 has the same functionality as the code in Figure 11.4 but it uses the `Runnable` interface to specify the code that will be executed by the thread.

```
/**
 * Illustrate how to create an additional thread in a Java
 * program by implementing the Runnable interface.
 */

public class ImplementRunnable implements Runnable {

    /**
     * This code will be executed after the thread has been
     * started. This method prints the message "I am a Thread"
     * on standard output and then terminates.
     */

    public void run() {
        System.out.println( "I am a Thread" );
    }
```

(continued)

FIGURE 11.5 Specifying thread code by implementing the `Runnable` interface

```
/**
 * Create an instance of this class and a thread to run it.
 * Then start the thread so that the run() method executes.
 *
 * @param args command line arguments (ignored)
 */

public static void main( String args[] ) {

    // Create the object that contains the run() method

    Runnable runnableObject = new ImplementRunnable();

    // Create the thread and tell it about the runnable object.

    Thread theThread = new Thread( runnableObject );

    // Start the thread.

    theThread.start();
}

} // ImplementRunnable
```

FIGURE 11.5 Specifying thread code by implementing the `Runnable` interface *(continued)*

There is only one hard-and-fast rule regarding the way in which you specify the code to be executed by a thread. Java does not support multiple inheritance; thus, if the class that contains the run() method for the thread already extends a class, it cannot extend Thread. In this situation, the class must implement the Runnable interface to execute the run() method in a separate thread. Many programmers prefer to specify the code a thread will execute using the Runnable interface because it separates the code the thread will execute from the state that must be maintained to manage the thread. The Thread object will contain all of the state information required to manage the thread, and the Runnable object will contain the code and application state that will be executed by the thread.

You may not have realized it, but you are already using threads in every Java program that you have executed. When the JVM starts executing a Java program, it creates a thread that invokes the main() method of the class specified on the command line that started the program. Thus, the programs in Figures 11.4 and 11.5 actually have at least two threads active: the thread running main() and the thread printing "I am a Thread". A Java program might have as many as a dozen threads active at any one time. So what happens in the program in Figure 11.4 if the main() method finishes before the run() method? To phrase this question another way: How does the JVM know when it is safe to terminate the entire program? Clearly, if multiple threads are still active in a program, you do not necessarily want the JVM to terminate when the main() method has completed.

The JVM terminates the execution of a program when one of two conditions occurs. Under normal circumstances, the JVM terminates when all user threads have terminated. Notice that we said "all" user threads. If the run() method in one thread returns or a thread throws an exception and terminates, the JVM will not terminate unless that thread was the last user thread being executed. The same applies to the main() method. The JVM will not terminate when main() returns unless there are no other user threads active in the program.

Threads can be marked as a nonuser or daemon thread. A **daemon thread** typically provides a service in a Java program. For example, in a chat program, you may want to have a thread scan the network to determine who is currently using the service. This way, I can be chatting with Laura and be notified when Linus logs on to the system. In the preceding paragraph, we stated that the JVM terminates when all the user threads have terminated, not simply when all the threads have terminated. In other words, the JVM does not wait for daemon threads to finish before it terminates. Threads by default are marked as user threads. You can mark a thread as a daemon thread when the thread is constructed or by invoking the setDaemon() method on the thread.

The other situation that will cause the JVM to terminate is when the exit() method of class Runtime has been called (e.g., System.exit(0)). In this case, the JVM will terminate immediately, regardless of the number of user threads that are active in the program. Essentially, the exit() method aborts the execution of the JVM. Because the consequences of executing the exit() method are so drastic, it should be used only in special situations. Typically, the only time it is appropriate to execute exit() is when an unrecoverable event has occurred in the program and all hope of continuation is lost. Perhaps the best example of a situation in which it is appropriate to invoke the exit() method is during the processing of command-line arguments in the main() method. If the command-line arguments are incorrect and the program cannot even be started, it may be appropriate to terminate the program by invoking exit().

There are other attributes associated with Thread objects that are useful when working with threads. One of these attributes is a String that can be used to associate a name with the thread. This can be useful when working with programs that utilize multiple threads. The name of a thread can be specified as an argument to the constructor when creating a thread or by invoking the setName() method in Table 11.1 on the Thread object after it has been created. Once a name is associated with a thread, that name will appear in diagnostic messages generated during run time, and it can be accessed by invoking the getName() method on the object. User-supplied thread names are optional. If you do not supply a name, a unique name for the thread will be generated when the thread is created. The program in Figure 11.6 creates five different threads, each with a unique name. When the threads execute, they print their name to standard output and terminate.

```
/**
 * Create five threads, each with a different name. Each thread
 * prints its name on standard output and terminates.
 */
```

(continued)

FIGURE 11.6 Example of a program with multiple threads

```java
public class MultipleThreads extends Thread {

    // The number of threads to create

    public final static int NUM_THREADS = 5;

    /**
     * Print the name of the thread on standard output.
     */

    public void run() {
        System.out.println( getName() );
    }

    /**
     * Create NUM_THREADS threads, start each thread, and terminate.
     * The name of each thread will be of the form "Thread #N" where
     * N will be replaced by a number from 0 to NUM_THREADS - 1.
     *
     * @param args command line arguments (ignored)
     */

    public static void main( String args[] ) {
        Thread newThread = null;   // Reference to new thread
        String name = "Thread #"; // Prefix for all thread names

        // Create the threads

        for ( int i = 0; i < NUM_THREADS; i++ ) {

            // Create a thread

            newThread = new MultipleThreads();

            // Set the name

            newThread.setName( name + i );

            // The name can also be specified in the constructor:
            //
            // newThread = new MultipleThread( name + i )

            // Start the thread

            newThread.start();
        }
    }

} // MultipleThreads
```

FIGURE 11.6 Example of a program with multiple threads *(continued)*

A reasonable question to ask about the program in Figure 11.6 is: What is the output generated by the program? Surprisingly, we cannot specify the exact output because it is dependent on the order in which the threads are executed, which is determined by the JVM at run time. In fact, the only thing the Java language specification guarantees is that statements within a single thread will be executed in the order specified by the program, but it says nothing about how the statements in different threads will be interleaved during the execution of a program. Figure 11.7 shows four different results that were generated by executing the program in Figure 11.6 four different times.

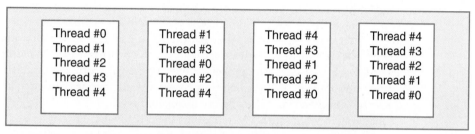

FIGURE 11.7 Possible output from the program in Figure 11.6

Using threads can be a little disconcerting because it makes the programs you write **nondeterministic**. When you wrote and analyzed programs that used only a single thread, you could trace the execution of the program and determine with 100 percent certainty the output that will be generated by the program for a given set of inputs. In a multithreaded program, you can trace the execution of each thread, and you can even determine the output that each thread will generate. However, you cannot determine how the scheduler will interleave the statements within the threads. Multiple runs of the same program may produce different results each time. This is a result of the decisions made by the scheduler each time the program executes.

With that said, you will often find that multiple runs of the same program, on the same machine, and under the same conditions will produce the same output. You are most likely to see different outputs if you run the same program on different platforms (e.g., UNIX, Windows, Macintosh) because their schedulers may use different scheduling algorithms. The crucial point to remember is that with a multithreaded program, you cannot, and should not, make any assumptions about the order in which the scheduler will execute the threads in your program. If there is a particular interleaving of the threads that is required for correct execution of a program, you will have to program that coordination using the thread synchronization features provided by Java, which is discussed in Section 11.3.

Threads allow you to write Java programs that appear to do more than one thing at a time. We cannot say that threads always allow you to do multiple things at the same time because most modern computers still have only one processor to execute user programs. Machines with a single processor can only do one thing at a time, but they can switch from one thread to another so quickly that to a human being it appears as though more than one thing is happening at once. The scheduler is the part of the JVM responsible for selecting which thread to execute and deciding when it is time to give another thread a chance to run. In the next section, we will discuss the life cycle of a thread and learn how the scheduler manages the execution of threads within a Java program.

◆ 11.2.2 Scheduling and Thread Priorities

A multithreaded Java program will have at least two active threads that require the use of the processor to perform their work. Since most modern computers typically have only a single processor, there must be a mechanism in place that allows both threads to share the processor. The scheduler, an integral part of the JVM, is responsible for allocating the processor in such a way that each thread can complete its work and the processor is utilized as efficiently as possible. At first glance, it might seem that the best way to do this is run each thread one at a time, one after another until they have all terminated. Each thread will get the processor time it requires to complete its work. However, the processor will not be fully utilized since there may be long periods of time during which the processor is idle because the current thread has to wait for some event to occur before it can continue.

The way in which the JVM schedules the threads in a Java program is not unlike the way patients are scheduled in a doctor's office. Several patients (threads) require the services of a single doctor (the processor). In a typical doctor's office, patients are not treated one at a time, one after another but instead are scheduled so that the doctor can see several patients at the same time. Patients are placed in different examination rooms; the doctor selects one of the examination rooms and treats the patient in that room. Should the current patient require tests, the doctor orders the tests and sees other patients until the tests are finished. When the tests are finished, the doctor continues the treatment of the patient whose tests are now complete. Even the waiting room is designed to improve the utilization of the doctor. Having several patients available in the waiting area almost always guarantees that when the doctor is ready to see a patient, one will be ready. The scheduling system used by a doctor has been designed so that each patient is treated within a reasonable amount of time, and the doctor's time is used as efficiently as possible.

What led computer scientists to develop scheduling algorithms, and perhaps the concept that makes scheduling possible, is the fact that the behavior of a typical thread follows a very specific pattern. Almost all threads will be in one of three different states while they are running. A thread is in the **ready state** when it is ready to utilize the processor but has not yet been given the processor. Once it is given the processor, it can start executing code immediately. A thread is in the **run state** if the processor is currently executing it. On a single processor machine, there will be only one thread in the run state. Multiple processor machines may have more than one running process. For the purposes of this text, we will assume that there is only a single running process. Finally, a thread that is waiting for an event to occur is in the **wait state**. A thread will remain in the wait state until the event it is waiting for has occurred.

These same states can be seen in the patients that are in the process of being treated by a doctor. The patients that have been placed in examination rooms and are prepared to see the doctor are in the ready state. The patient currently being seen by the doctor is in the run state. Finally, those patients waiting for test results or for paperwork to be completed are in the wait state. The doctor will be busy most of the time because it is likely there will always be at least one patient in the ready state. This way, when the doctor finishes with one patient, there will always be another one ready to be examined. The staff is responsible for monitoring the state of the patients and making sure that there will always be a patient for the doctor to see.

Like the staff in the doctor's office, the JVM scheduler is responsible for tracking the state of the threads in a Java program and managing the execution of these threads so that when the processor is ready to run a thread, one is always available. The scheduler utilizes two queues to keep track of the threads it is managing. The **ready queue** contains all the threads that are in the ready state and are prepared to utilize the processor. The **wait queue** contains all the threads that are blocked waiting for some event to occur. When the start() method of a thread is invoked, that thread is placed in the ready queue and competes with the other ready threads to gain access to the processor. This is the reason you cannot assume that a thread is executing code immediately after invoking its start() method.

By taking advantage of the fact that most threads run for short periods of time and then wait for an event to take place before they can continue, the scheduler can arrange things so that the processor almost always has useful work to do. If the scheduler is managing the execution of several threads, then when one of the threads blocks, the scheduler can move that thread to the wait queue and select the next thread from the ready queue to run. Things rarely work out as efficiently for the scheduler as we have shown in Figure 11.2. How effectively the scheduler can utilize the processor depends on the computing requirements of the threads it is managing.

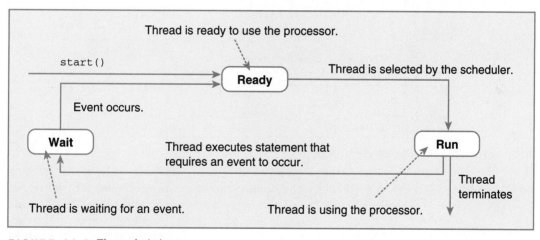

FIGURE 11.8 Thread states

The basic operations performed by a scheduler are illustrated in Figure 11.8. When the scheduler determines that the processor is idle, it selects one of the threads from the ready queue and prepares it for execution. The thread will then be allowed to run until it terminates or has to wait for an event to occur before it can continue. The scheduler will then either mark the thread as finished or move the thread to the queue of waiting threads. This means that the processor is once again idle, and another thread is selected from the ready queue and allowed to run. This cycle repeats until all the threads have terminated, at which time the JVM can terminate. In addition to keeping the processor busy, the scheduler also monitors the threads in the wait queue. The scheduler will move a thread from the wait queue to the ready queue when the event that the thread was waiting for has occurred.

The type of scheduler illustrated in Figure 11.8 is referred to as a **nonpreemptive** scheduler. The scheduler is called nonpreemptive because once a thread obtains control of the processor, it keeps control until it terminates, executes an instruction that causes the thread to wait, or yields the processor to another thread. Nonpreemptive schedulers are fairly easy to implement, but they allow a greedy thread to monopolize the use of the processor. A **preemptive** scheduler, on the other hand, will interrupt the execution of a thread so that other threads may use the processor. Figure 11.9 illustrates the actions of a preemptive scheduler. Note that the only difference between the two types of schedulers is the addition of a transition from the running state directly to the ready state. This occurs when the thread is interrupted by the scheduler.

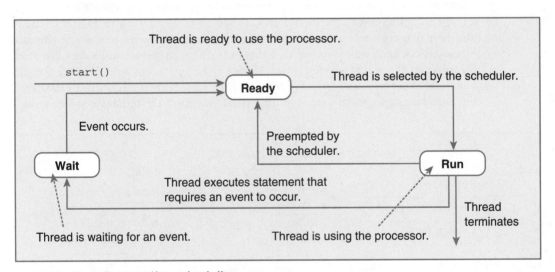

FIGURE 11.9 Preemptive scheduling

In a preemptive scheduler, the running thread can be preempted for a variety of reasons. Many preemptive schedulers assign a maximum length of time, called a **time quantum**, that defines the maximum amount of time a thread can remain in the running state. If the thread does not terminate or execute an instruction that initiates a context switch before the time quantum is exceeded, the scheduler preempts the thread and moves it to the ready queue. Instead of keeping track of the amount of time a thread has been executing, most Java schedulers count the number of instructions the current thread has executed. The thread is preempted if it attempts to execute more than the maximum number of instructions allowed by the scheduler. The use of preemption allows for a fairer allocation of processing time to all the ready threads.

Many schedulers also allow programmers to assign priorities to threads. The scheduler will then attempt to ensure that the highest priority thread in the system is always executing. Should a thread enter the ready queue, with a priority exceeding that of the currently running thread, the current thread will be preempted, and the higher priority thread is allowed to execute. Thread priority will affect the way in which the scheduler places threads in the ready queue. As was discussed in Chapter 6, a priority-based scheduler will often use a priority queue to hold the ready threads. The higher priority threads will be at the front of the queue and therefore will always have a chance to obtain the processor before the lower priority threads at the back of the queue. In the case of ties, the threads are selected based on the order in which they were placed in the queue. A major problem with priority-scheduling algorithms is **indefinite blocking** or **starvation**. Priority scheduling can leave some low-priority threads waiting indefinitely for the processor.

An integer priority is part of the state associated with every instance of the Thread class. When a new thread is created, it will have the same priority as the thread that created it. You can explicitly set the priority of a thread by invoking the thread's setPriority() method, and you can determine the priority of a thread by invoking its getPriority() method. Both of these methods are described in Table 11.1. Thread priorities range between the values specified by the class constants MIN_PRIORITY and MAX_PRIORITY defined in the Thread class (the class constant NORM_PRIORITY defines the default priority for a thread). High priorities are represented by large integer values, and low priorities are represented by small integer values. In Java, the maximum priority is currently ten, the minimum priority is zero, and the default priority is five. When programming, you should always use the class constants to specify the priorities because the actual values may change in future releases of the language.

Given the fact that all threads have a priority either explicitly assigned or set by default, you would think that the Java thread scheduler would be required to use priorities when making scheduling decisions. You would be wrong! As it turns out, the Java language specification states:

> When there is competition for processing resources, threads with higher priority are generally executed in preference to threads with lower priority. Such preference is not, however, a guarantee that the highest priority thread will always be running . . .

Thus, the scheduler may use the priority of a thread to help it determine which thread to run next, but it is not required to use priorities when making scheduling decisions. This allows the scheduler to have the flexibility it requires to ensure that all threads, regardless of their priority, receive some minimally acceptable level of service. Thread priorities serve as "hints" to the scheduler to help it determine the best way to schedule the threads and to avoid starvation. For this reason, use priorities to provide the scheduler with the information it needs to schedule your threads in the most efficient and beneficial way possible. For example, the thread in a word processor that writes a backup copy of the current document to the disk should have a lower priority than the thread that is accepting and interpreting keystrokes. Although both tasks are important, the word processor should spend most of its time examining the input. Otherwise, users will get frustrated with the noticeable time lag between when a key is pressed and the appearance of the corresponding character on the screen. Never assume that the scheduler will execute the threads in a program in priority order.

Some threads in a multithreaded Java program will need to coordinate their actions with other threads for the entire program to operate correctly. For example, in a word processing program, the thread that monitors keyboard activity should not add any new characters to the current document if the thread that automatically backs up the document is in the process of saving the current version of the document to disk. In this case, the keyboard thread should wait until the backup thread has completed the write operation before continuing. Without taking scheduling into consideration, you might have written code similar to that in Figure 11.10 to cause a thread to pause for a short period of time.

```java
public class BusyWait extends Thread {

    private static int DELAY = 100000; // Number of times to execute loop

    public void run() {

        // Code omitted

        // Delay execution of this thread for a few milliseconds
        // utilizing an empty for loop

        for ( int i = 0; i < DELAY; i++ ) {
            // do nothing
        }

        // Continue execution

        // Code omitted
    }

    public static void main( String args[] ) {

        // Create the thread and start the thread

        new BusyWait().start();
    }

} // BusyWait
```

FIGURE 11.10 Noncooperative thread

Consider what happens when the code in Figure 11.10 is executed in a multithreaded environment. The for loop in the run() method does not contain any instructions that cause the thread to relinquish the processor, thus providing the scheduler with the opportunity to perform a context switch. In fact, if the execution of this code were being managed by a nonpreemptive scheduler, no other threads would be able to execute until the for loop terminated. Effectively, this program waits by keeping the processor busy doing useless work, and since nothing can be scheduled during the wait, this thread will delay the execution of the entire program. Instead of monopolizing the processor, a better coding strategy would be to have the thread voluntarily relinquish control of the processor so that the scheduler could effectively utilize the processor during the wait period. In **cooperative multitasking,** a thread voluntarily yields control of the processor, allowing other threads to execute. The next section will look at some of the methods defined in the Thread class that can be used by the programmer to write cooperative threads.

◆ 11.2.3 Cooperative Multitasking

When writing code for a multithreaded environment, it is important to write it in such a way that the various threads do not interact in unexpected ways. Even though we cannot determine the exact order in which the threads will be executed by the scheduler, we must still be able to determine if the program will work correctly. Consider the program in Figure 11.11. The main thread, created and started by the JVM, starts a user thread that performs some complex computation, whose details are not important to this discussion. The main thread waits for the computation to be completed and then prints the results. The isAlive() is used by the main thread to determine when the scheduler is finished with the user thread.

```java
/**
 * Use a user thread to perform some complicated time consuming
 * computation.
 */

public class WorkerThread extends Thread {

   private static int result = 0; // Result of computation

   public void run() {

      // Perform a complicated time consuming calculation
      // and store the answer in the variable result

      // Code omitted . . .

   }

   /**
    * Create and start thread to perform computation. Wait until
    * the thread has finished before printing the result.
    *
    * @param args command line arguments (ignored)
    */
```

(continued)

FIGURE 11.11 Example of a busy wait loop

```
    public static void main(String args[]) {

        // Create and start the thread

        Thread t = new WorkerThread();
        t.start();

        // Wait for thread to terminate

        while ( t.isAlive() );

        // Print result

        System.out.println( result );
    }
} // WorkerThread
```

FIGURE 11.11 Example of a busy wait loop *(continued)*

The program in Figure 11.11 contains a busy wait loop. The busy loop in this program takes the form of a `while` loop that continues to execute until the user thread that was created by the program terminates (i.e., when `t.isAlive()` becomes false). Unfortunately, the scheduling problem that occurred in the program in Figure 11.10 can also happen here. Once the processor starts the busy loop in `main()`, the user thread will not be able to gain control of the processor until the busy loop terminates. However, in this program, the situation is considerably worse. In Figure 11.10, you know that the wait loop will eventually terminate. The wait loop in Figure 11.11 will not terminate until the user thread is no longer active. The user thread will remain active until its `run()` method returns. For the `run()` method to return, the user thread must obtain sufficient processor time to do its work. But if the busy loop is executing, it will never terminate because it is monopolizing all of the processor time and preventing the user thread from doing any work at all. The result is that we will never get our answer.

You must realize that events have to occur in a very specific order to produce this situation. For example, if the scheduler decided to make the main thread wait until the user thread terminated, the deadlock would be eliminated. However, even if a deadlock is only possible rather than certain, it still means that the program cannot be relied on to perform correctly at all times. Therefore, the code is useless. Imagine for a moment if a similar deadlock *might* occur in the flight control software of an aircraft that you are in. I certainly would not want to fly if there was even a tiny possibility of a deadlock occurring in midflight. Restarting the flight control computer is not an option when the plane is cruising at 37,000 feet above the earth.

The reason this problem occurred in the first place is that the scheduler does not have enough detailed information about the threads to execute them in the right order and thus prevent deadlock. The scheduler cannot, on its own, prevent deadlock. It is up to the programmer to avoid writing code that may potentially deadlock the system. One way to accomplish this is to provide hints to the scheduler about how threads should be scheduled. In the example in Figure 11.11, the deadlock could have been avoided if the while loop contained an instruction that forced a context switch to occur. During the context switch, the scheduler can give the processor to the user thread and allow it to do useful work. So this brings up the question: How can the running thread tell the scheduler to switch to another thread? We will look at three methods defined in the Java Thread class—sleep(), yield(), and join()—that can cause a context switch to take place.

The sleep() method, a static method of the Thread class, causes the current thread to cease execution for a user-specified time interval. The sleep() method takes a single integer parameter that specifies the amount of time to sleep in milliseconds (a millisecond is one-thousandth of a second, so there are 1,000 milliseconds in a second). Figure 11.12 shows how the sleep() method could be used to prevent the deadlock situation that arises in the program in Figure 11.11.

```java
/**
 * Use a user thread to perform some complicated time consuming
 * computation. The main thread will wait for the worker thread
 * using the sleep() method.
 */

public class SleepingMain extends Thread {

    private static final int DELAY = 1000;   // Milliseconds to sleep
    private static int result = 0;           // Result of computation

    public void run() {

        // Perform a complicated time consuming calculation
        // and store the answer in the variable result

        // Code omitted . . .
    }

    /**
     * Create and start thread to perform computation. Wait until
     * the thread has finished before printing the result.
     *
     * @param args command line arguments (ignored)
     */

    public static void main(String args[]) {

        // Create and start the thread

        Thread t = new SleepingMain();
        t.start();
```

FIGURE 11.12 Using sleep() to delay

```
        // Wait for thread to terminate

        while ( t.isAlive() ) {
            try {
                Thread.sleep( DELAY );
            } catch ( InterruptedException e ) {}
        }

        // Print result

        System.out.println( result );
    }

} // SleepingMain
```

FIGURE 11.12 Using `sleep()` to delay *(continued)*

By invoking the `sleep()` method within the `while` loop, the running processor will give up, or yield, the processor each time it executes the loop. When the `sleep()` method is executed, the scheduler places the current thread in the wait queue for the number of milliseconds specified by the argument, 1,000 in this case. The use of `sleep()` in Figure 11.12 eliminates the situation that arose in the code in Figure 11.11. That situation cannot occur now because `main()` will give up the processor for at least 1 second whenever it determines that the user thread is still active. During this sleep period, the scheduler is free to run the user thread, which means that the user thread should eventually terminate.

A thread can be interrupted by invoking the `interrupt()` method on the thread. If the thread is sleeping when it is interrupted, the `sleep()` method will throw an `InterruptedException` that must be caught or declared as discussed in Chapter 10. Should the user thread in the program in Figure 11.12 be interrupted, the `InterruptedException` will be caught but ignored.

The `sleep()` method causes only the current thread, the one that invoked the method, to sleep. You cannot use `sleep()` to put another thread to sleep. The `sleep()` method is `static`, so the sleep behavior is associated with the `Thread` class and not with any one of its instances. The parameter passed to `sleep()` is used to specify the duration of the sleep period, making it impossible to specify which thread should sleep.

Like any `static` method, `sleep()` can be invoked by specifying the class in which the method is defined or by using a reference to an instance of the class. When using an instance reference to invoke `sleep()`, it is easy to get confused about which thread will be put to sleep. Consider the program in Figure 11.13 that sleeps for a total of 3 seconds by invoking `sleep()` three times. In each statement, the `sleep()` method is invoked in a different way. Also notice the use of the `static` method `currentThread()` to obtain a reference to the thread currently being executed by the processor.

The first time the `sleep()` method is invoked in Figure 11.13, the class name `Thread` specifies the class that contains the method we wish to invoke. The second

```
/**
 * Demonstrate different ways to invoke sleep.
 */

public class SleepingMain {

    public static final int ONE_SECOND = 1000;

    public static void main() {

        Thread t = new Thread();              // Create a thread
        Thread me = Thread.currentThread();   // A reference to the thread
                                              // executing main()


        // Sleep for a total of 3 seconds.

        try {
            Thread.sleep( ONE_SECOND );
            me.sleep( ONE_SECOND );

            t.sleep( ONE_SECOND ); // This puts main to sleep - NOT t!!
        }
        catch ( InterruptedException e ) {}
    }
} // SleepingMain
```

FIGURE 11.13 Invoking `sleep()`

time the reference to the current thread, obtained previously in the program, is used to suspend execution of the thread. Both are valid ways to put the current thread to sleep. However, the third time `sleep()` is used might be a little confusing. Remember that `sleep()` is a `static` method, so even though it looks like we are invoking t's `sleep()` method, in actuality, the current thread is the one that will be suspended. The `sleep()` method is `static`, so regardless of how we access it, we are referring to the same `sleep()` method, and no matter how `sleep()` is called, the current thread is always the one that is suspended.

You might be tempted to use `sleep()` to introduce delays that last for a specific period of time in your programs. Figure 11.14 contains a crude clock program written in Java. The program consists of an infinite loop that uses `sleep()` to delay execution for 1 second and then prints the number of seconds that have elapsed since the program was started. It turns out that the clock provided by this program is far from accurate. In fact, if you execute this program on almost any machine, you will notice that it starts to lose time almost immediately.

For the program in Figure 11.14 to keep the time accurately, the amount of time between successive updates of the variables that represent time must be exactly one second. Unfortunately, this program was doomed from the start because it does not take into account the time required to update the variables and print the time. The

```
/**
 * Once every second print the elapsed time since the program
 * was started.
 */

public class Clock {

    public static final int ONE_SECOND = 1000; // Millisecs in a second
    public static final int SECS_PER_MIN = 60; // Seconds in a minute
    public static final int MINS_PER_HR = 60;  // Minutes in an hour

    /**
     * The main program consists of an infinite loop that sleeps for
     * one second, updates the current time, and prints the result.
     *
     * @param args command line arguments (ignored)
     */

    public static void main( String args[] ) {
        int secs = 0, mins = 0, hrs = 0; // Elapsed time

        while ( true ) {

            // Sleep for one second

            try {
                Thread.sleep( ONE_SECOND );
            }
            catch ( InterruptedException e ) {}

            // Update the time

            secs++;

            if ( secs >= SECS_PER_MIN ) {
                secs = 0;
                mins++;

                if ( mins >= MINS_PER_HR ) {
                    mins = 0;
                    hrs++;
                }
            }

            // Print the current time

            System.out.println( hrs + ":" + mins + ":" + secs );
        }
    }

} // Clock
```

FIGURE 11.14 Computation of elapsed time using `sleep()`

total time required for one iteration of the loop is the sum of the time required to evaluate the Boolean expression, update the variables, and print the current time, plus the 1-second delay for the sleep() call. However, even if we carefully adjusted the sleep interval so that the loop lasted 1 second, the program would still lose time.

The reason the program cannot keep accurate time has to do with the fact that the sleep() method only guarantees that the thread will be in the wait queue for the specified period of time; it does not make any promises about when the thread will be scheduled. When a thread invokes sleep(), the thread is placed in the wait queue for the specified interval. When the sleep interval is over, the thread is moved to the ready queue and now must compete with all the other ready threads in the queue. So even though the thread will be in the wait queue for the specified time interval, some additional time may pass before the thread is selected for execution. Add to this the possibility that the scheduler may preempt the thread at any time (e.g., to run a higher priority thread) and it becomes clear that the program in Figure 11.14 cannot accurately record the passage of time.

In the programs we will discuss in this book, it is not important how accurately they maintain the time. Even the clock program in Figure 11.14 is probably good enough to keep track of time for a human being. However, a special type of program, called a **real-time program**, must produce the correct results within an allotted period of time. If the timing constraints imposed by the requirements are not met, the program is considered incorrect. Consider, for example, the flight control software for the space shuttle, which issues a command for a thruster burn for a specific period of time. If the thruster does not burn for the exact amount of time specified, or if there is a delay between the time the command is issued and the burn starts, the shuttle may end up hurtling out of orbit or burning up in the atmosphere. Standard implementations of Java would not be suitable for this type of real-time programming.

The Thread class defines another static method, yield(), that causes the currently executing thread to pause temporarily and allow other threads to execute. Like sleep(), yield() affects only the thread that is currently executing. However, unlike sleep(), which puts the process in the wait queue, when the current thread executes yield(), the scheduler immediately places the thread back in the ready queue and then selects the next thread that will be executed. Note that since the current thread is placed into the ready queue before the next thread is selected, it is entirely possible that the thread that was just preempted will be selected for execution. The program in Figure 11.15 illustrates the use of the yield() method.

```
/**
 * Use a user thread to perform some complicated time consuming
 * computation. The main thread will wait for the worker thread
 * using the yield() method.
 */

public class YieldingMain extends Thread {

    private static final int DELAY = 1000; // Milliseconds to sleep
```
(continued)

FIGURE 11.15 Using yield()

```
    private static int result = 0; // Result of computation

    public void run() {

        // Perform a complicated time consuming calculation
        // and store the answer in the variable result

        // Code omitted . . .
    }

    /**
     * Create and start thread to perform computation. Wait until
     * the thread has finished before printing the result.
     *
     * @param args command line arguments (ignored)
     */

    public static void main(String args[]) {

        // Create and start the thread

        Thread t = new YieldingMain();
        t.start();

        // Wait for thread to terminate

        while ( t.isAlive() ) {
            Thread.yield();
        }

        // Print result

        System.out.println( result );
    }

} // YieldingMain
```

FIGURE 11.15 Using `yield()` *(continued)*

Although the use of the `sleep()` and `yield()` methods prevented the deadlock that occurred in the program in Figure 11.11, both solutions still require the use of a busy loop. In Figures 11.12 and 11.15, a `while` loop was used to determine if the user thread was still active, and if it was, either `sleep()` or `yield()` was invoked to give the other thread a chance to execute. Using a `while` loop to constantly check if the user thread is active is a waste of processor time. It would be much more efficient to pause the execution of the main thread until the user thread terminates. At this point, the main thread could be restarted and safely print the result of the computation.

The `join()` method from the `Thread` class does exactly what we want. A thread is paused after invoking the `join()` on another thread until that thread terminates. That is, if thread `a` executes the call `b.join()`, `a` is saying that it wants to pause until thread b terminates. At that time, a should be returned to the ready queue. Note that `join()` is not a `static` method. The current thread must have a reference to the thread that it wishes to join with. This is different from the other methods that we have discussed in this section. The program in Figure 11.16 illustrates the `join()` method.

```java
/**
 * Use a user thread to perform some complicated time consuming
 * computation. The main thread will wait for the worker thread
 * using the join() method.
 */

public class JoiningMain extends Thread {

    private static int result = 0;          // Result of computation

    public void run() {

        // Perform a complicated time consuming calculation
        // and store the answer in the variable result

        // Code omitted . . .
    }

    /**
     * Create and start thread to perform computation. Wait until
     * the thread has finished before printing the result.
     *
     * @param args command line arguments (ignored)
     */

    public static void main(String args[]) {

        // Create and start the thread

        Thread t = new JoiningMain();
        t.start();

        // Wait for thread to terminate

        try {
            t.join(); // Pause execution until t dies
        }
        catch ( InterruptedException e ) {}

        // Print result

        System.out.println( result );
    }

} // JoiningMain
```

FIGURE 11.16 Using `join()`

In Figure 11.16, the `while` loop has been replaced with a statement that invokes `join()` on the user thread. This will cause the main thread to be suspended until the user thread terminates. In terms of scheduling, the main thread will remain in the wait queue until the user thread has terminated. At that point, it will be placed into the ready queue and will eventually be selected for execution. By using `join()`, we are no longer wasting processor time checking to see if the user thread is active.

You will note that `join()` can throw an `InterruptedException`. If a thread is interrupted while executing a `join()`, an `InterruptedException` is thrown. There are three different versions of `join()`. The no argument version, illustrated in Figure 11.16, will wait indefinitely for the thread to terminate. There are two other versions that allow you to specify a maximum time that `join()` will wait for the termination of the thread. The parameters that specify the wait interval to be used by `join()` work exactly the same as `sleep()`. If the time period expires, the `join()` method will simply return. The `isAlive()` method can be used to determine if the other thread actually terminated or is still running.

Programs that utilize multiple threads can run into problems when the threads compete for resources. In this section, we have looked at what can happen in a program when two or more threads compete for the processor. The example program in Figure 11.11 illustrated how this competition can result in a program that does not execute as expected. This program was modified using `sleep()`, `yield()`, and `join()` to provide hints to the scheduler so that the program would execute correctly. Synchronization problems can also occur when concurrent threads access common memory locations. In this case, the program typically runs but gives an incorrect result. In the next section, we will look at how this situation can arise and explore the language constructs that Java provides to control the way in which threads execute.

11.3 SYNCHRONIZATION

◆ 11.3.1 Background

The processor is not the only resource that concurrent threads compete for. Other shared resources such as files, printers, and memory also need to be utilized carefully so that concurrent access to these resources does not have unexpected consequences. In this section, we look at the potential problems that can occur when two threads attempt to modify a common memory location at the same time.

To start our discussion, look at the code in Figure 11.17 that creates three threads that concurrently attempt to modify the class variable named `common`. Take a few minutes to try to determine the output that will be produced when this program is run.

```
/**
 * Add three to a variable in a strange way.
 */

public class ConcAccess extends Thread {
```

FIGURE 11.17 Concurrent access

```
    private static final int NUM_THREADS = 3;
    private static int common = 0;

    /**
     * Obtain a local copy of common, increment the copy by one
     * and store the result back in common.
     */

    public void run() {
        int local = 0; // Local storage

        // Add one to common
        local = common;
        local = local + 1;
        common = local;
    }


    /**
     * Create and start three threads that will each add one to
     * common. Print common when all threads have died.
     *
     * @param args command line arguments (ignored).
     */

    public static void main( String args[] ) {
        // Holds the references to the threads that
        // are created so that main can join with them

        Thread myThreads[] = new Thread[ NUM_THREADS ];

        // Create and start the threads
        for ( int i = 0; i < NUM_THREADS; i++ ) {
            myThreads[ i ] = new ConcAccess();
            myThreads[ i ].start();
        }

        // Join with each thread
        for ( int i = 0; i < NUM_THREADS; i++ ) {
            try {
                myThreads[ i ].join();
            } catch ( InterruptedException e ) {}
        }

        // Threads have terminated - print the result
        System.out.println( "Common is: " + common );
    }

} // ConcAccess
```

FIGURE 11.17 Concurrent access *(continued)*

Each of the threads in this program modifies the class variable common by incrementing it by 1. Since there are three threads in the program, the output from the program should be 3. As it turns out, about 95 percent of the time this program does print the correct answer, but it occasionally produces a wrong answer, such as 1 or 2. The program itself is correct, so let's concentrate on what is happening to the threads as they are scheduled and run. Remember that the scheduler is responsible for managing the execution of the three threads in this program and is free to interleave the execution of their instructions any way it sees fit. Consider what happens if the scheduler executes each thread one at a time until it terminates. The resulting instruction stream is shown in Figure 11.18.

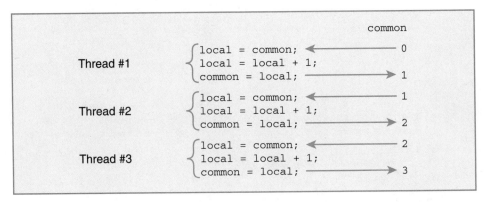

FIGURE 11.18 Serial execution

When each thread is run one at a time, the program produces the correct result, which is 3. As can be seen in Figure 11.18, each thread obtains a copy of the current value in the variable common, increments the local copy, and then stores the result back into common. This means that the next thread that accesses common will see the updates made by all the threads that ran earlier. The order of execution in Figure 11.18 ensures that only one thread is updating common at a time. This serializes the execution of the threads and effectively removes any concurrency from the program. When the threads are executed in this way, it is impossible for two threads to be in the process of updating common at the same time, and the program produces the correct result.

Now consider what happens if the scheduler runs the threads so that they are run one statement at a time. In other words, the scheduler executes the first statement from thread 1, the first statement from thread 2, the first statement from thread 3, the second statement from thread 1, and so on. The resulting instruction stream is shown in Figure 11.19.

When the threads are executed in this order, all three threads are updating common at the same time. From the very start, it is clear that this program will fail because each of the threads starts out by obtaining a copy of the value in common. Only one of the threads will see the "correct" value of common; the other threads will obtain the value that is stored in common before any of the threads have had a chance to store their results. If the threads are executed one instruction at a time, each thread will base its update on the original value stored in common. After the first statements in each thread are executed, it does not matter how the rest of the instructions in the

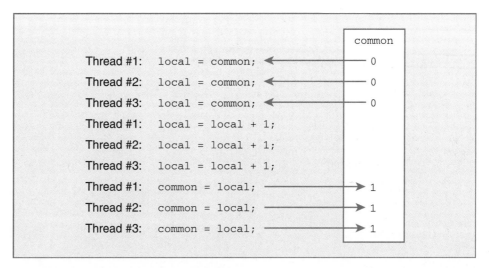

FIGURE 11.19 Concurrent execution

threads are executed; the final value that will be stored in common will be incorrect. This means the program will print the wrong answer. In the case of Figure 11.19, it incorrectly stores the value 1.

For this program to work correctly, the threads must be executed so that as soon as one of the threads retrieves the current value stored in common, the remaining threads are forced to wait until the newly updated value has been stored back into this shared variable. The block of code that starts with the statement local = common and ends with common = local must be executed as a single indivisible unit. As long as any one thread is in the midst of executing this block of code, all other threads must wait for it to finish this block before they can begin to execute. The block of code that updates common is referred to as a **critical section** because for the program to function correctly, it is critical that the code in this section of the program be executed by only one thread at a time.

The program in Figure 11.17 contained only a single critical section; however, a typical multithreaded program may contain many critical sections. For example, consider the code in Figure 11.20. This is the same program shown in Figure 11.17, but an additional class variable, other, is incremented by each thread. This program contains two critical sections: one that increments the variable common and another that increments the variable other.

```
/**
 * A program with two critical sections.
 */

public class TwoCritical extends Thread {
    private static final int NUM_THREADS = 3;
    private static int common = 0, other = 0;
```
(continued)

FIGURE 11.20 Two critical sections

```
/**
 * Increment both common and other by one
 */

public void run() {
   int local = 0; // Local storage

   // Add one to common

   local = common;
   local = local + 1;
   common = local;

   // Add one to other

   local = other;
   local = local + 1;
   other = local;
}

/**
 * Create and start three threads.
 *
 * @param args command line arguments (ignored).
 */

public static void main( String args[] ) {
   // References to the threads

   Thread myThreads[] = new Thread[ NUM_THREADS ];

   // Create and start the threads
   for ( int i = 0; i < NUM_THREADS; i++ ) {
      myThreads[ i ] = new ConcAccess();
      myThreads[ i ].start();
   }

   // Join with each thread
   for ( int i = 0; i < NUM_THREADS; i++ ) {
      try {
         myThreads[ i ].join();
      } catch ( InterruptedException e ) {}
   }

   // Threads have terminated - print the result
   System.out.println( "Common: " + common + "Other: " + other );
}

} // TwoCritical
```

FIGURE 11.20 Two critical sections *(continued)*

For the program in Figure 11.20 to function correctly, it is necessary to make sure that only one thread is executing within each critical section. It is only necessary to make sure that no more than one thread is executing the same critical section; there is no reason one thread could be updating `other` while another thread is updating `common`. What causes a program to fail is more than one thread attempting to update the same shared variable at the same time. Two threads cannot be in the same critical section at the same time, but two threads can be in two different critical sections at the same time without causing a problem.

When writing multithreaded programs, it is first necessary to identify all of the critical sections in a program so that the necessary actions can be taken to ensure that multiple threads do not attempt to execute the same critical section of code at the same time. It is often difficult to spot all of the critical sections in a program. Errors resulting from concurrent access to shared variables are one of the most common mistakes found in deployed software. You can typically identify critical sections by looking for code segments that modify shared resources such as variables, objects, or files. Although we have concentrated on concurrent access to variables in this section, all of the issues just discussed apply to almost any shared resource in a program.

Once the critical sections have been identified, appropriate steps can be taken to ensure that only one thread will execute this code at a time. Java provides a locking mechanism that allows a programmer to inform the scheduler that a particular section of code can be executed by only one thread at a time. By ensuring exclusive access to this critical section, we can be much more confident that the program will work as intended.

◆ 11.3.2 Locks

Every object in a Java program, whether it is a user-defined object or an object that is defined by a class in a library, is associated with a **lock** that provides a means of synchronization. It is only possible for one thread to hold a given lock at one time. If two threads try to obtain the same lock at the same time, only one will obtain it. The other thread will have to wait until the first thread releases the lock before it can obtain it. This type of lock is called a **mutually exclusive**, or **mutex**, lock. The name comes from the fact that access to the lock is exclusive.

Given our previous discussion about critical sections, it is not too hard to see how a mutex lock could be used to ensure that only one thread can be in a critical section at a time. We first associate a lock with a specific critical section. When a thread wishes to enter a critical section, it must obtain the lock for that block of code before it is allowed to execute it. After the thread has finished executing the code in the critical section, it releases the lock to inform other threads that might be waiting to enter the section that they may now attempt to obtain the lock and enter the critical section. This process is illustrated in Figure 11.21.

The Java programming language provides a syntactic construct called a **synchronized block** to control the access to critical sections of a program. The syntax of the `synchronized` statement is given in Figure 11.22.

Before executing any code in a synchronized block, the thread must first obtain the lock associated with the object specified by *expression* in Figure 11.22. The thread will hold the lock for as long as it is executing the code inside the synchronized block.

```
                         public void run() {
                             int local = 0;   // Local storage

┌─────────────────────┐      // Add one to common
│ Obtain lock for critical │
│ section              │      local = common;         ┐  ┌─────────────────────┐
└─────────────────────┘      local = local + 1;       ├  │ Only one thread can ever │
                             common = local;          ┘  │ be in the critical section │
                         }                                └─────────────────────┘
        ┌─────────────────┐
        │ Release lock    │
        └─────────────────┘
```

FIGURE 11.21 Using a mutex lock

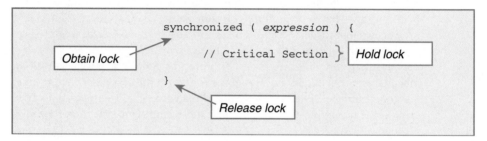

```
                      synchronized ( expression ) {

┌──────────────┐          // Critical Section  ┐  ┌────────────┐
│ Obtain lock  │                                ├  │ Hold lock  │
└──────────────┘                                ┘  └────────────┘
                      }
              ┌─────────────────┐
              │ Release lock    │
              └─────────────────┘
```

FIGURE 11.22 `synchronized` statement

When the thread executes the last statement in the block and leaves the block, the lock is released. Since only one thread can hold a specific lock at a time, only one thread can be in the critical section. If a thread cannot obtain the lock when it attempts to enter the synchronized block, it will be forced to wait until the lock is available. More than one thread can wait for a lock. When the lock is released, the JVM will select one of the waiting threads, give it the lock, and allow it to enter the block. The order in which the waiting threads are selected to obtain the lock is not specified and will be determined by the JVM at run time. Figure 11.23 contains a modified fragment of the program from Figure 11.17 that illustrates the use of the `synchronized` statement.

```
public class ConcAccess extends Thread {
    private static final int NUM_THREADS = 3;
    private static int common = 0;

    private static final Integer lock = new Integer( 0 );

    public void run() {
        int local = 0; // Local storage
```

FIGURE 11.23 Using `synchronized` in a program

```
        // Add one to common

        synchronized( lock ) {
            local = common;
            local = local + 1;
            common = local;
        }
    }

    // Rest of program omitted.
```

FIGURE 11.23 Using synchronized in a program *(continued)*

In Figure 11.23, a static Integer object is used to control access to the synchronized block. There is no particular reason an instance of Integer was used as the lock because the lock can be any type of object. The key to making the synchronized block work correctly is to make sure that all threads attempt to lock the same object when entering the block. If the threads obtain locks on different objects, multiple threads will be allowed to enter the synchronized block. This is the reason the variable lock is declared static in the program in Figure 11.23. Regardless of how many threads are created by main(), they will all attempt to obtain the same static variable lock when entering the synchronized block. The code in Figure 11.24 also arranges to have all of the threads lock on the same object. In this case, however, the reference to the lock is stored in an instance variable.

```
/**
 * Demonstrate object locking in Java.
 */

public class Locks1 extends Thread {

    private static final String PREFIX = "Thread #"; // For thread name
    private static final int N = 3;                   // Loop constant
    private static final int DELAY = 10;              // Sleep period

    private Object lock; // Object used for synchronization

    public Locks1( Object l, String name ) {
        // Store a reference to the lock and store name of the thread

        lock = l;
        setName( name );
    }

    public void run() {
```
(continued)

FIGURE 11.24 Synchronizing on a common lock

```
        // Get the lock before entering the loop
        synchronized( lock ) {
          for ( int i = 0; i < 3; i++ ) {

              System.out.println( getName() + " is tired" );

              try {
                 Thread.currentThread().sleep( DELAY );
              } catch ( InterruptedException e ){}

              System.out.println( getName() + " is rested" ); }
          }
        }

    public static void main( String args[] ) {
        // Create the object that will be used as the lock
        Integer lock = new Integer( 0 );

        // Create the threads and let them run
        for ( int i = 0; i < 3; i++ ) {
           new Locks1( lock, PREFIX + i ).start();
        }
      }
    }

} // Locks1
```

FIGURE 11.24 Synchronizing on a common lock *(continued)*

The critical section in the program in Figure 11.24 is the for loop in the run()
method that executes three times. Each time the loop runs, it prints a message that
states the thread is tired, sleeps for 10 milliseconds, and then prints a message that
states the thread is rested. Since this loop is inside a synchronized block, you might
be tempted to say that once any one of the threads starts executing the loop, all the
other threads will have to wait for the lock to be released. This will occur only if all of
the threads attempt to obtain the lock on the same object. Looking at the main()
method and the constructor for the class, you can see that indeed only one object is
being used as a lock in this program. The main() method creates an Integer object
and then passes a reference to that object to each of the threads it creates. The diagram in Figure 11.25 shows the object that each thread will use as a lock. Since the instance variables all refer to the same object, only one thread will be able to execute the
for loop at a time.

Although we have determined that the for loop will be executed by each thread
exclusively, we still cannot determine with 100 percent accuracy the behavior (output) of this program because we do not know the order in which the threads will be
executed. For example, assume for a moment that all three threads reach the synchronized statement at exactly the same time. Only one of the threads, we do not know
which one, will obtain the lock, while the other two will have to wait. When the first
thread leaves the loop, one of the two waiting threads will be able to obtain the lock,

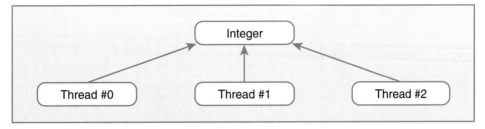

FIGURE 11.25 Threads and their locks

but again we do not know which one. So even though the `synchronized` statement made it possible to ensure that only one thread was executing the `for` loop at any one time, it is still not possible to determine the exact output of this program. Figure 11.26 shows three of the six possible outputs that can be generated by this program.

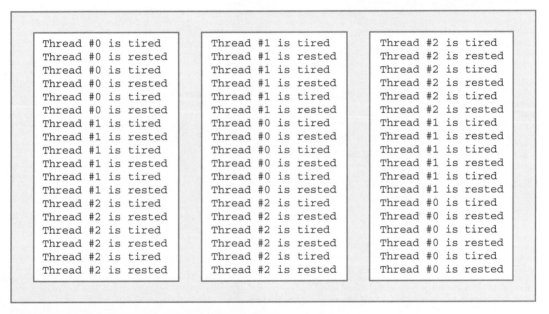

FIGURE 11.26 Three of six possible outputs

Now consider the program in Figure 11.27. This program is almost identical to the program in Figure 11.24 except for the way in which the lock is created and distributed to the threads. The `Integer` lock is now created in the constructor instead of being created in main and distributed to the threads as a parameter.

```
/**
 * Demonstrate object locking in Java.
 */
```
(continued)

FIGURE 11.27 Attempted synchronization using an instance variable

```
public class Locks2 extends Thread {

    private static final String PREFIX = "Thread #";   // For thread name
    private static final int N = 3;                     // Loop constant
    private static final int DELAY = 10;                // Sleep period

    private Object lock; // Object used for synchronization

    public Locks2( String name ) {
        // Store a reference to the lock and store name of the thread

        lock = new Integer( 0 );
        setName( name );
    }

    public void run() {

        // Get the lock before entering the loop
        synchronized( lock ) {
        for ( int i = 0; i < 3; i++ ) {

            System.out.println( getName() + " is tired" );

            try {
                Thread.currentThread().sleep( DELAY );
            } catch ( InterruptedException e ){}

            System.out.println( getName() + " is rested" ); }
        }
    }

    public static void main( String args[] ) {

        // Create the threads and let them run
        for ( int i = 0; i < 3; i++ ) {
            new Locks2( PREFIX + i ).start();
        }
    }

} // Locks2
```

FIGURE 11.27 Attempted synchronization using an instance variable *(continued)*

This small change in the program in Figure 11.27 dramatically changes the way the program runs. The for loop is no longer executed by the threads one at a time. Instead, all three threads can execute the loop at the same time. This is puzzling because the run() method has not changed from the previous program. The for loop is still in a synchronized block, and a lock still needs to be obtained to execute the loop. The difference between this program and the last lies in the locks. In the program in Figure 11.27, each thread creates its own lock when the constructor is called. So, as shown in Figure 11.28, each thread has a reference to a different lock. The synchronized statement still obtains the lock prior to executing the loop, but since each thread has a different lock, they can all execute the for loop at the same time. The synchronization that was present in the program of Figure 11.24 has been lost.

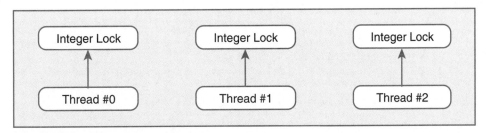

FIGURE 11.28 Different lock objects

Since every object is locking on different locks, there is no synchronization at all. The synchronized statement is still obtaining and releasing the lock as we have described, but each thread uses a different lock to control access to the loop. The output of this program will consist of the six lines of text printed by each thread interleaved in some random order as shown in Figure 11.29 below.

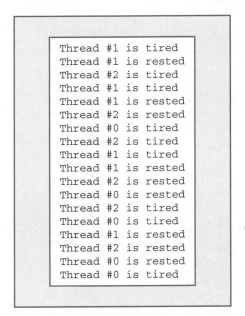

```
Thread #1 is tired
Thread #1 is rested
Thread #2 is tired
Thread #1 is tired
Thread #1 is rested
Thread #2 is rested
Thread #0 is tired
Thread #2 is tired
Thread #1 is tired
Thread #1 is rested
Thread #2 is rested
Thread #0 is rested
Thread #2 is tired
Thread #0 is tired
Thread #1 is rested
Thread #2 is rested
Thread #0 is rested
Thread #0 is tired
```

FIGURE 11.29 Random output resulting from multiple locks

One way to ensure that only one object is being used as a lock in the program in Figure 11.27 is to use a class variable as a lock. Since there is only one copy of a class variable, all of the instances of the class will be using the same object as a lock. The program in Figure 11.30 uses the class variable lock to synchronize the actions of the threads that it creates.

```
/**
 * Use a static lock for synchronization
 */

public class Locks3 extends Thread {

    private static final String PREFIX = "Thread #"; // For thread name
    private static final int N = 3;                   // Loop constant
    private static final int DELAY = 10;              // Sleep period

    // Object used for synchronization
    private static Object lock = new Integer( 0 );

    public Locks3( String name ) {
        // Store the name of the thread
        setName( name );
    }

    public void run() {

        // Get the lock before entering the loop
        synchronized( lock ) {
        for ( int i = 0; i < 3; i++ ) {

            System.out.println( getName() + " is tired" );

            try {
                Thread.currentThread().sleep( DELAY );
            } catch ( InterruptedException e ){}

            System.out.println( getName() + " is rested" ); }
        }
    }

    public static void main( String args[] ) {

        // Create the threads and let them run
        for ( int i = 0; i < 3; i++ ) {
            new Locks3( PREFIX + i ).start();
        }
    }

} // Locks3
```

FIGURE 11.30 Using a static lock

We said at the beginning of this section that every object in Java has a lock and that any expression that evaluates to a reference to an object can be used in a synchronized statement. Consider the code in Figure 11.31 that uses the this variable associated with an object to obtain a reference to the object whose lock will control access to the synchronized block.

```
/**
 * Using this to lock in Java.
 */

public class Locks3 extends Thread {

    private static final String PREFIX = "Thread #"; // For thread name
    private static final int N = 3;                   // Loop constant
    private static final int DELAY = 10;              // Sleep period

    public Locks3( String name ) {
        setName( name );
    }

    public void run() {

        // Get the lock before entering the loop
        synchronized( this ) {
            for ( int i = 0; i < 3; i++ ) {

                System.out.println( getName() + " is tired" );

                try {
                    Thread.currentThread().sleep( DELAY );
                } catch ( InterruptedException e ){}

                System.out.println( getName() + " is rested" );
            }
        }
    }

    public static void main( String args[] ) {

        // Create the threads and let them run
        for ( int i = 0; i < 3; i++ ) {
            new Locks1( PREFIX + i ).start();
        }
    }

} // Locks3
```

FIGURE 11.31 Attempted synchronization using `this`

Using `this` in the program in Figure 11.31 causes the program to behave in the exact same fashion as the program in Figure 11.27. The reason there is no synchronization in the program in Figure 11.31 is due to the fact that again each thread is locking on a different object. In this case, instead of locking on different `Integer` objects, the threads are locking on different `Thread` objects. At first glance, writing a method that locks on the object in which it is defined seems useless. Consider, however, the code fragment for a `Queue` class that is shown in Figure 11.32.

```
/**
 * A thread safe queue class.
 */

public class SyncQueue {

    // Instance variables go here

    public void enqueue( Object item ) {
        synchronized ( this ) {
            // Code to enqueue goes here
        }
    }

    public Object dequeue() {
        synchronized ( this ) {
            // Code to dequeue goes here
        }
    }

} // SyncQueue
```

FIGURE 11.32 Thread safe queue

In Chapter 7, you learned that the method enqueue() adds items to a queue, and the method dequeue() removes items from a queue. Clearly, these two methods should never be executed at the same time by two different threads since these methods access the shared state of the Queue object (i.e., size, front, and back). Unpredictable results could occur if an enqueue() and dequeue() operation occurred at the same time. By writing the enqueue() and dequeue() methods so that they have to obtain the lock on the Queue object prior to execution solves this problem. If an attempt is made to execute an enqueue() and a dequeue() at the same time, only one of the threads will be able to obtain the object lock. The other thread will have to wait until the first thread has released the lock.

It turns out that synchronizing methods in this way is so useful that the Java programming language allows you to define a method as synchronized. **Synchronized methods** are nothing more than a shorthand notation for a synchronization block that surrounds all of the code in the method as shown in Figure 11.33. The JVM must obtain the lock associated with the object on which the method is invoked before the statements in the instruction can be executed.

It is important when using synchronized methods that you keep in mind that the lock that controls access to these methods is the object itself. This means that there will be synchronization within the object; only one of the synchronized methods in the object will be able to execute at one time. The shorthand notation does not mean that the synchronization holds across all instances of the class. For example, in the Queue code in Figure 11.33 that uses synchronized methods, only one thread at a time will be able to place objects into or remove objects from any one queue. However, objects can be placed in different queue objects at the same time.

```
public synchronized void enqueue( Object item ) {

    // Body of method goes here

}
```

Shorthand notation for

```
public void enqueue( Object item ) {
    synchronized ( this ) {

    // Body of method goes here

    }
}
```

FIGURE 11.33 Synchronized methods

Whenever the JVM loads a class, it automatically instantiates a `Class` object that represents the class. A `Class` object can be used to obtain information about the class such as the full name of the class, the constructors provided by the class, or the methods associated with the class (for the complete specification of the class `Class`, refer to the appropriate Javadoc page in the Java API). An instance of a class can obtain a reference to its `Class` object by invoking the `getClass()` method that is defined in class `Object` as illustrated by the program in Figure 11.34.

```
/**
 * Use the class Class to obtain basic information about the
 * class Integer.
 */

public class UsingClass {

    public static void main( String args[] ) {

        // Create an instance of an integer

        Integer anInt = new Integer( 0 );

        // Obtain a reference to the class object associated
        // with an integer
```
(continued)

FIGURE 11.34 Using the class `Class`

```
            Class aClass = anInt.getClass();

            // Print out the name of the class and the package using
            // accessors provided by the Class object

            System.out.println( "Class: " + aClass.getName() );
            System.out.println( "Package: " + aClass.getPackage() );
        }

    } // UsingClass
```

FIGURE 11.34 Using the class `Class` *(continued)*

For every class that is loaded by the JVM, only one `Class` object will be created to represent the class regardless of the number of instances of the class that there might be in a program. Thus, when any instance of a particular class invokes the `getClass()` method, a reference to the same object will always be returned. Since an object is used to represent the class and every object has a lock associated with it, there is no reason instances of a class could not use the instance of the `Class` object returned by `getClass()` for synchronization. Figure 11.35 illustrates how the program in Figure 11.30 could be modified to use its `Class` object as a lock instead of a class variable.

```
/**
 * Using a class object for synchronization
 */

public class Locks4 extends Thread {

    private static final String PREFIX = "Thread #"; // For thread name
    private static final int N = 3;                   // Loop constant
    private static final int DELAY = 10;              // Sleep period

    public Locks4( String name ) {
        // Store the name of the thread
        setName( name );
    }

    public void run() {

        // Get the lock before entering the loop
        synchronized( getClass() ) {
            for ( int i = 0; i < 3; i++ ) {

                System.out.println( getName() + " is tired" );
```

FIGURE 11.35 Using a `Class` object for synchronization

```
            try {
                Thread.currentThread().sleep( DELAY );
            } catch ( InterruptedException e ){}

            System.out.println( getName() + " is rested" );
        }
    }
}

    public static void main( String args[] ) {

        // Create the threads and let them run
        for ( int i = 0; i < 3; i++ ) {
            new Locks4( PREFIX + i ).start();
        }
    }

} // Locks4
```

FIGURE 11.35 Using a `Class` object for synchronization *(continued)*

Figure 11.33 illustrated that when invoking a `synchronized` method, the JVM will use `this` to obtain a lock before any of the code in the method would be executed. It is possible to declare static methods as `synchronized` as shown in Figure 11.36. In a `static synchronized` method, the JVM will obtain the lock associated with the object returned by `getClass()` before executing the code in the method. A `static` method cannot use `this` to obtain a reference to a lock because a `static` method does not have a `this` reference.

```
/**
 * Static synchronized methods
 */

public class Locks5 extends Thread {

    private static final String PREFIX = "Thread #"; // For thread name
    private static final int N = 3;                  // Loop constant
    private static final int DELAY = 10;             // Sleep period

    public Locks5( String name ) {
        // Store the name of the thread
        setName( name );
    }

    public static synchronized void doIt( String name ) {
```
(continued)

FIGURE 11.36 Static `synchronized` methods

```
        for ( int i = 0; i < 3; i++ ) {

            System.out.println( name + " is tired" );

            try {
                Thread.currentThread().sleep( DELAY );
            } catch ( InterruptedException e ){}

            System.out.println( name + " is rested" );
        }
    }

    public void run() {
        doIt( getName() );
    }

    public static void main( String args[] ) {

        // Create the threads and let them run
        for ( int i = 0; i < 3; i++ ) {
            new Locks5( PREFIX + i ).start();
        }
    }

} // Locks5
```

FIGURE 11.36 Static `synchronized` methods *(continued)*

In this section, we discussed how to use locks to synchronize the behavior of concurrent threads in a Java program. Every object in a Java program has a lock associated with it, and using a `synchronized` block, it is possible to obtain a lock before executing the code within the block. Since a lock can be held by only one thread at a time, only one thread can be executing the code in a `synchronized` block. Locks and `synchronized` blocks provide the basis for synchronization in a Java program; however, as you will see in the next section, additional synchronization tools are needed to solve the synchronization issues faced by multithreaded programs.

◆ **11.3.3** `wait()` and `notify()`

Although the synchronization primitives that we have discussed so far in this chapter provide the ability to coordinate the activities of different threads, there are times when additional capabilities are required. To illustrate this, we will consider the interactions between a producer that produces items for a consumer and a consumer that consumes these items. In the program that we discuss in this section, the producer and consumer run as separate threads and are connected by a buffer. The producer places the items in the buffer, and the consumer removes them. The structure of this problem is shown in Figure 11.37.

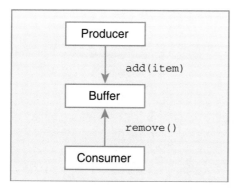

FIGURE 11.37 Producer/consumer

The `Buffer` class provides two methods: `add()` and `remove()`. The Producer invokes `add()` to place an item in the buffer, and the Consumer invokes `remove()` to retrieve the item. Clearly, the code that implements `add()` and `remove()` must be written in such a way that it is not possible for one thread to be adding an item while a second thread is removing an item at the same time. In terms of the producer-consumer problem, we do not want to allow a producer to execute the `add()` method at the same time the consumer executes `remove()`. Additionally, `add()` must work correctly if it is invoked when the buffer is full, and `remove()` must work correctly if it is invoked on an empty buffer.

The interface in Figure 11.38 defines the behavior associated with a finite `Buffer`. The interface requires that a `Buffer` provide two methods: `add()` and `remove()`. The method `add()` blocks until the item has been added to the buffer. In other words, if `add()` is invoked on a full buffer, the method will not return until the item has been added to the buffer. If the buffer is full when `add()` is invoked, the method will wait until there is room in the buffer for the additional item. Likewise, if `remove()` is invoked on an empty buffer, the method waits until an item is available for removal. So if a Consumer invokes `remove()` and there is no item available, it will wait until the Producer has placed an item in the buffer by invoking `add()`.

```
/**
 * A buffer that can serve as a connection between a
 * producer and a consumer.
 */

public interface Buffer {

    /**
     * Add an element to the buffer. If the buffer is full,
     * the method will block until the item can be placed in
     * the buffer.
     *
```
(continued)

FIGURE 11.38 `Buffer` interface

```
   * @param item the element to add to the buffer.
   */

  public void add( int item );

  /**
   * Remove an element from the buffer. If the buffer is empty,
   * the method will block until an item is available.
   *
   * @returns the next item in the buffer.
   */

  public int remove();

} // Buffer
```

FIGURE 11.38 Buffer interface *(continued)*

Given the constraint that at most one thread can execute add() or remove() in a single instance of a buffer at one time, it seems reasonable to implement these methods as synchronized methods (Figure 11.39).

```
/**
 * An implementation of a buffer that can lead to deadlock.
 */

public class DeadlockBuffer implements Buffer {

   private int currentItem; // Item currently in the buffer
   private boolean full;     // Is the buffer full?

   /**
    * Create a new buffer.
    */

   public DeadlockBuffer() {
      full = false;
   }

   /**
    * Add an element to the buffer. If the buffer is full,
    * the method will block until the item can be placed in
    * the buffer.
    *
    * @param item the element to add to the buffer.
    */

   public synchronized void add( int item ) {
```

FIGURE 11.39 Implementation of a buffer

```
        // Wait until there is room in the buffer for the item
        while ( full );

        currentItem = item;
        full = true;
    }


    /**
     * Remove an element from the buffer. If the buffer is empty,
     * the method will block until an item is available.
     *
     * @returns the next item in the buffer.
     */

    public synchronized int remove() {
        // Wait until there is something to remove
        while ( !full );

        full = false;
        return currentItem;
    }

} // DeadlockBuffer
```

FIGURE 11.39 Implementation of a buffer *(continued)*

Although the code in Figure 11.39 satisfies the synchronization constraints of this program (i.e., add() and remove() cannot be executed at the same time), it has a fatal flaw in that deadlock is possible. Consider what would happen if the consumer invoked the remove() method on an empty buffer. The consumer would obtain the lock associated with the buffer and execute the code in the remove() method. Since the buffer is empty, the consumer would execute the while loop until there is an item to remove (i.e., the buffer is no longer empty). However, as long as the consumer is executing the remove() method and is holding the lock, the producer cannot obtain the lock so that it can place an item in the buffer. The consumer will not give up the lock until the producer has added something to the buffer. The result is a deadlock. A similar situation can arise if a producer fills the buffer before a consumer has had a chance to remove an item.

It is possible to implement a buffer using only locks. The key is to write the code in such a way that when either the consumer or the producer is waiting, it does not maintain exclusive control of the lock. The code in Figure 11.40 contains a deadlock-free implementation of a buffer.

```
/**
 * An implementation of the producer/consumer buffer
 * that uses simple synchronization.
 */
```
(continued)

FIGURE 11.40 Deadlock-free implementation of a buffer

```
public class SyncBuffer implements Buffer {

    private int currentItem; // Item currently in the buffer
    private boolean full;     // Is the buffer full?

    /**
     * Create a new buffer.
     */

    public SyncBuffer() {
        full = false;
    }

    /**
     * Add an element to the buffer. If the buffer is full,
     * the method will block until the item can be placed in
     * the buffer.
     *
     * @param item the element to add to the buffer.
     */

    public void add( int item ) {
        boolean added = false;

        while ( !added ) {
            synchronized( this ) {
                if ( !full ) {
                    currentItem = item;
                    full = true;
                    added = true;


                }
            }

            Thread.yield();
        }
    }

    /**
     * Remove an element from the buffer. If the buffer is empty,
     * the method will block until an item is available.
     *
     * @returns the next item in the buffer.
     */

    public int remove() {
        int retval = 0;
        boolean removed = false;
```

FIGURE 11.40 Deadlock-free implementation of a buffer *(continued)*

```
        while ( !removed ) {
            synchronized( this ) {
                if ( full ) {
                    retval = currentItem;
                    full = false;
                    removed = true;
                }
            }

            Thread.yield();
        }

        return retval;
    }

} // SyncBuffer
```

FIGURE 11.40 Deadlock-free implementation of a buffer *(continued)*

The add() method in Figure 11.40 has not been written as a synchronized method; instead, it uses a synchronized block to obtain the lock only when it needs to look at the state of the buffer. If the item has not been added to the buffer, the method obtains the lock on the buffer and checks to see if the buffer has room for the item. If there is no room in the buffer, the lock is released and the thread invokes yield() to give the consumer a chance to check the buffer and remove the element. We should note that this implementation is not completely deadlock-free since Java does not guarantee that yield() will force the JVM scheduler to perform a context switch and run a different thread.

The implementation of the buffer in Figure 11.40 is not very efficient because both the add() and remove() methods use busy wait loops to check the status of the buffer. The processor will be spending the majority of its time executing these loops, waiting for items to be either produced or consumed. It would be much more efficient if the consumer, upon realizing that there is nothing in the buffer, suspended itself until the producer places the next item in the buffer.

In Java, it is possible for a thread that is currently holding a lock to pause its execution and release the lock that it is holding. When a thread invokes wait() on the lock it is holding, execution of the thread is suspended, the thread is placed in the wait set for the lock, and the lock held by the thread is released. An object has two sets associated with it that it uses to manage its lock: a set that contains the threads waiting to obtain the object's lock and a set containing the threads that are waiting on the object's lock. A thread that has been suspended will be placed in the set with the other threads waiting on the lock and will remain there until another thread invokes notify() or notifyAll() on the lock.

When a thread invokes notify(), the JVM will remove one of the threads from the wait set of the lock and place the thread in the set that contains the threads waiting to obtain the lock. There is no way to select which thread will be removed. It is important to note that after the thread is released, it still has to obtain the lock to resume its execution. The thread that was released is not treated much differently from any of the other threads trying to obtain the lock. The only difference is that once the released thread obtains the lock, it will resume execution at the point where it was suspended, as if the `wait()` call had simply returned. The `notifyAll()` is very similar to `notify()`, except that all of the threads that are waiting on the lock are notified instead of just one. It is important to realize that invoking `notifyAll()` will not cause more than one thread to enter the synchronized block because each thread must still obtain the lock before resuming execution. The diagram in Figure 11.41 illustrates how the locking mechanism works.

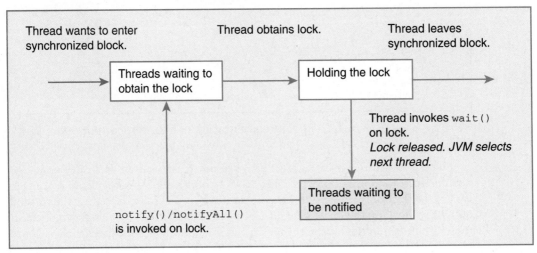

FIGURE 11.41 `wait()`/`notify()`

If you look at the Javadoc page for class `Object`, you will notice that `wait()` is overloaded. The alternative versions of `wait()` allow you to specify the maximum time that a thread is willing to wait before being notified. If the time-out period expires before the thread is notified, the thread will automatically be removed from the set of waiting threads and will be placed in the queue where it will wait until it re-obtains the lock. When the thread obtains the lock and resumes execution, an `InterruptedException` will be thrown to indicate that the time-out period had expired. A thread cannot invoke `wait()`, `notify()`, or `notifyAll()` on a lock unless it is currently holding the lock.

The methods `wait()` and `notify()` can be used to provide the synchronization required in the buffer that connects the producer and the consumer. Both the `remove()` and `add()` methods in the buffer would be written as synchronized methods. This time, instead of using a loop to constantly check the status of the buffer, `wait()` will be used to suspend the execution of the thread. In the `remove()` method, if the buffer is empty, the consumer will invoke `wait()` on the lock that it is currently holding. This will suspend the execution of the consumer so that it is no longer utilizing the processor and release the lock so that the producer can add an element to the buffer. The producer, after adding the item to the buffer, will invoke `notify()` to inform the consumer that it can safely remove the item and consume it. An implementation of the buffer using `wait()` and `notify()` is given in Figure 11.42.

```
/**
 * An implementation of the producer/consumer buffer
 * that uses wait/notify.
 */

public class MonitorBuffer implements Buffer {

    private int currentItem; // Item currently in the buffer
    private boolean full;     // Is the buffer full?

    /**
     * Create a new buffer.
     */

    public MonitorBuffer() {
       full = false;
    }

    /**
     * Add an element to the buffer. If the buffer is full,
     * the method will block until the item can be placed in
     * the buffer.
     *
     * @param item the element to add to the buffer.
     */

    public synchronized void add( int item ) {

       // If the buffer is full, wait until the consumer has removed
       // the element currently in the buffer.

       if ( full ) {
          try {
             wait();
          }
          catch ( InterruptedException e ) {};
       }

       // Place the item in the buffer

       currentItem = item;
       full = true;

       // There might be a consumer waiting for an element to consumer

       notify();
    }
```

(continued)

FIGURE 11.42 Using wait()/notify() to implement a buffer

```
/**
 * Remove an element from the buffer. If the buffer is empty,
 * the method will block until an item is available.
 *
 * @returns the next item in the buffer.
 */

public synchronized int remove() {
    int retval;

    // If the buffer is empty, wait until notified by the producer
    // that there is something to consume.

    if ( !full ) {
        try {
            wait();
        }
        catch ( InterruptedException e ) {};
    }

    // Remove the current element

    retval = currentItem;
    full = false;

    // There might be a producer waiting to produce.

    notify();

    // Return the item

    return retval;
}

} // MonitorBuffer
```

FIGURE 11.42 Using `wait()`/`notify()` to implement a buffer *(continued)*

It is possible, using `wait()` and `notify()`, to specify the order in which threads should be granted access to a synchronized block of code. Consider writing a program that models the behavior of customers and a cashier at a store. The program consists of two classes: `Customer` and `Cashier`. Each customer in the store must use an instance of a `Cashier` to pay for the items he or she wishes to purchase. A cashier services customers one at a time. The interface in Figure 11.43 defines the behavior that must be provided by an implementation of a `Cashier`.

```
/**
 * A cashier at a supermarket. When customers are ready to check out
 * they invoke readyToCheckOut(). The cashier will then determine
 * which customer will be serviced next. When the current customer
 * has finished checking out it will invoke done().
 */

public interface Cashier {

    /**
     * Invoked by a customer when they are ready to check out.
     * Contains the logic required to select the one customer
     * that the cashier will service. If the cashier is already
     * serving another customer, this customer will wait until
     * the other customer has finished with the cashier.
     */

    public void readyToCheckOut();

    /**
     * Invoked by a customer when they are finished with the
     * cashier. If customers are waiting for the cashier,
     * one of the waiting customers will be selected and
     * serviced by the cashier.
     */

    public void done();

} // Cashier
```

FIGURE 11.43 Interface for a Cashier

Given the interface for a Cashier, the code that implements a customer can be written. Each customer will run in a separate thread and will select the number of items that will be purchased randomly. The customer will invoke the readyToCheckOut() method on a cashier to indicate that it is ready to check out. When the method returns, the customer has the cashier, and they will proceed to check out. When the customer has completed the checkout process, they notify the cashier that they are finished by invoking the cashier's done() method. An implementation of the Customer class is given in Figure 11.44.

```
import java.util.Random;

/**
 * A simple example to demonstrate the use of notifyAll() in
 * java. This program simulates a number of customers who
```

(continued)

FIGURE 11.44 Customer class

```
 * wish to check out of a store. An instance of a cashier is
 * used to control the order in which customers are serviced.
 */

public class Customer extends Thread {
   public static int MAX_ITEMS = 25; // Maximum number of items a
                                     // customer may buy

   private int id;                   // This customer's id
   private int numItems;             // Number of items purchased

   private Cashier register;         // The only register in the store

   /**
    * Create a new customer with the specified id, wishing to
    * go through the specified register.
    *
    * @param id this customer's id
    * @param register the cashier who will service this customer
    */

   public Customer( int id, Cashier register ) {
      // Record state
      this.id = id;
      this.register = register;

      // Randomly determine the number of items
      numItems = new Random().nextInt( MAX_ITEMS ) + 1;

      // Indicate that a customer has been created
      System.out.println( "Customer " +
                          id +
                          " has " +
                          numItems +
                          " items." );
   }

   /**
    * This method simulates the behavior of a customer. The
    * customer requests to move to the head of the line. Once
    * there checks out, and then leaves the line.
    */

   public void run() {
      // Move to the head of the line
      register.readyToCheckOut();
```

FIGURE 11.44 Customer class *(continued)*

```
            System.out.println( "Customer " + id + " is checking out" );

            // I have the cashier so -- check out
            try {
                sleep( 500 );
            }
            catch ( InterruptedException e ) {}

            // That's it
            System.out.println( "Customer " + id + " has checked out" );
            register.done();
        }

        /**
         * Return the id associated with this customer.
         *
         * @return the customer's id
         */

        public int getId() {
            return id;
        }

        /**
         * Return the number of items this customer wishes to purchase.
         *
         * @return the number of items being purchased by this customer.
         */

        public int getNumItems() {
            return numItems;
        }

} // Customer
```

FIGURE 11.44 Customer class *(continued)*

Although the customers run as threads, the Cashier class will be responsible for synchronizing the threads in this program. The cashier must make sure that at most one customer is checking out at a time and is responsible for determining the order in which waiting customers will be serviced. The code required to synchronize the threads in the program will be contained in the readyToCheckOut() and done() methods of the cashier. The code in Figure 11.45 contains an implementation of a cashier that services one customer at a time; however, this implementation does not service the customers in the order they arrive (i.e., the order in which they invoke the readyToCheckout()).

```
/**
 * A cashier class that shows how to use java synchronization
 * primitives to gain access to a cashier.
 */

public class Cashier1 implements Cashier {
   private boolean busy = false; // Is the cashier busy?

   /**
    * Invoked by a customer when they are ready to check out.
    * Contains the logic required to select the one customer
    * that the cashier will service. If the cashier is already
    * serving another customer, this customer will wait until
    * the other customer has finished with the cashier.
    */

   public synchronized void readyToCheckOut() {
      // While the cashier is busy -- wait

      while ( busy ) {
         try {
            wait();
         }
         catch (InterruptedException e ){}

      // Move to the head of the line

      busy = true;

   /**
    * Invoked by a customer when they are finished with the
    * cashier. If customers are waiting for the cashier,
    * one of them will be selected to move to the head of
    * the line.
    */

   public synchronized void done() {
      if ( busy ) {

         // The cashier is no longer busy

         busy = false;

         // Let someone move to the head of the line

         notifyAll();
      }
   }

} // Cashier1
```

FIGURE 11.45 Simple cashier

The Cashier in Figure 11.45 maintains a Boolean variable, busy, that indicates whether a customer is currently checking out or not. If a customer is in the process of checking out, busy will be set to true. If busy is set to false, the cashier is idle. The readyToCheckOut() method uses busy to determine if the cashier is currently servicing a customer (i.e., is busy). If the cashier is busy, the customer will wait until the cashier is idle. The first customer that invokes readyToCheckOut() will determine that the cashier is idle, set busy to true, and proceed to check out. Any additional customers that invoke readyToCheckOut() before the first customer is done will wait.

When a customer invokes done(), indicating that it has finished checking out, busy is set to false and notifyAll() is invoked to signal any waiting customers that the cashier is now idle, which causes them to compete for the lock. The customer that obtains the lock first will resume execution of the while loop. Since busy is now false, the loop will terminate and the customer will be given access to the cashier. The remaining customers, after obtaining the lock, will find that busy is true and will wait again. This process continues until all of the customers have been serviced.

Figure 11.46 illustrates three customers working their way through the checkout process. After the threads are created, they all attempt to execute the readyToCheckOut() method and as a result need to obtain the lock. One thread, T_3, obtains the lock and proceeds to check out. The other two threads, T_1 and T_2, obtain the lock and determine that the cashier is busy and invoke wait. When T_3 finishes checking out, it invokes notifyAll() within the done() method, which releases T_1

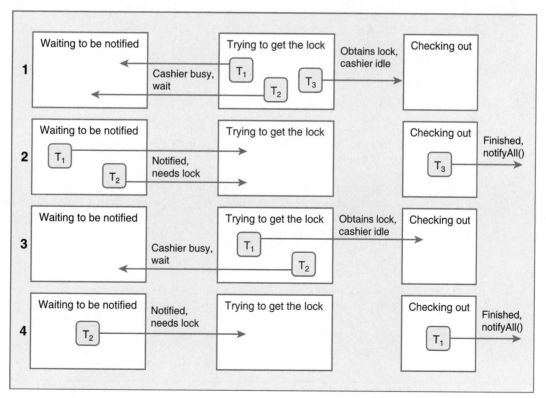

FIGURE 11.46 wait() and notifyAll() in the simple cashier

and T_2 and allows them to compete for the lock once again. This time, T_1 obtains the lock and checks out. T_2 once again determines that the cashier is busy and waits. Once T_1 is finished, it will notify the lock, which in turn will release T_2. Now that T_2 is the only thread in the program, it obtains the lock and checks out.

In this implementation of the cashier, the order in which the customers are serviced is not determined at all by the program. The order in which the customers will be serviced is determined by the JVM based on the way in which it assigns the ownership of the lock to the customer. The implementation of the Cashier interface given in Figure 11.47 will service all customers that are waiting and have 10 or fewer items first.

```
/**
 * A cashier that gives priority access to customers that have
 * ten items or fewer.
 */

public class Cashier2 implements Cashier {
    private boolean busy = false;  // Is the cashier busy?
    private int tenOrLess = 0;      // How many folks have 10 or fewer
                                    // items?

    /**
     * Invoked by a customer when they are ready to check out.
     * Contains the logic required to select the one customer
     * that the cashier will service. If the cashier is already
     * serving another customer, this customer will wait until
     * the other customer has finished with the cashier. Customers
     * with 10 or fewer items will be allowed to move ahead of the
     * other customers.
     */

    public synchronized void readyToCheckOut() {
        // Get a reference to the customer executing this code and find
        // out how many items they have

        Customer me = (Customer)Thread.currentThread();
        int items = me.getNumItems();

        // Make a note if they have 10 or fewer items

        if ( items <= 10 ) tenOrLess++;

        // As long as the cashier is busy, or there is someone in line
        // that has 10 or fewer items and I have more than 10 items, wait.

        while ( busy || ( tenOrLess > 0 && items > 10 ) ) {
            try {
                wait();
```

FIGURE 11.47 A cashier that gives priority to customers with 10 or fewer items

```
            }
        catch (InterruptedException e ){}

    // My chance to get out of this store!!

    busy = true;
    }


    /**
     * Invoked by a customer when they are finished with the
     * cashier. If customers are waiting for the cashier,
     * customers with 10 or fewer items will be allowed to get
     * to the head of the line before the other customers.
     */

    public synchronized void done() {
        if ( busy ) {

            // Get a reference to the current customer

            Customer me = (Customer)Thread.currentThread();

            // If they had 10 or fewer items, they have been taken care of

            if ( me.getNumItems() <= 10 ) tenOrLess--;

            // The cashier is no longer busy

            busy = false;

            // Let someone else move to the head of the line.

            notifyAll();
        }
    }

} // Cashier2
```

FIGURE 11.47 A cashier that gives priority to customers with 10 or fewer items *(continued)*

The Cashier class in Figure 11.47 has an additional state variable, tenOrLess, which keeps track of the number of customers that are in line with 10 or fewer items. When a customer that has 10 or fewer items to purchase invokes readyToCheckOut() the state variable tenOrLess will be incremented by 1. When a customer with 10 or fewer items invokes done(), the variable will be decremented by 1.

The while loop in the readyToCheckOut() method in Figure 11.47 uses the busy variable in the same way as in Figure 11.46; if the cashier is busy, the customer will wait. If the `readyToCheckOut()` method in Figure 11.47 discovers that the cashier is idle, it checks if there are any customers waiting in line that have 10 or fewer items. If a customer with more than 10 items is in line waiting to check out, the thread will wait. By making customers with more than 10 items wait, customers with 10 items or fewer will eventually obtain permission from the cashier to check out.

Like the previous version of the cashier, it is not possible to determine the exact order in which the customers will be serviced; however, all customers with 10 items or fewer will be serviced before customers with more than 10 items. In addition to showing how a program can influence the way in which threads are scheduled when using `wait()` and `notifyAll()`, it also demonstrates the more general problem of **starvation**. Note that in the cashier of Figure 11.47, as long as there are any customers with 10 or fewer items in the line, the other customers will not be serviced. Thus, it is possible in this program that some customers may never be able to check out.

11.4 SUMMARY

This chapter discussed how to write a program in Java that contains multiple threads of execution. A program written in this fashion can appear to be doing more than one thing at a time, a programming technique that is common in modern software systems. A thread in Java is represented by an instance of the `Thread` class, which contains all of the state that the JVM requires to manage the execution of a thread. A program specifies the code that a thread will execute by writing a class that either extends the `Thread` class or implements the `Runnable` interface. In either case, the code that the thread will execute is contained in the `run()` method that will be invoked by the JVM when the thread is scheduled to execute.

The order in which the threads in a program are executed is determined by the JVM. The programmer can utilize thread priorities to give the scheduler information on which it may base its decisions regarding the scheduling of the threads, but in the end, the decision is made by the JVM. Because the execution of multiple threads can be interleaved in an arbitrary number of ways, unexpected interactions between threads can result in programs that produce deadlock or incorrect results.

It is possible to synchronize threads within a program using the synchronization primitives provided by Java. The basic tool that provides synchronization is a lock. Every object in Java has a lock associated with it. A `synchronized` block can be used to associate an object's lock with a section of code in a program. To enter a synchronized block, a thread must obtain the lock for the associated object. Since only one thread can hold a lock at a time, you are guaranteed that only one thread will be executing the code in that block at a time. The `wait()` and `notify()` methods can be used within a synchronized block to suspend and resume the execution of a thread.

By placing support for threads in the JVM, it is possible to write a multithreaded Java program for a platform even if that platform does not support threads. Threads and synchronization in Java are just as portable as any of the other features of Java that we have discussed in this text. Another benefit of building support for threads and synchronization within the JVM is that special versions of the JVM can be built to provide additional support for parallelism within a Java program without making any changes to the code. Versions of the JVM already exist that take advantage of machines that have multiple processors. A multithreaded program using this version of the JVM on a machine with multiple processors will be able to take advantage of true parallel programming without making any changes to the code.

The next chapter will discuss how to use the classes provided in the standard Java library to build programs that interact with users through a graphical user interface.

EXERCISES

1. Look at a program that you run on a daily basis. Identify how that program might utilize threads.

2. Describe two reasons a thread might make a transition from the run state to the wait state.

3. Describe two reasons a thread might make a transition from the run state directly to the ready state.

4. Even if it were possible for an operating system to perfectly schedule the processes in a system so that the processor was executing user code all the time, the system will still not be utilized 100 percent. Why?

5. When using an interactive program on a computer, how can you tell when the system is busy? What happens to the performance of the program that you are running?

6. Imagine you are writing a program that uses a thread to perform some time-consuming calculation. You want the program to display a message on the screen indicating that the calculation has begun. Why can't you use `isAlive()` to do this? Give a brief description of the code that you would write to perform this task.

7. Write a Java program that prints the names and the total number of all the threads active in a Java program. You might find the `enumerate()` method defined in the class `Thread` useful for this exercise. After the program is working, modify it so that it prints information regarding the status of each of the threads (is it a daemon thread, the priority of the thread, whether or not the thread is alive, etc.).

8. Write a Java program that creates a number of threads, each of which will print a specific letter of the alphabet 10 times one character per line. Run the program several times on your computing system. Is the output the same each time? Try running the same program on a different computer system a number of times. Is the output the same each time? Does it match the output you obtain on the first system? Rewrite your thread code so that it invokes `yield()` or `sleep()` at various points in the program. Does the output change?

9. In a typical classroom setting, there is one professor and several students. If more than one student wishes to ask a question at a time, the professor must utilize a scheduling algorithm to service the students. How would you describe the algorithm used by your professor? Is it preemptive or nonpreemptive? Is it priority based?

10. In the area of road traffic, the computer science concept of deadlock is often called *gridlock*. In major cities whose roads are laid out in a gridlike fashion, it is possible for traffic to become gridlocked. Describe how this could occur. Describe some techniques that are often used by city planners to prevent such gridlock from occurring.

11. Conway's problem is defined as follows:

    Write a program to read a number of 80-character lines and write them to a file as 125-character lines with the following changes: A space is to be printed between each of the 80-character lines, and every pair of adjacent ** is to be replaced by a ^.

    Write two versions of this program. The first should not use any threads. The second version should use three different threads: One that reads in the 80-character lines that adds a space between consecutive lines, a second that looks for pairs of ** and replaces them with a ^, and a third that writes the resulting stream of characters as 125-character lines.

    Place a bounded buffer between the threads in the concurrent version of the program. Design your buffer so that you can easily change its capacity. Experiment with the program to determine if the size of the buffer affects the performance.

12. Some overly energetic students learn about threads and decide to use them in a sorting program they are writing. Their idea is to create a thread that will sort numbers at the same time the main program is executing. The program is acting weird. Sometimes the numbers print out sorted, sometimes they are partially sorted, and sometimes they are not sorted at all. What is the problem with the program that follows?

    How would you fix the problem making changes only to the code in the `main()` method? Note: Since the program sometimes prints the numbers in sorted order, you can assume that the sort routine is working correctly.

```java
public class Sorter extends Thread {
    private int data[] = null;

    public Sorter( int data[] ) {
        this.data = data;
    }

    public void run() {
        // Sort the numbers (the code is correct)
        for (int i = 0; i < data.length - 1; i++)
            for ( int j = i + 1; j < data.length; j++)
                if ( data[j] < data[i] ) {
                    int tmp = data[i];
                    data[i] = data[j];
                    data[j] = tmp;
                }
    }
}
```

```
public static void main( String args[] ) {
    int data[] = new int[ 10 ];

    // Generate some numbers to sort
    for (int i = 0; i < data.length; i++)
        data[i] = (int) (Math.random() * 100);

    Sorter x = new Sorter( data );
    x.start();

    for (int i = 0; i < data.length; i++)
        System.out.println( data[i] );
    }
}
```

13. Write a program to determine how accurate or inaccurate `sleep()` is on your computing system. After your initial tests, change the program so that it creates a number of threads that utilize the processor in some fashion (perhaps by executing a `while` loop). Does this change the accuracy of `sleep()` at all? Explain why or why not.

14. Write a method named `joinAll()` that takes as a parameter an array of `Thread` references. The method returns after joining with all of the threads specified in the array. Note that you cannot make any assumptions about the order in which the threads will terminate.

15. A good example of the problems that can occur with concurrent access to shared resources occurs when a team of programmers is working together to write a program. If two members of the team make changes to the same piece of code at the same time, one of the changes might be lost. CVS is a version control system that, among other things, tries to eliminate this problem. Look up the documentation for CVS on the Web at www.cvshome.org and discuss how it resolves the concurrent access problem.

16. Rewrite the program you wrote in Exercise 8 using locks and shared variables so that the order in which the threads are executed is deterministic (i.e., you specify the order in which they will execute).

17. What output is generated by the following program?

```
public class Foobar extends Thread {
    private static synchronized void method() {
        System.out.println( "→" );
        try {
            sleep( 1000 );
        } catch ( InterruptedException ex ) {}
        System.out.println( "←" );
    }
```

```
        public void run() { method(); }

        public static void main( String args[] ) {
            new Foobar().start();
            new Foobar().start();
            new Foobar().start();
        }
    }
```

18. What output is generated by the following program?

```
    public class Class2 extends Thread {

        private static class Class1 {
            private int n; private List a;

            public Class1( int x ) {
                a = new ArrayList(); n = x;
            }

            public synchronized void method1( int x ) {
                a.add( new Integer( x ) );
                n = n - 1;

                if ( n > 0 )
                    try {
                        wait();
                    }
                    catch ( InterruptedException e ) {}
                else {
                    Collections.sort( a );
                    notifyAll();
                }
            }

            public synchronized void method2( int y ) {
                boolean x = y % 2 != 0; // Is y odd?
                boolean p = false;

                while ( !p ) {
                    Integer i = (Integer)a.get( 0 );
                    p = i.intValue() == y;

                    if ( p && x ) {
                        a.remove( 0 );
                        a.add( i );
                        notifyAll();
```

```
                    x = false;
                    p = false;
                }

                if ( !p ) {
                    try {
                        wait();
                    }
                    catch ( InterruptedException e ) {}
                }
            }
        }

        public synchronized void method3() {
            a.remove( 0 ); notifyAll();
        }

    } // Class1

    private Class1 one; private int a;

    public Class2( Class1 one, int a ) {
        this.one = one; this.a = a;
    }

    public void run() {
        one.method1( a ); one.method2( a );
        System.out.println( a );
        one.method3();
    }

    public static void main( String args[] ) {
        Class1 one = new Class1( 10 );
        for ( int i = 0; i < 10; i++ )
            new Class2( one, i ).start();
    }

} // Class2
```

19. A semaphore is a classic synchronization tool provided by many operating systems. Look up the definition of a semaphore and then write a class named Semaphore that provides a Java-based implementation of a semaphore. Test your implementation by rewriting the producer/consumer code in this chapter so that it uses semaphores instead of Java locks.

20. A barbershop consists of a waiting room with N chairs and a barber chair. If there are no customers to be served, the barber goes to sleep. If a customer enters the barbershop and all of the chairs are occupied, the customer leaves the

shop without getting a haircut. If the barber is busy but chairs are available, then the customer will wait in one of the chairs for a haircut. If the barber is asleep, the customer wakes up the barber and gets a haircut. Write a Java program to simulate this barbershop.

20. Consider a system that consists of three smoker threads and one agent thread. Each smoker continuously rolls a cigarette and smokes it. But to roll and smoke a cigarette, the smoker needs three ingredients: tobacco, paper, and matches. One of the smoker threads has paper, another has tobacco, and the third has matches. The agent has an infinite supply of all three materials. The agent places two of the ingredients on the table. The smoker who has the remaining ingredient then makes and smokes a cigarette, signaling the agent when it is done. The agent then puts another two of the three ingredients on the table, and the cycle repeats. Write a Java program to simulate the smoker and agent threads.

CHAPTER 12

Graphical User Interfaces

12.1 INTRODUCTION

There is probably no single area of software development that has undergone a greater change over the last 10 to 20 years than the design of the interface between user and program. Although graphical user interfaces first appeared in the late-1970s,[1] their effective use required technologies such as high-resolution monitors and high-performance processors not yet available to the general public. Therefore, prior to the mid-1980s, virtually all program interaction was text based, and users were required to learn highly complex command sequences to manipulate their programs. For example, to delete a file in UNIX, a user might enter something like this:

rm -if /home/user/schneider/myFile

To get MS-DOS to produce a listing of all executable programs on drive A, a user would type the following cryptic sequence of characters:

A:\DIR *.EXE /P

One of the reasons for the widespread acceptance of these rather arcane command languages during the 1970s and 1980s was the fact that the overwhelming majority of computer users at that time were technical specialists (e.g., computer scientists, engineers, or physicists). They were intimately familiar with computers, so it was not inappropriate to ask them to master a complex, text-based command language. This was fairly standard practice for the first 30 to 35 years of software development.

All this changed with the appearance of personal computers and the rapid growth of email, word processing, and spreadsheets. By the mid-1980s, computing was beginning to open up to the general public. They wanted to take advantage of this exciting new technology, but they often had difficulty communicating with the applications. Although users eagerly flocked to email and word processing, many were unable to learn the complicated system commands necessary to get their programs to function correctly.

The Apple Corporation understood this, and in 1984 it released the Macintosh operating system, which popularized the use of graphical interfaces. Suddenly, even novices could communicate with computers and get them to do exactly what they wanted. Commands became visual and intuitive rather than textual and complex. To delete a file, users dragged the file icon into a trashcan; to list the files in their directory, they double-clicked its symbol on the desktop; to execute an application, they selected it from a drop-down menu. The impact of the Macintosh system and Finder was enormous, and within a few years, virtually all software packages started to incorporate graphical interfaces into their design.

Today, software projects almost always include a simple, intuitive, and easy to understand visual front end. Users will no longer tolerate cumbersome, confusing, and "clunky" textual interactions like those shown earlier. Even if your software package is well designed (as you learned in Part I) and uses efficient data structures and algo-

---

[1]The first graphical user interface and mouse were created by Xerox in 1978 at their Palo Alto Research Center (PARC). Unfortunately, Xerox never really appreciated the importance of this new development, and it was not until Steve Jobs, the founder of Apple, toured PARC in the early 1980s and incorporated these ideas into the design of the Apple Lisa (1983) and then the Macintosh (1984) that the enormous potential of GUIs finally came to be realized.

rithms (as you studied in Part II), unless it is simple to use, it will probably not be successful.

In this chapter, we investigate some of the basic concepts involved in designing and building a **graphical user interface** (GUI, pronounced "goo-ee"). There are three points we need to emphasize about this topic before diving into it:

1. It is a *huge* topic with an enormous amount of detail, far too much detail to cover in this one chapter. For example, the Java AWT package contains more than 80 classes with literally hundreds of constants, variables, and methods. Our goal here is not to provide encyclopedic coverage of this massive volume of code but, instead, to introduce some of the most important and fundamental concepts in GUI design. In this way, you will be well prepared to read about and study concepts not covered here.

2. It is a *volatile* topic. Software developers do not yet agree on exactly which methods should be included in a GUI toolkit or how they should behave, and the optimal design of a user interface package is still a point of debate. The original Java GUI package was the **Abstract Window Toolkit (AWT)**, and it was the standard toolkit used by Java programmers since Java was first released. Later versions of Java included a newer and more powerful package called **Swing** that added functionality and flexibility to the original set of AWT components. During your professional career, even more powerful GUI design packages will almost certainly appear.

   Therefore, this chapter focuses not on the details of a specific package (which will surely go out of date) but on those concepts that are part of virtually every graphical interface in the marketplace—concepts such as containers, components, layouts, events, and listeners. We present our examples using Swing, but the focus on basic ideas should allow you to migrate to whatever "new and improved" GUI package comes down the road.

3. It is a *conceptually interesting* topic. We motivated our study of GUIs by saying that any modern software project must include a well-designed visual front end or it will likely not be successful. That is true and, by itself, is a sufficient reason to study GUI design. However, there is another even more important reason, and that is because this topic will introduce us to some very important concepts in modern software development. For example:

   ◆ *The power of inheritance*. Inheritance is widely used in the classes that are used to instantiate the objects in a GUI. Studying how a GUI library is organized and using the classes within the library will help us better appreciate the many contributions that inheritance can make to software development.

   ◆ *Event-driven programming*. GUIs use a programming style that is quite different from the traditional sequential flow of control used in your first courses. In those programs, things happen because the program reaches a certain point. However, in a GUI, things happen because an **event** occurs, where an event represents an action that is external to the normal flow of control. An event could be, for example, a mouse click that was not directly caused by any of the statements you wrote. The graphical interfaces you build will use a control flow model called **event-driven programming**.

For all of these reasons, the topic of graphical user interfaces is both important and interesting. We begin our investigation of GUIs in the following section.

12.2 THE GUI CLASS HIERARCHY

◆ 12.2.1 Introduction

The package we use in this chapter to build our GUIs is named `javax.swing`, usually just referred to as *Swing*. It was developed at Sun in 1997 as part of a much larger collection of resources called the **Java Foundation Classes** (JFC), which are intended to help developers design and build sophisticated programs.

Swing is an extension of the AWT, and it enhances and extends the functionality of most AWT components. For example, in the AWT buttons only may have textual labels, but Swing buttons can display either images or text. There are many other examples of this type of Swing feature enhancement.

However, the most important difference between Swing and the AWT is that Swing components, such as menus and buttons, are all implemented directly in Java without using any of the native code of the processor on which the program is executed. These are referred to as **lightweight components**, and they allow all Swing components to be rendered in exactly the same way, producing a uniform "look and feel" regardless of the platform on which the program is run. AWT components, on the other hand, are mostly **heavyweight**, which means that they rely on the underlying system services of the local machine to help render the image. Different systems may do this in slightly different ways, so the same GUI running on two models of computer may have a slightly different look. In addition, because the AWT relies on the services of the local machine, the developers of the AWT had to take a "lowest common denominator" approach in the design of this package. This meant that they could only include components that they were absolutely sure could be correctly drawn by every machine on which the AWT could possibly be run. Although the AWT is still supported in Java 2 and later versions, the current recommendation is to use the Swing extensions for all future software development, and that is what we have chosen to do in this chapter.

The dozens of classes included in the `javax.swing` and `java.awt` packages are organized into a class hierarchy, a small part of which is shown in Figure 12.1. The first letter in the class name can be used to identify the Swing classes. The names of almost all of the Swing classes begin with a J. All other classes are members of the Abstract Window Toolkit.

Familiarity with the class hierarchy in Figure 12.1 is essential as it determines exactly what methods are available to an object in a user interface. For example, assume that an interface contains a `JFrame` object *f*. The hierarchy of Figure 12.1 shows that `JFrame` is a subclass of `Frame`, `Window`, `Container`, `Component`, and `Object`. Therefore, in addition to the methods available from the `JFrame` class itself, *f* inherits from all its parent classes, resulting in a large number of available methods. For example:

Inherited from Frame:

```
// specify a title for the top of the frame
public void setTitle(String title);
```

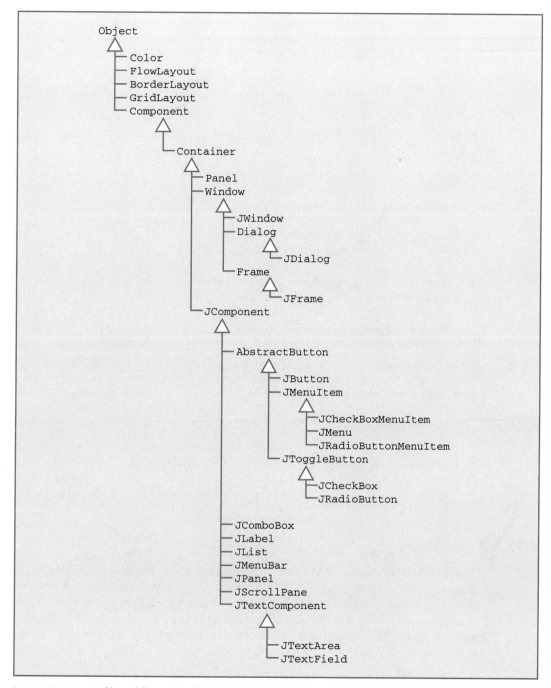

FIGURE 12.1 Class hierarchy in Swing and AWT

Inherited from Window:

```
// move this frame to the front of the screen
public void toFront();
```

Inherited from Container:

```
// Add component c to the frame
public Component add(Component c);
```

```
// Remove component c from the frame
public void remove(Component c);
```

Inherited from Component:

```
// Set height and width of this frame
public void setSize(int width, int height);
```

```
// Set the (x, y) location of this frame
public void setLocation(int x, int y);
```

```
// Set the background color of the frame
public void setBackground(Color c);
```

```
// Make the frame and its components visible
public void setVisible(boolean b);
```

Inherited from Object:

```
// Produce a textual description of the frame object
public boolean toString();
```

The following sections look more closely at the classes in the hierarchy of Figure 12.1.

◆ 12.2.2 Containers

The first class we examine is `Container`. A **container** is a GUI component that holds other components. `Container` itself is an abstract class, so you cannot instantiate it directly; instead, you instantiate one of its many subclasses. Every GUI is built from containers into which other objects are placed. Often, there will be multiple containers within a single user interface. In general, the steps involved in building a GUI are as follows:

1. Create a container into which we can put other objects and set the desired properties of this container.
2. Create a new object (called a component) to put into the container and set the desired properties of this component.
3. Add this new component to the container, specifying where it should be placed.
4. Go back to step 2 and continue until there are no more components to be added.

There are a number of `Container` classes in the Swing package. The most important ones are the following:

JWindow. A window is a container that can be displayed anywhere on the user's desktop. It does not have a title bar or window management buttons such as the close button or zoom box. It is a very general type of container, and for that reason, it is not widely used.

JPanel. A panel is essentially a "window inside a window." It is a general-purpose container that can be placed inside other containers. Panels are often used to simplify the process of building complex graphical interfaces. We create a single panel, place components into it, and then drop the panel, along with all its objects, into another container. This divides the task of constructing a single large container into smaller subtasks of constructing individual panels, which is yet another example of the "divide and conquer" strategy first mentioned in Chapter 1. This strategy is diagrammed in Figure 12.2, which shows a single `Container` object *c* and three `JPanel` objects *p1, p2, p3*.

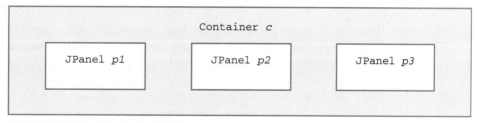

FIGURE 12.2 Example of using panels to simplify the creation of containers

JFrame. This class represents a resizable application window that is the most widely used `Container` class. A `JFrame` window looks like the following:

In addition to being resizable, it includes all the "bells and whistles" that we would expect from a GUI container such as title bar, close, resize, and iconify buttons, menu bar, and a range of other handy window features as shown in the diagram. Just about every Java program that contains a GUI will use a `JFrame` object to construct the main window. All of the examples presented in this chapter make use of a `JFrame`.

A `JFrame` object has two major sections, the **menu bar** and the **content** pane:

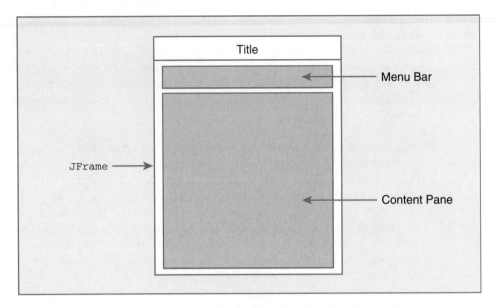

The menu bar is where the optional menu for this frame is placed. The content pane contains all other nonmenu components displayed by a JFrame object.

To create a new JFrame object, we typically use a one-parameter constructor, where the parameter specifies the title to be placed in the title bar at the top of the frame. For example, here is the declaration used to create the JFrame object shown on page 715.

```
JFrame f = new JFrame( "A JFrame" ); //put "A JFrame" in the title bar
```

JDialog. This is a pop-up dialog box that is often used to display special information or warning messages to the user. Here is an example of a JDialog container:

A dialog box can be **modal**, which means that it is possible to block user input to all other windows until the information in the dialog box has been read and the dialog box is closed. (This is the type of container object you often see when there has been an error or some other unusual event.) However, it is not only for warnings. A JDialog object is a fully functional container that can hold any type of component.

JScrollPane. This is a container object that is "attached" to another larger container object that is too big to display on the screen all at once. To handle this problem, we can create a JScrollPane object that is roughly the size of the visible portion of our screen and attach it to a larger container object. Now, the JScrollPane object is a scrollable component that allows the user to move around, horizontally and vertically, through the larger container viewing a section of it called a **viewport**. The following is an example of a JScrollPane object:

For example, assume that container *c* is 2,000 × 2,000 pixels. This will be too large for most screens. Instead, we can create a scrollable object, *jsp*, that is 500 × 500 pixels in size, attach it to *c*, and use *jsp* to view a 500 × 500 pixel "slice" of *c*. If the JScrollPane object is smaller than the container to which it is attached, then JScrollPane will automatically add horizontal and vertical scroll bars with which the user can navigate.

Although every GUI package will have its own distinct set of container classes, the concept of a container is universal. The containers you will encounter will be similar to those described in the preceding paragraphs: regular windows (e.g., windows, frames, dialogs), borderless windows (e.g., panels), and scrolling windows (e.g., scroll panes). As mentioned earlier, in the examples that follow, we will make the greatest use of the JFrame and JPanel classes.

◆ 12.2.3 Layout Managers

The previous section outlined the basic approach to GUI design, which is (a) create a container, (b) create a component, and (c) place the component into the container. An obvious question to ask is: Where will the component go? Specifically, how do we control the placement of component objects inside a container object? In GUI design, this is called the **layout problem**, and it addresses such issues as the physical arrangement of components in a window, the amount of blank space between components, and the resizing of components to make them fit into the available space.

There are two ways to handle the layout problem. The first is to explicitly do all layout operations yourself. That is, each time you create a component, such as a button, you specify exactly where it will go when added to a container. Every Swing component inherits from the Component class a layout method called setLocation():

```
public void setLocation(int x, int y);
```

The (x, y) location of a component is given in terms of the horizontal and vertical distance, in pixels, from the origin point, (0, 0), of the container. When identifying the position of a component, you give the (x, y) coordinates of the pixel located in the upper left corner of that component. Knowing that one point, along with the component's size, permits its proper placement within the container.

Pixel numbering begins in the upper left corner of a container and increases as you move to the right (the x-axis) and down (the y-axis). This pixel numbering scheme is diagramed in Figure 12.3.

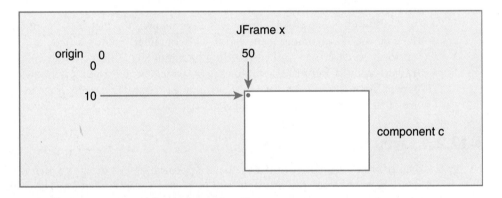

FIGURE 12.3 Pixel numbering scheme for containers

The following diagram shows a component c located at position (50, 10) in JFrame x. The point (50, 10) is the location of the uppermost left pixel of c.

After we have specified the position of the upper left pixel of component *c,* we then add it to our container using the getContentPane() method of the JFrame class and the add() method inherited from Container. If we assume that x is a JFrame object and c is a component whose location has been previously set, then the call:

```
x.getContentPane().add(c); // add c to the content pane of container x
```

first returns the content pane of frame x and then adds c to that object.

The values XMAX and YMAX in Figure 12.3 are set using the method

```
public void setSize(int width, int height);
```

that is inherited by all container objects from the AWT Component class. The following code creates a JFrame object that is 300 pixels wide × 400 pixels high, with the string "Example" contained in the title bar. It then makes the frame visible on the screen.

```
// Put "Example" into the title bar
JFrame f = new JFrame( "Example" );

// Set f to 300 pixels wide by 400 pixels high
f.setSize(300, 400);

// Make it visible on the screen
f.setVisible(true);
```

To place a button object b at position (50, 10) within this new JFrame object f, we do the following:

```
// Assume that b is a button object. We
// will see how to do this later

// Set the button size to 70 pixels wide by 90 pixels high
b.setSize(70, 90);

// Position the upper left corner of b to ( 50, 10 )
b.setLocation(50, 10);

// Put the button b into the content pane of the
// JFrame f that was created by the earlier declarations
f.getContentPane().add(b);
```

This will place the rectangular button object into pixel positions [50 . . . 120] along the x-axis and [10 . . . 100] on the y-axis. You repeat this sizing and placement process for every component that you put into your container.

As you can imagine, this is a difficult and rather cumbersome process because there may be literally dozens of components that have to be sized, located, and added to the container. Getting them all into the correct position, without overlap, can take a great deal of time, and it can require artistic and design skills that may not be the "strong suit" of many software designers. Therefore, there is a second approach to solving the layout problem, and that is to use a layout manager. This approach is by far the more popular.

A **layout manager** is an object that positions and sizes objects within a container. It automatically provides platform-independent layout services that can speed up the creation of a graphical user interface. The use of a layout manager allows a software developer to concentrate on the high-level look-and-feel design issues, while leaving the messy details of sizing and placing components to the layout manager. The LayoutManager interface defines methods for managing the way in which objects are arranged within a container. Every container object in Java comes equipped with a default layout manager that will be used if you do not specify a layout manager using the container's setLayout() method or you do not explicitly provide the location of components. You should establish the layout manager that you wish to use for a container before any components are added to that container.

There are five classes in AWT that implement the LayoutManager interface, and in this section, we describe three of the most popular. The first, called a **flow layout,** places components into the container in strict left-to-right, top-to-bottom positions in the order that they are added to the container. That is, components are stored in positions 1, 2, 3, 4, . . . as follows:

container f

| position 1 | position 2 | position 3 | position 4 |
| position 5 | position 6 | position 7 | position 8 |

. . .

Of course, the exact number of components that fit into a single row will depend on their size as well as the width of the container object. One of the most powerful features of a layout manager is that if a frame is resized, the position of all the components in the frame will be recomputed automatically based on the new height and width of the window. We can see this feature in Figure 12.4, which shows a window containing 12 buttons labeled one, two, three, . . . and whose layout is controlled by a flow layout manager. Notice that, as the width of the window is changed, the layout manager automatically determines how many of the 12 buttons can fit onto a single line.

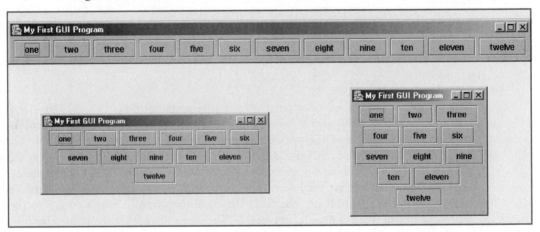

FIGURE 12.4 Flow layout

To associate a flow layout object with a container object f, we use the setLayout() method as follows:

```
// Container f is using a flow layout manager
f.setLayout( new FlowLayout() );
```

When f is a JPanel object, this statement is not necessary, as FlowLayout is the default layout manager for all JPanel objects.

In addition to the default constructor FlowLayout(), there is also a constructor FlowLayout(int align) that takes a single parameter, which specifies how to align objects in a row that is not yet filled. This alignment value can be any of the constants

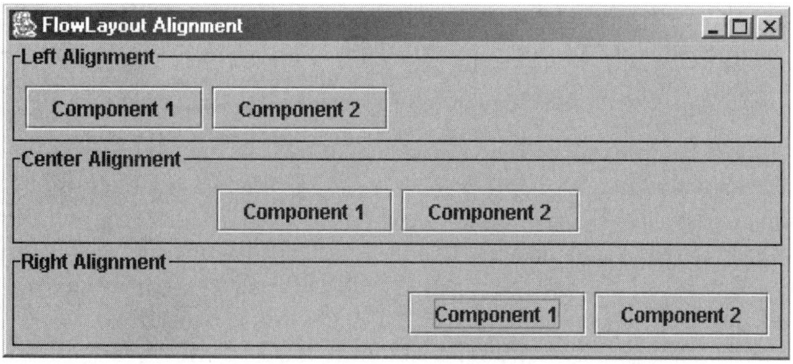

FIGURE 12.5 Alignment within a flow layout manager

LEFT, CENTER, or RIGHT. If we assume that a row can hold four components and it currently has only two, then these three constants behave as shown in Figure 12.5.

The second layout manager we will describe is the **grid layout**. This layout takes a container and divides it into *m* rows and *n* columns, much like a matrix, where each grid is a rectangle of equal size. Using a grid layout with four rows and four columns, the container would look like the following:

(0, 0)	(0, 1)	(0, 2)	(0, 3)
(1, 0)	(1, 1)	(1, 2)	(1, 3)
(2, 0)	(2, 1)	(2, 2)	(2, 3)
(3, 0)	(3, 1)	(3, 2)	(3, 3)

The number of rows and columns in a grid layout is specified by the grid layout constructor:

```
GridLayout( int rows, int columns );
```

The container is now divided into the specified number of rows and columns, with each rectangle of equal size. However, when the number of rows and the number of columns are both set to non-zero values, the value for the number of columns is ignored. Instead, the number of columns is determined dynamically from the specified number of rows and the total number of components that have been added to the container. For example, if you declare a grid layout with four rows and two columns and 12 components are added to the container, then they will be displayed in four rows of *three* columns each rather than two. (The only time that the column value is important is if a 0 is entered for the number of rows. Then we will explicitly use the specified number of columns.) In general, it is common to enter a 0 for the column field of the grid layout constructor.

The grid layout manager places the first component at position (0, 0). The next object is placed in the next available slot in the current row, position (0, 1), and we move to the right one position. The total number of objects placed in a row is determined by the layout manager from the number of rows declared in the constructor and the number of components placed in the container:

number of columns = total number of components / number of rows

When all the columns of a single row are filled, the layout manager moves to column 0 of the next row and begins filling it in the same left-to-right fashion. Because all grid slots are exactly the same size, the grid layout manager resizes all of the components to fit into the available area. In addition, if the number of rows is insufficient to handle the number of components added to the frame, the grid layout manager automatically increases the number of rows to the appropriate number.

To associate a grid layout with a container object f, we do the following:

```
// A GridLayout with m rows and n columns
f.setLayout(new GridLayout(m, n));
```

Figure 12.6 shows some examples of grid layouts that are storing 12 components using a different number of rows and columns. Note that the number of columns actually used is not necessarily the number declared. Also note that the grid elements are all the same size, and this size is recomputed as the dimensions of the container are changed.

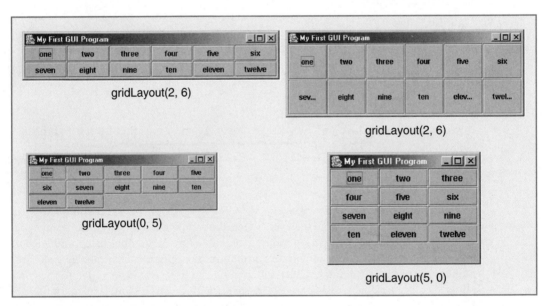

FIGURE 12.6 Examples of a grid layout

The final layout manager we present is the **border layout**. In this layout, there are five separate regions of the container called north, south, east, west, and center, and each of these regions can hold a single component. These five areas in the layout are defined by the static constants NORTH, SOUTH, EAST, WEST, and CENTER defined in the BorderLayout class. The north and south regions represent the top and bottom part of the container, respectively. They extend the full width of the container from left to right, and they are exactly as high as the component placed inside them. The west and east regions represent the left and right sides of the container, respectively, and they extend vertically from the north to the south regions and are exactly as wide as the component placed inside them. Finally, the center region holds all the space that is left. The center area is always resized to be as large as possible.

When adding a component to a container using a border layout, you must state which of these five regions it is to be placed in. For example, let's say that you want to place five buttons named North, South, East, West, and Center into a JFrame named win that is using a border layout. Furthermore, you want to place these buttons into their correspondingly named region. You could do this operation in the following way:

```
// Create a new JFrame called win
JFrame win = new JFrame( "My First GUI Program" );

// Get the content pane associated with the frame
Container content = win.getContentPane();

// Now add buttons to each of the five regions of the screen
content.add( BorderLayout.NORTH, new JButton( "North" ) );
content.add( BorderLayout.SOUTH, new JButton( "South" ) );
content.add( BorderLayout.EAST, new JButton( "East" ) );
content.add( BorderLayout.WEST, new JButton( "West" ) );
content.add( BorderLayout.CENTER, new JButton( "Center" ) );
```

Depending on the size of these five buttons, these operations will produce a frame that resembles one of those shown in Figure 12.7.

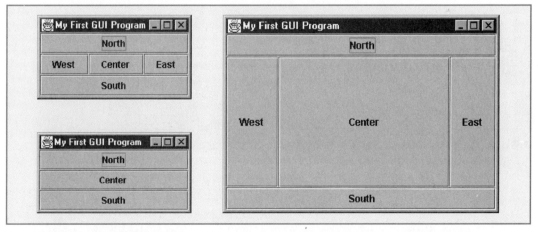

FIGURE 12.7 Border layout

We have now reached the point in our discussion where we can write a program to build our first graphical user interface, although it will be extremely simple and have no functionality. This program is shown in Figure 12.8.

```java
/**
 * Display a JFrame with a simple message.
 */

import java.awt.Color;
import java.awt.Container;
import java.awt.Dimension;
import java.awt.FlowLayout;

import javax.swing.JFrame;
import javax.swing.JLabel;

public class SwingFrame {
    // The size of the frame
    public static final Dimension FRAME_SIZE = new Dimension( 325, 150 );

    public static void main( String args[] ) {
        // Create the frame
        JFrame win = new JFrame( "My First GUI Program" );

        // Get a reference to the content pane
        Container contentPane = win.getContentPane();

        // Establish the layout, size, and color of the frame
        contentPane.setLayout( new FlowLayout() );
        win.setSize( FRAME_SIZE );
        win.setBackground( Color.LIGHT_GRAY );

        // Put the message in the frame
        contentPane.add(
            new JLabel("Programs for sale: Fast, Reliable, Cheap: choose 2"));

        // Make it visible
        win.setVisible( true );
    }

} // SwingFrame
```

FIGURE 12.8 First example of a graphical user interface

If you take a closer look at Figure 12.8, you will notice that we used the class JFrame to create win, the top-level window of our GUI. An instance of a JFrame is commonly used to create the main window for a Java application, and it includes all the functionality that we would want in a window. First, we set the layout manager of win to FlowLayout since the default layout manager for the content pane of a JFrame is a BorderLayout. Next, we set some of the properties of win. This includes its size, 325 pixels wide × 150 pixels tall, its background color, light gray, and the fact that it will be visible on the screen. The result of running the program in Figure 12.8 is shown in Figure 12.9.

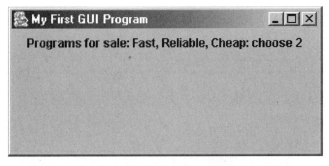

FIGURE 12.9 Our first graphical user interface

Compared to what you have seen before, this is certainly not a very exciting graphical user interface. The obvious reason is that we have not yet added any components, such as buttons, pull-down lists, or text fields. You learn how to do that in the next section.

12.3 GUI COMPONENTS

Components are the "things" that you put into your containers. (Note: Although it is a container, a JPanel is also a component, which means you can place panels inside other containers.) There are far too many components in the AWT and Swing packages to discuss in this one section. We will describe a few of the more interesting ones and then leave it up to you to read more about the components not discussed here. The components that we discuss in this section are summarized in Table 12.1.

TABLE 12.1 GUI Components

Component	Function
JButton	A push button that triggers an event when it is clicked.
JComboBox	A component that combines a button with a drop-down list of items. The user may select exactly one of these items.
JCheckBox	An on/off selection box that can be toggled.
JList	A list of items of which the user can select one or more.
JLabel	A display area for a short text string.
JTextField	An area where text can be entered, displayed, and edited.
JTextArea	A two-dimensional area for entering, displaying, and editing text.
JMenuBar	A menu bar across the top of a container.

Although there are many component types, the steps involved in creating and adding components to a container are similar for virtually all of them. The first step is to create a new instance of a component type using a constructor from the appropriate class. The constructor may or may not take parameters depending on the type of component being instantiated. Table 12.2 summarizes some of the constructors available for the components listed in Table 12.1.

TABLE 12.2 Constructors for the Components of Table 12.1

Component	Constructor	Action
JButton	`JButton();`	Creates a blank button.
	`JButton(String s);`	Creates a button with label s.
	`JButton(Icon i);`	Creates a button with icon i.
JComboBox	`JComboBox();`	Creates a drop-down list with no items.
	`JComboBox(Object[] i);`	Creates a drop-down list containing all the elements in the array i.
JCheckBox	`JCheckBox();`	Creates an unselected check box with no text.
	`JCheckBox(String s);`	Creates an unselected check box with label s.
	`JCheckBox(Icon i);`	Creates an unselected check box with icon i.
JLabel	`JLabel(String s);`	Creates a label with text s.
JList	`JList();`	Creates an empty list containing no items.
JTextField	`JTextField(String s);`	Creates a text field containing text s.
	`JTextField(int n);`	Creates a blank text field n columns wide.
	`JTextField(String s, int n);`	Creates a text field n columns wide containing text s.
JTextArea	`JTextArea(String s);`	Creates a text area containing text s.
	`JTextArea(int r, int c);`	Creates a blank text area containing r rows and c columns.
	`JTextArea(String s, int r, int c);`	Creates a text area with r rows and c columns containing text s.
JMenuBar	`JMenuBar()`	Creates a blank menu bar.

Once we have instantiated a new component, we set its attributes, called the **properties** of the component. There are some properties applicable to all components, and they are found in the AWT `Component` class. Some of the more interesting ones are:

Appearance Properties:

```
// Set the background color.
setBackground(Color c);
```

```
// Set the foreground color.
setForeground(Color c);

// Set font for the text.
setFont(Font f);

// Set the border type of this component.
setBorder(Border b);
```

Other Properties:

```
// Set the width (w) and height (h).
setSize(int w, int h);

// Set the (x,y) position of the upper left hand corner.
setLocation(int x, int y);

// Make the component visible or not visible.
setVisible(boolean b);

// Enable or disable (gray-out) this component.
setEnabled(boolean b);
```

Figure 12.10 illustrates some of these properties using a button labeled "Button Text."

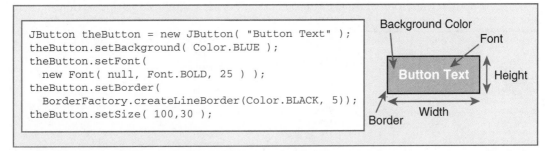

FIGURE 12.10 Example of component properties

In addition to the general properties just discussed, there are also properties that are unique to particular component types, and the methods that handle them will usually be found in the class for that particular component. Table 12.3 contains a sampling of operations that deal with properties associated with a specific component type.

Once we have set all the properties of our component (whether general to all components or specific to this one type), we are ready to add it to our container. In Swing, we must be careful how we do this. If our container is an instance of class JFrame, then the component must be explicitly placed into the portion of the frame called the **content pane**, which is a Container. This is done by first retrieving the content pane of JFrame f using the getContentPane() method in class JFrame:

TABLE 12.3 Sample Component Methods

Class	Methods	Purpose
JButton b	String s = b.getText();	Returns the label on this button.
JComboBox b	Object o = b.getSelectedItem();	Returns the currently selected item.
JLabel l	Component c = l.getText();	Returns the text associated with this label.
JTextField f	**int** i = f.getColumns();	Returns the number of columns in the text field.

```
f.getContentPane();
```

The addition of this component to the content pane is then accomplished using one of the add() methods in Container. For example:

```
add(Component c);            // add component c to the next available
                            // slot in this container.
add(String S, Component c); // add component c to region S. This is
                            // used to specify the region name in a
                            // border layout
```

Figure 12.11 shows a modification of the SwingFrame class of Figure 12.8 to include the addition of some of the component types introduced in this section.

```java
/**
 * Display a JFrame with a simple message and some components
 */

import java.awt.Color;
import java.awt.Container;
import java.awt.Dimension;
import java.awt.FlowLayout;
import javax.swing.JButton;
import javax.swing.JFrame;
import javax.swing.JLabel;
import javax.swing.JTextField;

public class SwingFrame2 {
    // The size of the frame
    public static final Dimension FRAME_SIZE = new Dimension( 325, 150 );

    // The length of the text field
    public static final int FIELD_LENGTH = 20;
```

FIGURE 12.11 Graphical user interface with components

```
public static void main( String args[] ) {
    // Create the frame
    JFrame win = new JFrame( "My Second GUI Program" );

    // Get the reference to the content pane
    Container contentPane = win.getContentPane();

    // Establish the layout, size, and color of the frame
    contentPane.setLayout( new FlowLayout() );
    win.setSize( FRAME_SIZE );
    win.setBackground( Color.LIGHT_GRAY );

    // Put the message in the frame
    contentPane.add(
        new JLabel("Programs for sale: Fast, Reliable, Cheap: choose 2"));

    // Add some more components to make things interesting
    JButton pushButton1 = new JButton( "Press here" );
    pushButton1.setBackground( Color.BLUE );
    contentPane.add( pushButton1 );

    JButton pushButton2 = new JButton( "No, Press here" );
    pushButton2.setBackground( Color.BLUE );
    contentPane.add( pushButton2 );

    JLabel lab = new JLabel( "The button that was pressed: " );
    win.getContentPane().add( lab );

    JTextField field = new JTextField( FIELD_LENGTH );
    win.getContentPane().add( field );

    // Make it visible
    win.setVisible( true );
    }

} // SwingFrame2
```

FIGURE 12.11 Graphical user interface with components *(continued)*

The program in Figure 12.11 produces a GUI with four components: two buttons that are blue in color and labeled "Press here" and "No, Press here." There is a label with the text "The button that was pressed: " and, finally, a 20-column text field, which currently is blank. Since we are using a flow layout manager to control positioning, these four components are added to the JFrame object in strict left-to-right sequence. If we did not like the layout that resulted, we could position each of the four ourselves using the setLocation() method. The program in Figure 12.11 will produce a graphical interface that resembles Figure 12.12.

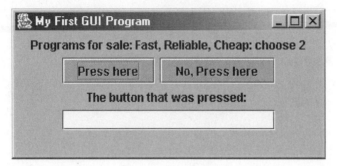

FIGURE 12.12 GUI produced by the program in Figure 12.11

The last component we present in this section is a menu, a common part of virtually every graphical user interface. Unlike the other components we have described, the menu is not added to the content pane of a JFrame object but, naturally enough, to the menu bar section using the setJMenuBar() method in the JFrame class.

Menus are a little more complex than the examples shown earlier. This is not because they work differently but rather because there are three separate pieces to a menu, and each piece must be correctly created and placed in just the right order. These three parts are the **menu bar**, the **menu**, and the **menu item**. The relationship between these three sections is shown in Figure 12.13.

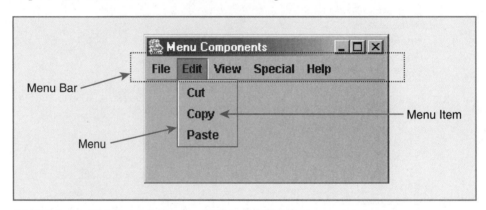

FIGURE 12.13 Three parts of a menu component

The first step in creating a menu is to create an empty menu bar and place it into the menu bar section of the frame. This is done using the constructor in the MenuBar class and then adding this new menu bar object to your frame with the setJMenuBar() method.

```
JMenuBar mb = new JMenuBar();   // create a menu bar mb
f.setJMenuBar(mb);              // Put it in the menu bar
                                // section of f
```

The second step is to add the names of the pull-down menus that will appear in this new menu bar. For example, in the application program MS Word, the menu names appearing across the top-level menu bar are File, Edit, View, Insert, and so on.

To create these new menus, you first invoke the constructor in the JMenu class. Then you use the add() method from the JMenuBar class to add these menus to the menu bar one at a time in order from left to right. These pull-down menus are initially empty. Here is how we might add the four menu items File, Edit, View, and Insert to the menu bar mb just created:

```
JMenu fileMenu = new JMenu("File");     // create a File menu
mb.add(fileMenu);                       // add it to the menu bar

JMenu editMenu = new JMenu("Edit");     // create an Edit menu
mb.add(editMenu);                       // add it to the menu bar

JMenu viewMenu = new JMenu("View");     // create a View menu
mb.add(viewMenu);                       // add it to the menu bar

JMenu insertMenu =
    new JMenu("Insert");                // create an Insert menu
mb.add(insertMenu);                     // add it to the menu bar
```

We now have a menu bar containing the names of four pull-down menus. The next step is to add the individual menu items to each of these pull-down menus. For example, in MS Word when you pull down the File menu, you will see such items as: New, Open, Save, and Quit. You create these menu items using the constructor in the JMenuItem class. (There also is a constructor that allows you to specify shortcut keys.) You then add these items to one of the pull-down menus using the add() method in the JMenu class.

Here is how we would add the four items New, Open, Save, and Quit to the File menu created earlier, without using the shortcut key feature:

```
JMenuItem mNew = new JMenuItem("New");
fileMenu.add(mNew);

JMenuItem mOpen = new JMenuItem("Open");
fileMenu.add(mOpen);

JMenuItem mSave = new JMenuItem("Save");
fileMenu.add(mSave);

JMenuItem mQuit = new JMenuItem("Quit");
fileMenu.add(mQuit);
```

We have now constructed a menu and added it to our frame. This menu will resemble Figure 12.14.

The only problem now is that, although the menu looks good, if we select and click New in the File menu, absolutely nothing happens! In fact, there is no functionality whatever associated with any of the menu items in Figure 12.14. We see the same problem in the GUI of Figure 12.12. In that program, when we clicked one of the two buttons, we would expect its label (either "Press here" or "No, Press here") to appear

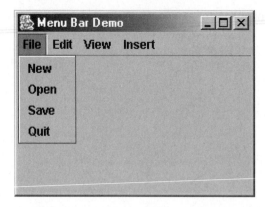

FIGURE 12.14 Example of a menu component

in the text field labeled "The button that was pressed: ". Unfortunately, when you run the program in Figure 12.11 and click either of the two buttons, no text appears anywhere. Similarly, if you click the window close box in the upper left corner of the frame, the program does not terminate.

We have created components, such as buttons, text fields, and menus, and added them to our frame but have not yet given them any behaviors. Adding functionality to a component is the last step in the GUI implementation process, and we discuss this important operation in the upcoming section.

12.4 EVENTS AND LISTENERS

◆ 12.4.1 Introduction

Things happen in a graphical user interface because of the occurrence of events, where an **event** is defined as an action or condition that occurs outside the normal flow of control of your program. An event could be, for example, a mouse click, a keystroke, or the selection of an item from a pull-down menu.

In the normal sequential style of programming, we can always determine exactly when a given statement is executed:

S_1;
S_2;
S_3;
. . .

Quite obviously, statement S_2 is executed at the completion of S_1. S_3 is executed next. However, we have no idea when an event will occur. We cannot possibly know when a user will stop staring at the screen and click a button or enter some data. Therefore, we cannot write GUI programs that assume that events occur in either a specific order or within some constrained time period. We may know that an event will occur, but we cannot plan for exactly when.

Instead, we use the fact that whenever an event occurs, it generates an **event object** instantiated from a class contained in either `java.awt.event` or `javax.swing.event`. Examples of classes in these packages are given in Table 12.4.

TABLE 12.4 Event Classes in `java.awt.event` and `javax.swing.event`

Event Class	Action That Would Cause This Event
`ActionEvent`	Clicking a button in the GUI.
`CaretEvent`	Selecting and modifying text on the screen.
`FocusEvent`	A component obtains or loses focus.
`KeyEvent`	Pressing a key.
`ItemEvent`	Selecting an item from a pull-down menu.
`MouseEvent`	Dragging the mouse over a component.
`TextEvent`	Changing text within a field.
`WindowEvent`	Closing a window.

The event object that is generated by an event is sent to your Java program. The question now is: What do we do with this event object, and how do we handle it? The answer is that we write special methods called **event handlers** that are automatically invoked by Java upon the receipt of an event object. This technique is called **event-driven programming**, and you will learn how to write these programs in the coming sections.

◆ 12.4.2 Event Listeners

To respond to an event object, we use an **event listener**. These listeners contain the actual methods, (i.e., event handlers) that deal with the different type of events generated by a GUI. There will usually be one event listener class associated with each different type of component that is added to your graphical user interface. However, not all GUI components have event listeners associated with them. Some components do not generate events (i.e., a `JLabel`), and in some cases, you may not be interested in processing certain events generated by a component. For example, your program may not be interested in obtaining mouse location information from a `JPanel`. In a situation such as this, you would not associate a listener with the panel, and you will not be notified when mouse events occur. The methods in an event listener class specify exactly what actions are to be taken for each event that can be generated by that component.

The process of creating an event listener for a component proceeds in three steps. The first step is to determine exactly what type of listener is needed for a particular type of component. Different components generate different types of events—you can click a button but you cannot click a label—so you must attach a listener that responds to the proper event types. Table 12.5 lists the components introduced in Table 12.1, the proper event listener type for that component, and the methods, or event handlers, included in that listener.

For example, to create an event listener for the two buttons labeled "Press here" and "No, Press here" in Figure 12.12, we first scan Table 12.5 to learn that Swing `JButton` objects generate an event type called `ActionEvent`, and the correct listener to respond to these action events is `ActionListener`. Similarly, if we want to handle window events for a `JFrame` object, we need a `WindowListener` that will properly respond to a `WindowEvent`.

TABLE 12.5 Listeners and Events Associated with Components

Component	Listener	Events Generated	Methods
JButton	ActionListener	ActionEvent	actionPerformed()
JComboBox	ActionListener	ActionEvent	actionPerformed()
	ItemListener	ItemEvent	itemStateChanged()
JCheckBox	ActionListener	ActionEvent	actionPerformed()
	ItemListener	ItemEvent	itemStateChanged()
JLabel	*None*	*None*	*None*
JTextField	ActionListener	ActionEvent	actionPerformed()
	CaretListener	CaretEvent	caretUpdate()
JTextArea	ActionListener	ActionEvent	actionPerformed()
	CaretListener	CaretEvent	caretUpdate()
JMenuItem	ActionListener	ActionEvent	actionPerformed()
	ItemListener	ItemEvent	itemStateChanged()
JFrame	WindowListener	WindowEvent	windowActivated()
			windowClosed()
			windowClosing()
			windowDeactivated()
			windowDeiconified()
			windowIconified()
			windowOpened()

The second step in building your event listener is to implement a class that can serve as the appropriate listener object. The listeners specified in Table 12.5 are all interfaces, not classes. That is, they specify the methods that must be implemented for a class to be "qualified" to function as a listener of that type, but they do not themselves contain any code. If you think about it, this makes obvious sense. A general-purpose listener for all buttons will certainly know that it must respond to a button click, but it cannot possibly have any idea exactly what it should do with that knowledge. That would depend on the specific GUI being built.

Instead, you write a class that implements the appropriate listener interface by coding all of the methods contained in the interface. This is the set of methods listed in the fourth column of Table 12.5. Often the interface includes only a single method, but in some cases (e.g., WindowListener), there are multiple methods that must be written. For example, Figure 12.15 shows a class called MyButtonListener that implements the ActionListener interface, which includes the single event handler method, actionPerformed(). This class implements the desired behavior of the two buttons shown in Figure 12.12, which is to put the name of the button that was clicked into the text field.

```
import java.awt.event.ActionEvent;
import java.awt.event.ActionListener;
import javax.swing.JTextField;
```

FIGURE 12.15 Example of a class that implements ActionListener

```
public class MyButtonListener implements ActionListener {
   // The text field used to display the button information
   private JTextField display;

   /**
    * Create a new button listener that will use the given
    * text field to display button information.
    *
    * @param textField the text field used to display button
    *     information.
    */
   public MyButtonListener( JTextField theDisplay ) {
      display = theDisplay;
   }

   /**
    * This method will be invoked whenever a button is pressed.
    * The label of the button that was pressed will be displayed
    * in the text field associated with this listener.
    *
    * @param e the event that caused this method to be invoked.
    */
   public void actionPerformed(ActionEvent e) {
      // Get the label of the button that was pressed
      String buttonName = e.getActionCommand();

      // Display the label in the text field
      display.setText( buttonName );
   }

} // MyButtonListener
```

FIGURE 12.15 Example of a class that implements `ActionListener` *(continued)*

The class `MyButtonListener` in Figure 12.15 implements the `ActionListener` interface. This means that it includes code for the one method specified in that interface, `actionPerformed()`. This method has a single parameter: the `ActionEvent` object e generated by the event of clicking the button. This event object e is automatically sent to the listener when the `actionPerformed()` method is invoked. In this case, the listener uses the `getActionCommand()` method located in the `ActionEvent` class in the `java.awt.Event` package to obtain the label of the button that was pressed. This method returns a `String` object that contains the name of the button that was pushed, either "Press here" or "No, Press here." We then take this text and store it into the `JTextField` display using the `setText()` method. Thus, the text field will display the name of the button that was selected.

However, how do we know that an object of class `MyButtonListener` is the one that should respond to button events? There may be two or more classes that implement the `ActionListener` interface, possibly for other buttons in the GUI. How do we associate an instance of the listener shown in Figure 12.15 with the button objects shown in Figure 12.12? The answer is that the third and final step in creating an event listener is called **registering** a listener object with a component. This means to create an association between components that can generate event objects and the listeners that will respond to them. This registration process is done using a listener registration method that is part of every component class or one of its superclasses. For example, the JButton class includes an instance method called addActionListener():

```
public void addActionListener(ActionListener al);
```

When this method is executed by b, an instance of the class JButton, the ActionListener al becomes the "official" listener object for b. Whenever b generates an event object, it is automatically sent to al for handling. In the case of the MyButtonListener class in Figure 12.15, we would register objects of this class as listeners for the two button objects pushButton1 and pushButton2 of Figure 12.11 in the following way:

```
MyButtonListener listener = new MyButtonListener( message );
pushButton1.addActionListener( listener );
pushButton2.addActionListener( listener );
```

Now, whenever a button event is generated by pushButton1, it will be sent to the MyButtonListener object registered earlier. Figure 12.16 adds the concept of button listeners to the GUI program from Figure 12.11. Note that instead of using a separate class to create the listeners, the class in Figure 12.16 implements the ActionListener interface itself, and it serves as the listener for the two buttons.

```
import javax.swing.JFrame;
import java.awt.event.ActionListener;
import java.awt.event.ActionEvent;
import java.awt.Color;
import java.awt.GridLayout;
import javax.swing.JLabel;
import javax.swing.JTextField;
import javax.swing.JButton;

public class ListenerDemo extends JFrame implements ActionListener {

    // Displays the label of the button that was pressed. This variable
    // needs to be accessed by the actionPerformed() method so it has
    // been declared to be part of the state of the object.
    private JTextField display;

    public ListenerDemo( String title ) {
        super( title );
```

FIGURE 12.16 GUI with action listeners

```
    // This GUI incorporates components such as buttons, labels,
    // and text fields. It also includes event listeners for these
    // objects.

    // Set up the main frame
    getContentPane().setLayout( new GridLayout( 0, 2 ) );
    setSize( 350, 100 );
    setBackground( Color.LIGHT_GRAY );

    // Create and configure the first button
    JButton pushButton1 = new JButton( "Press here" );
    pushButton1.setBackground( Color.BLACK );
    pushButton1.setForeground( Color.WHITE );
    getContentPane().add( pushButton1 );

    // Call the actionPerformed() method of this object whenever
    // the button is pressed
    pushButton1.addActionListener( this );

    // Create and configure the second button
    JButton pushButton2 = new JButton( "No, Press here" );
    pushButton2.setBackground( Color.BLACK );
    pushButton2.setForeground( Color.WHITE );
    getContentPane().add( pushButton2 );
    pushButton2.addActionListener( this );

    // This label is used to describe the contents of the text field
    JLabel lab = new JLabel( "The button that was pressed: " );
    getContentPane().add( lab );

    // When a button is pressed, the label that appears on the button
    // will be displayed in this text field.
    display = new JTextField( 20 );
    getContentPane().add( display );
}

/**
 * This method will be invoked whenever one of the two buttons in
 * the GUI is pressed. The label that appears in the button that
 * was pressed will be displayed in the text field on the screen.
 *
 * @param e the event that caused this method to be invoked.
 */
public void actionPerformed( ActionEvent e ) {
    // Get the label of the button that was pressed from the event
    String buttonName = e.getActionCommand();

    // Display the label in the text field
    display.setText( buttonName );
}
```

(continued)

FIGURE 12.16 GUI with action listeners *(continued)*

```
/**
 * Create an instance of a ListenerDemo and display it on
 * the screen.
 */
public static void main( String args[] ) {
   ListenerDemo win = new ListenerDemo( "Using Listener" );

   win.setVisible( true );
}

} // ListenerDemo
```

FIGURE 12.16 GUI with action listeners *(continued)*

When we run the program in Figure 12.16 and click one of the two buttons, we will get the desired behavior: The name of the button that was pressed will appear in the text field (Figure 12.17).

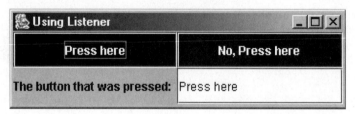

FIGURE 12.17 Execution of the GUI in Figure 12.16

To summarize, the following are the three steps involved in creating an event listener and attaching it to a component:

1. Determine the appropriate listener interface required by this component.
2. Build a class that implements this listener interface by writing code for all the methods in that interface. These methods, called event handlers, should implement the behaviors that you want to occur when this event is generated.
3. Register an instance of this class as the event listener for this component.

Selecting a menu item from a pull-down menu pane also generates an ActionEvent and uses an ActionListener. If we assume the menu structure shown in Figure 12.14, then one possible event listener for the items contained in the File menu is shown in Figure 12.18. This example assumes that if you select the menu item called New, the system will invoke a method called newProcedure(), not shown here, which handles all of the details associated with the creation of a new file. We assume that similar procedures exist for both the Open and Save options in the File menu pane. If the user selects Quit, then we execute the System.exit(0) operation, which terminates the Java Virtual Machine currently executing.

The class in Figure 12.18 was written specifically to handle events generated by menu items. Usually one class will handle the events from the same type of objects. For

```
public static class MyMenuListener implements ActionListener {
    public void actionPerformed( ActionEvent e ) {
        String command = e.getActionCommand();
        if ( command.equals( "New" ) ) {
            newProcedure();
        }
        else if ( command.equals( "Open" ) ) {
            openProcedure();
        }
        else if ( command.equals( "Save" ) ) {
            saveProcedure();
        }
        else if ( command.equals( "Quit" ) ) {
            System.exit( 0 );
        }
    }
} // MyMenuListener
```

FIGURE 12.18 Event listener for the menu of Figure 12.14

example, you might have a class that handles button events, one that handles menu events, and another that handles mouse events. It is also possible to write a listener that will handle events generated by different types of objects. The getSource() method defined in the Event class can be used to identify the particular object that caused this event. Then, using the **instanceof** operator, you can determine the class of the object that generated the event. This sequence of operations is quite common in event listeners because different types of objects can generate the same type of event. For example, looking back at Table 12.5, we see that both JButton and JMenuItem generate an ActionEvent. Similarly, both JCheckBox and JComboBox generate an ItemEvent. If you are writing an event listener that can potentially handle events coming from both button and menu items, you first need to determine exactly where the event came from and what type of object produced it. Most event classes contain methods for doing these operations. For example, the ActionEvent class includes these two methods:

getSource();	Returns the source object that generated this event
getActionCommand();	Returns a string naming the object that generated the event, either the button label or menu item name

Another useful command that can help you sort out exactly what is happening is:

getID();	Returns a constant that specifies the event type

Let's do one more example of creating and implementing an event listener. The screen shown in Figure 12.17 contains a small rectangular close box in its upper right corner. Most GUIs use this box as a quick and easy way to close a window and terminate execution of the thread running this GUI. However, if you were to click the close box on a JFrame, the default behavior is to hide the JFrame when the user closes the window (i.e., the program does not terminate). There are two ways to change the default close behavior exhibited by a JFrame. The first way to handle a window closing event is to attach a listener that will be invoked whenever the user clicks the close box.

According to Table 12.5, the listener interface that we must implement for a JFrame object is called WindowListener. (JFrame is a subclass of Window, as shown in Figure 12.1.) This interface contains seven methods, which handle all the different events that can be generated by containers like JFrame—events such as opening and closing the window, hiding the window, and iconifying it. The only method we care about in this example is WindowClosing, which is the one activated whenever the cursor is located inside the close box and we click the mouse button. The easiest and quickest way to terminate execution of a program is to invoke System.exit(0), and that is what we will do when the window is closed. However, when implementing an interface, you must write code for all the methods in the interface, not just the ones in which you are interested. Therefore, we also have to write do-nothing routines, called **stubs**, for the other six methods in the interface. If we do not, then the program will not compile. The MyWindowListener class in Figure 12.19 implements the WindowListener interface and can be used to instantiate a WindowListener that will terminate a program if the user closes the main window.

```java
import java.awt.event.WindowEvent;
import java.awt.event.WindowListener;

public class MyWindowListener implements WindowListener {
    // We put in stubs for all methods except WindowClosing.
    // The stubs are necessary since without them this class
    // will not implement the interface.

    /**
     * Invoked after a window has been closed and disposed of.
     */
    public void windowClosed( WindowEvent e ) {}

    /**
     * Invoked the first time a window is opened.
     */
    public void windowOpened( WindowEvent e ) {}

    /**
     * Invoked when a window is restored from the minimized state.
     */
    public void windowDeiconified( WindowEvent e ) {}

    /**
     * Invoked when a window is minimized.
```

FIGURE 12.19 WindowListener

```
    */
   public void windowIconified( WindowEvent e ) {}

   /**
    * Invoked when the window becomes the active window.
    */
   public void windowActivated( WindowEvent e ) {}

   /**
    * Invoked when the window no longer is the active window.
    */
   public void windowDeactivated( WindowEvent e ) {}

   /**
    * Invoked when the user attempts to close a window.
    */
   public void windowClosing( WindowEvent e ) {
      // Simply terminate the program
      System.exit(0);
   }

} //MyWindowListener
```

FIGURE 12.19 WindowListener *(continued)*

For most WindowListener classes that you will write, you will need to provide behavior for only one or two of the methods specified by the interface. For example, the WindowListener in Figure 12.19 specifies behavior for only the windowClosing() method. The remaining six methods are stubs. To make things more convenient for the programmer, the AWT includes adapter classes for some of the listener interfaces. **Adapter classes** provide stubs for all of the methods in the corresponding interface. You use the adapter class by writing a new class that extends the adapter and over-rides the specific methods that deal with the events that you are interested in han-dling. The WindowAdapter class can be extended to create listeners for window events. The MyWindowListener class in Figure 12.20 provides the same functionality as the listener shown in Figure 12.19, but since it extends the WindowAdapter, it needs to provide an implementation only for the windowClosing() method because the other methods in the interface are already implemented as stubs in the adapter class. Using adapter classes can help to simplify the task of writing listeners.

```
import java.awt.event.WindowAdapter;
import java.awt.event.WindowEvent;

public class MyWindowListener extends WindowAdapter {
   // We only need to override the methods that correspond to the
   // events we are interested in handling. The stubs are
   // provided by the super class.
```
(continued)

FIGURE 12.20 Using the WindowAdapter class

```
    /**
     * Invoked when the user attempts to close a window.
     */
    public void windowClosing( WindowEvent e ) {
       // Simply terminate the program
       System.exit(0);
    }

} //MyWindowListener
```

FIGURE 12.20 Using the `WindowAdapter` class *(continued)*

Finally, we register our listener using the `addWindowListener()` method in the `Window` class. Figure 12.21 shows the same GUI as Figure 12.17, but this time with the close box functionality working. (The new code is shown in boldface.) You might wish to enter and run this program, click the close box, and observe the results.

```
import javax.swing.JFrame;
import java.awt.event.ActionListener;
import java.awt.event.ActionEvent;
import java.awt.Color;
import java.awt.GridLayout;
import javax.swing.JLabel;
import javax.swing.JTextField;
import javax.swing.JButton;

public class ListenerDemo extends JFrame implements ActionListener {

   // Displays the label of the button that was pressed. This variable
   // needs to be accessed by the actionPerformed() method so it has
   // been declared to be part of the state of the object.
   private JTextField message;

   public ListenerDemo( String title ) {
      super( title );

      // This GUI incorporates components such as buttons, labels,
      // and text fields. It also includes event listeners for these
      // objects.

      // Set up the main frame
      getContentPane().setLayout( new GridLayout( 0, 2 ) );
      setSize( 350, 100 );
      setBackground( Color.LIGHT_GRAY );
```

FIGURE 12.21 Using a `WindowListener` to terminate a program

```
        // Use a window listener to terminate the program if the
        // user closes the window

        addWindowListener( new MyWindowListener() );

        // Create and configure the first button
        JButton pushButton1 = new JButton( "Press here" );
        pushButton1.setBackground( Color.BLACK );
        pushButton1.setForeground( Color.WHITE );
        getContentPane().add( pushButton1 );

        // Call the actionPerformed() method of this object whenever
        // the button is pressed
        pushButton1.addActionListener( this );

        // Create and configure the second button
        JButton pushButton2 = new JButton( "No, Press here" );
        pushButton2.setBackground( Color.BLACK );
        pushButton2.setForeground( Color.WHITE );
        getContentPane().add( pushButton2 );
        pushButton2.addActionListener( this );

        // This label is used to describe the contents of the text field
        JLabel lab = new JLabel( "The button that was pressed: " );
        getContentPane().add( lab );

        // When a button is pressed, the label that appears on the button
        // will be displayed in this text field.
        message = new JTextField( 20 );
        getContentPane().add( message );
    }


    /**
     * This method will be invoked whenever one of the two buttons in
     * the GUI is pressed. The label that appears in the button that
     * was pressed will be displayed in the text field on the screen.
     *
     * @param e the event that caused this method to be invoked.
     */
    public void actionPerformed( ActionEvent e ) {
        // Get the label of the button that was pressed from the event
        String buttonName = e.getActionCommand();

        // Display the label in the text field
        message.setText( buttonName );
    }
```

(continued)

FIGURE 12.21 Using a `WindowListener` to terminate a program *(continued)*

```
    /**
     * Create an instance of a ListenerDemo and display it on
     * the screen.
     */
    public static void main( String args[] ) {
        ListenerDemo win = new ListenerDemo( "Using Listener" );

        win.setVisible( true );
    }

} // ListenerDemo
```

FIGURE 12.21 Using a `WindowListener` to terminate a program *(continued)*

The second, and probably more convenient, way to handle the close window event is to use the `setDefaultCloseOperation()` method to specify what should be done when the user closes the window. The `setDefaultCloseOperation()` takes an integer parameter that specifies the action to take when the window is closed. The four constants that can be passed to the `setDefaultCloseOperation()` method and the action they specify are given in Table 12.6.

TABLE 12.6 Valid Arguments to `setDefaultCloseOperation()`

Constant	Action Specified
`WindowConstants.DO_NOTHING_ON_CLOSE`	Don't do anything. If the window closing event must be handled, the programmer must provide a `WindowListener` object to handle the event.
`WindowConstants.HIDE_ON_CLOSE`	Hides the frame after notifying any registered `WindowListener` objects.
`WindowConstants.DISPOSE_ON_CLOSE`	Hides and disposes of the frame after notifying any registered `WindowListener` objects.
`JFrame.EXIT_ON_CLOSE`	Terminates the program using the `System.exit()` method.

The remaining programs in this chapter will use the `setDefaultCloseOpera-tionMethod()`, passing it the constant value `JFrame.EXIT_ON_CLOSE` as an argument to specify that the program should be terminated when the user closes the window.

◆ 12.4.3 Mouse Events

The handling of mouse events is similar in most ways to the event handling discussion in the previous section. The primary difference is that mouse events may also include both motion and position information, and we may need to deal with (x, y) locations on the screen. Table 12.7 presents the listeners and events associated with the mouse.

TABLE 12.7 Mouse Events and Listeners

Event Listener	Events Generated	Methods
MouseListener	MouseEvent	mouseClicked() mouseEntered() mouseExited() mousePressed() mouseReleased()
MouseMotionListener	MouseEvent	mouseDragged() mouseMoved()
MouseWheelListener	MouseWheelEvent	mouseWheelMoved()

As you can see from Table 12.7, there are five methods that must be implemented by any class that wishes to implement the interface MouseListener. (The Swing interface MouseInputListener extends the two separate AWT listener interfaces MouseListener and MouseMotionListener.) The mousePressed() method is invoked when the mouse button is pressed and the cursor is within the boundary of some component. When the mouse button is clicked, a MouseEvent is generated and the mousePressed() method of the registered listener is invoked. In a similar fashion, the mouseReleased() method is activated whenever a mouse button is released over a component. Finally, the mouseClicked() method is called whenever the user presses and then releases a mouse button without any intervening movement.

The MouseEvent class inherits a method called getID() that will tell you what type of mouse event occurred, such as MOUSE_PRESSED or MOUSE_RELEASED. This allows you to differentiate between the different things that can occur. The methods getX() and getY() locate the x- and y-coordinates of the mouse event, and getClickCount() specifies how many times the button was clicked. (This last method is extremely useful if you want to do an operation only if the mouse button is double-clicked.) The method getButton() can be used to identify which button on the mouse changed state.

There are two methods associated with the movement of a cursor over a component. mouseEntered() is invoked whenever a cursor moves across the boundary of a component. mouseExited() is invoked when the cursor exits a component. Figure 12.22 indicates when these two routines will be called.

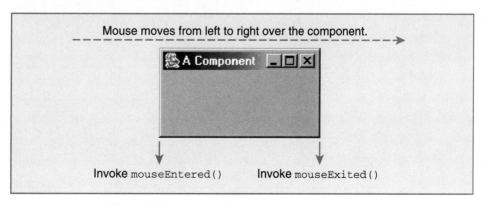

FIGURE 12.22 Mouse listener events

The method getComponent(), inherited from ComponentEvent, can be used to determine the specific component that has been entered or exited. The MyMouseListener class in Figure 12.23 illustrates how the MouseAdapter class can create a listener that will respond to mouse entry and mouse exit events. Because we are using an adapter class, we do not have to write stubs for the remaining three methods contained in the interface.

```java
import java.awt.event.MouseAdapter;
import java.awt.event.MouseEvent;
import javax.swing.JButton;
import javax.swing.JTextField;

class MyMouseListener extends MouseAdapter {

    private JTextField displayField; // Where button information is displayed

    /**
     * Create a new mouse listener that will display information using
     * the specified text fields.
     *
     * @param display where button information is displayed.
     */
    public MyMouseListener( JTextField display ) {
        displayField = display;
    }


    /**
     * Invoked when the mouse enters a component. This method assumes
     * only buttons are looking for this event and will display
     * the button text using the designated text field.
     *
     * @param e the event that caused this method to be invoked.
     */
    public void mouseEntered( MouseEvent e ) {
        // Get a reference to the button that generated this event
        JButton button = (JButton)e.getComponent();

        // Display the button text in the text field
        displayField.setText( button.getText() );
    }

    /**
     * Invoked when the mouse leaves a component. Causes the display
     * text field to be cleared.
     *
     * @param e the event that caused this method to be invoked.
     */
    public void mouseExited( MouseEvent e ) {
```

FIGURE 12.23 MouseListener

```
      // We have exited a component - blank out the text field
      displayField.setText( "" );
  }

} // MyMouseListener
```

FIGURE 12.23 MouseListener *(continued)*

Figure 12.24 shows a program that illustrates how the MyMouseListener class of Figure 12.23 can handle mouse events. This GUI contains two buttons and one text field. Whenever the cursor is positioned over one of the two buttons, the text field contains the label of that button; otherwise, the text field is blank. This example should give you an idea of how mouse event management is handled.

```
import java.awt.Color;
import java.awt.Container;
import java.awt.Dimension;
import java.awt.GridLayout;
import javax.swing.JButton;
import javax.swing.JFrame;
import javax.swing.JLabel;
import javax.swing.JTextField;

public class MouseDemo extends JFrame {
   // The size of the frame
   private static Dimension FRAME_SIZE = new Dimension( 300, 100 );

   // Length of the text field
   private static final int FIELD_SIZE = 20;

   /**
    * Create a GUI that demonstrates how to use a MouseListener.
    *
    * @param title the title of the frame.
    */
   public MouseDemo( String title ) {
      super(title);

      Container content = getContentPane();
      JTextField display = new JTextField( FIELD_SIZE );
      JButton button = null;

      // The listener that will handle mouse events
      MyMouseListener listener = new MyMouseListener( display );
```

(continued)

FIGURE 12.24 Using a MouseListener

```
        // Set up the frame
        setSize( FRAME_SIZE );
        content.setLayout( new GridLayout( 0, 2 ) );
        setDefaultCloseOperation( JFrame.EXIT_ON_CLOSE );

        // Create two buttons and add them to the frame
        button = new JButton( "Button one" );
        button.setBackground( Color.RED );
        button.addMouseListener( listener );
        content.add( button );

        button = new JButton( "Button two" );
        button.setBackground( Color.YELLOW );
        button.addMouseListener( listener );
        content.add( button );

        // Label and text field for the mouse information
        content.add( new JLabel( "Button entered" ) );
        content.add( display );
    }

    /**
     * Display a MouseDemo GUI.
     */
    public static void main( String args[] ) {
        MouseDemo win = new MouseDemo( "Mouse Listeners" );

        win.setVisible( true );
    }

} // MouseDemo
```

FIGURE 12.24 Using a `MouseListener` *(continued)*

Figure 12.25 illustrates the GUI displayed by the program in Figure 12.24. It assumes that right now the cursor is positioned over the button labeled Button two.

In the following section, we give some additional, and more significant, examples that illustrate concepts related to designing and implementing a graphical user interface.

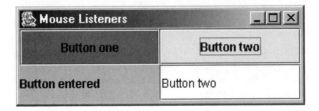

FIGURE 12.25 GUI produced by the program in Figure 12.24

12.5 EXAMPLES

These additional GUI programming examples will give you more experience with graphical interface design and show you techniques commonly used in building GUIs.

The first example demonstrates two components not used before: JCheckBox and JTextArea. A check box is a Boolean on/off component that can be in either a selected or a nonselected state but not both. A text area is a two-dimensional text field that has both rows and columns. In the following example, there is a separate check box for each computer science course for which a student might wish to sign up. Students can check the courses they wish to take up to a limit of three. When they are finished selecting courses, they click the button labeled Finished. At that point, the text area will either display all of the courses they have selected, or if they have checked more than three, it will display an error message saying that they have exceeded the limit.

A JCheckBox component requires an ItemListener that contains a single method: ItemStateChanged. Text areas and buttons both use the same ActionListener interface that you have seen a number of times. Notice that when we register our listeners, we use the reference this to indicate that this object itself will be the listener for the component. The program is shown in Figure 12.26.

```
import java.awt.BorderLayout;
import java.awt.GridLayout;
import java.awt.Color;
import java.awt.Dimension;
import java.awt.event.ActionEvent;
import java.awt.event.ActionListener;
import java.awt.event.ItemEvent;
import java.awt.event.ItemListener;
import javax.swing.BorderFactory;
import javax.swing.JButton;
import javax.swing.JCheckBox;
import javax.swing.JFrame;
import javax.swing.JLabel;
import javax.swing.JPanel;
import javax.swing.JTextArea;
import java.util.Iterator;
import java.util.Set;
import java.util.TreeSet;

/**
 * A data input screen that allows students to select courses. Students
 * select from 1 to 3 courses and then press the Finished button. The
 * names of the courses will be displayed in the text area.
 */
class GUIExample1 extends JFrame implements ItemListener, ActionListener {
```
(continued)

FIGURE 12.26 Example GUI using JCheckBox and JTextArea

```java
// The size of the frame
private static final Dimension = new Dimension( 500, 250 );

// The size of the text area
private static final int DISPLAY_ROWS = 10;
private static final int DISPLAY_COLS = 20;

// The names of the courses
private static final String courses[] = { "CS 101",
                                          "CS 102",
                                          "CS 210",
                                          "CS 215",
                                          "CS 217",
                                          "CS 302" };

// The courses selected by the student
private Set selectedCourses;

// Where the messages will be displayed
private JTextArea display;

/**
 * Create a new course selection screen.
 *
 * @param title the title to be placed in the frame.
 */
public GUIExample1( String title ) {
   super( title );

   // Use a TreeSet so the courses are displayed in alphabetical order
   selectedCourses = new TreeSet();

   // Set frame attributes
   setDefaultCloseOperation( JFrame.EXIT_ON_CLOSE );
   setSize( FRAME_SIZE );
   getContentPane().setLayout( new BorderLayout() );

   // Instructions for the user
   JLabel l1 = new JLabel( "Please select the courses you wish" +
                           " to take. Click on the Finished button " +
                           "when done." );

   getContentPane().add(l1, BorderLayout.NORTH );

   // The check boxes for course selection will go in a panel.
   JPanel checkPanel = new JPanel();
   checkPanel.setLayout( new GridLayout( courses.length, 0 ) );
   checkPanel.setBorder( BorderFactory.createEtchedBorder() );
```

FIGURE 12.26 Example GUI using `JCheckBox` and `JTextArea` *(continued)*

```
      // Create the check boxes and add them to the panel
      for ( int i = 0; i < courses.length; i++ ) {
         JCheckBox box = new JCheckBox( courses[ i ] );

         // This object will handle the state change events
         box.addItemListener( this );

         checkPanel.add( box );
      }

      getContentPane().add( checkPanel, BorderLayout.WEST );

      // Create the finished button
      JButton done = new JButton( "Finished" );
      done.addActionListener( this );

      getContentPane().add( done, BorderLayout.SOUTH );

      // Create the text box that will be used to display messages
      display = new JTextArea( DISPLAY_ROWS, DISPLAY_COLS );
      display.setBorder(
         BorderFactory.createTitledBorder(
            BorderFactory.createEtchedBorder(),
            "Courses Selected" ) );
      display.setBackground( getBackground() );

      getContentPane().add( display, BorderLayout.CENTER );
   }

   /**
    * This method will be called whenever the user clicks on a check
    * box. If the user is selecting a course it will be added to
    * the set of selected courses. If they are deselecting a course
    * it will be removed from the set.
    *
    * @param event the item event that caused this method to be invoked.
    */
   public void itemStateChanged( ItemEvent event ) {
      // The label on the checkbox is the name of the course
      String courseName = ((JCheckBox)event.getItem() ).getText();

      if ( event.getStateChange() == ItemEvent.SELECTED ) {
         // They are adding the course
         selectedCourses.add( courseName );
      }
      else {
         // They are dropping the course
         selectedCourses.remove( courseName );
      }
   }
```

(continued)

FIGURE 12.26 Example GUI using `JCheckBox` and `JTextArea` *(continued)*

```java
/**
 * This method will be invoked whenever the user clicks on the finished
 * button. If 1, 2, or 3 courses have been selected, the names of
 * the course are displayed in the GUI. If the incorrect number of
 * courses is selected an error message is displayed.
 *
 * @param event the action event that caused this method to be invoked.
 */
public void actionPerformed( ActionEvent event ) {
    // What will be displayed on the screen
    String text = "";

    if ( selectedCourses.size() < 1 ||
        selectedCourses.size() > 3 ) {
        // Too few or too many courses - display error message
        text = "You must select between 1 and 3 courses";
    }
    else {
        // Use an iterator to get the course names out of the
        // set and format them into a string separated by
        // newline characters
        Iterator i = selectedCourses.iterator();
        while ( i.hasNext() ) {
            text = text + i.next() + "\n";
        }
    }

    // Display the message
    display.setText( text );
}

/**
 * Run the course selection program.
 *
 * @param args command line arguments (ignored).
 */
public static void main( String args[] ) {
    // Create the GUI
    GUIExample1 screen = new GUIExample1( "Course Selection" );

    // Display it on the screen
    screen.setVisible( true );
}

} // GUIExample1
```

FIGURE 12.26 Example GUI using JCheckBox and JTextArea *(continued)*

When the program of Figure 12.26 is executed, it will produce the screen display shown in Figure 12.27.

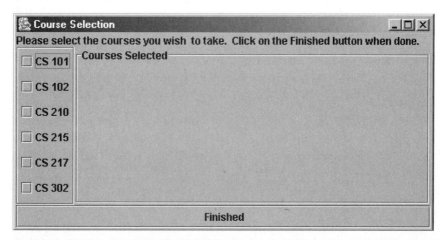

FIGURE 12.27 Screen produced by executing the program in Figure 12.26

Our second example is a demonstration of using a GUI for data entry. In this application, the user is asked to enter information about himself or herself, including name, department, university, state, and zip code. They type in these data, and when they are finished, they click the button labeled Store. The information entered will now be displayed in a text area. Of course, in real life, the information would not simply be displayed; it would also be stored as a record in a data file. These operations are typical of what happens when you register as a user on any number of online services.

The most important new feature presented in this example is the use of panels to simplify the GUI-building task. The interface in this example is not constructed as one large monolithic container; instead, it will be built from other containers of type JPanel.

Panels, first mentioned in Section 12.2.2, are borderless containers that are frequently used to simplify GUI construction. A JPanel is a fully functional container that has its own properties, layout manager, and components. For example, it is perfectly permissible for a JPanel object to use a FlowLayout manager and enter components in a strict left-to-right fashion. However, when the panel is added to a JFrame object, the frame itself may use a totally different scheme, such as a border layout.

We use JPanel objects to implement a divide and conquer GUI design strategy. Rather than think about the entire screen all at once, we can work on individual regions. For example, assume that we are designing a JFrame f containing a huge number of components. Instead of dealing with the entire collection, we could instead choose to construct a JPanel called ul that contains only the component layout for the upper left quadrant of f. When that is done, we can begin work on a second panel, ur, which contains the component layout for the upper right quadrant. We repeat this process for as many subproblems as we wish to create. When we are finished, we simply add the individual panels, which are components, to JFrame f. This process is diagramed in Figure 12.28.

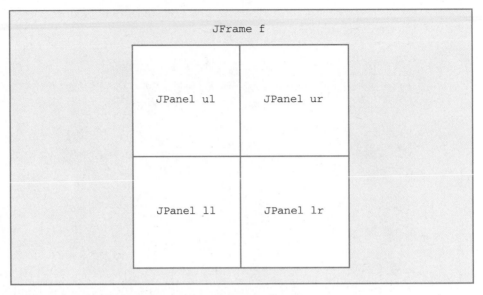

FIGURE 12.28 Using panels to construct a frame

This second example will also demonstrate another new component type that we have not seen or used before: a JComboBox. This is a drop-down list of items, only one of which can be selected at any one time. Originally, only the selected item is visible on the screen. When you place the cursor over the combo box and click the mouse, a list of all items appears. You may move the cursor through the list and select any one item, and the selected item will be displayed in the visible portion of the combo box component. The items included in the drop-down list are added to the combo box using the addItem() method in the JComboBox class or set to the values contained in an array passed to the JComboBox constructor. The item initially selected can be specified using the setSelectedIndex(), where the first item in the list has index 0.

In this example, the combo box is used to select the user's state. The label of the JComboBox is State. Assume that when the GUI is first created, we have selected the state MN. This is what you will see:

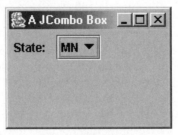

When the mouse is placed over this component and the mouse button is clicked, a drop-down list will appear containing, in this example, the three entries MN, WI, and IA. (We apologize to the other 47 states. A real example containing all 50 states would have been a bit too long!) You may now move the cursor up and down to select any one of the three items. For example, if you have selected the item WI, here is what you will see on the screen just before releasing the mouse:

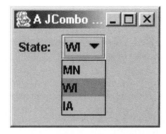

When you release the mouse button, the drop-down list will disappear, and the selected item, WI, will appear on the screen.

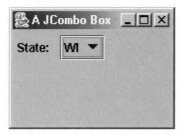

There is another Swing component that combines the look and feel of the visible multiselection JCheckBox components used in the first example with the single selection JComboBox component just described. They are called **radio buttons**. A ButtonGroup class represents a collection of visible radio buttons that operates under the rule that one and only one button can be selected at any one time. If the user selects a radio button that is part of a ButtonGroup, then the previously selected one will be automatically deselected. Radio buttons are added to the ButtonGroup object using the add() method in the ButtonGroup class. The button that is initially selected can be set using the setSelected() method.

We could use a ButtonGroup to implement the state input that has been described rather than a JComboBox. We would create three radio buttons that look something like this (assuming that the MN button is the one initially selected):

We would now add all three of the buttons to a ButtonGroup. If the user were now to change his or her mind and select the WI button, the selection indicator on the MN button will be automatically removed:

Although we will not use this component, it is a good example of the many different component types provided by a modern GUI design package. Our discussions in this chapter have only introduced you to a sampling of the many resources that can be found in packages like AWT and Swing.

A program to implement the data entry operation we have described appears in Figure 12.29. The output of this program is shown in Figure 12.30.

```java
import java.awt.BorderLayout;
import java.awt.Container;
import java.awt.Dimension;
import java.awt.FlowLayout;
import java.awt.GridLayout;

import java.awt.event.ActionEvent;
import java.awt.event.ActionListener;

import javax.swing.JButton;
import javax.swing.JComboBox;
import javax.swing.JFrame;
import javax.swing.JLabel;
import javax.swing.JPanel;
import javax.swing.JTextArea;
import javax.swing.JTextField;

/**
 * Display a simple data entry screen. This program illustrates the
 * use of listeners and a JComboBox.
 */
public class DataEntryGUI extends JFrame implements ActionListener {

    // Size of the main frame
    private static final Dimension WINDOW_SIZE = new Dimension( 775, 250 );

    // Size of a prompt
    private static final Dimension PROMPT_SIZE = new Dimension( 75, 15 );

    // Number of characters allowed in a data entry area
    private static final int DATA_LENGTH = 30;

    // Number of data entry fields in this GUI
    private static final int NUM_FIELDS = 5;

    // Constants used to identify the data entry fields
    private static final int NAME = 0;
    private static final int SCHOOL = 1;
    private static final int MAJOR = 2;
    private static final int HOMETOWN = 3;
    private static final int STATE = 4;
```

FIGURE 12.29 GUI that demonstrates data entry operations

```java
// The states that will be listed by the JComboBox
private static final String stateList[] = {
    "AK", "AL", "AR", "AZ", "CA", "CO", "CT", "DE", "FL", "GA",
    "HI", "IA", "ID", "IL", "IN", "KS", "KY", "LA", "MA", "MD", "ME",
    "MI", "MN", "MO", "MS", "MT", "NC", "ND", "NE", "NH", "NJ",
    "NM", "NY", "NV", "OH", "OK", "OR", "PA", "RI", "SC",
    "SD", "TN", "TX", "UT", "VA", "VT", "WA", "WI", "WV", "WY"
};

// The names of the fields on the GUI
private static final String fieldName[] = {
    "Name:",
    "School:",
    "Major:",
    "Hometown:"
};

// This component will allow the user to select a state
private JComboBox stateSelector;

// The input areas will be stored in this array
private JTextField field[];

// Where the completed information will be stored
private JTextArea displayArea = new JTextArea( NUM_FIELDS, DATA_LENGTH );

/**
 * Create a data entry screen.
 *
 * @param title the frame title.
 */
public DataEntryGUI( String title ) {
    super( title ); // Let the JFrame initialize things

    // Get a reference to the content pane for convenience
    Container contentPane = getContentPane();

    // Create the array that will hold the text fields
    field = new JTextField[ fieldName.length ];

    // Create the data entry panel
    JPanel dataEntry = new JPanel();
    dataEntry.setLayout( new GridLayout( 0, 1 ) );

    // For each field on the GUI, create a panel that will
    // hold the name of the field and the text field associated
    // with the field. This way we can be sure that the description
```

(continued)

FIGURE 12.29 GUI that demonstrates data entry operations *(continued)*

```
// of the field and the text area where the information is entered
// will be in the same row.
for ( int i = 0; i < field.length; i = i + 1 ) {
   JPanel row = new JPanel();

   // Create the text field
   field[ i ] = new JTextField( DATA_LENGTH );

   // Create the description for the field
   JLabel prompt = new JLabel( fieldName[ i ] );
   prompt.setPreferredSize( PROMPT_SIZE );

   // Put them in the panel
   row.add( prompt );
   row.add( field[ i ] );

   // Put the panel in the main frame
   dataEntry.add( row );
}

// The state is handled differently because it is a combo box
// and not a text field like the others

JPanel row = new JPanel();
row.setLayout( new FlowLayout( FlowLayout.LEFT ) );

JLabel prompt = new JLabel( "State" );
prompt.setPreferredSize( PROMPT_SIZE );

stateSelector = new JComboBox( stateList );

row.add( prompt );
row.add( stateSelector );

dataEntry.add( row );

// The data entry panel and the display area will be
// placed in a single panel so that they occupy the
// center area of the frame
JPanel centerPanel = new JPanel();
centerPanel.setLayout( new FlowLayout() );

centerPanel.add( dataEntry );
centerPanel.add( displayArea );

// The buttons go in a separate panel and will
// eventually be displayed in the south area of the frame
JPanel buttonPanel = new JPanel();
buttonPanel.setLayout( new FlowLayout() );
```

FIGURE 12.29 GUI that demonstrates data entry operations *(continued)*

```
        JButton button = new JButton( "Store" );
        button.addActionListener( this );
        buttonPanel.add( button );

        button = new JButton( "Clear" );
        button.addActionListener( this );
        buttonPanel.add( button );

        button = new JButton( "Quit" );
        button.addActionListener( this );
        buttonPanel.add( button );

        // Setup the main frame
        setSize( WINDOW_SIZE );
        setDefaultCloseOperation( JFrame.EXIT_ON_CLOSE );

        // Add the subcomponents to the main frame
        contentPane.setLayout( new BorderLayout() );
        contentPane.add( BorderLayout.CENTER, centerPanel );
        contentPane.add( BorderLayout.SOUTH, buttonPanel );
    }

    /**
     * This method will be invoked whenever one of the buttons
     * on the GUI is pressed.
     *
     * @param e the event that caused this method to be invoked.
     */
    public void actionPerformed( ActionEvent e ) {
        // Get the label on the button that was pressed
        String arg = e.getActionCommand();

        // Determine which button was pressed
        if ( arg.equals( "Store" ) ) {
            // If the store button was pressed, display the data entered
            // in the display area of the GUI

            // Erase any text currently being displayed
            displayArea.setText( "" );

            // Copy the contents of the text fields and put them in
            // a single string separated by newline characters
            for ( int i = 0; i < field.length; i = i + 1 ) {
                displayArea.append( field[ i ].getText() + '\n' );
            }

            // Get the state from the combo box
            String s = (String) stateSelector.getSelectedItem();
```

(continued)

FIGURE 12.29 GUI that demonstrates data entry operations *(continued)*

```
         // Display the results
         displayArea.append( s );
      }
      else if ( arg.equals( "Clear" ) ) {
         // Erase any text currently being displayed
         displayArea.setText( "" );
      }
      else {
         // Terminate the program
         System.exit( 0 );
      }
   }


   /**
    * Create an instance of a DataEntryGUI and make it visible.
    */
   public static void main( String args[] ) {
      DataEntryGUI mainWindow = new DataEntryGUI( "Student Information" );
      mainWindow.setVisible( true );
   }

} // DataEntryGUI
```

FIGURE 12.29 GUI that demonstrates data entry operations *(continued)*

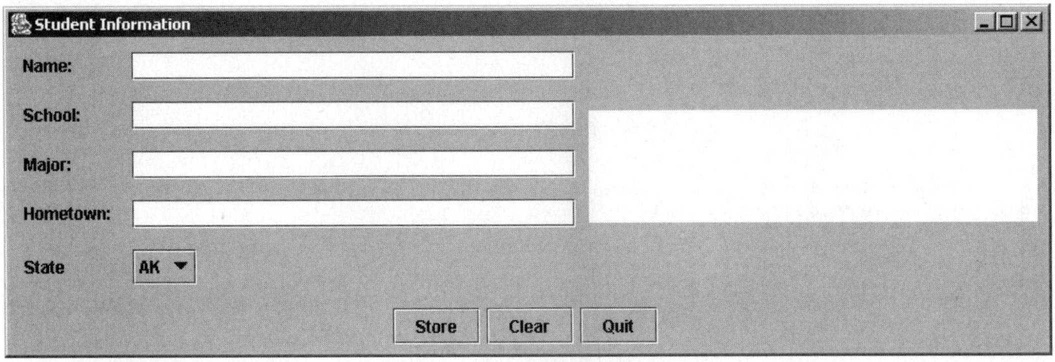

FIGURE 12.30 Output of the GUI program in Figure 12.29

For our final example, we will do a classic GUI-based application that is part of virtually every computer system sold today: a four-function calculator. This example will utilize a good number of the components and event listeners that we have been discussing throughout the chapter, including frames, layout managers, labels, panels, and buttons. An image of the calculator interface we will be building is shown in Figure 12.31.

We will construct our calculator using a JPanel, named buttonPanel, that holds the 16 buttons of the calculator—10 number buttons and 6 function buttons—and a

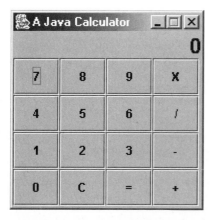

FIGURE 12.31 GUI for a four-function calculator

JLabel that holds the result to be displayed. Looking at the button panel in Figure 12.31, it seems reasonable to use a grid layout manager that will place the buttons into a grid that is four rows by four columns in size. It also seems reasonable to use a border layout for the entire frame, with the JLabel that contains the display going into the NORTH region just above the button panel that we can place into the CENTER region.

The code presented in Figure 12.32 implements the visual aspects of this interface. The actual arithmetic functionality of the calculator, which is implemented in the class CalcLogic, is left as an exercise.

```java
import java.awt.BorderLayout;
import java.awt.Container;
import java.awt.Dimension;
import java.awt.Font;
import java.awt.GridLayout;
import java.awt.event.ActionEvent;
import java.awt.event.ActionListener;
import javax.swing.JButton;
import javax.swing.JFrame;
import javax.swing.JLabel;
import javax.swing.JPanel;

/**
 * A simple four-function calculator.
 */
public class Calculator extends JFrame implements ActionListener {
    // The labels on the buttons
    private static final String labels = "789X456/123-0C=+";

    // The size of a button
    private static final Dimension WINDOW_SIZE = new Dimension( 200, 200 );
```

(continued)

FIGURE 12.32 GUI visualization code for a four-function calculator

```
// The font to use in the display
private static final Font DISPLAY_FONT = new Font( null, Font.BOLD, 20 );

// Number of rows and columns to use when displaying the buttons
private static final int NUM_ROWS = 4;
private static final int NUM_COLS = 4;

// The object that knows how to do the arithmetic
private CalcLogic myCalc;

// The display portion of the GUI
private JLabel display;

/**
 * Create a new calculator.
 */
public Calculator( String name ) {
   super( name );

   Container content = getContentPane();
   JPanel buttonPanel = new JPanel();

   // The object that knows how to process keys. This GUI
   // will simply catch button presses and pass them on to this
   // object that knows what to do with them
   myCalc = new CalcLogic();

   // Configure the frame
   setDefaultCloseOperation( JFrame.EXIT_ON_CLOSE );
   content.setLayout( new BorderLayout() );
   setSize( WINDOW_SIZE );
   setResizable( false );

   // Create the button panel
   buttonPanel.setLayout( new GridLayout( NUM_ROWS, NUM_COLS ) );

   // Create the buttons and place them in the panel
   for ( int i = 0 ; i < labels.length() ; i = i + 1 ) {
      JButton b = new JButton( labels.substring( i, i + 1 ) );
      b.addActionListener( this );
      buttonPanel.add( b );
   }

   // Create the display
   display = new JLabel( "0", JLabel.RIGHT );
   display.setFont( DISPLAY_FONT );
```

FIGURE 12.32 GUI visualization code for a four-function calculator *(continued)*

```java
        // "Assemble" the calculator
        content.add( BorderLayout.NORTH, display );
        content.add( BorderLayout.CENTER, buttonPanel);
    }


    /**
     * Return the current contents of the display portion of the
     * GUI.
     *
     * @return the contents of the display.
     */
    public String getDisplay() {
        return display.getText();
    }


    /**
     * Set the contents of the display.
     *
     * @param text the value to place in the display.
     */
    public void setDisplay( String text ) {
        display.setText( text );
    }


    /**
     * Invoked whenever a user presses a button. The button press
     * is simply passed on to the calculator engine which processes
     * the button and updates the display if required.
     *
     * @param e the event that caused this method to be invoked.
     */
    public void actionPerformed( ActionEvent e ) {
        // Get the name of the button that was pressed
        String s = e.getActionCommand();

        // Let the logic object handle it
        myCalc.handleButton( s, this ) ;
    }


    /**
     * Create and display a calculator.
     */
    public static void main( String args[] ) {
        Calculator calcGUI = new Calculator( "A Java Calculator" );
        calcGUI.setVisible( true );
    }

} // Calculator
```

FIGURE 12.32 GUI visualization code for a four-function calculator *(continued)*

12.6 SUMMARY

This concludes our all-too-brief discussion of the design and implementation of graphical user interfaces. As we have said many times, it is a huge topic, and the material in this chapter has some of the same properties as an iceberg—a great deal is hidden from view to be uncovered at a later time! For example, we did not introduce the capabilities of the `Graphics` class, which allows you to create arbitrary line drawings, polygons, icons, and images as well as do a range of graphical manipulations such as shading, area filling, clipping, and image painting. This information would fill another chapter or, indeed, an entire book. We leave these and the many other interesting capabilities of typical GUI toolkits to both later classes in computer science as well as to your future work in the public or private sector.

However, remember that what is really important to take away from this discussion is not the myriad of details introduced in the preceding pages: What is the event listener type attached to a `JComboBox`? What is the default layout manager for a `JPanel` object? When answers to these types of questions are needed, they can be located in a good reference manual for the toolkit that you are using or found online at http://www.java.sun.com/j2se/1.4/docs/api/. Instead, what is really important are the basic ideas stressed throughout the chapter. You should understand the inheritance hierarchy that is used to organize GUI components; you should feel comfortable creating GUI components and placing them into containers; you should be knowledgeable about the properties of components and how to set them—size, location, color, font, and visibility. You should be able to deal with issues of component layout, and you should understand the concepts of events and listeners and be able to write event-driven programs. If you are comfortable doing all this, then as we said at the very beginning of the chapter, you will be well positioned to deal with whatever "new and improved" GUI package comes down the road.

EXERCISES

1. Describe the differences between the following pairs of GUI objects:

   a. panels and frames

   b. buttons and radio buttons

   c. text fields and text areas

2. The standard Java distribution includes a number of demonstration programs. One of these programs is `SwingSet2`. You can find this program in the `demo/jfe/swingSet2` directory in the directory where Java has been installed on your computer. The `SwingSet2` program displays all of the components that are supported by Swing and provides source code listings that show you how to use the components. Find a copy of the `SwingSet2` program and use it to explore the Swing components that were not discussed in this chapter.

3. Event-driven programming might be new to you, but the idea of handling events is not. Describe three different events that you are capable of handling. Describe the actions that will cause these events to occur.

4. Describe, in words, the process that you would have to go through in Swing to create and lay out the components displayed in the following figure:

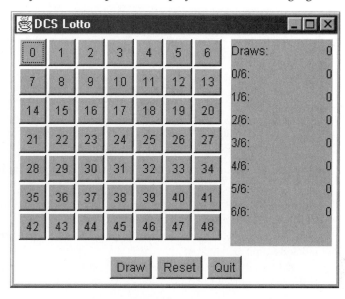

Exercises 5 through 9 all refer to the same GUI. They should be done in sequence.

5. Create and display on the screen a `JFrame` object `f` that is 200 pixels wide × 250 pixels high and labeled " My First Attempt ". Set its background color to blue and its layout manager to flow layout. After you have displayed it on the screen, change the size of `f` to 500 × 500 and its color to red. Try some other size and color values as well. This will give you initial experience with the properties of `Container` objects.

6. Now place a label inside frame `f` that says " This is a Label Object ". Use the `setFont()` and `setLocation()` methods to change both the appearance and the location of this label. This will give you some experience with label components.

7. Now add four buttons, labeled B1, B2, B3, and B4, to frame `f` created in Exercise 6. (You do not have to write event handlers for them just yet.) Notice where the flow layout places these buttons. Now resize the window and observe how the layout manager automatically determines the proper position of these buttons.

8. Now change the layout manager for frame `f` to grid layout. Notice where the buttons are placed within the frame. How does this compare with the flow layout of Exercise 7? What happens to the buttons when the frame is resized?

9. This time change the layout manager for frame `f` to border layout. Place the label from Exercise 6 in the North area, and place the four buttons B1, B2, B3, and B4 into the West, Central, East, and South areas, respectively.

10. Create a GUI with seven buttons located vertically up and down the left side of the frame. These buttons are labeled RED, BLUE, GREEN, PINK, ORANGE, CYAN, and MAGENTA. Initially, the frame has a white background. However,

when any one of these seven buttons is clicked, the background changes to the color specified by the button that was clicked.

11. Create a GUI with three text fields labeled Number 1, Number 2, and Sum, one button labeled Add, and a label field that is entitled My First Adder. The layout of the GUI should be as follows:

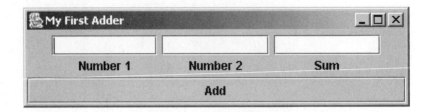

Now add the following functionality to your GUI: Enter an integer into the text field labeled Number 1 and another into the field labeled Number 2. When you click the Add button, the sum of those two values appears in the text field labeled Sum.

Add another button labeled Clear just to the right of the existing Add button. When this button is clicked, it clears all three fields to blanks.

12. Build a GUI that looks like the following:

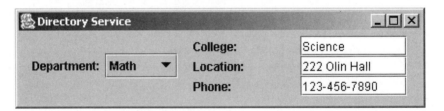

The GUI contains a JComboBox listing all the departments in your school. (You can keep it to a manageable number if your institution has a huge number of departments.) You select any one of them, and information about that department appears in the text fields to the right of the combo box. For this GUI, you should display the name of the college in which the department is located, the building and room number of the department office, and its phone number. This is a simple example of an application called a Directory Service.

13. Build a GUI for totaling a customer's bill in a convenience store. The GUI contains two text areas. The one on the left, labeled ITEM, contains a preset list of all the products sold in the store. The one on the right, labeled BILL, itemizes the cost of each of the items purchased and the total bill. There is also a button labeled Done under the text areas. The clerk first selects the items in the ITEM area that the user has purchased (there may be many). After highlighting every item purchased, click the Done button, and an itemized bill for all the items purchased is displayed in the text area labeled BILL along with a 4 percent sales tax. The GUI looks like the following:

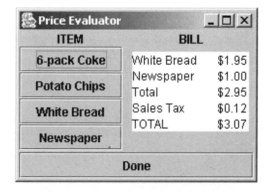

14. Repeat the GUI described in Exercise 10, which changes the background color setting of a frame, but this time have the list of color options be part of a menu. Your menu bar should contain the following two menu items:

    Application   Color

    The application menu has two items, Reset and Quit. The color menu contains a list of the same seven colors in Exercise 10. The frame starts with the background set to a default color (which you determine). When one of the colors in the color menu is selected, the frame's background color is reset to that color. In the application menu, the Reset option resets the frame to its default color. The Quit option terminates the GUI.

15. Write a GUI that tracks the behavior of a mouse. Put three buttons on the screen labeled B1, B2, and B3. Also include three text fields labeled X, Y, and Button. The idea of this GUI is that the X and Y text fields will constantly be displaying the (x, y) coordinates of the cursor. The Button field will either be blank, if the cursor is not inside any one of the three buttons, or it will contain the name of the button, B1, B2, or B3, in which the cursor is currently located. Overall, your mouse tracking GUI should look something like the following:

16. Implement the functionality of the four-function calculator whose visualization was given in Figure 12.31.

17. A student wrote the following program to experiment with the mouse listener interface. The student wanted the program to print the word "Click" whenever the user clicked the mouse anywhere inside the window. The program compiles and runs, but it does not print anything when the mouse is clicked. What is wrong with the program? Correct the program and run it to verify that it now works correctly.

```
import javax.swing.*; import java.awt.event.*;

public class Mouse extends JFrame implements MouseListener {
   public Mouse( String title ) {
      super( title ); setSize( 200, 200 );
   }

   public void mouseClicked( MouseEvent e ) {
      System.out.println( "Click" );
   }

   // Here to satisfy the MouseListener interface
   public void mouseEntered( MouseEvent e ) {}
   public void mouseExited( MouseEvent e ) {}
   public void mousePressed( MouseEvent e ) {}
   public void mouseReleased( MouseEvent e ) {}

   public static void main( String args[] ) {
      Mouse win = new Mouse( "A Cheesy Program" );
      win.show();
   }
}
```

18. Modify the program in Exercise 17 so that it prints the current X and Y coordinate of the mouse.

19. The code following this question creates and displays a simple graphical user interface. Take a few minutes to look over the code and then answer the following questions.

    a. Sketch what the GUI will look like when it is displayed by the computer.

    b. What happens to the GUI when the user presses the JButton labeled Grumpy?

    c. What happens to the GUI when the user presses the JButton labeled Mouse?

    d. How would the appearance of the GUI change if a flow layout was used instead of a grid layout in the JPanel panel2?

```
import javax.swing.*;
import java.awt.*;
import java.awt.event.*;

public class Grumpy extends JFrame implements ActionListener {
   private static final String
       BUTTONS[] = { "Buster", "Grumpy", "Mouse" };

   private static final String
       LABELS[] = { "Woof", "Meow", "Feed me" };

   private JLabel theLabels[] = new JLabel[ BUTTONS.length ];
```

```java
        private int lastButton = 0;

        public Grumpy( String title ) {
            super( title );

            JPanel panel1 = new JPanel();
            JPanel panel2 = new JPanel();
            Container contentPane = getContentPane();
            JButton button = null;

            panel1.setLayout( new FlowLayout() );
            panel2.setLayout( new GridLayout( BUTTONS.length, 0 ) );

            for ( int i = 0; i < BUTTONS.length; i++ ) {
                button = new JButton( BUTTONS[ i ] );
                button.addActionListener( this );
                theLabels[ i ] = new JLabel( LABELS[ i ] );
                theLabels[ i ].setForeground( Color.BLACK );
                panel1.add( theLabels[ i ] );
                panel2.add( button );
            }

            contentPane.setLayout( new BorderLayout() );
            contentPane.add( BorderLayout.CENTER, panel2 );
            contentPane.add( BorderLayout.SOUTH, panel1 );

            setSize( 150, 250 );
        }

        public void actionPerformed( ActionEvent e ) {
            int pressed = -1;

            for ( int i = 0; pressed == -1; i++ ) {
                if ( BUTTONS[ i ].equals( e.getActionCommand() ) ) {
                    pressed = i;
                }
            }

            theLabels[ lastButton ].setForeground( Color.BLACK );
            theLabels[ pressed ].setForeground( Color.RED );
            lastButton = pressed;
        }

        public static void main( String args[] ) {
            Grumpy win = new Grumpy( "Cats Rule" );
            win.show();
        }
} // Grumpy
```

20. The GUI shown in Exercise 4 is the interface for a simple lottery program. You play the game by selecting six lucky numbers. The computer then draws six numbers at random. If the computer selects the same six numbers that you selected, you win. The interface of Exercise 4 allows you to select a number by clicking the numbered button that contains the number you want. When you select a number, the button turns blue. You can unselect a number by clicking it a second time. Once you have your numbers selected, click the Draw button. The computer will select six numbers at random and display them on the board. If you and the computer selected the same number, the corresponding numbered button will turn yellow. Any numbers the computer selected that you did not will turn green. You can click the Draw button as many times as you wish. The game maintains statistics that let you see how well you are doing. Write a Java program that implements this game.

CHAPTER 13

Networking

13.1 INTRODUCTION

Looking over the technological innovations of the past century, one could reasonably argue that the development of computer networks was one of the most significant and important advances. A short 30 years ago, when networks first appeared, only a few, highly technical, users had access to this new technology. Today, networks are a common sight in schools, government buildings, and libraries. Even many private homes are beginning to install their own local area computer networks connected via high-speed links to the Internet. If you look at the advertising on television and radio, or even the placards on the sides of buses, you will see evidence of how much networking has become a part of the mainstream world.

The idea of a computer network was first conceived in 1962 when J. C. R. Licklider of MIT proposed a "Galactic Network" in which he envisioned a globally interconnected set of computers.[1] Leonard Kleinrock, also at MIT, developed the theory of **packet switching** that forms the technical basis for all modern computer networks. In a packet-switched network, messages are broken up into pieces called **packets**. The individual packets are then sent separately to their destination where the original message is reassembled. The primary advantages of a packet-switched network are that multiple users can share a common communications channel, and if one part of a message is lost or damaged during transmission, only that part of the message needs to be resent, not the entire message.

Near the end of the 1960s, the U.S. Defense Advanced Research Projects Agency (DARPA) initiated a research program to develop the technologies required to interconnect packet-switched networks. The U.S. Department of Defense was interested in building a communication system that would be able to withstand a nuclear attack. Unlike the telephone network, which is unable to function if one of its switching centers is damaged, a packet-switched network can automatically route packets around damaged nodes, allowing communication to continue. The ARPANET, developed as a result of DARPA funding, was brought online in 1969 and connected computers at four major organizations (UCLA, Stanford Research Institute, UCSB, and the University of Utah). The very first packets on the ARPANET were sent from UCLA to Stanford on October 29, 1969. (Rumor has it that the system crashed after the first three letters of the message were sent.) In addition to developing the hardware, work was also being done on creating the protocols that would allow computers to communicate across linked packet-switched networks. The protocols that were developed over the course of this research effort became known as the **TCP/IP protocol** suite, named after the two most important protocols that were developed.

There was nothing friendly or easy about the early Internet. The network was designed for and used by computer engineers, physicists, and librarians. There was very little in the way of documentation or support. By 1973, the only network applications available were email, Telnet, and FTP. Email provided a way for users to send messages to each other electronically, Telnet allowed users to log on to a remote computer on a network and use it as if it were local, and FTP (for File Transfer Protocol) provided a mechanism to transfer files between computers. During this time frame, the ARPANET

[1]Much of the information in the following pages is taken from the 1997 article "A Brief History of the Internet," B. Leinter et al., www.isoc.org/internet-history/.

had grown to 23 hosts connecting universities and government research centers around the country. Since the primary funding for this work was coming from the military, only government installations or groups doing research for the Department of Defense were allowed to connect to the ARPANET.

Due to the restricted nature of the ARPANET, other networking projects were started in order to provide a way for nonmilitary organizations to connect their computers to a network. In 1980, the BITNET and CSNET networks were started. BITNET (Because It's Time Network) provided mail services to IBM mainframes. CSNET (Computer Science Network) was initially funded by the National Science Foundation (NSF) to provide networking services to university, industry, and government computer science research groups. These were just two of the dozen or so packet networks that were designed and built during the early 1980s. Most of these networks were very specialized and intended for a restricted group of people. There was little effort to standardize the protocols used and little motivation to interconnect these separate networks.

In 1986, the National Science Foundation announced a program to develop a national communication infrastructure that would interconnect packet-switched networks to support the needs of the general academic and research community. NSF decided to use the same networking technology developed by DARPA. This meant that the new network would use the organizational infrastructure already in place in the ARPANET, and its primary protocols would be TCP/IP. The result was a major new communication service called the NSFnet, which served as the primary conduit for all network traffic. The NSFnet, shown in Figure 13.1, provided a cross-country 56-Kbps network that composed the core of the Internet. NSF encouraged regional networks to connect to NSFnet and expand their services to commercial, nonacademic customers. NSF maintained their sponsorship of NSFnet for nearly 10 years, establishing rules for noncommercial, government, and research use. By 1988, a 1.5-Mbps network had been established that connected the six original NSF supercomputer centers plus seven additional research sites. The NSFnet now connected 217 networks, and network traffic began to double approximately every 7 months.

During the mid 1980s, inexpensive minicomputers and personal computers became widely available. This combination of inexpensive desktop machines and powerful network servers fueled the rapid growth of the Internet. Many companies were now able to purchase and maintain their own computing systems and were interested in connecting them to the Internet. One problem that many companies faced during this period was the fact that since funding came primarily from the government, the use of the Internet was limited to research, education, and government applications. Commercial use of the Internet was prohibited unless it served the goals of education and research.

In 1990, the ARPANET was officially dissolved, and the responsibility for the Internet passed to the NSFnet. The network continued to spread among research and academic institutions throughout the United States, including connections to networks in Canada and Europe. As the network grew, so did the pressure to allow commercial use. In March 1991, the NSFnet modified its acceptable use policy to allow commercial use. With the introduction of commercial traffic, the growth of the NSFnet over the next 2 years was explosive. By 1994, the traffic on the network broke the 10-trillion bytes a month level. At its peak, the NSFnet connected more than 4,000 institutions

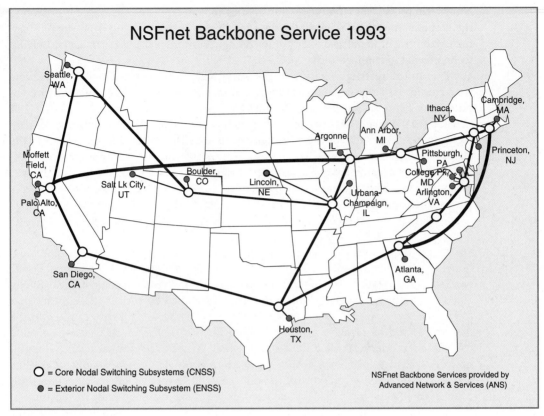

FIGURE 13.1 NSFnet
Source: Copyright Merit Network, Inc.

and 50,000 networks across the United States, Canada, and Europe. On April 30, 1995, NSFnet was officially dissolved, and administration of the Internet was turned over to the private sector. Since that time, the Internet has grown from a secretive cold war technology to a user-oriented technology that has profoundly changed the world in which we live.

The phrase "the network is the computer" epitomizes the importance of networking technology. Networks are one of the least visible and least apparent parts of a modern computing system, and yet they provide an indispensable resource. Networks are the conduits used for sharing and communicating data. Almost every computer program in use today uses a network in some way. For example, the word processor that I am using to write this text has a feature that allows me to access a collection of clip art that resides on remote machines attached to the Internet. Collaborative games, productivity tools, and Web browsers are all examples of programs that rely on a network to function properly. Organizations of all sizes are dependent on enterprise software that consists of distributed servers and databases. Knowledge of networking and the ability to develop software that effectively utilizes networks have become basic skills that every programmer must have.

In the programming languages of the 1960s, 1970s, and 1980s, there was usually no direct support for networking. Instead, programmers had to rely on the services of the underlying operating system. This made network programming complex and hard to implement. Java, developed in the mid-1990s, appeared at a time when it was becoming obvious how important networking would be to software development. From the very beginning, Java included library support for networking and data communications, and it did so in a way that was simple and easy to understand.

The goal of this chapter is to introduce you to the basics of networking, explain the protocols that make network communication possible, and show how to use the classes in the `java.net` package to develop programs that communicate across a network. This chapter will only scratch the surface of the huge topic of computer networking. However, after reading this chapter, you will be able to develop Java programs that can fully and effectively utilize a TCP/IP network.

13.2 NETWORKING WITH TCP/IP

◆ 13.2.1 Protocols

Probably the best place to start a discussion about computer networking is to ask the question: What is a network? If you look up the term *network* in a technical dictionary, you are likely to find a definition similar to the following:

> *A computer network is a set of computers using common protocols to communicate over connecting transmission media.*

Although most of the words in this definition will make sense to you, it still does not intuitively explain what a computer network really is. Some parts of this definition are relatively easy to understand. For example, the phrase "set of computers" clearly implies that there will be more than one computer in a network. The phrase "connecting transmission media" indicates that these machines will be connected in some way via wires, fiber optic cables, or radio waves, and they will have the ability to exchange messages across this media. The phrase "common protocols" may need a little more explanation.

Again, if we turn to a technical dictionary and look up the term *protocol,* we are likely to find a definition similar to the following:

> *A protocol is a formal description of message formats and the rules two or more machines follow to exchange messages.*

Consider, for example, what you do to call a friend on the telephone. You pick up the receiver and listen for a dial tone. After hearing the dial tone, you enter your friend's number into the telephone. If you hear a busy signal, you know that you cannot establish a connection and hang up. If you hear a ringing tone, you wait until someone picks up the phone on the other end and says "Hello." This sequence of events is nothing more than the "telephone protocol" used in the United States to make a phone call. It is essential that the entities on both sides of the connection understand and use the same protocol. That is what allows communication to proceed in an orderly way. For example, what would happen in our telephone protocol if the receiver did not know he or she was supposed to say "Hello" and instead just picked up the receiver but said nothing. The caller may become confused and hang up.

A protocol in a computer network functions in the same way. It defines the messages that can be sent, the possible replies to these messages, and the actions that should be taken upon receipt of a particular message. The only real difference between a computer and a human protocol is that the computer protocol will be much more detailed. The computer protocol has to cover every possible sequence of messages, and it must define what actions to take in each one of those situations. For example, the sequence of messages exchanged between two computers when sending electronic mail using the Simple Mail Transport Protocol (SMTP) is shown in Figure 13.2.

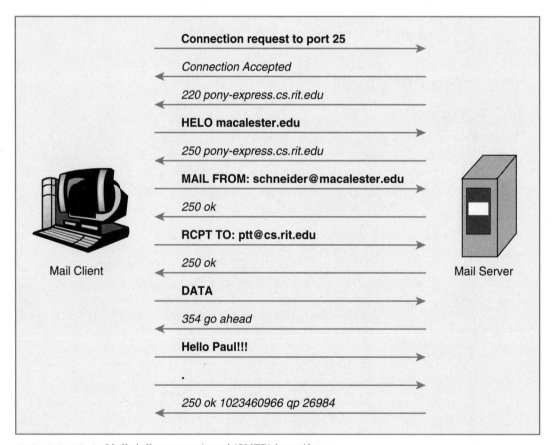

FIGURE 13.2 Mail delivery protocol (SMTP) in action

Returning to the definition of computer network, the phrase "uses common protocols" basically means that the set consisting of the sending and receiving computers is speaking the same language and following the same set of procedures. A computer network thus consists of a set of computers that are connected together and use a common language to exchange data.

In the world of computer networks, standardization is extremely important. Without standardization, it would be impossible to build a network that allowed different types of computers, made by different manufacturers, to communicate and exchange information. All official standards in the Internet community are published as a Request for Comments document, commonly referred to by the acronym RFC. Every RFC is assigned a unique number and serves as a standard for a particular aspect of Internet computing. An RFC contains the detailed technical information required by a programmer either to use, or to write, a network protocol. We will be including references to the appropriate RFCs so you can obtain detailed information about the protocols that will be discussed in this chapter. RFCs are available via electronic mail, FTP, or the Web. One of the best sites to obtain RFCs is www.rfc-editor.org.

◆ **13.2.2** The OSI Model

To help manage the complexity of a computer network, models have been developed that describe the functions the software must perform. The best-known model is the International Organization for Standardization (ISO) Open Systems Interconnection (OSI) reference model, which is shown in Figure 13.3.

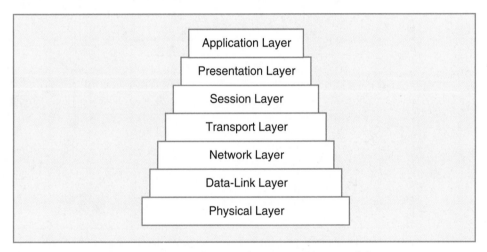

FIGURE 13.3 The ISO Open Systems Interconnection model

The OSI model consists of seven layers. Each one of the layers performs a specific, well-defined function within the network. The bottom layer of the OSI model is the physical layer. The **physical layer** provides a raw, unreliable channel across which data in the form of binary digits, or bits, can be sent from one machine to another. You can think of the physical layer as a bit pipe and the bits that it carries as Ping-Pong balls. The sending machine drops a Ping-Pong ball into the pipe, and it rolls down the pipe until it comes out the other end. Since this is an unreliable channel, there are times when you drop a ball into the pipe, but it disappears and never comes out.

The next layer in the OSI model is the data-link layer. The **data-link layer** provides a reliable point-to-point service. It uses the physical layer to transmit data from one machine to another. The data-link layer adds information to the message so that it can detect if information is lost during transmission and then retransmit it if necessary. Like the physical layer, you can think of the data-link layer as a pipe, but this time you are guaranteed that every Ping-Pong ball dropped into the pipe comes out correctly at the other end and in exactly the same order in which they were inserted. An important aspect of the data-link layer is that the connection is point to point, which means that it only guarantees the delivery of data between two machines directly connected by a physical link.

The **network layer** is on top of the data-link layer and provides end-to-end delivery within the network. In other words, the network layer makes it possible for two machines that are not directly connected to exchange data. The network layer will determine how to route a message through the network so that it arrives at its intended destination. Given the network depicted in Figure 13.4, it is the network layer that is responsible for delivering messages from machine A to machine D and for deciding if the message should be sent along the route A→B→D or the route A→C→D. The network layer uses the services of the data-link layer to transmit the message from one machine to another until it has arrived at its destination.

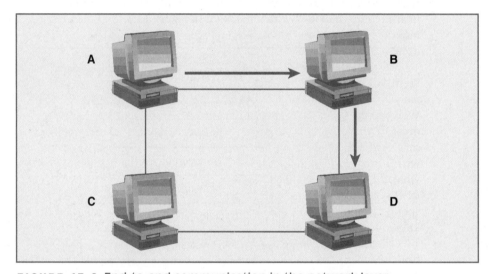

FIGURE 13.4 End-to-end communication in the network layer

The network layer, like the physical layer, does not guarantee that the data will be delivered correctly. Even though the network layer uses the reliable services that the data-link layer provides, it is possible that as the data pass through a machine they might be lost. You can think of the services provided by the network layer as analogous to the services provided by the physical layer. Both layers provide an unreliable delivery service. The difference is that the network layer deals with the issues of delivering messages between machines that may not be directly connected to each other, whereas the physical layer delivers bits between machines that are directly connected. The network layer deals with end-to-end delivery, whereas the physical and data-link layers deal with point-to-point delivery. The network layer also deals with the issue of addressing and includes a mechanism to identify the final destination of a message.

The **Internet Protocol** (IP) implements the services of the network layer within the Internet. IP is truly the workhorse of the Internet. Almost every message sent within the Internet is handled by IP. IP provides an unreliable, connectionless, datagram-based delivery service. This means that any message sent using IP must be broken down into units called **datagrams**. When a datagram is sent across the network, IP will make every effort to deliver the datagram, but there is no guarantee that it will be delivered correctly. Every datagram is treated separately, so there is no notion of ordering associated with the datagrams that are sent. Thus, datagrams sent to a common destination may not arrive in the same order in which they were sent. RFC791 is the official specification of the Internet Protocol.

Although routing is an important IP function, you do not need to understand how IP routes datagrams to write a Java program that uses a network. You can think of the network layer as a black box into which you put your messages, and most of the time, the messages magically appear at their intended destination.

Every machine on the Internet is assigned a unique IP address. An IP address is 32-bits long[2] and is organized in a way that simplifies the routing process. Normally, IP addresses are written in dotted decimal notation. An address written in dotted decimal notation consists of four decimal numbers separated by a period. Each of the numbers in the address represents 1 of the 4 bytes in the IP address. An example of a dotted decimal address is 129.21.38.169.

IP identifies machines using 32-bit addresses. However, human beings prefer to identify computers using symbolic names. For example, if I were to ask you the name of the machine in the Computer Science Department at RIT that is running its Web server, you would probably reply with www.cs.rit.edu instead of the IP address of that machine, 129.21.30.99. The Domain Name System (DNS), one of the services within the Internet, provides the ability to look up the IP address associated with a particular symbolic name. DNS does for computer names and IP addresses what the telephone book does for people's names and their telephone numbers. A DNS server accepts queries from clients that contain a machine name, and it responds by sending the IP address associated with the name, assuming the name is known to DNS.

The next layer in the OSI model of Figure 13.3 is the transport layer. The primary function of the **transport layer** is to deliver data received from the network layer to its ultimate destination. A typical computing system will be running several applications that are using the network to communicate. The network layer knows how to get a message from one machine to another; what it does not know is how to get the message to the specific application on that machine. Delivering the message to its final destination is one of the main jobs of the transport layer.

You can think of the transport layer as performing a function similar to that of a mailroom in a large organization. For example, when the post office receives a letter addressed to

Ms. Cathy Vandelay
Computer Science Department
Rochester Institute of Technology
102 Lomb Memorial Drive
Rochester, New York 14623-5680

---

[2]The new version of IP, IPv6, has addresses that are 128-bits long. This provides an addressing space large enough to assign 10^{24} addresses to every square meter of the earth's surface.

it does not deliver the letter directly to Ms. Vandelay; instead, the letter is delivered to the central mail handling facility at the Rochester Institute of Technology (RIT). The staff within the mail facility will sort all of the letters sent to RIT and deliver the letter to the intended recipient, in this case Cathy Vandelay. In a computer network, the network layer performs the function of the post office in that it delivers a message to the destination machine. The transport layer performs the function of the central mail facility, which sorts all the messages arriving at this computer and delivers each message to its intended application.

The transport layer usually provides two different types of service: connection-oriented and connectionless. A **connection-oriented transport protocol** provides a reliable, end-to-end, stream-based transfer of data. This means that when you send data, you are guaranteed that the data will be correctly delivered to the machine on the other end of the connection. Furthermore, you are guaranteed that the information will be received in the exact same order that it was sent. With a connection-oriented transfer, a connection must be established before data can be sent, and once the data transfer has been completed, the connection must be terminated.

A **connectionless transport protocol**, as the name implies, does not require a connection to be established before communication can begin. A connectionless protocol provides an unreliable datagram-based transfer. This means that there is no guarantee that the data that are sent will ever be delivered and no guarantee about the order in which the datagrams are received.

The services provided by connection-oriented and connectionless transport protocols are very similar to the types of services offered by the telephone system and the post office, respectively. The telephone system provides a connection-oriented transfer service for words. Before you can start transmitting a stream of words to someone using a telephone, you must establish a connection by dialing the number of the person to whom you wish to speak. Once the connection has been established, you speak your words into the phone, and these words are delivered to the person on the other end of the connection in the same order that you speak them. When you are finished, you terminate the connection by hanging up.

The post office, on the other hand, provides a connectionless transfer service for letters. To send a letter to someone, you place that letter into an envelope (a datagram) and put the address of the recipient and the correct amount of postage on the envelope. You then drop the letter into a mailbox for delivery. About 99.9 percent of the time, the letter is successfully delivered. However, there is a small chance that your letter will be damaged or lost. The post office makes no guarantee about the order in which letters will be delivered. Furthermore, if I mail 10 letters all with the same address, it would be foolish to believe that they will be delivered to the recipient in the exact order that they were sent. Even if I mail only one letter per week, there is still no absolute guarantee that they will arrive in order.

Within the Internet, the **Transmission Control Protocol** (TCP) and the **User Datagram Protocol** (UDP) are the two primary protocols used within the transport layer. TCP is a connection-oriented protocol, and it provides a reliable stream-oriented delivery service. UDP, on the other hand, provides an unreliable datagram-based delivery service. The official specification for TCP is in RFC793, and UDP is described in RFC768.

Both TCP and UDP use the concept of a **port** to identify the ultimate destination of a message (like "Ms. Cathy Vandelay" in our earlier example). You can think of a port as being similar to the apartment number in an address. The apartment is identified by the single address of the building that houses all of the apartments (e.g., 123 North Main Street). This would be like the single IP address of a machine running a number of applications. The apartment number (e.g., Apartment 3c) identifies the specific apartment in the building to which the mail will be delivered. This would be like the TCP port number identifying the specific application to which that data should be delivered. Any application that uses either TCP or UDP must first obtain a port assignment from the operating system before it can communicate on the network. A TCP or UDP port is nothing more than an unsigned 16-bit integer.

To send a message to an application program using either TCP or UDP, you must know both the IP address of the machine on which the application is running and the port number that has been assigned to that application. When a client application, such as a Web browser, requires a port number, it really does not matter what number it is assigned. The only important thing is that it is not currently being used by another application on this machine. A server is a different story. If a server is assigned a random port number, how does a client that wants to communicate with the server learn what port number has been assigned? This is not unlike trying to call someone you just met using a telephone. How do you obtain the phone number?

One of the most common techniques to assign port numbers to services is to use **well-known ports**. The idea is a simple one: A list of port numbers used by important services on the Internet has been compiled and published in RFC1700. When a client wishes to communicate with a specific service on a remote machine, it looks up the well-known port for that service and sends the message to the specified port. Table 13.1 lists a few of the well-known ports defined in RFC1700.

For example, let's say we start up a Web browser and wish to view the home page for the Computer Science Department at Macalester College. Our Web browser would be assigned a random port number by the operating system. It would then attempt to establish a connection to the machine www.cs.macalester.edu on port 80, the well-known port for a Web server as shown in Table 13.1. On most computing systems, the port numbers between 0 and 4,096 are reserved for system services, and it is impossible for a user process to request a port in that range.

TABLE 13.1 Examples of Well-Known Ports

Port	Service	Description
7	Echo	Echos back whatever message is sent.
13	Daytime	Returns a string that gives the current time on the remote machine.
19	Chargen	Upon connection, the remote host sends back a stream of random characters until the connection is closed.
20	ftp-data	Used by the FTP service to transfer data.
21	ftp-control	The port that an FTP client connects to initiate a file transfer.
23	Telnet	The port where the Telnet server listens for remote terminal connections.
25	SMTP	The port where the mail delivery agents listen for incoming mail.
80	WWW	The port where a Web server will listen for HTTP requests.

The next two layers in the OSI model are the session and presentation layers. The **session layer** provides enhanced services that are useful in some applications. The **presentation layer** deals with the way in which data are presented to the network. This layer might be responsible for converting data to a network standard form before they are transmitted or for encrypting the data before they are placed on the network. However, these two layers are not implemented in any of the Internet protocols. An application that requires session or presentation services must implement these services itself.

The application layer is the final layer in the OSI model. The **application layer** provides the interface that applications use to access the network. For example, the classes within the `java.net` package provide the API that we will use to access the network.

Although the ISO/OSI reference model is commonly used to describe the various software layers that constitute a network, very few networks actually implement the model exactly as shown in Figure 13.3. For example, most software used to implement the Internet protocols is organized into four layers instead of seven. Figure 13.5 illustrates how the seven layers in the OSI model map to the four layers in the Internet model. It also shows the major protocols used in each of the layers in the Internet model. When developing software in Java, our primary concern will be the transport layer and TCP and UDP. The next section discusses the classes provided by Java that can be used to access the resources available on a network.

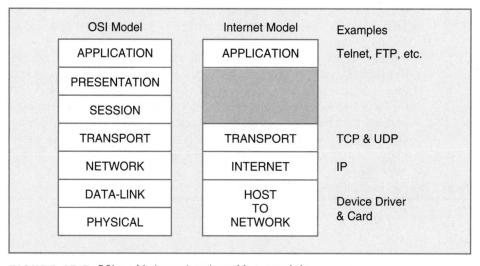

FIGURE 13.5 OSI and Internet networking models

13.3 NETWORK COMMUNICATION IN JAVA

The classes in the `java.net` package provide a variety of networking services that can be utilized in a Java program. These classes can be divided into roughly three categories. The first category, which we will refer to as the **socket classes**, provide access to the transport layer of the network and are listed in Table 13.2. These classes pro-

TABLE 13.2 Socket-Level Classes in `java.net`

Class	Description
DatagramPacket	Represents a datagram, the unit of transfer used by UDP.
DatagramSocket	Represents a socket for UDP (i.e., unreliable connectionless transport).
InetAddress	Represents an IP address. Provides the capability to look up an IP address for a given host name.
ServerSocket	Represents a socket for TCP (i.e., reliable stream-oriented delivery). Usually used by a server since it provides the ability to listen for incoming requests (i.e., perform a passive open).
Socket	Represents a socket for TCP (i.e., reliable stream-oriented delivery). A connection is established when a socket is created.

vide direct access to the fundamental building blocks of communication in the Internet, such as datagrams and TCP and UDP. The design of these classes is based in part on a package called Berkeley Sockets, which is a networking API introduced in the Berkeley UNIX Software Distribution from the early 1980s. In the socket API, network communication is modeled as taking place between two endpoints called **sockets**. An application plugs into the network using a socket in the same way that a toaster plugs into an electrical socket to obtain electrical power.

The second category, the **URL classes**, consists of classes that participate in HTTP and can be used to communicate directly with a Web server. The URL classes are listed in Table 13.3.

The URL classes provide higher level access to network services. These classes utilize both the socket classes and their knowledge of specific protocols (e.g., HTTP) to allow a program to deal with the content of a Web server. For example, using these classes, it is possible to transfer an entire Web page. Although you could perform the same function using the lower level socket classes, you would have to write the code

TABLE 13.3 URL Classes in `java.net`

Class	Description
HttpURLConnection	A subclass of URLConnection that implements HTTP.
JarURLConnection	A subclass of URLConnection that is capable of downloading and extracting information from a Java Archive (JAR) file.
URL	Represents a Uniform Resource Locator (URL).
URLClassLoader	A class that can load classes and resources from a list of URLs.
URLConnection	An abstract class that represents a connection between an application and a Web server. The openConnection() method of this class returns a subclass that implements the protocol specified in the URL.

to implement the protocols that accomplish the transfer. The URL classes simplify the process of writing programs that utilize the Web.

The third category of classes in `java.net` consists of a variety of utility classes and classes that implement basic security mechanisms utilized in the Internet. While these classes are important, we will not discuss them in this chapter. Instead, we focus our discussion on the socket and URL classes. The next section discusses the socket classes and illustrates how they can be used to write programs that utilize TCP and UDP.

13.4 THE SOCKET CLASSES

◆ 13.4.1 Representing Addresses in Java

The `InetAddress` class in the `java.net` package creates an object that represents an IP address, and it provides the ability to convert symbolic machine names to numerical IP addresses. An instance of the `InetAddress` class consists of an IP address and possibly the symbolic name corresponding to that address.

The `InetAddress` class does not have a public constructor. Instances of an `InetAddress` object are obtained using one of the static class methods listed in Table 13.4. All of these methods will throw an `UnknownHostException` if the parameters do not specify a valid address. The `getLocalHost()` and `getByName()` methods are the most common ways to obtain instances of this class.

TABLE 13.4 Methods to Create `InetAddress` Objects

Signature	Description
`InetAddress[] getAllByName(String host);`	Creates `InetAddress` objects for the known IP addresses for the given name.
`InetAddress getByAddress(byte[] addr);`	Creates an `InetAddress` given an IP address.
`InetAddress getByAddress(String host, byte[] addr);`	Creates an `InetAddress` for the given name and IP address. No check will be made to determine if the name and address are valid.
`InetAddress getByName( String host )`	Creates an `InetAddress` for the given host.
`InetAddress getLocalHost();`	Creates an `InetAddress` for the local host.
`String toString();`	Returns a string representation of this address. Includes the IP address in dotted decimal notation and the symbolic name associated with the address.

Using the `InetAddress` class to obtain IP addressing information is very easy to do. The program in Figure 13.6 uses the `getLocalHost()` method to obtain the IP address for the machine on which the program is run. The `InetAddress` class overrides the `toString()` method to print the name associated with the address along with the IP address in dotted decimal notation. Note the use of the `try` block to handle the situation where an IP address could not be found for the local host. This might happen, for example, if TCP/IP have not been configured on the local host.

```java
import java.net.InetAddress;
import java.net.UnknownHostException;

/**
 * Print out the IP address of the local host using the
 * getLocalHost() method from the InetAddress class.
 */

public class HostInfo {

    public static void main( String args[] ) {

        // Must be executed in a try block since getLocalHost()
        // might throw an UnknownHostException

        try {

          // Attempt to print the local address

          System.out.println( "Local address: " + InetAddress.getLocalHost() );
        }
        catch ( UnknownHostException e ) {

            // Will be thrown if the local address cannot be
            // determined. This might happen for example if
            // the machine has not been assigned an IP address

            System.out.println( "Local address unknown" );
        }

    }

} // HostInfo
```

FIGURE 13.6 Determining the IP address of the local host

The program in Figure 13.7 is a slight modification of the program in Figure 13.6. The revised version of the program prints the IP addressing information for any symbolic machine name that is specified on the command line. The program uses the `getByName()` method to do the name resolution. The `getByName()` method uses the

Domain Name Service of the Internet, discussed in the previous section, to convert symbolic names to numerical IP addresses. Again note the use of the `try` block to handle exceptions caused by machine names that cannot be resolved.

Now that we know how to represent the address of a machine, we will look at the `Socket` and `ServerSocket` classes that provide reliable stream-oriented delivery using TCP.

```java
import java.net.InetAddress;
import java.net.UnknownHostException;

/**
 * Print out the IP address for each machine name on the
 * command line.
 */

public class Resolver {

   public static void main( String args[] ) {

      // Iterate over the command line arguments

      for ( int i = 0; i < args.length; i++ ) {

         // Must be executed in a try block since getByName()
         // might throw an UnknownHostException

         try {

            System.out.print( args[ i ] + ": " );

            // Attempt to print the IP address of the
            // current host

            System.out.println( InetAddress.getByName( args[ i ] ) );
         }
         catch ( UnknownHostException e ) {

            // Will be thrown if the current machine name
            // is not known

            System.out.println( "Unknown host" );
         }

      }

   }

} // Resolver
```

FIGURE 13.7 Determining the address of an arbitrary host

◆ **13.4.2** Reliable Communication

The `Socket` and `ServerSocket` classes provide reliable stream-oriented delivery using TCP. The first step in a TCP communication is to establish a connection between the two machines that wish to exchange messages. When establishing a connection, one machine actively establishes the connection (i.e., places the phone call), whereas the other machine takes a passive role and waits for a connection request (i.e., answers the phone). The term **client** denotes the machine that actively opens the connection, while the term **server** denotes the machine that takes the passive role. The steps taken by the client and server to establish a connection are illustrated in Figure 13.8.

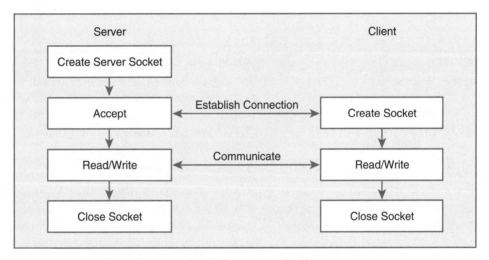

FIGURE 13.8 Connection-oriented communication

The words to describe the events that must take place to establish a connection between machines may sound foreign to you, but the process should be familiar. Consider the events that take place when you decide to call a friend on the telephone. Your friend must be near the phone and willing to answer it; otherwise, there is no sense in placing the call! You pick up the phone and dial your friend's number, taking an active role in establishing the connection. When your friend hears the phone ring, he or she answers the phone, says "Hello," and the connection is established. You took the active role in establishing the connection, whereas your friend took a more passive role. You were playing the role of a client, and your friend was playing the role of a server.

In Java, a server uses an instance of the `ServerSocket` class to obtain a port number to which clients can connect. There are two parameters that can be passed to the constructor of a `ServerSocket`. The first is the port number to which the server wishes to connect this socket. Normally, a server will specify the number of its well-known port when creating a `ServerSocket`. However, if this parameter is set to 0, the socket will be connected to any available port number on the system. The second parameter sets the size of the queue that holds pending connection requests to a `ServerSocket`. When a `ServerSocket` receives a connection request, it is placed in this queue. When the server indicates that it is willing to accept connections, the requests in the server queue are processed one at a time on a first-come, first-served basis. If the ServerSocket receives a connection request, and the queue is full, the connection will be refused.

A server indicates its willingness to accept a connection request by invoking the accept() method on a ServerSocket. The accept() method checks the pending request queue for a connection request. If there is a request in the queue, the request at the front of the queue is removed, the connection is established, and accept() returns a reference to a Socket that can be used to communicate with the client on the other end of the connection. If there are no pending connection requests in the queue, accept() will wait indefinitely until one arrives. It is possible to set a timeout that limits the length of time the accept() method will wait for a connection request.

Some of the methods provided by the ServerSocket class are listed in Table 13.5.

TABLE 13.5 ServerSocket methods

Method	Description
Socket **accept**();	Waits for a connection to be established. Returns a socket that can be used to communicate with the client.
void **close**();	Terminates the connection and releases all system resources associated with the socket.
InetAddress **getInetAddress**();	Returns the IP address that the socket is bound to.
int **getLocalPort**();	Returns the port on which the socket is accepting connections.
void **setSoTimeout**(int timeout);	Determines the length of time in milliseconds that the accept() method will wait for a connection request.
String **toString**();	Returns a string representation of the socket.

A client establishes a connection with a server using an instance of the Socket class. When the client creates a Socket, it specifies the host and port number that identify the server that it wishes to connect to. The constructor for the Socket class will use this information to contact the server and take the necessary steps to establish a connection. Once the Socket has been created, it can be used to communicate with the server.

A step that is often overlooked when developing network programs is closing the connection when it is no longer needed. It is important to terminate a connection, whether it is active or not, because a connection utilizes resources within the operating system. If connections are not closed, the networking resources of a computing system will slowly be consumed until a point is reached where the system is no longer usable and may have to be restarted. Invoking the close() method on the Socket being used for communication is all that is needed to close the connection. Note that, for the connection to be completely closed, both sides of the connection, client and server, must each close their own socket.

Once a connection has been established, instances of the Socket class serve as the endpoints of the connection. Since TCP provides reliable stream-oriented transport, standard Java streams are used to read information from and write information to the network using a `Socket`. After a `Socket` has been created, a programs uses the `getInputStream()` and `getOutputStream()` methods of the `Socket` class to obtain references to the streams associated with the connection. The next step is to wrap the appropriate streams around the socket. Once that is done, you can read and write to a `Socket` in the same way that you read or write to a file. Some of the methods provided by the `Socket` class are listed in Table 13.6.

TABLE 13.6 `Socket` Methods

Method	Description
void **close**();	Terminates the connection and releases all system resources associated with the socket.
InetAddress **getInetAddress**();	Returns the IP address of the host that the socket is connected to.
InputStream **getInputStream**();	Returns an InputStream that can be used to send data across the network.
InetAddress **getLocalAddress**();	Returns the IP address that the socket is bound to.
int **getLocalPort**();	Returns the port assigned to the socket.
OutputStream **getOutputStream**();	Returns an `OutputStream` that can be used to read data from the network.
int **getPort**();	Returns the port on the remote machine that this socket is connected to.
String **toString**();	Returns a string representation of the connection the socket is associated with. The string includes the names, IP addresses, and ports used by both hosts.

To illustrate how to use the `Socket` and `ServerSocket` classes, we will write Java programs that implement the TCP day/time service. This service provides a way for a client to obtain the current date and time on a remote host (the time returned is the local time as recorded by the host, not universal time). The protocol for this service is very straightforward. Table 13.1 specifies that a day/time server accept connections on TCP port 13 for connections from a client. When a connection is established, the server sends a string to the client that contains the current date and time as recorded on the server. After sending the string, the server closes the connection.

A client program that wished to use the day/time service would create a `Socket` to establish a TCP connection to port 13 on the host running the day/time server. Once the `Socket` is created, the client wraps a character-based reader around the `InputStream` associated with the `Socket`. The reader is used exactly as described in Chapter 11 to read the string sent by the server from the stream and print the result. The Java program in Figure 13.9 implements a day/time client.

```java
import java.io.BufferedReader;
import java.io.InputStreamReader;
import java.io.IOException;

import java.net.Socket;
import java.net.UnknownHostException;

/**
 * A simple client that will query the day/time service on a
 * remote computer to determine the date and time at that location.
 */


public class DayTimeClient {

    public static final int DAYTIME_PORT = 13; // Port day/time service

    public static void main( String args[] ) {

        if ( args.length != 1 ) {
            System.err.println( "Usage: java DayTimeClient host" );
        }
        else {
            try {
                // Attempt to connect to the specified host

                Socket sock = new Socket( args[ 0 ], DAYTIME_PORT );

                // Wrap a stream around the socket so we can read the
                // reply

                BufferedReader in =
                    new BufferedReader(
                        new InputStreamReader( sock.getInputStream() ) );

                // Read and print the reply sent by the server

                System.out.println( in.readLine() );

                // All done close the socket

                in.close();
                sock.close();
            }
            catch ( UnknownHostException e ) {
                System.err.println( "DayTimeClient: no such host" );
            }
```

FIGURE 13.9 A Java day/time client

```
            catch ( IOException e ) {
                System.err.println( e.getMessage() );
            }
        }


    }

} // DayTimeClient
```

FIGURE 13.9 A Java day/time client *(continued)*

The program in Figure 13.9 follows the steps outlined earlier in this section to establish a connection with a server. The creation of an instance of a `Socket` in the first line inside the `try` block actively establishes a connection with the server whose name is specified on the command line. Should something prevent the connection from being established (e.g., the host name is invalid, the server has crashed, the server is refusing connections), an exception is thrown and the program terminates. After the `Socket` has been created and the connection established, the program wraps an `InputStreamReader` around the socket's `InputStream` and a `BufferedReader` around the `InputStreamReader`. The `InputStreamReader` is required to convert the bytes being read from the `Socket` into characters. The program reads the response from the server by invoking the `readLine()` method on the `BufferedReader`. After the response has been printed, the program closes the socket and terminates.

When reading information from a socket using a stream, you might wonder how the program detects that there is no more information to read. A client detects that a server has closed its connection when it encounters an EOF in the input stream. In other words, the act of closing a network connection is mapped to the presence of end of file in a stream.

What is remarkable about the `DayTimeClient` is the fact that the same streams that are used to read information from a file, a keyboard, or even a serial port are being used to read information from the network using TCP. The program in Figure 13.9 is similar to the programs in Chapter 11 that illustrated how to use streams. Because TCP provides a reliable stream-oriented connection, Java streams are the obvious choice to read the stream data from the socket. Polymorphism makes this all possible. The `InputStream` returned by the `getInputStream()` method of the `Socket` class has had its `read()` method overridden so that instead of reading from a file, it uses TCP to read from the network.

Writing a Java day/time server is almost as easy as writing a day/time client. The only issue that needs to be addressed is the fact that the Java day/time server you write cannot listen for incoming connections on port 13 because there may already be a day/time server running on your machine, or more likely, you will not have permission to use a port number in the range 0–4,095. The Java day/time server in this chapter does not run on the well-known day/time port. Instead, it allows the operating system to select the port to which it will bind. The server will print the port that it was assigned so that a modified client can learn this port number and access the server.

The first action the day/time server must take is to create a `ServerSocket` that will accept incoming requests. The server will then enter an infinite loop, where it will invoke the `accept()` method on the socket to express its willingness to accept a connection from a client. The `accept()` method will block until a connection has been established and will return an instance of a `Socket` that can be used to communicate with the client. After the server has the socket, it wraps an output stream around the `Socket` and prints its message (i.e., the current date and time) to the stream. Once the message has been sent, the server closes the streams and the socket and repeats the process. The code in Figure 13.10 is a Java implementation of a day/time server.

```java
import java.io.IOException;
import java.io.PrintWriter;

import java.net.Socket;
import java.net.ServerSocket;

import java.util.Date;

/**
 * A Java implementation of a day/time server. This program
 * does not accept connections on the well-known port for the
 * day/time service.
 */

public class DayTimeServer {

    public static void main( String args[] ) {

        try {

            // Create the server socket that will be used to accept
            // incoming connections

            ServerSocket listen = new ServerSocket( 0 ); // Bind to any port

            // Print the port so we can run a client that will connect to
            // the server.

            System.out.println( "I am Listening on port: " +
                listen.getLocalPort() );

            // Process clients forever...

            while ( true ) {

                // Wait for a client to connect
```

FIGURE 13.10 Java day/time server

```
            Socket client = listen.accept();

            // Wrap streams around the socket so a reply can be sent

            PrintWriter out =
                new PrintWriter( client.getOutputStream(), true );

            // Print out the current date

            out.println( new Date() );

            // That's it for this client

            out.close();
            client.close();
        }

    } catch( IOException e ) {
        System.err.println( e.getMessage() );
    }


    }

} // DayTimeServer
```

FIGURE 13.10 Java day/time server *(continued)*

Rarely are servers implemented using a single thread. Imagine for a moment a Web server that used a single thread to service requests from clients. Once one client established a connection to the server, it would have exclusive use of the server until the connection was terminated. Any other client that wished to access the server would have to wait until the current client has finished and the server is ready to accept a new connection. This might be a long wait. Instead, most modern network servers handle each client's request in a separate thread. The server waits for a client to establish a connection and then creates a separate thread to process that client's request using the concepts presented in Chapter 11. Once the client thread has been created and scheduled, the server is ready to accept a connection from another client.

It is quite easy and natural in Java to create a multithreaded server. At a very basic level, the design of a multithreaded server consists of two classes: one class that implements the server itself and a second class that will be used to create the threads that handle requests from clients. The UML diagram in Figure 13.11 illustrates the design of a simple multithreaded server.

The server consists of two classes: TdayTimeServer and Connection. The Connection class is a subclass of Thread and contains the code required to process a request from a client. The TdayTimeServer class accepts new connections and then creates an instance of the Connection class to handle the request.

Note that not all servers should be designed to use multiple threads. A server such as the day/time server in Figure 13.10 should probably not be implemented

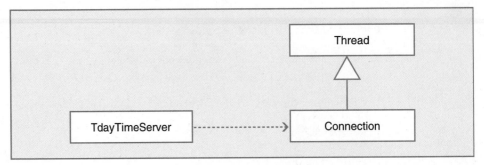

FIGURE 13.11 Design of a multithreaded server

using threads. The tiny amount of time it takes the day/time server to process a request is probably less than the amount of time it would take the JVM to create and schedule a new thread to service the request. Clearly, a server that takes a considerable amount of time to process its requests, such as an FTP or Web server, should be implemented using threads.

To illustrate how easy it is in Java to write a multithreaded server, we will modify the day/time server from Figure 13.10 to create a multithreaded version. The multithreaded day/time server consists of two classes: `Connection`, which processes a request from a client, and `TdayTimeServer`, which implements the server proper. The `Connection` class is shown in Figure 13.12.

```java
import java.io.IOException;
import java.io.PrintWriter;

import java.net.Socket;

import java.util.Date;

/**
 * This class handles a client connection to the day/time service
 * in a separate thread.
 */

public class Connection extends Thread {

    private Socket myClient; // The client this thread will service

    /**
     * Create a new connection.
     *
     * @param client the socket connected to the client.
     */
```

FIGURE 13.12 Thread to handle day/time requests

```
    public Connection( Socket client ) {
       myClient = client;
    }


    /**
     * Send the current date and time to the client.
     */

    public void run() {

       try {

          // Wrap streams around the socket so a reply can be sent

          PrintWriter out =
             new PrintWriter( myClient.getOutputStream(), true );

          // Print out the current date

          out.println( new Date() );

          // That's it for this client

          myClient.close();

       } catch( IOException e ) {
          System.err.println( e.getMessage() );
       }
    }

} // Connection
```

FIGURE 13.12 Thread to handle day/time requests *(continued)*

You should notice that the code in Figure 13.12 is almost identical to the code in Figure 13.10. The only significant difference between the two classes is that `Connection` extends `Thread`. The constructor for the `Connection` class takes as a parameter the `Socket` that will be used to communicate with the client. The `run()` method contains the code to process the client's request. Once the client has been serviced, the streams and sockets are closed and the thread terminates.

The code that implements the threaded day/time server is shown in Figure 13.13.

```
import java.io.IOException;

import java.net.Socket;
import java.net.ServerSocket;
```

FIGURE 13.13 Threaded day/time server

```
/**
 * A multi-thread Java implementation of a day/time server. This program
 * does not accept connections on the well-known port for the
 * day/time service.
 */

public class TDayTimeServer {

    public static void main( String args[] ) {

        try {

            // Create the server socket that will be used to accept
            // incoming connections

            ServerSocket listen = new ServerSocket( 0 ); // Bind to any port

            // Print the port so we can run a client that will connect to
            // the server.

            System.out.println( "Listening on port: " +
                listen.getLocalPort() );

            // Process clients forever...

            while ( true ) {

                // Wait for a client to connect

                Socket client = listen.accept();

                // Create and start the thread to handle the client

                Connection newThread = new Connection( client );
                newThread.start();
            }

        } catch( IOException e) {
            System.err.println( e.getMessage() );
        }

    }

} // TDayTimeServer
```

FIGURE 13.13 Threaded day/time server *(continued)*

The multithreaded day/time server invokes the `accept()` method on a `Server-Socket` to establish a connection with a client. Once the connection has been established, an instance of the `Connection` class is created to process the request. Before going back to the top of the loop and waiting for another connection, the server invokes `start()` on the `Connection` to schedule execution of the thread that will process this request.

In this section, we have looked at how the `ServerSocket` and `Socket` classes can provide reliable network communication in Java. The next section will discuss how a datagram, the basic unit of transfer in UDP, is represented in Java.

◆ **13.4.3** Representing Datagrams

Every message sent using UDP is carried inside a datagram. You can think of a datagram as the envelope in which UDP messages are placed. When using the postal service, the letter that you wish to send must be placed inside an envelope. The envelope shows the address of the individual to whom the letter is being sent, the address of the person who sent the letter, plus the proper amount of postage. To have UDP deliver a message, the message must be placed in a datagram, which is the UDP version of an envelope. In addition to the message, a datagram contains the IP address and port number of the destination and the IP address and port of the sending machine (no postage required!).

The `DatagramPacket` class represents datagrams in Java. Some of the methods that are part of `DatagramPacket` class are listed in Table 13.7.

TABLE 13.7 `DatagramPacket` Methods

Method	Description
InetAddress **getAddress**();	Returns the address of the machine to which the datagram will be sent or the address of the machine that sent the datagram.
byte[] **getData**();	Returns a reference to the byte array that contains the message within the datagram.
int **getLength**();	Returns the length of the data within this datagram.
int **getPort**();	Returns the port to which the datagram will be sent or the port from which the datagram was sent.
void **setAddress**();	Sets the destination address of the datagram.
void **setData**();	Sets the message that will be sent in the datagram.
void **setLength**();	Sets the length of this datagram.
void **setPort**();	Sets the port to which this datagram will be sent.

Although the datagram sent on the network contains the addressing information for both the source and destination machines, a `DatagramPacket` object only contains the addressing information for the *other* machine involved in the transfer. If a program creates a `DatagramPacket` to be sent to another machine, the IP address and port associated with the `DatagramPacket` will be that of the destination. If a program receives a `DatagramPacket`, the `getAddress()` and `getPort()` methods will return the address and port from which the datagram was sent. The `setAddress()` and `setPort()` methods, however, only affect the address and port of the destination.

Datagrams transfer messages as an array of bytes, which means that any message sent using UDP must first be converted into bytes. Some messages, such as strings, are easy to convert to bytes since a string is nothing more than a sequence of character codes, which are usually bytes. Converting messages that contain other types of information, such as integer or floating-point values, is a little more difficult. Internally, the JVM stores everything as a sequence of bytes, so it is clearly possible to convert an integer value to bytes, but the question remains how do you do it?

Perhaps the easiest way to deal with this issue is to use the DataInputStream and DataOutputStream classes in the java.io package. These classes provide a number of methods that can convert different types of information into a sequence of bytes. For example, the writeInt() method of DataOutputStream will take an integer value and convert it into the equivalent sequence of 4 bytes. The DataInputStream and DataOutputStream classes can be used in conjunction with the ByteArrayInputStream and ByteArrayOutputStream classes to read and write the bytes directly to or from a byte array. These four classes make it relatively easy to create messages in byte format that can be sent using UDP. As an example, assume a program is using a UDP-based protocol whose messages consist of a single integer value followed by the 11-character string "Hello World" (Figure 13.14).

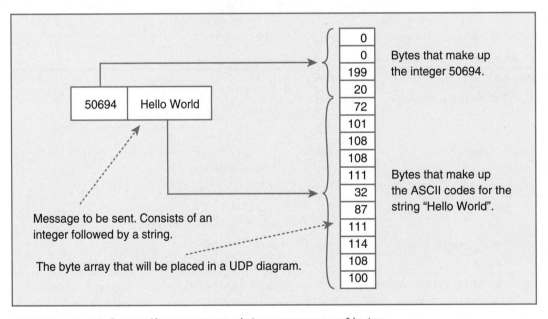

FIGURE 13.14 Converting a message into a sequence of bytes

The code in Figure 13.15 shows how to use a DataOutputStream and a ByteArrayOutputStream to convert the message of Figure 13.14 into a byte array for transmission across a network. The program uses the writeInt() and writeBytes() methods to send the data into the stream. The DataOutputStream converts the data into a sequence of bytes that is sent to a ByteArrayOutputStream to be written to a byte array. Invoking toByteArray() on the ByteArrayOutputStream returns a byte array containing the message as a sequence of bytes.

```
public static DatagramPacket makePak( int number, String message )
    throws IOException {

    DatagramPacket retVal = null;
    byte data[] = null;

    // Streams used to do the conversion

    ByteArrayOutputStream bytes = new ByteArrayOutputStream();
    DataOutputStream out = new DataOutputStream( bytes );

    // Write the message into the stream. Make sure to flush
    // the stream so that all the bytes are sent to the
    // byte array. Note these methods may throw an exception.

    out.writeInt( number );
    out.writeBytes( message );
    out.flush();

    // Get the message in byte form

    data = bytes.toByteArray();

    // Close the streams

    out.close();
    bytes.close();

    // Create the datagram

    retVal = new DatagramPacket( data, data.length );

    return retVal;
}
```

FIGURE 13.15 Using a `DataOutputStream` and a `ByteArrayOutputStream`

Converting the byte form of the message created by the program in Figure 13.15 back to an `int` and a `String` is also not hard to do. The easiest way to obtain the integer value from the message is to use a `ByteArrayInputStream` and a `DataInputStream` stream to extract the information from the data portion of the datagram (Figure 13.16).

Since the characters that comprise a string can be expressed in a variety of different character codes, you have to be very careful to interpret the byte form of a string using the correct character encoding to reconstruct the string correctly. Internally, Java uses Unicode to represent the characters in a string, whereas the characters in the message are represented using U.S. ASCII coding. Unfortunately, the `DataInputStream` class does not provide a method that can be used to read a sequence of U.S. ASCII codes and convert the bytes to the Unicode that is used by Java. Fortunately, the `String` class provides a constructor that can do the necessary translation.

```
public static int getNumber( DatagramPacket packet )
  throws IOException {

    // Wrap streams around the data portion of the packet so
    // that the integer in the first part of the packet can
    // be extracted

    DataInputStream data =
        new DataInputStream(
            new ByteArrayInputStream( packet.getData() ) );

    // Read the number and return

    return data.readInt();
}
```

FIGURE 13.16 Extracting an integer from a datagram

The program in Figure 13.17 extracts the string from the message using one of the constructors of the String class. The constructor in this program takes as parameters a byte array that contains the string in byte form, the length of the string, the index of the array where the first character code may be found, and the name of the character code that represents the characters in the string. The character code used in the message is ASCII and is represented in Java by the string "US-ASCII".

```
public static String getString( DatagramPacket packet )
  throws IOException {

    // Extract the string using one of the constructors of
    // the string class.

    return new String( packet.getData(),         // Where the codes are stored
                       4,                         // Where the codes start in
                                                  //   the array
                       packet.getLength() - 4,    // Length of the string
                                                  //   (subtracting 4 because of
                                                  //   the integer at the front)
                       "US-ASCII" );              // Coding used
}
```

FIGURE 13.17 Extracting an ASCII string from a datagram

As you can see, in Java it is easy to place data into datagrams and extract data from the datagrams that you receive. These techniques are not difficult, just tedious, when compared to the ease of dealing with data in a TCP stream. The next section will discuss how the DatagramSocket class sends and receives datagrams.

◆ 13.4.4 Unreliable Communication

The `DatagramSocket` class in the `java.net` package allows UDP to send and receive packets over a network. UDP provides a connectionless, unreliable, datagram-based delivery system. So unlike TCP, when using UDP, you must first convert your messages to byte form and place them into a datagram for them to be correctly transmitted. Furthermore, you can never be certain that when you send a datagram it will reach its destination. Even though UDP is unreliable, you do not have to worry about checking datagrams to see if they were corrupted in some way during transmission because corrupted datagrams will not be delivered.

Since UDP is a connectionless protocol, you do not have to establish a connection before sending a datagram. As soon as a client has created a socket, that socket can transmit datagrams even if the server is not ready to receive them. The general steps required for communicating using UDP are illustrated in Figure 13.18.

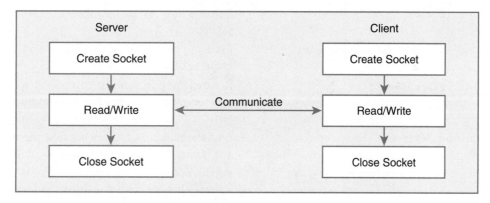

FIGURE 13.18 Connectionless-oriented communication

Writing programs that communicate using UDP is more tedious than writing programs that communicate using TCP. Since TCP is reliable, a program that uses it does not have to worry about lost packets. Furthermore, because TCP is stream oriented, you can use standard Java streams to send and receive data. On the other hand, when using UDP, a program has to worry about what to do in the presence of errors. Lost packets are typically handled in a UDP-based application using **time-outs**. The concept of a time-out is straightforward. When a client sends a packet, it is usually possible to determine the average amount of time that it will take for the message to be delivered and a reply to be received. As the client waits for the reply, it keeps track of the elapsed time. If the reply does not come within the expected period of time, the client will time out and assume that either the request or the reply was lost. The original datagram can then be re-sent. This process will be repeated until a correct copy of the message gets through.

You might be wondering why anyone would use UDP. The answer is that the UDP protocol is much less complicated than TCP. The amount of overhead associated with UDP, both in terms of the computer and the network, is small compared to that of TCP. In situations where you want to take full advantage of the speed of your network connection, UDP is the protocol of choice. For example, most networked game applications use UDP to transmit game status between players because of the low overhead associated with UDP. Also, UDP might be used to implement audio and video streaming where speed is more important than an occasional missed packet.

The DatagramSocket class is used to create a UDP communication endpoint in a Java program. Since UDP is connectionless, the addressing information is associated with each datagram, not with the socket as is the case with TCP. A single instance of a DatagramSocket can communicate with several different applications, whereas a Socket can only communicate with the application at the other end of the connection. There is no special datagram server socket class, so both a client and a server use a DatagramSocket to communicate. Some of the methods of the DatagramSocket class are given in Table 13.8.

TABLE 13.8 DatagramSocket Methods

Method	Description
void **close**();	Releases any system resources associated with this socket.
InetAddress **getLocalAddress**();	Returns the IP address that this socket is using to receive datagrams.
int **getLocalPort**();	Returns the port number this socket is bound to. A −1 is returned if the socket is not bound to a port.
int **getSoTimeout**();	Gets the number of milliseconds a call to receive() will wait until throwing a time-out.
void **receive**(DatagramPacket p);	Retrieves the next datagram sent to this socket. If a time-out has been set, this method will block until a datagram is received or the time-out period expires.
void **send**(DatagramPacket p);	Sends a datagram.
void **setSoTimeout**(int timeout);	Set the time-out for this socket. The time-out is expressed in milliseconds. A value of zero disables time-outs.

If you look at the Javadoc pages for the DatagramSocket class, you will notice there are a number of methods that seem to imply that it is possible to establish a "TCP-like" connection using a DatagramSocket. A connected DatagramSocket can only send and receive datagrams to or from the application whose address and port are specified when the connect() method is invoked. A connected DatagramSocket will filter out—in other words, discard—any packets that are sent to or received from a source other than that specified in the connection. However, a connected DatagramSocket does not provide any of the value added services that you might expect from a connection-oriented protocol, such as ordered delivery or guaranteed delivery.

There are several parameters than can be specified when creating a DatagramSocket. When the socket is created, it is possible to specify the port to which the socket will be bound. Typically, a server uses this form of the constructor to bind the `DatagramSocket` to a well-known port. The default constructor for the class will bind the socket to any available port. The other constructor parameters allow the programmer to specify the address and port on the remote machine to which the `DatagramSocket` should be bound. Again, remember that a connected `DatagramSocket` only filters out datagrams from unwanted hosts. A connected `DatagramSocket` does not provide reliable stream-oriented delivery.

The `send()` method of the `DatagramSocket` class is used to transmit a datagram on the network. The datagram must contain the IP address and port number of the application that it is being sent to. Since UDP is an unreliable protocol, the `send()` method provides no information about the success or failure of the transmission. The `send()` method will throw an `IOException` if an IO error occurs. This exception indicates that the local machine encountered an error while placing the datagram on the network. The absence of an `IOException` does not indicate that the datagram was correctly received by the destination.

A program reads incoming datagrams by invoking the `receive()` method on a `DatagramSocket`. The `receive()` method will block until a datagram has arrived at the socket. It is possible to enable time-outs by invoking the `setSoTimeout()` method on the socket prior to invoking `receive()`. If time-outs are enabled, `receive()` will block until a datagram arrives or the time-out period expires. The `receive()` method will throw a `SocketTimeoutException` if a time-out occurs.

The datagram that is read by the `receive()` method is copied into the `DatagramPacket` object that is passed to the method as a parameter. Recall from Section 13.4.3 that the state of a `DatagramPacket` includes a byte array that holds the data portion of the datagram. When reading datagrams using the `receive()` method, you must ensure that there is enough room in the `DatagramPacket` parameter to hold the incoming datagram. If the `DatagramPacket` does not have enough room to hold the datagram, only that portion of the datagram that will fit in the `DatagramPacket` will be read. The remaining bytes of the datagram will be read the next time `receive()` is invoked. For most datagram-based protocols, you will know the size of the largest datagram that your application might ever receive. Therefore, you can create a `DatagramPacket` object that is big enough to hold the largest datagram and pass that object to `receive()`. This way, no matter what size packet is received, as long it adheres to the protocol, it will fit in the `DatagramPacket`.

You can now appreciate the importance of the `getLength()` method associated with the `DatagramPacket`. The byte array that holds the datagram may be larger than the packet just read. The only way to determine the true length of the packet is not to use the length of the byte array parameter but to invoke the `getLength()` method.

To illustrate the use of the `DatagramPacket` and `DatagramSocket` classes, we will rewrite the day/time service from Section 13.4.2 so that it uses UDP instead of TCP to receive requests and send replies. It is very common for a machine to provide servers that use both TCP and UDP to communicate. A UDP-based day/time server creates a socket and then waits for a datagram to arrive. The arrival of the datagram causes the day/time server to obtain the current time, places the string that represents the time into a datagram, and then sends the datagram to the machine that sent the original request. The day/time server ignores the contents of the request packet. It only uses the datagram to obtain the IP address and port to which it will send the reply. The program in Figure 13.19 implements a UDP-based day/time server.

```java
import java.io.IOException;

import java.net.DatagramPacket;
import java.net.DatagramSocket;
import java.net.SocketException;

import java.util.Date;

/**
 * A Java implementation of a UDP day/time server. This program
 * does not accept connections on the well-known port for the
 * day/time service.
 */

public class UDPDayTimeServer {

    public static int MAX_PACKET_SIZE = 1024;

    public static void main( String args[] ) {

        // Create the server socket bound to any port

        DatagramSocket sock = null;
        try {
            sock = new DatagramSocket();
        }
        catch ( SocketException e ) {
            System.err.println( "UDPDayTimeServer: unable to create socket" );
        }

        // Create the datagram that messages will be read into

        byte data[] = new byte[ MAX_PACKET_SIZE ];

        DatagramPacket packet = new DatagramPacket( data, MAX_PACKET_SIZE );

        // Print the port so we can run a client that will connect to
        // the server.

        System.out.println( "Listening on port: " + sock.getLocalPort() );

        // Process clients forever...

        while ( true ) {
            byte now[] = null; // Current time as bytes

            // Wait for a client to send a request
```

FIGURE 13.19 UDP day/time server

```
try {
    // Need to reset the size back to the full size
    // The size will be reset everytime a packet is
    // read.

    packet.setLength( MAX_PACKET_SIZE );
    sock.receive( packet );

    // Got something. Put the current date and time into
    // the packet and send it back.

    now = new Date().toString().getBytes( "US-ASCII" );

    for ( int i = 0; i < now.length; i++ ) {
        data[ i ] = now[ i ];
    }

    // Null terminate the string

    data [ now.length ] = 0;

    // Set the size of the packet

    packet.setLength( now.length + 1 );

    // Send the reply

    sock.send( packet );
}
catch ( IOException e ) {
    // Ignore anything that goes wrong. This is perfectly
    // acceptable since UDP is an unreliable protocol
}
    }
  }

} // UDPDayTimeServer
```

FIGURE 13.19 UDP day/time server *(continued)*

The program starts by creating a socket and a `DatagramPacket` that is capable of holding the largest datagram that might ever be sent by a client. The server then enters a loop where it waits for the arrival of a request from a client. Upon receipt of a datagram, the server obtains the current time and places the character codes that represent the time into the `DatagramPacket` that it received. The datagram is then sent back to the client. By reusing the `DatagramPacket` that holds the client's request, the addressing information for the reply is already stored in the state of the datagram. You will notice that the server invoked the `setLength()` method two times within the program. The length of the byte array and the length of the packet are not necessarily the same. The DatagramSocket relies on the getLength() method to determine the size of the datagram to be sent, not on the length of the byte array. Setting the length of the DatagramPacket after copying in the time ensures that only the portion of the byte array that actually contains data is sent to the client. The program in Figure 13.20 provides an implementation of a UDP-based day/time client.

```java
import java.io.IOException;

import java.net.DatagramPacket;
import java.net.DatagramSocket;
import java.net.InetAddress;
import java.net.SocketException;
import java.net.SocketTimeoutException;
import java.net.UnknownHostException;

/**
 * A simple client that will query the day/time service on a
 * remote computer to determine the date and time at that location.
 */

public class UDPDayTimeClient {

    public static final int MAX_PACKET_SIZE = 1024;
    public static final int TIMEOUT_PERIOD = 3000; // 3 seconds

    public static void main( String args[] ) {

        if ( args.length != 2 ) {
            System.err.println( "Usage: UDPDayTimeClient host port" );
        }
        else {
            try {
                // Create a socket to send and receive on

                DatagramSocket sock = new DatagramSocket();

                // Determine the IP address of the server

                InetAddress server = InetAddress.getByName( args[ 0 ] );

                // Get the port

                int port = Integer.parseInt( args[ 1 ] );

                // Assemble an empty packet to send

                DatagramPacket packet =
```

FIGURE 13.20 UDP-based day/time client

```
                new DatagramPacket( new byte[ MAX_PACKET_SIZE ],
                                    MAX_PACKET_SIZE,
                                    server,
                                    port );

        // The message from the server

        String serverTime = null;

        // Send an empty message to the server

        sock.send( packet );

        // Wait for a reply from the server, but only
        // for the specified timeout period

        sock.setSoTimeout( TIMEOUT_PERIOD );
        sock.receive( packet );

        // Convert the message to a string and print it

        serverTime = new String( packet.getData(),
                                 0,
                                 packet.getLength() - 1,
                                 "US-ASCII" );

        System.out.println( serverTime );

        // All done close the socket

        sock.close();
    }
    catch ( UnknownHostException e ) {
        System.err.println( "UDPDayTimeClient: no such host" );
    }
    catch ( SocketException e ) {
        System.err.println( "UDPDayTimeClient: can't create socket" );
    }
    catch ( SocketTimeoutException e ) {
        System.out.print( "No response from server" );
    }
    catch ( IOException e ) {
        System.err.println( e.getMessage() );
    }
  }

 }

} // DayTimeClient
```

FIGURE 13.20 UDP-based day/time client *(continued)*

The day/time client of Figure 13.20 takes two command-line arguments: the name of the host to send the day/time request to and the port number assigned to the server on the remote machine. In the TCP-based version of the day/time service, the server responded with the current time when the client established a connection. In the UDP-based version, the server waits for the client to send a packet. The content of the packet is ignored. The receipt of the packet causes the server to assemble a packet containing the current time, which is then sent to the client. The server uses the addressing information in the UDP datagram sent by the client to determine the address to which the reply should be sent.

It is possible that the client may send a request to a server and never receive a reply. Remember this is a UDP-based day/time service, which means that the delivery of messages is not guaranteed. The request that the client sends or the reply sent by the server may be lost. The client uses a time-out to ensure that it does not wait indefinitely for a reply. Prior to invoking `receive()`, the client invokes `setSoTimeout()` to establish a time-out of 3 seconds (1,000 milliseconds is equivalent to 1 second). This means that the `receive()` method will throw an exception if a reply is not received within 3,000 milliseconds. It is not necessary to reset the time-out period after invoking read. Once set, the time-out period will remain the same until it is changed by a subsequent invocation of `setSoTimeout()`.

The datagram sent by the server contains the current time as a sequence of ASCII characters terminated by a line feed character. The length of the datagram that contains the server's response can be used to determine the number of characters in the reply (including the line feed). Since we do not want to include the line feed character in the string version, the program uses `packet.getLength() - 1` when converting the bytes in the reply into a `String`.

This section discussed the socket classes in the `java.net` package. The socket classes provide direct access to the transport protocols available within the Internet. The `ServerSocket` and `Socket` classes provide TCP-style delivery, whereas the `DatagramPacket` and `DatagramSocket` classes provide UDP-style delivery. The `InetAddress` class provides a representation of IP addresses and name resolution within a Java program. In the next section, we will discuss the URL classes. The URL classes provide high-level access to data stored on a Web server.

13.5 THE URL CLASSES

The URL classes in the `java.net` package provide high-level access to information stored on a Web server. In a typical transaction with a Web server, a client establishes a TCP connection with the server and then issues a request to the server using the Hypertext Transfer Protocol (HTTP). The server then returns the requested page. The interaction between a client and a Web server is shown in Figure 13.21. You could use the socket classes discussed in the previous sections and write the code necessary to implement HTTP, but that has already been done for you in the URL classes. The URL classes not only provide a way to access a Web server, but they also provide classes that can recognize and manipulate different types of information downloaded from a server.

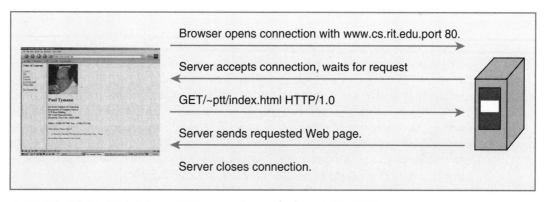

FIGURE 13.21 Obtaining a Web page from a server with HTTP

The HttpURLConnection class can deal with forms that are found on many Web sites. The class provides methods that allow you to obtain information about a Web page and, in the case of a form, provides methods to fill in the fields on the form. The JarURLConnection class can manipulate Java Archive Files (JAR). JAR files are similar to a Zip file in that they contain a collection of files that are transported as a unit and then extracted at their final destination. Using the JarURLConnection class, you have the ability to determine what files are stored in an archive and extract them if desired. Finally, the URLClassLoader class loads class files so that they may be executed by a JVM.

The URL classes are used to represent a resource on the network, and they can be used to obtain information directly from a Web server. The next section will define the term URL and illustrate how the URL classes access information stored on a Web server.

◆ 13.5.1 Representing a URL

URL is an acronym for Uniform Resource Locator. URLs are used to identify resources available on the Web. People often mistakenly think that a URL refers only to a file. However, a URL can refer to many different types of network resources. A URL consists of two parts: a protocol identifier and a resource name. A colon and two forward slashes separate the two components in a URL from each other. For example, in the URL

```
http://www.cs.rit.edu
```

the protocol identifier is http and the resource name is www.cs.rit.edu.

The protocol identifier determines the type of protocol that will be used to access the resource. For Web pages, the protocol identifier is almost always http, which specifies that HTTP will access the resource. Another commonly used protocol identifier is ftp, and this indicates that the File Transfer Protocol should obtain the resource that, in this case, is a remote file. When accessing the Web, the resource identifier provides both the resource name as well as the path that must be followed to access the resource. For example, the URL

```
http://www.cs.rit.edu/~ptt/index.html
```

specifies that the file `index.html` can be found in the home directory of the user `ptt`.

A URL in a Java program can be represented by an instance of the URL class. There are several constructors provided by this class, but the one you will use most often takes a single parameter, a string containing the URL. If the URL is not properly formatted or specifies an invalid protocol, it will throw a `MalformedURLException`. Some of the other methods in the URL class are described in Table 13.9.

TABLE 13.9 URL Methods

Method	Description
Object **getContent**();	Returns the object referred to by this URL. If the Java system knows about the type of object being referred to, the object will be converted into the appropriate Java type.
String **getFile**();	Returns the name of the file that this URL refers to.
String **getPath**();	Returns the path to the file referred to by this URL.
int **getPort**();	Returns the port associated with this URL.
String **getProtocol**();	Returns the protocol identifier of this URL.
URLConnection **openConnection**();	Returns a URLConnection object that can be used to access the resource identified by this URL.
InputStream **openStream**();	Returns a stream connected to the URL. This can be used to obtain the data associated with this URL.

Many of the methods in Table 13.9 are simple accessor methods that return the various parts of the URL: the protocol, port, and name of the resource. However, some of the methods provide the ability to obtain the information associated with the resource identified by the URL. The next section will discuss how the `openStream()` method can read the data associated with a URL.

♦ 13.5.2 Reading from a URL

Once you have created a URL, you can use it to read the data associated with the resource that it identifies. The `openStream()` method of the URL class returns a stream that, when read, will return the bytes contained in the resource. If the URL refers to a Web page, the bytes that will be read from the stream are the characters contained in the Web page. For example, the program in Figure 13.22 prints the contents of a Web page, the HTML codes that make up the page. The URL that identifies the Web page to be printed is obtained from the command line.

```java
/**
 * Use the URL class to read the HTML associated with a
 * Web page. The URL for the Web page is taken from the
 * command line.
 */

import java.net.URL;
import java.net.MalformedURLException;

import java.io.BufferedReader;
import java.io.InputStreamReader;
import java.io.IOException;

public class ReadHTML {

    public static void main( String[] args ) {

        // Usage

        if ( args.length != 1 ) {
            System.err.println( "Usage: java ReadHTML url" );
        }
        else {
            try {
                // Create the URL

                URL webPage = new URL( args[ 0 ] );

                // Connect the streams

                BufferedReader in =
                    new BufferedReader(
                        new InputStreamReader( webPage.openStream() ) );

                // Used to store lines as they are read

                String line = null;

                // Read and print the HTML

                while ( ( line = in.readLine() ) != null ) {
                    System.out.println( line );
                }

                // Close the streams

                in.close();
```

(continued)

FIGURE 13.22 Using `openStream()` to print a Web page

```
        }
        catch ( MalformedURLException e ) {
           System.err.println( "ReadHTML: Invalid URL" );
        }
        catch ( IOException e ) {
           System.err.println( "ReadHTML: " + e.getMessage() );
        }
     }
   }

} // ReadHTML
```

FIGURE 13.22 Using `openStream()` to print a Web page *(continued)*

The `openStream()` method returns the stream of data associated with the URL; it does not allow you to initiate and control an HTTP dialog with the server. The `openConnection()` method, on the other hand, opens an HTTP connection with the server, and this connection can be used to communicate with a resource using HTML. Using the `openConnection()` method, for example, you can interact with Web forms or other GUI objects on the server.

In this section, we discussed the URL classes that provide high-level access to resources on the Web identified by URLs. Using the classes in this section of the text, it is relatively easy to write a Java program that can obtain a range of different types of information stored on a Web server. In all modern computer applications, especially applications that make use of a network, security is a vital consideration. You have probably read story after story about poorly designed software that contained security flaws exploited by hackers to gain unauthorized access to a computing system. You may even have had the misfortune to experience such an attack firsthand. Security has always been a major concern of software developers, but the rapid growth of distributed applications has made it even more essential for all software designers to be knowledgeable of its basic concepts. To familiarize you with some of the issues that need to be taken into consideration when developing software that utilizes a network, we conclude this chapter with an introduction to the basic security mechanisms provided by Java.

13.6 SECURITY

Computer security, and network security in particular, is a very broad area that includes topics such as encryption, authentication, digital signatures, and protocol design. Java provides support for some of these features in the `java.security` and `javax.crypto` packages. These packages provide classes that implement authentication mechanisms and have the ability to encrypt and decrypt data. Thorough coverage of these topics is well beyond the scope of this text, and we will leave a discussion of these topics for future courses in computer networking and computer security. What is appropriate, and important, to discuss in this chapter are the basic security mechanisms built into the Java Virtual Machine (JVM).

From its very inception, Java was designed to dynamically load programs, in the form of applets, from a variety of different sources. Java's ability to download and execute programs from anywhere is one of its strengths, but it is also inherently unsafe. Whether the program file is local or comes from the network via an untrusted source, giving it full access to all the system's resources could wreak havoc on a computer system. An applet, for example, could erase system files, generate forged email, or launch attacks on other systems.

The JVM serves as a barrier to protect the underlying computer system from the execution of Java programs in the form of class files. The JVM does not allow a program to directly access any aspect of the computing system on which it is running. Any attempt by a Java program to access resources on the local system, whether to access memory or erase a file, must be done through the JVM. This gives the JVM the opportunity to check any operations that a program wishes to perform and prevent them if it deems them to be unsafe.

When the JVM loads a class file, it goes through a process known as **bytecode verification**. During bytecode verification, the JVM checks the bytecodes of the class file it is about to load and verifies that they are valid. Bytecode verification is designed to prevent the JVM from executing class files that might make it crash or put it in a state where it would be vulnerable to attack by malicious code. Since every class file executed by the JVM goes through this verification process, you can be almost 100 percent certain that the bytecodes interpreted on your system have been generated by a trusted Java compiler and cannot bypass the JVM. Bytecode verification ensures that only legitimate Java code is executed by a JVM.

However, even programs that pass the bytecode verification process can cause damage to a computing system. For example, given what you have learned in this text, you could easily write a Java program that deletes all of the files on a computer. **Access control** policies are the second line of defense that the JVM provides against malicious code. These policies specify exactly what operations a Java program can and, more important, cannot do. The basic idea behind access control is that a user can explicitly enumerate what operations a program is allowed to do. If the program attempts to do something that is not allowed, the attempt is aborted, and the JVM throws an exception to indicate what happened.

In the basic Java security model, trusted code is allowed full access to the system via the JVM, whereas untrusted code is forced to execute in a restricted environment referred to as the **sandbox**. The access control policies of the sandbox are established by an instance of the `java.lang.SecurityManager` class. A security manager provides a number of methods that can be invoked to determine if a particular operation is allowed. For example, the `checkWrite()` method of the `SecurityManager` class can be invoked to determine if a program has permission to write to a file. If the `checkWrite()` method determines that the program cannot access the file, it throws a `SecurityException`; otherwise, the method simply returns. The sandbox model is illustrated in Figure 13.23.

The classes in the Java API have been written so that they invoke the appropriate methods in the `SecurityManager` class before executing potentially dangerous code. For example, when you are using a `FileWriter` to write to a file, the `write()` method in the `FileWriter` class will invoke the `checkWrite()` method of the current `SecurityManager` to determine if the operation is allowed. You do not have to worry

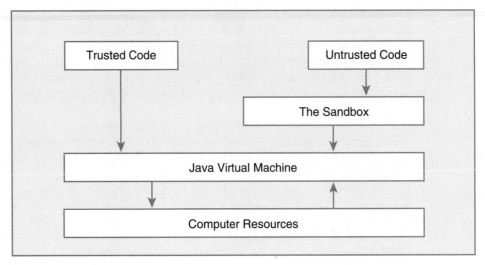

FIGURE 13.23 Sandbox

about making any of these checks in the programs you write because the checks are done for you in the classes that you use to access system resources.

A **policy configuration file** specifies the operations that are permitted for code from specific sources. For a program to be allowed to perform an operation, such as read the contents of a file, it must be granted permission for that operation. A policy file consists of zero or more entries. Each entry specifies the permissions for one or more classes that form a domain. A **domain** is a group of classes that have the same set of permissions.

An entry in a policy configuration file starts with the keyword grant, which may be followed by the keywords signedBy and codeBase. The keyword codeBase is used to define a domain based on the source of the code. A **code base** is a URL that specifies the directory from which the classes are loaded. For example, the URL:

```
file:/c:/classes/ptt
```

refers to the files that were loaded from the directory

```
c:/classes/ptt
```

on the local machine. The URL that identifies the source of the classes in the domain follows the keyword codeBase in an entry. The keyword signedBy is used to define a domain based on the authority that signed the code. The **signer** of a class identifies the organization that digitally signed the class file. Java provides the ability to attach digital signatures to a class file so that the author of a class may be verified.

The keywords codeBase and signedBy are optional and, if omitted, signify any code base or any signer. Figure 13.24 contains a policy file that grants all permissions to all classes.

```
grant {
    permission java.security.AllPermission;
}
```

FIGURE 13.24 A policy file that grants all permissions to all classes

The body of an entry lists the operations that classes in the domain are allowed to do. The permissions in an entry are string representations of a Java `Permission` class. The Java `Permission` classes represent access to system resources and specify what is allowed for their specific resource. The top-level class in the permission class hierarchy is the abstract class `Permission`. New permissions are entered as either subclasses of `Permission` or one of its subclasses. Like the exception classes, the subclasses of `Permission` are stored in the package whose permissions they describe. The UML diagram in Figure 13.25 shows the `Permission` class hierarchy.

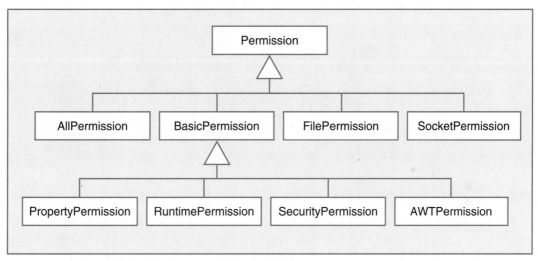

FIGURE 13.25 `Permission` class hierarchy

The policy file in Figure 13.25 uses the `AllPermission` class to specify that classes in the domain have access to all system resources. The entry in Figure 13.26 refers to all classes because both the keywords `codeBase` and `signedBy` have been omitted. The syntax used by the `Permission` classes to specify what operations are allowed varies slightly from class to class. The Javadoc pages for each of the individual `Permission` classes specify the format used by each class. The policy file in Figure 13.26 illustrates how to use the `FilePermission` class.

The policy file in Figure 13.26 defines two domains. The first entry defines a domain that consists of code coming from `c:/classes/RoadMap`. The classes in this domain are allowed to read the files `"roads.txt"` and `"cities.txt"`. Any other file

```
grant codeBase "file:c:/classes/RoadMap/" {
    permission java.io.FilePermission "roads.txt", "read";
    permission java.io.FilePermission "cities.txt", "read";
};

grant codeBase "file:c:/classes/MapDatabase/" {
    permission java.io.FilePermission "roads.txt", "read,write";
};
```

FIGURE 13.26 Using the `FilePermission` class in a policy file

operations are not allowed. The second entry defines a domain whose classes have been given permission to both read from and write to the file `"roads.txt"`. Note that if a class is in more than one domain, the permissions from the domains are combined. For example, if I were to add a third entry to Figure 13.26 that granted all permissions to all classes, the third entry would in essence override the other entries in the file.

When running an application using the JVM, you may specify from the command line whether or not the application should be run with a security manager installed, and you can specify the policy file to be used to define run-time permissions. The command

```
java -Djava.security.manager some-application
```

will run the program *some-application* using the sandbox model described earlier in this section. You can modify the default security policy by specifying a policy file in the command line as follows

```
java -Djava.security.Manager -Djava.security.policy=file application
```

where *policy-file* is the name of the policy file that defines the domains for *some-application* and the operations that they are allowed to perform. Java provides the ability to define systemwide and user-specific policies. You may want to check with the administrator of the machine you use to find out what security policies, if any, are in effect.

13.7 CONCLUSION

This chapter completes our discussion of networking and, indeed, of the entire topic of modern software development. We hope that the material presented in the preceding chapters has made you aware of the many steps involved in the creation of a large, complex software system.

In Part I, Chapters 1 through 4, we introduced the requirements, specifications, and design phases that must be successfully addressed before the issue of implementation is ever raised. These phases specify the exact problem to be solved and the design of the software to solve the problem. The most widely used design methodology today is object-oriented design, and the most popular way to express an object-oriented design is with the Unified Modeling Language (UML). Software developers must not only be familiar with implementation issues but also program specification and design.

The object-oriented design methodology divides a problem into many smaller units called classes. We must decide on the data structures that represent the information in our classes and the algorithms that our methods will use to access and modify these structures. In Part II, Chapters 5 through 9, we introduced a taxonomy of data structures and also showed that many of these data structures already exist as part of the Java Collections Framework. Today, it is more common to use libraries, such as the Java Collections Framework, than to design and implement these data structures from scratch. Software developers today must be comfortable using the facilities of libraries provided by the language they are using to write programs.

Finally, once you have selected your data structures and algorithms, you must implement them in Java. This phase will, of course, use all the basic programming concepts you learned in your first course—things like iteration, conditionals, declarations, scope, methods, and parameters. However, software implementation involves much more than these basic issues, and Part III, Chapters 10 through 13, introduced some important programming techniques widely used in software development. These include exception handling, streams, threads, GUIs, network programming, and system security. Many of these topics had been considered "advanced subjects" and were not even introduced until much later in the computer science curriculum. However, their central importance today makes it essential that these subjects be introduced in the earliest courses, with future classes building on this base and providing more advanced material. Students must, from the very beginning, be comfortable writing simple fault-tolerant, multithreaded, distributed software with a powerful visual interface.

Thus, the key points we have presented in this text include:

◆ Familiarity with requirement and specification documents.

◆ Knowledge of object-oriented design and representation of that design in a formal notation such as UML.

◆ The ability to implement an object-oriented design in a language like Java that supports object-oriented programming.

◆ Understanding the basic data structures in common use, including lists, stacks, queues, trees, sets, maps, and graphs.

◆ The ability to use data structure resources provided by a package like the Java Collections Framework.

◆ The ability to use modern programming concepts such as exception handling, streams, threads, networking, and toolkits for building user interfaces.

This is what modern software development is all about!

EXERCISES

1. The session and presentation layers were described briefly in this chapter. Use the Web to find out more about these layers.

2. Clearly, one of the advantages of building a network as a series of layers is that it makes the software easier to understand. Can you name some disadvantages to this approach?

3. Many people add an eighth layer to the OSI model. The layer is called the Media Access Control (MAC) layer and it fits between the data-link and network layers. What services does the MAC layer provide?

4. Obtain a copy of RFC768 that defines UDP. How many bytes are in the header of a UDP datagram? Describe what a checksum is and how the checksum is computed in UDP.

5. What is Dynamic Host Configuration Protocol (DHCP)? How is it used in a computing system?

6. Search the Web for information on the transport protocols used in a Novell network. How are the protocols in a Novell network similar to TCP/IP and how do they differ? Give advantages of each family of protocols.

7. An echo server "echoes" any packets it receives back to the sender. An echo server provides a way to test basic network connectivity. Write a UDP-based echo client (you may want to base your program on the UDP day/time client in Figure 13.20). Use your echo client to determine the average amount of time it takes to get a response from a variety of different echo servers.

8. The chargen service on many UNIX machines can be used to generate a stream of data to test the basic operation of a network. Like the day/time service, chargen is available for both UDP and TCP. The TCP chargen server accepts connections on port 19 and will generate a constant stream of character data until the connection is terminated. The UDP-based version of the service waits for the arrival of a datagram on port 19 and in reply sends a datagram that contains a random number of characters. Write a TCP- and a UDP-based chargen client and test them on your system.

9. Write a TCP- and a UDP-based chargen service. Test your servers using the clients you wrote in the previous exercise.

10. Obtain a copy of RFC1288 that describes the finger service. After reading RFC1288, write a finger client that is capable of retrieving user data from arbitrary finger servers. Write your program so that it reads the query information from the command line.

11. UDP is an unreliable protocol. How unreliable do you think UDP is? Devise a way to measure how many packets are dropped in a UDP transfer. Write a set of programs in Java that implement your testing scheme and run them on your network. Be sure to run your tests on a pair of machines that are on the same network and then on a pair of machines on different networks. How do the error rates compare?

12. In the text, we stated that there was more overhead associated with TCP than there was with UDP. Devise a way to measure the overall speed of a UDP and a TCP connection. For UDP, be sure to take into account the fact that packets might be lost. Write a suite of programs that implements your testing strategy. What conclusions can you draw from your experiments?

13. Using the URL classes described in Section 13.5, write a program that will print the title of a Web page given its URL. Write the program so that it reads the URL from the command line.

14. Get a copy of the RFC that describes HTTP, the protocol used to transfer hypertext information. After studying HTTP, write a Java program that serves as a simple Web server. Once you have your Web server completed, test it using one of the Web browsers available on your system.

15. A hacker could potentially misuse the Web server you wrote in the previous exercise to obtain unauthorized access to files on your computer. Design a Java security policy that will prevent this from happening. Run your Web server using your policy and attempt to misuse your server. Are you successful?

16. Trivial File Transfer Protocol (TFTP) uses UDP instead of TCP to transfer files. Obtain a copy of the RFC that defines TFTP and name some common uses of the protocol. Why do you think it is designed to use UDP instead of TCP?

17. Write a TFTP server and a TFTP client and test them on your system. Be sure to define a security policy for your server to prevent unauthorized access.

18. The class `MultiCastSocket` in the `java.net` package provides the ability to do multicasting. In multicasting, a host can send a message to a multicast group, and that message will be delivered to all machines in the group. Write a multicast version of the echo program. What are the advantages and potential disadvantages of multicast?

Basic Java Syntax

A.6 Methods

A.7 Summary

A.1 INTRODUCTION

In this text, we assume that the reader has completed an introductory programming course and is familiar with elementary programming concepts such as declarations, scope, assignment, conditionals, iteration, procedures, and parameters. However, we realize that the language covered in a first course varies from one school to another, and it may not have been Java, the language used throughout this book. To provide support for students with knowledge of an alternative programming language such as C++, Visual Basic, or Scheme, we have included this Appendix to review the basic elements of the Java language. It introduces the overall structure of a Java program and summarizes its basic data types, declarations, and statements. This material is expanded in the main body of the text with discussions of advanced features of the language. This includes the object-oriented capabilities of Java (Chapters 2 and 3), the Java Collection Framework (Chapter 9), exceptions (Chapter 10), streams (Chapter 10), threads (Chapter 11), the AWT and Swing graphical user interface libraries (Chapter 12), and networking (Chapter 13).

This Appendix is not a replacement for the in-depth coverage of the language that would be found in a typical introductory Java text. For students who want more detailed information and more guidance and assistance in learning the language, we suggest that you purchase and read one of the many good introductory Java programming books available in the marketplace to supplement the information presented in the following pages.

A.2 THE STRUCTURE OF A JAVA PROGRAM

In its most basic form, a Java program consists of a class declaration that defines a single method named `main()`. The method `main()` contains the code that is executed when the program is run. A Java class declaration is placed in a **source file**. The name of the source file and the name of the class that it contains must be the same. By convention, files that contain Java source code use the suffix `.java`. The general structure of a Java program is shown in Figure A.1.

A typical Java program will use several different classes as it executes. Some of these classes will come from prewritten classes libraries, and other classes will be ones that you write yourself. In this Appendix, we only discuss how to write a single top-level class that can be used to build simple Java programs. However, this single class is permitted to use all of the classes found in the Java class library that is part of every standard Java development kit. Chapters 2 and 3 explain in detail how to write complex object-oriented programs that are composed of many classes.

The Java class library that is included with Java contains hundreds of classes that can perform many useful operations. These classes are organized into about 135 **packages**. A package is nothing more than a collection of related classes. Table A.1 lists a few of the packages that are part of the Java API.

```
/* Here is an example of the general structure
   of a Java program */
import packageName;
public class ClassName {
    public static void main( String args[] ) {
        // Your program goes here
    }
}
```

FIGURE A.1 General structure of a Java program

TABLE A.1 Some of the Packages Defined in the Java Class Library

Package Name	Description
java.lang	Contains classes that implement many of the fundamental concepts of the Java language. Almost every Java program will use a class from this package.
java.math	Contains classes that provide infinite precision (i.e., big) numbers and other useful numerical routines.
java.util	Contains several utility classes that are useful in most Java programs. For example, this package contains the Date class that represents dates and time in a Java program.

To use a class that has been placed into a package, you use an import statement, as shown in Figure A.1. The import statements must appear at the very top of the program. (Note: The package java.lang is considered so essential that it is automatically imported into every Java program. It is the one package that does not need an explicit import statement.) The import statement allows you to access either a single class or a set of classes within a given package. For example, to use the Date class located in the package java.util, we would write:

```
import java.util.Date;    // allow access to class Date in
                          // package java.util
```

To access all of the classes in the java.util package, we use the following shorthand notation:

```
import java.util.*;       // allow access to every class in java.util
```

Note, however, when using the * notation, you gain access to every class inside this package but not to the contents of any other packages that are nested inside it. Although the * notation is a convenient way to import all of the classes in a package, it is considered good practice to explicitly import each class that will be used in a program. This way it is possible, just by looking at the import statements, to determine which classes in a package are actually being used by the program.

In addition to providing you with access to the public classes inside a package, the `import` statement also allows you to refer to a class by its class name alone rather than by its fully qualified name. In general, when referring to a class, you must use its **fully qualified name,** which is:

```
packageName.ClassName
```

So, for example, the fully qualified name of the `Date` class in the `java.util` package is `java.util.Date`. However, the `import` statement allows you to refer to the class solely by its class name, which is `Date`.

Another part of the Java programming language that can be seen in the program of Figure A.1 is the format of a comment. Java supports two types of comments. The first, a **multiline comment,** begins with the characters `/*` and ends with `*/`. Anything between the starting `/*` and the terminating `*/` is ignored by the compiler. The second type of comment, a **single-line comment,** starts with the characters `//` and terminates at the end of the line. Everything on the line following the `//` is ignored by the compiler. Comments do not nest, which means that the characters `/*` and `//` have no special meaning inside a comment. The program in Figure A.2 illustrates comments in a Java program.

```java
/**
 * This program will print the message "Enjoy reading this book!!"
 * when executed by the JVM.
 */

public class MyFirstProgram {

    public static void main( String args[] ) {

        // This statement will print the message
        System.out.println( "Enjoy reading this book!!" );
    }

} // MyFirstProgram
```

FIGURE A.2 Java program with comments

To "execute" a class from the command line, the class must define a method called `main()` that is defined as:

```
public static void main(String args[])
```

The **Java Virtual Machine (JVM)** starts the execution of a Java program by invoking the `main()` method contained in the class specified on the command line. The program begins execution with the first executable statement in `main()`. The program terminates when the last statement in `main()` is executed. If the file named on the command line does not contain a method called `main()`, the JVM will flag this as an error and not run the program.

For additional information about how to compile and run Java programs, you will have to refer to documentation provided by your instructor, as this will depend on exactly which compiler and hardware are in use at your installation.

A.3 JAVA DATA TYPES

Java, like most programming languages, allows a programmer to define a variable that refers to a memory location within the computer. Once a variable has been defined, the programmer can store and retrieve values to and from this memory location. An **identifier** is a name used to identify a variable, class, method, or symbolic constant in a program. The rules for forming identifiers are the same, regardless of how the identifier will be used:

◆ It may contain uppercase letters (A–Z), lowercase letters (a–z), digits (0–9), the underscore (_), and the dollar sign ($).

◆ It may not start with a digit. (You should also avoid starting an identifier with either an underscore or a dollar sign. These names are often used by the system for special purposes, and they can sometimes cause strange problems.)

◆ It can be any length, although to be useful the name should fit on a single line.

◆ It is case sensitive, so ABC, Abc, AbC, and abc are all different names.

◆ It cannot be equal to any of the 59 reserved words listed in Figure A.3.

abstract	default	goto	operator	synchronized
boolean	do	if	outer	this
break	double	implements	package	throw
byte	else	import	private	throws
byvalue	extends	inner	protected	transient
case	false	instanceof	public	true
cast	final	int	rest	try
catch	finally	interface	return	var
char	float	long	short	void
class	for	native	static	volatile
const	future	new	super	while
continue	generic	null	switch	

FIGURE A.3 Reserved words in Java

In addition to these restrictions, there are long-established stylistic guidelines followed by Java programmers when selecting identifiers. Although not enforced by the compiler, it is considered good practice to follow them to enhance the readability of your code.

◆ Class names begin with a capital letter, whereas variable and method names begin with lowercase letters. So, `Mathematics` is fine for a class name, but `sort` and `compare` would be used for the names of methods in this class.

◆ When names are composed of two or more separate words strung together, you capitalize the first letter of each of the words, except possibly for the first word to adhere to the previous rule. So, the name `MyFirstExample` would be fine for a class name, and `sortByKey` would be a good method name.

♦ Choose a name that is highly indicative of the function of this entity, such as `setRate` or `getAccelerationValue`. Meaningless names like `x32` or `zzz` should be avoided.

♦ Use all capital letters for constants and separate the words in an identifier with an underscore, such as `PI` and `FIXED_RATE`.

Every variable in a Java program is identified by a unique identifier and has a data type associated with it. The **data type** of a variable determines the kind of values that can be stored in the variable. A **declaration statement** defines a variable and specifies the identifier and data type of the variable. Every variable in a Java program must be declared and initialized before it can be used. The two formats for a variable declaration follow (the symbols [ ] indicate that a particular construct is optional and may be omitted)

```
[ final ] data-type identifier [ = expression ];
[ final ] data-type identifier-list;
```

where `identifier-list` is a list of valid identifiers separated by commas. Here are some valid variable declarations:

```
int count = 0;
float root, xValue, yValue;
double temperature, humidity;
boolean done = false;
```

You may add the optional reserved word `final` before any declaration. This means that the identifier can be initialized once but never changed. Essentially, this makes it a constant, and any attempt to assign it a new value will be flagged as a fatal error. The word `final` is an example of a **Java modifier** that is used to set the characteristics of a variable. There are a number of other modifiers that can be added to a Java declaration, including `public`, `private`, `protected`, and `static`. These modifiers are discussed and explained in detail in Chapter 3. The use of the `final` modifier to define symbolic constants in a Java program is shown in the following examples:

```
final double PI = 3.1415927;
final double FREEZING_POINT = 32.0;
final int MONTHS_PER_YEAR = 12;
```

There are two quite different categories of data types in Java: primitive types and reference types. We describe each of these two types in the following sections.

♦ A.3.1 Primitive Types

The **primitive types** have their value stored directly in a variable. For example, given the declaration

int x = 5;

the primitive value will be stored in memory as shown:

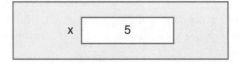

In Java, there are eight primitive types, and they are summarized in Table A.2. Each of these primitive types has a fixed size (in bits), regardless of the platform on which the program is being run. Note that primitive types in Java are used for only the simplest and most basic of data values: integers, reals, characters, and Boolean. These are the types that are often implemented directly in hardware by most processors.

TABLE A.2 Java Primitive Types

Type	Description
boolean	Has two values, true and false.
byte	8-bit signed two's complement integers, range: −128 to 127
short	16-bit signed two's complement integers, range: −32768 to 32767
int	32-bit signed two's complement integers, range: −2147483648 to 2147483647
long	64-bit signed two's complement integers, range: −9223372036854775808 to 9223372036854775807
char	16-bit unsigned values from 0 to 65535, representing Unicode characters
float	Single-precision, 32-bit format IEEE 754 floating-point values, range: 1.40239846e−45 to 3.40282347e +38
double	Double-precision, 64-bit format IEEE 754 floating-point values, range: 4.9406564581246544e−324 to 1.79769313486231570e+308
	There are special floating-point values: positive infinity, negative infinity, and not a number (NaN).

Primitive literals refer to specific primitive values in a Java program such as +4 or −7.3. Although we present a number of rules in this section that describe how to construct valid literals, the basic rule of thumb you should follow is that literals in Java are written in the same way that you would write numbers on a piece of paper. For example, a series of digits with no decimal point is an integer, whereas a series of digits with a decimal point is of type double. Character literals consist of a single character surrounded by single quotation marks. The Boolean literals are the words true and false. Table A.3 lists all of the literal values recognized in the Java language.

Note that decimal integer literals use the standard 32-bit format, unless they end with the letter L or l, in which case they are stored in the long, 64-bit format. Alternatively, integers can be expressed in hexadecimal (base-16) and octal (base-8) notation. An integer that begins with the symbols 0x is interpreted as a hexadecimal number, and an integer that begins with the character 0 is interpreted as octal.

Floating-point constants must have at least one digit to the right of the decimal point, but it is optional whether or not to include digits to the left. All floating-point literals are stored as 64-bit double values by default. To represent a number as a

TABLE A.3 Java Literals

Type	Examples
`byte, short, int`	0, 123, −456, 55665, . . .
`long`	0L, 123l, -456l, . . .
	`long` literals are denoted by appending L or l to any integer literal.
`char`	'a', 'A', 'b', 'B', . . . 'z', 'Z' '0', '1', '2', . . . '9' '!', '@', '#', . . . '\b', '\f', '\n', '\r', '\t', '\\', '\''
`float`	1.2345f, 1234.423F, 0.1f, −1.23f, . . . 1e10f, 1.234e−10f, 3.456e2f, −1.2345e12f, . . .
	By default, floating-point literals are of type `double`. If an F or f is added to the end of a floating-point literal, it will be of type `float`.
`double`	1.2345, 1234.423, 0.1, −1.23, . . . 1e10, 1.234e−10, 3.456e2, −1.2345e12, . . .
`boolean`	`true, false`
`String`	"This is a String", "Hello World\n"
`Object`	`null`

32-bit single-precision `float` value, you follow the literal by the character F or f. Finally, real numbers can be written in scientific notation using the letter E or e to represent the phrase "times 10 to the power of . . . ".

Java will automatically convert one primitive type into another whenever it can be sure that no information will be lost in the conversion. This would be done, for example, to convert an `int` to a `double` or a `byte` to an `int`. This is called a **widening conversion**. However, Java will not do this when the conversion is to a smaller data type and information might be lost. This could happen, for example, if we were to convert a `float` to an `int` or a `short` to a `byte`. This is called a **narrowing conversion**, and the Java compiler will flag this as a fatal error. However, if you still wish to force Java to carry out this conversion, you can do so using a **casting operation**. This is done by writing in parentheses, before the expression to be converted, the name of the type into which you wish the value to be cast. For example, if x is an `int` and we wish to convert it to a `byte`, we can write:

```
(byte)x
```

Java will do the cast, but you should realize that if x > +127 or x < −128, the maximum and minimum values that can be represented in a byte, then this conversion will produce an incorrect value. Narrowing conversions should be done with the utmost of caution.

In Java, characters are stored using the 16-bit Unicode set. To indicate a character, it is placed inside single quotation marks—for example, 'A'. There are also special escape characters to represent nonprinting control characters, such as:

\r	carriage return
\f	line feed
\n	new line
\t	tab

◆ **A.3.2** Reference Types

Reference types are used for every data value in Java other than the eight primitive types listed in Table A.2. With a reference type, the values associated with object x are not stored directly in memory location x. Instead, location x holds *a reference to* that object—that is, a pointer to where in memory this object will be found (Figure A.4).

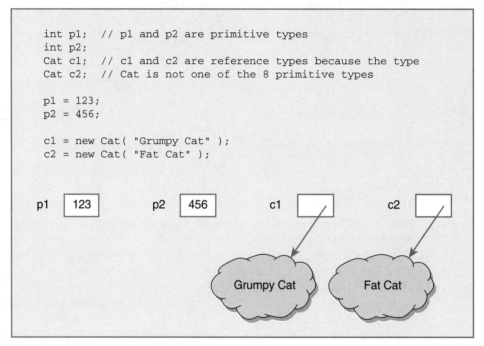

```
int p1;   // p1 and p2 are primitive types
int p2;
Cat c1;   // c1 and c2 are reference types because the type
Cat c2;   // Cat is not one of the 8 primitive types

p1 = 123;
p2 = 456;

c1 = new Cat( "Grumpy Cat" );
c2 = new Cat( "Fat Cat" );
```

| p1 | 123 | p2 | 456 | c1 | | c2 | |

Grumpy Cat   Fat Cat

FIGURE A.4 Reference types in Java

The eight primitive types in Table A.2 can be converted into reference types using **wrapper classes** that have exactly the same name as the primitive type. These wrapper classes are all found in the package `java.lang`. For example, to convert the primitive integer value x into a reference type, we use the class `Integer`. To convert the double value y into a reference, we use the class `Double`. This capability is important, as there are a number of places in Java where only reference types are permitted. You will see how to do this in the following section.

The last data type we discuss in this section is an array. An **array** is a structure that holds multiple values of the same type. In Java, arrays are considered reference types, and they behave slightly differently from array types in languages like C or C++. A declaration for an array specifies the name that will identify the array and the type of elements that will be stored in the array as shown next. The square brackets in the declaration indicate that x refers to an array.

```
int x[];
```

This declaration statement allocates storage for a reference to an array; it does not actually create the array itself. An array is created using operator new as follows:

```
x = new int[ 10 ];
```

The type specifies the type of the elements that will be stored in the array, and the number inside the square brackets indicates how many elements can be stored. The elements in the array will automatically be initialized to the appropriate initial value for its type: 0 for integers, 0.0 for reals, the null character for characters, and null for references.

The size of an array is fixed and cannot be changed. Given a variable that contains a reference to an array, it is possible to determine the size of an array using the length operator:

```
int size = x.length;
```

Elements within the array are accessed using the following syntax:

```
x[0] = 10;    // Set element x[0] to 10
int z = x[1]; // Set z to element x[1]
```

In Java, array indexes are 0-based, which means they start at 0 and run to 1 less than the length of the array. For example, the index of the first element in the 10-element array x would be 0 and the last index would be 9. At run time, the JVM checks all array accesses and verifies that the indexes are valid. If an attempt is made to use an invalid index (i.e., a negative index or one greater than the length of the array), an exception is raised, which may cause the program to terminate.

◆ A.3.3 Identifiers, Variable Declarations, and Scope

Every variable and constant declaration has a **scope**—the region of the program where it is visible to the programmer and can be used. A variable is said to have **class scope** if it is declared within a class but outside the methods contained within this class. An identifier with class scope can be accessed by any of the methods in the class that follow its declaration. An example of class scope is shown in Figure A.5. The constant PI can be accessed by any method that follows its declaration, specifically areaOfACircle() and circumferenceOfACircle().

```
public class ClassScopeExample {
    final double PI = 3.14; // this has class scope
    public double areaOfACircle() { . . . }
    public double circumferenceOfACircle(){ . . . };
    . . .
}
```

FIGURE A.5 Example of class scope

An identifier is said to have **block scope** if it is declared within a block. A block is a construct that begins with a { and ends with a }. The code inside a Java method is an example of a block. The scope of a variable declared inside a block is from the point where the declaration is made to the end of that block. For example, Figure A.6 expands the example in Figure A.5 to show a variable called area with block scope.

```
public class BlockScopeExample {
    final double PI = 3.14; // this has class scope
    public double areaOfACircle(double radius) {
        double area;  // this has block scope
        area = PI * (radius * radius);
        return area;
        // and its scope ends here
    }
    public double circumferenceOfACircle() { . . . };
    . . .
}
```

FIGURE A.6 Example of block scope

The declaration double area on the second line of areaOfACircle is declared inside a block that begins with the immediately preceding {. This variable has a scope that extends from the point of the declaration to the } character that occurs four lines later.

When a primitive type, such as an int or float, is declared, the JVM allocates enough memory to store the specified value and initializes its value either to a default value or to an initial value provided by the user. However, when a reference variable is declared, something quite different happens. We said that a reference variable points to or refers to an object. However, the object to which it refers has not yet been created. For example, if Circle is a class, then the declaration

```
Circle x;
```

creates a reference variable x that can point to objects of type Circle, but right now it does not refer to anything. After making this declaration, the variable x looks like this:

To create an object for x to refer to, we use the new operator in Java. This operator allocates memory for a new object of the type that x refers to (Circle, in this case) and returns a reference (i.e., a pointer or memory address) that we can store into the reference variable. The methods that create new objects are called **constructors**, and they have exactly the same name as the class to which they belong. So, for example, to create a new Circle object, we would use a constructor called Circle. A constructor may have zero, one, or more parameters.

Here is an example of how to use a constructor with no parameters, called the **default constructor**, to initialize x that was created using the preceding declaration:

```
x = new Circle();    // assume no parameters
```

This creates a new `Circle` object and has it referenced by the variable x:

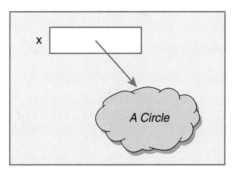

It is also possible to combine into a single step the declaration of a reference variable and its initialization as follows:

```
Circle x = new Circle();
```

This is also the way to convert a primitive type, such as an `int` or `double`, into a reference type. We use the constructor from the corresponding wrapper class, passing it the primitive type as its only parameter. What we will get back is the primitive type now represented as an object. For example:

```
int x;                  // x is a primitive object
double y;               // so is y
Integer xAsAnObject;    // x as a reference value
Double yAsAnObject;     // y as a reference value
xAsAnObject = new Integer(x);
yAsAnObject = new Double(y);
```

When a variable goes "out of scope," the memory allocated to the variable is returned to the **heap**, the area of memory used for dynamic allocation of space to variables. To keep track of when objects are no longer needed and the memory allocated to them can be returned to the heap, the JVM keeps track of the number of references to every object in memory. Whenever a new reference to an object is created, the reference count of the object is incremented by 1. When a reference to an object is removed, the reference count of the object is decremented by 1. When the reference count of an object reaches 0, the object can no longer be accessed, and it is called "garbage." Periodically, Java invokes a **garbage collector** that collects all the objects that can no longer be accessed and returns the memory allocated to those objects to the heap.

A.4 EXPRESSIONS

Java **expressions** are composed of variables, constants, operators, method invocations, and the grouping symbols (and). All variables and constants in the expression must have been declared, initialized, and in scope; otherwise, the compiler will flag this as an error. In addition, the user must be careful to use values of consistent data type within the expression. If you use values of different type within a single expression, the compiler must be able to convert them, either automatically or via a user-specified cast, into a single data type so that they can be operated on in a consistent manner. For example, if i is an int and f is a float, then the expression (i + f) mixes values of different types. This is called a **mixed mode expression**, and Java must deal with it in a reasonable way. In this example, the compiler will automatically perform a widening conversion on the integer i and convert it to a float so that the addition can be performed using real numbers. We could also write this expression in either of the following two ways:

```
(float) i + f      // behaves the same as not doing a cast
i + (int) f        // this is a narrowing conversion.
```

Note that the second example may cause the loss of information because we are discarding the fractional part of f.

Some mixed mode expressions cannot be rectified. For example, if b is a boolean and f is a float, then the expression (b + f) makes no sense because Boolean values cannot be cast into real numbers, or vice versa. In this case, the compiler will produce an error message. The bottom line about writing expressions is to be very careful of the data types you use within the expression and use only a single type or a set of types that can be meaningfully cast into a single type.

The arithmetic operators in Java are listed in order by precedence in Table A.4. The operators with the highest precedence are listed first, followed by the operators with lower precedence. All of the operators with the same description have equal precedence.

You should be familiar with most of the operators in Table A.4 because they are, for the most part, quite similar to what is found in a number of other programming languages. The ones that you may not have seen before are:

a % b	remainder	The remainder left after doing an integer division of a by b. For example, 9 % 5 is 4.
a++	postincrement	Use the value of a to evaluate the expression and, when that is completed, increment a by 1. If a currently has the value 4, then (a++) * 2 will evaluate to 8, and a will be 5.
++a	preincrement	First increment a and then use that new value to evaluate the expression. If a currently has the value 4, then (++a) * 2 will evaluate to 10, and a will be 5.

(Note: The pre- and postdecrement work in a similar fashion but subtract 1.)

TABLE A.4 Java Operators and Their Precedence

Description	Syntax	Meaning	Associativity
Unary postfix	[]	Array access	Left to right
	.	Object member access	
	()	Method invocation	
	++	Postincrement	
	--	Postdecrement	
Unary prefix	++	Preincrement	Right to left
	--	Predecrement	
	+	Unary plus	
	-	Negation	
	~	Bitwise complement	
	!	Logical NOT	
Object creation and Cast	new	Object creation	Right to left
	(type)	Cast	
Multiplicative	*	Multiplication	Left to right
	/	Division	
	%	Remainder	
Additive	+	Addition	Left to right
	-	Subtraction	
Shift	<<	Left shift	Left to right
	>>	Right shift	
	>>>	Right shift with zero fill (unsigned shift)	
Relational	<	Less than	Left to right
	<=	Less than or equal	
	>	Greater than	
	>=	Greater than or equal	
	instanceof	Instance of	
Equality	==	Equal	Left to right
	!=	Not equal	
AND	&	Bitwise AND	Left to right
XOR	^	Bitwise exclusive OR (XOR)	Left to right
OR	|	Bitwise OR	Left to right
Logical AND	&&	Logical AND	Left to right
Logical OR	||	Logical OR	Left to right
Conditional	?:	Ternary conditional operator	
Assignment	=	Assignment	Right to left
	+=	Assignment combined with an operator	Right to left
	-=		
	*=		
	/=		
	%=		
	<<=		
	>>=		
	>>>=		
	&=		
	^=		
	|=		

`a && b`	Boolean AND	`&&` is the standard Boolean AND with which you are familiar. The operator `&` is a bitwise AND, where each bit of `a` and `b` is separately ANDed together.
`a || b`	Boolean OR	The standard Boolean OR. The operator `|` is a bitwise OR, where each bit of `a` and `b` is ORed together.

Since Java includes a Boolean data type, the Boolean operators like && and || will only work with Boolean types. This is different from programming languages like C or C++ that use integer values to represent Boolean values.

The Boolean operators perform what is called **short-circuit evaluation**. For example, when evaluating an expression such as `(a && b && c && d)`, the JVM will evaluate each of the Boolean variables one at a time starting from the left. As soon as one of the Boolean expressions evaluates to `false`, the evaluation stops since the overall value of the entire expression must be `false`. This means that some of the variables in the expression may never be evaluated (Boolean OR works in a similar fashion). It is also possible to use the bitwise AND and bitwise OR operators with Boolean types. These operators never short circuit, which means all of the variables in the expression will be evaluated.

The **precedence level** of an operator determines the order in which operations are carried out in the absence of grouping symbols that change the order. The rule is that, in the absence of parentheses, an operator with a higher precedence is always done before an operation of lower precedence. The symbol pair `( )` changes precedence because anything inside parentheses is done first. For example, the expression

```
a++ + b > --c
```

uses the following four arithmetic operators:

`++`	postincrement
`+`	addition
`>`	greater than
`--`	predecrement

Since we do operations in strict order of their precedence level, we can determine from Table A.4 that this expression will be evaluated as if it had been written as:

```
((a++) + b) > (--c)
```

One of the characteristics of a well-written program is that it is easy to read. Since it is unrealistic to expect a reader of your program to be familiar with all of the precedence levels in Java, you should use the grouping symbols (and) whenever required to make your intentions clear. Not only will your program be easier to read, but you are likely to prevent yourself from making errors. Therefore, when writing a complex expression, be sure to use parentheses whether or not they change the actual order of computation. This will make your program far more readable.

The **associativity** value given in Table A.4 specifies how operators of the same precedence level will group. For example, the subtraction operator groups left to right. Therefore, the expression a − b − c is interpreted as (a − b) − c. The assignment operator groups right to left, so the expression a = b = c is evaluated as a = (b = c).

Here are some examples of arithmetic expressions and their Java equivalents. The examples assume that all variables have been correctly declared and properly initialized (all expressions are assumed to use real values):

Arithmetic Expression	*Java Representation*
a. $\dfrac{sum}{number+1}$	`sum / (number + 1.0)`
b. $\dfrac{a}{2}+bc^4$	`(a / 2.0) + (b * Math.pow(c, 4.0));` (Note: `pow()` is in class `java.lang.Math`)

c. $\dfrac{-b+\sqrt{b^2-4ac}}{2a}$	`(-b + Math.sqrt((b * b) -`
	`    (4.0 * a * c))) / (2.0 * a)`
	(Note: `sqrt()` is in class `java.lang.Math`)

A.5 JAVA STATEMENTS

◆ A.5.1 Assignment Statement

The Java assignment behaves in much the same fashion as the assignment statement in other imperative languages such as C, C++, and BASIC. The syntax of the statement is

```
variable = expression;
```

where `variable` is the name of a declared variable currently in scope, `=` is the assignment operator, and `expression` is any valid Java expression formed according to the rules described in Section A.4. The behavior of this statement is exactly what you would expect: The expression on the right side of the assignment operator is evaluated, and the resulting value is stored in the variable on the left side. The previous value stored in this variable is lost.

Assignment statements themselves have a value. That is, the statement a = b + c will not only compute the sum of b and c and store that value in a, but it also evaluates to the value that is stored into a. Since an assignment statement produces a result, you can treat it as if it were an expression and use the result of that expression in other computations. For example:

```
a = b = c + d;
```

You can see in Table A.4 that the assignment operator groups right to left. So, the computer will begin by evaluating b = c + d, which computes the sum c + d and stores the result in b. Now the next assignment expression is evaluated, which causes the variable a to be assigned the value of the assignment statement b = c + d or the value that was stored in b. The end result is that the sum c + d is placed into both a and b. This is a good way to initialize a group of variables to the same value with a single statement:

```
a = b = c = 0;        // initialize a, b, and c to 0.
```

Here are two examples of Java assignment statements:

Algebraic Representation   *As a Java Assignment Statement*

a. $C = \dfrac{5(F-32)}{9}$

```
double centigrade, fahrenheit;
. . .
centigrade = (5.0*(fahrenheit-32.0)) / 9.0;
```

b. $\dfrac{-b \pm \sqrt{b^2 - 4ac}}{2a}$

```
double a, b, c; // the three coefficients
double root1, root2; // the two real roots
. . .
root1 =
  (-b + Math.sqrt((b*b)-(4.0*a*c)))/(2.0*a);
root2 =
  (-b - Math.sqrt((b*b)-(4.0*a*c)))/(2.0*a);
```

In example b, we used the Java method `Math.sqrt()`, which is found in class `Math` in package `java.lang`. However, as mentioned earlier, it is not necessary to import any classes in the `java.lang` package because they are automatically imported into every program you write. It would not be wrong, though, to include the following:

```
import java.lang.Math;
```

Finally, a common statement in Java is an assignment that looks like the following

```
a = a + b;
```

in which you take a value `a`, perform some arithmetic operation on it (in this case, adding `b`), and put the result back into `a`. Java provides variations of the assignment operator to make it easier to write this type of assignment statement. These variants all have the format `op=`, where `op` is one of the following 11 operators: `+ - * / % & | ^ << >> >>>`. The meaning of this construct is exactly the same as if you had written `var = var op expr;`. Examples of these variations are:

Example   *Meaning*

```
a += b         a = a + b
a -= b         a = a - b
a *= b         a = a * b
```

◆ A.5.2 Conditional Statements

The **conditional statements** are the decision-making statements of Java. The two conditional statements in the language are the `if/else` and the `switch`. There is also a **ternary conditional operator**, `?:`, that allows you to imbed a conditional test inside a Java expression. This conditional operator is written:

```
boolean expression ? expression1 : expression2
```

The meaning of this is to first evaluate the `boolean expression`. If it is `true`, then evaluate `expression1`, and that is the result of the overall expression; if the `boolean expression` is false, then evaluate `expression2` and that becomes the result of the overall expression. So, to find the bigger of `a` and `b` and store that value into `c`, we could write:

```
c = a > b ? a : b
```

This operator is not used very often, and we will not say any more about it.

A.5.2.1 The `if/else` Statement

This is the most important conditional statement in Java, and it is the one that is used the overwhelming majority of the time. The syntax of the `if/else` (where the [ ] mean that something is optional) is shown in Figure A.7.

```
if (boolean expression)
    statement1;
[else
    statement2; ]
```

FIGURE A.7 Syntax of the `if/else` statement

The meaning of this statement is to first evaluate the `boolean expression`. If it evaluates to `true`, then execute `statement1` and skip `statement2` (if it is present) and continue execution with the next statement. If `boolean expression` evaluates to `false`, then skip `statement1` and execute `statement2` if it is present. If the `else` clause has been omitted, then do nothing at all and continue with the next statement. Pictorially, we can view the `if/else` statement as shown in Figure A.8.

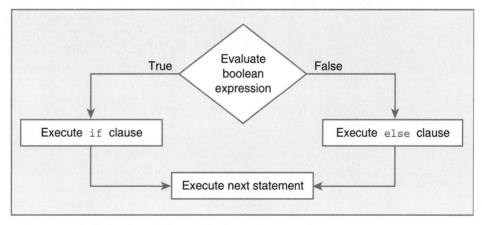

FIGURE A.8 Behavior of the `if/else` statement

Note that the syntax of the `if/else` explicitly allows only a single statement in either case, but we often want to do much more. To accomplish this, we must use the concept of a **compound statement**, also called a **block**. This is a group of declarations and/or statements that begins with a `{`, includes any number of declarations and/or statements in a row, and ends with a `}`. For example,

```
{       int b = 53;        // example of a compound statement
        b = x * 45;
        int c = b - 101;
}
```

The rule is that anywhere in Java where only a single statement is allowed, you may place a compound statement. Thus, if you need to do more than a single thing in an `if/else` (or anywhere else for that matter), this will not be a problem. Just surround the statements with `{` and `}`, and they will now function as if they were one statement.

In the last section, we showed how to write two assignment statements to compute the real roots of a quadratic equation. However, it is not possible to compute these roots if either a = 0, because the denominator of the formula will be 0, or if $b^2 - 4ac < 0$, because the roots will then be imaginary. We can handle this situation as follows:

```
boolean errorFlag = false;
if ((a == 0) || ((b*b) - (4.0 * a * c)) < 0.0 ) {
    errorFlag = true;
}
else {
    root1=(-b + Math.sqrt((b*b)-(4.0*a*c)))/(2.0*a);
    root2=(-b - Math.sqrt((b*b)-(4.0*a*c)))/(2.0*a);
}
```

Note that we did not need to put curly braces around the assignment of the value `true` to `errorFlag` because it is only a single statement. The curly braces are needed, however, in the `else` clause to allow us to include the two assignment statements. If you accidentally omitted the curly braces in the `else` clause, then only the first assignment statement (`root1 = . . .`) will be inside the `else` clause, and the second one (`root2 = `) will become the statement that follows the entire `if/else`. That is, leaving out the `{}` will produce the following (we are formatting it to more clearly indicate the structure):

```
boolean errorFlag = false;
if ((a == 0) || ((b*b) - (4.0 * a * c)) < 0.0 ) {
    errorFlag = true;
}
else
    root1=(-b + Math.sqrt((b*b)-(4.0*a*c)))/(2.0*a);

root2=(-b - Math.sqrt((b*b)-(4.0*a*c)))/(2.0*a);
```

If `a == 0`, you will correctly set the `errorFlag` to `true`, but then you will try to compute the value of `root2`, producing a fatal divide by zero error. Always remember to bracket `if` or `else` clauses with curly braces even if the clause contains a single statement. In fact, many coding standards encourage you always to place curly braces around the statements in an `if` or `else` clause regardless of the number of statements in the clause.

Since the `else` clause is optional in Java, you may get yourself into the following ambiguous situation, called the **dangling else problem**:

```
if (condition1)
    if (condition2)
        statement1;
    else
        statement2;
```

The ambiguity comes from not knowing if the `else statement2` clause goes with the `if (condition1)` test or the `if (condition2)` test. You cannot tell from the indentation alone because we could also have formatted these statements as:

```
if (condition1)
    if (condition2)
        statement1;
else
    statement2;
```

The rule in Java is that an `else` clause is always associated with the nearest `if` statement. Thus, in the preceding situation, the statements will be interpreted as shown in the first example, not the second. That is, `statement2` is associated with the test `if (condition2)`.

Java is a free format language, and you are explicitly allowed to format a cluster of statements in whatever way you want, including the second example. Since indentation is transparent to the compiler and does not change the flow of control, you should always use indentation to show how statements are nested and to make your programs easier to read. (Many Java editors will do this for you automatically.) Grouping statements as shown in the second example would be highly confusing to a reader of your program. You are strongly encouraged to avoid this type of misleading indentation.

A conditional construct that is quite common is a series of nested `if/else` clauses that select exactly one of n blocks of code. For example, assume that `yearInSchool` is a variable that specifies a student's year in school. We could handle all the different possibilities as shown in Figure A.9.

There is nothing special or different about the block of statements in Figure A.9, as it is simply a series of nested `if/else` statements of the type just discussed. However, this pattern occurs quite often, and a familiarity with this particular statement sequence can be very useful.

```
if (yearInSchool == 1) {
    // handle freshman students
}
else if (yearInSchool == 2) {
    // handle sophomore students
}
else if (yearInSchool == 3) {
    // handle junior students
}
else if (yearInSchool == 4) {
    // handle senior students
}
else {
    // handle all other cases here
}
```

FIGURE A.9 Nested `if`/`else` statements

A.5.2.2 The `switch` Statement

There is another way to handle the sequence of decisions shown in Figure A.9. We can use the second type of Java conditional statement called the `switch` statement. The syntax of this statement is given in Figure A.10.

```
switch (expression) {
    case c₁:   // code block 1
               break;
    case c₂:   // code block 2
               break;
    case c₃:   // code block 3
               break;

    . . .

    default:   // default code block
}
```

FIGURE A.10 Syntax of the `switch` statement

The `switch` statement is a multiway conditional. We first determine the value of the expression on the top line, which must evaluate to a value of type `byte`, `char`, `short`, or `int`. We then determine if this value is equal to any of the constant values c_i, which are of the same type as the expression on the first line. If the value equals the constant c_1, we execute code block 1. If the value equals constant c_2, we execute code block 2 and so on. Finally, if the value does not equal any of these constant values, then we execute the `default` code block.

After finishing the indicated code block, the `switch` statement code continues with the next code block; that is, after doing code block 1, it would start executing block 2, block 3, and so on. This is rarely what we want to happen. To indicate that after completing execution of a code block we wish to terminate the entire `switch` statement, we must use a special Java statement called `break`. Executing this statement will cause you to immediately exit the block in which the `break` statement is contained and continue execution with the first executable statement after the block. In this case, it will cause you to immediately exit the `switch` statement and continue with the statement that follows it.

Figure A.11 shows how we could use the `switch` to implement the year in school computations that were done in Figure A.9 using nested `if`/`else` statements.

```
switch (yearInSchool) {
case 1:     // handle freshman students
    break;
case 2:     // handle sophomore students
    break;
case 3:     // handle junior students
    break;
case 4:     // handle senior students
    break;
default:    // handle all other conditions
}
```

FIGURE A.11 Example of the `switch` statement

A `switch` statement can have more than one case clause labeling a single code block. For example, let's say that juniors and seniors are handled using the same block of code. Then we could rewrite these two cases from Figure A.11 in the following way:

```
case 3:   case 4:   // handle juniors and seniors
    break;
```

Every constant value in a `switch` statement must be unique. The following structure

```
case 1:     // code block 1
    break;
. . .
case 1:     // code block 2
```

is ambiguous. If the `switch` expression evaluates to a 1, we will not know whether to execute code block 1 or code block 2. The compiler does not allow this, and it will flag the condition as an error.

◆ A.5.3 Simple Input/Output

The easiest way to output text in Java is with the `print()` and `println()` methods, both of which can be found in the class `PrintWriter` in the package `java.io`. These two routines produce a character stream that is usually directed to the standard output stream. The syntax of these two methods is as follows:

```
System.out.print(expression₁+expression₂+ . . . +expressionₙ);
System.out.println(expression₁+expression₂+ . . . +expressionₙ);
```

These two routines behave in very similar ways: Each of the expressions, which can be of any type, is evaluated and converted to a character string. Then the individual strings are concatenated together, using the concatenation operator +, and the string that results is displayed on the standard output device, usually the screen. The only difference between the two methods is that, after the output has been displayed, the `println()` variant generates a carriage return. Thus, the following output operation will begin on the next line. With the `print()`, the next output operation begins from wherever this one left off.

For example, here is how we could display the two real roots of a quadratic equation, called `root1` and `root2`:

```
System.out.println( " The two roots of the equation are " +
                    root1 + " and " + root2 );
```

If the equation has no real roots, here is how we might display an error message on the screen rather than setting an error flag to true as was done earlier:

```
System.out.println(" *** ERROR. No real roots. ***");
System.out.println();
```

A `println()` command with no arguments generates a blank line, and it can be used to control the horizontal spacing of the output.

Basic character output is rather easy in Java using the `print()` and `println()` commands, but the same cannot be said about character-based keyboard input. Java was intended for use in a visual environment that supports a graphical user interface. Therefore, it does not have simple character-oriented keyboard input commands analogous to the `print()` and `println()` output methods just described.

Obviously, input is a fundamental part of most programs. Therefore, to solve the problem of providing basic input operations, most introductory Java textbooks include their own Java classes for reading primitive numerical and character data types from the keyboard. These classes typically include methods with names such as `readInt()`, `readDouble()`, `readChar()` that allow a user to enter these primitive data types via the keyboard. Unfortunately, these classes are nonstandard, and a method used by students with one textbook will almost certainly not operate in exactly the same way as an input method provided by another text.

A second solution is to immediately learn how to build graphical user interfaces so that you can design and use GUIs for all program input. Although this is a wonderful solution, the time required to adequately cover this huge and complex topic could take significant amounts of time away from other critically important concepts. In this text, we discuss in detail how to design and build graphical user interfaces, but not until Chapter 12, after we have covered other important ideas, such as software design, object-oriented programming, and data structures.

A third way to support keyboard input is to write your own input methods using the stream classes included in the package `java.io`. We explain at length how to do this in the main body of the text, but again, not until much later (see Chapter 10).

Therefore, if you are currently unfamiliar with how to build a GUI and are not comfortable using the `InputStream`, `InputStreamReader`, and `BufferedInputStream` classes, then none of these solutions will work for you right now. In this case, you will either need to use a nonstandard keyboard input class provided by your instructor, or you will need to use the fourth method that we will mention: **command-line arguments**.

To start the execution of a Java program, you must provide the name of a public class that contains a method called `main()`. For example, given the program in Figure A.2, we could begin its execution with a command line that looks like the following, although the exact format will depend on which Java environment you are using:

```
java  MyFirstProgram
```

In addition to the file name, this command line may also contain a series of command-line arguments, which are entered immediately following the file name. For example, here is how we might include three command-line arguments, an integer, a real, and a string:

```
java  MyFirstProgram  1  2.3  file.data
```

These command-line arguments are passed into the program using the `String` parameter `args` that is the standard parameter for every `main()` method.

```
public static void main(String args[])
```

The first parameter on the command line (the 1 in this example) is passed in as `args[0]`, the 2.3 is stored in `args[1]`, and the string "file.data" will be located in `args[2]`. You can determine exactly how many arguments were entered on the command line using the length operation `args.length`. Once you have these parameters stored in a `String` variable, you can use the methods contained in the wrapper classes `Integer`, `Float`, `Double`, and so on to convert these string representations to data values of the proper type. For example, the method `parseDouble()` found in class `Double` will convert the string representation of a double into a numeric value of type `double`.

Suppose that we wanted to input the three coefficients of a quadratic equation on the command line in the following way:

```
java  Quadratic  3.1  -1.2  4.0
```

This corresponds to the equation $3.1x^2 - 1.2x + 4.0 = 0$. Our program could use these inputs in the following way:

```
if (args.length != 3)
    System.out.println("Wrong number of parameters");
else {
```

```
double a, b, c;      // the 3 coefficients
a = Double.parseDouble(args[0]);
b = Double.parseDouble(args[1]);
c = Double.parseDouble(args[2]);

// now go ahead and solve the equation
// ax² + bx + c = 0
. . .
```

If needed, this technique can serve as a temporary way to do keyboard input until you become more comfortable with one of the more general and more flexible techniques—either GUIs or streams.

◆ A.5.4 Iterative Statements

The most basic method of looping in Java is **iteration**: the repetition of a block of statements either a fixed number of times or until a specific condition occurs. There is another method, called **recursion**, to execute a block of statements repeatedly. Recursion is the invocation of a method by the method itself, and there are some languages (e.g., LISP and Scheme) in which recursion is the only method of implementing a loop. Recursion is explicitly allowed in Java, and if you are familiar and comfortable with it, go ahead and use it. In fact, we show numerous examples of recursive algorithms in the body of the text, such as the merge sort and quicksort examples in Chapter 5.

However, by far the most common method of looping in Java is iteration using one of the three iterative control constructs: while, do, and for. We will discuss these statements in the upcoming sections.

A.5.4.1 The while Statement

The while statement is the most common and widely used iterative statement in Java. The while statement repeats a block of statements, called the **loop body**, until a given Boolean condition become false. The syntax of the while statement is shown in Figure A.12(a), and its behavior is diagramed in Figure A.12(b).

The while statement is a type of looping construct called a **pretest loop**. In this type of loop, we *initially* test the Boolean condition to see if it is false. If so, we immediately exit the loop, and the statement is never executed. Thus, the loop body can be executed zero, one, or more times. Note that the syntax of the while permits only a single statement. However, as we mentioned in the previous section, that is not a problem. If you want the loop body to be longer than a single statement, then make it a compound statement by encasing the loop body within the characters { and }.

As with any loop based on iterating until a condition becomes true (or false), it is essential that at least one statement in the loop body changes the value of a variable such that the Boolean expression will eventually become false. Otherwise, you have the unfortunately all-too-common programming error called an **infinite loop**. (Note: If you want to write a program that runs forever, or at least until the user does something to stop it, then it is acceptable to write while (true) . . . . However, be very careful when using this construct.)

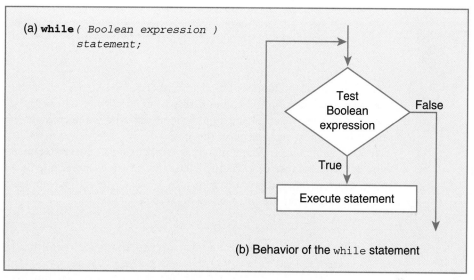

(a) while (*Boolean expression*)
     statement;

(b) Behavior of the `while` **statement**

FIGURE A.12 `while` statement in Java

There are a number of other things to be careful of when using the `while` construct that can lead to errors. The first concern is that, because the Boolean expression is immediately evaluated, you must be sure that all variables in the expression have a value when the loop is first entered. For example, let's say you want to read input values until the occurrence of the special sentinel value 999, at which time you exit the loop. (Assume that `getInput()` returns the next input value.) The following code has errors:

```java
while (num != 999) {
    num = getInput();
    // now process the input value num
}
```

The problem is that `num` is given a value by the `getInput()` method on the first line of the loop. However, we initially test `num` to see if it is 999 when we start the loop, before it is ever assigned an input value. (We could rely on the fact that all integer variables are automatically initialized to 0, but we should write the program correctly in the first place rather than rely on Java to fix our mistakes.) Another problem is that, once the `while` loop is entered, it will continue executing to the end of the loop body, even if the boolean expression becomes true somewhere in the middle of the loop. So, when we input the sentinel value 999 on the first line, we will still continue with the rest of the loop body and will process the value 999 as if it were "real" data, which it is not.

The correct way to write the loop is as follows:

```java
num = getInput();  // read the first data value
while (num != 999) {
```

```
    // process this input value,
    // and then get the next
    num = getInput();
}
```

This version of the loop will read a number before we ever start the loop so that the variable num has an initial value. If this value is 999, we will skip the entire loop. If it is not 999, then we enter the loop, process this data value, and get the next input to set up for the next pass through the loop.

Another common programming error when using iterative statements is the **off-by-one error**. It is caused by writing a loop that executes either one time too many or one time too few. The program in Figure A.13, for example, is supposed to input N real numbers and compute the average of all these numbers.

```
float sum;                // the sum of all numbers
float number;             // the next input value
final int N = 100         // the number of input values
int count;                // a count of how many values
                          // have been read in so far


count = 0;
sum = 0.0;
while (count <= N) {
    number = getInput();
    sum = sum + number;
    count++;
}

float average = sum / (float) count;
```

FIGURE A.13 Program that should read in N real numbers

There is an off-by-one error in this code, although it is certainly not obvious. The problem is that we start counting the number of times we have done the loop at 0 and continue up to *and including* the value N. This represents a total of N + 1 iterations, one more than desired. The correct test to use in the Boolean expression is (count < N) rather than (count <= N). Our choice of the wrong relational operator has led to an off-by-one error and an incorrect program. The moral of this example is that every time you write a loop, be sure to check that it starts at the place you want and ends at exactly the place you want—not one time too many or one time too few.

A.5.4.2 The do/while Statement

The do/while statement is similar to the while described in the previous section in that it repeats a block of statements as long as a Boolean expression remains true. The main difference is that the do/while is a **posttest** looping construct. The body of the loop is executed, and then the Boolean condition is tested at the end of the iteration. This means that the body of a do/while loop must be executed at least once. The syntax of the do/while statement is shown in Figure A.14(a), and its behavior is diagramed in Figure A.14(b).

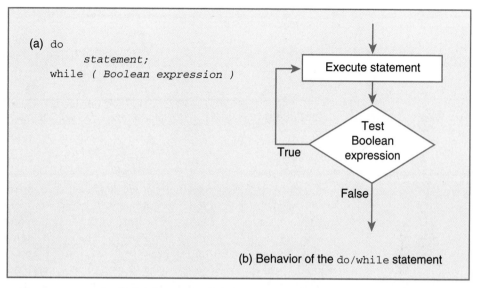

(a) do
　　　　 statement;
　　　 while (Boolean expression)

Execute statement

True   Test Boolean expression

False

(b) Behavior of the do/while **statement**

FIGURE A.14 do/while statement in Java

The other difference between the do/while statement of Figure A.14 and the while statement of Figure A.12 is that the entire do/while construct is terminated with a semicolon.

The while is used more often than the do/while because it is somewhat unusual to construct a loop that must always be executed at least once. With most loops, there is the possibility that the loop will be skipped entirely. However, if a loop does have the characteristic that it must execute at least once, then the do/while can be an appropriate control structure.

The code fragment in Figure A.15 shows the outline for a block of code that inputs a value from a user, computes an answer (not shown), prints that answer, and then asks the user if they want to repeat this operation. The do/while is quite appropriate because the computation must be done at least once.

```
// This is a loop that solves a problem and asks the
// user if they want to do it again. The computation
// of the answer is not shown
do
    value = getInput();      // get the data

    // Compute the answer
    answer = . . . ;
```
(continued)

FIGURE A.15 Obtaining user input using a do/while loop

```
// Print the results
System.out.println(" Answer = " + answer);

// Find out what the user wants to do
System.out.println(" Do it again, Y or N?" );
response = getAnswer(); // get the user's answer

while (response == 'Y') || (response == 'y');
```

FIGURE A.15 Obtaining user input using a do/while loop *(continued)*

A.5.4.3 The for Statement

The for statement is an extremely powerful iterative construct, and for certain situations, it is by far the most convenient looping statement. It works best when there are four specific components in the loop: (a) an *initialization* expression executed exactly once before the loop begins, (b) a *test* to see if we are done before the loop body is executed (i.e., a pretest looping condition), (c) the *loop body*, and (d) an *update* operation that is executed at the completion of each iteration. The general model for this type of loop structure is shown using a while statement to construct it:

```
initialization
while (test)    {
    loop body
    update
}
```

While sounding somewhat specialized, this type of loop structure is rather common and occurs quite often in computer science problems. We have just shown that it is possible to implement this loop using a while statement. However, note that in addition to the loop body, you need three separate statements to construct this loop: the initialization, test, and update commands. The Java for statement simplifies writing this type of loop by combining all three of these operations into a single construct. The resulting for behaves in an identical fashion to the while loop shown but with less work and fewer statements. The syntax of the for is given in Figure A.16(a), and its behavior is summarized in Figure A.16(b).

Although the initialization expression can be any statement in Java, it is almost always an assignment statement that initializes either a loop counter or another variable that controls how many times the loop is executed. The test is a Boolean expression that determines when the loop has completed. Finally, the update expression indicates that the loop body has been done one more time. It is often implemented as an increment (or decrement) of a counter that tallies the total number of times the loop has been done.

For example, the following for loop evaluates the series $1^3 + 2^3 + 3^3 + \ldots + N^3$. (It assumes that N has already been assigned a value.)

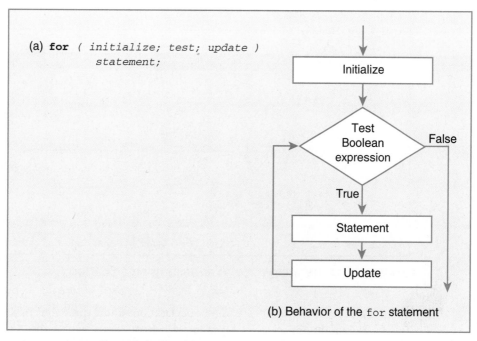

(a) **for** (*initialize; test; update*)
        statement;

Initialize

Test
Boolean
expression

False

True

Statement

Update

(b) Behavior of the `for` statement

FIGURE A.16 `for` statement in Java

```
double sum = 0.0;
for (int i = 1; i <= N; i++) {
    sum += (double) (i * i * i);
}
```

Notice how easy it is to understand the behavior of this loop because all its parameters appear in a single place: at the very top of the loop. In this case, we can determine that the loop counter i starts at 1, the loop continues as long as i is less than or equal to N, and the loop counter i is incremented by 1 after each pass. Thus, it is simple to determine that this loop executes exactly N times. Notice also that the loop counter i has been declared inside the `for` statement itself. The scope of i is the body of the `for` loop, which means the final value of i will not be available after the loop terminates. While not required, this is quite common since we no longer need this counter once the loop has exited.

The `for` loop in Figure A.17 iterates through an array x[] of integer values, counting how many elements in the array are negative, how many are zero, and how many are positive. The length of the array determines the total number of times the loop body is executed.

The increment and update expressions can contain a comma-separated list of expressions. This makes it possible for a programmer to specify that more than one action occur during the initialization or update phases of the `for` loop. The update expression can consist of any valid expressions; however, the initialization expression can be either a comma-separated list of declaration statements or expression state-

```
negatives = zeros = positives = 0;

for (int k = 0; k < x.length; k++) {
   if (x[ k ] < 0) {
      negatives++;
   }
   else {
      if ( x[ k ] == 0) {
         zeros++;
      }
      else {
         positives++;
      }
   }
}
```

FIGURE A.17 Iterating through an array using a `for` loop

ments. In other words, you cannot mix declarations and expressions in the initialization portion of the `for` loop. So, for example, we could incorporate the initialization of the three counters—`negatives`, `zeros`, and `positives`—into the initialization expression of the `for` statement itself (Figure A.18).

Note in Figure A.18 that we had to declare the variables `k`, `negatives`, `zeros`, and `positives` outside the `for` loop because we cannot mix declarations with expressions in the initialization expression of a `for` loop.

```
int k;
int negatives;
int zeros;
int positives;

for (k=0, negatives=0, zeros=0, positives=0; k < x.length; k++ ) {
   if (x[ k ] < 0) {
      negatives++;
   }
   else {
      if (x[ k ] == 0) {
         zeros++;
      }
      else {
         positives++;
      }
   }
}
```

FIGURE A.18 Using the comma operator in a `for` loop

The program fragment in Figure A.19 contains a `for` loop that reverses the contents of an array `x` and uses multiple expressions in both the initialization and update portions in the `for` loop. Since `i` and `j` are only needed within the loop itself, they are declared in the initialization expression of the `for` loop, which means the scope of these variables is limited to the body of the loop.

```java
// The array that will be reversed
int x[] = new int[10];

// The variables i and j identify the elements to reverse.
// i starts out at the front of the array and j starts at
// the back. The loop continues as long as i and j have
// not passed each other.
for ( int i = 0, j = x.length-1; i < j; i++, j--) {
    // Swap the elements
    int temp = x[i];
    x[i] = x [j];
    x[j] = temp;
}
```

FIGURE A.19 Reversing an array

A.6 METHODS

The last topic that will be introduced in this Appendix is how to write methods. The general structure of a Java method is given in Figure A.20, where [] indicates an optional construct:

```
[modifiers] return-type method-name( [parameter list])
{
        local declarations
        method body
}
```

FIGURE A.20 General structure of a Java method

The optional *modifiers* are zero, one, or more keywords that describe characteristics of how this method can be used. These modifiers, such as `public`, `private`, `protected`, and `static`, are introduced and described in detail in Chapter 3, and they will not be dealt with any further in this Appendix.

The *return-type* specifies the data type of the value that is returned by this method. If the method does not return an explicit value, then the reserved word `void` is used as the return type.

Finally, the *parameter list* is a list of zero, one, or more parameters separated by commas. The syntax of this list is:

```
(type name, type name, . . . , type name)
```

If the method has no parameters, then we use the notation (). In Java, all parameters are passed by value. This means that a copy of the value is passed to the method rather than the value itself.

Here is the first line of a method called myMethod that contains three parameters—an integer and two floats—and returns a String:

```
String myMethod(int x, float y, double z)
```

The **signature** of a method is a listing of the data types of all of the method's parameters. Thus, the signature of method myMethod just shown is:

```
int, float, double
```

The signature of a method is an extremely important characteristic for the following reason: It is permissible to have two or more methods with the same name as long as they have different signatures. This is called **method overloading**. Thus, it would be acceptable to declare the following two methods, with the same name myMethod, within your program:

```
String myMethod(byte b, double d);
void myMethod(float f)
```

This is because the signatures of these methods

```
byte, double
```

```
float
```

are all unique and can be distinguished from each other. A Java compiler would not have a problem determining which of these three versions of myMethod() you wish to execute. It would simply examine the data types of the parameters contained in the parameter list.

The body of a method is a single compound statement that can contain any of the Java declarations and statements that have been introduced and discussed in the previous sections. The one new statement that will appear within a method is the **return** statement, which specifies the return value of the method. The syntax of this statement is

```
return expression;
```

where expression evaluates to a value of the same data type as the return type of the method. In addition to providing a return value, the return statement also terminates execution of the current method and returns control to the method that invoked this one. If the method has a void return value, then the return statement is written as:

```
return;
```

Figure A.21 shows a method that computes the discriminant of the quadratic equation $ax^2 + bx + c$. The discriminant is the value $b^2 - 4ac$.

```java
// preconditions: three double values a, b, c
// postconditions: returns the value b² -4ac
public double discriminant(double a, double b, double c) {
    double disc;
    disc = (b * b) - 4.0 * a * c;
    return disc;
}
```

FIGURE A.21 Example Java method

Note that we started out with some helpful comments that describe the overall behavior of the method, namely, its pre- and postconditions. This can be extremely useful to anyone reading your program, and it is a habit that you should immediately adopt. In Chapter 1, we talk more about the use of comments in Java, especially a special form of comment called the **Javadoc comment**.

Note that the method in Figure A.21 includes the declaration of a double variable called disc. As we mentioned earlier, the scope of this declaration is the block in which it is declared, which in this case is the body of this method. Variables declared within a method are called **local variables**, and they only exist for the life of the method. When the method terminates, these variables disappear, and they are no longer available. Finally, note that the method returns the value disc using a return statement. This is because the declaration of the method indicated that it returns a double value. Failure to return a value of the correct type will cause an error.

To use a method, you must invoke it. If the method has a nonvoid return value, then you can place a call to the method anywhere that you could legally place a data value of the specified return type. In the case of the method discriminant() in Figure A.21, which returns a double, you can place a call to this method anywhere in the program that you could legally place a variable of type double.

For example, here is how we might invoke the method discriminant() in a program that evaluates quadratic equations:

```java
double x = getInput();    // assume getInput reads a
                          // single input value
double y = getInput();
double z = getInput();

double d = discriminant(x, y, z);   // compute the discriminant

if (d < 0.0)
    System.out.println("*** Complex roots ***");
else
    // compute the real roots here
```

If a method has a `void` return value, then you invoke it by writing the method name with the appropriate parameters. For example, if you have written the following `void` method

```
void exampleMethod(int j)
```

then it could be invoked in the following way:

```
int a;
. . .
exampleMethod(a);    // invoking a void method
```

It is also possible to invoke a method with a nonvoid return value in the same way. All that happens is that the return value of the method is discarded and not used. For example, the method `discriminant()` in Figure A.21 returns a `double` value. However, it would be permissible to write

```
discriminant(x, y, z);
```

which invokes `discriminant()` but does not keep the value it returns. This is not very useful because in this case we invoked the method specifically to compute a result. However, there are methods that return an "optional" value in the sense that you may or may not wish to keep it.

A.7 SUMMARY

This Appendix has been a brief overview of the basic procedural constructs of Java. This treatment has included coverage of primitive data types, reference types, declarations, expressions, assignment, control statements, simple input/output methods, and parameters. As was mentioned earlier, this coverage is not meant to replace the comprehensive treatment of the language that would be found in a beginning Java text. However, if you come into the course with a good knowledge of a language similar to Java (e.g., C++, Visual Basic), then the material in this Appendix should be adequate to allow you to read and understand all the programming examples that are presented.

In addition to the material in this Appendix, a number of important advanced features of Java are introduced within the main body of the text. These concepts include support for object-oriented programming, exceptions, streams, threads, GUIs, and networks. Together with the Appendix, they provide a relatively thorough overview of the Java language.

INDEX